CAPE CARIBBEAN STUDIES

An Interdisciplinary Approach

JENIFFER MOHAMMED
School of Education
The University of the West Indies
St Augustine
Trinidad & Tobago

Consultant Editor: Dr Anthony Luengo

CAPE® is a registered trade mark of the
Caribbean Examinations Council (CXC).
CARIBBEAN STUDIES for CAPE® EXAMINATIONS
is an independent publication and has not
been authorised, sponsored, or otherwise
approved by CXC.

MACMILLAN
CARIBBEAN

Macmillan Education
Between Towns Road, Oxford, OX4 3PP
A division of Macmillan Publishers Limited
Companies and representatives throughout the world

www.macmillan-caribbean.com

ISBN: 978-1-4050-6297-8

Designed by Oxford Illustrators and Designers
Typeset by 𝓣\Tek-Art, Croydon, Surrey
Cover design by Clare Webber

The authors and publishers would like to thank the following for permission to reproduce their photographic material:
Cover: EnjoyLife/Bigstockphoto

Alamy/ p2(br), Alamy/ Rubens Abboud 198(tm), Alamy/ Ace Stock Ltd p268(bl), Alamy/ Bill Bachmann p126(bl), Alamy/ Black Star p166(ml), Alamy/ Richard Broadwell p2(bl), Alamy/ Danita Delimont p2(tml), Alamy/ Paul Doyle p268(br), Alamy/ Mike Goldwater p26(tr), Alamy/ Jeff Greenberg p375(bl), Alamy/ Robert Harding Picture Library p207, Alamy/ Blaine Harrington III p2(tl), Alamy/ Jennie Hart pp26(br), 198(ml), 205, Alamy/ M. Timothy O'Keefe p345, Alamy/ Tom Kidd p375(tr), Alamy/ Wilmar Photography p375(mr);
The Art Archive/ Monastery of the Rabida, Palos, Spain / Dagli Orti p93(m), The Art Archive / National Palace Mexico City / Dagli Orti p93(tr);
Art Directors and Trip/ Mary Jelliffe p23(br), Art Directors and Trip/ Helene Rogers p403;
Aurora Photos/ Bill Bachman p166(bl), Aurora Photos/ Robert Caputo p44(bl), Aurora Photos/ Scott Warren p375(tl);
Bridgeman Art Library p93(bm), Bridgeman Art Library/ Private Collection p93(ml);
Camera Press/ Bilderberg/ Rainer Drexel p166(tl);
Corbis pp49(tr), 213(r), 335, 375(ml), Corbis/ Bettmann pp217(l), 217(m), 268(m), 330(tl), 330(r), 330(mr), 330(bl), 337(b), 339, Corbis/ Pablo Corral V p208, Corbis/ Alejandro Ernesto/ EPA p126(tr), Corbis/ Najlah Feanny p394(l), Corbis/ Natalie Fobes p23(tl), Corbis/ Franz-Marc Frei p375(br), Corbis/ Stephen Frink pp126(ml), 145, Corbis/ Sergio Gaudenti/ Kipa p343(l), Corbis/ Philippe Giraud p126(tl), Corbis/ Hulton-Deutsch Collection p121(bl), Corbis/ Michael Kim p198(br), Corbis/ Kit Kittle p166(mr), Corbis/ Chris Kleponis/ ZUMA p394(r), Corbis/ Istian Liewig/ Liewig Media Sports p298(ml), Corbis/ Gilbert Iundt/ TempSport p298(tmr), Corbis/ Wally McNamee p375(blt), Corbis/ Ed Quinn p126(br), Corbis/ Reuters pp23(bl), 126(mr), 268(tr), 298(mm), 298(ml), 298(tr), Corbis/ Dennis M Sabang/ EPA p268(bm), Corbis/ David Turnley p44(br), Corbis/ Underwood & Underwood p334, Corbis/ Werner-Forman p103;
Gamma Press p198(tl), Gamma Press/ Fotoblitz/ Stills p209, Gamma Press/ Laurent Maous p343(r);
Getty Images/ AFP/ Thony Belizaire p298(bm), Getty Images/ AFP/ Assif Hassan p198(tr), Getty Images/ AFP/ Antonio Levi p49(bl), Getty Images/ AFP/ Adalberto Roque pp26(bl), 198(mr), Getty Images/ Hamish Blair p298(bl), Getty Images/ Stephen Dunn p198(bl), Getty Images/ Hulton Archive pp93(mr), 121(t), 212, 330(tr), 330(br), 337(t), Getty Images/ The Image Bank p29(t), Getty Images/ Mike Powell p298(bml), Getty Images/ Steve Pyke p350, Getty Images/ Time & Life Pictures pp93(br), 217(r), 330(ml), Getty Images/ Roger Viollet p354;
Green Globe International p225;
Robert Harding Picture Library pp136(r), 166(br), 375(bm);
Lonely Planet Images/ Jerry Alexander p26(tl), Lonely Planet Images/ Chris Barton p136(l);
Mary Evans Picture Library p93(tl);
NASA/ GSFC/ Jacques Descloitres, MODIS Rapid Response Team p152;
Panos Pictures/ Andy Johnstone pp2(r), 161, Panos Pictures/ Guy Mansfield p268(tl), Panos Pictures/ Caroline Penn p2(tmr);
Penguin Publishers p343(m);
Popperfoto pp298(tl), 298(m);
Rex Features p49(br), Rex Features/ Image Source p408(br);
Devon Shaw pp23(tr), 29(b), 36, 44(tr), 166(tr), 408x7;
Alex Smailes pp2(bm), 375(m);
Still Pictures/ Achim Pohl p39;
Topham Picturepoint pp93(bl), 121(t), 121(br), 213(l), 298(tml), 355(l), Topham Picturepoint/ Jeff Greenberg/ The Image Works pp49(l), 298(br), Topham Picturepoint/ UPPA p213(m), 353;
Triniview p44(tl)

Printed and bound in Malaysia

2016 2015 2014 2013 2012 2011
10 9 8 7 6 5

This book is dedicated to
SYLVIA, CURT, MIKHAIL, NIKOLAI AND ISABEL
────────────

CONTENTS

Preface   ix
List of abbreviations and acronyms   xi

MODULE 1   CARIBBEAN SOCIETY AND CULTURE   1

CHAPTER 1   LOCATING THE CARIBBEAN   3

1.1   Geography, geology and the Caribbean   3
1.2   The historical Caribbean: the colonial Caribbean experience   8
1.3   The political Caribbean: the many Caribbeans   10
1.4   Caribbean identity and culture: exploring the bases of identity   17
      Practice tests   22
      Research topics   24

CHAPTER 2   UNDERSTANDING SOCIETY AND CULTURE   27

2.1   The social   27
2.2   Society: multiple meanings   35
2.3   Culture: multiple meanings   43
2.4   Caribbean 'society' and 'culture'   53
      Practice tests   58
      Research topics   58

CHAPTER 3   INVESTIGATING FEATURES OF CARIBBEAN SOCIETY AND CULTURE   61

3.1   Cultural diversity   61
3.2   Hybridization   70
3.3   Social stratification   83
3.4   Social mobility   88
      Practice tests   90
      Research topics   90

CHAPTER 4   TRACING HISTORY IN CARIBBEAN SOCIETY AND CULTURE   93

4.1   Migrations   93
4.2   The development of systems of production   111
4.3   Resistance   114
4.4   Movements towards independence   119
      Practice tests   124
      Research topics   124

CHAPTER 5 DEVELOPING GEOGRAPHICAL AWARENESS   127

5.1 Geographical perspectives: the environment, society and culture   127
5.2 Environmental hazards   130
5.3 Environmental disasters   132
5.4 Impacts on society and culture   161
   Practice tests   164
   Research topics   164

CHAPTER 6 ANALYSING SOCIAL INSTITUTIONS   167

6.1 Social institutions   167
6.2 The social institution of the family   170
6.3 The social institution of education   176
6.4 The social institution of religion   183
6.5 The social institution of the justice system   188
   Practice tests   195
   Research topics   195

CHAPTER 7 INTERACTING WITH THE WIDER WORLD   199

7.1 Imperialism and colonialism   199
7.2 Influence of extra-regional countries on the Caribbean   202
7.3 Caribbean influences on extra-regional countries   226
   Practice tests   232
   Research topics   232

MODULE 2 CARIBBEAN DEVELOPMENT   235

CHAPTER 8 CONCEPTUALIZING DEVELOPMENT   237

8.1 Conceptions of development   237
8.2 Approaches to development   239
8.3 Factors influencing development   247
   Practice tests   265
   Research topics   265

CHAPTER 9 CONTEXTUALIZING DEVELOPMENT: GLOBALIZATION AND REGIONALISM   269

9.1 Defining globalization   269
9.2 Multilateral agencies   276
9.3 Regional integration   281
9.4 Achievements and challenges of regional organizations   287
   Practice tests   296
   Research topics   296

CHAPTER 10 PROMOTING DEVELOPMENT: SPORT AND THE MASS MEDIA 299

    10.1 Sports, leisure and recreation   299
    10.2 Sport and development   301
    10.3 The mass media   313
    10.4 The mass media and development   316
          Practice tests   327
          Research topics   327

CHAPTER 11 THEORIZING CARIBBEAN DEVELOPMENT 331

    11.1 Ideology   331
    11.2 Black Nationalism: pan-Africanism   333
    11.3 Economic perspectives   344
    11.4 Caribbean feminist perspectives   354
    11.5 Indo-Caribbean thought   362
    11.6 Indigenous perspectives   366
          Practice tests   371
          Research topics   371

CHAPTER 12 HUMANIZING DEVELOPMENT: SOCIAL JUSTICE 375

    12.1 Defining social justice   375
    12.2 Social injustice   380
    12.3 Ageism   384
    12.4 Sexism   389
    12.5 Racism, classism and creedism   399
          Practice tests   406
          Research topics   406

MODULE 3 RESEARCHING SOCIAL LIFE 407

CHAPTER 13 RESEARCHING SOCIAL LIFE 409

    13.1 What is research?   409
    13.2 Alternative ideas about research   415
    13.3 Beginning a research project   419
    13.4 Collecting data   429
    13.5 Analysing the data   438
    13.6 Wrapping up the study   440
          Practice tests   449

          Glossary   450

          Index   461

with society, culture, youth and development but has not had much experience in reflecting on his/her own preferred ways of thinking and prejudices. Thus, the text emphasizes important specific details of different Caribbean countries and proposes or provokes some deeper thinking and self-introspection. Teachers too should welcome a text where there is not only a focus on content but also activities and end-of-chapter review questions and detailed suggestions for research.

- *Interdisciplinary nature of the syllabus.* The approach used in the text underscores the interdisciplinary nature of the subject, Caribbean Studies. Since most teachers have been trained in well-defined disciplines, the interdisciplinary nature of Caribbean Studies poses a challenge in constructing and delivering the curriculum. It is indeed quite unique that such a subject should find its way into post-secondary education, which has traditionally been the domain of systematic knowledge with strong disciplinary boundaries and specialization into compartments of knowledge – be it science, modern studies or languages. The introduction of a subject like Caribbean Studies, with 'weak boundaries', is perhaps symptomatic of a postmodern curriculum that celebrates the inter-connected nature of knowledge and people and tries to downplay the hitherto dominant view of knowledge as comprising separate and distinct disciplines. To facilitate the interdisciplinary approach, related themes and core concepts have been used to structure each module. The thematic approach is very useful in organizing teaching and learning materials that are integrated in an attempt to promote meaning in the real world rather than just disciplinary knowledge.

- *Pedagogy.* Elements of a constructivist approach have been used in writing the text. The main thrust of the course is about helping students to continue to develop a sense of Caribbean identity and a greater appreciation of the region's potential and problems. Thus, it is highly affective. As much as possible, the factual, definitional aspects of content are used as a platform to encourage students to engage in reflective and analytical thinking. The activities represent a major area of stimulation in developing these skills and competencies, especially bringing to the fore the role that the individual plays in society, culture and development.

Jeniffer Mohammed

PREFACE

Caribbean Studies is focused on developing Caribbean citizens with a keen awareness of the potential and challenges of the region. It is written especially for the post-secondary and tertiary student in mind, targeting those issues threatening human development in the region. This emphasis is addressed through a number of strategies and approaches that are detailed below.

- *Content.* The expository part of the text emphasizes issues important in generating and developing knowledge of the past, present and future of the region. It deals specifically with the challenge of human and economic development in small states, especially within a context of global interaction. While factual content is provided, this is subservient to the main intention of engaging the student in thinking through important issues.
- *Activities.* These are both lower-order knowledge items as well as activities designed to deepen the reflective spirit and encourage analytical and critical thinking. There is some focus on helping a person to understand his or her own role in shaping the region.
- *Boxes.* These give greater detail to issues introduced in the text and may highlight the unique experience of specific Caribbean countries. Within the general Caribbean region it is important to realize that experiences may differ from one territory to another. Boxes may also be used for showcasing divergent and controversial views to provoke thought and discussion about our developing understanding of ourselves.
- *Glossary.* The glossary provides brief definitions of important terms used in the text and will serve as a useful revision aid. These terms are highlighted in **bold** at their first mention in each chapter. Additional terms, plus the names of important people, organizations and movements are shown in ***bold italics*** at their first mention in each chapter.

STRUCTURE

The text has a three-part modular structure:

- Module 1 – Caribbean society and culture
- Module 2 – Caribbean development
- Module 3 – Researching social life

A student can begin at any point as there is no obvious scaffolding of Module 1 on to Module 2. However, to be able to research social life competently, much of the content explored in Modules 1 and 2 will be relevant.

- *View of the learner.* The text is expected to be a major source of information for both students and teachers. It has been conceptualized and written with a particular view of the learner in mind. For example, the student is envisaged as one who has an interest in the Caribbean and its links with the wider world, but little specific pre-knowledge of other Caribbean countries. At the same time, the learner has the desire to discuss controversial and provocative issues dealing

LIST OF ABBREVIATIONS AND ACRONYMS

AAPRP All-African People's Revolutionary Party

ABB African Blood Brotherhood

ACL African Communities League

ACP African, Caribbean and Pacific

ACS Association of Caribbean States

ALP Antigua Labour Party

ALSC Amerindian Legal Services Center

APA American Psychological Association

APA Amerindian Peoples Association

ASEAN Association of South East Asian Nations

ASJA Anjuman Sunnat-ul-Jamaat

AWOJA Association of Women's Organizations of Jamaica

BITI Belize Indigenous Training Institute

BVI British Virgin Islands

CAC Central American and Caribbean

CAFRA Caribbean Association for Feminist Research and Action

CAPE Caribbean Advanced Proficiency Examinations

CARICOM Caribbean Community and Common Market

CARIFTA Caribbean Free Trade Area

CBI Caribbean Basin Initiative

CBU Caribbean Broadcasting Union

CCN Caribbean Communications Network

CERD Committee on the Elimination of Racial Discrimination (UN)

CGDS Centre for Gender and Development Studies, UWI

CIA Central Intelligence Agency (US)

CMO Caribbean Meteorological Organization

CNN Cable News Network

COIP Caribbean Organization of Indigenous Peoples

CROSQ Caribbean Regional Organization on Standards and Quality

CSEC Caribbean Secondary Examinations

CSME CARICOM Single Market and Economy

CTO Caribbean Tourism Organization

CXC Caribbean Examinations Council

ECCB Eastern Caribbean Central Bank

ECCM Eastern Caribbean Common Market

ELDC Economically Less Developed Country

EMDC Economically More Developed Country

ENSO El Niño and the Southern Oscillation

EU European Union

FBI Federal Bureau of Investigation

FTAA Free Trade Area of the Americas

GATT General Agreements on Tariffs and Trade

GDP Gross Domestic Product

GNP Gross National Product

IAAF International Association of Athletics Federation

IACHR Inter-American Commission on Human Rights

IADB Inter-American Development Bank.

IBRD International Bank for Reconstruction and Development (World Bank)

ICTs Information and Communications Technologies

IOC International Olympic Committee

ISER Institute for Social and Economic Research

ITUC–NW International Trade Union Committee of Negro Workers

LAFTA Latin American Free Trade Association

LAI League Against Imperialism (and for Colonial Independence)

LDC Less Developed Country

MAVAW Men Against Violence Against Women

MDC More Developed Country

MERCOSUR South American Common Market

MNCs Multinational Corporations

NAACP National Association for the Advancement of Colored People

NAFTA North American Free Trade Association

NBC National Broadcasting Company

NGC National Garifuna Council

NGOs Non-governmental Organizations

NJAC National Joint Action Committee

NJM New Jewel Movement

NWCSA Negro Welfare Cultural and Social Association

OAU Organization of African Unity

OECS Organization of Eastern Caribbean States

PNC People's National Congress (Guyana)

PNM People's National Movement (Trinidad and Tobago)

RSS Regional Security System

SAP Structural Adjustment Policy

SAT Scholastic Assessment Test

SMMA Soufrière Marine Management Area

SNCC Student Nonviolent Coordinating Committee

TATT Telecommunications Authority of Trinidad and Tobago

TIA Tackveeact ul Islamic Association

TMCC Toledo Maya Cultural Council

TML Trinidad Muslim League

TNCs Transnational Corporations

UDHR Universal Declaration of Human Rights

UNDP United Nations Development Programme

UNESCO United Nations Educational, Scientific and Cultural Organization

UNIA Universal Negro Improvement Association

UNICEF United Nations Children's Fund

UNIFEM United Nations Development Fund for Women

USSR Union of Soviet Socialist Republics

UTEC University of Technology (Jamaica)

UTT University of Trinidad and Tobago

WAND Women and Development

WICB West Indies Cricket Board

WID Women in Development

WIPA West Indies Players Association

WISA West Indies Associated States

WTO World Trade Organization

MODULE

1 CARIBBEAN SOCIETY AND CULTURE

One of the goals of Caribbean Studies is the development of a Caribbean citizen who has a deep awareness and understanding of the challenges and possibilities of the region. Module 1 seeks to develop this awareness and understanding through a study of Caribbean society and culture.

To grasp the opportunities and avoid the pitfalls of development, Caribbean citizens should be thoroughly knowledgeable about how their societies were created and developed – and indeed are continuing to develop – in contexts of constant change, conflict and contradiction. Most important is knowledge that relates to how groups and individuals interact to create the world they live in. Such knowledge can equip Caribbean people to make, both individually and collectively, better decisions, which enhance the possibilities and potential of their own lives and that of the region.

MODULE OBJECTIVES

On completing this module, you will be able to
1 understand how Caribbean societies have grown and developed and are still evolving
2 appreciate how history and geography have shaped the culture and society of the region
3 assess the dilemmas that Caribbean society and culture experience in their intra-regional and extra-regional relationships
4 develop an awareness of the commonalities across the region, as well as its marked diversity
5 construct an understanding of how an individual can contribute to enhancing the development of society and culture in the region.

Look for common historical links and similar heritage?

Only include lands washed by the Caribbean Sea?

How do we locate and define the Caribbean Region?

Look for common, deep structures/ processes e.g. the Caribbean Plate?

Countries perceived to have a common destiny e.g. the ACS?

How do Caribbean people define and locate their own space?

How do persons outside the region perceive the Caribbean?

1 LOCATING THE CARIBBEAN

Before we can attempt a meaningful study of the society and culture of the Caribbean, it is necessary to define and locate the region we will be studying. Sometimes, the society and culture of a people define and locate where they live more than some physical or geographical feature, such as water that surrounds them or a mountain range that separates them from another people. For example, if we had to locate and define Lapland the most we could say is that it is a region in northern Scandinavia where the Lapps – a distinct social and cultural group – live. Trying to define and locate the Caribbean may well lead us to evaluate the part played by physical and geographical boundaries as well as culture and society as dimensions that define and locate a region.

EXPECTED LEARNING OUTCOMES

On completing this chapter, you will be able to

1 treat 'definition' and 'location' as problematic concepts in relation to the Caribbean
2 locate and define the Caribbean using different criteria
3 discuss the advantages and disadvantages of different criteria – geographical, historical, geological and political – in helping to define and locate the Caribbean
4 address culture and society as issues related to the definition and location of a region
5 locate territories, subregions and water bodies on maps of the Caribbean.

1.1

GEOGRAPHY, GEOLOGY AND THE CARIBBEAN
A geographic definition: the Caribbean Basin

A *geographic* basis for delimiting the Caribbean region is a familiar idea. It is based on the concept of a 'Caribbean Basin' where the central identifying feature is the Caribbean Sea, rimmed by islands and the mainland territories of Central and South America. This is the traditional geographic definition of the Caribbean region, which is usually described as 'lands washed by the Caribbean Sea', or it can be thought of as the 'West Indies' and the surrounding mainland territories.

Another geographical way of defining the Caribbean is to use coordinates such as lines of latitude and longitude to locate the region. Fig. 1.1 shows the Caribbean stretching from 60°W to 90°W (of the Greenwich Meridian). These are approximate coordinates used in defining the Caribbean and are fairly well accepted in establishing the breadth of the region. However, the map also shows the region as stretching from near the Equator (Guyana is 5°N of the Equator) to beyond 25°N. This northernmost limit is debatable and is sometimes extended to 30°N to accommodate Bermuda. Perhaps a more realistic northern cut-off point would be the Tropic of Cancer at 23½°N, which passes through the Bahamas and between Cuba and Florida. Thus, the geographical delimitation of the Caribbean Region is not fixed; the idea of the 'Caribbean Basin' and even the coordinates of latitude and longitude are interpreted subjectively.

Fig. 1.1 The geographic Caribbean

Fig. 1.1 also shows the main territories, islands, archipelagos, subregions and water bodies found in the Caribbean. We must be careful to distinguish between islands and continental countries and not overly generalize, as in statements such as 'the islands of the Caribbean'. For example, the territory of Belize in Central America is a large landmass that is considered to be as 'Caribbean' as any of the islands. An *archipelago* is a chain of islands that is usually closely related at a subterranean level. For example, the *Lesser Antilles* forms a chain of small islands that exhibit similar volcanic features. The *Greater Antilles* is an older archipelago of much larger islands. The Bahamas is also an archipelago. The water bodies found in the Caribbean and its environs are the Caribbean Sea, the Gulf of Mexico and the Atlantic Ocean. Fig. 1.1 also shows how close the Pacific Ocean is to the Caribbean at the isthmus of Panama. An 'isthmus' is a narrow neck of land separating two water bodies, and thus the Pacific Ocean is also considered to be part of the 'environs' of the Caribbean.

It is possible to demarcate *subregions* because the region is so large. The Lesser Antilles is further subdivided into the Windward and Leeward Islands. The *Windward Islands* are Grenada, St Vincent and the Grenadines, St Lucia, Martinique, Dominica and Guadeloupe. They are larger than the *Leeward Islands*, located further north – Antigua, St Kitts, Nevis, Montserrat – to name a few. There is no valid geographical reason to explain why the southern end of this chain has been called 'Windward' and the northern end 'Leeward'. The whole chain is subject to the impact of the prevailing north-east trade winds.

The geographic conception of the Caribbean shown in Fig. 1.1 is based on a view of the Caribbean Sea as a basin with the surrounding territories representing the limits of the basin. However, a closer look at this understanding of the Caribbean reveals some issues still to be resolved. For example, such a definition is not comprehensive in that it excludes countries that are normally accepted as Caribbean countries. Guyana, Barbados and the Bahamas are not located within the Caribbean Sea. Barbados and the Bahamas are located in the Atlantic Ocean and Guyana's coast also borders the Atlantic Ocean. However, they are very close by. (An interesting case is Bermuda, discussed in Box 1.1.)

BOX 1.1 Caribbean identity: the case of Bermuda

Fig. 1.1 does not show Bermuda, which is in the Atlantic Ocean, about 950 km (600 miles) off the North Carolina coast. Bermuda is an archipelago of some 200 islands, 20 of which are inhabited. They are the tops of submarine ridges on which coral has grown. Britain has been in control of Bermuda since 1609, making it the oldest British colony. It became an international centre for shipping and trading because of its strategic location in the mid-Atlantic. Although slavery existed there, the slaves worked mainly as sailors, traders and artisans.

Approximately 40 per cent of Bermuda's population is white (descendants of English and Scottish settlers, and of Portuguese immigrants) and 60 per cent black. There are tensions between these groups, with the whites owning most of the means of production. However, Bermuda has the third highest per capita income in the world, with no unemployment and no income tax, and Bermudians are full British citizens. They are responsible for their internal self-government, foreign affairs being overseen by the Governor, who represents the British monarch.

How do Bermudians feel about being identified as Caribbean people?

- Bermuda lies some 1600 km (1000 miles) north of the Lesser Antilles so that there is very little communication of any kind between those islands and the Caribbean.
- Bermudians continue their education in the US and Britain, much more so than other Caribbean people.
- The 1995 independence referendum indicated that 70 per cent of the voters were against independence.
- Joining CARICOM has been a heated national issue and at present Bermuda is only an Associate Member, for various reasons:
  - The main argument is that CARICOM cannot do much for a country that is already the third richest country in the world.

- There is fear that there will be a mass migration from those Caribbean countries struggling with poverty and scarce resources if full membership of CARICOM is sought, especially now that the CSME (CARICOM Single Market and Economy) is being implemented.
- Becoming a member of CARICOM may mean giving up colonial status.
- There is a minority opinion which views the issue in terms of race and ethnicity – Bermudians of Portuguese descent have strong ties with the Azores, and those of British descent maintain links with the mother country, but black Bermudians have no strong ties with Africa or even the Caribbean, where there are people with a similar history, culture and ethnic make-up

Identity and culture are indeed complex and contentious. Today we see the interplay of economic blocs and sanctions forcing closer ties with groups that were perhaps ignored in the past. For example, recently the US threatened to deny federal contracts to American companies locating in offshore havens. And CARICOM as a bloc has been able to garner foreign assistance in fighting crime, most significantly the drug and narcotics trade. Bermuda is not in control of its foreign policy and thus has to rely on the UK for assistance. What this points to – and there are those who hold this opinion in Bermuda – is that although Bermuda is enjoying prosperity and a high standard of living because of its ties to the UK and its importance as a tax haven for big corporations, that link may be precarious in this age of globalization, as shown recently by efforts to change US corporate law. To be mindful of the well-being of Bermudians in the future, it may make good sense to forge closer alliances of all kinds with the Caribbean.

ACTIVITY 1.1

Read over the previous section and look again at Fig. 1.1 in attempting the following exercise.

1. Identify FOUR countries shown on Fig.1.1 which are defined as part of the geographic Caribbean, but which are not widely accepted as 'Caribbean' by people in the region.

2. Suggest ONE reason to explain why the geographic definition of the Caribbean conflicts with popular perceptions.

Therefore there are some countries which have long been considered to be part of the Caribbean but are excluded if a strict *geographical* definition is applied. The opposite is also the case. There are some countries which are not widely accepted as 'Caribbean' although they are 'washed by the Caribbean Sea'. Activity 1.1 invites you to examine this issue.

Using the Caribbean Sea as the central organizing feature in distinguishing the Caribbean region is only partially successful, as we have seen in attempting to define and locate the Caribbean. Physical geography can only define and locate a space in terms of landforms and water bodies. Trying to delimit Caribbean society and culture using physical geography criteria results in obvious anomalies. For example, Guyana is considered to be Caribbean although it borders the Atlantic Ocean because the social and cultural experiences of its people are similar to those of the people of the islands in the Caribbean Sea.

The geographic concept of space derived from physical geography is that of a neutral expanse of land or sea delimited by physical features. Space is just a 'container' for the natural features of the Earth's surface. The way a people interpret their space and other people's space, the way they shape their space, and the way they feel about it are not the concerns of physical geography. If we define the Caribbean using the boundaries of physical geography, such as the Caribbean Basin, we thus define a different Caribbean than if we were using human geography. The latter takes into account the historical, social and cultural lives of peoples in a particular region and often the differences among them are used to define the limits of their territory.

Thus, countries such as Mexico, Honduras, Panama or Nicaragua may be perceived by West Indian peoples as belonging to the wider Latin American mainland, and not the Caribbean at all, even though they may have a coast on the Caribbean Sea. As a matter of fact, Mexicans may not regard themselves as belonging to the Caribbean, even though physical geography places them there. These are large countries, many with coasts also on the Pacific, so that to include them as Caribbean at all suggests that we have some way of saying where Caribbean begins and ends in these lands. Trying to apply strict physical limits to social and cultural perceptions leads us into this kind of predicament.

Interestingly, in recent times we have seen international agreements such as the Caribbean Basin Initiative (CBI) and regional organizations such as the Association of Caribbean States (ACS) include these countries as part of the 'Wider Caribbean' Region. It seems, then, that when outsiders view the region and when we who are inside need to assume a broad or holistic view, as in trade and economic cooperation initiatives, we adopt something closely resembling a geographic conception of the region. We therefore seem to hold different conceptions of the Caribbean at the same time and use them for different purposes! If geography is taken as playing a defining role for the Caribbean, then, it may well be that the interpretation of the Caribbean by international bodies (the Wider Caribbean) may emerge as a more accepted version of 'what is the Caribbean' in the future – accepted, that is, by the international community. Locally, there will always be differences of opinion.

Geological conceptions of the Caribbean: the Caribbean Plate

There is another conception of the Caribbean that is not widely known – the entity considered 'Caribbean' by geologists and seismologists. The defining feature here is the ***Caribbean Plate***, which has marked boundaries or margins where it meets other plates. A 'plate' is a subterranean feature that is part of the Earth's crust and on which land and oceans are found. Much of the Caribbean region lies on the Caribbean Plate, one of the smaller plates to be found on the Earth's crust. Its boundaries are shown on Fig. 1.2 and define the Caribbean Region in terms of tectonic activity. **Tectonic activity** refers to earth movements that impact and influence the surface of the Earth. Earthquakes, volcanic activity and mountain building are examples of tectonic activities that occur along plate margins as they move and interact with other plates. More detail is given on **plate tectonics** in Chapter 4.

You will notice on Fig. 1.2 that the western edge of the Caribbean Plate is in the Pacific Ocean. While the other margins of the plate may conform largely to traditional geographic conceptions of the Caribbean, this western edge alerts us to the fact that surface geography may well delude us as to what is happening at a subterranean level. Since earthquake, volcanic and mountain-building activities directly and indirectly impact human beings, and since these activities and processes are linked deep in the Earth's crust, we need to become more aware of the Caribbean as a geological entity.

While the Caribbean Plate is a significant entity on which to build our conception of a Caribbean region, it does not include Guyana, the Bahamas, and much of Cuba. Like geography then, geology alone cannot give us a comprehensive organizing framework to define the Caribbean.

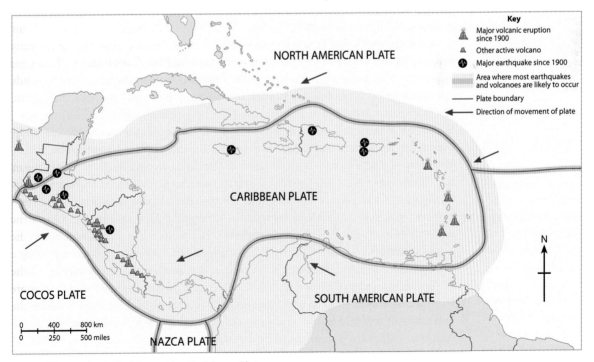

Fig. 1.2 The geologic Caribbean: the Caribbean Plate

Summary

From the geographic and geologic conceptions of the Caribbean we have emerging a picture of a 'Wider Caribbean Region' that is built on the natural, physical features of the Earth's crust. We have also seen that this view of the Caribbean is akin to that of contemporary global and regional organizations, and even that of the tourist. At the same time, people in the West Indies are somewhat reluctant to embrace only geography (the geological factor is largely unknown) in defining the Caribbean. They feel that geography is important but not as important as history.

1.2

THE HISTORICAL CARIBBEAN: THE COLONIAL CARIBBEAN EXPERIENCE

Defining and locating space only according to geography and geology does not acknowledge the importance of human activities and relationships in demarcating a region. The view of space inherent in physical geography and geology is virtually that of a container in which objects occur. Those who view history as the important dimension in locating the region choose to emphasize *how* people regard their space and *what* they regard as their space. For example, the following factors can transcend geographical barriers:

- long and continuous occupation over time
- a sense of belonging to a place
- the building of a way of life or culture.

Thus, although Barbados, Guyana and the Bahamas are located in the Atlantic Ocean, that is of minor importance because the historical processes that shaped these territories were similar, and in many ways identical, to those experienced on the islands of the Caribbean Sea.

These historical processes include occupation of the area by the indigenous peoples, European exploration and settlement, **genocide** and war waged against the indigenes, African slavery and Indian **indentureship**, **colonialism**, the development of the plantation economy and **plantation society**, independence, and the forging of a free society out of such experiences. One may well remark that the entire New World was subject to such developments. In fact, the whole area known as 'Latin America' (Central and South America and the Caribbean) had a very similar history. Yet today the Caribbean is considered to be separate and distinct from Central and South America. Only part of Central America is sometimes included in the Caribbean. If the history of the New World had so many similarities one must wonder why the countries developed so differently. Not only is the Caribbean different from Central and South America, but within the Caribbean there are marked variations as well. Activity 1.2 addresses this issue so that we are able to assess how historical criteria can be used to define and locate the Caribbean.

While history is concerned with describing and analysing significant events, trends and processes over time, it also examines how such phenomena are experienced differently in different locales and contexts. The entire sweep of Central and South America underwent the historical experiences mentioned above, but the Caribbean is considered a region apart largely because it reflects the legacy of a particular

ACTIVITY 1.2

1. Taking your country as an example, identify at least ONE factor or aspect that differentiates it from the historical experiences of Central or South America.

2. Explain why, even with a common history (and geography), Caribbean countries are marked by so much social and cultural diversity.

combination of European nations who were intruders into the original Spanish Main. While the heritage of the majority of Latin American countries is rooted in the Iberian Peninsula (Spain and Portugal), the countries of the Caribbean represent the varied legacies of Britain, France, Holland and Spain, and to a lesser extent, Denmark. Language embodies these cultural differences and presents the major distinguishing factor that delimits the Caribbean region within the Latin American region.

Using such an argument, the history and cultural heritage of Cuba and the Dominican Republic, and to a lesser extent Puerto Rico, ought to place them squarely with the mainland territories of Latin America. Geography locates them in the Caribbean but history links them to the Spanish-speaking countries of Central and South America. So, while language can be used to differentiate the countries of the Caribbean from the mainland territories of Central and South America, we must also know that exceptions occur. Just as in physical geography, where traditionally the Caribbean Sea has been used as a central unifying feature, one factor alone cannot be expected to locate and define the Caribbean. There are always anomalies and exceptions.

Notice that we are defining and delimiting regions based on the legacy of *Europeans*. Whether they are Spanish and Portuguese on the one hand, or British, French or Dutch on the other, the fact remains that in defining the Caribbean using historical criteria, the European influence looms larger than that of the indigenous peoples, or even those who were brought here later as enslaved and indentured labourers.

To address social and **cultural diversity** in the Caribbean, a region described as having a common history, we must first take a closer look at the West Indies and see how West Indians define and locate their space. In doing so, we again find cleavages along the lines of the European legacy. So, we can define and locate a *British* West Indies, a *French* West Indies, a *Dutch* West Indies (commonly called the Dutch Antilles) and the *Spanish*-speaking West Indies. Governance, trade and migration under colonialism occurred in the Caribbean as if geographical proximity did not exist and only the historical ties were important. Thus, the British islands and territories developed relationships with each other and Britain and had minimal involvement with nearby French, Dutch or Spanish islands and territories. Life under colonialism was such that the French and Spanish colonies also only developed deep cultural ties with their own **metropolitan countries**. Thus, culture largely embodied as language has proven to be an impenetrable barrier that defines and locates different 'Caribbeans'.

We see then that in the West Indies the historical and cultural ties which people acknowledge as more important than geography in defining their region are aligned mainly along the differences wrought by the European legacy – one of the most evident and immediate being language. If that is so, then it is hardly likely that people in the French, Dutch or British West Indies will readily include the people of Venezuela, Colombia and Central America as part of their region. How people perceive space and what they regard as theirs as opposed to others' space represents an important tension in how they receive attempts from outside to prescribe, locate and define their region.

For instance, in the deliberations of the CBI, the ACS and the FTAA (Free Trade Area of the Americas) and, as we mentioned before, in the tourist industry's perception of what constitutes the Caribbean, these cultural and linguistic differences are not recognized as significant enough to carve up the region. And to people outside the region, Mexico, Colombia and Panama appear to be a logical part of the Caribbean. To people inside the region, particularly the West Indies, it is quite another matter.

Summary

There is something of a consensus that history represents the best possible guide in defining the Caribbean. Even though there are many variations in historical and cultural experiences from one country to another, these variations stem largely from the influence of Europeans in the region and are significant in how Caribbean people define themselves today in relation to the region as a whole. The legacies of the British, French, Spanish, Dutch and Danes in the relatively small area of the Caribbean compared to the overwhelming presence of the Spanish and Portuguese in Central and South America probably goes furthest in trying to delimit the Caribbean from its Latin American counterparts.

1.3 THE POLITICAL CARIBBEAN: THE 'MANY CARIBBEANS'

At present the political entities comprising the Caribbean are diverse and show varying stages in achieving political autonomy from the colonial powers that were once dominant in the region. The Caribbean as a single political entity is as yet only an ideal raised by Caribbean visionaries, statesmen and those deeply involved in the integration movement. The notion of a Caribbean citizen or CARICOM citizen, often heard in rhetoric, is really a cultural yearning rather than any indication of present political reality.

Citizenship in the Caribbean today represents a varied set of relationships between citizens and their governments, *and* sometimes with governments outside the region. This diversity in political arrangements, even within CARICOM, stands in marked contrast to the political entities of Central and South America, the majority of which have had a long history of being independent, of being republics, with a succession of dictators, and struggles with democratic rule. While the Caribbean has not been entirely free of dictatorships, revolution, armed interventions and *coups d'état*, these have been limited in impact and generally the region as a whole has been politically stable. In the Latin American region, then, the Caribbean can be defined by its diverse and complex political relationships.

Many Caribbean countries are now politically independent, favouring different forms of governance. For example, Cuba is a communist country while Guyana has opted for republic status based on socialist principles. Both **communism** and **socialism** are theories of governance and society. They advocate public ownership of the means of production. Socialism is regarded in **Marxist** thought as a stage preceding that of communism. The former emphasizes distribution of resources based on one's abilities and deeds, and the latter, more utopian, is based on distribution according to needs.

The official name of Guyana (formerly British Guiana) is the Cooperative Republic of Guyana and its **constitution** is based on a socialist transformation of the institutions of the country. The principle of *cooperativism* through which this will be accomplished envisages members of the society eventually owning and sharing in the means of production. This socialist orientation has in the past incurred the disapproval of the US and there have been intrigues and political interference in order to destabilize the regime. This has also been the experience of the communist state of Cuba.

Haiti was the first country in the Caribbean to achieve independence through revolution in 1804, described since then as the Black Republic. A **republic** is a form of governance where the head of state is not a monarch but a president. Some countries, though, have preferred to retain stronger ties with the metropolitan country, for example Barbados: although independent, and a **parliamentary democracy**, it still has the British sovereign as the official head of state.

It is important to mention here that the countries of the English-speaking Caribbean have long been members of the **Commonwealth** – a worldwide group of territories that were once part of the British Empire. All are independent but continue to recognize the British monarch as the head of state (represented by a Governor General). In the English-speaking Caribbean, only Trinidad and Tobago, Guyana and the Commonwealth of Dominica are republics, where the head of state is a president, but they continue to be members of the Commonwealth.

Curaçao, Bonaire, Saba, Sint Eustatius and Sint Maarten are five *self-governing* territories of the Dutch Antilles. (It is interesting to note that Sint Maarten occupies only part of an island; St Martin, a French territory, occupies the other part.) Aruba has a different arrangement with the Kingdom of the Netherlands from the other five islands, but they are all associated with the Netherlands and their foreign policy and matters of defence are controlled by the government of the Netherlands. They are thus *colonies* of the Netherlands. The Dutch monarch is head of state and represented by a governor. The Republic of Suriname, once a part of the Kingdom of the Netherlands, is today a fully independent state.

Britain too has colonies in the Caribbean. For example, Anguilla, the British Virgin Islands, Montserrat, the Turks and Caicos Islands, the Cayman Islands and Bermuda are still colonies of Britain. In contrast, the French Caribbean territories are not colonies at all, but an integral part of the operations of France. Cayenne (formerly known as French Guiana), Guadeloupe, Martinique, and the smaller French islands, all belong to a *département* of France, meaning that they function *as if they are a part of France*. St Martin, occupying only half an island, is administered through Guadeloupe. Guadeloupe itself is an archipelago including the islands of Marie Galante, La Désirade, and Îles des Saintes. They all belong to the *Département d'Outre-Mer* (DOM or overseas *departement*).

The 'many Caribbeans' arise from this diversity in political arrangements today. This diversity has a historical basis for it is bound up in European **colonization** and the efforts by Caribbean people to either garner their independence or to develop viable relationships with the 'mother country' for growth and development. Activity 1.3 helps you to continue to explore political diversity in the Caribbean.

ACTIVITY 1.3

Table 1.1 shows some Caribbean countries in one column and a range of political statuses in the other. Match each country with its present political status.

Table 1.1 Diverse political arrangements in the Caribbean

	COUNTRY		POLITICAL STATUS
1	Belize	A	A federation
2	Anguilla	B	An Associated State of the US
3	Puerto Rico	C	An independent country
4	Dominican Republic	D	A British Overseas Territory
5	St Barth's	E	Part of an independent state, the other members being Petit Martinique and Grenada
6	Barbuda	F	Administered through St Martin
7	Carriacou	G	Member of a multi-island independent state
8	Montserrat	H	Seceded from a three-member Associated State to regain colonial status
9	St Kitts–Nevis	I	An independent state that does not recognize a monarch as head of state
10	Bequia	J	Part of a twin-island state

Citizenship

The section above called attention to the diversity of political forms in the Caribbean. Of the independent countries, some are republics and some constitutional democracies with the British or Dutch monarch still as head of state. There is also an array of dependencies, colonies, crown colonies, internal self-governing countries, associated states and *departements*. This diversity is significant not only because it differentiates the Caribbean as a distinctive region within Latin America, but also because it has implications for citizenship. Clearly what it means to be a Caribbean citizen in a dependency or a *departement* will vary considerably from what it means to be a citizen in an independent country. Box 1.1 presented the case of Bermuda, a British colony, and we will now go on to further explore how citizenship varies in the 'many Caribbeans'.

The term *colony* describes a territory owned and administered by a metropolitan country, historically designated the mother country. However, colonies differ according to how much autonomy or freedom they have in controlling their affairs. In a colony all the laws, regulations and procedures must be in accordance with those of the metropolitan country. Even if it is self-governing, its laws cannot run counter to those of the colonizer. In the colonies mentioned above the people are automatically British or Dutch citizens. However, as we saw in the case of Bermuda (Box 1.1), while this may be considered advantageous at present, there is no guarantee that such a relationship will continue.

To be a citizen in a colony often means that there is constant tension and on-going debate about continuing in a historically dependent relationship with a European country. Since many independent Caribbean countries are struggling with poverty, crime and unemployment, the protective link with Europe seems advantageous and so there is an ambivalence about seeking independence and joining CARICOM. At the same time, citizens are well aware that conditions change and that the European metropolitan countries may experience ultimatums within the European Union (EU) that might force them to abandon their colonies. Citizenship in these countries then is hotly debated, with the fate of political parties depending on their stance on this issue.

While the term *dependency* is generally used for a colony, it is sometimes reserved specifically for a colony where all economic and political activities are controlled through the metropolitan country. The economic condition of the colony is usually the deciding factor in whether it is spoken of as a dependency or not. A dependency is not considered to be economically viable on its own and can only survive through substantial grants from the **metropole**. For example, the Turks and Caicos Islands are a British colony, sometimes described as a dependency. Officially, the Turks and Caicos, the Cayman Islands, the British Virgin Islands (BVI) and Montserrat are all **crown colonies** of Britain. They are not all dependencies as some have flourishing tourist and offshore industries (especially the Caymans and the BVI) and need less overseas development aid than, say, the Turks and Caicos. However, crown colony status means that there is limited internal self-government and defence, foreign affairs, internal security, and various financial and administrative matters are controlled by Britain. The people are British citizens.

Note though that Anguilla is a fully self-governing territory, described as an *associated state* of Britain (Box 1.2) and that Bermuda, because of its long history as a colony and its economic prosperity, enjoys more autonomy than the other territories. This array of terms describing stages on the road to self-government and full independence may be confusing, especially when the same term, for example 'crown colony', does not mean exactly the same thing each time it is applied. Thus, the Turks and Caicos, the Caymans, the BVI and Montserrat are not governed in exactly the same way. There are variations because each country's governance system evolved differently according to historical circumstances. Recently the UK announced that the term *British Overseas Territory* should be used for all its dependent territories.

The Commonwealth of Puerto Rico is a *free state in association* with the United States of America. It is not fully independent and is described by the US as an *unincorporated territory* of the US, like the US Virgin Islands. It has internal self-government and is a 'free' state in that it has a legal identity in international law. (Compare this with a colony, which is considered to be part of the territory of the metropolitan country, and thus not 'free'.) Puerto Ricans and US Virgin Islanders are citizens of the US but they cannot vote in US elections. However, they do not pay taxes to the US government and receive unique access and facilities denied citizens of other countries. Foreign affairs are under the control of the US.

As elsewhere in the Caribbean, citizenship is hotly contested. Perhaps it is stronger in Puerto Rico, which is a large territory with strong nationalist sentiment and enjoying more autonomy than a colony. The debate concerns the relative advantages and disadvantages of (1) remaining as an Associated State of the US or (2) pressing for complete statehood within the US, or (3) seeking independence. The US is a major superpower and 'owning' Caribbean territory gives it certain geopolitical or strategic advantages, which it would not easily relinquish. Citizenship in Puerto Rico will continue to be a contentious issue, perhaps less so in the US Virgin Islands.

The French Caribbean is unique in that its territories all belong to an overseas *departement* of France (Box 1.3). The French possessions in the Caribbean are not colonies;

association with Europe and later on with the US. Their status, such as dependency or *departement*, describes different theories about colonialism (Box 1.3). Even the countries that are independent today embody a colonial relationship. Many were granted **independence** at a time when it was increasingly inconvenient for Britain to bring its sugar-producing colonies with it when it entered the Common Market and, later, the European Economic Community. Today, its deepening relationships within the European Union put all its dependent territories in the Caribbean in an ambivalent position. It is interesting to note that in the independent countries of the Caribbean citizenship is as contentious an issue as in colonies and *departements* struggling for and against the idea of independence.

Britain next formed the *Windward and Leeward Islands Associated States*. Associated statehood involved developing *full internal self-government,* while Britain retained control of defence and external affairs. By 1967 the unit of St Kitts, Nevis and Anguilla was undergoing the transition to associated statehood with Britain. However, Anguillans voiced increasing discontent about the close ties with St Kitts. They knew that in the arrangements being made for associated statehood and then independence they would be controlled by St Kitts. By 1969, through much political unrest and violent uprisings, it was quite clear that Anguilla was seceding from the union. They held a **referendum** to decide on independence. At this time, Anguilla was not only locked in conflict with St Kitts, which opposed its secession, but also with Britain, who did not want a colony back on its hands. In defiance at one point Anguilla declared itself a republic. Eventually, through the intervention of the United Nations, good sense prevailed and the British government toned down its position. In 1980 Anguilla officially reverted to being a colony (an associated state, this time) of Britain. In 1983 St Kitts and Nevis became an *independent federation*, provision being made in its constitution for Nevis to secede if it wished to do so in the future. Recently, a referendum in Nevis to decide on seceding from the union was only narrowly defeated.

The British model of colonization emphasized the inculcation of British culture and then graduating the colony to independence through a series of stages. Often overlooked is the fact that there was no deep-seated thrust towards helping the territories to develop shared partnerships large enough to put them on a better footing with other nations of the world. The unions and associations that were tried by Britain were merely expedient solutions, not very mindful of the cultural differences between the colonies or their fear of being dominated by larger partners.

The many abortive attempts at union attest to this failure.

In trying to understand the political Caribbean and citizenship issues in the English- speaking territories today, we need to be look more closely at the ideas underlying British colonization. Spreading British culture across the globe was its major goal. At the same time there was a clear understanding that 'natives' (e.g. West Indians) *could not become Britons*. While Britain was prepared to teach us its customs and ways of life, helping us to develop in the image of the 'mother country', there was a line that kept us apart. We see this, for example, in how citizenship was granted and how colonies were graduated into independent existence.

British citizenship was a temporary thing granted only until the colony was graduated to independent status. For example, Montserratians are British citizens today but they are not Britons – and they can never become Britons; they remain Montserratians even though they have British citizenship. But they could become independent, if they so choose. Thus, the process of 'graduation' is really one of becoming more entrenched in a British way of life, until the ultimate is reached when one can become independent of the mother country. Where very small colonies are concerned, the normal course can only occur if various unions and associations are found acceptable. And, as we have seen, Britain has tried to force unions on us in the past, many of which have collapsed. Continuing to maintain and govern small dependent territories indefinitely is contrary to the British conception of colonization.

Compared to the French Antilles then, the English-speaking territories today display much variation in status and labels. Independence marked the culmination of a long process of **acculturation** into British values and customs. Of interest to us is that having gone through this process, we were not considered eligible to be British, but rather were graduated into independence. In Box 1.3 we look at the quite different approach the French took to colonization.

BOX 1.3 French colonialism in the Caribbean

Compared to the British (Box 1.2), the French had quite different ideas about colonial rule. Each, however, was concerned with the supremacy of its own culture in civilizing people and lands won through empire-building. The British felt that although such people could never become Britons, they could come to appreciate British culture and institutions through a long process of acculturation. Thus, in the British philosophy of colonialism these lands and nations would be graduated through a series of stages, showing that they were becoming increasingly competent to govern themselves. Implicit in this is the assumption that British culture is so pre-eminent and incomparable, and that whilst others could benefit by prolonged interaction with its customs and institutions, they could never truly become Britons.

While the French position is quite different, they are both 'supremacist' positions and represent different theories of colonization. The French are of the opinion that they have developed a *civilization* that is unique. Through immersion in its way of life anybody anywhere can not only develop an appreciation of it or be able to practise it, but they can *become French*. The French colonial mission was to civilize the world through a philosophy of cultural **assimilation**. Thus we see in the Caribbean that the French territories are literally that; they belong to an overseas *departement* of France. (A *departement* is a unit of local government similar to a county or parish.) The territories of Cayenne, Guadeloupe, Marie Galante, Îles des Saintes, La Désirade, Martinique, St Martin and St Barth's *are France*. All the people are French citizens without any qualification of being 'overseas citizens'. As a result they are 'ultra-peripheral' regions of the European Union. They have the right to vote in national elections. There are no restrictions on travel and many have migrated to France. Many native, white French people have also migrated from France to live in Martinique and Guadeloupe. Within a business or government department one can be transferred from Marseilles to Basseterre and vice versa.

The *independence movement* is small but at times such sentiments run high. French Caribbean citizens enjoy the economic advantages and opportunities that stem from being a part of France. Yet it rankles that Martinique or Guadeloupe is not recognized as an identifiable country with its own customs and ways of life that are quite distinct from those of France. There is no official flag, for instance. As far as France is concerned, Martinique does not exist – what is important is France. Compare the position in the British Overseas Territories, where the colonies *are* recognized as separate entities and the citizens can never become Britons!

Of serious concern too is the racism French Caribbean people experience in France. Officially policies stress equality but in reality migrants from the Caribbean and elsewhere report racial undertones. France has long been receiving migrants from its Caribbean territories, so that today there is a huge Caribbean population. The resulting problems between host and migrants occur in a similar manner to that of Puerto Ricans in New York and Jamaicans in Liverpool, attesting to the hollowness of French claims that French Caribbean people are equal to the native French population in all respects. This conflictual notion of citizenship within a colonial relationship that purports not to be colonial, that is shaped by ethnicity but is said to be colour blind, is probably the strongest argument for those groups seeking independence.

'The Wider Caribbean'

Even though there are many 'Caribbeans', there are continuing efforts to demarcate a *Wider Caribbean Region*. Mentioned before are the CBI, the FTAA and the ACS, which are largely economic responses to a **globalized** world well on the way to integration in huge alliances and blocs. Examples include the South American Common Market (Mercosur), the Latin American Free Trade Association (LAFTA), and the European Union (EU). Having had a chequered history, the *Caribbean Community (CARICOM)* now encompasses the independent English–speaking countries of the Caribbean as well as Haiti, Suriname and the Netherlands Antilles.

Interestingly, the *Organization of Eastern Caribbean States (OECS),* founded in 1981, and comprising both independent (Antigua and Barbuda, Dominica, Grenada,

St Kitts–Nevis, St Lucia, St Vincent and the Grenadines), and dependent countries (Montserrat, Anguilla and the British Virgin Islands), has led the way in establishing elements of functional cooperation between the different countries of the Eastern Caribbean. Their goal is to create a single economic space.

The economic pressures which globalization is bringing to the region should induce Caribbean countries to find a rationale for transcending the geographic, historic and political differences that have divided them in the past. Although a political entity called 'the Caribbean' may be a long way ahead, economic cooperation could change the configuration of the Caribbean in the not too distant future. In fact, the image of the Caribbean that is beginning to prevail, emanating from international agreements on trade and economic cooperation, is one of a Wider Caribbean Region.

Summary

The issue of citizenship in the Caribbean is an explosive one and experiences vary markedly from the Caribbean person born in Martinique who is French to the Puerto Rican who is a US citizen but cannot vote in US elections to British Overseas Citizens who are regarded quite differently from British citizens. History looms large in how political arrangements and citizenship were constructed across the Caribbean. This variety of independent, self-governing and associated states, colonies, and dependent territories, existing as republics, parliamentary democracies, federations, and even as an administrative department of a European country, or a communist enclave, attest to the fact that the 'political Caribbean' is a diverse entity. This is not surprising considering the impact of the many different European colonizers in the region and the varied responses of Caribbean people in trying to attain their independence − through revolution, negotiations with the colonizer, regionalism, and on-going dialogue and protest. History then provides a rationale for defining the Caribbean as a region that is difficult to dispute.

1.4

CARIBBEAN IDENTITY AND CULTURE: EXPLORING THE BASES OF IDENTITY

In the previous section we discussed the 'many Caribbeans' largely in terms of the varied legacies of Europe in the Caribbean. In this section on Caribbean **identity** and culture, the 'many Caribbeans' continue to be relevant. Many people say that the Caribbean is an extremely diverse region, and from our understanding of the legacies of Europe in the Caribbean, we find no hesitation in agreeing. To speak of a Caribbean identity against this background of diversity is an extremely complex undertaking, and some say that it may even be a figment of the imagination. At the same time, there is an equally strong view that although the Caribbean is a region of marked diversity, there is much that is common, leading to the existence of a 'culture sphere'. In this section we want to explore these ideas as we try to flesh out our understanding of Caribbean identity and culture.

A good way to start is with ourselves. How do we, as individuals, identify with the space where we live? Two views about how people form their identity with a place are given below and Activity 1.4 calls on you to reflect on your own thinking about who you are in the world. There are no right or wrong answers.

ACTIVITY 1.4

Two views describing how a person may form his or her Caribbean identity are given opposite.

1. Critically analyse each view and assess how close it comes to your own understanding of yourself as a Caribbean person.

2. Suggest ideas that you think are relevant in forming an identity that may have been omitted in the two views reported.

3. Draw a labelled diagram that portrays how you think your identity as a Caribbean person was formed and is continuing to be formed.

A. In constructing our identities as Caribbean people we emphasize (for some individuals this may mean excluding all others) our own nation-state first. This we strongly identify with, and moving outwards with somewhat less intensity we then identify with those Caribbean territories that are nearest to us and where our own language is spoken. Still moving outwards, we may then recognize other territories, such as the French or Dutch Caribbean, as part of what we identify as our region or the wider Caribbean region. If we are an English-speaking country which had a long French presence in the past, it is quite likely that we will feel an affinity with the French-speaking Caribbean before that of the Dutch or the Spanish. We may feel the least sense of belongingness with those countries on the periphery of the region, the Spanish mainland territories.

B. People develop a sense of place as they grow up in a particular locality. They identify with their immediate environs – their village or town – and the region around. They develop relationships to these places and people with whom they share a culture. These relationships are really connections, grounded in that place, to other people and other places, and describe how a person is socially located. For example, a person of Maroon descent in Jamaica today identifies with Jamaica and the Caribbean in ways that differ from someone in mainstream Jamaican society. He or she may feel more strongly rooted in Jamaica because of how his or her ancestors forged a lifestyle in defiance of the colonial overlords and won recognition by treaty to their lands. So that, within Jamaica there are different Caribbean identities depending on connections and relationships.

The first view suggests that because there are so many 'Caribbeans' confronting people, they are forced to construct their identity based on what is close and familiar first and then move outward. Thus, to make sense of the 'many Caribbeans' we as human beings need to focus on what is common and with which we readily identify in order to develop a sense of solidarity, loyalty and belongingness.

The second view seems similar to the first. It also refers to ways of building a sense of identity beginning with what is close and familiar and then moving outwards. However, it challenges the idea that in building a Caribbean identity we begin with a well-developed sense of the complexity of the region. For example, do we make decisions about our own sense of identity based on historical knowledge and the existence of the Dutch, Spanish and French 'Caribbeans'? Do we necessarily identify with the labels that have been assigned to us – for example, our **nationality** – as our identity? We saw in the previous section that a Caribbean person from the island of Martinique may not identify with France at all, despite being a French citizen, but with his or her Caribbean heritage. Similarly, an Amerindian growing up in the interior of Guyana may primarily identify with his or her own **ethnic group** rather than with Guyana. A *nation-state* is something that has been declared – it has political reality. For people, other realities and issues may be closer and more immediate and influence their sense of identity.

The discussion so far is leaning towards the notion that developing an identity with a place is perhaps more strongly influenced by the *relationships* and *connections* that you have learned about yourself and the people around you, rather than your nationality. This suggests that **ethnicity** looms large in developing an identity. 'Ethnicity' refers to your membership in cultural groups such as racial, religious, language, gender, and even national groups. You can be described in terms of your

ACTIVITY 1.5

This is a private reflective exercise.

1. List all the ethnic groups to which you belong. Which ethnic group seems to be the most significant in identifying how *you see yourself* in the world?

2. Is there more than one type of ethnicity that you believe important in describing or explaining how you see yourself at this time? Identify those ethnic groups that seem to be most important in shaping your identity.

ACTIVITY 1.6

This can be done as a class exercise or project.

1. Select a few persons from various walks of life – a fellow student, a housewife, a blue-collar and a white-collar worker, among others. Ask them the following question: 'If you had to describe your identity as a Caribbean person, what is ONE thing that you would stress?'

2. Summarize the main points and compare with the findings of class members.

3. Using all the data from class members, list the major perceptions on the issue. Also compile a list of minority opinions.

4. Critically analyse in class discussion what Caribbean people seem to understand about their Caribbean identity.

ethnicity. However, each may exert a different 'pull' on you in terms of how *you* would want to be described. Activity 1.5 continues to probe this aspect of how your identity may be constructed.

Trying to sort out how membership in different ethnic groups shapes the identity of others is also difficult. Think of the Maya in Belize, the whites of Cuba and Martinique, the mulattoes of the Dominican Republic, the Rastafari of Jamaica, the Indians of Trinidad, the Carib community of Dominica, the Amerindians of Guyana, and the Bush Negroes of Suriname. Smaller but still significant communities are the Javanese in Suriname, the Portuguese in Guyana, the Chinese in Trinidad and Jamaica, and the Garifuna in Belize. In each case, ethnicity is very complex because of membership in a myriad of ethnic groups. For example, in Dominica the Caribs *are also* Dominicans and they may be Roman Catholic. How each Carib person constructs his or her sense of identity may or may not emphasize Carib heritage.

So far we have been exploring the bases of identity formation. We sought explanations in terms of ethnicity, which covers a wide range of identities, even one's nationality. However, we have not yet adequately tackled the question of *Caribbean* in the formation of our identity. While we understand what we identify with and whom we identify with in terms of our own ethnicities, the discussion has been at a personal and local level. How do we make the leap towards our *Caribbean* identity? Activity 1.6 begins to focus on this issue.

The findings of Activity 1.6 should provide interesting background to keep in mind as we continue to explore the term 'Caribbean identity'. Let us return to the ethnicity factor. Consider the point of view that ethnicity of any kind (e.g. race, religion, language and so on) has a dimension to it that is not only a personal or a shared group experience limited to one's region or territory, *but could be part of a Caribbean-wide experience*. For example, is a Jamaican Rastafari or Maroon wholly a product of being born and bred in Jamaica? Is there a way in which we can discuss such a person as having a *Caribbean* identity? To begin to think of the Rastafari or any of the ethnic groups that were mentioned before, we need to go back to *origins*. All the people of the Caribbean are **transplanted peoples,** the exception being the Amerindians. This is one commonality, whether the Europeans who initiated the transplanting were Dutch or French. One common identifier throughout the Caribbean, then, is that we have a 'homeland' in another place.

The diversity then could be said to begin here, in that once transplanted we developed differently in our different situations. So, from a common experience of *European colonization* we developed institutions, languages, political systems and customs that reflected those of a *specific* colonizer. However, there continued to be commonalities. For example, African slavery was a common denominator whether it was experienced in Haiti, which threw it off as early as 1804, or in the British colonies where it was abolished in 1834 or in the Spanish territories where it persisted till 1888. The Europeans' need for labour also explains the presence of a diverse assortment of people in the Caribbean – Africans, Indians, Chinese, Portuguese, Madeirans, Javanese, and even Europeans also came as labourers. Thus, the presence of various ethnicities in the Caribbean has a common root cause – these groups were brought here originally for a specific purpose. Even the Amerindians were not spared as they too were forced into the production machine of the Europeans. Since then the fortunes of all these groups may have developed differently but the circumstances of their origins bind them together in an experience that is distinctly 'Caribbean'.

The responses by Caribbean people to slavery, **indentureship** and colonialism were very similar. *Resistance, rebellion, revolution, resilience* and *independence* were in evidence throughout the region. **Syncretism,** *adaptation* and **hybrid forms** were created as various cultures met and clashed. We see this today in languages, **religions**, education, politics, fashion and, among other things, cultural expressions such as art, craft, literature, music and dance. **Cultural erasure, cultural retention** and **cultural renewal** were experiences of all Caribbean people as they tried (and are still trying) to work out vexing questions of identity and culture (these concepts are discussed in Chapter 3). For example, a part of your Caribbean identity, whether you are an Indian in Guyana or a Rastafari in Jamaica, is the problematic relationship that you have developed with your *original culture and homeland*. Whether you value it and continue to make links with it in a public and visual way, or whether you don't think much about it, describes how you have chosen to deal with a challenging issue of Caribbean identity. The debates that arise in Caribbean countries about an ethnic group being more loyal to a foreign country than their Caribbean country of citizenship are outcomes of a colonial condition that goes back to the original purposes of bringing people here from all over the world.

Experiences that are Caribbean-wide, even though they played out differently in different countries, foster a Caribbean identity and culture. We all belong to a region where the great shapers of who we are were the processes of transplantation, forced labour and colonialism. We did not just acquiesce but resisted and applied resilient strategies. A *culture of overcoming* is part of out identity and culture. For example, the strong *migration ethic* in the Caribbean is a strategy for bettering our chances, something that preoccupied our forebears. The Caribbean people of the **diaspora** have a strong sense of this culture of overcoming. They know that they are not American, Canadian or British. Understanding their origins leads to high aspirations for success and they often take advantage of the opportunities abroad to excel in education, sports, culture, health and business. For generations of Caribbean people, migration has meant an opportunity to achieve **social mobility**.

Summary

In this section we have explored the bases of how our Caribbean identity is constructed. We have looked at how our own identities developed through our location in a specific place and the relationships and connections we made, such as our membership in different ethnic groups. We have seen, however, that these relationships and connections were not something unique to us. Other people in the Caribbean were also engaged in doing the same thing. In each case these relationships and connections resulted from the common purposes and conditions that placed us in this region in the first place. Thus, as we were growing up and developing a sense of who we are (our identity), *we were also developing our Caribbean identity*. For some people the immense diversity in the Caribbean overshadows what is common. We have seen, though, that common origins and purposes are at the root of diverse responses. Thus, diversity results from specific differences in contexts and conditions, not any deep-seated divergence that makes it possible to say that there is nothing like a Caribbean identity, that it is merely a figment of some people's imagination. In summing up Caribbean identity and culture, then, we acknowledge the area as a culture sphere where a great deal of the manifest difference is but a complex working out of common themes – origins, purposes and processes.

WRAP UP

The chapter has presented an analysis of the location of the Caribbean region showing that 'location' changes according to the criteria used. A geographical concept of the Caribbean, for example, differs from that of a historical or geological understanding. The political Caribbean is a fragmented reality where a great many political models and varying understandings of citizenship co-exist. The geographical, geological, historical and political Caribbeans each paint a picture of immense diversity. It is easy, therefore, to be sceptical about claims for the existence of something called Caribbean identity and culture. However, if we view the region as a culture sphere where the descendents of transported peoples are developing ways of life to assist them in overcoming the conditions of their origins, we can discern common patterns and themes.

PRACTICE TESTS

Fig. 1.3

Mapwork

1 On the blank map of the Caribbean region provided (Fig. 1.3), locate the following:
   (a) water bodies – the Caribbean Sea, the Gulf of Mexico, the Pacific Ocean
   (b) territories – Belize, Bahamas, Barbados
   (c) the isthmus of Panama.
2 On the blank map of the Eastern Caribbean provided (Fig. 1.4):
   (a) locate the subregions of the Leeward and Windward Islands
   (b) draw in the eastern margin of the Caribbean Plate
   (c) identify the islands of Antigua and Barbuda
   (d) locate the Atlantic Ocean.

Fig. 1.4

Photograph recognition

The following photographs (Figs 1.5–1.8) were taken in certain Caribbean countries. Identify each country – some clues are given in the captions.

Fig. 1.5 These people belong to an indigenous cultural group

Fig. 1.6 River rafting is a growing tourist activity

Fig. 1.7 A remote but famous waterfall

Fig. 1.8 Goat racing

Structured response

1   Describe TWO ways in which an area such as the Caribbean region can be geographically located. (4 marks)
2   List FOUR geographical subregions of the Caribbean. (4 marks)
3   Explain what is meant by each of the following:
   (a) geological definition of the Caribbean region
   (b) historical definition of the Caribbean region. (4 marks)
4   Identify TWO forces that are influencing the Caribbean which are urging a definition of the Caribbean as the 'Wider Caribbean' region. (4 marks)
5   For an identified Caribbean country, examine THREE ways in which its sense of Caribbean identity has been constructed. (9 marks)

Essay questions (20 marks)

1   Explain what criteria you would use in defining and locating the Caribbean.
2   Describe what is meant by having 'a Caribbean identity' and show how that varies from place to place within the Caribbean.
3   Identify the geographical factors that may make it difficult for Caribbean people to develop a shared sense of identity.
4   Distinguish between the different political forms found within the *British* Caribbean.

Challenge essay questions (30 marks)

1   Examine the extent to which one can speak of 'Caribbean culture and identity'.
2   Account for the conflicting conceptions of a place called 'the Caribbean'.
3   Discuss the differing philosophies of colonialism of the British and French.
4   For a country such as Belize, examine the factors that facilitate and those that discourage the building of a sense of Caribbean identity.

RESEARCH TOPICS

Conducting well-conceptualized research is a necessary skill for students pursuing Caribbean Studies. Each chapter in this text explores some ideas for deepening the issues discussed by outlining possible research projects that you might want to take up. The following is suggested as a research topic based on the theme of the mass media but emphasizing ideas related to locating and defining the Caribbean.

Conceptions of the Caribbean region in the mass media

(a)   An interesting exercise you may carry out that could develop into a research project is to survey any form of the mass media that is available to you to describe and analyse what is presented as 'Caribbean' news or images. For example, it may be easiest to take a national newspaper and count the number of stories on the Caribbean that appear over a certain period, categorize the type of story, analyse the images, and present such information using bar graphs, pie charts or tables. Your findings should give a good portrayal of 'the Caribbean' from that media source. You may want to compare different newspapers or even different media as you deepen the inquiry.

(b)   Another way of deepening the exercise is to research the news that is occurring over the entire Caribbean, especially in countries that do not seem to appear very much in your initial survey, and suggest why such news is not considered newsworthy for your national media. Consider the implications of such a practice in your country.

(c)   To balance the inquiry, if possible, you can interview media people to find out their perspectives on which Caribbean countries are reported on and which are not. If you do not have access to media persons, you may ask the people around you about how they feel about the extent of news coverage given to the Caribbean, and consider the implications of what they have to say.

REFERENCES

Brereton, B. (Ed.) (2004). *General history of the Caribbean, Volume 5: The Caribbean in the twentieth century.* Paris: UNESCO and London: Macmillan Caribbean.

Brereton, B., & Yelvington, K. (Eds) (1999). *The colonial Caribbean in transition.* Mona, Jamaica: UWI Press.

Honychurch, L. (1995). Caribs, creoles and the concepts of territory: the boundary between France and Dominica. *Caribbean Geography*, 6(1), pp. 61–70.

Nettleford, R. (1978). *Caribbean cultural identity.* Kingston, Jamaica: Institute of Jamaica.

Palacio, J. (1995). Aboriginal peoples: their struggle with cultural identity in the CARICOM region. *Bulletin of Eastern Caribbean Affairs*, 20 (4), pp. 25–40.

Society is everything about a people and that includes their culture.

You can talk about a society, yes, but you must realize that there will not be one culture. There are many cultures in a society.

Society and culture are one and the same you cannot separate them. It makes more sense to talk of the socio-cultural.

What about Caribbean people throughout the world, in the diaspora? Do they not belong to Caribbean society? Are they not part of Caribbean culture? Are they included in conventional definitions?

Look at Caribbean society – how many cultures are involved? Do we unify them and speak of them *all* as Caribbean culture? How can we justify this?

2

UNDERSTANDING SOCIETY AND CULTURE

'Society' and 'culture' are terms in everyday use and many of us believe that we understand them correctly. A quick way of verifying this is to reflect on whether we do indeed know the difference between the two. In this chapter you will not only learn conventional definitions of society and culture, some of which you may know already, but we will move beyond that to question what definitions say about society and culture. Definitions are popular, shorthand ways of *re-presenting* knowledge which, instead of clarifying meaning may obscure it, especially in the social sciences. 'The social' is a concept that is introduced in this chapter, which attempts to portray the variety and variability of the ways in which people interact and make meaning of their experiences. Understanding 'the social' will help you in approaching conventional definitions of society and culture in a critical light.

EXPECTED LEARNING OUTCOMES

On completing this chapter, you will be able to

1 evaluate typical definitions of society and culture
2 describe the relationship between knowledge in the social and natural sciences
3 explain how knowledge of 'the social' deepens an understanding of society and culture
4 analyse the relationship between society and culture
5 appreciate the role of the individual in the development of society and culture
6 discuss different portrayals of Caribbean 'society' and 'culture'.

2.1

THE SOCIAL

In attempting a deep understanding of society and culture, 'the social' is a concept that becomes all-important. It is *the totality of explanations describing how people interact and make meanings of their experiences.* It has no existence in itself – what we call 'the social' is a **construct** that we create and use to represent all the many ways through which people make meaning in their lives. A 'construct' is a label given to some idea or way of thinking that people use in order to better explain and describe social life. If we take this as our starting point in understanding *society* and *culture,* we will have to begin with the complexity, variability and uncertainty that characterize the social world. If we start at any other point – for example, a definition – we will most likely obscure meaning, as definitions tend to 'tidy up' reality. Thus, our study of society and culture will not begin with conventional definitions; it will begin with a study of 'the social' so that later we can see the definitions in a more critical light.

'The totality of explanations describing how people interact and make meanings of their experiences' includes:

- the variety of perspectives and explanations people have for the same phenomena
- the tendency to prefer order and precision and to feel safer when definitions are used.

Explaining 'the social': definitions

Certain knowledge

A starting point for the study of any subject invariably begins with a *definition* – a concise description of some phenomenon where enough information is given to clarify what it is and at the same time to distinguish it from something else. For example, 'a depression is a low-pressure system where winds are in-blowing' says what a depression is and what it is not – it is not a high-pressure system and its winds do not blow outwards. We can draw on other examples from the natural and physical sciences to begin a general discussion about the problematic nature of definitions:

- ***osmosis*** – the diffusion of fluids through a semi-permeable membrane from a less concentrated solution to that of a higher concentration until there is equal solute concentration on both sides of the membrane.
- ***oxidation*** – the process by which a mineral combines with oxygen, loses electrons, and reduces to form oxides.

In the above examples, ambiguity is reduced to a minimum and explanations are given as precisely as possible. This means that the terms used are clear and have precise technical meanings that do not overlap. Each component can be defined exactly. Many people accept such knowledge as *uncontested,* especially those who regard the findings of scientific research as dependable and verifiable. This way of characterizing knowledge – as clear, precise and unambiguous – tends to be typical of how many people (layperson and scientist alike) regard knowledge of the physical or natural sciences. It paints a picture of the natural and physical environment as predictable and orderly, where patterns are repeated as prescribed by previous knowledge. Definitions then play a well-established and logical role as the starting point for the study of any topic in the natural and physical sciences. However, in a study of 'society' and 'culture' that may not be the best place to begin.

Certain knowledge: a social construction

The **scientific method** describes the **norms** and guidelines that natural and physical scientists follow in conducting research to produce new knowledge. It is a logical process developed from careful experimentation, observation and analysis of regularly repeated occurrences of a phenomenon (e.g. osmosis) so that a truthful *generalization* can be revealed about such a phenomenon (Fig. 2.1). Thus osmosis tends to occur in the same way over and over again whenever certain conditions prevail. Knowledge that is produced by the scientific method to explain and predict the natural and physical world tends to be regarded as certain knowledge, uncontested, and therefore 'truth'. 'Certainty' here refers to knowledge that is permanent in that it will not change.

Conclusions – may verify or reject the initial hypothesis. A **theory** may be offered to explain the phenomena observed which would be able to predict similar relationships in the future. This is called a **natural law** or a **generalization**.

Data analysis – all the findings are studied to determine significant trends and relationships.

Data collection – observations and experiments are conducted on the variables to try to establish the correct relationship between them.

A **hypothesis** is put forward to be tested. It states the relationship that the researcher feels exists between the variables.

An **observation** that you find intriguing and would like to investigate further. It usually involves a relationship between two variables.

Fig. 2.1 The scientific method

These **beliefs** about the certainty of scientific knowledge are strongly held by many people to the point where science is regarded as factual knowledge. This view, though, is only a **social construction** – ways people have of giving meaning to something and then coming to believe in it. For example, groups of people over time have rendered this 'opinion' of the knowledge produced by natural and physical scientists because they had utter *faith* in the use of *empirical* or *sensory* data (phenomena that can be seen, touched, tasted, heard and smelled),

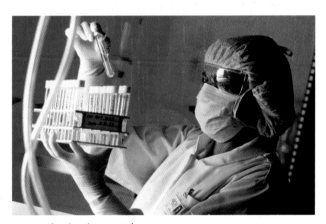

Fig. 2.2 A scientist at work

Fig. 2.3 A social scientist at work

and the rigorous process of experimentation involved. The emphasis on tangible realities (that is, sensory data) affirmed people's belief that knowledge produced in this way was certain and factual. These social constructions can be easily unmasked when we study the history of science and learn of the many 'truths' that have been disproved over time as investigations became more sensitive to alternative approaches, and especially to *anomalies* – phenomena that could not be explained by existing theories (Box 2.1)

BOX 2.1 Beliefs and knowledge

Thomas Kuhn in his book *The Structure of Scientific Revolutions*, first published in 1962, showed that over time scholars and scientists developed strong *beliefs* in the knowledge they had derived and which to them represented *truth*, or *certain knowledge*. Kuhn called their way of deriving knowledge a **paradigm** – a coherent set of theories that can explain and predict reality; scholars and scientists work within its parameters. However, *anomalies* occur from time to time and if the present paradigm of research and inquiry cannot explain the phenomenon it may be ignored. If, though, anomalies continue to recur until they cannot be denied any longer a crisis then ensues among scholars, affecting other social groups as well. Kuhn calls this a 'revolution' because a 'paradigm shift', which has to happen, is often intellectually traumatic and accompanied by turmoil.

These revolutions and paradigm shifts show that there has *not* been a steady build-up of scientific knowledge in smooth increments leading eventually to some universal principles of the natural and physical world. It is a *social construction* to believe that scientific knowledge has been slowly but surely progressing or evolving to deeper truths. Rather, what happens is that scholars and scientists may go along for centuries using the same sets of procedures, instrumentation and theories. This is a period of what Kuhn calls 'normal science', where scientists solve problems and consolidate their knowledge using existing theory; that is, until anomalies build up that threaten their conventional ways of operating. Rival schools of thought develop with a different understanding of how the physical and natural world operates. Their theories can explain the 'anomalies' more satisfactorily. Then, a shake-up occurs where those who contest the conventional wisdom triumph over those locked into the old paradigm.

Reputations and livelihoods founder amidst the ensuing controversy and hullabaloo. For example, 'societies' of scholars who form and control university departments, conferences and journals find their credibility in jeopardy. Research and development business interests withdraw funding from projects that now seem to be based on some wrong concepts. Completed projects, and policies and programmes already in place, are now regarded as deficient or useless. It is not easy to accept this and often the character and reputations of those in the rival school of thought are attacked.

Box 2.1 highlights the fact that scientific knowledge is only 'true' until disproved – it is therefore provisional and uncertain. However, when definitions are given, the usual provisos about temperature and pressure remaining constant (which suggest that the context is important and that if conditions change so will the phenomena) are either ignored or downplayed. The social then maintains a picture of the natural sciences as producing certain and predictable knowledge and facts, and not being unduly affected by context.

In our study of the social the point we need to understand is that we cannot get away from social constructions and ways of seeing that are socially constructed. We have seen that even science, which has historically been portrayed as an objective and rational activity, has only been portrayed that way because people (both scientists and others) have constructed it in that image. There is nothing, then, like a science that is not enmeshed in a social context. However, while scientists today may be more inclined to show that what they do is really an act of 'interpreting nature' and that that has its fair share of hunches, intuition, imagination and value-laden judgements (in other words, a social side), the dominant view remains that knowledge of the natural sciences is still somehow 'stronger' and more 'scientific' than knowledge of the social world.

A famous example of this was the confirmation by Galileo (1564–1642), using the recently invented telescope, that the sun is indeed the centre of the universe. The conventional wisdom of the times was based on Ptolemy, who had said that the sun revolved around the Earth. This view was defended for centuries, and staunchly upheld by the Roman Catholic Church, even in the face of opposing evidence brought up from time to time. For example, there was a rival conception by Copernicus indicating that the Earth revolved around the sun. Galileo, in investigating the movements of the tides, found support for a *heliocentric* rather than a *geocentric* model of the heavens, and this was confirmed by his observations through the telescope. Physical evidence and incontrovertible proof were not enough to get the authorities of the day to accept his findings. He was denounced as a heretic and denigrated in publications; his works censored, he was arrested and brought before the Inquisition. It is important to note that it was not only the Church that vilified Galileo but his colleagues at the universities as well. However, other mathematicians, physicists and astronomers, who felt that Galileo's work had more explanatory power than the traditional paradigm, continued to deepen this new paradigm. Newton's laws of gravity, based on Galileo's principles, inspired a whole body of work now relying on Newtonian laws. And so the story of science unfolds in a series of paradigm shifts and revolutions.

Kuhn was able to show through the experiences of Galileo and many other scientists that 'though the world does not change with a paradigm, the scientist afterwards works in a different world' (1996, p. 121). Thus, the image of science as offering strong factual bodies of uncontested knowledge, and that of scientists as neutral and impartial observers of the truth, are only social constructions. This myth about science is transmitted to us via textbooks, for example, which often summarize the false starts, anomalies and contradictions in the history of science as a steady stream of progress, deepening and consolidating a body of knowledge 'out there' to be discovered. As we have seen, there is no body of knowledge out there waiting to be discovered; a scientist can only work within the traditions of his or her paradigm until that gives way to another.

Contested knowledge: a variety of perspectives

Concepts such as 'society', 'culture', 'family' and 'education' are examples of social science knowledge and defy definition. They are difficult to reduce to precise and fixed meanings. This is usually the case with ideas and concepts that describe the social world. Any one of these concepts or ideas occurs in varied forms that change over time and, moreover, change in different ways in different places. As an example, let us examine the social institution of education.

Education is a **contested concept**; there is little agreement on what it is. Some equate it with the process of schooling, some with the inculcation of skills and knowledge that goes on throughout life, some with learning to be human, and still others with freedom. We even find the same people holding conflicting views about it. While they may acknowledge the emancipating aspects to being educated, they still see it in a utilitarian or **instrumental** way – that the main reason to be educated is to get a job, and a good job. Moreover, at different times in our history, social groups alternately championed different ideas about education. With such a background, and amidst continuing disagreement about what it is, any definition of education can only be partial and at best a 'working definition'. Lined up against how we have come to view physical and natural scientific knowledge, such knowledge appears to be imprecise and that is often seen in a negative light.

Perhaps this negative portrayal of social science knowledge comes from it being obviously enmeshed in contexts – whether meaning different things to different social groups or its meaning changing over time. (Compare contexts in natural science knowledge, where temperature, pressure and other factors tend to be downplayed.) In understanding the social we have to recognize the variety of perspectives that may co-exist and oppose each other. The views people hold tend to stem from their *social location* (for example, their context). The social world comprises many kinds of groups in which we hold multiple memberships. Belonging to a group often means that you tend to identify with certain views that that group has of social life and this describes your social location. Social groups include women, the disabled, students, out-of-school youth, scientists, tourists, the elderly, and many others, as well as ethnic groups of all kinds and socio-economic groups. It is easy to see that our multiple memberships influence us to hold different, and sometimes competing, perspectives.

The natural sciences: the dominant image

Because there is so much approval and positive acclaim for the 'strong' and 'certain' knowledge of science, efforts have been made to define social science phenomena in a similar way. So, concepts that describe the social world, such as society and culture, are often cast as precise definitions, as if other meanings did not exist. For example:

- *society* – a collection of people living in the same area over time
- *culture* – the ways of life of a people

These definitions are acceptable only if one understands that they are not comprehensive and leave out much more than they can say about the phenomena they attempt to describe. However, we do not seem to be comfortable with definitions that give only a partial picture. There is an urge to paint over what we know with a veneer of certainty. Perhaps this is because human beings only seem to be comfortable with certainty, with the perception of how knowledge is viewed in the natural sciences, and find human or social science knowledge, which is characterized by *uncertainty* and tentativeness, as unsettling and disconcerting. This is an understanding of the social that we have met already – a tendency to cast knowledge that is complex and variable in an image that seems to be more acceptable (a social construction).

This way of thinking about knowledge stems from the *Age of Enlightenment* in western civilization when reason, logic and the scientific method were seen as the hope for mankind. Since the eighteenth century science and technology have held a dominant place in how we regard knowledge and explain much of our positive feelings for 'hard' and precise data (Box 2.2).

The point is that when we model human or social science knowledge on dominant images from the natural and physical sciences we are likely to confer on it a static, certain, orderly and predictable veneer. Definitions of society and culture (or any other social science concept), if understood in this light, describe phenomena that are taken as precise and therefore capable of being fully defined. This is misleading and is not helpful to us as we study society and culture.

BOX 2.2 Knowledge and the Age of Enlightenment

Europe in the seventeenth and eighteenth centuries was undergoing rapid changes in social life. Earlier, the *Renaissance* had brought about renewed interest in the arts, learning, and the possibilities of mankind. It was an era when there were rapid strides in the development of knowledge about the natural and physical worlds. This knowledge facilitated inventions and discoveries that enabled people to live a better life; it was known as the 'Age of Enlightenment'.

The **industrial revolution** ushered in the manufacturing age; goods and services were cheaper and more widespread, and thanks to the *agrarian revolution* food was now produced in bulk for the burgeoning urban industrial centres. Engineering breakthroughs helped to build machines that made possible large-scale manufacturing, shipping, railroads, road and canal construction and the damming and diversion of rivers to control and regulate floodwaters. There were great strides as well in the knowledge of the human body; vaccinations were developed to ward off disease and better information was available about cleanliness and hygiene through germ theory.

Scientific experiments led to inventions and innovation that helped to tame nature and to give people a better life. From then to now science and technology have held pride of place in how we regard knowledge. 'Development' eventually came to be equated with what industrial nations did, and there was a focus on **economic development** and 'modernization' as the hallmarks of progress.

The beliefs and values that imbue science, industry and technology came to be prized and have since configured our ideas about reality. From the Age of Enlightenment in seventeenth- and eighteenth-century Europe until the present day, increasing value has been placed on having qualities such as logic, rationality, objectivity and efficiency, and being able to establish and maintain cost-effectiveness,

order, neutral decision-making and profits. These values and beliefs, important in the world of science, business and industry, have come to characterize the 'modern era'. (Today there is a reaction by some who say we have now entered the **postmodern era** and they are calling for recognition of the importance of the emotions, humanity, empathy, the environment and the spiritual in how social life is organized.)

No wonder then that science, from which all this knowledge has sprung, has been regarded as a model or standard by which we should view *all* knowledge. No wonder then that the social sciences and humanities came to be seen through these social constructions of science. The social sciences are relative newcomers. Sociology, economics, anthropology and political science only began to be organized as separate disciplines in the nineteenth and twentieth centuries. They are still continuing to grow and develop. Much of their early development was influenced by the dominance of the natural sciences. Early sociologists, for example, felt that the social world was a mirror of the natural and physical world, and that the quest by natural and physical scientists to discover laws by which the universe was governed (e.g. Boyle's Law) could be duplicated in sociology by studying society to find out the 'laws' of social interaction. Needless to say, they modelled their way of investigating on the *scientific method* (Fig. 2.1); to this day, this school of thought in sociology (**functionalism**) remains the dominant one.

Thus, the dominant images of science have not only constructed our view of scientific knowledge but also our view of the *social* sciences. Definitions such as 'society is a collection of people living in the same area over time' and 'culture is the ways of life of a people' are constructed with an image of knowledge in mind where facts and essential characteristics are stated as if they summed up the story in its entirety.

Statics versus dynamics: the problem of change

The social world is characterized by constant change. So too is the natural world; for example, rivers, earth movements, the sub-atomic world, diseases, viruses and so on present a dynamic, highly interactive and constantly changing milieu. Yet knowledge in the natural sciences continues to be portrayed as if only predictable patterns and processes take place. What we are seeing, then, is that knowledge of social life and its processes *as well as* knowledge of the natural world are portrayed as orderly and predictable. Thus, the major aspects of life in the social *and* natural worlds – dynamism, change, interaction – tend to be wiped out by the bias that has operated in how we treat with knowledge. Particularly important for us in the study of the social is how definitions of concepts in the social world, such as society and culture, deny them their dynamic character. Let us look again at these two definitions:

- **society** – a collection of people living in the same area over time
- **culture** – the ways of life of a people

ACTIVITY 2.2

Describe any features of 'society' that can be regarded as being dynamic.

We do not see anything that is dynamic and changeful (having an innate tendency to change). Neither do they seem to be problematic or unduly complex. Again we need to note how an understanding of the social helps us to see the ways in which people attempt to construct a reality that is solid and predictable.

'A collection of people living in the same area over time' seems to be saying that 'society' is a quantitative measure referring to numbers of people living in a place over a long time period. What is only inferred, and never made explicit in this definition, is that for a society to exist there must be arrangements, interactions and relationships that make social life possible. The natural sciences model of knowledge, as we have seen, is not comfortable with terms such as 'interaction' or 'relationships' that are not clearly prescribed, so any definition will tend to omit these dynamic aspects and focus on what cannot be disputed or considered uncertain. Social scientists who have closely followed what is considered legitimate knowledge, as laid down by the natural scientists, persist in offering these static portrayals of the social world as definitions.

The idea of a definition is not itself being questioned here. Definitions *are* useful, particularly in the natural sciences where they carry important information in a nutshell. However, because of the understandings we now have of 'the social', we can see that in the social sciences definitions tend to reduce important information to static relationships that do not give a true picture of the social world. On the other hand, if a comprehensive definition were to be attempted it would be much too long; it would no longer constitute a definition but an extended *explanation*. Thus, we have to be aware that when we use definitions of social phenomena they are of limited value as explanations.

The problem arises when we come to believe that the 'shorthand' ways of describing the world are absolutely true, in a similar manner to how we read and interpret definitions of osmosis or oxidation. If we commit this error then our attempts to study society and culture, and to deepen our understanding, will only give us an unreal picture of these phenomena. If we are to reflect on the role of the individual in the development of society and in the creation of culture or cultures in our region, we must have a clearer picture with which to work. It may not be too far fetched to claim that many of the intentions to improve society expressed by governments, international bodies, churches, and other organizations and individuals suffer from an overly static understanding of social life.

Summary

In this section, 'the social' has been portrayed through illustrations that attempt to capture how people tend to view and develop explanations for phenomena in social life. We have focused on knowledge and definitions, as they are especially important in beginning a study of the concepts 'society' and 'culture'. In examining the social we found that people tended to:

- develop social constructions to make reality more meaningful (these seemed to downplay the complexity, variation and changeability of social life)
- hold multiple and conflicting views based on their social location.

We will now turn our attention to the specific study of 'society' and later we will examine 'culture'. If our intention is to study society, faithful to its dynamic nature, we cannot begin with a traditional definition and we will also use what we have learned about 'the social' in examining definitions.

SOCIETY: MULTIPLE MEANINGS

The strategy here is to come to an understanding of what 'society' is not through a definition, but by mapping out all its various meanings. To do this we will:

1 examine popular ways of using the term
2 analyse how it is understood in different disciplines of knowledge.

We may notice, for example, that while a definition such as 'society is a collection of people living in an area for a long time' is accepted, the ways in which people use the term assume far deeper meanings. By surveying the ways in which the term is used we may get closer to a more meaningful interpretation.

Popular ways of portraying 'society'

Let us look at other ways in which the term is used and see if we can discern themes similar to those you identified in Activity 2.3, or even different understandings. Especially common today is the term *information society*, describing a society where maximum use is made of information and communications technologies (**ICTs**). Groups in society employ the new technologies to lead lives of utmost efficiency and enjoyment. ICTs imbue all aspects of life: businesses are networked into large databases, financial transactions are flexible and can take place in multiple locations, shopping can be done on the internet, teletext messages offer just one of many alternatives to quick communication, and computers are found if not in every home, certainly in companies and associations of all kinds. The term 'information society' is thus saying that the ways in which information is managed, stored and communicated in these times deeply influence and alter *relationships* among groups of people and permeate the whole society, making it palpably different from, say, ten years ago.

We can easily understand this if we focus on groups of people such as the elderly, the poor, technophobes, and citizens of countries with a low per capita income, who have all somehow been left out of the computer age. They suffer all kinds of disadvantages in trying to live lives to the best of their ability. They find that they do not have the requisite skills for work, for study, and even for conducting business or simple transactions in the public domain. Operating in the everyday environments in which they are required to remember pin numbers, interpret computerized transactions, and communicate via voice mail, email, cellular telephones and text

2.2

ACTIVITY 2.3

Below are three examples of how the term 'society' appears in social life.

- Society for the Prevention of Cruelty to Animals (SPCA)
- The National Audubon Society
- Civil society

1. Explain how 'society' is understood in each of the above?

2. Which TWO of the three listed above share the same understandings of 'society'?

3. Identify another understanding of 'society' in popular use that is not evident in the examples given.

Fig. 2.4 Growing up in the information society

ACTIVITY 2.4

1. Using your country as an example, reflect on the nature of the digital divide. Which groups are enabled, and which groups disadvantaged, by the dominance of ICTs in society?

2. On an international level, identify countries on either side of the digital divide. Suggest reasons why the gap may be widening rather than closing.

messaging, and so on, leaves them with a diminished confidence in themselves as effectively functioning adults. Such groups of people, some of who may actually live in high-tech information societies and some who may live in developing societies, experience social life differently from others who are literate in computer and information technologies. The **digital divide** is a term that calls attention to the different relationships that the haves (the computer savvy) and the have-nots (those who do not know how to make use of the technologies or have little access to them) experience in society. Contrary to what some people think, it is not a continuum but a gap that is widening.

Today the rhetoric on human development calls for the need for another kind of society, a *learning society*. Reform efforts visualize the whole society as one that actively promotes and enhances learning. This is seen as necessary in today's world of rapid and unprecedented change, where learning has to be continuous. Those who advocate the concept of a learning society see that even normal participation in church, work and leisure should involve learning. It should be among the principles that characterize how the media operate, as well as the health sector and government departments. Everyone should see themselves as a learner. A focus on continuous learning in society has the potential to deepen the knowledge and understanding we have of each other and help us to share that knowledge in more meaningful ways that help to improve our relationships.

What is the understanding of *society* in the term 'learning society'? Like the 'information society', it refers to the *quality of the relationships* that structure *interaction* in a group of people living together. There is also a stress on something of **value** that you may also have discovered when you attempted to describe *civil society* (see Activity 2.3), where society is seen to be working towards the attainment of some ideal. The idea of a civil society is one with a certain vision of society where the citizenry operates and benefits from lawful and just relationships. The 'learning society' is similar. It is a way of visualizing society where through an emphasis on learning a more humane society results.

In mapping out the various ways in which the term 'society' is used in everyday life, we have seen that they extend far beyond 'a group of people living together in a place over a long period of time'. The most important aspects seem to have been left out of such a definition. Let us now bring the concept of 'the social' back into the discussion. Remember that the social is 'the totality of explanations describing how people interact and make meaning of their experiences'. What have we understood about the social that has helped us to better discuss the concept of society?

Firstly, as we saw in the previous section, in social life there are *a variety of perspectives* depending on the group to which one belongs or one's social location.

Thus, one term can have multiple and conflicting meanings. For example, 'society' has all of the following meanings:

- a group of people living together in a place over a long period of time
- a group which shares a common purpose that structures their relationships and interactions
- an ideal which a group of people is striving to achieve; society is always becoming, we cannot say that we have achieved it as yet.

All these meanings are in popular use, and although no distinction is made when we are using the term in the various senses, people usually know how to interpret it. For example, they know when the term is being used to indicate the social institutions of the land, as in 'The society today is in need of healing' or when it is used in a narrow and circumscribed sense of a common purpose as in 'The Audubon Society will hold its annual general meeting on . . .'. Understanding the social helps us to see that 'society' will continue to be a contested concept and any definition chosen is merely that, a choice. In other words, understanding the social shows us that there is no one definition of the concept 'society'.

Secondly, the social helps us to better understand how people attribute meanings as they *construct an image* of what society is like. There is no law written anywhere that we have to follow that says definitively what a society is. People living in groups from time immemorial have tried to construct their day-to-day living on an image of what their society *should* be like. The three meanings of society listed above are *social constructions* of the term:

- *A group of people living together in a place over a long period of time.* There are those of us who conjure up an image of space and place where the group is 'contained', and such a construction of society has a strong historical, political, geographical and ecological perspective. (This view ignores the idea that members of a society – for example, Caribbean society – can live in areas that are far removed from the Caribbean.)
- *A group which shares a common purpose that structures their relationships and interactions.* This definition stresses the common bonds – 'values' – that group members share, which must necessarily structure their interaction and relationships. The social construction popular here is in terms of consensus, harmony and order that *ought to* prevail in society. In sociology, this is a *functionalist* (see Fig. 2.6 and p. 39) understanding of society and is fairly widespread. It portrays an image of society as stable and peaceful.
- *An ideal which a group of people is striving to achieve; society is always becoming, we cannot say that we have achieved it as yet.* This definition sees society as actually having a life of its own and evolving towards some ideal; it is always becoming. Visions of civil society and the learning society fit into this conception of what the term 'society' means.

All the above are social constructions about what a society is, and people can hold different and conflicting images of society quite comfortably. Nevertheless, not all these images are held with the same intensity. There tends to be a dominant image that is shared, and apparently it is the least complex version that often has widespread acceptance.

Disciplinary perspectives

Let us now move from popular understandings of society and focus on how various disciplines, particularly the social science disciplines, view society. A 'discipline' is an organized body of knowledge such as biology or economics. In the western traditions of Europe and North America knowledge is classified into the physical or natural sciences, the social sciences, and the arts and humanities. There are certain subdivisions and overlaps but generally the three-way classification is accepted by scholars and academic and professional communities as representing the broad divisions of knowledge.

All social science disciplines study society, emphasizing different aspects. Thus, a body of perspectives has grown up among students and scholars that emphasizes certain views of society according to their subject speciality. Examining some of the ways in which society is perceived in the different social science disciplines deepens our understanding of the diversity and divergence of opinions associated with it. One meaning that we are interested in clarifying is its perceived relationship with 'culture'.

- *Geographical* ideas are one of the many elements underlying the everyday use of the term 'Caribbean society'. It assumes that the groups of people who live in a region develop ways of interacting that are significantly influenced by the place or space in which they live. Caribbean society will thus differ from American society or social life in the Amazon. This notion of society also has an *ecological* perspective where people develop ways of adapting to their environmental conditions as well as adapting the environment using their own unique knowledge and expertise. For example, the Dutch were able to bring their skills of land reclamation to the low-lying Guiana coastlands to create the conditions necessary for society to develop. Given the strong linkages between people *adapting their ways of life* in a specific location and the concept of society, a social construction of society has evolved in geography that blurs the boundaries between 'Caribbean society' and 'Caribbean culture'.

- *History* locates societies in time. Roman society flourished at a certain time and no longer exists; the relationships that structured that society are long gone. Historians think of a society as located in time and belonging to a certain period. They study how the society changes over time. Historians thus have a notion of society as a set of dynamic relationships between and within different groups. When historians speak of a society they tend to stress the *social formation* – the structure of groups and their relationships. They do not necessarily need to separate out culture for their purposes – though they do study culture as the expressive arts in different periods – and thus their discussions about society *are inclusive of culture.*

- *Anthropology* is the study of the societies that human beings have formed from earliest times to now. Of primary interest is the culture of these societies. An anthropological study of Caribbean society today may emphasize traditional societies such as that of the Amerindians or small communities such as the Rastafarians or the Chinese community in Jamaica. Anthropologists thus study societies focusing on the *culture* of those societies, *making virtually no distinction between the two.*

ACTIVITY 2.6

If we agree that Roman 'society' no longer exists as it did during the Roman Empire, then how do we explain the persistence of Roman 'culture' to the present day? Some examples of Roman cultural forms are still evident in language (Latin), drama, law, government and engineering, among others.

● *Political science* studies politics, government, political systems and power relationships among the interest groups in society. The state is traditionally seen as the limit of the society. Society thus has a geographical basis and is understood as a 'container' in which power relationships occur. Definitions, which say that society is a 'defined territorial space' or 'citizenship within a space', illustrate a political science conception of the term 'society'. Compared to the other social science disciplines discussed above, there seems to be less of a tendency to bring society and culture together as one indivisible whole. On the other hand, society seems to be *fused or equated with the state*.

● *Sociology* is defined as the study of society and so it attempts to distinguish between 'society' and 'culture' and to specify the relations between the two. The dominant way of studying society is through an understanding of its social structure. **Social structure** refers to the organized patterns, arrangements and interactions between groups who comprise the various **social institutions** and **social organizations** making up a society. Examples of social institutions are religion, the **economy**, politics, education and health. Examples of social organizations are churches, the labour market, political parties and so on, based on the different social institutions. Patterns of behaviour describe how members with different **roles** interact with each other. Thus, the meaning of society in sociology is bound up with social structure and social organization.

  ● *Functionalist* sociologists tend to view social structure as working in such a way as to ensure peace and stability. The structures that organize relationships and interactions make certain that the *collective will* of members is satisfied. Undesirable behaviours are discouraged through social structures such as laws, norms, rules, roles, values and **sanctions**. For example, churchgoing is a strong Caribbean norm encouraging conformist behaviours (Fig. 2.5). The processes of **socialization** and *education* are the major ways through which respect for these laws and norms are taught (Fig. 2.6).

Fig. 2.5 Churchgoing in the Caribbean

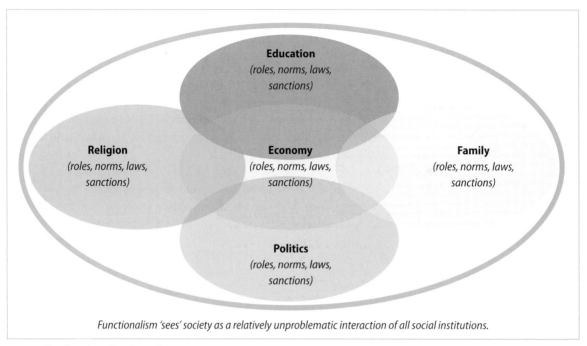

Functionalism 'sees' society as a relatively unproblematic interaction of all social institutions.

Fig. 2.6 The functionalist view of society

- *Marxist* sociologists also understand society in terms of its social structure but do not hold the harmonious view described above. They say that the structures in **capitalist** societies are enabling for the wealthy and coercive for poorer groups. This means that since the economic structure of the society dominates interaction and relationships, the interests of the **elites** are always taken care of. Gross inequalities occur in the society and the poor do not have the power to change societal arrangements. According to Marxists, the processes of socialization and education support these inequalities (Fig. 2.7). Thus, even within sociology, there are different perspectives on society.

Social science disciplines study the same phenomenon – 'society' – but differently, as no one discipline can seemingly capture all its various facets. However, it is often the case that a social scientist becomes deeply socialized into the discipline in which he or she has specialized, and ignores or plays down the understandings of society put forward by the other disciplines. For example, the political scientist emphasizes the political system of society and a Marxist sociologist emphasizes the economic system in explaining society. Having some understanding of the social enables us to recognize the tendency to reduce and simplify what 'society' means to the specific aspects studied by a particular discipline (Box 2.3). Also, the difficulty of extricating culture from understandings about society has tended in most social science disciplines to conflate the two terms.

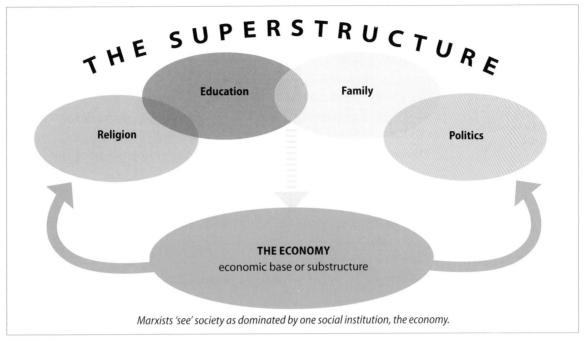

Marxists 'see' society as dominated by one social institution, the economy.

Fig. 2.7 The Marxist view of society

BOX 2.3 Scholarly societies

It is ironic (and instructive) that in promoting a particular view of society (and excluding others), scholars in the disciplines portray themselves *as a society*. The National Geographic *Society* or the American Psychological *Society* provide examples of how disciplines, through their journals, subject associations, conferences and departments attempt to map out *their territory* of the study of society and establish boundaries with other social science disciplines. In so doing they create a 'society' of scholars and students (an academic community). Commitment to a set of cherished norms and values is fostered through on-going efforts at refining and outlining their shared interests – a distinctive body of language and concepts, accepted ways of studying, researching and reporting, and strong opinions about what is considered valid knowledge. In these ways a **community of discourse** (a society) is built up around a particular discipline based on consensus. This process is continuous as new scholars are always being inducted by the old guard into the concepts and preferred ways of understanding the term 'society' in a particular discipline. Rivalries tend to develop between the different societies representing each discipline, competing for universal recognition that each one is better than the other in the kinds of authentic and unique insights about society that they can generate.

Exploring perspectives on the disciplines shows us that within the organization of knowledge there are various conceptions of society and each one becomes a sort of lens or a preferred view for adherents of a particular discipline. For example, political scientists conceive of the state as the basis of a society, whilst geographers focus on the land and its resources. What is remarkable, however, is that in trying to refine and present their discipline to the world, scholars form what are called 'societies' where they quite inadvertently demonstrate a shared meaning of what a society is. This is interesting to think about as it gives us some deeper insights into the social.

For example, while scholars answer the question 'what is society?' quite explicitly from their various disciplinary viewpoints, implicitly they emphasize *in the societies they form* generally accepted understandings about society – shared norms, goals and purposes which structure relationships and interactions. Thus, what they say a society is differs from what *they do* in forming a society. Trying to understand the social has alerted us to this before – that people seem to be able to hold multiple and conflicting beliefs and act from the various positions according to the context.

ACTIVITY 2.7

Ten definitions of society are listed in Table 2.1. Some of them overlap to a certain extent, some say the same thing in different words, and a few are unique. Answer the questions below based on the definitions given.

Table 2.1 Definitions of 'Society'

(a) All the social relationships found among human beings.

(b) A group of people who have mutual interests, certain forms of interaction, characteristic relationships, shared institutions, and a common culture.

(c) A concept that describes how people who live together as a group develop a commitment to a shared set of norms for living and interacting.

(d) A group of people who have developed certain social structures that prescribe appropriate behaviours and relationships.

(e) Relationships and arrangements in a group which represent ways of ensuring that members remain loyal to its purposes, shared aims and values by attention to consensus building; for example, through the concept of society as a moral police.

(f) A set of relationships and arrangements in a group which are constantly changing and re-configuring how social life is organized.

(g) Certain norms, values and behaviours characteristic of a people who live in a place and shaped that space.

(h) The set of social relationships that an elite group or groups have organized and try to maintain against the competing interests of other groups.

(i) An ideal that we are always striving to achieve in our relationships and arrangements for social life; e.g. the 'good' society.

(j) A social system where members share a common history, heritage, language and social institutions, and which occupies a defined geographical space.

1. Identify ONE definition of society from the list in Table 2.1 that you think will be helpful as you continue to deepen your understandings of society and culture. Justify your choice.

2. Select ONE definition that seems to be limited in some way in attempting to define society. Analyse the definition to show what it emphasizes and what it downplays. In analysing the definition, to what extent did your opinion change about its limitations?

3. Create your own definition of society (in about three or four lines) that includes all the aspects of society that you deem important.

For our purposes, what is especially important is what the disciplines emphasize in their various explicit definitions of society. What is emphasized and what is downplayed refer yet again to our growing understandings of the social – that people speak about things from their own experience and their own social location, and often ignore the experiences of others. For us, their different definitions serve to question each other and provide a more comprehensive understanding of what 'society' means.

Summary

'The social' is the totality of explanations describing how people interact and make meanings of their experience. Understanding the social shows us that social constructions of knowledge have come to imbue how people think of the natural and social sciences. Accordingly, 'society' has traditionally been defined in static and simple terms. To challenge these ideas, the complexity of society has been presented here as fully as possible, mapping out popular perceptions of the term as well as the emphases given by the different disciplines. This strategy tends to yield commonalities across disciplines referring to a composite view of society as 'a group of people who have interacted over time in a specific place, developing certain shared purposes and goals that structure their relationships in dynamic ways'. Certain disciplines, such as geography, history and anthropology, focus more on the socio-cultural, and from these we get a good picture of how society and culture are embedded in each other. Sociology is the only discipline that seeks to differentiate between the two. In sociology the social structure is stressed when describing society. Social structure refers to the organized patterns, arrangements and interactions between groups that comprise the various social institutions and social organizations making up a society.

2.3 CULTURE: MULTIPLE MEANINGS

We begin our study of culture by working through the variety of perspectives that are in popular use, as well as those found in the more formal world of academic disciplines. We will continue to maintain our vigilance where understanding of the social is concerned, and to identify how that understanding influences the meanings we attribute to culture. And, particularly because our understanding of the social can contribute to blurring the boundaries between 'society' and 'culture', we want to be mindful of the distinction between these two concepts.

Popular ways of portraying 'culture'

Culture as 'ways of life'

Perhaps the best-known definition of culture is the one that describes it as *the ways of life of a people*. Reducing something that is so complex to a few words is entirely understandable, given what we understand about the social. People tend to speak in terms of labels, definitions and shorthand ways of describing something, especially if the phenomenon is complex. Understanding the social helps us to see how complexity is treated in everyday life and discourse. Culture, interpreted as 'ways of life', is a concept, then, that needs to be deconstructed.

For example, students who have been weaned on an understanding of knowledge as primarily factual may be likely to interpret 'ways of life' as representing predictable patterns and behaviours. Ways of worshipping, celebrating, voting, earning a living and interacting with the different social groups in the country will qualify as the culture of those people in that country. This is an 'omnibus' version of the concept, carrying the understanding that all patterns and processes in which a people engage are eligible to be described as its culture. While this is not wrong, it reduces culture to a set of patterns of behaviour, and this is quite inadequate, as we will see if we want a deeper understanding.

Let us focus on a specific 'way' of life – *worshipping*. When we say that this form of behaviour is cultural, what do we mean? Worshipping may occur in many forms and guises; people belong to different religions and some do not value the ways of other groups; many persons only worship on special occasions; and some may never do so. In revealing broad patterns or ways of life, are we revealing their 'culture'? If a certain pattern can be discerned in how people live their lives, is it this pattern that makes it 'cultural'? Or is the 'display' of a rite, for example, what is considered 'cultural'?

ACTIVITY 2.8

Examine the questions in the paragraph opposite. Suggest what might be the limitation in the definition of culture that reduces it to 'a set of patterns of behaviour or, the ways of life of a people'. Use the photographs in Figs 2.8 to 2.11 to help you think about this aspect of culture.

Fig.2.8 A Hindu wedding ceremony in Trinidad   **Fig. 2.9** A Rastafarian gathering in Jamaica

Fig. 2.10 An Aucaner Maroon dance in central Suriname   **Fig. 2.11** A Spiritual Baptist ritual: river baptism in Haiti

Culture as products

Certain terms in everyday use tend to equate culture with cultural *products*. 'Popular culture', 'high culture' or 'elite culture', 'mass culture' and 'global culture' are examples.

- *Popular culture* refers to the music, visual and performing arts, literature, festivals, cuisine, poetry and artistic and designer creations that are promoted mainly through the efforts of the **mass media**, and even the foreign mass media. Here we see one understanding of culture that tends to get overlooked – that the culture of a people is not necessarily only about things *indigenous* to them.

The term 'mass culture' refers to the lifestyles and values promoted through the mass media. And in this era of **globalization**, where through ICTs we are all becoming increasingly like each other, there is talk of a 'global culture'.

● *High culture* is an elitist understanding of culture and was first put forward by Matthew Arnold in the nineteenth century. It refers to values that promote the best thoughts and ideas that human beings have developed and perfected. For example, classical music, philosophy, literature and the arts are thought to represent beauty, intelligence and truth. Human society, then, can be transformed by contact with these products of high culture. It is undoubtedly an **ethnocentric** view, as it seems to value only the cultural products of western society – primarily, the legacies of Greece and Rome, but also of Europe and the European influence in North America. This understanding still persists in statements like 'he is highly cultured', and refers to certain refined tastes or aesthetic accomplishments.

Culture as ordinary

In 1958 Raymond Williams put forward the view that culture is ordinary. He was opposing both 'the ways of life' and the 'cultural products' view of culture by stressing its *symbolic* nature. In his view what should be emphasized is the process by which common meanings come to be accepted, debated and modified by people in a society. People develop or do not develop a commitment to the values and norms of their society through contact with them and the varied experiences each has had with them. Thus, culture is ordinary because it develops in every individual according to his or her experiences. In addition, it is not something that has a tangible existence. Culture is the meanings people have for something and those meanings are represented in ordinary life through behaviours, acts, rituals, norms and so on. In this view culture is not just what is manifest but the *deep personal meanings* that ordinary people develop and externalize in different ways. Perhaps you had thoughts along this line in responding to Activity 2.8.

Culture as learned behaviour

This is another very popular way of defining culture – that culture is learned and shared. It improves on the equally popular notion of 'ways of life of a people' by focusing not on the specific patterns of behaviour but on how people come to develop those behaviours in the first place. It builds on Williams's ideas by deepening an understanding of the symbolic.

People who live together develop symbols that each member has to learn about and these symbols represent significant *shared meanings* for something. Language, gestures, habits, religion, marriage and aspirations act as symbols for a set of shared meanings and values, which for people in that society represents their culture. Language and gestures are easy to understand. A word in any language – for example 'house' – bears no real connection to an actual building. The word 'blue' could have been used instead. A word is an arbitrary thing with no meaning in and of itself. It is the shared understandings among a people that confer meaning on a word so that it goes without saying what a person means when he or she uses that word. Any word is therefore merely a symbol to represent something, and because its meaning is shared, *communication* is possible. Different cultures generate different languages, dialects, idioms, and even accents.

Learning the shared agreements of a culture, in this view, is at the heart of how culture is created and maintained. Communication, then, is all-important in how a culture is learned and shared. For a society **cultural reproduction** becomes a major goal and this is ensured through different ways of teaching the culture to members so that the shared values and norms are constantly being reproduced. **Enculturation** describes the process through which we learn culture and is part of the more general process of socialization – the process through which we become human. Becoming human refers to learning the rules of the society, many of which are based on the need to have a common understanding of social life. **Diffusion** is another term that describes how culture spreads from one society to another. Migration and the effects of the mass media are two ways by which diffusion can occur.

Culture had to pre-date our entry into it. We were born into a society that already had a set of behaviours that were really symbols signifying shared meanings. We had to learn all the subtle meanings that we as a cultural group shared. For example, growing up in the Caribbean we learned that planting the land was a valuable pursuit but also, paradoxically, that farmers did not enjoy high social **status**. If we decided to become farmers we would have to deal with the set of shared meanings for our work that we had learned and opted to reject. Thus, although the ways culture is taught tend to reproduce it, that may not always be the case. The shared meanings are *negotiated meanings* and these are subject to alteration and change. If, for example, an entire graduating class with BSc qualifications in agriculture went to work as farmers, the shared meanings of who a farmer is would undergo some change.

ACTIVITY 2.9

1. What do you consider to be *your* culture?

2. What were (and are) the processes through which you learned (and are learning) about your culture?

ACTIVITY 2.10

Explain what is meant by 'culture' in the subcultures listed below:

1. drug culture

2. cyberculture

3. literary culture.

Culture as subculture

Understanding the social has shown us that one way people have of making meaning is to reduce complexity. A popular way of using the term 'culture' is to refer to a characteristic set of values and attitudes shared by a specific group or **subculture** within a larger group. We hear about organizational culture, political culture, an examinations culture, migration culture, and so on. This shows us that for something carrying so many varied and contested meanings as 'culture', it is perhaps more meaningful when it is specifically defined and applied to a subculture.

We continue to gain a deeper understanding of 'the social' by examining popular ways in which the concept of 'culture' is used or has been used. Focusing on something tangible is often an easy way out in trying to describe phenomena as complex as culture. Others reduce it differently, for example, as 'cultural products' or only applicable in specific subcultural contexts. However, running through most of the ways culture is described in popular use is the understanding of having common customs and values and deriving meanings in similar ways. And, while society and culture may seem fused in certain interpretations (for example, *high culture* can also be thought of as *high society)*, there is a strong sense in which culture is believed to be occurring *within a society*. Thus, 'the culture of a society' makes sense, and not vice versa.

Disciplinary perspectives

Geography

The study of the interaction between the physical landscape and human activity invites us to view culture as the ways people have found to adapt to, and adapt, the environment in which they live. In this view, then, a particular location is the important factor in *generating culture*, and adaptations are the public and shared ways in which culture is manifest. For example, economic activity is directly related to the physical and human resources in a locality, and how such activities are developed and organized depends on the skills and expertise of the people. Thus, agricultural organization – be it subsistence, peasant or **plantation economies** – describes a particular way of adapting the skills of people and the possibilities of the landscape. The determinant of culture, then (or what *causes* it), is the *adaptive capacity* of the people and the land. There is no real distinction in geography between studying a society and studying its culture.

History

Periodization is the emphasis of history. 'Ways of adapting' or 'ways of life' or 'shared meanings' are studied, but under the guise of politics, religious organization, diplomacy, economic activity, or any other aspect of social life in a specific historical period. And they are studied in terms of the social forces and processes evident in society that are changing these aspects of social life over time. History therefore studies culture as aspects of social organization. For example, politics is studied in terms of how power and influence are distributed among social groups and how the present arrangement is influenced by the legacies of previous generations. In addition, it looks at how politics is adapting and changing in the present era. Thus, although the historian does not specifically focus on *culture*, he or she *is* studying culture when the focus is on the political system, for example, and how it has changed and adapted over time.

Biology

In biology, the term 'culture' refers to quite different things. It refers to the growing of micro-organisms in some medium or the raising of plants and animals as in *agri*culture. Less well known is its role in human evolution, and that touches on two views we have already encountered – that culture is learned and shared, and that it is adaptive. Cultural knowledge enabled humans to survive over millennia in that technical and other knowledge was passed on to each new generation, who adapted and improved upon it. *Evolutionary biology* cites culture (mainly language, facilitating communication) as the major factor enabling early humans to survive in greater numbers, enjoy better health, and develop physical attributes that made them better able to protect and reproduce themselves, compared with other creatures.

As with history and geography, we again see an understanding of culture as an adaptive mechanism. The popular view that culture is learned and shared seems to be a necessary first step, though, in understanding culture as an adaptive mechanism rather than a separate and different explanation. However, we need to turn to another discipline, anthropology, to understand the processes whereby culture becomes an adaptive mechanism.

Anthropology

People usually summarize the work of anthropologists as 'the study of everything pertaining to a society'. Anthropologists study all societies from the earliest to the present day. While their work overlaps with that of the sociologist, they tend to keep their focus on culture. However, because culture is an ineffable and contested concept, anthropologists have found it necessary to subdivide it into specific areas for specialized study. For example, some anthropologists study *material culture* – the objects that a group produces and which differ significantly from the material culture of other groups. These artefacts include clothing, art in its various expressions, architecture, fashion, technological products, utensils, and the products known as 'popular culture'.

The ideas, beliefs, values, assumptions and behaviours of a people refer to its *non-material* or *symbolic culture*, and include language and other characteristic forms of interaction. This subdivision of culture focuses on the **meaning systems** that a group has for the symbols mentioned above. Within the meaning system is what anthropologists call a group's 'ideal culture' (the ideal values and norms of that society) and its 'real culture' (actual behaviours, which may fall short of its ideals). Thus, a society may value democracy and have symbols and practices to uphold it, such as general elections. Yet some groups, perhaps marginalized groups, remain persistently unrepresented. The meaning system for democracy in that culture includes both the ideal and a recognition that it is not being realized for all.

Cultural anthropologists like Clifford Geertz study symbolic culture and help us to extend our understanding beyond the contribution of Raymond Williams and those who define culture as learned and shared behaviour. By putting forward an understanding of culture as *the interpretation of meaning systems*, Geertz emphasized the *signs* or *symbols* that we *learn, share* and *adapt* in everyday life (our acts and behaviours). Thus, 'what we learn' or 'the meaning or significance something has for someone', cannot be obtained by simply labelling the process as 'enculturation' or by assigning fixed and precise meanings to acts or behaviours.

To mine the deep significance of an act for someone, Geertz introduced the concept of **webs of significance**. A person exists within a context of different layers or webs of meaning, which he or she has helped to spin. If we want to understand the 'deep structure' of culture we need to make a greater effort to find out the significance of behaviours or acts *to the people engaged in those acts* (as in Figs 2.12, 2.13, 2.14 and 2.15).

This is not a view from the outside. It deliberately seeks the perspectives of the group being studied. According to Geertz, what we learn about culture through this process of intense observation and interviews about everyday life in a society is that *people interpret their culture*. They choose from a range of signs or symbols within their webs of significance in making decisions about how to act or behave in the innumerable situations of everyday life. They choose from a set of values and beliefs (Box 2.4) that are interpretable by other members of the community. 'Values' refer to how something is ranked or judged. For example, theft may be regarded negatively and punctuality is rewarded. People choose their behaviours based on how they interpret the set of values and beliefs that are meaningful and intelligible to other members. Common *systems of meanings* thus exist, but they are continually created and re-created because culture is adaptive.

ACTIVITY 2.13

Using the understanding of culture put forward by Geertz, discuss the significance of a decision by someone of marriageable age not to get married. (The following questions address different aspects of this topic and may be helpful in the discussion.)

1. Would this decision be interpreted differently depending on whether the person not wishing to get married was male or a female?

2 What are images and social constructions of the 'married' or 'unmarried'?

3. Why are there so many acts, ceremonies, rituals and practices associated with marriage?

4. What are the underlying values and beliefs in your society about marriage?

Fig. 2.12 Conversation

Fig. 2.13 Courting

Culture then is the context in which people interact within webs of significance. Living in these webs means that one is continually interpreting signs and symbols – language, gestures, habits, ceremonies, rites of passage (for example, going to school), or shopping. Definitions of culture, which say that it is learned, shared or adaptive, need a deeper explication, possibly through greater attention to the meaning systems in which people are embedded. Thus, a more authentic representation of culture will go beyond it being learned, shared or adaptive, and emphasize how people actively interpret it according to some meaning system (values and beliefs) that is publicly intelligible. Values and beliefs, then, seem to be at the heart of culture.

Fig. 2.14 A schoolroom

Fig. 2.15 A family outing

BOX 2.4 Beliefs and values

The academic disciplines, rather than popular conceptions of culture, try to get at what generates or causes culture. We have seen that at the heart of culture is a set of beliefs and values. It is these beliefs and values that confer meanings on any act or behaviour. Because people share common understandings based on common beliefs and values they are able to interpret each other's acts and behaviours intelligibly. In another culture, such acts and behaviours may have altogether different meanings because they are based on a different set of values and beliefs. To understand what causes culture we therefore need to acquire a deeper understanding of beliefs and values.

Beliefs

To have a belief is to have deep faith and trust in something. There is utter conviction and confidence that what the belief says is certain. One can count on it. There are many kinds of beliefs that you may be able to identify in the culture of schooling. For example, there are beliefs that:

- high marks in school show that one is 'bright' or 'intelligent'
- certain types of schools are 'better' than others
- certain subjects are more important than others.

Examples drawn from different aspects of life in society show how beliefs are deeply embedded in how we live our lives.

- If a family goes to church every Sunday, this shows that they are basically 'good' people.
- Someone without a job and not actively looking for one is at risk of a host of negative consequences.
- Motherhood is a state far more sacred, precious and cherished than fatherhood, or being childless.
- Visiting friends or relatives where we are not offered food or drink signifies that something is wrong – they are being either mean or unfriendly for some reason.

Values

You will have noticed that it is extremely difficult to speak of beliefs without bringing in values. In each of the examples above there is a value involved. Values refer to how some quality, act, behaviour, disposition, image, and so on, is *ranked* by people sharing a culture.

Looking at the examples of beliefs linked to the culture of schooling in this light we see that scoring high marks on tests is not valued because the tests were well constructed and matched what was taught, but rather that it indicates who is 'intelligent'. The latter quality is highly prized and often rewarded. Tests and their educational significance have thus been subverted by a belief that they can identify those who are 'bright' because that is valued in the society.

Similarly, there are different types of secondary schools, usually offering different curricula to a different clientele. While there is the view that students have different needs and interests and that the curriculum should be tailored with this in mind, there is a dominant belief that some schools are 'better' than others. Such a belief is based on a value or a high rank placed on a particular kind of curriculum, perhaps one affording access to higher-status jobs and advanced areas of study.

What is being shown is that we have a system of values that is really a set of beliefs that ranks certain things (qualities, acts, behaviours, dispositions, images) as better than others. Thus, going to church regularly is highly regarded, as is being gainfully employed. Motherhood is beset with so many positive beliefs and values that fathers (and women who do not have children) feel that they are almost discriminated against by the dominant beliefs and values of their society.

There is also a strong belief among Caribbean people that we must show hospitality to our friends, neighbours and relatives. This rests on values that cherish family life, friendship and camaraderie, an ethic of helping others, as well as the desire to look good in the eyes of others. We also seem to value oral communication a great deal, and humour, so that visitors give us a chance to talk and make jokes as we relax. The significance placed on visiting friends and relatives as regularly as we can is based on all the values mentioned above. You may note, though, that visiting friends and relatives, for example, on a Sunday, is becoming less and less important as we become more and more enmeshed in the cultures of today's urban living and influences from abroad. Thus, values undergo change.

Sociology

Sociology sees culture as a social phenomenon. The 'social' is a construct of sociology that helps us to see that various explanations of culture have different emphases because of the difference in social location between groups. There are three aspects to this.

(1) Reducing complexity

For example, understanding the social shows us that complexity is glossed over in favour of short, precise, all-encompassing statements like 'ways of life', 'learned behaviour', 'shared meanings' and 'adaptive mechanism'. While these statements seem to summarize a lot, they need to be deconstructed to understand their usefulness – and their limitations. That this seldom happens is not difficult to believe; most people feel they understand the summary version and do not need to explore in-depth explanations of culture. In addition, notions of change and dynamism are not evident in these statements, except for 'adaptive mechanism'.

Understanding the social also helps us to question the emphasis put on cultural products in explaining culture. 'High culture', 'mass culture' and 'global culture' refer to art, creative expressions, artefacts, media and technology, and are attempts to understand culture through its products. However, the attempts do not really get off the ground as the processes behind their production are not examined. Similarly, attempts to simplify culture by pinpointing only some aspects of social life for study – for example, the drug culture, student culture, the culture of poverty – are clearly saying that studying the culture concept is too large and unwieldy an undertaking. In trying to understand the social and its impact on 'culture', what we see are clear attempts to simplify complexity in various ways.

(2) Social constructions

Understanding the social also means that we have to acknowledge that culture exists in a social context and inevitably people will construct a view of culture that takes into account the interaction and relationships of social groups. There are those who see culture as reflecting social life, as a mirror of the society. In this view, culture has a structural dimension in that it is the *social structure* which is seen to generate (or cause) the kind of culture experienced by different social groups. For example, the rich and famous will experience a different culture to that of the poor. Thus, 'high culture', 'mass culture' and the 'culture of poverty', are *social constructions* of culture built up by those who emphasize social distinctions in explaining culture.

(3) Multiple perspectives

Understanding the social means that we know that there is a variety of perspectives that exist about almost any issue. We also know that persons can hold multiple and conflicting views of reality. Attempts to understand culture that recognize this social context must acknowledge variation, complexity, change and interaction. Thus, explanations themselves will be complex because what they are attempting to do is to understand how people make meaning, how they interpret their actions and those of others, and how they communicate meaning. Explanations of culture that stress the symbolic – for example, 'ordinary culture', 'non-material culture' and 'webs of significance' – show that culture is not easy to understand, mainly because our understanding of the social prevents us from seeing it clearly.

ACTIVITY 2.14

Let us examine some aspect of our own culture, for example, drinking alcohol.

1. Reflect on how you came to hold the values and beliefs you do about drinking.

2. Identify some of the mainstream views about drinking in your society? If you hold minority or unpopular views, explain how as an individual you can derive meanings that are at odds with how others derive meanings and interpret 'drinking'.

3. If you do not have any strong views on drinking alcohol, whether for yourself or for others, do you still think that you hold values and beliefs about drinking? If an anthropologist were trying to understand the significance of your views in studying the culture of your society, how would you explain your interpretation of 'drinking'?

Geertz has offered an *interpretive view of culture*. If we agree that people interpret symbols to make meanings of the messages of others, to communicate their own meanings through various media (for example, speech, writing, gestures, structures and procedures, and the mass media), then we acknowledge the variety of views and perspectives that are likely to occur. In a way we are also acknowledging the impossibility of acquiring a complete understanding of culture. People are enmeshed within this context – this is perhaps why Geertz chose the analogy of the web to interpret culture. Attaching meanings and deriving understandings is not straightforward, yet we all do it. What are the processes we put ourselves through to interpret our actions and those of other people? If we can identify such processes then we can come close to a complex understanding of culture. Activity 2.14 seeks to clarify such processes in creating culture.

The main objective of this activity was to engage you in trying to unravel the webs of meaning in which you are enmeshed and which you have helped to spin. It may have helped somewhat to deepen your understandings of yourself as a social being and it certainly would have shown that the study of culture, and attempts to define it or unravel it to unearth its processes, meet only with partial success. Although we will have to give explanations of culture from time to time, we should be aware that such explanations speak of it largely in a finished and complete way, as if fully understanding culture was something that was even possible. When anthropologists have completed a study of some culture they know that they have not captured as much as they would have liked, and what is even more intriguing is that in helping you to understand their culture, people are limited by their own social location.

As we close this section, let us consider some of the different levels at which people speak about culture. You will be able to recognize and categorize some of the statements in Table 2.2 based on the different perspectives on culture that we have already explored in this chapter.

ACTIVITY 2.15

Suppose that you are an anthropologist or sociologist who has to analyse the following statements that people have made about someone's culture. Match each statement in Table 2.2 with what you consider an appropriate analysis based on the understanding of culture being expressed.

Table 2.2 Analysing statements about culture

DESCRIPTION OF CULTURE	ANALYSIS
1 'Those children only interested in wearing fancy footwear, nothing else.'	A This description of culture enters into the shared meanings attached to an act. It goes on to describe how the person feels from an insider's perspective by referring to his or her 'webs of significance'.
2 'Among youth having things that others value gives them social capital – prestige.'	B This description of culture merely states a behaviour. It can be used as an example of 'ways of life'.
3 'The latest and most expensive sneakers make the wearer feel good, successful, and capable of success.'	C This description goes a step further where someone gives a theory about why people act the way they do. It is still a view from the outside. It could be an example of an understanding of culture as the 'shared meanings' people have for something.

Summary

Popular conceptions of 'culture' are mediated by our understanding of the social. We come to an understanding of culture through the social. Thus, we have tended to build social constructions of culture emphasizing a static, straightforward and uniform portrayal because that is a dominant way that we regard knowledge. Deeper investigations of culture, largely through disciplinary perspectives such as anthropology and sociology, try to explicate its symbolic nature. The symbolic can easily accommodate the traditional understandings of culture as 'ways of life', 'shared meanings', 'learned behaviours', and as an 'adaptive mechanism', because all rely on an interpretation and communication of meanings. Those meanings, however, seem to be generated by sets of beliefs and values that give significance to something. It is these beliefs and values that encourage a society to adapt, change or stand still. Beliefs and values, then, are at the heart of culture.

2.4   CARIBBEAN 'SOCIETY' AND 'CULTURE'

Let us now apply what we have learned about 'society' and 'culture' in the previous sections to analysing the ways that Caribbean society and culture have been portrayed. Scholars have studied Caribbean social life and attempted to capture what they believe are the important aspects of its society and culture.

ACTIVITY 2.16

Examine each of the statements in Table 2.3, keeping in mind our previous attempts to map out the terms 'society' and 'culture', and our understanding of the social. Then answer the questions.

Table 2.3 Portrayals of Caribbean society

AUTHOR	PORTRAYALS OF CARIBBEAN SOCIETY
Vidia Naipaul	The Caribbean, and Trinidad in particular, has 'no society'. The people are transients (*The Loss of El Dorado*), have created nothing of value and are always hankering after what others have (*The Mimic Men*).
Derek Walcott	Ours is a creative society and uniquely so. There is nothing like what we will and can create.
Edward Kamau Brathwaite	Caribbean society is a creole society. Different social groups came here from elsewhere. They met, mixed, developed, transformed and changed their original ways of interacting.
R.T. Smith	*Plural* society exists in the Caribbean where different ethnic groups met but led separate lives under an ethic of toleration.

1. 'Although this list shows various labels for Caribbean "society", it is really "culture" that is emphasized'. Discuss the significance of this statement.

2. In the statements listed, **identity** seems to be an issue in describing Caribbean society and culture. Explain why 'identity' is an important component of a society and culture.

3. If values and beliefs form the core of a culture, suggest how the shared beliefs and values evident in Caribbean society and culture were formed.

Table 2.3 lists a selection of views attempting to portray Caribbean society, and hence its culture. There are many other views; one that is widely respected is Beckford's analysis of Caribbean society as **plantation society** (Box 2.5). Examining the statements in Table 2.3 we see repeated references to the *beliefs and values* of Caribbean people. For example, Caribbean people are variously described as valuing ethnocentric, indigenous, **creolized** and separatist beliefs. Our earlier discussions (Box 2.4) led us to reason that beliefs and values were at the heart of culture. At this point, though, we come close to uncomfortably deep questions about culture. For example, if we have beliefs and values, why are they ethnocentric or creolized, or even separatist? We met this debate earlier when certain disciplines such as history and geography attempted to offer the *determinants* of culture. This is when people try to explain the *causes* of culture – why do we hold the beliefs and values we do, and how do our beliefs and values shape *how* we adapt and *what* we adapt?

BOX 2.5 Plantation society

George Beckford (1972) portrayed Caribbean society as 'plantation society'. His emphasis focused on the legacy of slavery and **indentureship** and the system of economic organization, the plantation, which used this form of labour. To him the most significant characteristic of Caribbean society today is its stratified nature and he used the term 'plantation society', although the era of the large plantations dominating economic and social life is long gone. **Social stratification** today in this analysis continues to reflect the historical divisions among the various groups where **caste** (race and colour) and **class** (occupation) were rigidly tied.

Whites and people of lighter colour were the wealthier members of the society historically and they continue to be so, although other groups – blacks, those of mixed heritage and Indians – are increasingly accessing **social mobility**, mainly through education. Even though these other groups are now moving into better-paying jobs and enjoying higher status and prestige, they are relatively few, and large numbers are still at the poorest levels of the society. Thus, essentially the society is unchanged from its stratified nature during the colonial era of the plantation economy, when interactions and relationships among social groups were bounded largely by race, colour and class.

This portrayal of Caribbean society emphasizes its social structure. It analyses the characteristics of, and relationships between, the various social groups. For example, it shows that there is an unwillingness by the elites to allow other social groups to access social mobility. Groups of similar **ethnicity**, wealth, status or education level intermarry and associate with each other rather than with other groups. It can be thought of as a Marxist view of social relations as all the patterns and relationships are dominated by the ideas and values of the elites. The poorer classes do not have the power to challenge these interactions and usually comply with such arrangements, often not seeing how they are being deprived.

Although this view admits that change has occurred and is occurring, it tends to emphasize a static social structure suggestive of the colonial era. The notion of dynamism and change is also under-emphasized in certain other views of society, as portrayed in Activity 2.16: for example, **plural society** or *no society*. Beckford's analysis views culture as mirroring social structure. Thus, the culture of the elites will differ from the culture of those at different socio-economic levels in the society. The values and beliefs of each group occupying a particular socio-economic level will reflect their social location. For example, beliefs and values are at work in matters such as marriage and occupation, where those who enjoy privileged status seek to only bring those they favour into profitable alliances. They have the power to hire and fire and the criteria they use are often linked to beliefs and values attached to caste and class.

A consistent belief among lower socio-economic groups in society is that social mobility is necessary to live a better life. Thus, we are familiar with parents working very hard to secure a higher **standard of living** for their children. These beliefs and values seem to stem directly from the menial positions that their ancestors were forced to endure in the colonial era. Among the wealthier classes, beliefs and values do not necessarily focus on working hard and self-sacrifice but on strategies to consolidate their position and exclude others.

ACTIVITY 2.17

This is a debating exercise. Each statement can be used for a separate debate where students construct arguments that can uphold or reject the position in the statement.
• Our culture is really an amalgam of beliefs and values arising from our historical and geographical experiences.
• Our culture arises from our identity.
• Our culture is what causes us to be creative and adapt or to not do so.
• Our culture is being re-created every day.

However, precisely because we find many questions about culture to be quite unanswerable we need to engage in continuing dialogue to clarify what we can, rather than take it for granted that we know all about it. Activity 2.17 focuses on several issues related to the creation of culture which, as Caribbean people trying to better understand ourselves and our region, we should deliberately debate and ponder.

Having gone through the debates of Activity 2.17 you should be better prepared to interpret the insights offered by Nettleford (2004) in Activity 2.18. You can, for instance, compare some of your key ideas from Activity 2.17 about how culture is created with the connections that Nettleford makes. Although the ineffable nature of culture remains, you will have a sense of making some headway in understanding the concept of culture.

Culture is a social phenomenon. One cannot keep the concepts 'society' and 'culture' apart for very long, although we have been attempting to do just that in this chapter in order to clarify what each means. The difficulty with studying 'society' and 'culture' is that they are so tightly intertwined that we have to find ways to separate them to better understand each one and how they interrelate (Box 2.6).

ACTIVITY 2.18

Read the passage and then answer the questions below.

The clear and established 'Caribbean expressions', which have been the subject of anthropological investigation and tourist curiosity and have served as mild entertainments for an outside world that expects minstrelsy from exotic climes, must now be seriously put into perspective. For in contemporary life, identity goes beyond jump-up and calypso, beyond reggae, and beyond exteriorities of dreadlocks, red-green-and-gold woollen cap and the smoking of marijuana as a sacrament, regarded by many as the essence of exotica Caribbeana.

It goes, in fact, into the interiorities of self-determination, sovereignty (both territorial and cultural) and independence for individuals and nations alike. And it is precisely for this reason that the centuries of popular cultural expression by the mass of the population, who were always central to the process of creolization or indigenization, must be taken into account. After all, it is that historical experience which now informs existential reality, giving to the Caribbean well-articulated

parameters of concern in building nations and shaping societies as part of a still-emerging civilization.

Contemporary identity in Caribbean terms must therefore take into consideration not only the notions or theories that have been employed to articulate, explain and comprehend the phenomenon itself, but also the divisive forces of geography, colonization and the distinctive 'culture-spheres' resulting from the geo-politics of superpower rivalry over centuries of plantation slavery and mercantilist greed. (Nettleford, 2004, pp. 544–545)

1. According to the popular conceptions of culture that were outlined earlier in this chapter, identify those which seem to fit Nettleford's claims about how Caribbean culture has been regarded by others.

2. List some of the beliefs and values that Nettleford thinks should inform identity.

3. What part do history and geography seem to play in the creation of culture and identity?

BOX 2.6 Cultural sensitivity

The view is sometimes expressed that understanding culture helps us to better understand our society. What does this mean? What have we understood about culture so far that can help us to clarify this statement?

First, we have seen that culture is ineffable, indescribable and elusive when we attempt a study of it and try to define and explain it. We never seem to truly grasp it. Secondly, we come to our understandings of culture through *the social*, so that we are constantly fielding social constructions, varied perspectives, and attempts to simplify it. Thus, what we understand of it is conditioned by our *social location* and *relationships*.

If we are unclear about it, then, it is these unclear understandings of our own culture that we use to view and assess the culture of others, and what we use to try to understand our own. Outsiders too have a similar problem in trying to understand *our* culture because they have to do so through the lens of their own culture. It is interesting to note that anthropologists who go to live in certain cultures to study them better find that the longer they stay and become comfortable, the more difficult it is to make insightful observations.

If a study of culture such as that encountered in this chapter helps you to grasp these points, then it is likely that you will be somewhat wary of describing or judging your ideas and views, as well as the ideas and views of others, too easily. What such understandings confer is a degree of 'cultural sensitivity' that enables us to better understand the society. For example, if we examine any issue in our society today we see that there are competing views from different social groups. The urge to pronounce a judgement on the views of others must now be stayed while we acknowledge our imperfect cultural understandings as well as the knowledge that others (as well as ourselves) act from their own social location. Thus, issues of religion, youth, race and ethnicity, which rage in the society from time to time, can be better understood if we do not judge and assess from our individual viewpoint as if it were the only reference point in resolving the issue. Such cultural sensitivity can only come about through a study of culture and the recognition that we are hampered in finding out much about it because we are too deeply embedded in it. Yet it is all that we have to help us understand our society.

Anthropologists call for us to 'understand our understandings', meaning that we should attempt to acknowledge how partial and incomplete they are. A good way of checking this is to reflect on the views of people in the society about a topical issue, perhaps in the newspapers or on talk shows. You will notice that among those who do not have a well-developed sense of cultural sensitivity there are strong views based on the person's social location and experience. There is no recognition that they may have only a partial view; rather they give the impression that what they believe is right and others should recognize how right they are.

Someone who is less certain that they have a thorough understanding, or the only true and correct understanding of the issue, will make a greater effort in trying to make sense of oppositional views based on the nature of culture. They will be able to consider what they know of the beliefs and values of a group and reflect on how they are conditioned by time and place, by conflict, by consensus, and by change. They will be increasingly wary of statements that declare a bias as if it were an unshakable truth – for example, 'the government does not help poor people', 'you have to know somebody to get a job', 'Muslim groups in the society have a hidden agenda', 'the US is the greatest country on earth', 'voodoo is hocus-pocus', 'homosexuals are vile', and so on.

An orientation based in cultural sensitivity enables you to see that nothing is a 'given'. Everything should be challenged to determine as best as we can the extent to which someone in the grip of their own beliefs and values is relating to others in ways that suggest that these beliefs and values are universal and are a 'given'. If such is the case among groups in the society, then communication closes down. No one will be able to hear what others are saying because what is said will be screened through a set of beliefs and values deemed to be superior.

The student of culture, however, brings a certain awareness to an understanding of issues in the society that is conditioned by the very nature of culture. It is so elusive, some say, that all we see is the tip of the iceberg, yet we all live in it, act on it, and are quite comfortable with it. Thus we lead a somewhat ambiguous existence. If we are prepared to admit that we live out acts, beliefs and values that we ourselves understand imperfectly, then we are better able to deal sensitively with issues in the society as they arise, and in so doing deepen our own understandings.

Summary

When we analyse some of the ways in which Caribbean 'society' and 'culture' have been portrayed, our understanding of the social helps us to see that some representations reflect the social location of the writer and some reduce complexity so that only certain aspects, for example, creativity, are emphasized. As students attempting to understand Caribbean society and culture the many perspectives are valuable, because for us they represent different dimensions of a phenomenon. We have also learned that while we may separate the study of 'society' from 'culture' in attempting to get a clearer picture of each concept, when we apply it to a specific place we find that in reality they are embedded in each other. A study, for example, of the ways that Caribbean society has been portrayed emphasizes history and conceptions of identity, thus incorporating culture. Thus, to study Caribbean society means to study its culture.

WRAP UP

Traditional definitions of 'society' and 'culture' tend to give us an unreal picture of these concepts because of our habitual ways of regarding knowledge. Understanding the social enables us to see that our definitions tend to downplay the variety of perspectives that exist, reducing meanings to those of our own social location, and employing social constructions which we then proceed to regard as facts. To develop a more authentic understanding of each of these concepts, both have been considered in all their complexity. This analysis has revealed the concepts as having more dynamism than was apparent in traditional definitions. It has also showed that definitions tend to give the impression that one can know all about something, but the study of culture has revealed its ineffable aspects – for example, how do beliefs and values form in the first place? Finally, specific portrayals of Caribbean society and culture have shown that in real life both concepts are deeply embedded in each other. Thus, the strategy used in this chapter, of studying the two separately, was only done to deepen understanding and awareness of both concepts.

PRACTICE TESTS

Structured response

1 (a) Define society. (2 marks)
   (b) Define culture. (2 marks)
   (c) Identify ONE reason why it is difficult to separate the two concepts, 'society' and 'culture'. (2 marks)
2 Give TWO criticisms of the definition of society as 'a group of people living in an area for a long time'. (4 marks)
3 Suggest TWO reasons to explain why definitions of culture are often inadequate. (4 marks)
4 Explain what is meant by the 'socio-cultural'. (2 marks)
5 (a) Identify ONE cultural act or behaviour in Caribbean society. (1 mark)
   (b) Explain why the act or behaviour you identified is 'cultural'. (2 marks)
6 Explain how social institutions and social organizations help to explain the concept of 'society'. (6 marks)
7 Describe what is meant by an 'interpretive view of culture'. (2 marks)
8 Identify TWO ways that Caribbean writers have used to describe Caribbean society and its culture. (4 marks)
9 Explain what is meant by (a) 'the information society' and (b) 'the learning society'. (4 marks)
10 Distinguish between material and non-material culture. (4 marks)

Essay questions (20 marks)

1 Examine different understandings of the term 'society' and give a reasoned account of what aspects should be included in a definition of society.
2 Explain the differences and areas of overlap in the terms 'society' and 'culture'.
3 Identify the definitions of society and culture that you think are appropriate for a study of Caribbean society and culture.
4 Explain what is meant by 'the social'.

Challenge essay questions (30 marks)

1 Discuss the complexity of the culture concept by analysing TWO portrayals of Caribbean society and culture.
2 Assess the statement that 'there is not one Caribbean culture but many cultures'.
3 To what extent do Caribbean people in the diaspora still belong to Caribbean society?
4 Examine the view that definitions of 'society' and 'culture' have been influenced by how knowledge is conceived in the natural sciences.

RESEARCH TOPICS

The following is suggested as a research topic that you may wish to conduct. It is based on the theme of religion, emphasizing ideas related to understanding society and culture.

Conceptions of religion and culture

In this chapter you have come across several levels and different ways in which culture is understood. Using religion as a focus you can interview several persons (or you may use a questionnaire) to find out what ideas they have on the relationship between religion in the society and culture. For example, in an interview your main question might be:

'When religion is described as an aspect of the culture of a country, what does that mean?'

This will be a qualitative type of study eliciting what people feel, think or believe and it may take them quite a while to compose an answer as it is a complex issue. Their varied responses should give you a cross-section of views of what people think culture is (through the lens of religion). You can use the various definitions and emphases highlighted in the chapter to organize their responses. You will want to be able to summarize their points of view and then categorize them according to the ways in which people describe or explain culture. You may also display or present the data as verbatim quotes that will show the spread of ideas.

Your findings may lead you to reflect on what people tend to think about culture and the extent to which that may be problematic for Caribbean societies. For instance, there may be a lot of disagreement about what culture actually is, and as a researcher reflecting on the findings you will want to discuss the implications for multi-cultural Caribbean states.

REFERENCES AND FURTHER READING

Beckford, G. L. (1972). *Persistent poverty: underdevelopment in plantation economies of the Third World*. New York: Oxford University Press.

Geertz, C. (1973). *The interpretation of cultures*. New York: Basic Books.

Henslin, J. M. (2001). *Sociology: a down-to-earth approach* (5th ed.). Boston: Allyn & Bacon.

Kuhn, T. (1996). *The structure of scientific revolutions* (3rd ed.). Chicago, IL: University of Chicago Press.

Nettleford, R. (2004). Ideology, identity, culture. In B. Brereton (Ed.), *General history of the Caribbean, Volume 5: The Caribbean in the twentieth century*. Paris: UNESCO and London: Macmillan Caribbean.

Williams, R. (1958). *Culture and society, 1780–1950*. London and New York: Columbia University Press.

The Caribs, Arawaks and others lived in this space

The Europeans, a diverse crew, came as conquerors to exploit the land and people

Different African ethnic groups brought as enslaved labour

Indians, Chinese, Portuguese, Madeirans, Javanese brought as indentured labour

creolization hybridization

Syncretism

cultural erasure

social stratification

cultural retention

social mobility

cultural renewal

ethnicity

class colour

race

The Caribbean Basin

3

INVESTIGATING FEATURES OF CARIBBEAN SOCIETY AND CULTURE

An ever-present debate rages about Caribbean society and culture. Some say that the region is so culturally diverse that reference to a Caribbean consciousness or a Caribbean culture, or even a Caribbean region, exists only in the imagination. Another equally strong view refers to the common historical experiences forged in colonization – genocide, slavery, the plantation system, indentureship – and later migration, independence and attempts at regional integration. This is perhaps the most enigmatic thing about Caribbean society and culture – that there is so much difference amidst admittedly common experiences. We will explore this debate by investigating how ethnicity, hybridization, cultural change, social stratification and social mobility impact cultural diversity and identity in Caribbean society and culture.

EXPECTED LEARNING OUTCOMES

On completing this chapter, you will be able to

1 explain terms such as cultural diversity, hybridization, social stratification and social mobility
2 examine diversity and commonality in the Caribbean
3 analyse the phenomenon of cultural change
4 discuss the issue of identity and cultural diversity.

3.1

CULTURAL DIVERSITY

Culture is diverse

When people use the term **cultural diversity** we get a clear picture that differences are being emphasized. The *social* (Chapter 2) portrays a view that 'culture' is holistic and uniform so that in some places like the Caribbean, where there are many apparent distinctions, culture appears to be unusual in its diversity. As we saw in Chapter 2, **social constructions** sometimes obscure the meanings of terms and this is the case with 'cultural diversity'. What is not emphasized is the fact that culture *is* diverse, wherever it occurs. People *interpret* their culture and act from their *social location*, so that even if **ethnicity** seems to be homogeneous, that does not necessarily mean that culture is uniform.

Take *your culture* for instance. You are a bearer of your culture. And so is your brother and so is your neighbour down the road. But you do not live it and experience it in the same way. Suppose you are a Jamaican, then you belong to an **ethnic group** based on **nationality**. However, you may differ from your neighbour by virtue of **race** (Box 3.1); that is an ethnic difference that may influence how you live and experience Jamaican culture. Perhaps, within your family, one member has chosen to join the Rastafari. Then you will also differ based on ethnic categories of **religion, traditions** and **customs** (Box 3.2). On the other hand, suppose you lived in a neighbourhood where everyone is black, middle class and professional, do you think that because they belong to the same ethnic categories of colour, class and occupation, they live and experience the culture in the same way?

Often when we talk and think about complex issues we simplify matters and polarize them into neat categories. With culture, people tend to focus on either similarities or differences. The black, middle-class professionals would be generalized into having some similar behaviours to typify them. This is easier to do than to search for how they genuinely live their lives and what **beliefs** and **values** they hold. If we had a view of culture that focused not only on the beliefs and values people share, but also on their unique ways of expressing and experiencing these beliefs and values, even interpreting them, then it will not be so easy to have an image of culture as something that is uniform and unvarying.

BOX 3.1 Cultural diversity and race

Biology was used in the past as a scientific way of differentiating the races. One racial group was separated from another using criteria supposedly based on genetic inheritance – distinctive hair, eye and skin colour, as well as other facial characteristics, and perhaps height and stature. However, these physical characteristics seem to occur along a continuum, as over time the ancestors met and mated with other groups who are no longer in the picture. There is no telling what is in the gene pool!

Negroid, Caucasoid and *Mongoloid* are the most well-known racial categories that have been used to classify the world's peoples on the basis of physical appearance. This classification, though, cannot accommodate the Australian **aboriginal** peoples and those of mixed heritage, so a large array of sub-types and sub-categories had to be created. In addition, the varieties of people who did occur *within* one category or racial type were bewildering. Most importantly, no consistent scientific way has been found to justify this classification – for example, by blood type, cell structure, and the like. And so, after a century or two of intense scientific investigations, there appears to be no consistent *biological* difference among the races that can be used to name and distinguish them.

Thus, 'race' has no existence in biology or science. It is, though, ever present in social life and is thus a *social construction*. In our societies we have accustomed ways of classifying and labelling people and these categories have a semblance of solidity because we all more or less agree on the categories, or we know what someone means when

they use them. This is known as 'social race', to underscore the notion that we have created the categories based largely on *phenotype* (outward physical characteristics).

Using the three-way classification in the Caribbean we see that the *pre-Columbian* or aboriginal peoples had distinct physical characteristics that distinguished them from the European invaders. They were categorized as Mongoloid and the Europeans were said to belong to the Caucasoid racial grouping. The Africans were then added, bringing Negroid racial characteristics to the region. Those are the main racial groupings. Any group coming afterwards represented some sub-grouping of the races already present. Thus, the Chinese and Indians are also categorized as Mongoloids, and the Syrians, Jews and Lebanese (who are more recent immigrants) are Caucasoid. These categories are not very meaningful as all these people vary a great deal in appearance.

When we say that cultural diversity is extremely marked in the Caribbean because of the many races and racial groupings that are present, this use is really based on categories of 'social race' and can better be described as 'ethnicity'. Sometimes we use 'race' as a synonym for nationality or genealogy. Thus, if we speak of the 'Indian race' we are identifying a group of people who are linked through bloodlines and **kin** (genealogy) and who reside in a particular geographical area. In this case, it is more accurate to speak of ethnicity than race. And that may well be the case for most discussions that tend to want to focus on race, because it is an ill-defined social phenomenon.

BOX 3.2 Cultural diversity and ethnicity

Cultural groups are identified using several criteria: for example, race, colour, religion, heritage and language. Cultural differences are referred to as 'ethnic' differences. Other cultural dimensions are also used to differentiate groups – for example, wealth, kin, education, urban/rural residence – but these are more like fine distinctions laid upon already existing differences. Groups do not necessarily differ according to only one characteristic, say race. For example, people may be of the same race but of different religions. 'Ethnicity' refers to social and cultural 'belongingness' – the ties that bind people who see themselves as similar in some way, and who regularly interact.

Ethnic groups can be based on *race*, though many times it is not very meaningful. Lumping whole groups of people who may look similar as belonging to one ethnic category based on race is fraught with difficulty. For example, the British and French may be of the same race but culturally they are quite distinct. And for many the race factor may be less important than the cultural life they share with others. People of African descent (or Negroid ancestry) comprise the largest racial grouping in the Caribbean. It is difficult to differentiate between an African person from Guyana and one from Barbados, but they may belong to different cultural groups, have certain ideas, values and beliefs that are similar to those of people in their nation-state, and those people do not have to be African. They therefore belong to different ethnic groups based on *nationality* though they belong to one racial grouping. Thus, ethnic categories overlap in ways that may be indecipherable to people from outside the region.

And we must also be aware of the many who are of mixed descent and identify with, say, their African origins, even though their physical characteristics may proclaim otherwise. Further, people of *mixed race* may not identify with any one race, may actually discount race as important to them, and may actually feel more comfortable belonging to an ethnic group that celebrates their nationality – for example, being Belizean rather than mestizo. In addition, there are African people who identify more closely with Africa as a homeland and are therefore culturally or ethnically different from other people of African descent in the society. The Maroons, the Bush Negroes and the Rastafarians are all ethnic communities that are mainly of African descent but their *cultural practices* and *beliefs* set them apart. Cultural diversity deepens immensely when you realize that there may be, as in Suriname, different Maroon groups, with their own traditions, customs and languages.

If we look at the *Amerindian* groups of Guyana we find a similar situation. They have recognizable physical traits or features, but belong to very different ethnic groups because of their cultural heritage and geographical location. There are about nine distinct Amerindian ethnic groups comprising 7 per cent of the Guyanese population. They live for the most part in separate communities in different areas of the country and speak their own languages. Those on the coast tend to interact and live together – the Arawaks, Warau and Caribs. However, the Akawaio, Patamona, Arekuna, Makushi, Wapishana and Waiwai live over the vast interior hinterland of forests, plains, savannas, plateaux and mountains.

Let us look at a culture that *appears* to be less diverse than others within the Caribbean – the twin island state of St Kitts and Nevis. The people are mainly of African origin and their cultural practices are similar. They have had common historical experiences. If we are using the typical social construction of culture – that culture is a uniform way of life for people – then the people of St Kitts and Nevis would appear to be one people. Activity 3.1, however, gives an alternative view.

Culture, then, *is* a diverse phenomenon but we have become accustomed to speaking and thinking about it in a static way. This social construction put on the concept 'culture' is at the centre of the debate about whether it is diverse in some places and uniform in others. To go beyond this way of thinking, it may be helpful to visualize how an outsider would *see* the culture of a place as opposed to how people in that place experience their own culture.

ACTIVITY 3.1

Read the excerpt from Hubbard (2002) analysing events in St Kitts and Nevis in the 1990s and then answer the questions below.

Early attempts at a compromise failed and as a result, Premier Amory of Nevis called for a secession referendum pursuant to the constitution. Feelings ran very high in Nevis. All the slights, real or imagined, which Nevis had suffered through the years under the administration of St Kitts were recalled in detail. For over two centuries there had been disagreements between the two, including but not limited to the payments Nevis was called upon to make in 1782 to the victorious French, the failure to rebuild the Nevis hospital after the 1899 hurricane, the Bradshaw years, and finally what Nevis called an unwarranted intrusion into its local affairs in connection with its offshore business. Additionally, it had been felt for years that St Kitts retained development money for itself when some of it should have gone to Nevis.

(Hubbard, 2002, p. 159)

1. What does the passage indicate about loyalties and identities among the people of St Kitts and Nevis?

2. Compare what you think a Caribbean person would say about cultural diversity in St Kitts and Nevis with what a citizen of that country would say.

Commonalities and differences

The truth is that there are both commonalities and differences in Caribbean culture and in others. However, we need to pause a moment and consider how we think about difference. For us to be able to speak of differences between two things there must be something that is common. It is only among things that share basic similarities that we can speak of differences and make sense. For example, the differences between two individuals, male and female, are only recognizable because they are accepted as persons. Other than that we would not be able to speak of the differences between them, as it wouldn't make sense. We would not ask for differences between the sea and a dog or a man and a planet. We only seek out difference when the entities being compared are recognized as similar. That is the only context within which seeking difference or 'diversity' makes sense. Thus, when we speak of 'cultural diversity' in the Caribbean, *we are acknowledging* that there are similarities and commonalities amongst the cultures of the Caribbean.

The *balance* between difference and commonalities, however, is what is problematic in this whole debate. The term 'balance' here does not refer so much to two things occurring equally, each offsetting the other, but any equilibrium that exists is a 'balance'. Thus, a dynamic that occurs in cultural life is the relation between its similar and different elements. Activity 3.2 explores this theme.

A brief historical, sociological and anthropological reading of the Caribbean situation follows. Together these disciplines furnish us with a more insightful understanding of how commonalities and differences can be better understood.

ACTIVITY 3.2

All societies have different and common cultural elements. However, over time and place in one country there will certainly be changes in the 'balance' between differences and commonalities. Think of your country in terms of its racial or ethnic composition. To what extent did that change between 1900 and 2000?

History – what happened?

Caribbean society formed out of the meeting and mixing of different groups of people from societies and cultures in different parts of the world. These groups were forcibly uprooted or coerced into leaving their homelands. The aboriginal inhabitants suffered violent confrontations with the Europeans and were severely decimated. The sole purpose for importing these groups was to provide manual labour for the plantations. Europeans, Africans, Indians, Chinese and the Amerindian population all met and interacted within the context of European dominance and plantation life. It was a mixing of cultures.

Historians tell the story of a period of time. They seek to give a chronological account of what has occurred divided into significant time periods. They focus on structures and processes impacting on people *generally speaking*. Even when they study something unique, such as the Haitian revolution, they look for what is *general in the unique*. They compare it with other like events – for example, the American, French and Russian revolutions – to distil greater understanding about revolutions. While they do study the unique or different, there is no stress on just recognizing exceptionality. Rather, the unique is used as an opportunity to better understand what is general or common. Thus, Maroon societies are studied not primarily because of their differences to mainstream society but to learn more about **cultural retention, cultural erasure** and **cultural renewal** and how cultures change. (These are important concepts to which we will return.) History, then, gives us a perspective on cultural diversity where differences are important in illuminating commonalities.

Sociology – what kind of society?

Sociology is the study of society. The groups who came to the Caribbean varied in their cultural orientations and posed problems for organizing the society. There were differences in religions, languages (Box 3.3), customs and other ethnicities, leading to the existence, then and now, of distinct cultures in the Caribbean. However, they shared common experiences such as being uprooted, transported, transplanted and colonized. **Colonization** consisted of policies for the control and cultural transformation of the different groups through conquest, settlement, the plantation system and colonial laws. In this way, some kind of common or assimilatory process took place across the diverse groups, leading to a different set of relationships between the cultures as they settled down in their new home.

Sociology, while not ignoring the passage of time, focuses on the relationships among the various groups making up the society. For example, it shows that **social stratification** occurred in all societies – in Carib and Arawak society, in **plantation society**, and in 'free' society. There was always a ranking of social groups though the criteria differed. In aboriginal societies **status** could be because of fighting prowess or descent; in plantation society it depended on race/colour, and in societies of the post-**emancipation** era social status turned on race, colour, class, wealth and/or education. In Caribbean life today, sociologists will point out that education is the primary means of accessing **social mobility** throughout the region. Previously disadvantaged groups, such as those of African, Indian and Amerindian descent, can now attain greater wealth and prestige than their parents and move to a higher socio-economic class position by virtue of being educated. This changes the traditional stratified picture and increases diversity in social relations. For example, in some countries (Barbados, Jamaica) the descendants of Europeans continue to own wealth and occupy the highest rungs of the social hierarchy. Increasingly, though, they have to share their position with other ethnic groups achieving professional status. In some Caribbean countries, such as Dominica and St Vincent, the old white **elite** is virtually non-existent and Africans make up the majority in all socio-economic levels. Cultural diversity then is a normal part of the relationships that characterize cultural groups who share a society.

BOX 3.3 Languages of the Caribbean

A mosaic of languages contributes to cultural diversity in the Caribbean. In some countries language is not a major issue, in others it is extremely contentious. In the region as a whole though, language is seen as a divisive force militating against efforts at integration. This comes home very quickly when we realize that even when most Caribbean countries have become independent, and arbiters of their own destinies, there are very few ties between countries where different languages are spoken. Our levels of interaction, then, are still largely determined by whether we speak the same language or not.

This macro picture is echoed in various ways within the different Caribbean countries. When one is speaking generally, it is easy to think of a Caribbean country in terms of one language, and the European language of the colonial power at that. While the European languages persist – for example, English, Dutch, French and Spanish are the official languages of various Caribbean countries – the reality is that in many cases they are rarely spoken. They are the languages for official business, for written communication and for formal situations. In each country a **creole** language has evolved which has become the first language of many Caribbean persons. Thus, in a country like Barbados where English has been thought to be the main language for centuries, today Barbadian English is acknowledged as the first language. Standard English is mainly for written communication and specialized contexts.

However, the plural ethnic situation in some Caribbean countries results in an array of languages, and the creole may not be the first language for some people. For example, Guyana has nine pre-Columbian languages (West Indian Commission, 1992), and in Belize the Kekchi and Mopan are Maya languages spoken today. In these linguistic communities the aboriginal languages will be their first or home language. Almost all of them will become bi- and trilingual speakers. In Guyana, they will almost certainly learn the creole as a second language. In Belize, the Kekchi and the Mopan usually learn the Belizean Creole (*Kriol*) as

well as Spanish, which is spoken widely.

There are still other Caribbean countries with even deeper linguistic diversity. In Suriname strong multi-ethnic traditions persist and a multiplicity of languages co-exists. Many nationals only know one or two of these languages. For example, Dutch is the official language, English is widely spoken and Surinamase (the creole or *sranan tongo*) is the lingua franca (for those who cannot speak each other's language). However, about 15 per cent of the population is Javanese (originally from Indonesia) and they speak a hybrid language known as Surinaams–Javaans. Hindustani (or Hindi) is also spoken, mainly by the East Indians. And there are also Bush Negro or Maroon communities which include the Ndjuka, Saramacca and Matawai – and other smaller groups, such as the Kwinti, all considered ethnically different. They have their own languages, many of which differ considerably from the creole spoken by the majority population on the coast, sranan tongo.

The Indians of Trinidad, Guyana and Suriname brought Hindi, Urdu and Bhojpuri (a variant of Hindi), and Arabic is the language of prayer for Muslims. Chinese is spoken in newly immigrant families. To a large extent, though, in these countries these languages are not widely spoken and are reserved for special occasions, such as prayer meetings. However, in Trinidad the creole tends to be liberally sprinkled with words from Hindi and Bhojpuri, particularly for foods and vegetables – *bodi* (a type of string bean), *bhaggi* (spinach), *bhaigan* (melongene), *channa* (garbanzo beans, chickpeas) and *alloo* (potato), among others.

The issue of language is one of cultural identity. The difficulties experienced in multilingual Caribbean countries stem from the unwillingness of some groups to recognize the languages of other groups as of equal status. There have been some really heated national debates about what is chosen as a national language. Minority groups feel particularly vulnerable to becoming **encultured** by the dominant culture and eventually losing their language.

Anthropology – what experience?

Anthropologists focus on understanding how in a society and culture the group develops a sense of self and **identity**. These are issues of culture. They study how people in a group at a particular time and in a particular space come to learn what they stand for or represent. Thus, the experiences they share are important as well as how they are perceived by others in the society. Their behaviours and the meanings they attach to them give insights about the symbolic aspects of that culture.

For example, how a person perceives himself or herself is very much influenced by how his or her ethnic group experienced the transplanting process within the new societies of the Caribbean. Indians were brought to Trinidad, Guyana and Suriname, as well as to other territories, virtually as 'scab' labour to set up a competitive situation with the freed Africans, who were unwilling to work on the plantations for a menial wage. The Africans had other options. As new immigrants, the Indians, with customs, religions and languages very different from those of the African and European populations, were relegated to the bottom of the social hierarchy. Within this diverse milieu of different ethnic groups, occupying different social strata, the anthropologist is interested in how the self is built and how the group sees itself among others.

Indians had their own cultural resources, more or less intact, to help them deal with the hardship and oppression they experienced. In a foreign land amidst strange people who were long established, they clung to their customs and remained in the rural areas even after their period of **indentureship**. Being social outcasts they formed a virtually closed community. However, their children, born in the Caribbean, sought education and soon after that competition for the rewards of the society. They used any means – education, land, business and family contacts – to better their social and economic position.

Occupying the same space meant that accommodations had to be made between the different ethnic groups. For example:

- In similar places where different groups had been brought in as labour (for example, Mauritius and Sri Lanka) **cultural pluralism** was the form of accommodation that resulted (Box 3.4).
- Particularly in the Caribbean more than other places, from the very first contact of Europeans and the First Peoples, **hybridization** (discussed on pp. 70–80) or mixing of the races became a form of accommodation.
- Another option also exercised from the beginnings of the Conquest was *maroonage* – running away and attempting to build a different society and culture (Box 3.5).

All these accommodations reflect the perceptions and understandings of the self in relation to their experiences. All groups used their cultural resources to help them adapt in the Caribbean environment. In the options they exercised about Caribbean space, and thus their relationships with other groups, they were forging an *identity* (Box 3.6). When speaking of cultural diversity, then, we should be mindful of what lies behind the different customs, values and traditions. And what lies behind all these diverse outcomes is remarkably similar. It lies in the experiences a people have had which have shaped their perceptions of themselves and others in the space they occupy. It lies in the cultural resources they have used and adapted to survive.

History, sociology and anthropology, then, give us some insights into how the study of cultural diversity is approached by different disciplines. History shows us that differences are studied to understand commonalities better. Sociology indicates that the same cultural processes occur in all societies and that differences arise because of how groups relate to each other. Finally, anthropologists focus on the common experiences of people that shape their concept of 'self' and influence them to choose different options.

ACTIVITY 3.3

'In the options they exercised about Caribbean space, and thus their relationships with other groups, they were forging an *identity*.' Explain what this statement means in relation to ONE of the following (see also Box 3.6):

1. the Chinese population in an identified Caribbean country

2. the aboriginal population in an identified Caribbean country.

BOX 3.4 Cultural pluralism

Cultural pluralism is a term associated with the cultural diversity resulting from European colonization, when different groups were brought either forcibly, or under contract, as labour for plantations. It describes culture and society not only in the Caribbean but in Mauritius, Sri Lanka, Fiji and other ex-colonies. In a **plural society** there are two or more ethnic groups who share the same space but do not mix to a significant extent. They may meet and mingle at school, at the workplace, and in different groups and associations, but to a large extent they live in different areas, work in different occupations (one may be largely rural based), celebrate different festivals, and do not intermarry.

In Fiji, the British brought in labourers from India to work on the plantations. Today their descendants and the native Fijians make up a plural society where not only do they not mix but there is much hate and mistrust between them. In Sri Lanka the British also brought in workers from India as labour for the tea plantations in what used to be known as Ceylon. Today, the native population (Sinhalese) and the Indians (Tamils) have been engaged in unending civil strife and open violence. In the Caribbean, societies that seem to be somewhat similar are Guyana, Suriname and Trinidad and Tobago. In Guyana relations are polarized between those of African and Indian descent and there have been incidents of ethnic violence in the past. Trinidad and Tobago teeters on the brink of this from time to time. Suriname, however, presents a special case.

The two major ethnic groups in Suriname are the Indians (36 per cent), whose ancestors were brought by the Dutch as contract labour, and the Creoles (descendants of Africans and Europeans), comprising 31 per cent. However, there are substantial minorities such as the Javanese from Indonesia (15 per cent, also brought by the Dutch on contract) and the Maroons (10 per cent). The rest of the population is made up of Amerindians, Chinese and others. The Indian, Javanese and Chinese elements together make Suriname a predominantly 'Asian' country. Alliances of the major ethnic groups functioned well in Suriname (once independence had been achieved) in an elaborate system of checks and balances, though there were instances of ethnic tensions. The military takeover in 1980 disrupted this delicate peace by removing the checks and balances that had been established between all the major ethnic groups. The Maroons or Bush Negroes were increasingly discriminated against. Economically difficult times intensified conflicts with the Maroons, who held a relatively autonomous position in the interior, claiming large areas as their homelands given to them by treaty with the Dutch in the eighteenth century. Of significance, too, is the strong feeling by other Surinamers that the Maroons were a backward people.

The dictatorship was made up mainly of the Creoles. What followed was akin to **genocide**: the military were dispatched to forcibly remove the Maroons from their homeland and relocate them. A bloody civil war and untold atrocities ensued. What is remarkable was that this was a war waged on Africans by Africans. It tells us that the possibility of ethnic conflict is an ever-present reality in plural societies. Yet some countries have been able to avoid it entirely, as did Suriname until power was grasped by a group unconcerned with achieving a 'balance' of representation by the different groups.

The 'us' and 'them' syndrome

Cultural diversity is a term that emphasizes the differences among people. It is both a call to 'celebrate' and recognize difference and at the same time to be aware that cultural difference is a potentially explosive reality (Box 3.7). We have surveyed different ethnicities in this section, and tried to go beyond seeing difference as 'just difference'. Here we want to go a bit further to interrogate ourselves to reveal the social constructions that we have inherited which can lead people from different ethnic groups to keep a distance from each other. Thus, the problems we associate with cultural diversity do not necessarily arise out of people being so unalike, but because we have been **socialized** to behave in a 'them versus us' way. Activity 3.4 explores this theme.

BOX 3.5 Maroonage

Throughout the history of the Conquest and the colonization period in Caribbean history, individuals and groups sought freedom from oppression by running away. The Amerindians tried it and so did the enslaved Africans. They were only successful in hiding from capture in those terrains that were inhospitable and proved challenging to the European military forces sent to bring them back. They sought refuge in mountainous territories in the Caribbean and in the interior forests of the Guianas. In Jamaica, in the Blue Mountains and the Cockpit Country, and in British, Dutch and French Guiana they settled and formed viable stable communities.

Running away was one way of responding to the harsh reality of their existence. In the communities they founded, resistance and resilience were core values and this was reinforced by the practise of African religions and the healing arts, as well as family life and organization according to kin. Land was communally owned and decision-making was participatory and based on kinship networks. They were able to develop self-sufficiency in agriculture and raided the plantations mainly for women, weapons and gunpowder. They were so successful in waging war on the Europeans that in both Suriname and Jamaica peace treaties were signed, giving them lands on which they could live without interference.

Communalistic values were essential to their survival in the wild and in this they drew on their African roots and culture. They therefore set up a rival society based on values at odds with the individualistic, **capitalist** enterprise of the plantation economy. Their presence – communities of free black people existing long before the abolition of slavery and actively engaging the European in combat – proved invaluable as an alternative model or ideal on which enslaved blacks could base their self-concept. It laid to rest the notion that the European was the superior power and, although the enslaved had to defer to the European in daily interaction, in their gatherings and celebrations he was mocked. The history of the enslaved Africans (and Amerindians) shows that for the most part they did not accept their fate passively; they resisted, and some of them, such as the Maroons, resisted successfully (see Chapter 4).

BOX 3.6 Ethnic identity

Box 3.4 discussed the fragile nature of plural societies, where different ethnic groups live in a tenuous peace that sometimes deteriorates into civil war. These societies are an outcome of colonization and the plantation system. The groups brought to the Caribbean at different times had to work out accommodations and rules for living together. What loomed important in these accommodations was maintaining ethnic pride.

The plantation was the most important, if not the only, economic unit under colonization. It was also a social unit, each plantation being a mini-society in itself. There was not much communication between plantations for non-Europeans, whose lives were severely restricted. Europeans brought in enslaved labour from Africa to work on the sugar plantations, and after emancipation, Indian, Chinese, Portuguese and Javanese were also brought in where a labour shortage was experienced. The groups were naturally distrustful of one another, each having its own cultural norms and customs. It was an artificial situation constructed by Europeans who maintained a highly stratified system of social relations that effectively separated the groups. While the British were in control of the colony they thought it in their own best interests to keep the races divided. Unity would have threatened the position of the few whites who were in control.

Indians and Africans began their relationship in mutual antipathy. While some Africans were willing to work on the plantations for wages, the influx of Indians drove down the price of labour. They therefore resented the newcomers, who were looked on as social outcasts and remained locked into an isolated existence on the plantations. In this artificial situation to which they were brought, where they met other groups but were not expected to mix, where they were of low social status, each group tried as best as it could to forge an ethnic identity of which it could be proud.

In Guyana and Trinidad each sought to lay claim to their new society: Africans claimed a superior education, a sophisticated urban existence and long residence in the colony; Indians claimed that their propensity for hard work, thrift and business acumen helped to develop the country. These self-characterizations spoke to the need to find a place in a situation that was not of their making but in which they had to live. Thus, these ethnically based conceptions of themselves were accommodations that Africans and Indians employed to show that they belonged. They had to do this because no one *really* 'belonged'. The issue of 'belongingness' always looms large in plural societies where different ethnic groups have been imported over time.

ACTIVITY 3.4

One argument that encourages the 'them versus us' condition is that 'no one can really understand a culture if he or she does not belong to it'. This statement is suggesting that you need to become an insider to totally understand someone's way of life. If this is so, then different ethnic groups in a country are fated to remain suspicious and distrustful of each other. To what extent do you agree that you cannot understand others if you don't belong to their ethnic group?

1. Explain how socialization encourages the 'them versus us' syndrome.

2. Do you believe that people can transcend their socialization?

3. For all the points given in Box 3.7 suggest concrete Caribbean examples.

Summary

'Cultural diversity' is a term that emphasizes the idea of difference, invites a celebration of differences, and at the same time is wary of the problems that may result. However, it conceals something about the true nature of culture as culture is in itself a diverse entity. People do not just *bear* their culture but interpret and choose their actions and behaviours. It also conceals something about diversity or difference – that for something to be different there must be some things that are common. History, sociology and anthropology show us that underlying the obvious ethnic differences are some very strong similarities between those groups. However, the idea of difference is so strongly emphasized, and indeed there are so many ethnicities in the Caribbean to reinforce this idea, that the common human experiences of all Caribbean people tend to be overlooked and discounted as a source of Caribbean identity and solidarity.

3.2 HYBRIDIZATION

'Hybridization' refers to processes of cultural and ethnic mixing to produce new or 'creole' forms (Box 3.8). Meeting and mixing in the Caribbean region have been going on for more than five hundred years. Prior to the Conquest the aboriginal inhabitants of the New World migrated through the Caribbean from South America. They captured each other and adopted each other's languages and adapted cultural practices. Thus, when Columbus arrived there is no telling how 'hybrid' the cultures of the peoples he met already were. The term 'hybridization' is borrowed from biology and refers to one species being cross-fertilized with another to produce a new species. It is used in Caribbean life to describe many levels of meeting and mixing and creating something new, especially fusion between different races to produce hybrid peoples and cultures.

BOX 3.7 Positive and negative effects of cultural diversity

Studying the relations between different ethnic groups in culturally diverse societies, especially plural societies created as a result of colonization, reveals that many of them have erupted into ethnic violence from time to time. They are generally felt to be 'fragile' societies because of the seeming impossibility of getting different groups to appreciate each other's point of view. However, some plural societies have managed to avoid outright ethnic violence, and some have had periods where the groups, solidified by political alliances, have worked peaceably together. Nevertheless, they live all the time with the understanding that deep-seated ethnic prejudices can be stirred up (usually in times of economic downturn) and threaten social stability. While discussions about ethnic relations in culturally diverse and plural societies tend to take on a negative tone, people who live in such societies do still speak of a more positive side.

Positive effects of cultural diversity

- Members enjoy a variety of foods, festivals, music and celebrations, as well as fashions, handicraft, and other cultural expressions such as dance. Even though some persons do not participate in another group's ethnic celebrations, the fact is that they occur, presenting citizens with a variety of alternatives and experiences.
- Day-to-day living in such societies provides instances enabling one to reflect on the values and customs of others: for example, the furore created when a Roman Catholic school in Trinidad refused to enrol a student wearing a hijab, and at a later date a Rastafarian student because of the dreadlocks hairstyle. These situations present opportunities for national dialogue which may or may not occur as civilized discourse – they are opportunities nevertheless.
- One can learn to appreciate other cultures and an array of perspectives by just growing up in the society: for example, by having close friends in other groups and being invited to religious celebrations and festivals, or by just observing family life in another culture.
- Diverse and plural societies provide unique conditions under which experiments in cultural hybridization may take place to create wholly different forms of music, art, literature and poetry, which speak to the experience of more than one ethnic group.

- As members of associations and unions of all kinds in these societies, including the government, persons learn from an early age that conflict is endemic and that they need skills of negotiation, alliance-building and brokering peace to accommodate all the many perspectives that arise. They recognize the importance of maintaining 'balance' between the ethnicities, which is the essence of democracy – letting all voices be heard.
- Persons of mixed race, themselves a product of cultural diversity, who do not feel such strong affiliation to any specific ethnic group, provide interesting alternatives in behaviour that may act as mirrors for some members of the wider society to reflect on and evaluate their own views and reactions.

Negative effects of cultural diversity

- Ethnic prejudices are perpetuated through socialization within the family, which is reinforced in interaction with friends and acquaintants; differences appear to be so profound that myths and misconceptions of the other race or ethnic groups are believed as fact.
- Ethnic hate may arise out of feelings of ethnic superiority (the 'Us versus Them' syndrome), compounded by perceptions that one group is getting more of the national pie than one's own group.
- Ethnic politics develops, with political parties becoming polarized according to race. In such situations politics becomes a contest between ethnicities. The ethnic lines harden and jobs, promotions, opportunities and gifts are limited to people of the same ethnicity as that of the ruling party. This sort of discrimination exacerbates an already potentially unstable situation.
- Continued feelings of discrimination, of being exploited, and that one's lifestyle and means of earning a living may be in jeopardy, lead to social unrest – spontaneous demonstrations, labour riots and outbreaks of ethnic violence.
- Inability on the part of the ruling group or any other power to intervene and restore order may lead to civil war and genocide.

BOX 3.8 The meanings of 'creole'

Jolivert (2003), in the following passage, discusses the derivation and meaning of the term 'creole'.

It comes from 'criollo' which in the sixteenth century was used by the Spanish to designate their children born in the West Indies. That was always the definition of the word 'criole' in the Furetière dictionary, dated 1690. For the French who quickly transformed it into 'créole', the term became synonymous with any white person born in the colonies. However, a distinction began to appear between the definition used in Europe (and in the dictionaries) and local practice. From the end of the seventeenth century, in fact, in his New Voyage to the Islands of America, Father Labat . . . spoke of creole slaves as opposed to traded slaves. In a more general sense, the term describes the local 'descendant' of anything imported: one speaks of 'creole corn' or 'creole livestock'. Applied to people, it describes a person born locally of immigrant parents and, thus, also distinguishes native peoples from newcomers. (p. 214)

Later in the chapter, in speaking of the situation in French Guiana (or Guyane, sometimes referred to as Cayenne), Jolivert mentions that the people who regard themselves as Creoles do so in order to maintain distinctions between themselves and the Amerindians, new immigrants and the Bush Negroes, who are also African. One distinction they prize is the adoption of a European way of life, with its connotations of urban lifestyles.

However, in Trinidad and Tobago the term 'creole' is used to describe persons of African descent. Paradoxically (and more aligned to Jolivert's explanation in the passage above), the term 'French Creole' refers to the descendants of French settlers who came to Trinidad in the late eighteenth century. But there is a world of difference in calling someone a 'French Creole' and a 'creole'. The former are descendants of white colonials and still carry names such as de Verteuil, de la Bastide, Farfan and de Montbrun. They were large landowners and today have considerable business and industrial interests. It would be incomprehensible in Trinidad and Tobago's culture and society to describe a person of Indian or Chinese descent as a 'creole', though elsewhere in the Caribbean that will be entirely acceptable in the general use of the term according to Jolivert.

Labelling the hybrid languages of the Caribbean as 'the creole' follows the traditional meaning of the term as 'something born or created in the Caribbean'. There is also widespread use of the term in the Caribbean and the southern US to describe specific culinary arts as 'creole cooking'. Today the term is also used to refer to the environment – the 'creole environment' or 'creole space' – an acknowledgement by scholars of the themes of hybridity, creativity, resistance and resilience, which have characterized much of the interaction between groups in the Caribbean.

The convention used here about capitalizing the first letter of 'creole' is fairly standard. If reference is to a specific place or group or thing, capitals are used, as in the 'Haitian Creole' or 'Caribbean Creole' cooking. For general reference, lower-case 'c' is used, as in 'creoles', or 'the creole spoken in the Caribbean'.

Racial and ethnic hybridization

Amerindian, African, and to a lesser extent Indian women, were forced to cohabit with and have children for the European conquistadors, slave masters and overseers. This went on for centuries so that a mixed or coloured 'race' of people grew up. Sexual unions between persons of different races, resulting in children of mixed race, is called **miscegenation**. Many of the children of such unions had physical features proclaiming their 'white' inheritance and sometimes, if they too cohabited with white men, their offspring looked virtually 'white'. By inference, according to the racial ideologies prevailing, these lighter-skinned children were somehow 'better' than their maternal ancestors, they were dealt with more leniently, and some were educated, all because they had biological/physical traits publicizing their European connection. A **pigmentocracy** evolved, in which persons of fairer complexion wielded more prestige and power in the society than others. Thus, skin colour, and to a lesser extent hair texture and facial features, loom large in any discussion of society and culture and identity in the Caribbean. It is a *social construct* tacked on to biological characteristics.

It is not difficult to understand the role that skin colour played (and still plays) in the development of society and culture in the Caribbean. From the very beginning of the Conquest, the Spaniards regarded the aboriginal inhabitants as subhuman. This notion of racial superiority was extended to encompass the enslaved and, later, indentured populations who were of a different race. Although Europeans came to the Caribbean as indentured labourers at different times, they were never regarded as subhuman. That category was reserved for non-whites. Racial and ethnic hybridization, then, underscored and emphasized the prevailing ideologies in the society, equating skin colour with social constructions of superiority/inferiority.

However, there was much variety in this coloured group. A continuum of colour and shade came to characterize Caribbean people, with each colour and shade coming to have social meanings. Those at the 'almost white' end of the continuum looked forward to better prospects and life chances than those at the 'darker' end of the continuum because 'high' colour was often rewarded with more lucrative employment and entry into exclusive social circles. This respect accorded to colour pervaded the society. It was not only a matter of preference for European-type features but also that alliances with whites or lightly coloured persons were a means of social betterment. Thus, a black man who was educated and had good prospects would look for a light-skinned wife, even one of lower socio-economic status, as their children would move in higher social circles than he had when growing up. The lighter-skinned wife would be something akin to a status symbol. Such a woman would be optimistic that this marriage would move her into a higher social bracket where her light skin would be an asset.

Today, skin colour continues to weave its fascination among Caribbean people. However, preference for lighter-skinned persons – be it as spouses, friends or employees – is very much underground. Fewer persons today own to these prejudices publicly because the populace at large now has a more balanced understanding of how skin colour has been socially constructed.

Although persons of mixed race form an ethnic group, they are so diverse in their characteristics that we cannot quite pinpoint their sense of cultural 'belongingness'. Some countries have more 'coloureds' than others (Trinidad, St Lucia, the French Caribbean). Some countries may only have two majority races (black and white) producing their coloured population (Jamaica, Barbados, Antigua). Others have more players (African, European, Indian, Amerindian and Chinese) so that the varieties and combinations are innumerable. They are found at all socio-economic levels of the society, but perhaps because of the deliberate effects of privileging light colour by better jobs and marrying 'upward', the higher socio-economic groups tend to have larger numbers of coloured persons today. Thus, the student of cultural diversity will remark on the alignment of coloured persons with the more affluent groups in the society.

At the same time, though, skin colour is not the only characteristic of the mixed-race groups that contributes to cultural diversity. The actual physical characteristics of such persons provide a spectrum of blends of other characteristics as well, such

ACTIVITY 3.5

To what extent do you agree that skin colour is no longer an important factor in Caribbean society and culture, in determining life chances – for example, courting and marriage, or employment? Is it an important factor in establishing friendships or in everyday activities?

as height, hair texture, body types, eye colour and facial features. And in different Caribbean countries the same groups may occupy different social and cultural positions. Here we want to look in somewhat more detail at the different hybrid groups produced by the meeting and mixing of people.

Although various terms have been coined for the offspring of some of these unions, there are not enough terms to match all the varieties and combinations that have occurred. Europeans first encountered the Amerindians in the fifteenth century, and in that violent impact between the powerful and the powerless the mixed race of **mestizos** was born. Among Hispanic scholars in the Caribbean the term 'mestizo' has been used to label all people of mixed race in the Caribbean – Euro-Amerinidan mestizo, Afro-Amerindian mestizo, Afro-European mestizo, and so on. In the terminology of British historians, enslaved Africans and their white European overlords produced the ethnic group known as **mulattoes**. The preoccupation with lighter skin colour as a mark of superiority has led to some fine distinctions being calculated about one's ancestry. A mulatto was half-black and half-white. A child of a mulatto and a black person was called a *sambo*; a child of a mulatto and a white person a *quadroon*; and a child of a quadroon and a white an *octaroon*. Continued unions of Africans, coloureds and whites over several hundred years produced the continuum of colour apparent amongst coloured and African ethnic groups today in the Caribbean. Contributing to the diversity is the geography of this distribution. Some countries, such as Cuba and Puerto Rico, have large creole (locally born descendants of Europeans) and mulatto populations, while the Dominican Republic is mainly mulatto, and Haiti black.

Other unions were also taking place: for example, Africans (especially those who ran away from the plantations) and Amerindians, forming the Afro-Amerindian category of mestizo. The Misquito Indians of the Nicaraguan coast are an ethnic group comprising persons of mixed heritage. Their African ancestors were completely assimilated, fully adopting the language and customs of the Amerindians. The Garifunas of Belize, on the other hand, are descendants of Black Carib rebels (see Chapter 4) deported from St Vincent by the British in 1797 and relocated on the coast of Honduras, where they met and bred with the local Africans and Amerindians. Their mainly Arawakan language persists, as well as their kinship networks and religious beliefs. This hybridized culture of Africans and Caribs from St Vincent is considered among anthropologists to be a remarkable example of cultural retention.

The **polyglot** peoples of the Caribbean showcase the rich racial and ethnic diversity of the region resulting from hybridization. However, a full account of hybridization, especially as it relates to cultural diversity, must take a deeper look at how cultures meet and mingle, and how cultural erasure, retentions and renewal occur.

Cultural hybridization

The development of new cultural forms out of existing ones through a period of contact and interaction is referred to as 'cultural hybridization'. The term **creolization** is used if this hybridization took place in the context of European colonization. Thus hybridization and creolization mean virtually the same thing in the Caribbean context. One of the effects of cultural hybridization is cultural diversity. This is manifest in the Caribbean in the hybrid forms that are created and which emerge when two or more racial or ethnic groups or cultures meet and interact. These cultural hybrids can be any mixture and combination of the original cultural forms. Cultural hybridization is itself a process, and so the hybrids themselves change and develop over time. We now look at specific examples of cultural hybridization.

Religion

The major religions of the world met in the Caribbean region and underwent considerable hybridization or **syncretism** into creolized forms. Some of these expressions were not very different from the original mould, and others were quite the opposite. The longer-established Christian religions have undergone more of a process of syncretism than, say, Islam or Hinduism. Christianity, and its many denominations, came to the Caribbean with the Conquest and later through missionary activity. African religions came with the enslaved peoples and lived in their memories and imagination as they had limited opportunities to worship together, and much of that was in secret. Living in the Caribbean context and looking for a way to worship meaningfully – trying to fill the vacuum left in their cultural life when they were forcibly removed from their homeland – Africans created many syncretic religious forms that were adapted to their conditions of life. While they incorporated elements of the dominant religion, namely Christianity, the way they perceived a creator and even the purpose of religion differed in significant ways from European **cosmology** (beliefs about the nature of the universe and reality).

Myal is an early Caribbean religion that developed in Jamaica where Christian elements were blended with African world views. When Baptists fleeing the American War of Independence settled in Jamaica, bringing that religion with them, they soon realized that their congregation, as well as the native ministers, not only also belonged to the Myal faith, but were actively incorporating, transferring and transforming Christian doctrine and concepts into a Myal world view. The Holy Spirit was deemed important as an intercessor for the faithful, and from then to now spirit possession has played a key role in all Afro-centric religions in the Caribbean. Later, *Revivalism, Pukumina* (or *Pocomania*) and *Kumina* all flowered in Jamaica. Myal and Revivalism were influential in the development of *Rastafarianism* in Jamaica in the 1930s.

These Caribbean religions are very similar to the **Shouter Baptists** (otherwise called 'Spiritual Baptists' or 'Shakers') in Trinidad and Tobago and St Vincent. Again, these faiths are derived from a meeting and mixing of Baptists from the south of the US who settled in Trinidad in the nineteenth century, and whose beliefs were syncretized with existing traditional African belief systems such as *Rada, Shango* and *Obeah*. Migration between Trinidad and St Vincent served to strengthen the faith and increase membership. Both the Shouters in Trinidad and the Shakers in St Vincent were persecuted by the British government. Officially they were deemed a public nuisance because of their noisy services, shouting, bell-ringing and drumming.

Today, African elements in these religions include drumming, chanting, shouting and dancing; music is integral to worship. The religious ceremony tends to be highly emotional compared to a Sunday service in the established churches. Christian

ACTIVITY 3.6

Suggest reasons why the white planter class, and other groups in the society (black and mixed), wanted these religions outlawed.

elements are found in the use of the Bible, the feast days of the saints, and recognition of the Holy Spirit. **Rastafarians** believe that they and members of the black race belong to one of the twelve tribes of Israel and that one incarnation of Jah was Jesus Christ. They re-interpret the Bible, especially the Old Testament, and believe that it is the route to spiritual freedom (from Babylon).

On a much deeper level we see syncretism in the ways that the Christian religions have been adapted to recognize the sacred in all aspects of life. African cosmologies acknowledge the spiritual in all places and activities of everyday life such as in rivers, dancing, stories, dreams, visions, healing and wholeness. It is a belief system woven into a way of life that is holistic; there are no differences between what is secular and what is sacred. To speak of this as a 'cultural retention' is not strictly true, as the ways in which African cosmology itself underwent change and adaptation in confronting the dominant Christian beliefs resulted in something quite new, a true hybrid.

Hybridization must be understood as a creation where the extent of fusion can vary. Thus, Myal, Revivalism, Rastafarianism, the Shouters and Shakers are Caribbean religions that are primarily Christian and syncretized with African elements. However, more Afro-centric Caribbean religions also occur as hybrids. They are more African in orientation than Christian but still have some elements of Christianity. Examples are the *Orisha* faith of Trinidad and Tobago, with variants such as *Shango*, also found in Grenada and Carriacou, the *Santeria* of Cuba, the *Winti* of Suriname, and the *Vodun* of Haiti. The fusion of Christianity and African cosmologies finds common ground in that both recognize a spirit world populated by angels, archangels, the forces of good and evil, supernatural powers and other entities.

Many of these syncretic religions share similar beliefs, rituals and practices. Differences can sometimes be attributed to their historical evolution under varying colonial conditions. For example, Santeria survives in Cuba with a host of saints renamed in Yoruba because the Spanish colonizers felt that it was only a local and harmless expression of Roman Catholicism. Thus, the god *Shango* is associated with St Barbara, Our Lady of Mercy becomes *Obatala*, and *Oshun*, the goddess of rivers, is worshipped as the Virgin of Cobre. The Yoruba and Roman Catholic names are used interchangeably.

In the Afro-centric Caribbean religions there is a greater emphasis on going into trance-like states, spirit possession, being a medium for the spirits, animal sacrifice and magic of various kinds, as well as occult practices, than in those where Christianity is more dominant. The magic that is practised is called *sympathetic magic* – a connection is made between physical objects and one's life: for example, reading cards, the palms of the hands, the stars, or something you throw that falls into a pattern. There is a magical connection between the physical world and one's past, present and future lives.

Syncretism is a complex process. Whether traditional African elements are dominant in a Caribbean religion or whether it is the Christian element that is dominant, they do not exist side by side. They develop as *integrated* entities. Practitioners have blended the inputs from Africa and Europe in ways that are difficult to deconstruct and explain. It is not correct to refer to these elements as merely cultural 'retentions'. There may in fact be pockets of cultural retentions, but the hybrid Caribbean religion is just that, a hybrid, something new, created in the Caribbean under certain conditions of subjugation where resilience and resistance played a part in building an identity.

ACTIVITY 3.7

Practitioners of Vodun say that it suffers from its 'Hollywood image'.

1. Explain what this may mean. Suggest reasons why Vodun has been stereotyped by non-practitioners.

2. Discover some more about the main tenets of Vodun by researching its beliefs and practices.

ACTIVITY 3.8

Investigate the existence of syncretic religious forms in your country. Identify elements that belong to the original or 'parent' religions and elements that seem to be completely new. (To develop some in-depth understandings of at least *one* of these religions, you may need to speak to a practitioner of this religion or have that person come and speak to the class. Some students in class can also be resource persons for this exercise.)

The 'openness' of these religions can be seen when practitioners say that they are Roman Catholics or belong to established Christian churches and attend mass or traditional services. There is no division as they see it – the devotee can often see a different time and place for orthodox Christian worship and the folk or the syncretic religion. Thus, in Suriname bereaved family members make the journey home from the Netherlands to attend Winti burial rites, which in many instances occur in addition to burial services in the traditional churches. And it is said that in Santeria the devotee sees the orisha in the Christian saint. It is this blending, co-existence and integration that constitute creole culture.

Not surprisingly, the major religious denominations within Christianity, such as Roman Catholicism and Anglicanism, also went through (and are going through) a creolizing and hybridizing process. Clapping, drumming and a great deal of music, of the folk variety, are now typical of mainstream Christian services. While traditional hymns persist, many are now written by Caribbean persons and sung to local rhythms. The homily, delivered by local priests, uses language (intonation, gestures and expressions) in ways that only those who are accustomed to an oral language culture can produce. These are subtle creolizing processes.

The development of hybridized and creolized religions in the Caribbean is discussed further on pages 183–187.

Language

Caribbean languages are also replete with hybridities, mainly of the dominant European language liberally sprinkled with words from other languages, and transformed in unique ways by oral culture. The fact that the creole languages of the Caribbean largely exist in an oral tradition often makes them far more expressive and vivid than the European forms from which they grew. The African languages that the enslaved population remembered were usually not written languages, so that the creole forms which mixed, emerged and evolved differ greatly from the European 'master' language. These hybrid forms are variously referred to as **patois** or the 'creole'.

ACTIVITY 3.9

1. Compare traditional and present-day attitudes in your country to hybrid forms of language, such as the creole.

2. Contrast the relative usefulness of the creole and standard forms of the language (e.g. Standard English) in your society and culture.

Jamaica has an English-based patois and St Lucia a French-based patois, and they are languages in their own right, having been forged through a process of creolization to produce something of immense hybridity, which continues to evolve and change. In each language the grammar has a typical structure, which differs remarkably from the standard, and there are words and expressions that have been created, used in unique ways, or adopted from other languages. They are considered to be fully developed languages because they meet all the needs of their speakers in functioning in society. The creole is the first language (or 'mother tongue') of almost all the people resident in a Caribbean country.

In each English-speaking Caribbean country it is fair to say that the creole exists as a continuum. At one end is the 'extreme' form of the creole (the *basilect*) and at the other is Standard English (Fig. 3.1). Between are all manner of hybridities, appropriate for communicating in a host of different situations. In this 'zone of language use' the *mesolect* tends to be the language used by most creole speakers and it is easier to shift between different forms of the creole than to the standard form of the language (Craig, 1980).

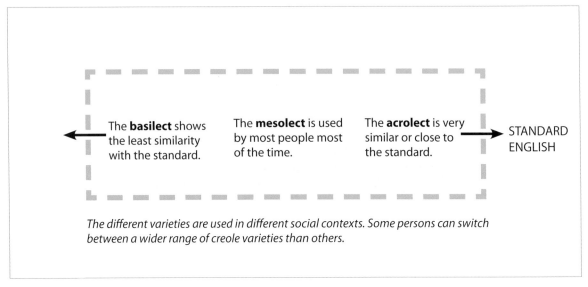

The **basilect** shows the least similarity with the standard.

The **mesolect** is used by most people most of the time.

The **acrolect** is very similar or close to the standard.

STANDARD ENGLISH

The different varieties are used in different social contexts. Some persons can switch between a wider range of creole varieties than others.

Fig. 3.1 The creole language continuum

ACTIVITY 3.10

1. Demonstrate the use of different forms of the creole (for example, the *basilect, mesolect* and *acrolect* – see Fig. 3.1) by speaking in ways that may be appropriate
(a) at home amongst members of your close family
(b) for responding to the teacher in class
(c) in communicating with a foreign-based English speaker.

2. Linguists argue that Standard English is hardly ever spoken in the Caribbean. Even in very formal situations, such as giving a speech in parliament, it is not Standard English that is used. To what extent do you agree with this view?

Since the words used in English-lexicon creoles (that is, the vocabulary is based on English), such as Trinidadian Creole or Jamaican Creole, are very similar to those of Standard English, the view has come about that the creole is a bastardized or corrupted form of 'proper' English. This is a social construction arising from ideologies that privilege European culture and regard creole or hybrid cultural forms as inferior. Recently, however, there has been more of an inclination to accept the creole as a language in its own right and we see its widespread use in the media. Great efforts have been made in trying to standardize its written form and to compile dictionaries so that it can move from being purely oral to becoming a literary culture.

French-lexicon creoles are found in the patois of Dominica and St Lucia, and those of the French territories of Martinique, Guadeloupe and Guyane (French Guiana), as well as in Haiti. In Haiti it is known as the *kreyòl* and in Dominica as the *kwéyòl*. The French-lexicon creoles of Trinidad, St Vincent and Grenada, which are not widely spoken today, are similar to the patois spoken in St Lucia, Dominica, Martinique and Guadeloupe. However, the Haitian Creole is very different, no doubt because French was removed as an active influence by 1804 through revolution, so there was more scope for African linguistic forms and structures to be incorporated into the language. The structure of the language varies so considerably from French that in the past it has been argued that the Haitian Creole is actually a West African language (Ewe) with a French lexicon.

How did creoles develop?

During the era of slavery, different cultural groups were brought to the Caribbean from all over West Africa, where they spoke different languages. The peoples of Dahomey, Sierra Leone, Liberia, the Gold Coast and Nigeria were all distinct ethnic groups. In the Caribbean, communication between Amerindians, Europeans and Africans had to depend on the development of a common language. This is known as a **lingua franca**.

ACTIVITY 3.11

1. Usually French or English speakers from Europe cannot fully comprehend French- or English-based creole languages even though the lexicon is based on French or English. Suggest why this may be so, and give examples of words, phrases or grammar from a creole that you know.

2. Discuss what may be problematic in the special language situation of St Lucia and Dominica, which are English-speaking countries with a French-based creole.

3. Persons from two Caribbean countries having English-based creoles (for example, Jamaica and Barbados) may find difficulty in communicating. Suggest why that may be so.

ACTIVITY 3.12

Conduct independent research to answer the following questions.

1. For the creole in your country, describe TWO ways in which it has been influenced by African languages, giving examples.

2. Explain the relationship between creoles, pidgins and dialects.

3. Describe the language of the Rastafari, discussing its lexicon, syntax and special features.

Pidgins first developed as rudimentary forms of communication largely for conducting business – slaving, trading, giving orders. Pidgins were just a set of words (usually only nouns and verbs) borrowed from the vocabulary of different language speakers that over time became mutually intelligible. Gradually pidgins developed into whole, complex languages, mixing the lexicon of the European language (and sometimes more than one European language) with that of West African languages (and sometimes with that of the Amerindians too), and evolving their own syntax (the rules of grammar and arranging words in sentences), with structures and expressions borrowed from both the Europeans and the Africans. The common West African linguistic device of repetition is identifiable in the creole: for example, instead of saying that 'it is very big', we often hear 'it big big'. We also notice that a verb is sometimes not necessary for meaning to be communicated.

The processes of cultural hybridization

An understanding of the processes of cultural erasure, cultural retention and cultural renewal is important in any discussion of the hybridization of cultures. These are terms used to describe *cultural change* and can help us to begin to put our understandings of processes such as creolization and hybridization of cultures in perspective.

- *Cultural erasure* refers to practices that have died out or are dying out. Some debate whether a culture can be erased, given the extent of mixing that has gone on amongst the world's peoples. Remember that in Chapter 2 we learned that culture was both *material* and *non-material.* Thus, a culture can survive based on the artefacts it has left behind. Non-material or symbolic culture is more difficult to trace. The language of the Tainos or Arawaks of the Greater Antilles, for example, still survives in place names and in local dialects to some extent. However, even if we could not detect a trace, it is still problematic to say that a culture has been erased. The hybridity that would have resulted amongst different aboriginal groups over the centuries before the Conquest makes it extremely difficult to even think of Taino or Ciboney culture, or Carib culture, as separate and distinct. Thus, some Taino practices could have survived and be hybridized within local contexts in the Caribbean.
- *Cultural retention* refers to practices that have survived even when most other forms and symbols of a culture are no longer evident. Traditional Carib basketry designs and technologies continue in Dominica and elsewhere even as the surviving Carib populations change and adapt to modern life. A cultural retention usually refers to some specific aspect of a culture, for example within a language or religion. Cultural retention does not necessarily mean survival in an intact form. For example, in Belize, Garifuna culture is described as one where there are a remarkable number of cultural retentions. It was hybridized to begin with and it has since undergone some elements of mixing and hybridizing with other cultures in Belize, but it is still sufficiently different to be regarded as an ethnic minority.
- *Cultural renewal* occurs when a group goes through a conscious rejuvenation process and returns to some elements of its culture, which it believes have been ignored or suppressed. It comes about largely through a change of

ACTIVITY 3.13

Using music as an example in any Caribbean country, identify any one form that you believe is a hybrid. Describe how that type of music evolved and whether on the present music scene the hybrid exists alongside the original forms as well as other forms that are difficult to classify.

ACTIVITY 3.14

1. Reflect on any aspect of culture and society in your country where you can identify examples of (a) cultural erasure and (b) cultural retention.

2. Explain your reasons in labelling some aspect of cultural life as a 'retention' rather than a 'hybrid'.

consciousness brought on by historical forces of change at a certain time. The advent of Garveyism early in the twentieth century not only provided a core for the development of black consciousness in Jamaica but also in the wider Caribbean and North America (see pp. 333–344). Mobilization of black people into understanding that they were arbiters of their own destiny led to the development of labour unions, which eventually emerged as political parties challenging colonial rule. The ***Black Power*** movement of the 1970s in the Caribbean and elsewhere continued these themes of commitment to African consciousness and a re-interpretation of history to promote a Caribbean view of Caribbean history rather than an ethnocentric view. African ethnic garb, hairstyles and names accompanied such efforts at cultural renewal, as well as interest in learning African languages, notably Swahili and Yoruba. There was also a heightened consciousness of Africa, and what was happening on the African continent – for example, the resistance movements and civil wars in the liberation of Angola and the apartheid struggles in South Africa.

These terms 'cultural erasure', 'cultural retention' and 'cultural renewal' give us a broad understanding of cultural change. They are concepts that describe what is happening in a particular aspect of a culture. You will meet other terms in this chapter – **enculturation, acculturation, assimilation, transculturation** and **interculturation** – which will serve to address *how* cultures change. They help to provide possible explanations for cultural erasure, cultural retention and cultural renewal, as well as hybridization or creolization.

Cultural change

Enculturation

'Enculturation' is a process of socialization whereby a person becomes part of another's culture. A person can become enculturated through processes of acculturation or assimilation, which have been policies tried by the various European colonizers in the Caribbean. One has to be wary, though, of accepting the view that whilst being enculturated, one's culture can actually be *erased*. During your own lifetime it is possible that you remember practices that were once important and you do not see much of them any more. Perhaps they were related to preparing for a festival such as Christmas, and while your family still celebrates Christmas, some of the traditions have disappeared, to be replaced by others. Perhaps you remember the ways of life you enjoyed growing up in a village that you no longer observe. In each case, one cannot say that the practice has been erased if it continues to live in your memory and imagination, and may still be continued by others. Enculturation alerts us to the idea that accepting a dominant culture may lead to cultural erasure – but not of everything – and that cultural retentions (and possibly, at a later date, cultural renewal) will be part of the picture. This is further explained below in reference to British and French colonizing efforts.

In Chapter 1 we discovered that one of the main ideas influencing British colonization in the Caribbean was to develop an appreciation of British culture in the people. This was done through a policy of *acculturation* – the adoption of English as the official language; the use of an English curriculum in schools, espousing

English stories, values and customs; as well as the institution of English laws and systems of governance. In this way the colonized people would be *socialized* into a deep appreciation of British culture and follow many of its practices and customs. There was no expectation that Caribbean people would become British but that their original cultures would be sufficiently enculturated to produce a hybrid culture in which a British way of life was dominant.

Acculturation meant that some aspects of the culture of the Amerindians and Africans, especially, were erased. However, a unique culture was also born, a hybrid culture, where there was reverence and legitimacy given to British values and customs but at the same time Afro-centric and other cultural forms were also embraced, such as in religion and language. *Cultural retentions* also persisted, as in African knowledge and use of herbal medicines, and cooking traditions. In some societies cultural retentions are stronger than in others – notably, the Maroons and the Garifuna. Thus, the creole culture developed, as a thoroughly hybridized culture, alongside cultural retentions.

Assimilation

'Assimilation' occurs when a dominant group makes a bid to enculturate another by attempting to supplant all aspects of its culture and make it over into the image of the dominant group. Our study of French colonization in Chapter 1 (see Box 1.3) is a case in point. Compared to British policy, the French intended to convert their colonized people into French people, culturally speaking. Thus local and indigenous customs, beliefs and yearnings were ignored. The countries Martinique and Guadeloupe, for example, are considered to be part of France. This has created an ambivalent situation where the people, having undergone a creolizing process, identify both with their Caribbean nationality and their place as French citizens. In spite of the efforts and policies to enable Martiniquans and Guadeloupeans to think of themselves as French, a persistent theme in these countries is national identity and autonomy. Aimé Césaire is a celebrated Martiniquan who popularized **négritude**, a philosophy of black consciousness and racial pride (see pp. 342–343), which could be regarded as an example of cultural renewal.

Thus Caribbean people under conditions of acculturation and assimilation have not succumbed in their entirety to the dominant culture. They may have become enculturated, but only to a certain extent. Hybridizing processes show that culture is not a passive entity that can be easily erased. In fact it seems to be highly reactive and absorptive. While in the Francophone Caribbean French customs, curricula, laws and ways of life are generally evident, in each case they are hybridized forms, if not on paper, then in practice. The French-based Creole is a case in point, and certain festivals and celebrations, which are in fact cultural retentions, seen in villages and local communities are clearly evident as well. Thus hybridization has occurred, but aspects of cultural retentions can still be identified, and cultural renewal as a heightened creole awareness and consciousness is receiving a lot of support in the French Caribbean.

Transculturation

'Transculturation' describes the process whereby a culture changes drastically, actually overcoming itself and translating into something new. Cuba, before and after the revolution, exemplifies this process. The customs and ways of life of pre-revolutionary Cuba were fundamentally different from the socialist perspectives which prevailed after 1962. However, amidst sweeping social change and collectivization of the economy, there were cultural beliefs and practices that continued almost unchanged. One of these was the attitude towards blacks in Cuban society. Even as late as 1948, Granados (2000) says that 'blacks basically remained condemned to manual labour and, . . . to being second class citizens' (p. 131). While under the revolutionary regime their lot improved, Granados goes on to ask: 'How is it possible that after 35 years of socialism 90 per cent of the prison population is black?' (p. 135). This is especially damning when we realize that blacks comprise less than 15 per cent of Cuba's population.

The experience of slavery to newly arrived Africans and creole Africans in the Caribbean could be described as a process of transculturation. Yet even amidst comprehensive attempts at cultural erasure, the African was able to retain elements of language and religion that were fashioned into complete fully functioning hybrid cultures. 'Transculturation' is thus a broad, all-encompassing term referring to whole cultures, and in the case of slavery involves the experience, for newly arrived Africans, of moving from being steeped in African cultures to a hybrid culture. In the later history of the Caribbean we witness attempts to reverse this process through efforts at cultural renewal, largely through black consciousness. One can even argue that opposition to transculturation was going on from the very onset of slavery, where runaways set up maroon communities – a rival culture based on cultural retentions.

Interculturation

'Interculturation' refers to the mixing of cultures that goes on between groups who share a space. The groups do not necessarily give up their own culture but participate in various ways in each other's lives. Culturally plural societies are often described as societies where the groups meet but only limited mixing occurs. This is correct, but misleading; there is often much interaction between persons of different ethnicities within such cultures, which feed off each other, producing some degree of incorporation and merging. The extended example given in Box 3.9 clarifies how interculturation may be evident in a culturally plural society.

Summary

Hybridization is a process that occurs in creole societies where different groups have met and forged relationships under conditions of oppression. Forced to live under conditions that suppressed their culture or their freedom to interact, they developed ways of coping and integrating that produced distinctly new cultural forms. While scholars have long recognized the existence of cultural hybridization, they are not sure about how the process occurs. Thus terms like 'cultural erasure', 'cultural retention' and 'cultural renewal' have been used to describe elements of Caribbean society and culture, as well as terms that attempt to provide more explanatory power – 'enculturation', 'acculturation', 'assimilation', 'transculturation' and 'interculturation'. Whether racial or cultural hybridization, creole varieties of people, religions, customs and languages have contributed enormously to cultural diversity in the Caribbean.

BOX 3.9 Interculturation

Trinidad and Tobago is described as a culturally plural society where the major ethnic groups, namely Africans and Indians, meet but do not mix. Fairly rigid family and ethnic codes concerning marriage, voting patterns and sometimes business partnerships discourage the mixing of races or ethnic groups. While that is mainly so, it denies the complex and subtle mixing that goes on, which we can best describe as 'interculturation'. In Trinidad the Indians, Africans and Mixed groups, especially, meet in their workplaces, schools, churches and when pursuing leisure. They form friendships and tend to appreciate certain areas of each other's culture. For example, Indian foods and 'creole' dishes are part of the diet of all ethnic groups. Festivals and celebrations of each group are appreciated, mainly for their culinary aspects and the accompanying holidays. Food seems to be a cultural value that transcends racial lines and unifies the people.

Almost all religious groups celebrate Christmas and there seems to be a widespread feeling that it is a national holiday rather than a Christian celebration. Hindus, Muslims and others have appropriated Christmas in ways that do not necessarily endorse its religious nature, regarding it as something akin to a national celebration. And there is widespread participation of all ethnic groups in carnival, and that includes playing pan, designing and building costumes, singing calypsos and chutney, and participating as masqueraders and fête-goers. In parts of the country where the ethnic groups live side by side, there is closer community and intermixing. Among urban, Christian Indians there is more intermixing with Afro-Trinidadians

than among traditional Hindus and Muslims. It is important, too, to recognize that Hindus and Muslims are two distinct ethnic groups, with different customs, beliefs, languages and celebrations. Where these two ethnic groups intermarry there is a form of interculturation that springs up in religious observances and customs generally. The Mixed population has to a larger extent than other ethnic groups intermixed with all other ethnic groups in the country. The Chinese population has long intermarried or had liaisons with Afro-Trinidadians. Thus, even though there are social and cultural norms that keep the ethnic groups from integrating, a significant amount of mixing still occurs.

This mixing has produced a level of interaction and knowledge about each other's ways that can be deepened or remain superficial. Soca and calypso have been hybridized with Indian rhythms to form *chutney* and *chutney soca*. *Parang*, the traditional Christmas music sung in Spanish and a cultural retention from the days of Spanish colonization, has also been hybridized into *parang soca*, and there is on-going experimentation. It may be rather early to say that these are hybridized forms because they are still emerging, but clearly attempts at hybridity arise from an initial interculturation phase.

Interculturation, then, is occurring ceaselessly but deep-seated changes are only evident in certain areas of cultural life. In those areas genuine hybridizations seem to be in the making. In trying to analyse cultures and cultural change, a degree of mixing may be discerned that can best be described as interculturation.

3.3   SOCIAL STRATIFICATION

Another characteristic feature of Caribbean societies, indeed almost all societies, is social stratification. This refers to the ranking of social groups according to one or more criteria deemed important in the society. The ranking indicates that some groups have more and some have less of what the society values – for example, money, power and/or prestige. Thus, they are unequal. Wealthy groups occupy the highest positions in the social hierarchy. The different levels of the hierarchy are called 'social strata' (singular 'stratum'). A 'status' is a rank or position in the social hierarchy. The lowest strata, occupied by the poorest groups, have low status. A system of social stratification indicates that the groups in society are unequal and the pattern of inequality that forms persists from one generation to the next.

ACTIVITY 3.15

Investigate how the caste system functions among the descendants of Indian indentured labourers in the Caribbean today. To what extent is there evidence of cultural erasure, and cultural retention? Suggest reasons why certain rituals or practices are no longer evident and why others persist.

Stratified societies vary in the criteria they regard as important. In *closed systems* of social stratification, such as Caribbean society during the era of slavery (see Box 2.5, Plantation society), the criteria determining a person's position in the social hierarchy were race and colour. Thus, the system was effectively closed to those below trying to move up because their race and colour proclaimed their low status. Similarly, in India where the **caste** system is also closed, you are expected to interact and intermarry within your caste, keeping the social strata distinct. Castes are relatively strong and stable categories that have existed for centuries and they effectively separate groups who follow different traditions of ritual purity, who engage in certain related occupations and who have different ethnicities and lineage. (However, in India today these rigid caste prescriptions have been breaking down for some time.) Closed systems of social stratification are based on **ascribed** criteria that allocate persons to the different social strata. Ascribed criteria are those categories that you were born into and cannot change, such as your race and colour or the caste to which your family belongs.

Social inequality

A stratified system or ranking of social groups is a form of **institutionalized** inequality. That means that persons have less or more access to the rewards of the society (for example, wealth, status and prestige) according to their social standing. Thus, even with qualifications a poor person may lose a job he seeks to a wealthy applicant, who may not have such good qualifications, simply because the latter may have powerful family connections. In the Caribbean, as already noted, persons of lighter skin colour or of white or mixed race have traditionally been held in high regard. These traits had the stamp of social approval. It often happened that such persons obtained better jobs, and had better marriage prospects and opportunities than others in the society who were ranked lower on those traits.

ACTIVITY 3.16

Suggest at least THREE ways that the more influential groups in your society attempt to restrict members lower down the social hierarchy from moving upwards.

These are examples of how the system of social stratification in a country maintains the inequalities between the groups. Although some of the examples described above are illegal and officially regarded as forms of discrimination today, there are usually ways to get around such charges so that inequalities are actually maintained. These inequalities, then, are actually part of how the society is organized and how it functions. This is what is meant by inequalities being 'institutionalized'. As a result, groups with more money, status and power tend to obstruct other groups from moving upwards in the society. They act as **gatekeepers**, preventing the progress of other groups.

Social stratification under slavery

Plantation society in the Caribbean during the seventeenth, eighteenth and nineteenth centuries was a closed system of stratification based on the ascribed criteria of race and colour. Fig. 3.2 represents its social structure, showing the occupations and the relative positions of each group. It was a rigid and inflexible system based on institutionalized **racism**.

Race and colour were tied to one's occupation in the society. Black or coloured persons could be either slaves or free people of colour, and the latter was a relatively

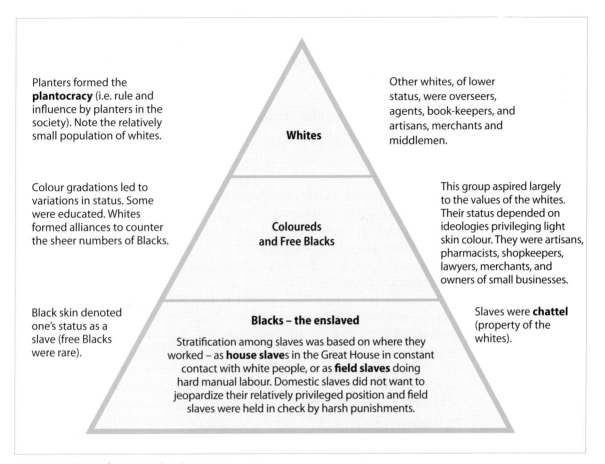

Planters formed the **plantocracy** (i.e. rule and influence by planters in the society). Note the relatively small population of whites.

Other whites, of lower status, were overseers, agents, book-keepers, and artisans, merchants and middlemen.

Whites

Colour gradations led to variations in status. Some were educated. Whites formed alliances to counter the sheer numbers of Blacks.

This group aspired largely to the values of the whites. Their status depended on ideologies privileging light skin colour. They were artisans, pharmacists, shopkeepers, lawyers, merchants, and owners of small businesses.

Coloureds and Free Blacks

Black skin denoted one's status as a slave (free Blacks were rare).

Slaves were **chattel** (property of the whites).

Blacks – the enslaved

Stratification among slaves was based on where they worked – as **house slave**s in the Great House in constant contact with white people, or as **field slaves** doing hard manual labour. Domestic slaves did not want to jeopardize their relatively privileged position and field slaves were held in check by harsh punishments.

Fig. 3.2 Social stratification under slavery

small group. Thus, it was evident just by looking at someone what his or her station in life was. White persons were never of low social status, though white indentured labourers from time to time strained these social boundaries. One's race said clearly what one's social position was. This was an oppressive social system that one could not escape unless one had some bargaining power. Persons of mixed ancestry and light-coloured skin were the most fortunate in this regard; by virtue of their appearance they were rewarded with lighter work as domestic slaves. Many, too, were freed by their white fathers and even educated, so that their prospects were considerably better than others who were not free and not mixed. The coloureds worked as an efficient buffer group between the whites and the blacks as they shared European values and would hardly risk losing their 'privileged' status by uniting with blacks to overthrow the oppressor. The only hope for many an African slave lay in escaping.

However, on much closer inspection the three levels were also subdivided. Among the whites, those who were European by birth were usually of higher social standing but they were often 'absentee', so the creole whites were at the top of the social hierarchy. The poorer whites (the tradesmen, overseers, book-keepers) were somewhat removed but ranked above the free coloureds, by virtue of race. Among the free coloureds there was a complicated ranking based on the degree of whiteness (octaroon, quadroon), the degree of education, wealth, and the extent to which one had the protection of a white relative. And amongst the African slaves there was the 'house' and 'field' distinction.

Social class and social stratification

Today in the Caribbean social **class** is used to distinguish the different levels or strata of society based on those who have the same social and economic resources and therefore the same social status. The 'class structure', as it is sometimes called, refers to how modern societies are stratified into the upper, middle and lower social classes. Contrary to the social structure in plantation society or under the Indian caste system, social class in modern societies is based on **achieved** criteria. This refers to a person's performance in being able to earn what the society values – wealth, status and prestige. Any system of social stratification, though, is based on inequalities. Thus, within the population there are unequal chances of *achieving* these rewards.

Social class is a concept that was used by *Karl Marx* (see p. 347) in his analysis of the inequalities in modern capitalist society. He saw society as having two main social classes – the **bourgeoisie** who were the capitalists and owned the **means of production** and the **proletariat** who were the workers and sold their labour. In between, there was a smaller group known as the **petite bourgeoisie**, who were mainly farmers and small business owners. The capitalists and workers were in ceaseless conflict because their goals were mutually incompatible. The capitalist or bourgeois class focused on making as much profit as possible at the expense of exploiting the workers. Marx claimed that the wages being paid to the proletariat were minimal compared to the profits that their labour made possible. Consequently, the workers were bent on forcing the bourgeoisie to pay a more realistic wage.

Max Weber challenged Marx's portrayal to show that social class was also based on *power* (those having the resources to impose their will on others) and *prestige* or *status* (those having something that was held in high esteem in the society). For example, a poor lawyer could move in high social circles because of his or her status as a lawyer, a respected profession. Similarly, a politician may be from the poorer classes but by virtue of the power inherent in such a position he or she will have access to the highest social classes. Additionally, Weber argued that the growth of a capitalist economy enables a third class, the *middle class*, to evolve, and become differentiated into several layers (upper middle class, lower middle class), which are not necessarily locked in ceaseless conflict with workers. For example, the new **intelligentsia** (those who have had the benefit of higher education) may not own much property, but certainly do not match Marx's concept of the proletariat. They are the intellectual elite and comprise the managerial and professional class. Then there are 'white-collar' workers who work in all types of businesses, industry, and the service sector generally, including 'dot com' economies.

Marx saw the *working class* as mainly unskilled, manual labour earning a low wage with minimal levels of education and training. This lower social class category is widely known as the working class today but it is much more complex than Marx's original ideas. At various levels within this social class there are blue-collar workers,

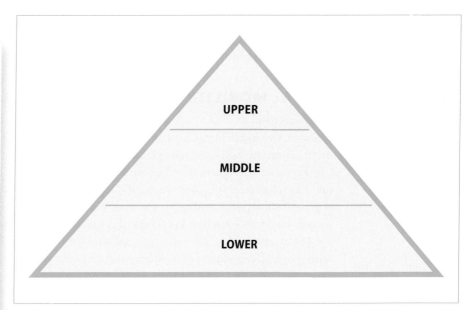

Fig. 3.3 Social class divisions in a typical Caribbean country

skilled workers, semi-skilled, unskilled and self-employed non-professionals. One may even find an extremely skilled tradesman earning much more than a white-collar worker, who enjoys higher status. The **underclass** is defined as those who belong to the lowest social stratum, and although some may be employed, for the most part they live below the poverty level.

It is important to note that whilst society in the Caribbean today is stratified according to social class, that situation has evolved gradually from plantation society, where status was ascribed and based on race and colour. Indeed, there are still many similarities in the structure of the society that echoes the past. A comparison of Figs 3.2. and 3.3 should reveal some of these. However, there have also been changes. The next section tries to account for the continuance of inequalities based on race and colour and discuss how a ranking of social groups based on achievement criteria has changed the structure of the society.

Summary

Social stratification is a system of inequality that may be based on ascribed or achieved criteria. Contrary to plantation society and the Indian caste system, social class in modern-day capitalist societies is based on achieved criteria. A 'social class' refers to a group in the society who share the same access to economic opportunities and social status. Based on the criterion of achievement, individuals are located in the social hierarchy based on what they or their family have achieved. While Marx painted a simple picture of capitalists and workers forming the main social classes in capitalist society, Weber showed that money, and sometimes power and prestige, were important in explaining one's social class location. Thus, income or wealth were not the only criteria in determining social class. Additionally, Weber showed that as capitalism grew, each social class (upper, middle and lower) developed its own subdivisions. Thus, the system of social stratification in modern capitalist economies based on social class is an extremely complex way of institutionalizing inequalities.

3.4 SOCIAL MOBILITY

The movement of individuals and groups from one social class to another, either up or down the social hierarchy, is called 'social mobility'. In closed systems of social stratification, mobility was not possible, or was extremely limited. In modern-day Caribbean society, where membership in a social class is 'open' and depends on what one has achieved – for example, wealth, status or prestige – upward social mobility is prized and equated with perceptions of success. A society where one can advance socially based on what one has achieved is called a **meritocracy**.

The main ways of achieving upward social mobility are by marrying someone with money, by acquiring enough educational credentials to secure a well-paying job, or by owning a successful business and investing wisely. Persons already in the higher social classes have more or less inherited family wealth or married into such families. They are the owners and managers of business and industry. In many cases social mobility is intergenerational; that is, a family may move to a higher socio-economic bracket because of the hard work, diligence and foresight of the older generation. The elders in a family may have been poor but by being thrifty, perhaps opening a small business and making wise investments, such as buying land, they were able to educate their children to tertiary levels, positioning them to access social mobility.

The most popular route to social mobility for the majority of people today lies in education. In modern societies education has been made more accessible to everyone in all income groups. For many, especially those of the lower social classes, education is the only route to social mobility. Education has been responsible for entirely new class formations – for example, the intelligentsia and the workforce involved in the new occupations proliferating in business, technology and micro-electronics. There has been a tremendous expansion in occupational types and sub-types, resulting in many different kinds of white-collar and blue-collar jobs. Education and training up to secondary and post-secondary levels opens up access to these opportunities and represents a path to upward social mobility for those in the lower income groups. Such a movement, though, is usually only from one level to another (for example, manual labour to skilled labour within the working class, or from lower middle class to higher levels within the middle class).

ACTIVITY 3.18

1. Several ways of accessing social mobility are described here. Discuss the point of view that it is difficult for persons in the lower income groups to access any of them

2. Choose THREE persons from among your circle of family and acquaintances who are employed. Compare their occupations with those of their parents. Where social mobility has occurred, identify the factors you believe were important. Similarly, where it has not occurred try to account for the factors that may be responsible. (Note that since we are dealing with individuals a host of personal factors may apply: for example, individual drive and determination, and gender-based factors such as women having to give up jobs to look after children, and so on.)

ACTIVITY 3.19

An interesting case is presented by the Portuguese, Chinese and the Syrian–Lebanese community in different Caribbean countries. Not very long ago they were at the bottom of the social hierarchy as newly arrived poor immigrants, but today many are in the highest social classes. Suggest reasons why, in perhaps two generations, these groups have become upwardly mobile to such an extent, while groups that have been here for centuries have not been able to do the same.

Money, wealth or income remain the main criteria that stratify the society into different social groups, and thus to a large extent social class depends on occupation. Social mobility is possible and many have accessed it, especially through education, but it happens within a stratified society based on social class. Thus, there are inequalities and for some people they are **entrenched** inequalities.

While the structure of Caribbean societies today shows that many descendants of Africans and Indians are in the higher social classes, it also shows that large numbers of these same groups have not been successful in accessing social mobility. They still comprise the poorest groups in the society and are at the bottom of the social hierarchy. The wealthier and more powerful groups (white, near-white and coloureds) continue to be found almost exclusively in the higher social classes. They do not seem to have experienced any significant downward social mobility over time. Thus, although the society is said to be structured on achieved criteria and is a meritocracy, there are large numbers of people who cannot access (and some believe, are prevented from accessing) the means to become socially mobile.

Summary

Social mobility is a characteristic of modern-day capitalist societies that is based on achievement criteria. Persons are able to access membership in higher social classes largely through their efforts in education and the chance to secure better-paying jobs or occupations. Such a society is referred to as a 'meritocracy'. In many cases a person becomes socially mobile owing to the efforts of the older generation in either amassing wealth that is passed on or ensuring that educational opportunities are taken up; this is 'intergenerational mobility'. Certain social groups have been able to access social mobility to a greater extent than other groups. However, social class is a system of stratification and it is not easy to move upwards in the social hierarchy, even with advanced educational credentials. Thus, while there have been changes to the social structure, there are still many similarities to the social stratification experienced in plantation society.

WRAP UP

In this chapter certain characteristic features of Caribbean society and culture, such as cultural diversity, hybridization, social stratification and social mobility, have been investigated. Each has been analysed in order to show its usefulness in describing Caribbean society and culture. Cultural diversity has been deconstructed to reveal certain assumptions that tended to privilege the notion of difference over commonalities, and show how an emphasis on difference prevents us from recognizing our common experiences in the Caribbean. Hybridization has been explored, showing its contribution to cultural diversity in the many ethnic and cultural hybrids evident in Caribbean society and culture. The process of creolization that produced these hybrids has been portrayed as something unique, created in Caribbean societies, and thus a common theme across the region. Studying social stratification has revealed the persistence of common elements inherited from historical experience. While social mobility played a role in changing this traditional social structure, strong commonalities are still evident between Caribbean societies then and now.

Structured response

1 (a) Explain what is meant by the term 'cultural diversity'. (1 mark)
   (b) For an identified Caribbean country, describe ONE way in which it is culturally diverse. (2 marks)

2 (a) Define the term 'ethnicity'. (1 mark)
   (b) Explain why 'race' and 'ethnicity' are often used interchangeably. (2 marks)

3 It is believed that cultural diversity poses several problems for Caribbean society and culture. Account for TWO of those beliefs. (4 marks)

4 (a) Explain what is meant by a plural society. (1 mark)
   (b) Account for the relationships experienced between groups in plural societies in the Caribbean. (2 marks)

5 Describe TWO advantages and TWO disadvantages of living in culturally diverse societies. (4 marks)

6 (a) Explain what is meant by (i) hybridization and (ii) creolization. (2 marks)
   (b) Describe ONE way in which hybridization has contributed to cultural diversity in the Caribbean. (2 marks)

7 (a) Explain what is meant by 'cultural erasure'. (1 mark)
   (b) Give an example of cultural retention in Caribbean society and culture. (2 marks)

8 (a) Explain the difference between transculturation and interculturation. (4 marks)
   (b) Describe what is meant by a 'creole society'. (2 marks)

9 (a) Explain why the Maroons are considered to be an ethnic group. (1 mark)
   (b) Describe ONE way in which the Maroons are similar to and ONE way in which they are different from mainstream Caribbean society and culture. (4 marks)

10 (a) Explain the difference between ascribed and achieved status. (2 marks)
   (b) Account for ONE difference that has occurred in the social structure of Caribbean society from the plantation era to the present. (2 marks)

Essay questions (20 marks)

1 Compare and contrast cultural diversity in TWO Caribbean countries. Account for the differences and similarities.

2 Examine the processes of cultural hybridization in Caribbean society and culture.

3 Choose ONE ethnic group in an identified Caribbean country and discuss the extent to which it has been able to access social mobility today.

4 Explain what is meant by cultural erasure, cultural retention and cultural renewal, drawing examples from society and culture in the Caribbean.

Challenge essay questions (30 marks)

1 'The Caribbean is a region where cultural differences far outweigh any commonalities that might exist. These differences occur within and between the various societies and cultures of the Caribbean.' Assess this statement.

2 Discuss the nature of the challenge in Caribbean society and culture in finding ways to mediate group differences.

3 'Creolization leads to the development of entirely new cultures.' Evaluate this point of view using examples of religion, language and music in Caribbean society and culture.

4 Choose ONE ethnic group in Caribbean society and culture and show how its members' sense of cultural identity has been influenced by the experiences they have had.

Language is a topical issue you can identify for further investigation, focusing on the attitudes different groups have towards the creole in your country. You could design a questionnaire about the appropriateness of using the creole in a variety of contexts. You may select individuals from different 'populations' – teachers, students, parents, employers, older persons, and so on – and use some of the ideas listed below.

- Which language do you speak most of the time – Standard English or the creole?
- When do you tend to use each form – at school, with friends, giving a speech, in writing (these are choices you give them).
- Which do you prefer to use?
- Give reasons for your preference.

You can choose a method of presenting the data graphically. Pie charts could be used to summarize and present the information for the first question based on the categories of people who answer – students, teachers, adults and so on. A bar graph could be used to present the data for question 2 and a table could summarize the information from the third and fourth questions. Then as researcher you will need to interpret the trends and patterns that the statistical graphs and diagrams reveal.

REFERENCES AND FURTHER READING

Craig, D. (1980). Language, society and education in the West Indies. *Caribbean Journal of Education,* 7(1), pp. 1–17.

Granados, M. (2000). Notes on the history of blacks in Cuba … and may Elegguá be with me. In C. James, & J. Perivolaris (Eds), *The cultures of the Hispanic Caribbean,* pp. 127–135. London: Macmillan Caribbean.

Hoogbergen, W. (1992). Origins of the Suriname Kwinti Maroons. *New West Indian Guide,* 66(1&2), pp. 27–60.

Hubbard, V. (2002). *A history of St Kitts – the sweet trade.* London: Macmillan Caribbean.

Jolivert, M. (2003). Creolization and intercultural dynamics in French Guiana. In S. Puri (Ed.), *Marginal migrations: the circulation of cultures within the Caribbean,* pp. 212–239. Oxford: Macmillan.

Stewart, R. (2004). Religion, myths and beliefs: their socio-political roles. In B. Brereton (Ed.), *General history of the Caribbean, Volume 5: The Caribbean in the twentieth century,* pp. 559–605. Paris: UNESCO and London: Macmillan Caribbean.

The West Indian Commission (1992). *Time for action: the report of the West Indian Commission.* Barbados: West Indian Commission.

<table>
<tr><td>4</td></tr>
</table>

TRACING HISTORY IN CARIBBEAN SOCIETY AND CULTURE

Until recently, Caribbean history was written by scholars with a distinctly ethnocentric outlook; that is, everything was judged by mainstream ideas in developed countries. Today those views of what happened in the past have been repeatedly challenged by Caribbean scholars more sensitive to the notion that history is largely an interpretive exercise, greatly influenced by who is doing the interpreting. Such insights are more likely to come from people who were colonized and are seeking ways of establishing their identity or identities. They offer alternative explanations and analyses to those presented in the past, largely by Europeans. This chapter is an attempt to dispel ideas that history is only about understanding the past and is of limited value in the here and now. The history of the Caribbean is related to present-day society and culture, and a major concern throughout the chapter relates to these ethnocentric ideas we have been taught as history and how they have influenced our understanding of the contemporary Caribbean.

The chapter begins with the earliest peoples in the Caribbean, people who have been virtually ignored in the historical account. It then moves through significant themes in the development of Caribbean society and culture – namely migration, systems of production, responses to oppression and genocide, and political and economic movements towards independence. The emphasis is not so much the re-telling of history as an analysis of its significance in Caribbean society and culture.

EXPECTED LEARNING OUTCOMES

On completing this chapter, you will be able to
1 describe the main historical events and processes in Caribbean history
2 relate historical events and processes to contemporary Caribbean society and culture
3 critically analyse traditional accounts of Caribbean history
4 apply historical knowledge in describing diversity and complexity in Caribbean society and culture
5 appreciate how a knowledge of history deepens an understanding of Caribbean social life.

4.1 MIGRATIONS

The movement of people from place to place also means the movement of society and culture, as well as their meeting and mixing with other societies and cultures. The great migrations that have occurred over the Earth's surface from time immemorial have always signalled fundamental changes and adaptations in both the migrants and in the groups amongst whom they eventually settled. The Caribbean is a region that

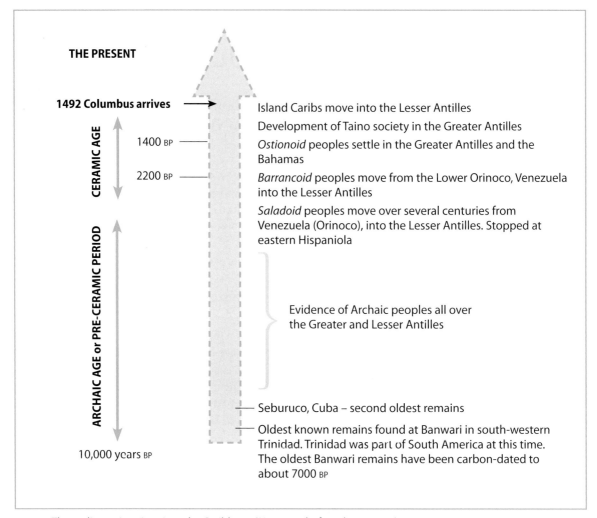

Fig. 4.1 The earliest migrations into the Caribbean (*Note*: BP = before the present)

has experienced significant migrations, each impacting on social life, even today. In this section, the focus is on the major movements of people *into* the Caribbean (***immigration***).

Earliest Caribbean migrations

A popular misconception about Caribbean history is that it is 'short' and that the society is 'relatively new'. These are **ethnocentric** ideas in that emphasis is given to Columbus and the influx of Europeans into the region, dating all that is significant in the Caribbean region from 1492, with the first voyage of Columbus. Some attention has been given to Caribs and Arawaks but much of that account too is flawed, being informed largely by European interpretations of the life of native peoples.

A more accurate picture of the history of the Caribbean region must reverse these misconceptions. Fig. 4.1 shows the long habitation of people in the region,

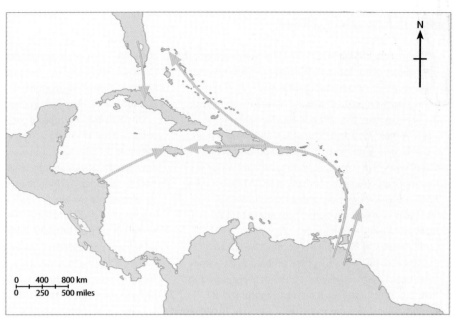

Fig. 4.2 Early migratory routes into the Caribbean

dating from over 10,000 years before the present (BP). Today archaeology is revealing more of their lives and challenging many of the assumptions we have come to accept as Caribbean history. For example:

- The fact that the earliest remains of habitation are found in both Trinidad and Cuba suggests that migrations into the Caribbean were not just from south to north but also that people entered the region from Central America, and even Florida (Fig. 4.2).
- These earliest peoples, of the *Archaic* or *pre-Ceramic period* (they had not yet discovered the use of pottery), spread out and lived in the Greater and Lesser Antilles for over 5000 years *before* other groups migrated into the region. Thus, the region already had a long history before *Ceramic* groups moved in and long before Columbus arrived.
- From about 2400 years BP different cultural groups, distinguished by distinctive styles of pottery, ornamentation and lifestyles (occupations, diet, ceremonies, **beliefs** and practices) began to migrate from South America into the Lesser Antilles. They did not settle the islands chronologically from south to north, but bypassed some altogether. The Archaic peoples who were already there experienced **acculturation** into the *Saladoid, Barrancoid* and *Ostionoid* cultures (Box 4.1), showing that the meeting, mixing and **hybridization** of peoples and cultures have been going on in the Caribbean for millennia.
- One aspect that has been played down in the historical record of life amongst these early peoples is the amount of contact and mobility they enjoyed. While we have learned about the prowess of the Caribs with the dug-out canoe, we did not learn that trade, for example, was something that was long established between the early island dwellers and mainland communities. Thus, it was not

---

BOX 4.1 Early Caribbean cultures

Europeans brought writing and the means whereby the history of the Tainos, the Caribs and other indigenous people could be recorded for posterity. It is only through archaeological evidence that we can reconstruct the everyday lives of people of the earlier cultures. The labels 'Archaic', 'Saladoid', 'Barrancoid' and 'Ostionoid' are archaeological terms given to groups who each shared similar styles of pottery, tools and implements, which put them at a particular level of organization and development. All the knowledge we have of these peoples derives from what archaeologists can discern from artefacts of the *material culture* they left behind.

The *Archaic* or *Pre-Ceramic* peoples have left an extensive record throughout the Caribbean in their stone tools, implements and middens (rubbish heaps) showing that they were hunters, gatherers and consumers of shellfish. Fluctuating sea levels over a period of 10,000 years sometimes created shallow expanses of sea conducive to the growth of shellfish. Archaeologists feel that the Caribbean provided an optimal environment for the growth and survival of these early migrants.

The *Saladoid*, *Barrancoid* and *Ostionoid* were more advanced cultures using pottery and cultivating manioc (cassava). Being experienced navigators, they traded between the islands and the mainland and had simple, egalitarian societies. Through acculturation they eventually developed into the highly organized chiefdoms of the Tainos, ruled over by *caciques*. The people of the Caribbean at the time of the Conquest comprised the relatively advanced Taino societies, groups of Archaic peoples, other groups still at the Saladoid stage, and the most recent migrants, the Caribs. The Europeans used the terms 'Taino' or 'Carib' to include all these various groups.

---

just a matter of migrant groups moving northwards into the Caribbean; they frequently backtracked and kept in constant communication with suppliers of raw materials for pottery, ornaments, and various tools of stone, shell, coral and bone. The historical picture, then, is one of intense interaction between the peoples of the northern coast of South America and the Antilles.

- We have been taught about 'Amerindians' as if they were (and are) a uniform group. The reality is that hybridization developed differently in different parts of the Caribbean, and these hybrid groups co-existed with Archaic peoples still living in large communities in western Cuba and remote parts of Hispaniola (they were called *Ciboneys*) in 1492.

- European historians used labels for native peoples that were later revealed to be wrong. The people of the Greater Antilles at the time of Contact (coming of the Europeans) were labelled 'Arawak'. They spoke a language similar to that of the 'true' Arawaks of the Orinoco valley and Trinidad, people who are still found today in coastal Guyana and Suriname. However, they did not regard themselves as allied with any **ethnic group** in South America. In fact, they did not even regard themselves as one uniform cultural group throughout the Greater Antilles. The people of the Greater Antilles did use the term 'Taino', but historians are unsure about how they used it. Today we use it as a label to describe them instead of 'Arawak'.

- The *Tainos* evolved out of cultural mixing amongst the earlier peoples of the Greater Antilles; they did not come as a separate wave of migration. At the time of Contact they had developed a highly organized civilization of chiefdoms governed by *caciques*, in the process of becoming city-states similar to those of the Maya and other mainland societies. In fact, Jaragua in Santo

Domingo was almost a city-state as its *cacique*, Behechio, had united many of the nearby *caciques* into a confederation, on the basis of which there was a surplus economy (Chanlatte Baik, 2003). What the Spaniards emphasized, and what has come down to us in the traditional account, is that these peoples were 'simple, primitive and peace loving'. This is an interpretation of the Spanish dating from the fifteenth century, yet this perception remains amongst Caribbean people today.

- The last wave of migrants from South America before the Contact was the **Island Caribs**, so called to differentiate them from the present-day Caribs in Venezuela and the Guianas. The label 'Carib', too, was created by the Spaniards. The Island Caribs spoke an Arawakan language (no doubt derived from capturing so many 'Arawak' women) while the Caribs of the mainland speak a Cariban language. The Island Caribs may have only entered the Caribbean a few hundred years before Columbus and were regarded as very different from the Tainos. However, historians today see both groups as having evolved from a common Saladoid culture.

- Historians today also question the judgement handed down by the Spaniards of the 'peaceful Tainos' and 'warlike, cannibal Caribs'. The Tainos may have been peaceful initially, but they vigorously resisted their extermination and even allied with the Caribs, as in 1511 in Puerto Rico to stage an uprising against Spanish rule. If we employed less ethnocentric thinking we might describe the Caribs as 'daring, fearless and mighty warriors'. One can even say that the Spaniards were 'warlike' as they were wresting territory from their rightful owners. The charge of cannibalism is also debated. While certain beliefs may have called for rituals involving cannibalism, the Spaniards distorted these religious practices to cast the Carib as bestial and deserving of enslavement or annihilation. It is argued that the Europeans needed slave labour to replace the dwindling Taino population and used the 'myth of cannibalism' as a justification for waging war on the Caribs, with the intention of subjugating them as slaves. In 1511, Bartolomé de Las Casas protested Trinidad's indigenous peoples being classified by the Spanish Crown as 'Carib' for this very reason; yet many were enslaved and sent to Margarita for pearl fishing.

- Finally, we have all learned that the Tainos were completely wiped out in the Greater Antilles and that the earlier inhabitants are long gone. Today, however, DNA evidence is throwing new light on our connections to our prehistory (Box 4.2).

Patterns of early migrations in the Caribbean show that the region has had a long history of settlement, much of which is unknown to students. In schools, emphasis is given to the study of the Caribs and Tainos, as these were the people living in the region when the Europeans arrived and about whom there is a written record. Archaeology helps us to discover more about the earlier inhabitants, but even with some of this knowledge already unearthed many Caribbean people still date our history to the advent of Europeans into the region. Diverse groups of Amerindians in the Caribbean today are aggressively trying to reverse this misconception by researching their own history, forming associations to publicize their lifestyles and that of their ancestors, and reminding us that they are the

BOX 4.2 DNA versus the historical record

Our *DNA* is found in the nucleus of our cells and we inherit it in equal parts from our mothers and fathers. However, *mitochondrial DNA* (mtDNA) is not found in the nucleus of the cell with our DNA; it is found separately as an *organelle*. Recently it has been discovered that our mtDNA is inherited only from our mothers, and they inherit it intact from their own mothers, and so on, going back throughout history. Thus, the mtDNA within your body carries clues about your early maternal ancestors.

In 1990 a study of ancestral inheritance was conducted in Puerto Rico by genetic testing of a random sample of people. The results were startling in that 61 per cent of Puerto Ricans were shown to have mtDNA characteristic of Amerindians, while 27 per cent had mtDNA characteristic of Africans and 12 per cent had mtDNA characteristic of Caucasians. Puerto Ricans usually regarded themselves as descended from the Spaniards, with some admixture of African and Amerindian heritage. While that may be true in terms of their DNA, governing how they look (their *phenotype*), their mtDNA showed their genetic history over many hundreds of years (their *genotype*), and that many of them were descended from Amerindians (Kearns, 2003).

This is interesting in that it shows the amount of *miscegenation* occurring in the early days of the Conquest. Amerindian mtDNA, too, will undoubtedly show the miscegenation which occurred between Archaic and Ceramic peoples and the Taino. What all this really shows is that much of our genetic ancestry may be hidden from us. We may have physical characteristics that tend to characterize us as belonging to an ethnic group – African – but our genetic record may show that we have had Amerindian ancestors.

ACTIVITY 4.1

1. Suggest how an Amerindian version of the 'Coming of the Europeans' would differ from the traditional account.

2. Reflecting on what you learned about early Caribbean history as a younger student, how has that historical account influenced your understanding of Caribbean society and culture today?

original inhabitants of these lands, still alive and well. For example, the Carib community of Dominica has staged canoe trips to Trinidad and Guyana to meet other Carib communities.

European migrations

Columbus may not have been the first European to visit the Americas but he was the first to carry back tangible evidence of gold to show their Catholic Majesties, Ferdinand and Isabella. If Columbus had not found gold and precious stones it is hardly likely that the Caribbean would have stirred up so much interest and expectations amongst Europeans. As soon as he returned to Spain after his first voyage of 1492, wave after wave of Spaniards came out to 'seek their fortunes'. Conquistadors and soldiers came to plunder, priests came to convert the 'heathen', and administrators came to organize society and arrange that the gold and silver of the Spanish Main be directed solely at Spain.

The Caribbean was the springboard for all this activity, which was launched mainly at Central and South America, with the island of Hispaniola being a particular focus. The fact that gold had been found on Hispaniola and that it had a large resident population of Tainos suitable for conversion into slave labour made it the first official, administrative Spanish settlement in the Americas. Spanish migrants came to satisfy a lust for riches and therefore they made war on the Tainos, enslaved them, took their wealth, killed off their leaders, and exploited the mines until the metals were exhausted. The Spanish, more than any other European power, were responsible for the **genocide** of the native peoples of the Caribbean.

Hispaniola became the established hub of this very large Spanish American empire, stretching from Mexico to Patagonia, including the Caribbean (but excluding Brazil,

BOX 4.3 Treaty of Tordesillas, 1495

The two nations of the Iberian Peninsula, Spain and Portugal, were fairly advanced in exploration and navigation by 1492, when Columbus arrived in the New World. They were also rivals. Some intervention was thought necessary to map out territory between these two European countries – even yet undiscovered territory – lest rivalry and hostility erupt into war. The Pope at the time, Alexander VI, drew an arbitrary line on the map of the Atlantic, 370 leagues (about 1300 miles or 2000 km) from the Cape Verde Islands, and decreed that any newly found territories west of this line would be considered Spanish territory and any to the east of it would go to the Portuguese.

Referring to Fig. 4.3 we see that by this papal decree Portugal received the large territory of Brazil, making it today the only Portuguese-speaking country within Latin America.

While the Iberian nations obeyed the Pope, the Protestant countries of Britain and the Netherlands had no reason to do so, and France, a Roman Catholic country, was wary of Roman authority in France in secular matters. Thus, the maritime nations of Europe – France, Britain and the Netherlands – ignored papal authority and chose to regard the Caribbean as fair game; they would encroach on Spanish territory through whatever means – raids, piracy, smuggling, trade, and later settlement.

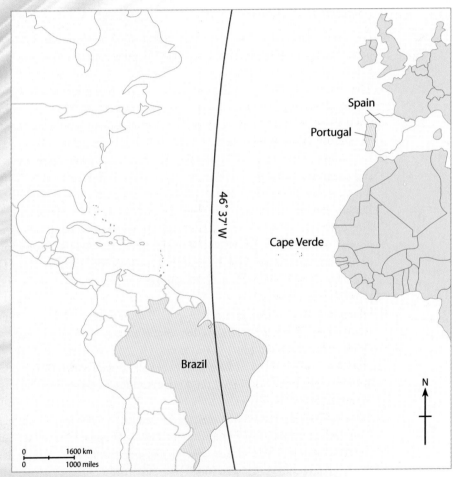

Fig. 4.3 The Treaty of Tordesillas – dividing the New World

see Box 4.3). The migrants who continued to come from Spain after the initial spate of explorers, adventurers, priests and conquistadors came to settle, to become ranch- or estate-owners, or to get involved in the business and trading life of the new colonies. Many were royal officials sent to make sure that the business of the empire remained in Spanish hands. But Spain could not keep the 'riches of the Indies' a secret or monopolize it for very long. Indeed, the vast expanse of the empire made it impossible to patrol effectively. The greed that spurred the first migrations of Spaniards now spread to all the capitals of Europe where adventurers gathered, prepared to take what they could from the Spanish. The maritime nations of Europe – Britain, France, the Netherlands and Portugal – were best suited for this contest.

In histories of the Caribbean, the Europeans are usually treated as if they were a uniform group. A more sensitive reading of our own history will show that the differences amongst Caribbean nations today initially stemmed from the old hostilities and rivalries amongst European nations. It is important then that we are aware of some of the differences between the various groups of Europeans and how they impacted the Caribbean.

- For over a hundred years after Columbus claimed the Americas for Spain, no other European nation was able to establish a permanent settlement in the Caribbean.
- The British and French in the sixteenth and seventeenth centuries came to raid, pillage and capture the rich Spanish galleons carrying gold and silver back to Spain or to lay siege to and destroy Spanish settlements and steal their treasures. They were called 'buccaneers', 'privateers' and 'pirates' (Box 4.4).
- According to the Treaty of Tordesillas, Spain was not given territory in Africa and therefore had to rely on the Portuguese for a supply of slaves. This took the form of a licence, the *asiento*, granted at first to the Portuguese, then to the Dutch, French and British. Portuguese fortunes waned in Africa when their forts and slaving connections were gradually usurped by the growing maritime powers of the Dutch, British and French. There was intense rivalry for the licence and they undermined each other at the point of supply along the African coast. No longer gold and silver but human cargo was now proving to be a way to profit from Spain's empire.
- Smuggling was another means whereby all the European nations sought to encroach on the empire. The holders of the *asiento* could never satisfy the demand for slaves and other goods needed by the colonists. The Portuguese and Dutch, in particular, assisted Spanish colonists, as well as the British and French settlers who illegally occupied the Lesser Antilles, by providing them with smuggled goods and slaves.
- Once the British and French managed to establish a permanent settlement in St Kitts (1624), migrants spread quickly to Nevis, Antigua, Montserrat, Guadeloupe and Martinique. These islands were virtually ignored by the Spaniards and the Amerindian populations were small and easily overcome.

It has been calculated that in 1650, 56,900 Europeans lived in the British Caribbean and around 15,000 in the French and Dutch Antilles. This means that on average around 2,000 to 3,000 Europeans per year came into the Caribbean

BOX 4.4 Challenging Spain

As soon as word filtered back to other European nations that Spain had come upon untold wealth and riches, nobleman, merchant and commoner alike vowed to have a share as well. Settlement was not yet a dominant idea; robbery was the most pressing concern. Throughout the sixteenth century and for part of the seventeenth, Spain's empire in the New World was constantly harassed by privateers, buccaneers and pirates.

● *Privateers*. French and British monarchs gave the captain of an armed ship the authority to patrol coastal areas to protect merchant vessels or to commit acts of reprisal against any ship or territory that was owned by a rival European nation. These privateers were given *letters of marque* by the monarch as their official permission to attack, loot and pillage enemy possessions in the Americas. They were rewarded by a portion of the spoils. Famous privateers included *Sir Francis Drake* and *Sir Henry Morgan*.

● *Buccaneers*. Initially these were French runaways who lived a hand-to-mouth existence on Tortuga and nearby islands, killing wild pigs, and inventing the 'barbecue' in the process. The term *boucanier* means 'one who hunts wild pigs'. Spain tried to dislodge them from the small islands on which they had settled, and many joined the ranks of privateers and pirates in revenge. The term 'buccaneer' has come into general use to describe privateers and pirates and all those who sought to rob Spain of its treasure in the Americas.

● *Pirates*. These were groups of men who sailed the high seas generally to rob and plunder. Their attacks were usually directed at the laden Spanish galleons en route to Spain with gold and silver, but they would attack any ship perceived to be the enemy of their country, or even a ship belonging to their own country if it was believed to be carrying valuable goods. *Blackbeard* was a famous (or infamous) pirate who frequented the waters of the Bahamas.

during the period, 1624–50. . . . These regular, massive migrations from Europe created a drastic change from the previous situation: the sparsely-populated Spanish Caribbean counted perhaps one European to 10 square miles; around 1650 the islands of the English Caribbean had become one of the heaviest populated areas in the world, with more than 50 Europeans per square mile. (Emmer, 1999, p. 16)

● Many of the colonies established by the French and British in the early seventeenth century were **proprietorships.** The European monarch gave to noblemen, highly favoured persons, or even companies, the sole right of settling and developing such colonies. These were the Lord Proprietors who bore the expenses of the colony and in return taxed the profits of the colonists.

● The Dutch settled on the Guiana coastlands and the small islands of Aruba, Curaçao, Bonaire, St Maarten, Saba and Sint Eustatius. They were less interested in agriculture, preferring to be traders, supplying the colonies with slaves and other goods. They used the islands as massive warehouses and places where slaves were kept en route to their final destination.

● Unlike the Spanish, the British, French and Dutch did not enslave the native populations. Poor and unemployed persons from Europe came out as **indentured** or contracted labour for the tobacco farms before sugar cultivation became widespread.

● Denmark settled St Thomas in 1672 and later St Croix and St John, while Sweden bought St Barth's from the French in 1784 and sold it back in 1878.

Whatever their nationality, Europeans first came to the Caribbean for economic gain. Spain attempted to prevent other Europeans from sharing in the riches of the Indies but was unsuccessful. After a turbulent period of piracy in the sixteenth century, Spain was unable to stop the flow of British, French and Dutch migrants who succeeded in establishing settlements in the Caribbean; these grew into substantial colonial societies. In a manner very similar to Spain in the fifteenth century, the British, French and Dutch tried to keep their colonies as separate and distinct entities. Communication and trade between colonies of the different European countries were discouraged through laws and regulations. Not only geographical borders separated the islands but political, linguistic and cultural barriers as well. By the close of the nineteenth century, the period of large-scale European migrations had come to an end, and the Caribbean was subdivided into enclaves owned by different European empires. Even today, in the twenty-first century, there is minimal interaction between the islands and territories of the French, British, Dutch and Spanish Caribbean. In each island a society and culture has developed heavily influenced by the European **metropolitan country**. Efforts at cooperation and regional integration across all these cultural groups are still proving to be very difficult.

Forced migration of Africans

It is a matter of some considerable interest whether Africans came to the Americas long before Columbus (Box 4.5). We do know that Africans came with the first expeditions of the Spanish as free men. While slavery had existed in Spain for centuries, slaves were of different races and ethnicities – Jews, Moors and Canary Islanders. Slavery also existed in Africa long before the Europeans organized the infamous Atlantic **slave trade**. Yet how Europeans eventually organized the capture, transport, distribution and servitude of Africans in the seventeenth, eighteenth and nineteenth centuries remains unprecedented in world history. The sheer numbers involved, its economic basis as a **capitalist** enterprise, the unspeakable brutality, as well as the racial **stereotyping** that accompanied the Atlantic slave trade, involved a totally new understanding of slave trading and slavery.

In Europe and Africa people were enslaved for many different reasons – religious persecution, captives of war, as payment, as part of a dowry – or they could be kidnapped and traded. In many cases there was little difference in **ethnicity** between master and slave. Even in the organized systems of capture and distribution, as in the trans-Saharan caravan trade, the numbers involved were very small, and no country's **economy** depended wholly on enslaved labour. What made the Atlantic slave trade unique was not only the forced migration of millions of Africans into a lifetime of captivity and servitude, or that it continued for centuries, or that it supported an economy overseas that could only survive on enslaved labour, but that the foundation of this trade was based on **race**. 'Over time, whatever positive images that had also constituted a part of the perception of Africa and its peoples were filtered out and a full blown racist ideology emerged, particularly in the 18th and 19th centuries' (Palmer, 1997, p. 12).

Enslaved Africans were imported into the Caribbean in small numbers from as early as 1503. By 1520 the Spanish Crown had given permission to import Africans as slaves to supplement the dwindling Taino population. The Portuguese, who held

BOX 4.5 Africans in the Caribbean before Columbus?

Some archaeological finds in central Mexico are difficult to explain without allowing for the possibility that Africans came to the Americas at different times long before Columbus. *Ivan van Sertima*, a world-renowned Guyanese historian, first put this theory forward in his 1976 book *They came before Columbus*. He proposed that Africans had made contact with the Americas as long ago as 3000 years BP and then again more recently in the twelfth century, when the Mandingo and Songhai went on long trading voyages. Other equally renowned scholars vigorously dispute these claims.

The *Olmec civilization* of Central Mexico is at the heart of the controversy. Fig. 4.4 shows an example of the huge stone sculptures that were carved by the Olmecs. To many they indicate unmistakably Negroid physical features. Olmec writing too bears close similarities to that of the Vai people of West Africa and the Mende of Sierra Leone. Their language is also somewhat similar to that of the Malinke–Bambara peoples of the Senegambia region of West Africa. Additionally, examination of some of the human skulls at Olmec sites show similarities to skulls found in West Africa. And there continue to be the yet unexplained similarities of the calendars and pyramids of Egypt and those of the Aztec and Maya civilizations of Central America. However, all this 'evidence' is dismissed as only circumstantial by critics of van Sertima.

Other explanations put forward (other than direct contact in the pre-Christian era and in the twelfth century) suggest that Africans were among the first peoples to enter the New World, when the continents were placed differently

Fig. 4.4 An Olmec stone head

to how they are now (see Box 5.8). Hence, they have left some influences behind. At the moment, then, some scholars are willing to admit that the presence of Africans in the Americas before Columbus is not that far fetched, but without the necessary archaeological evidence it can only be judged as a strong possibility.

the *asiento* and controlled large tracts of territory in Africa, supplied the Spanish Empire with African slaves. Spain could not be an active player in the slave trade because of the Treaty of Tordesillas (see Box 4.3). In turn, the Dutch, French and British each dominated the Atlantic slave trade from the sixteenth through to the nineteenth century, when it was abolished.

The organization of the Atlantic slave trade illustrates how differently it developed compared with previous forms of slave trading or slavery:

- The trade was highly organized on a business footing. European merchants, banks and chartered companies put up the necessary capital to finance the undertaking. It was hardly likely that a lone sea captain could stand the costs of such a venture by himself or with a few partners.
- European governments took an active role in the commercial aspects of the slave trade. They founded by charter *joint stock companies*, of which the best known are the Royal African Company, the Company of Senegal (French) and the

Dutch West India Company. These companies were given a **monopoly** to trade in slaves and other goods for certain time periods. They were responsible for defending their forts and warehouses in Africa and could harass other European traders on the African coast by capturing their merchandise.

● West Africa was integral to the operations of these companies. Each European country involved in the trade built forts at different points on the coast. The Portuguese built the massive fort at Elmina, which was captured by the Dutch in 1650. (Ghana has restored many of these forts today as historical sites.) The Royal African Company built its fort at Cape Coast Castle on the Gold Coast, Ghana. The forts were used to store the merchandise brought from Europe for trading purposes – cloth, iron, weapons, cowrie shells, trinkets and beads – and to house those Africans who were to be sold as slaves in the Americas. Europeans at the forts were also responsible for conducting delicate negotiations with African chiefs and their emissaries. Indeed, members of these chartered companies acted on behalf of their governments, offering gifts and bribes to tribal chieftains who sometimes proved uncooperative. The forts had armed guards to ward off dissatisfied African traders and European rivals.

● Conservative estimates put the total numbers of Africans forcibly taken from Africa and sent to the Americas at 15 million. The Portuguese were mainly active along the Gold Coast (Fig. 4.5) and then shifted operations to present-day Angola. The Dutch established forts and small settlements on the Gold Coast, the Slave Coast and the Ivory Coast. France's main areas of activity were Angola, Benin, Senegal and the Gold Coast. Britain traded along the Gold Coast, Whydah, Guinea, Benin and later Angola. Each country carved out a sphere of influence on the African coast and nurtured delicate relations with the tribal chieftains for the good of the trade but also to safeguard their own persons.

● Wherever slave trading took place on the coast, it affected a region hundreds of miles inland. Initially the Europeans conducted their own raids to capture Africans, sometimes with help from rival African groups. Later, as they found it necessary to go deeper inland, they formed alliances with African groups willing to capture and sell fellow Africans. Eventually, although they were only involved in bartering or buying slaves, they were constantly drawn into the internal, domestic intrigues of the coastal kingdoms, providing guns and ammunition to their allies.

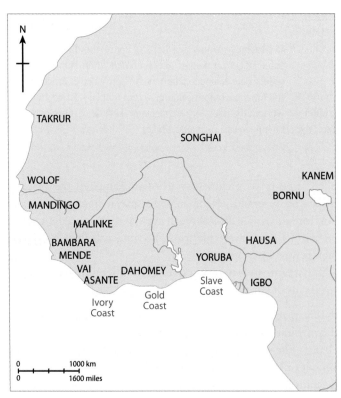

Fig. 4.5 The kingdoms of West and Central Africa

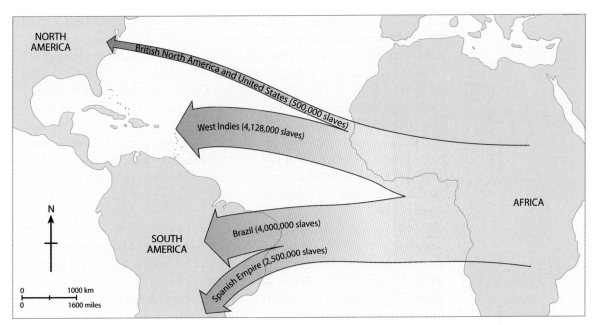

Fig. 4.6 The Atlantic Slave Trade

- Once the slave ships left the African coast they embarked on the second leg, the **Middle Passage**, across the Atlantic to the Caribbean or North America (Fig. 4.6). The conditions of life aboard a slaver were terrible. Many died from suffocation in the hold because there was only enough room to lie down with another layer of captives above and below. The more slaves a ship could carry, the higher the profits, and if a certain number of fatalities were to be expected then even more were taken on to offset that occurrence. The journey lasted roughly two to three months.
- When the enslaved Africans were sold, the ships took on a cargo of sugar, rum and molasses and headed for Western Europe, to ports such as London, Amsterdam and Bordeaux. This was the third and final leg of the **triangular trade** route, showing that the slave trade was a complex, economic enterprise that required financing and coordination on three continents.

The forced migration of millions of Africans to the Americas is the single most important historical process impacting the Caribbean today. It totally changed the demographic structure of the Caribbean. Caribbean societies became **slave societies** because of the sheer numbers of the enslaved in the society. They were not just societies where slaves existed but slavery became the basis for the economy and society. However, it impacted Caribbean countries in different ways:

- The slave trade was directly tied to the need for *labour*. Thus, colonies where plantations were first established tended to develop large African populations before others. In the British, French and Dutch territories, the African segment of the population became dominant.
- The Spanish, on the other hand, were slow to introduce plantations into Cuba, Puerto Rico and Santo Domingo, and so over the centuries fewer Africans were

imported. However, in the late nineteenth century they imported African slaves at a time when other European countries had already abolished the slave trade and slavery. For example, in 1750, while the slave population of St Domingue (present-day Haiti) was 164,859 and Jamaica's was 127,881, Cuba had only 28,760 slaves. Yet in 1880 Cuba had 199,094 slaves (Engerman and Higman, 1997), brought mainly by the Spanish, who had only recently become active slave traders.

- The British, French and Dutch *abolished* the slave trade and slavery before the Spanish. In 1804 Britain abolished the slave trade; the Dutch followed suit in 1814 and France in 1818. Slavery itself was abolished by the British in 1834, by the French in 1848 and by the Dutch in 1863. Slavery was finally abolished in Cuba in 1886.

- Although slavery was completely abolished in 1886, people of African descent do not comprise a majority in the Hispanic Caribbean. Cuba today is approximately 66 per cent white, 22 per cent mixed and 12 per cent black (Iglesias Garcia, 2004). (Census and other statistics vary by a few percentage points.) The people of Puerto Rico and the Dominican Republic are mainly mixed, usually mulatto (African and white admixture).

- The forced migration of African peoples created a **diaspora** – people or migrants who have a homeland elsewhere to which they share an emotional attachment. This 'in-betweenity' (of living in the Caribbean as the largest ethnic group, while at the same time having only a short history in the region and actually belonging elsewhere) continues to impact Caribbean society and culture as identity issues in many different ways.

- We should be aware that in speaking of the Caribbean as an 'African' diaspora we are smoothing over all the ethnic differences of the people who were forcibly brought here. They did not identify themselves as African but as Wolof, Ewe or Ashanti. Thus, some of the cultural differences evident in Caribbean society and culture today are due to large numbers of people from the same African ethnic group being found only in certain islands. For example:
  - The French traded a great deal in Dahomey (Benin) and supplied mainly their own colonies, so the strong influence of voodoo (*Vodun*) in Haiti is easy to understand; it is the official religion of Benin today.
  - Most Africans taken to Cuba were of the Bantu peoples. The Bakongo, a Bantu group from northern Angola, practise a religion very similar to the Palo Monte found today in Cuba. And, although there were not as many Yoruba in Cuba, the religion they practised, Santeria, is now widespread throughout that island.
  - The Big Drum and Nation Dances in Carriacou, usually performed at Easter, are strongly associated with the Ibo and Koromanti of West Africa.

Migrations of indentured servants

Slavery was abolished in the British Caribbean over a period of time (1834–1838). Some smaller territories became free overnight (for example, Antigua and the

ACTIVITY 4.3

1. Identify the arguments someone might use to show that the Atlantic slave trade was a **racist** enterprise.

2. It is likely that you are a member of one (or more than one) of the diasporas affecting the Caribbean.

(a) What kind of ties would you like with your homeland or homelands?

(b) To what extent do you feel that acknowledging a homeland or homelands elsewhere affects the ties you may have to your Caribbean country?

British Virgin Islands); others went through a compulsory transition period (termed **apprenticeship**), ending in 1838. The crucial issues after **emancipation**, confronting both European and African, centred on the price of labour. How those issues were resolved fundamentally affected society and culture in the Caribbean.

In the smaller islands such as Antigua, St Kitts and Barbados, Africans had fewer options and so had to return to the plantations and accept the wages offered. In British Guiana (present-day Guyana) the ex-slaves could make a living by moving into the interior and becoming small farmers. Trinidad never developed into a classic slave society as slave imports took place mainly between the 1790s and 1806 (Brereton, 2002). Europeans made the case that especially in British Guiana and Trinidad, which had only recently become large-scale sugar producers, more labour was needed for expansion of the industry. In the transition years after emancipation Europeans were on the search for a reliable source of cheaper labour. Any new labour supply coming into Caribbean society and culture, however, was bound to encounter hostility from the Africans, who wanted wages increased. They felt that while Europeans were making claims of a labour shortage, it was they who created that shortage by refusing to pay Africans a fair wage

'Indentureship' was an old idea brought back to solve the labour problems in the British West Indies. Indentured servants agreed to enter into a contract to work in the Caribbean for a period of five to seven or ten years, for a minimum wage. Their outward passage would be provided and they had the option of either accepting a return

BOX 4.6 Experiments in indentured immigration

Europeans were first tried as indentured labourers to help 'whiten' the ethnic balance in the British West Indies. Between 1834 and 1846 Portuguese from the Azores and Madeira came in several thousands to Trinidad and British Guiana, and British and German immigrants went to Jamaica. The Lesser Antilles received much smaller numbers. However, the Europeans could not perform satisfactorily as manual labourers in tropical conditions and gradually drifted off the plantations into the towns. The Portuguese were more successful as shopkeepers.

Planters in British Guiana, Trinidad and Jamaica then looked to the other islands of the British Caribbean, offering higher wages. By 1850 thousands of Africans had left Barbados and Grenada for Trinidad and British Guiana; Jamaica received several hundred. This internal migration heightened the labour shortage in the Eastern Caribbean but it gradually declined when migrants realized that the wages were not much better.

A short-lived scheme then involved attracting indentured labour from West Africa, particularly Sierra Leone and Liberia. However, Africans did not seem interested in voluntarily migrating and the majority of Africans who entered the Caribbean as a labour force by the 1860s were those who had been liberated from ships still plying the slave trade. Since the British had abolished the trade in 1804 they had been policing the high seas to prevent other nations from bringing slaves into the New World. Very few of these liberated Africans were repatriated; instead they were dropped off in the British Caribbean to swell the labour supply. However, they too drifted off the plantations in search of other work.

In 1838 the experiment involving indentured labour from India began in a small way when 396 Indians arrived in Guyana (Box 4.7). Europeans had no way of knowing that this was to be the only group to show signs of realizing planter expectations and would continue until 1917. They were trying several alternatives simultaneously, including recruiting Chinese labour from Canton and Hong Kong, mainly for British Guiana, Trinidad and Jamaica. When they too drifted off the plantations as they found business and commerce more suited to their talents, the planters focused exclusively on India.

BOX 4.7 'Indians' in the Caribbean

In the Caribbean, particularly Guyana and Trinidad, which received the largest numbers of immigrant labour from India, Indians have often been referred to as 'East Indians'. It is a local use of the term that sometimes confuses persons from outside the area. We can only suppose that it grew out of a desire to differentiate them from the native 'Indians' or Amerindians, who were not Indians at all, but a case of mistaken identity on the part of Columbus, who had gone in search of a new route to India and the spice islands of the east. When it was realized that Columbus had stumbled on islands that were not the sought-for spice islands, a distinction was drawn by simply putting 'east' or 'west' before the term 'the Indies'. 'The Indies' was a term probably long used by Europeans to describe the islands to the east of India (mainly what is present-day Indonesia). Thus, the *East* Indies and *West* Indies came into being and have been a source of confusion ever since. For example, today there is no country or group of countries one can identify as the *East* Indies; the term has fallen into disuse. However, the *West* Indies remains very much in use. That gives rise to the interesting fact that more than half the population of Guyana and Trinidad are East Indian West Indians!

passage to their country of origin once the period of indentureship was completed or receiving a grant of land. Various experiments were tried. Europeans looked first to Europe, then to other Caribbean islands, Africa, India and China (Box 4.6).

India proved to be the most satisfactory source of labour, and in 1845 both Trinidad and Jamaica (Box 4.7), following the lead of British Guiana, began importing Indian indentured labour. While immigrants came in small numbers from time to time to virtually all of the Caribbean territories (Fig. 4.7), immigration into British Guiana and Trinidad was heavy and continuous. By the time the experiment in Indian indentureship ended in 1917, approximately 239,000 had gone to British Guiana, 144,000 to Trinidad and 36,000 to Jamaica.

The price of labour was the crucial factor governing the entry of Indians into Caribbean society and culture. They came from conditions of extreme poverty mainly in northern India – Bengal, Uttar Pradesh, and various other parts of British India (Fig. 4.8) – and were willing to work for the small wage offered. The Africans did not trust a people who accepted such poor conditions of work, and who thereby excluded them from making effective wage demands on the planters. The Indians

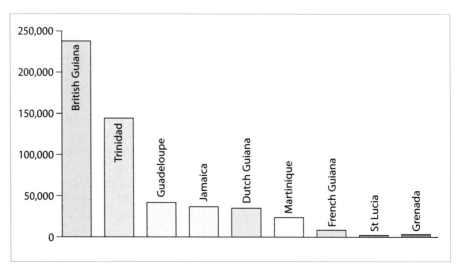

Fig. 4.7 Indentured immigrants to Caribbean countries

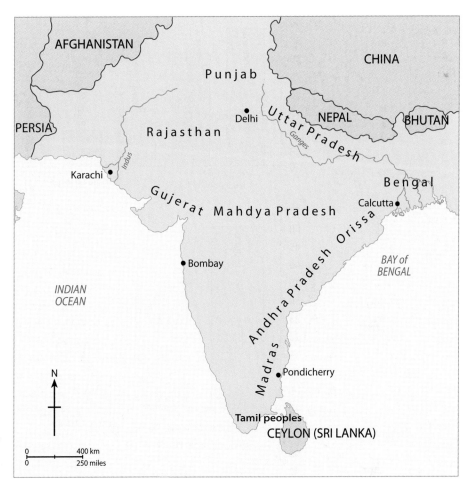

Fig. 4.8 Origins of Indian immigrants in the nineteenth century

for their part, in an alien environment where their customs found disfavour, remained apart on the plantations.

Indentured migrants added to the diversity and complexity of Caribbean society and culture:

- Although the societies of the Caribbean are described as **plural**, the influx of indentured immigrants, particularly in Guyana, Trinidad and Suriname, created sizable additional groups and sub-groups. As was discussed in Chapter 3, the tensions amongst them go largely unresolved to this day.
- After 1848 planters in the French Caribbean brought labourers from Pondicherry, a French colony in India (Fig. 4.7), to work in the cane fields. The Kali ceremony and other examples of Tamil or Madrasi culture (from South India) can still be found in Guadeloupe today.
- The Dutch had an extensive empire in the East Indies and brought labourers from the island of Java to their colony Dutch Guiana (Suriname). They also imported Indians from British India, who are referred to in Suriname today as 'Hindustanis' or East Indians. The Javanese comprise 15 per cent of Suriname's population and are mostly Muslim, while the 'Hindustanis', comprising about

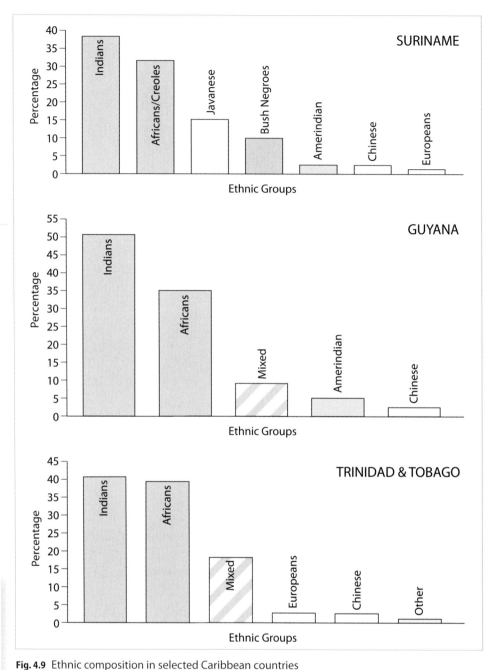

Fig. 4.9 Ethnic composition in selected Caribbean countries

ACTIVITY 4.4

There is a complaint sometimes heard in Trinidad and Tobago that whilst it is acceptable to speak of Afro-Trinidadians and Indo-Trinidadians, other groups are still referred to as 'Chinese', 'white' or 'Portuguese', even though they are also nationals. Discuss the issues that may be important here. Is there a similar situation in another Caribbean country that you may know about?

37 per cent of the population, are mainly Hindus with a Muslim minority. However, Javanese and 'Hindustani' Muslims practise different traditions in Islam.

- Today, the Indian populations in Suriname, Guyana and Trinidad are larger than the other ethnic groups (Fig. 4.9).
- Compared to the Indians, Chinese indentured immigrants readily assimilated into Caribbean society and many married African women and became Christian.

Summary

The Caribbean has been a destination for migrants over many thousands of years. Each group has contributed to the creation of Caribbean society and culture. Migrants came through normal processes of diffusion and expansion of cultures, through voyages intent on discovering new trade routes, as well as through force by being enslaved, and through worker indentureship schemes. Each group added to the increasing diversity of Caribbean society and culture, especially as each group impacted the various territories differently. Today both diversity and complexity deepen as we see the resurgence of groups thought to have long died out, namely the Amerindians, with a demand to be recognized as a vibrant part of Caribbean society and culture. And we also see Africans, Indians, Chinese and whites not only as Caribbean people, but also as part of the various diasporas, having homelands elsewhere and learning to forge an identity under such circumstances. The complexity deepens considerably when Caribbean people migrate to metropolitan countries and live in 'a double diaspora'.

4.2

THE DEVELOPMENT OF SYSTEMS OF PRODUCTION

A system of production refers to the ways in which an economy is organized to produce commodities to sustain society. Early societies had simple systems of production such as hunting and gathering or subsistence agriculture. Once surpluses occurred, trade became important. Amerindian societies were at different stages of economic organization when the Europeans arrived in the Americas. The Tainos, the most advanced, were producing agricultural surpluses and trade was mostly organized around feeding and providing for the wants of their increasingly urban communities. The Spaniards, however, brought ideas about systems of production in which wealth in the form of gold and silver (bullion) was the desired goal. They believed that if Spain had access to its own gold and silver mines, then it would be the most powerful country in Europe. Thus, the driving force behind Spain's **colonization** of the Americas was the lure of precious metals.

Encomienda

The Spanish monarchs decided that the native population should be divided up amongst Spaniards, who had the right to exact from them some form of tribute – produce, gold or personal service. In return, the Spaniards would guarantee religious instruction in the Roman Catholic faith. This system was known as the **encomienda**. In reality, the Amerindians were treated as slaves and put to work in the mines. They quickly died out from hunger, overwork, harsh punishments and European diseases. Many committed suicide. The system of production was a get-rich-quick scheme where precious metals were taken from a conquered people by forced labour and sent to Spain to increase Spain's power and prestige in Europe.

Slavery

African slavery was then introduced throughout the Americas. Other Europeans had begun to encroach on Spain's empire, settling territories they had captured such as

Jamaica and the western part of Hispaniola, or islands of little importance to Spain, namely the Lesser Antilles. In the British, French and Dutch Caribbean, slavery as a system of production was primarily bound up with the cultivation of sugar and the social and economic organization of the plantation.

Slavery as a total institution

Slavery was a **total institution** in that it determined all aspects of the lives of African people, as well as the social and economic arrangements of the plantation and, by extension, the society. Slavery as a total institution formed the basis of **plantation society** (Box 2.5 and Fig. 3.2) and this was the system of production in the Caribbean associated with sugar cultivation. One fundamental way in which slavery shaped the lives of Africans was by the attempt to *dehumanize* the African. Africans were regarded as 'chattel' (property like land or buildings) and were thus owned by Europeans who had paid for them. This attempt at dehumanization was done through suppressing the social and cultural ties which helped to form an identity and a sense of belonging. For example:

- Choosing Africans from different tribal groups for the plantations to minimize communication and bonds of kinship between them was based on a fear of Africans banding together.
- Giving the Africans European names and forbidding the practice of their religions, customs and traditions, so that any semblance of social and family life was discouraged, was also based on a fear of developing solidarity and identity.
- Meting out harsh physical punishments, torture, and even death, was done to force the African to submit to the will of the European.
- Playing one group of Africans against others was meant to promote European values and ways of life. (The domestic or house slaves or lighter-skinned, partly European slaves, were accorded higher status and prestige because of their constant and intimate contact with Europeans.)
- Rigidly stratifying the society according to race and colour, relegating black people to the bottom of the social strata, was dehumanizing because the very characteristics identifying Africans as a race were the same ones identifying them as slaves, and therefore the property of others.

The plantation system

The plantation was a system of production that Europeans had devised in their colonial empires. They brought different ethnic groups to live and work on plantations far from their homelands; the groups were encouraged to distrust each other; and they were encouraged to look on the European as superior. Labour was coloured and the whites were the owners, managers and supervisors. When coupled with slavery as a total institution the plantation system became a sophisticated economic mechanism that dominated the culture and society of the Caribbean, locking it into European economies. For example, the plantation system:

- relied on the Atlantic slave trade for its labour supply and provided the raw materials for the third leg of the triangular trade – sugar, rum and molasses for the port cities of England, France and Holland

- provided the basis for the growing manufacturing and industrial strength of Europe (plantations were a form of investment financed from the capitals of Europe)
- was so valuable that in 1651 Britain instituted the Navigation Laws whereby only English ships could trade with English colonies. This prevented other nations from getting a share of the profitable trade arising from the slave plantations of the Caribbean. France followed in 1664 with similar laws.

Europeans brought systems of production to the Caribbean that began to take the shape of capitalist enterprises. The emphasis lay in amassing huge profits that were repatriated to the metropolitan country. The basis of such wealth depended on the enslavement of people who, for the purpose of profit and prosperity, were regarded as subhuman. Values stressing exploitation of the environment and people for economic gain and an ideology of European superiority became part of the system of production.

Indentureship

After emancipation, the planters sought a reliable source of labour, particularly in the larger territories where the ex-slaves refused to work for what they regarded as very low wages. The system of production in the British, French and Dutch Caribbean was thus thrown into jeopardy. Indentureship has been described as another form of slavery, though the Indian and Chinese immigrants were not regarded as chattel and they continued to practise their religions, speak their languages and maintain their traditions as best they could. The charge of slavery comes from how they were treated. They were paid extremely low wages and their accommodation was crowded, substandard and unsanitary. They were always in debt to the company store where they were forced to buy goods. In addition, they were not allowed to move about freely, and if caught some distance from the plantation to which they had been assigned they were charged with vagrancy, flogged, and jailed. If they tried to escape they were hunted down and jailed for breach of contract, then returned to the plantation. For minor offences they were charged exorbitant fines. Many died from poor nutrition and they suffered from malaria, yaws, typhoid and dysentery. They were in a continual state of poor health and the rate of suicide was high.

As a system of production, indentureship was very much related to African slavery and, indeed, plantation society survived because of this new supply of labour. The socio-economic influences of the plantations still pervaded the whole society even though some Africans had opted to move away. For example, the Indians were a non-white group of labourers who now occupied the lowest stratum of the society and were encouraged to see the European bosses as superior. They were also encouraged to keep themselves apart from the Africans, thus continuing disunity amongst workers. Although a new group had entered Caribbean society, the system of production – the plantation – continued to influence social and economic affairs in the same ways.

However, times had changed. Towards the end of the nineteenth century Caribbean plantations were no longer as important to European economies because they now had worldwide empires. In addition, the sugar plantations had to contend

ACTIVITY 4.6

Some Caribbean scholars have described the impact of systems of production in this way. They say that elsewhere, such as in colonial New England, a society was developed with strong and vibrant institutions. *Here in the Caribbean, though, the economy developed society.* Explain your understanding of this interpretation of Caribbean society and culture.

with cheaper sugar produced by larger sugar producers, some of them still using slave labour – notably Brazil and Cuba. When the nationalist movement in India brought pressure to bear on the British authorities who were in control of India at this time to discontinue immigration schemes because they were dissatisfied with how their nationals were treated, the British ended indentureship in 1917. (The Chinese government had ended indentureship in 1885 for similar reasons.)

As a system of production Indian indentureship did save the sugar plantations in the British, French and Dutch Caribbean in the aftermath of emancipation. The very low wages they were paid exploited the labour force and enabled the plantations to survive through some turbulent times when the price of sugar on the world market was falling. However, the long association with enslaved and indentured labour predisposed Caribbean planters into a preference for exploitative systems of production. In the twentieth century, however, the number of plantations quickly decreased as the planters found that they could not survive by paying a fair wage. In addition, the reliance on forced or indentured labour had created a mindset that refused to implement labour-saving techniques and cost-effective technologies. The cost of production in Caribbean territories was thus very high and this legacy was bequeathed to Caribbean societies struggling with independence and self-determination later on in the century.

Summary

The systems of production established by Europeans in the Caribbean have continued mainly intact, even though centuries have passed since they were first introduced. Whilst the *encomienda* system, slavery and indentureship were all eventually abolished, the plantation is still seen as the main organizer of society and culture in the Caribbean. The plantation is a synonym now for highly stratified, ex-colonial societies where labour was brought in and now forms rival groups, in an economy that is still largely based on **monocultural** (one main product) exports. Europeans did not develop the economic institutions of Caribbean societies. Their emphasis was on producing agricultural products by monoculture and exporting the raw materials to Europe to be manufactured. Today, Caribbean societies continue to struggle with systems of production that are not geared towards developing a vibrant, indigenous manufacturing sector and food production.

4.3   RESISTANCE

Since the coming of the Europeans the history of the Caribbean has been steeped in violence and genocide. This oppression is a direct outcome of the systems of production that were established for economic gain – *encomienda*, slavery and indentureship. Whilst it may seem that the European will prevailed – for example, witness the divisions of the French, British, Dutch and Spanish Caribbeans today – this was achieved only amidst continuous wars, rebellions, revolution, maroonage, and other more subtle forms of resistance. It is a common belief that because plantation society was organized to keep the Amerindians and Africans in an inferior position, where not only prevailing attitudes but the actual laws of the country kept them powerless and vulnerable, they were mostly resigned to accepting their lot.

This is borne out by the fact that whilst Amerindians and Africans far outnumbered the whites at all times, they were not successful in overthrowing them.

This is a traditional version of Caribbean history. It is an account that usually refers to the Africans as 'slaves', whereas more sensitive renderings today acknowledge that Africans did not think of themselves as slaves but as people who were *enslaved* by others. What we have had as 'history' is an edited account that gave us the European perspective of events. This distinction between *slaves* and *the enslaved* helps us to gain some alternative insights into the nature of the resistance from the captive peoples' point of view. In fact, they resisted the oppression by any means possible.

The native peoples

The Tainos

The coming of the Europeans with their weapons of iron and steel, and their tracker dogs and horses, was an unprecedented experience for the native peoples. Yet almost from the inception of the Spanish invasion they resisted the newcomers. The people, described by the Spaniards themselves as 'peaceful' and 'gentle', realizing that they were facing genocide, were roused into open warfare. The earliest account dates from 1493, when they killed the men that Columbus had left at La Navidad in Hispaniola because of their ill treatment of native women. A series of conflicts continued throughout the Spanish occupation of the Greater Antilles and their imposition of the *encomienda*. Important native leaders in the struggle were the *caciques*, such as **Guarionex** in Hispaniola, **Hatuey** in Cuba and **Agueybana** in Puerto Rico.

Although the Spaniards had superior military might, their conquest of the Greater Antilles was not easy. By 1503 they had brought much of the active rebellions in Hispaniola to a close, but that was a long time considering their advantage of advanced weapons technology. It was not until 1513 that the Spaniards actually won the war for possession of Puerto Rico, and as late as 1520 they were still fighting a guerrilla war in Cuba. Other than open warfare, the Tainos also resisted the Spaniards by running away and withdrawing from settled areas so that the *encomienda* could not be enforced. They also resorted to sabotage and suicide.

The fierce resistance put up by the Tainos, a people at a relatively early form of technological development compared with the Spaniards, is hardly mentioned in the historical record. The Caribs are more likely to be mentioned in this regard, emphasizing the European myth that the inhabitants of the Greater Antilles were 'peaceful' and the Caribs were 'warlike'. Our history texts do not dwell on the heroes and heroines, tragic though they might be, the *caciques* and *cacicas*, who first engaged the Spaniards, yet we are well acquainted with Columbus, his brother Diego, Ponce de Leon, Magellan, Ovando, Las Casas and so on.

Perhaps one way we can *resist* this ethnocentric version of Caribbean history today is to tell these tales and write about them in textbooks and story-books where young Caribbean children will learn not only about the exploits of male *caciques*, but also of the powerful **Anacona** in Hispaniola, and other *cacicas*. Millions of people who inhabited the Greater Antilles at the time of the Conquest should not be rendered silent by history. In this way, and others, resistance continues as a theme in Caribbean society and culture.

The Caribs

The Caribs of the Lesser Antilles met the Spaniards' offensive with implacable resistance. Their tactical responses were well suited to the mountainous terrain of their islands, where they could engage in protracted guerrilla warfare indefinitely. Their social organization permitted flexibility as they did not have a traditional noble line with hereditary power; instead leadership resided in the best warriors. They were highly mobile, especially with the dug-out canoe enabling them to elude capture time and time again. Very soon the Spaniards left them alone, believing it was too much trouble defending islands where no gold was to be found.

However, the Caribs had to deal with the interlopers in Spain's empire – the British, French and Dutch who sought to colonize the Lesser Antilles. When they arrived in large numbers to settle, the Caribs would usually retreat into the interior. From there they waged continuous raids on the settlements, even forming alliances with one European power against another. Carib and European often lived on the same island in an uneasy co-existence. Gradually, however, the constant influx of Europeans and their superior weapons drove the Caribs out of most of the islands to their remaining strongholds in Dominica and Grenada. In St Vincent they mixed with Africans to form the Black Caribs, who after much bloody warfare with the British were deported to the coast of Belize. Their descendants today comprise the *Garifuna* people of Belize. In Dominica, Caribs persist in the north, occupying territory won by treaty with the British.

The Caribs never let up in their resistance to the Europeans who took their territory, captured their people and were bent on exterminating them. It is only because the Europeans could not fully subdue the Caribs that treaties were finally signed that ensured their survival as a race. By this time, though, they were severely decimated and only found in large numbers in Dominica and in Belize. Their fighting spirit and attitude of resistance continue today in efforts to draw all the aboriginal populations of the Caribbean together, to re-create aspects of their ancestry such as the re-enactment of historic voyages, and to collaborate with archaeologists in interpreting the historical record. Today they use modern technologies such as the internet to maintain websites about their culture, past and present.

ACTIVITY 4.7

Using the internet, find websites which support Amerindian peoples and showcase their activities and culture. What examples of *resistance* do you discern in how Amerindians portray themselves?

The Africans

Millions of Africans were imported into Caribbean society, where the whites, their oppressors, formed a minority. To be able to keep so many people in subjugation for centuries meant that it was not only the threat of physical violence and death that was employed but also some degree of psychological 'brainwashing' occurred. Resistance has to be understood against this peculiar background – that it would take both active and passive forms, and that sometimes it would not even be understood as resistance. One has to be able to enter the world of the enslaved to assess and judge whether their efforts succeeded or not.

Passive forms of resistance included acts of sabotage such as damaging tools, equipment and other property belonging to the planter, malingering (as in protracting an illness or delaying or avoiding work), deliberately misunderstanding instructions, suicide and induced abortions. These acts were committed in situations where all power had been taken away, and although they might not greatly cripple operations on the plantation they served to make the powerless feel that they could still control the events of their lives to some extent. Actually, such acts proved expensive to the planter. For example, the deliberate abortions and the killing of babies denied the planter a continuous source of slaves so that the enslaved labour supply always had to be replenished by the slave trade.

Running away was also an option, and in territories where there were mountainous interiors prohibiting the Europeans from effective pursuit, sizeable *maroon* communities were established (see Box 3.5). In Guyana, Suriname, Jamaica and Hispaniola the presence of Africans living freely in the interior acted as a beacon or symbol of what was possible to those on the plantations. This was the main reason why the Europeans tried every strategy, even importing troops, to destroy these settlements. The symbolic power of freed Africans living nearby acted as a tremendous psychological boost to enslaved Africans. It demonstrated that one could escape the oppressors. It also resurrected hopes that African customs and ways of life could be restored.

It was a priority with Europeans that the different aspects of African culture should be wiped out so that European culture could be substituted, making the Africans more subservient and controllable. This form of psychological brainwashing required some cunning responses from the captives. They continued to use African words where possible, they hybridized African religions onto Christianity, they told their *Anansi* stories as they recounted their oral folklore, and they made up songs and performances that ridiculed the white man. Although banned in several territories, their drumming continued as a major **cultural retention**. Africans, then, made great efforts to protect and practise their traditions as a form of resistance to cultural oppression.

More active forms of resistance did occur, on a regular basis, but the Africans had few weapons and could not communicate effectively between the various plantations. Nevertheless, revolts and rebellions made life in the colonies unsafe and risky for Europeans. Sporadic and isolated incidents were common (for example, an African killing a white man), and all whites lived with the ever-present threat of being poisoned by their house slaves. Rebellions that grew into full-scale revolutions, involving the whole territory and continuing for a protracted period, did erupt from time to time but were largely suppressed with great cruelty. The most famous and successful was the Haitian Revolution of 1791 (Box 4.8).

Superficially it may seem that the African responses to centuries of oppression were largely ineffective. Historians today are of the view, though, that the continued violence in the colonies was one of the main reasons why the slave trade and then slavery was abolished. The traditional account emphasized the activities of the Quakers and other humanitarian groups in England in bringing about the end of slavery. Many influential members of the British House of Commons were sympathizers and the case against slavery was widely debated in the British parliament. Nowadays more credit goes to the part that the enslaved Africans played in ending their own servitude. The continued violence and the high costs of maintaining the slave system made sugar plantations uneconomic to operate. Eventually European governments were prepared to abandon their commitment to actively supporting the costly sugar producers of the Caribbean and did away with the Navigation Laws, opening up markets to **free trade**.

ACTIVITY 4.8

Identify THREE other major slave rebellions that took place in the Caribbean, their dates and the major figures involved.

BOX 4.8 The Haitian Revolution

Under French rule Haiti was known as St Domingue. It was the largest sugar producer of the French Caribbean and in the late eighteenth century the most valuable plantation economy in the world. A socially stratified plantation society had developed where half a million Africans lived in bondage, with many thousands of Free Coloureds (*gens du coleur*), who were the children of Frenchmen and their slaves, who were also dissatisfied. These people were free, often educated, and had careers as doctors, pharmacists, teachers, and even slave owners. However, in the rigidly stratified society, they suffered discriminatory practices because they were not white – neither *Grands Blancs* nor *Petits Blancs*.

It is the activities of this relatively privileged group that actually began the revolt against the whites and provided the opportunity that was quickly grasped by the enslaved Africans. It mushroomed into a full-scale slave rebellion that was further expanded into a revolution, which wiped out society as it was known. An estimated 350,000 people died in this revolution before Haiti was declared a free **republic** in 1804.

This revolution saw Haiti fighting France (Napolelon) and Britain at different times and even forming alliances with Spain. Caribbean historians today accredit the success of this revolution to:

- the role of maroon communities in mounting guerrilla-type offensives against the Europeans
- *vodun* in providing a unifying force
- the genius of African leaders such as *L'Ouverture*, *Christophe* and **Dessalines**.

The existence of a Black Republic in 1804, where the slaves freed themselves and were now governing themselves, reverberated throughout the slave societies of the Caribbean.

ACTIVITY 4.9

There are African peoples who are opposed to the reparations movement. Suggest TWO arguments to justify their position.

The end of slavery did not mean the end of resistance. After emancipation Africans had to struggle to establish viable systems of production and political arrangements that would make 'freedom' into more than just a hand-to-mouth existence. All attempts by African people in the Caribbean to downplay the emphasis on European ideas and ideals and supplant them with more Afro-centric ones are examples of resistance in the modern era. The **reparations** movement (Box 4.9) is a bold move that continues this theme of resistance.

BOX 4.9 The reparations movement

The reparations movement is an example of the resistance to slavery that is going on even now. The word 'reparations' means that it is necessary to make amends, that some compensation is being asked for, for some damage or injury that has occurred. African groups and organizations today have set up committees in different countries to publicize their intention of seeking compensation for:

- the deaths of millions of Africans in the slave trade
- the forced labour expended by millions of slaves over hundreds of years
- the value of resources taken out of Africa during colonial rule (e.g. copper).

They seek compensation in monetary terms from the countries that profited from the slave trade, slavery and colonialism. However, they feel that some acknowledgement of guilt and an apology from European countries is equally important. This spirit of resistance and defiance today they see as necessary. They feel that African people need to be aware that some redress has been put in train for the racism that they have suffered at the hands of Europeans.

We see here a bold and innovative gesture through which we learn that history does not just 'happen' but apparently we can be held accountable in the here and now. This kind of thinking is a good example of 'tracing history in Caribbean society and culture' today. It has not yet met with a serious response from the developed countries but it is provocative and shows that slavery is still very much part of the issues being debated and analysed in contemporary life.

Indentured immigrants

The Indian labourers also experienced great hardship on the plantations and the Indian government actually stopped immigration several times because of reports of the cruelty being suffered by their nationals. Although a Protector of the Immigrants was appointed in each colony where there were indentured servants, most of them were biased in favour of planter interests. Because of their bonded state the labourers could not resort to collective bargaining to seek redress about their low wages and conditions of work. Inevitably then, protests and widespread unrest resulted in Guyana and Trinidad. This culminated in the serious outbreak on Leonora Estate in Guyana in 1869. In 1870 the British responded by setting up a commission of inquiry but this did not substantially address the problems of the labourers.

While some of the indentured servants resisted their condition by running away or refusing to work, most of them were able to establish some other small business on the side, usually market gardening, and invest its proceeds in land, small-scale trade enterprises, and shopkeeping concerns. Their efforts at **entrepreneurship** represent an extraordinary resilience amidst every kind of hardship and were a very productive form of resistance. They quickly became independent of the plantation, and if they chose to work there after their period of indenture, they usually had other economic interests as well. These strategies succeeded largely because of the **joint household** structure (households comprised two or three generations and extended family members) where everyone worked in the family business and it was the business rather than individual success that was important.

Summary

In the history of the Caribbean the themes of genocide and oppression are emphasized and so are resistance and survival. Genocide, slavery and indentureship are each by themselves horrific forms of oppression. For all three to have occurred in this region is an extraordinary circumstance. Yet the oppressed have forged lives, and even family life, under these conditions. Some **cultural erasure** might have occurred but the processes of acculturation, **interculturation** and **transculturation** have come together in the Caribbean to create some unique, culturally hybrid forms. Resistance occurs in many ways, as we have seen, and this dynamic, cultural fusion is a response that says culture is resilient and it will re-surface in different guises. One of the major elements, then, of Caribbean culture is its resistant response to domination or oppression.

ACTIVITY 4.10

1. List the ways that Caribbean people have resisted oppression and continue to do so today.

2. What role do you see for young Caribbean people today in resisting oppression?

4.4

MOVEMENTS TOWARDS INDEPENDENCE

From emancipation until the end of the nineteenth century Caribbean people were shaking off the mental, psychological and emotional trauma associated with enslaved and bonded labour. This process of 'realizing freedom', however, took place within a colonial society that at times seemed as oppressive as it had been in the era that had gone before. By the dawn of the twentieth century Caribbean people were increasingly coming to understand what 'freedom' meant and beginning to challenge the very basis of colonialism, particularly in the aftermath of two world wars. We may look at the entire period after emancipation until the first half of the twentieth century as a time when Caribbean people were preparing for self-determination, for finally throwing off European domination.

Economic enfranchisement

Economic **enfranchisement** is the condition whereby a country or nation achieves the right to determine how it will develop its systems of production. While under colonialism the economy was largely organized by the European power, Caribbean people also tried to resist and develop their own ways of making a living.

Plantation economies were based on large quantities of cheap, unskilled, manual labour, and monoculture – the production of one cash crop, namely sugar cane. Almost all the harvest was exported to Europe to be processed. Food production was haphazard and it was mainly left up to the ex-slaves and indentured labourers to grow fruit, vegetables and provisions for subsistence and sale in local Sunday markets. During the nineteenth century, as it became clear that the downturn in sugar prices would mean a decline in plantation economies, Caribbean small farmers or peasants turned more and more towards developing alternative cash crops for export. Cocoa, bananas, coffee, ginger, cotton, coconuts and arrowroot were grown by peasant farmers on their smallholdings. They also grew food crops and reared farm animals. In so doing they developed a diversified local economy – different types of cash crops, food crops and livestock. This strategy of economic diversification attempted to make small farmers self-sufficient and resilient in the face of economic hardship. It kept them independent of the planter and the low wages offered on the plantations. It introduced them to an outward focus by having to organize themselves for the export market and to develop some sophistication in making trading connections with the wider world.

They were largely on their own, however. They received little support and encouragement from the colonial authorities, who would have preferred a more subservient peasantry that was easy to control. The peasants were charged high rents for land and were frequently evicted. The planters sometimes refused to sell land to the peasants and blocked their efforts to seek credit facilities. The peasant proprietors also experienced sabotage. In the face of such **discriminatory** practices they resorted to different strategies. They banded together and bought whole plantations where impoverished planters could not afford to refuse the sale. Baptist ministers assisted them in buying land, especially in Jamaica, establishing free villages. Others, with few alternatives, squatted on crown lands, as in Trinidad and Guyana, for example.

It must be remembered that the peasantry's efforts to establish an economic basis for their independence from the planters was done under colonial rule. It could have been more successful and helped to develop a prosperous peasantry if the colonial authorities had not been deliberately obstructionist. They tended to side with planter interests. Efforts at economic diversification did assist the colony in establishing a more balanced economy and provided the peasants with a sense of independence, but it was ad hoc and could not raise the peasants far from poverty.

ACTIVITY 4.11

The entrepreneurial spirit amongst the Caribbean peasantry led to the development of savings societies and building and loan societies. Find out about these forms of economic organization from older persons, as their functions have been largely taken over by commercial banks today.

Fig. 4.10 Uriah Buzz Butler

Political enfranchisement

'Political enfranchisement' refers to the right of a people or nation to determine their own affairs. Under colonialism the Caribbean colony was under the control of the European power. However, once emancipation had been achieved it was only a matter of time before Caribbean people would develop the skills and expertise necessary to challenge the status quo.

Caribbean people in their thousands, in the years after emancipation, migrated to different regional destinations for work and better wages. The Panama Canal, the modern sugar plantations of Cuba, Puerto Rico and Santo Domingo, the oil refineries of Curaçao and Aruba, and the oilfields of Venezuela, helped to develop a consciousness of political and economic conditions in these countries and exposed workers to new and different ideas. Returning soldiers who had served Britain in the world wars in far-flung reaches of the empire were unwilling to resume a lowly status in the social hierarchy because they had been exposed to different ideas and political philosophies. Moreover, the ideas and speeches of Marcus Garvey of Jamaica pervaded the entire Caribbean. Black consciousness and nationalist sentiments began to seem enabling strategies of resistance.

In the 1930s economic conditions had deteriorated to such a level that the region was wracked by labour riots, strikes and wide-scale protests. Violence and mayhem followed. This period saw the rise of charismatic leaders in the labour movement who, riding on their mass popularity, made the successful transition to political leaders. ***Uriah Buzz Butler***, ***Adrian Cola Rienzi*** and ***Captain A. A. Cipriani*** of Trinidad and Tobago, ***Alexander Bustamante*** and ***Norman Washington Manley*** of Jamaica, ***Grantley Adams*** of Barbados (Figs 4.10–13) and ***Nathainel Crichlow*** of Guyana organized and developed the trade union

Fig. 4.11 Alexander
Bustamante

Fig. 4.12 Norman Manley

Fig. 4.13 Grantley Adams

BOX 4.10 Political development

The form of government that was widespread throughout the British Caribbean was called the *Old Representative System*. A 'governor' was appointed from England who transmitted the dictates of the Colonial Office to the colonies. He ruled with the help of a nominated council and an elected assembly. The latter proved troublesome to the governor on many occasions. However, for a long time their quarrels were largely between whites from England and creole whites (planters) about how best to run the colony.

During the nineteenth century Britain took more direct control of many of the colonies by eliminating the elected assembly. The governor and a legislative council, with official and nominated unofficial members, now ruled. This was called **crown colony** government and proved oppressive to a population of ex-slaves and ex-indentured labourers who were economically distressed and looking for ways to improve their condition.

Widespread unrest in the 1930s forced the colonial authorities to reinstate elected representation. It occurred gradually, but from 1944 onwards, Caribbean territories were granted **universal adult suffrage**. There were no restrictions put on the population (except that of age) in being eligible to vote and elect members to the **legislature**. Once this occurred it was only a matter of time before these territories sought *internal self government.* They remained colonies with Britain's interests being overseen by a governor general, but a chief minister and members of the legislature were now elected from the ranks of Caribbean people of all ethnicities. This could be viewed as a period of transition to full *independence*, as once it became possible to supplant white or European persons in positions of control, colonialism no longer made any sense (see also Box 1.2).

ACTIVITY 4.12

Suggest why *enfranchisement* is an important concept in discussing the economic and political developments of the Caribbean in the nineteenth and twentieth centuries.

movement in the Caribbean. While some Creole whites were involved in the early stages it quickly became a working-class movement dedicated towards better working conditions for the poor as well as improvements in health and education. This concern with social welfare made it inevitable that the trade unions would be the birthplace for Caribbean political parties.

It also became clear to many of the trade union leaders that the interests of labour had to be represented in the government so that laws could be passed to protect trade unions and their activities as well as the rights of workers. The traditional make-up of the legislative bodies comprised persons who were of the planter class and sympathetic to the needs of that group. The strategy was to get the trade union leaders elected to office so that they could form a lobby agitating for internal self-government and then full independence. Thus, once the trade union movement began, it was the whole colonial system in the Caribbean that was being challenged. Colonialism depended on social class divisions, with European governors, planters, supervisors and property owners exploiting labour and people of a different colour and race. Once Africans and Indians were elected to office, the writing was on the wall for the colonial system (Box 4.10).

Summary

Economic and political enfranchisement of Caribbean people in the nineteenth and twentieth centuries was won out of their continued resistance to the planter class and control of the colony from the mother country. The resilience of Caribbean people in developing vibrant and diversified peasant economies came out of a spirit of resistance. They could not change the economic structures, however, and Caribbean societies remained very much plantation economies dominated by whites trying to stifle any initiative that was not solely concerned with their own welfare. This lack of interest on the part of the whites led to economic distress, and in response to the rise of trade unionism and political parties. Behind all this was a growing awareness of black consciousness and nationalism, both deeply embedded in a spirit of resistance. Thus, the end of enslaved and bonded labour did not see a minimizing of resistance; it changed focus as it grappled with bringing down colonialism itself. Since independence it has occurred in myriad ways as history continues to impact society and culture today.

WRAP UP

Analysing the history of the Caribbean shows how ethnocentric ideas have pervaded the traditional account. *Resistance* is a central theme in Caribbean history and uncovering ethnocentrism is a form of resistance. Hybridization is also a process of resistance where the culture of the captors, the enslaved and the indentured come together today in unique forms. The struggle of Caribbean nations to achieve sustainable economies is a continuing act of resistance to overcome the underdeveloped state in which the European countries left their colonial possessions. Independence – political, economic and psychological – continues to be important to ideas of resistance. Tracing history in Caribbean culture and society shows the extent to which historical events and processes arise in contemporary social life in the Caribbean.

PRACTICE TESTS

Structured response

1 Explain what is meant by 'ethnocentric ideas' and give ONE example. (1 mark)
2 Identify the relationship of these terms to each other:
   (a) The Middle Passage
   (b) The Triangular Trade
   (c) The Atlantic Slave Trade. (3 marks)
3 Describe TWO aspects of a slave society. (4 marks)
4 List FOUR ways in which indigenous Caribbean peoples resisted the Europeans invaders. (4 marks)
5 Identify FOUR indigenous groups that lived in the Caribbean before the coming of Columbus. (4 marks)
6 Explain why the European interlopers in the Spanish Empire did not settle in Cuba, Hispaniola and Puerto Rico? (4 marks)
7 Define the following terms: (a) encomienda (b) diaspora (c) apprenticeship and (d) enfranchisement. (8 marks)
8 Summarize the main differences and similarities between slavery and indentureship. (6 marks)
9 Distinguish between slavery as practised in the New World (the Americas) and the Old World (Europe and Africa). (6 marks)
10 Explain why Indian indentured labourers went mainly to Guyana and Trinidad. (4 marks)

Essay questions (20 marks)

1 Outline the major migrations into the Caribbean region that greatly affected society and culture.
2 Explain why it was possible for so few Europeans to dominate plantation society in the era of slavery.
3 Describe the legacies of slavery on Caribbean society and culture today.
4 Describe the strategies used by African, Indian and Amerindian groups in resisting oppression.

Challenge essay questions (30 marks)

1 Justify attempts by Caribbean historians and scholars to re-write the history of the West Indies.
2 Examine the debate that says emancipation was largely due to the efforts of the enslaved in seeking freedom rather than to the humanitarian movement in England.
3 Discuss how economic life today is influenced by the plantation economy created by Europeans in the Caribbean.

4 Analyse selected aspects of resilience shown by Caribbean people in the transition from a slave to a free society.

RESEARCH TOPICS

Older persons, especially the very old, are good sources for the history of the immediate past. They will be able to recall events and ways of life that their grandparents spoke about so that you can have access, by speaking to them, to around a hundred years of history. This should make for a meaningful research study where the main source of information is oral history. You should focus on a specific topic or issue you want to investigate about the past in your country or district. Here are some examples to start you thinking about this:

- If there is a school that has at least a century-old history then you can research its background, its links with the metropolitan country, the kind of curriculum it used and the values that were thought important. These could all be compared with ethnocentric ideas about what was 'good' for the colonies, whether the school had elitist or democratic agendas, how many of its teachers were local and how that changed over the years, and was that in response to independence and other historical forces? Old school records as well as interviews with past students or even past principals would be helpful.
- If there are indigenous groups in your country, their members could give you insights as to their traditions and practices as well as those they know about through their ancestors that are no longer practised today. They will be able to tell you about how other more dominant groups in the society have interacted with them and what their position is now – one of resurgence, of marginalization?
- Persons in rural areas who perhaps worked on large sugar estates or banana plantations in the past, or who had parents and grandparents who did, can give you information on how the economic landscape has changed in a specific local area, how it was organized then, who were the bosses and who were the workers, what the relationships between them were like, and if any significant events occurred to change the mode of production and/or these relationships. Their information can be cross-checked by you and related to the general historical trends that you know about in the Caribbean.

REFERENCES

Brereton, B. (2002). Histories and myths: the case of Trinidad and Tobago. Speech given at the Rudranath Capildeo Learning Resource Centre, Couva, Trinidad, 8 May 2002.

Chanlatte Baik, L. (2003). Agricultural societies in the Caribbean: the Greater Antilles and the Bahamas. In J. Sued-Badillo (Ed.), *General history of the Caribbean, Volume 1: Autochthonous societies*, pp. 228–258. Paris: UNESCO and London: Macmillan Caribbean.

Emmer, P. (1999). The creation of a new Caribbean society, 1492–1650, Part 2: The creation of a second expansion system. In P. Emmer (Ed.), *General history of the Caribbean, Volume 2: New societies – the Caribbean in the long sixteenth century*, pp. 1–28. Paris: UNESCO and London: Macmillan Caribbean.

Engerman, S., & Higman, B. (1997). The demographic structure of the Caribbean slave societies in the 18th and 19th centuries. In F. Knight (Ed.), *General history of the Caribbean, Volume 3: The slave societies of the Caribbean*, pp. 45–104. Paris: UNESCO and London: Macmillan Caribbean.

Iglesias Garcia, F. (2004). Demographic and social structural changes in the contemporary Caribbean. In B. Brereton (Ed.), *General history of the Caribbean, Volume 5: The Caribbean in the twentieth century*, pp. 401–433. Paris: UNESCO and London: Macmillan Caribbean.

Kearns, R. (2003). Indigenous Puerto Rico: DNA evidence upsets established history. *Indian Country Today*, posted 6 October 2003. Retrieved from http://www.indiancountry.com/content.cfm?id=1065462184 on 25 January 2006.

Palmer, C. (1997). The slave trade, African traders and the demography of the Caribbean to 1750. In F. Knight (Ed.), *General history of the Caribbean, Volume 3: The slave societies of the Caribbean*, pp. 9–44. Paris: UNESCO and London: Macmillan Caribbean.

5 DEVELOPING GEOGRAPHIC AWARENESS

Geography is the study of the interaction between people and their environment – whether it is the natural physical or the built environment. A sense of place is stressed in geography – the spatial location and relationships between people and places. We need to develop our geographic awareness because the nature of these relationships and interactions are sometimes not fully grasped. On the whole, our attitude to the environment is a good indicator of our level of geographic awareness. In this chapter, we will examine some of the understandings about nature that we have inherited and the part they play in creating environmental problems such as soil erosion, drought and the destruction of coral reefs. Where, in turn, the environment wreaks destruction on human life and habitation, it is important to realize that instead of feeling vulnerable and resigned there is much that we can do to mitigate disasters.

EXPECTED LEARNING OBJECTIVES

On completing this chapter, you will be able to

1 evaluate various perspectives on the relationship between Caribbean peoples and their environment
2 show how human activity determines whether an environmental hazard becomes an environmental disaster
3 discuss soil erosion, drought and the destruction of coral reefs as examples of environmental degradation
4 describe the nature, occurrence, and the social and economic consequences of hurricanes, earthquakes and volcanic eruptions
5 explain the theory of plate tectonics with reference to the Caribbean
6 suggest mitigation strategies to control and/or reduce the adverse effects of environmental disasters on Caribbean society and culture.

5.1 GEOGRAPHICAL PERSPECTIVES: THE ENVIRONMENT, SOCIETY AND CULTURE

A study of geography opens up the debate about whether the environment determines how a society and its culture develops, whether it is the society and culture which impacts the environment, or whether the two – people and the environment – are bound together in a dynamic relationship which 'produces' or 'creates' the environment. Each view has implications for how space or place, and thus society and culture, are portrayed. Traditional geography teaching, especially physical geography, tends to emphasize the dominant role that landscape plays in influencing society and culture. The settlement patterns in the Lesser Antilles, for example, show relatively dense settlement on the drier west coasts, where the main towns are also found, because the north-east trades bring heavy relief rainfall to the east coasts, which are also the first places where hurricanes make landfall. Fig. 5.1

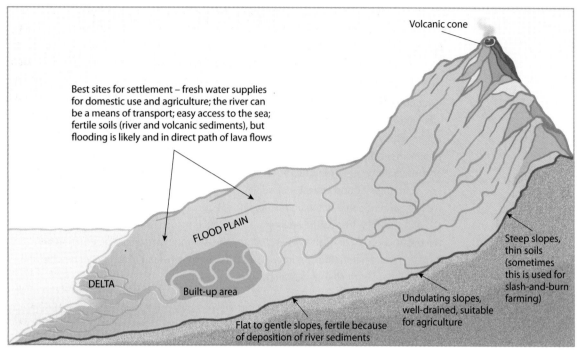

Fig. 5.1 Environmental determinants of settlement

shows how the landscape influences decisions people make about where to settle. Human and cultural geography, on the other hand, stress an opposite view, showing that human beings impact and shape the landscape through technology and scientific breakthroughs, whereby people have been able to adapt different environments for human habitation and sustenance.

Recently, a **postmodern** perspective has developed which goes beyond this simple polarity of people and environment as determinants of the landscape. Postmodernism is a way of thinking that asks us to deconstruct traditional explanations and look for more authentic descriptions of what really happens. This view suggests that the term 'people' is not a single, neutral category. There are *power relations* in all societies and cultures that will inevitably affect how each group lays claim to the environment. **Aboriginal** peoples often create a geography that is very different from, say, that of urbanized Caribbean residents, but the latter tend to be more powerful than other groups in Caribbean society and culture. They comprise, among others, the highly educated, the wealthy and the political **elite**, and hence their view and influence become dominant in shaping the environment. So, in the Caribbean today we have ever-growing cities and suburban areas, depopulation of the countryside, industrial estates, hotels and marinas – an organization of space and place stemming from the interests of powerful groups in urban society.

The postmodern outlook also emphasizes that the traditional category of 'environment' is also not a single, fixed entity in a primordial state of being 'untouched'. What is regarded as 'the environment' is constantly changing, based on historical interactions between human beings and the space where they live. Thus, the environment right now, for you, may be a townscape, a built environment. This environment (although built by people in the past) constrains the present inhabitants and the possibilities for development. The colonial tendency to build ports as capital cities in the Caribbean islands, to facilitate exports to the **metropole**, has for a long time been constraining national development because the capital has become a *primate city* – an over-large urban area with a disproportionate level of goods and services. The capital city houses the headquarters of all the economic, commercial, financial, political, social and cultural organizations, and people from far-flung areas either journey into the city for work or to go to school or must come to town to transact business. The rest of the country remains poorly served with these goods and services. Similarly, how our forebears organized the agricultural environment into large plantations constrains us today as we seek to find more viable livelihoods. For example, the profits to be had from traditional plantation crops such as sugar cane and cocoa have dwindled but poor small farmers cannot buy estates or plantations as they go out of production.

The environment, then, is an arena of contestation – between social groups having different amounts of power. It is therefore a *social* space that has already been moulded by certain groups for their own purposes. A postmodern outlook is therefore useful in examining the power relations in society and culture to explain how the environment as a social space is perceived.

Perspectives on the Caribbean environment

The colonial experience has left us with perspectives on the land in which human beings dominate and control the environment. This contrasts directly with the perspectives held by the pre-Columbian inhabitants and their descendants today. In certain areas of the world – for example, lands inhabited by Native American Indians, Amerindians and Australian Aborigines – there are places considered to be sacred and devoted to worship and left virtually untouched. They are associated with stories, myths and legends.

A different world view altogether came with the Europeans. As conquerors they did not regard the land in the same way as the native peoples did. The advances that the Europeans had made in science and technology enabled them to work wonders in controlling nature to provide more food, better medicines and production tools that made manufacturing more efficient. The idea of the environment as something to be controlled and dominated came with the Europeans and became entrenched through colonial rule. The early forms of **capitalist** enterprise – the plantations, the mines and the ranches – organized Caribbean space for economic gain. Land was conceived as merely a backdrop for the activities of powerful social groups. It was the source of raw materials.

Perspectives on the environment are directly related to how aware people are of the importance of the Earth to their very existence. This awareness may be at a spiritual and religious level. It can also be at the level of geographical awareness – through an examination of the relationships between human beings and the environment that can lead to sustainable practices benefiting both the environment and human life and livelihood.

ACTIVITY 5.1

Identify at least two websites dedicated to building awareness of indigenous peoples in the Caribbean. Describe how their relationship to the natural environment is portrayed.

ACTIVITY 5.2

1. How did the religion of the aboriginal inhabitants influence their perspectives on the environment?

2. Would you also say that religion was a factor in the perspectives that Europeans held for the environment? Explain your answer.

Summary

The impact of human beings on the environment is to a large extent related to their world views about the land, about the significance of mankind and progress, and their spiritual beliefs. Thus, aboriginal peoples, the European invaders, and today's affluent urban dwellers in the Caribbean all have or have had varying perspectives on how land should be utilized. The societies and cultures developed by different peoples in the Caribbean over time put in train beliefs about land use that supported their world views. Thus the original inhabitants had a strong nurturing relationship with the land (a relationship their descendants still have today), the Europeans a strong exploitative relationship that favoured the primacy of human beings over nature, and today affluent Caribbean folks tend to regard land as merely a social space for capitalist enterprise. This then shows that how landscape is shaped is as much a cultural and social creation as an environmentally determined creation. Developing our geographical awareness therefore entails understanding the relationships, historical and otherwise, between the environment, society and culture.

5.2 ENVIRONMENTAL HAZARDS

Hurricanes, soil erosion, volcanic eruptions, earthquakes and droughts are only termed **environmental hazards** when they have the potential to destroy human life and property. If they occur in places far away from human habitation they are termed 'natural events'. Only when people and property are harmed do we refer to them as **environmental disasters.** Thus, people and their activities are central to whether a *hazard* becomes a *disaster*. We will study some of these environmental hazards to understand better how, through social and cultural practices, Caribbean people actually create risky environments and thereby intensify the nature of environmental disasters. Perspectives on the land become important, because if our relationship to the land is one of protection, then we would be less likely to put it and ourselves at risk.

Environmental degradation

Environmental degradation is a general way of describing the loss of some degree of quality in the air, land or waters around us. It describes soil that has lost its fertility, hillsides that are severely gullied, air that is full of emissions from factories, rivers that have a reduced flow because the water is channelled away for human use, and a reduction in the numbers of species of flora and fauna in an area. **Pollution** is a more specific term referring to the ways in which human beings have caused the contamination of the environment through adding pollutants that harm human, animal and plant life. *Pollutants* are substances such as poisonous gases or emissions and effluents released into the air, land and waters around us by vehicle exhausts, factory fumes, and industrial, agricultural and household waste, including sewage (Fig. 5.2).

Pollution and other processes of environmental degradation that are caused by human activity tend to disrupt the balance and harmony found in ecosystems. An **ecosystem** refers to the dynamic and complex interactions between plants, animals

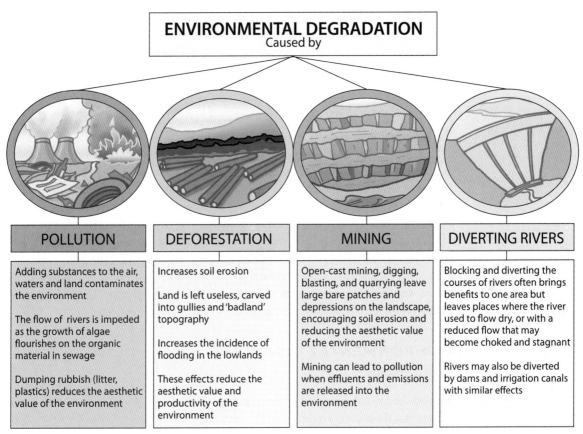

Fig. 5.2 Environmental degradation

and micro-organisms and their non-living environment at a particular location. It is well known, for example, that the increasing population pressure on land in the Caribbean has influenced urban populations to fill in shallow parts of the coasts for much-needed residential areas. In so doing they have disrupted the delicate ecological balance of coastal wetlands (mangroves, marshes and swamps), destroying the habitats of the flora and fauna of the area and often endangering certain species in the process. Attempts to remedy or reverse the effects of pollution and other forms of environmental degradation and restore the environment as close as possible to its natural state are referred to as **conservation**.

Natural processes of environmental change

The environment has always experienced change, even destruction, caused by *natural* events. These changes, though, are part of the natural cycles of the Earth. For example, according to the theory of **plate tectonics** continents have been moving for millions of years, causing volcanic activity and earthquakes. Also, over millennia separate Ice Ages came and went, with ice covering a large percentage of the Earth. The melting of the ice raised sea levels, drowning many lowland areas. Soils which take hundreds of years to develop are always being washed away by heavy storms, especially soils on steep slopes. Hurricanes continue to wreak havoc on the landscape. But the likelihood is that the natural environment will recover from these events. However, human habitation often aggravates these natural processes of environmental change.

Summary

Natural events and processes such as erosion, flooding, hurricanes, volcanic eruptions and earthquakes are termed environmental hazards and they are a normal occurrence. The environment usually recovers over a period of time if left undisturbed. When they threaten human life and property, however, they are termed natural disasters. It is more and more the case that human activity turns what may have just been a hazard into a disaster. Environmental degradation exacerbated by human activity leads to soil erosion, flooding and the disruption of ecosystems, contributing to many forms of pollution. Dense settlement on fragile coastal ecosystems puts wetlands and coral reefs at risk as well as human lives and property. We continue to see that our perspectives about land and about how we use it – whether we have a conservationist stance towards it or not – goes a long way in explaining how an environmental hazard is converted into an environmental disaster.

5.3 ENVIRONMENTAL DISASTERS

Soil erosion

Soils are formed by the breakdown of rocks over hundreds of years. The rocks break down into their constituent minerals forming the *inorganic* (the physical medium) basis of a soil. This material combines with vegetation such as roots and leaves, as well as with water and air to form the biochemical entity known as 'soil'. Earthworms and other soil organisms bore passages through the soil, allowing air to circulate, and grind up the soil into finer particles. It is quite complex and fragile and much more than just the sum of its parts. For example, *humus* – a substance formed by the decomposition of animal and vegetable matter through the action of bacteria – is a vital component of any soil because it helps to maintain good soil structure and has the capacity to retain and exchange nutrients. It thus plays a major part in all the soil processes (especially chemical reactions) that maintain the fertility of a soil.

The removal of soil by wind, water or moving ice is known as **soil erosion**. It is a natural process but human activity has made it easier for larger amounts of soil to be removed in a shorter period of time, known as 'accelerated soil erosion'. Once removed, soil is hardly likely to be recovered and reused. Nevertheless, it is not as dramatic or sudden as other environmental hazards (such as hurricanes or earthquakes) and the loss of soil may go undetected for long periods of time. Soil erosion is described as a 'creeping' hazard and an example of environmental degradation that may lead eventually to an environmental disaster (as in Haiti, Box 5.1).

Social and cultural practices that accelerate soil erosion

Deforestation

The roots of plants and trees hold the soil together. The leaves and branches intercept rainfall, slowing down the impact of raindrops on the soil below, thus reducing the chances of loosening and displacing soil particles. When the vegetation is removed, the soil is left bare and can be blown or washed away. Deforestation occurs as a result of various activities.

- **Slash and burn** is a widespread practice to remove undergrowth. Burning helps to increase fertility because the ash is rich in minerals, but leaving the land bare for even short periods encourages soil erosion.

BOX 5.1 A case study: soil erosion in Haiti

The island of Hispaniola is one of the most mountainous in the Caribbean. The central mountains contain the highest peak in the region, Pico Duarte, in the Dominican Republic (Fig. 5.3). The physical landscape consists mainly of mountains, plateaux and hilly terrain, with the minimum of flat land. In fact, it is estimated that only 20 per cent of the country is considered *arable* – a major area being the Artibonite Valley – but 50 per cent is under cultivation.

Soil erosion is so severe in Haiti that it is an ecological disaster. A small elite own the most productive lands and the masses of the poor are *subsistence farmers* who cultivate steeply sloping lands of only marginal fertility to provide for their families. Although Haiti took the dramatic step in 1791 of overthrowing the French as colonial rulers, the local dictators and heads of state since then have done little to redress a situation where the poor continue to eke out a miserable existence.

The soil erosion problem that results from farming on steep slopes is compounded by the fact that firewood (from trees) is the major source of fuel in Haiti – in both rural and urban areas. Vast areas of the country have been deforested to supply its energy needs. Gullies and bare rock surfaces are evidence of the environmental degradation that resulted.

It is well known that Haiti is 'the poorest country in the western hemisphere'. Inevitably this poverty, of both urban and rural dwellers, has a severe impact on the environment. When daily survival is of paramount importance, the controls and careful husbandry that are necessary to protect the environment go by the wayside. There have been many attempts by international agencies to implement soil conservation schemes but they have failed largely because they relied on the government to force farmers to adopt the techniques with few apparent rewards. Today there is a concerted effort to expand *agroforesty* as a conservation technique, using grassroots meetings and community groups that also discuss issues dealing with poverty, health and women's rights. Thus, soil erosion is now on the agenda as a socio-political issue.

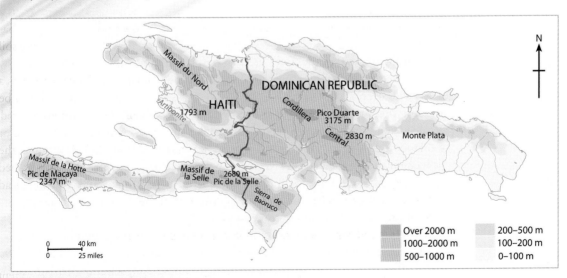

Fig. 5.3 Hispaniola: physical features

- *Overgrazing* is likely to occur when the number of animals on a piece of land exceeds its 'carrying capacity'; the likelihood is that the animals will remove all the vegetation, leaving the soil bare. The carrying capacity of a plot of land refers to a minimum number of animals that can graze without leaving the land bare.
- *Bulldozing hillsides and clearing lands* for housing developments, roads, quarries and mines, and for urban development projects – malls, shopping plazas, commercial complexes and industrial parks – leaves land unprotected while construction is in progress.
- *The making of charcoal* is a common practice where fuel is expensive; people have long relied on trees and woody shrubs for firewood as a household and industrial fuel. This is the case over large expanses of Haiti (Box 5.1), where the wood is burnt to convert it to charcoal, which burns cleanly.

Farming practices

- Shifting **cultivation** is a traditional practice of small farmers all over the Caribbean. Plots are cleared and cultivated for a few years and then left in *fallow* (under grass to recover fertility) while another plot is cleared for use. Now that populations have grown, the land is in continuous use so that there is little time for recovery and the soil fertility deteriorates.
- *Ploughing* up and down a hillside helps to form natural grooves which channel water (carrying soil) from the top of the hill downwards.
- *Planting* in neat, straight rows leaves exposed soil in between the rows as well as an uninterrupted path for the wind to blow the soil away.

The effects of deforestation and farming practices are intensified by climatic conditions. *Convectional rainfall*, occurring just after the noonday heat in the Caribbean, is usually a short episode of torrential rain. The raindrops in a thunderstorm are large (compared to drizzle) and they hit the soil with great impact. This is called 'raindrop splash' and increases the chances of soils being eroded from deforested areas.

Effects of soil erosion

The effects of soil erosion are widespread:

- With the removal of the nutrient-rich topsoil, the immature soils below cannot sustain crop production at similar levels. The productivity of land thus decreases as yields decrease.
- Some land may go out of use entirely and become covered in secondary vegetation (scrub, bush) or carved into gullies and deep ravines.
- Flooding in lowland areas occurs when soil is removed from the hillsides and accumulates on the beds of rivers, thus building up the beds and reducing the capacity of rivers. In times of heavy rainfall, the rivers cannot hold as much water as before and flooding results. This may occur over wide areas that may be far from the original sites of soil erosion (Fig. 5.4).
- There tends to be a close relationship between environmental degradation and hazards. For example, during hurricanes, or even an earthquake, eroded hillsides are more prone to landslides and mudslides, causing destruction to human lives and property (an environmental disaster).

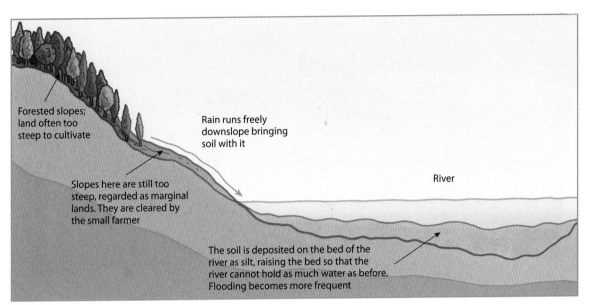

Forested slopes;
land often too
steep to cultivate

Rain runs freely
downslope bringing
soil with it

River

Slopes here are still too
steep, regarded as marginal
lands. They are cleared by
the small farmer

The soil is deposited on the bed of the
river as silt, raising the bed so that the
river cannot hold as much water as before.
Flooding becomes more frequent

Fig. 5.4 Soil erosion and flooding

Soil conservation

Conservation is designed to prevent environmental degradation or restore lands that have been degraded. The following measures are useful to address the specific problem of soil erosion.

- *Afforestation*. Deep-rooted trees and other types of vegetation are planted in areas where the vegetation was removed and topsoil is brought in from outside. Fast-growing trees are desirable rather than the original cover, which might take too long to reach maturity. The aim is to produce a dense network of roots to bind the soil together and produce a substantial amount of organic material to help in the production of more soil. The effectiveness of the plant cover in reducing soil erosion depends on its type, extent and quantity. Forests and grasses which completely cover the soil, and which intercept all falling raindrops at and close to the surface, are efficient in controlling soil loss.

- *Landscaping*. Sometimes an eroded hillside is carved into deep gullies and ravines so that the whole area has to be bulldozed and sculpted into an undulating landscape before afforestation.

- *Agricultural practices*
  - *Contour ploughing*. Tilling land around the hillslopes along the height contours breaks up the natural channels and grooves in the soil which may channel water directly downslope (Fig. 5.5).
  - *Planting shelter belts*. To break the force of the wind, lines of trees are planted at intervals along flat expanses of land where the speed of the wind may otherwise take up loose soil particles.
  - *Intercropping/strip cropping*. Clean, neat rows between crops are avoided when different crops are cultivated together, at different angles to each other.
  - *Agroforestry*. Crops such as cocoa, coffee, fruit trees and bananas can be grown in the forest, co-existing with the trees and other vegetation.

Fig. 5.5 Contour ploughing in Costa Rica   **Fig. 5.6** Terracing in Haiti

ACTIVITY 5.3

1. Identify the causes of soil erosion for any ONE area in your country.

2. What conservation measures, if any, are being employed?

- *Crop rotation.* Each crop depletes the soil of certain minerals so if different crops are planted in succession, rather than the same crop continuously, the depleted nutrients will regenerate naturally.
- *Terraces.* Building small walls, ridges and channels around sloping land helps to prevent rainfall from running freely downslope and reduces the chances of soil being removed (Fig. 5.6).
- *Stubble mulching.* Leaving stubble or residues after harvesting on the field as long as possible helps to reduce evaporation and keeps the soil covered.

Soil erosion and poverty

While soil erosion is a natural phenomenon, *accelerated soil erosion* on the scale that is being experienced in Caribbean countries today is a social and cultural phenomenon. Box 5.1 describes the horrific state of soil erosion in Haiti and also the relationship of soil erosion to poverty. Countries that are very poor (and poorer groups in a seemingly affluent country) are driven by the need to survive and fulfil their basic needs. Preserving the environment is a long-term goal to which they cannot commit because they are more concerned with short-term survival. Deforestation, especially to gather fuel, and farming lands of only marginal fertility, put the environment at risk, but such practices also represent a means of making a livelihood to people with few options.

The reduction in yields that these people experience, and the resultant flooding that farmers on the lowlands experience, are too often ignored as issues of national importance. They are seen as the plight of poor people. Thus, soil erosion is an environmental problem that is exacerbated by poverty, but because the poor do not have much power in the society, soil conservation does not have a high profile. Affluent groups, too, contribute to soil erosion as owners and investors in large-scale construction projects, timber industries and tourist development sites which require the removal of vegetation over large areas. Although these people are the powerful groups in the society, soil erosion is still not seen as an issue because these ventures are not based on farming.

ACTIVITY 5.4

1. Suggest how the alleviation of poverty can lead to conservation of the environment.

2. How can wealthy and elite groups also be involved in conservation efforts?

Suggestions that are sometimes offered to combat soil erosion go far beyond the conservation measures listed above. They see the basic problem as how the society and culture is organized. Population control, productive employment, meeting basic needs for health care, housing, and food, as well as a better income distribution, may well be the fundamental solutions to the problem of soil erosion and environmental degradation.

Drought

A drought is a temporary feature of the climate. It is an unusually long period when rainfall is below the 'normal' levels for that region, causing the severe depletion of the water available to plants, animals and human beings. It is difficult to define drought more precisely because it depends on the climate of a particular place. A month of low rainfall in *equatorial* latitudes will be considered a drought because the high temperatures maintain high rates of evaporation and transpiration, thus reducing the supply of water. In a *semi-arid* climate, or one with a pronounced 'dry' season, as in the Caribbean, a month without rainfall would, however, constitute a normal pattern of rainfall. *Arid climates* (those that are normally dry, like deserts) would also not be said to be experiencing a drought.

Drought as a natural phenomenon

The **tropical marine climate** experienced in the Caribbean has definite wet and dry seasons. Fig. 5.7 for Belize City gives a general picture of the annual distribution of rainfall where average rainfall is 2000 mm (80 inches) a year. Some areas may be drier than normal in the dry season because of local conditions of *size, relief* and *location*. Also, naturally occurring dry spells brought on by global changes in weather patterns exacerbate the dry season (see below).

Size, relief and location

- Anguilla, located at 18°N latitude, receives only 800 mm (35 inches) of rainfall annually, much of that in October to December. The island is small (about 91 square km or 35 square miles) and because of its size does not generate much *convectional* rainfall, though hurricanes and tropical storms periodically bring

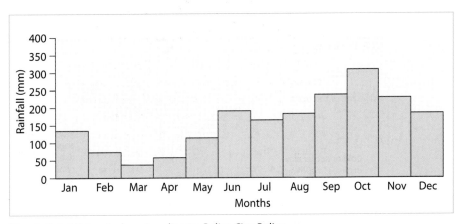

Fig. 5.7 Rainfall, tropical marine climate: Belize City, Belize

heavy rainfall. The landscape is also flat and low lying so that rain generated from *relief* or *orographic* effects is negligible. Some of the rainfall is *cyclonic* in origin, especially in the winter months (Box 5.2). Anguilla, then, is at risk of drought because it is highly dependent on passing weather systems from North America to bring rainfall.

BOX 5.2 Types of rainfall

When air is forced to rise, the water vapour in it cools, condenses and changes to droplets of water. Clouds are masses of water droplets. When the clouds become saturated and no more water droplets can be held, rain occurs. The trigger action for rain to fall then is for the air to rise. The different types of rainfall – convectional, relief and cyclonic – occur because air is forced to rise for different reasons.

Cold air usually comes into the Caribbean in the winter months of the northern hemisphere. Cold air flows out of North America bringing cooler temperatures and cyclonic rain (sometimes called *frontal rain*) to the Greater Antilles, the Bahamas, Anguilla and the northern Leewards. The zone of interaction between the cold and warm air is called a *cold front* or *norther*.

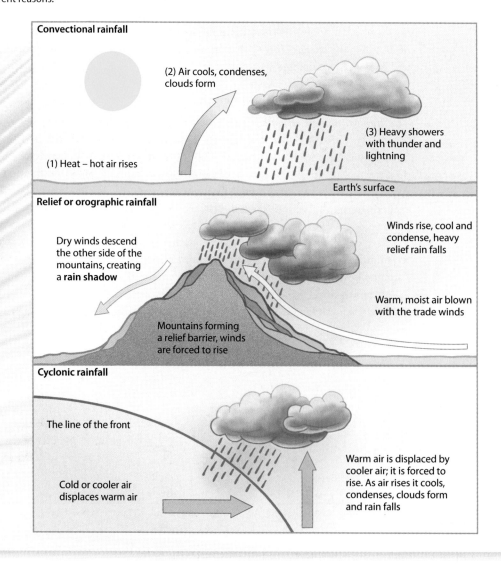

Convectional rainfall

(2) Air cools, condenses, clouds form

(3) Heavy showers with thunder and lightning

(1) Heat – hot air rises

Earth's surface

Relief or orographic rainfall

Dry winds descend the other side of the mountains, creating a **rain shadow**

Winds rise, cool and condense, heavy relief rain falls

Warm, moist air blown with the trade winds

Mountains forming a relief barrier, winds are forced to rise

Cyclonic rainfall

The line of the front

Cold or cooler air displaces warm air

Warm air is displaced by cooler air; it is forced to rise. As air rises it cools, condenses, clouds form and rain falls

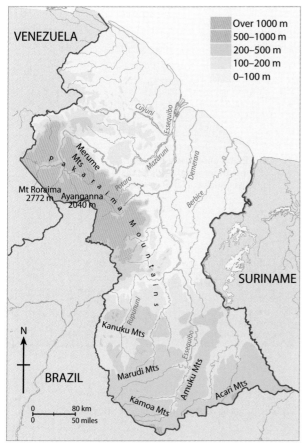

Fig. 5.8 Guyana: physical landscape

- A country such as Guyana, on the other hand, located in the equatorial latitudes (stretching from 1°N to 6°N), represents a marked contrast (Fig. 5.8). Rain falls throughout the year, with a definite rainy season from May to July. Coastal areas have a second rainy season from November through to January. The average annual rainfall is 2525 mm (about 100 inches). However, because the country is so large there are regional variations. The Rupununi savannas in the interior, far from the rain-bearing effects of the trade winds, are much drier, and in recent years have suffered from drought. So although Guyana is in the hot and wet equatorial latitudes, it is also at risk of drought in certain areas.

- In the Greater and Lesser Antilles rainfall distribution is determined by size, relief and the orientation of mountains to the prevailing north-east trades. The average rainfall is about 1140 mm (45 inches). But where the winds are forced to rise over mountains, there is extremely heavy relief rainfall. For example, Port Antonio on the north-east coast of Jamaica receives 3082 mm (150 inches) of rain per annum as the moisture-bearing north-east trades are forced to rise over the Blue Mountains. The mountains themselves record as much as 5000 mm (nearly 200 inches) of rainfall a year, while in the lee of the mountains, Kingston receives only 813 mm (32 inches) (Fig. 5.9). In the Greater and Lesser Antilles coastal plains in

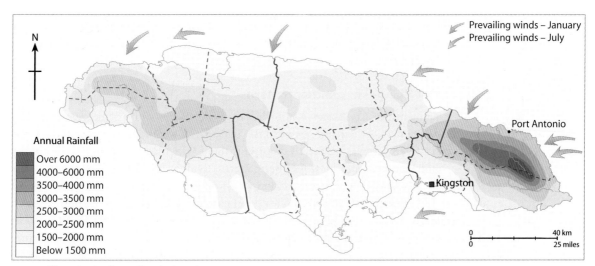

Fig. 5.9 The rain shadow effect in Jamaica

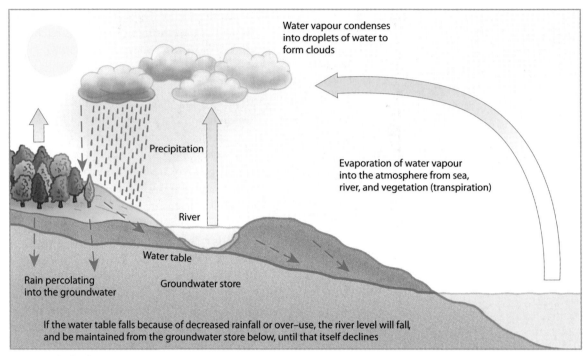

Fig. 5.10 The hydrological cycle.

the south, usually where plantation agriculture takes place, experience a similar *rain shadow* effect.

The dry season, and the even drier conditions brought on by size, relief and location, make Caribbean countries susceptible to drought. Fortunately, the physical environment conserves and stores water that can be available for use in the dry season. This is referred to as the *groundwater store* (Fig. 5.10). Groundwater seeps into and maintains rivers at a certain 'base level' (lower than the levels at the height of a rainy season) and can be tapped by wells. Drought is really pronounced when this store is affected. Like soil erosion, drought is a 'creeping hazard'; its onset may not be detected when rainfall supplies decrease because the groundwater store acts as a 'back-up' for a while.

Global changes in weather patterns

Drought in the Caribbean is also linked to global shifts in weather patterns. The **El Niño** effect is the name given to the periodic upwelling of warm waters off the coast of Peru, displacing the cold currents there, which adversely affects the fishing economy and disrupts local weather patterns. Evidence for El Niño is found in the historical records left by Spanish colonists, as well as in geological evidence. In the past the El Niño effect has been implicated in extreme weather events worldwide, such as floods, hurricanes and droughts. However, researchers say that the El Niño effect is only a local part of a more global shift in the pattern of sea surface temperatures and atmospheric pressure that occurs over the breadth of the Indian and Pacific Oceans. This increase in sea surface temperatures and the fluctuations in atmospheric

BOX 5.3 ENSO effects in Guyana

The worldwide ENSO events of 1997–8 resulted in a prolonged and intense drought in Guyana, not only in the interior Rupununi savannas but throughout the whole country. The rainy season of November 1997 to January 1998 did not arrive. Rivers were greatly reduced in volume, groundwater stores were depleted, and in the remote areas springs and wells dried up. The effects on the country included:

- a shortage of drinking water, causing many families to use unsafe or untreated supplies, thus risking waterborne diseases
- a substantial fall in the acreage under rice and sugar. Rice needs a plentiful supply of water for sowing. These are the major export crops, indicating a significant loss in earnings
- saltwater intrusions on some rivers, making the water unfit for irrigation purposes
- soil erosion, especially in the savannas of the interior.

Mitigation measures

Emergency measures were put in place to bring *short-term relief* to the population and to agriculture, especially:

- water conservation strategies – rationing of water, delivery of water to stricken areas, extension services
- increasing the supply – use of pumps to supply water to reservoirs and irrigation channels and the drilling of wells
- relief assistance to families.

A longer-term plan was an assessment of the needs of the country in addressing a drought of this nature. It was decided that in Amerindian settlements hand pumps were needed and in the Georgetown area submersible pumps, as well as the drilling of additional wells, would ensure a more reliable supply. In addition, farmers who had lost their crops would be supplied with seeds for the next season. The assessment showed that greater attention had to be paid to land use such as deforestation and human activities that lead to soil erosion and land degradation. These activities prevent the groundwater store from being replenished. Thus, any drought mitigation strategy must take into consideration human impacts on the environment.

pressure over the oceans occur every two to seven years. This combined air and sea anomaly is called the **Southern Oscillation**. El Niño and the Southern Oscillation (**ENSO**) together are responsible for the prolonged droughts experienced in the Caribbean, Central America, Venezuela and Brazil, as well as in Africa, Australia and India, in certain years. The ENSO events of 1982–3 and 1997–8 were particularly severe. In 1998 Guyana experienced a seven-month drought linked to ENSO (Box 5.3). ENSO events are also believed to be responsible for unusually active hurricane seasons. The ENSO phenomenon is being extensively studied, especially because of its negative impacts on the natural and human environment (Box 5.4).

BOX 5.4 Predicting ENSO

Scientists have been collecting empirical data for some years now on atmospheric pressures over the oceans and sea surface temperatures and studying how the two are connected. On a daily basis, moored buoys in the equatorial Pacific Ocean measure sea surface temperature, ocean currents and air pressure. This is the first place where an ENSO event begins so that this region is now rigorously monitored and all stages of an ENSO event can be studied. Scientists can tell us a year in advance whether the next year will have an unusually active hurricane season or drier than normal conditions.

In the Caribbean ENSO forecasts can help countries to anticipate and plan for periods of drought and floods, and prove useful in agricultural planning. However, national systems of disaster preparedness such as early warning systems for droughts and floods should be put in place. The bodies running these will be able to use the ENSO forecasts to devise timely strategies to assist in mitigating the impacts of such disasters. Drought is a creeping disaster, so forewarning may greatly assist countries in reducing its impact.

Not all ENSO events are severe, but Caribbean people need to be aware that the drier part of the year can be prolonged and intensified through natural causes. When we add the knowledge that through size, relief and location some parts of Caribbean countries are already very dry, we realize that drought is an ever-present hazard.

Drought and human activity

The depletion of the supply of fresh water in rivers, which contributes to drought-like conditions, is caused by many human activities. For example, deforestation practices contribute to the silting of rivers and drying up of water courses (see Fig. 5.4). Polluting rivers with sewage encourages algae to flourish and this chokes streams, which eventually become stagnant. The groundwater store also becomes depleted through human activities. For example, channelling and paving stretches of rivers interferes with the *infiltration* of rainwater to replenish the underground water supply. Deforestation, too, often leads to soil erosion, leaving the ground hard and impermeable and preventing infiltration of rain for underground water storage. The water supply held in lakes, dams, wells and reservoirs tends to be severely depleted in the dry season as it is used for irrigating crops, and for urban demands such as drinking, other domestic uses, watering gardens, washing cars and industrial uses. The growth of population and improvements in living standards also put a strain on the water supply. Caribbean populations, particularly urban populations, are growing, and therefore the demand for water is also growing. At the same time, the supply from rainfall in the dry season is inadequate and that from groundwater stores is being greatly reduced.

Effects of drought

Water shortages and a lower than normal water supply have both short-term and long-term effects on agriculture, human beings and the environment. For example:

- as soil moisture decreases, vegetation wilts and eventually dies
- low soil moisture prevents or delays germination of crops, leading to low yields
- when vegetation dies the bare ground encourages soil erosion
- the reduced groundwater store takes a long time to be replenished (sometimes years); some rivers may dry up permanently
- competition for water tends to lead to conflict, with rationing of water for different socio-economic groups and conflicts over who decides how water should be apportioned between irrigation, recreation and urban supply.

Caribbean people have adapted their social and cultural practices to the dry and wet seasons of the tropical marine climate. Reaping, building, fixing roofs, kite flying and cricket tend to be left for the dry season. Planting of the major cash and food crops is done in the rainy season, which is also the football season. Social and cultural life, then, has adapted to the climatic regime. However, there is a need now to raise the consciousness of Caribbean people that increasingly the dry season may be more severe than it has been in the past and that the rainy season may not necessarily restore groundwater supplies. Social and cultural life, then, should reflect an increasing geographic awareness about something as fundamental and taken for granted as the climate.

Destruction of coral reefs

Until recently the major hazards coral reefs faced were hurricanes, earthquakes and volcanic eruptions, or in the longer term an Ice Age. Since the 1950s population growth has occurred on such an unprecedented scale, mainly in the tropical and subtropical latitudes (where coral reefs are located), that there has been massive reef destruction in certain areas. Human beings pose a major threat to coral reefs, killing the reefs and causing environmental degradation. This is paradoxical, because coral reefs provide conditions on which social and cultural life depends in many coastal communities. The threats faced by coral reefs are considered further below.

What are coral reefs?

They are living communities. *Coral polyps*, tiny marine creatures, secrete a calcium carbonate (limestone) shell around their bodies, which remains when they die. The long, tubular shells become cemented together to form the physical structure of the reef, on top of which the live coral polyps grow. The reef structure is a complex physical haven where many kinds of flora and fauna find a refuge. The presence of so many organisms means that it is rich in food supply. There are many coral reefs in the Caribbean.

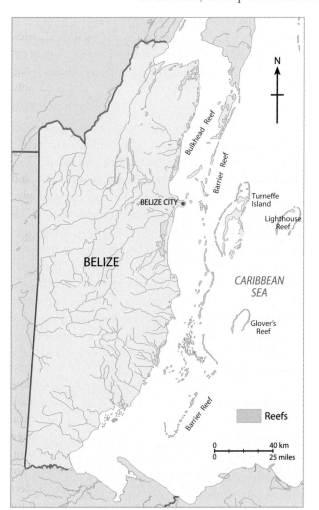

- Off Belize is the second largest **barrier reef** in the world, stretching for some 320 km (200 miles). The reef is separated from land by a lagoon that is 16–30 km (10–20 miles) wide. On the landward side of the reef the lagoon is quite shallow. On the seaward edge, the reef drops suddenly, plunging thousands of metres to the ocean floor and forming massive coral canyons (Fig. 5.11). Another long barrier reef, almost 200 km (120 miles) long, is located east of the island of Andros in the Bahamas. The longest barrier reef in the world (the Great Barrier Reef) is found off the east coast of Australia, stretching for over 1900 km (1200 miles).

- *Fringing reefs* are more common in the Caribbean and occur around or partially around most of the islands. Buccoo Reef off Tobago is one example (Fig. 5.12). These reefs are built by corals growing on shallow rocks near the shore and extend gradually seawards. Waves break on the reef, ensuring that a calm lagoon or stretch of sea occurs between the reef and the coastline.

Fig. 5.11 The barrier reef off Belize

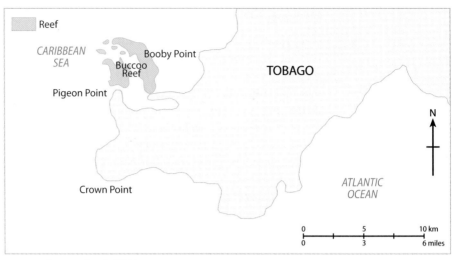

Fig. 5.12 Buccoo Reef off Tobago

- Coral *atolls* are rare in the Caribbean. They are coral islands, oval or almost circular, built around a central lagoon. They were formed by the growth of corals on top of sinking volcanoes, the lagoon marking the site of the ancient crater. Some are found in the hundreds of islands forming the barrier reef off Belize.

Growth of coral reefs

Between 30°N and 30°S of the equator, the tropical and subtropical latitudes (Fig. 5.13), conditions are optimum for the growth of coral. Salty and shallow water, around 68°F (20°C), which is clear of sediment, provides the best conditions. The shallow environment allows sunshine to penetrate freely. Inside each coral polyp grow algae, which produce food and oxygen for the polyp. The algae are protected by being inside the polyp, and feed off nutrients in the coral's waste products. This *symbiotic* relationship (they are of mutual help to each other) is similar to many kinds of 'living arrangements' found on the reef between the different types of flora and fauna that have to cohabit and co-exist within the reef. Any *turbidity* in the water reduces the efficiency with which these processes take place and also reduces the amount of sunlight that can penetrate to the coral. Thus, corals will not be found where major rivers bringing a large sediment load reach the sea. The coastal waters of Guyana, for example, where the Essequibo, Demerara, Berbice and Corentyne rivers bring down sediment, silt and nutrients from the interior, do not offer favourable conditions for the growth of coral.

Coral reefs and society and culture

Biodiversity

In addition to the many different types of coral found on reefs (hard coral, black coral, sea plumes, stony corals, soft corals and fans), there are thousands of species of marine flora and fauna. There are fish species of all sizes, sponges, molluscs, oysters, crabs, lobsters, shrimps, sea worms, eels, octopuses, sea urchins, clams, jellyfish, sea anemones, turtles, and a host of others (Fig. 5.14). The protection the reef structures offer to plant and animal life encourages great *biodiversity* (many different species)

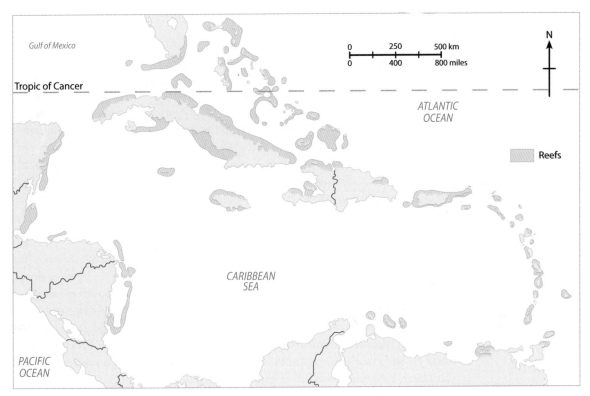

Fig. 5.13 The location of coral reefs in the Caribbean

and some species are millions of years old. Some species are *endemic* (they are found nowhere else in the world), and some are rare.

Coral reefs are therefore ecosystems that support an immense variety of life and also have great potential to produce new medicines for mankind. The relatively new drug for the treatment of AIDS – AZT – was developed from chemicals in a sponge found on Caribbean reefs. There is on-going research into producing sunscreen derived from chemicals found in corals and into synthesizing a bone-building substance for injuries involving broken bones.

Fig. 5.14 Some flora and fauna of the coral reef

Tourism

The reef provides a wonder world of colours, shapes and sizes, in addition to the immense variety of marine fauna and flora. The Belize Barrier Reef has been designated one of UNESCO's World Heritage Sites. In addition to travelling out to observe the reefs through glass-bottomed boats, tourists can snorkel, or go scuba-diving or fishing. These are becoming increasingly popular pursuits as tourists now have developed tastes for *adventure tourism* and **ecotourism**. The typical white, sandy beaches that traditionally lured the tourists are formed by waves smashing coral fragments to powder. The coral reef, then, is an important part of the 'Caribbean package' in which the tourist is interested, and thus contributes a great deal towards the income from tourism – easily the highest income-generating activity for most Caribbean countries today.

Fisheries

Since the reefs are a haven for all kinds of life, they provide valuable fisheries. For hundreds of years Caribbean fishermen have been depending on the reefs to sustain the livelihoods of many coastal villages. Seafood provided an important source of protein and the basis of a healthy lifestyle. The fishermen were aware of the part that nearby mangroves and sea grass beds played as a nursery for fish. The fish were spawned in these environments, where they spent some time, but sooner or later they made for the coral reef structures, which offered better protection from predators. Caribbean fishermen, with their traditional practices, did not disturb the valuable connections between sea grass beds, mangroves and coral reefs. Social and cultural life in these coastal villages depended on the local knowledge fishermen had about coral reefs and their ecological connections.

Coastal protection

The fringing reefs found throughout the Caribbean play an important role in protecting the coasts from erosion. The reefs break the force of the waves, thereby providing an expanse of calm waters between the reefs and the coast. This enables ports, harbours and settlements to enjoy sheltered locations on a calm sea. It also facilitates fishing, and tourist activities such as beach and sea sports. Mangrove and other wetlands thrive as they are dependent on the accumulation and deposition of silt, which is more likely to occur under calm conditions. Caribbean society and culture, then, have been shaped in many ways by proximity to the coast, especially to coral reefs, where sea food is plentiful and coastal protection is given.

Threats to coral reefs

Natural threats

- The ENSO event of 1997–8 generated higher than normal sea surface temperatures and this led to the bleaching of corals in the Caribbean and elsewhere. Bleaching occurs when the warm temperatures kill the algae living in the coral polyp, causing the polyp itself to weaken, whiten and die. There was extensive damage done to certain species of coral (namely the elkhorn coral) on the Belize reef and elsewhere in the Caribbean. An earlier ENSO episode occurred in 1982–3, with similar effects.

- Scientists today seem more committed to the phenomenon known as **global warming** than a few years ago, though there are still some who maintain that it does not exist and any warming detected is due to the natural variability of the climate. Global warming, in the long term, will result in higher sea surface temperatures and the likelihood of bleaching. There is the likelihood too that global warming will contribute to the melting of the polar ice caps, causing sea levels to rise and coral reefs to be destroyed if sunlight can no longer reach the reef.
- Sometimes in the dry season Caribbean countries receive large amounts of dust from the Sahara, blown over the Atlantic Ocean. Researchers believe that the increasing incidence of drought and **desertification** in the Sahel region of Africa will bring more African dust to the Caribbean. The dust brings with it soil fungi that are believed to be detrimental to some reef species such as sea fans.

Human threats

In Caribbean society and culture, small coastal communities have made a livelihood by fishing off the reefs and their impact on the reefs has been negligible (see above). For example, the remoter cays and islands within the barrier reefs off Belize and the Bahamas show healthy corals with an abundance and great variety of flora and fauna. However, there is a direct relationship between the growth of population and an increase in the pace and extent of their economic activities and coral reef degradation. As populations have grown and economies have been expanded, reefs have come increasingly under threat, thereby threatening the sustainability of the fishing industry. For example:

- Inland activities such as blasting hillsides and deforestation have led to an increase in the sediment load brought down by rivers, increasing the turbidity of coastal waters. The silt smothers the coral, preventing sunlight from reaching the algae within the coral polyp.
- Building of marinas, hotels and urban settlements on the coast disturbs the fragile coastal ecosystems because wetlands and mangrove areas are drained, cleared and filled in, artificial beaches are created, and the contours of the coast are changed, often disturbing the ecological connections between fish nurseries and the reefs.
- Harvesting coral for building material physically destroys the reef and reduces the effect of the protection from storms that coral reefs offer.
- Improper sewage treatment for coastal settlements, particularly large hotels, allows raw or partially treated sewage to flow into the sea. This is nutrient rich and algae grow in abundance, covering the reef and choking corals.
- Industrial effluents such as mine run-off, and agricultural effluents rich in pesticides and insecticides, prove poisonous to corals and other forms of life on the reef. Fertilizers in agricultural run-off also provide nutrients, which again lead to the overgrowth of algae.
- Hot water emissions from power plants lead to bleaching of coral in a manner similar to an ENSO event.

- Overfishing, especially of 'target fish', depletes certain species. People tend to develop a taste for certain fish, which then become target fish and are caught in such large numbers that they are endangered. This is also the case for specialty fish for the pet trade, such as aquarium fish. The methods employed, such as trawling using small-sized nets, capture many other types of fish that are merely discarded. These activities threaten the sustainability of the fishing industry. Jamaica's reefs, especially those to the north of the island, where there is the heaviest tourist presence, have become degraded largely because of overfishing.
- Destructive fishing methods physically destroy the reef and reef species when explosives are used to kill fish. Cyanide is used to poison and stun fish so that they can be captured live – often for the pet trade. It also succeeds in killing the corals and other fish species. Fish traps set for larger fish also kill smaller fish and thus endanger the fish supply for the following years.
- Tourism contributes to the physical destruction of the reef when tourists trample on it during sight-seeing expeditions. Boats carrying tourists indiscriminately drop anchor, again destroying the reef structure. Where the tourist trade is well developed, local people rob the reef to make jewellery, handicrafts and trinkets from coral. Shells of all kinds, too, are a specialty item.

A study of coral reefs shows us how a resource that has been important in maintaining society and culture in the Caribbean is being progressively destroyed by 'development' activities. Although there have been calls for **sustainable development**, awareness of the problem is still largely confined to a few environmental groups. 'Sustainable development' refers to the way a resource is used so that it can continue to provide for human beings from one generation to the next (Box 5.5). It calls for geographic awareness and an attitude of environmental conservation and protection.

BOX 5.5 Sustainability and coral reefs

St Lucia has moved swiftly to rehabilitate its coral reefs, which were severely degraded. To do so compromise and partnerships had to be forged with the very people who had been guilty of destroying the reefs – fishermen, poachers, tourists and divers. It is a continuing struggle, though, to control the behaviours of the owners and operators of factories and hotels and inland developers.

In St Lucia the Soufrière Marine Management Area (SMMA) was formed in 1994, making the fringing reefs of the south into a *marine park* or *reserve*. This became necessary because of pollution and overfishing in the area. Sustainability is a complex issue as it involves the livelihoods of people; the environment cannot just be protected from human beings without the latter being given some way of continuing to maintain their standard of living. To establish the marine park the SMMA had to enter into delicate negotiations and constant dialogue with the residents of the area, especially those who were directly affected – dive-shop operators, fishermen, yacht owners, farmers, and those offering a range of tourist services. Through an extensive consultative process, workshops, a public awareness campaign, and the involvement of business interests, stakeholders were gradually won over to the need for user fees, for controls and monitoring of fish populations and water quality, for rangers to enforce restrictions, for re-stocking of fish, and the management of land based sources of pollution. It is an on-going development which has resulted in an increase in fish and healthy corals. The model of a marine park has been used by other countries in the Caribbean, namely Bonaire and the Dominican Republic, to preserve the coral reef environment and to sustain the fishing industry by providing a profitable livelihood for those who depend on it.

Hurricanes

Hurricanes are environmental hazards in the face of which we tend to feel helpless. While we know that our behaviour affects us (as in the case of soil erosion, drought and the degradation of coral reefs) and that we can change our behaviour, meteorological or atmospheric phenomena seem beyond our power to control. From 1 June to 30 November, as the tropical Atlantic warms up, the tropical marine climate in the Caribbean experiences a number of *low-pressure systems*, some of which grow into fully developed hurricanes (Box 5.6). In 2005, however, the hurricane season lasted until January 2006 and it became necessary to use the Greek alphabet as the names assigned for the season using our normal alphabet were exhausted. This indicates that the hurricane season may be becoming longer with more hurricanes per season than in previous years.

What is a low pressure system?

Normal **atmospheric pressure** at sea level is 1013 millibars (mb). On a warm, sunny day in the Caribbean the pressure readings will be close to this measurement. Atmospheric pressure is the weight of the air pressing down on the Earth's surface and would therefore be greater nearer sea level than on top of a high mountain. An area that is extremely warm will also experience low pressure because the tendency of warm air is to rise. Atmospheric pressure is measured by a *barometer* and recorded on maps as lines joining places of equal pressure at sea level – **isobars** (Fig 5.15).

The difference in atmospheric pressure between one place and another generates winds. If the pressure drops considerably, the isobars are drawn close together (Fig. 5.15c), showing that there is a steep *pressure gradient* generating a strong wind. Generally speaking, winds blow from high-pressure areas to low-pressure areas. Sometimes the north-east trades bring weather systems into the Caribbean which have pronounced low pressure. These are systems where the air is rising (hence, low pressure) because of unusually warm ocean temperatures (the tendency of hot air is to rise). Such systems may develop into hurricanes – areas of intense low pressure, causing strong in-blowing winds (Box 5.6).

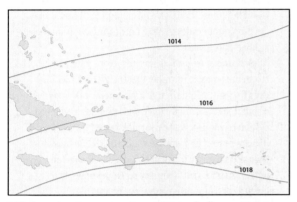

(a) Isobars showing pressure increasing gradually over an area

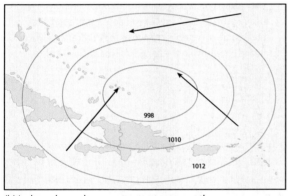

(b) Isobars show a low-pressure system, a gentle pressure gradient. Gentle winds blow from high pressure to low pressure

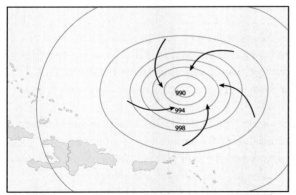

(c) A hurricane, an intense low-pressure system, very low pressures, a steep pressure gradient and strong winds, spiralling inwards

Fig. 5.15 Atmospheric pressure on weather maps

BOX 5.6 Low pressure systems

Extremely high sea surface temperatures in the Atlantic from June to November generate localized areas of low pressure where warm, moist oceanic air rises and cools, producing heavy convectional rains.

- An *easterly wave* or *tropical wave* is merely an area of unstable weather that dissipates over one or two days. It brings a slight lowering of pressure, an increase in wind strength of perhaps a few knots and cloudy and rainy weather.

- A *tropical depression* results if the easterly wave forms a system – the isobar pattern becomes closed – and pressures are lower than normal in the centre of the system. Winds begin to strengthen as they blow from high-pressure areas outside the system into the lower pressures inside the system. Winds may increase to about 20–34 knots (23–39 mph) and cloudy and rainy conditions are experienced. Again, conditions may dissipate over one or two days. At this point the National Hurricane Center in Miami gives the system a number.

- A *tropical storm* forms once the winds increase to 35 to 64 knots (39 to 74 mph). This means that the air pressure is continuing to decrease, generating stronger winds. Shown on a weather map, the isobars are drawn closer together, indicating steep pressure gradients and an increasingly organized system around a central area of low pressure. At this point the authorities issue a name for the storm. Such storms are likely to bring limited damage to buildings; for example, roofs may blow off and power and telephone lines may be brought down by falling trees. There is the likelihood of floods. It may develop rather quickly into a hurricane, so it is intensively studied and tracked.

- A *hurricane* or *tropical cyclone* develops when a tropical storm becomes so unstable that the warm air within rises to great heights in the atmosphere. It then derives a spin from the Coriolis Force and becomes a whirling system of winds spiralling in, maintained by the supply of warm, moist air from the waters below. Pressures drop considerably to 880 mb and lower. Powerful winds (in excess of 74 mph or 65 knots) now blow inwards and around a central eye or area of calm. The hurricane becomes an environmental disaster when lives, livelihoods and property are lost through strong winds, heavy rainfall and floods. In addition, a *storm surge* (a high dome of water) is created as the hurricane moves inland, intensifying the danger for coastal lowlands.

How hurricanes form

Off the coast of Africa in the period June to November each year the high temperatures of the oceans spawn local convectional disturbances, usually areas of unstable weather (winds and rain), which are brought into the Caribbean by the prevailing winds. Only a few of these go through all the developmental stages from being a tropical or easterly wave, a tropical depression and a tropical storm to become a hurricane. The process is described below.

- In all these systems *convection* (the uplift of air) is the main process at work, producing thunderstorms and heavy convectional rainfall. However, when the convection is so strong that there is continuous uplift of air and cooling to produce tall clouds, a weather system of great vertical extent starts to emerge.

- As the water vapour in the rising air cools, high in the atmosphere, to produce clouds (water droplets), enormous energy is released by the *latent heat of condensation* (the energy that was originally used in evaporation to convert water to water vapour). This produces warm conditions at great heights, thereby encouraging air to continue to rise long after the point where it would have normally condensed to form clouds.

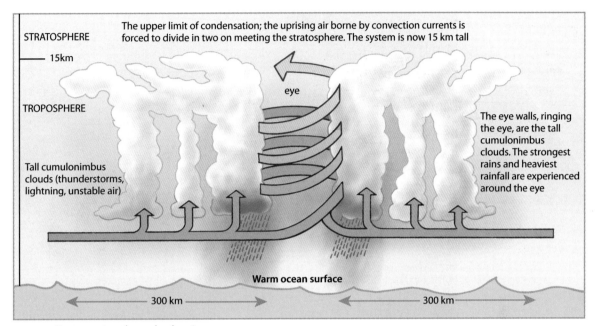

Fig. 5.16 Cross-section through a hurricane

Labels within figure:

STRATOSPHERE

15km

The upper limit of condensation; the uprising air borne by convection currents is forced to divide in two on meeting the stratosphere. The system is now 15 km tall

eye

TROPOSPHERE

Tall cumulonimbus clouds (thunderstorms, lightning, unstable air)

The eye walls, ringing the eye, are the tall cumulonimbus clouds. The strongest rains and heaviest rainfall are experienced around the eye

Warm ocean surface

300 km   300 km

- Air in such a system is buoyant, continuing to rise and forming towering *cumulonimbus* clouds (producing thunderstorms).
- Pressure continues to drop because of the rising air (Figs 5.16 and 5.17). This system is unstable and it can be perpetuated if it continues to travel over warm waters. It develops into a tropical storm or a hurricane once its vertical extent is large enough to be affected by the *Coriolis Force* (the force that is exerted on an air mass because of the spinning of the Earth).
- The Coriolis Force imparts a spinning effect to the entire weather system.
- Within the system pressure is so low that a steep pressure gradient occurs from outside to inside the system. Inside a hurricane pressures may reach 880 mb.
- Consequently, very strong and powerful winds are generated across the steep pressure gradients.
- If the winds are between 40 and 74 mph (65–120 kph), the system is labelled a tropical storm. Once the winds are over 75 mph a Category-1 hurricane has formed. The ***Saffir–Simpson Scale*** classifies hurricanes according to wind speed:
  - Category 1: 75–95mph (120–150 kph)
  - Category 2: 96–110mph (150–175 kph)
  - Category 3: 111–130mph (175–210 kph)
  - Category 4: 131–155mph (210–250 kph)
  - Category 5: over 155mph (over 250 kph)

The Coriolis Force is not felt strongly at the Equator and so hurricanes do not form or travel routes that are close to the Equator. Guyana and Trinidad, then, are at a low risk for hurricanes. However, in 2004 Hurricane Ivan devastated Grenada and affected Tobago, showing that they can sometimes follow routes that are very southerly. At such times Trinidad usually feels the effects of the outer bands.

Fig. 5.17 A satellite photograph of Hurricane Ivan over Cuba and the Yucatan Peninsula, 2004

Features of a hurricane

A hurricane has three major characteristics:

- extremely low pressure
- strong winds
- heavy convectional rainfall.

In addition, the strong winds may create huge waves that can devastate the coast (*storm surges*).

Hurricanes are well-organized low-pressure systems that may be several hundred kilometres across. They move at only about 12–15 mph so there is potential for extreme destruction as they take several hours to pass over an area. There is a sequence in how a hurricane affects an area.

- The first half of the hurricane normally has winds spiralling in from the north-west and west, with increasing intensity of rainfall and winds as the eye wall approaches.
- Then the eye passes, an area of relative calm, with winds sinking rather than rising.
- The second half of the hurricane then arrives, with winds now blowing from the south-west and south-east (Figs 5.16 and 5.17).
- The area of most intense pressures, strongest winds and heaviest rainfall is the eye wall – the tall cumulonimbus clouds ringing the eye of the hurricane.

ACTIVITY 5.7

1. Conduct independent research to fill in the blanks in the Table 5.1.

2. On a blank outline map of the Caribbean, plot the tracks of TWO of the hurricanes listed in the table.

• For ONE of the hurricanes you have plotted, explain how it increased and decreased in strength along its course.

• Identify the countries which were most seriously affected and describe how they were affected

Table 5.1 Hurricanes in the Caribbean

YEAR	NAME	HURRICANE CATEGORY *
1980	Allen	4
	Gilbert	
2004	Ivan	
	Andrew	5
	Hugo	4
	Katrina	

* The highest category reached.

Hurricane tracks are an interesting area of study for meteorologists and provide vital information for Caribbean people. Most of the hurricanes affecting the Caribbean originate off the coast of Africa, in the Atlantic Ocean, and are brought by the prevailing winds westwards into the Caribbean. The Lesser Antilles are usually the first areas of landfall for a hurricane making its way into the Caribbean. Every year at least one island in the Lesser Antilles is likely to be affected by a hurricane. However, the islands in the archipelago are located so close to each other that if an island does not score a direct hit, it will certainly feel the winds and rains in the outer or feeder bands, as well as the high waves and storm surges. From the Lesser Antilles, meteorologists have to rely on computer models and up-to-date weather information from inside the hurricane (usually from satellites, or special airplanes and ships) to make forecasts about the possible tracks that a hurricane might take. They usually adopt a north-westward route, which may take them straight to Jamaica and other islands in the Greater Antilles. From there they may threaten the Bahamas, Florida and the Gulf States of the US, or they may move westward, reaching Belize and Central America. This was a major reason why the capital of Belize was moved from Belize City on the coast to Belmopan in the interior. It is not very common, but sometimes hurricanes form in the Caribbean Sea or the Gulf of Mexico.

Forecasting the route a hurricane will take is now an extremely specialized skill and it can help significantly in reducing the dangers posed to people and property. Accurate forecasts serve as the basis for evacuating people from risky environments. However, hurricanes are erratic and there may only be a 12-hour period before it is certain that a hurricane will come ashore at a certain place. Generally, forecasts help to forewarn and prepare people to batten down and safeguard their property as best they can and to stock up on essential supplies to ease the chaos in the aftermath of a hurricane.

Hurricanes are thus environmental *hazards*, potentially dangerous to human beings and property. They become environmental *disasters* when they exact a heavy toll on the people who live in these risky environments. It is thus in the interests of Caribbean people to be proactive about putting in place strategies that may help to mitigate the effects of a hurricane rather than just hoping for the best (Box 5.7).

BOX 5.7 Disaster mitigation

Mitigation is a term used to describe strategies undertaken to prevent or reduce death, damage or hardship either for a hazard that has already occurred or for one that is likely to occur in the future. The focus of mitigation is to reduce risk and even modify the hazard where possible. Mitigation occurs at different levels and different time frames.

- Individuals, communities and national groups have different and complementary roles to play. Coastal populations have grown over the last two decades and tall buildings have been constructed on newly reclaimed lands. The majority of the population now lives on the most hazard-prone areas at risk of storm surges, tsunamis, hurricanes and earthquakes.
- Individuals can institute their own mitigation strategies (buying insurance, structural reinforcement of roofs and walls, and plans for evacuation, stocking supplies, and charting emergency escape routes).
- Communities can organize the safest shelters possible in the area. They can mobilize certain trained individuals to check on the elderly, the handicapped, and others who may be at risk for different reasons. They can inform national bodies about areas likely to flood and the best evacuation routes, and promote a sense of awareness in the persons in the community about what options they have in the event of a disaster.
- National emergency management disaster organizations occur in virtually all Caribbean countries but their level of efficiency varies. One of the most important mitigation

strategies that they undertake is public awareness campaigns to enable people to know how they can best prepare their homes for an emergency such as a hurricane, and how they can ensure their health and safety during and after a disaster. Unfortunately, there is very little liaison with urban planning departments, land use development projects and the like, which are all involved in mitigation. Most organizations of this kind remain at the level of managing a disaster.

Comprehensive mitigation is organized into phases:

- *Pre-disaster.* A proactive outlook that seeks to minimize the country's vulnerability by examining land use planning, implementation of building codes, dredging rivers, building dams, and ensuring that the greatest concentrations of people are on the least risky areas.
- *During the disaster.* Communication networks are kept open via amateur radio operators and other mechanisms; search and rescue teams are mobilized; emergency shelters are provided with food, supplies, medical assistance. International relief assistance may be needed.
- *Post-disaster.* This too can be divided into phases. Relief assistance must continue to provide basic needs even as the reconstruction phase begins. Restoration of water, power and gas is a priority. Clean-up measures give a sense of returning normalcy. Property must be protected from looters and criminal elements. People are given building supplies to use in self-help projects, a strategy that helps in reducing the trauma of dislocation and begins the process of getting busy building back their lives.

ACTIVITY 5.8

1. Brainstorm the range of strategies and measures that you and your family can put in place to mitigate the effects of a hurricane.

2. Suggest difficulties that any ONE group of people may face in putting these measures into effect.

3. Conduct independent research to determine the reasons why Hurricane Katrina was so devastating in its effects on New Orleans in August 2005.

It is imperative that each Caribbean country today has a well-thought-out *national disaster preparedness plan.* Such a plan depends on effective coordination between various community, district and national groups. This is perhaps the most difficult hurdle that such a plan has to overcome. Usually it is well-meaning amateurs who first agitate for disaster preparedness – people who have an interest in the environment, those who are concerned about the effects of a disaster on the poor and squatter communities. It is unfortunate, but it is usually a looming crisis that will finally attract the attention of national bodies and make them see the need for a plan of action. Even when a plan is put in place, it does not necessarily mean that the general population is any more aware of what they should be doing to avert a disaster. For example, many persons may not exert themselves to find out where their nearest hurricane shelter is or even put up in their homes the telephone numbers of emergency relief organizations. Any plan, then, must take into account ways of dealing with the mindset of people, especially when changes in habits and behaviour are involved. Disaster preparedness is much more of a human issue than it is an environmental one.

ACTIVITY 5.9

In preparing a national disaster preparedness plan for hurricanes or flooding in your country, suggest what might be the 'sticking points' in the development of such a plan?

Earthquakes and volcanoes

The Caribbean is also at risk from environmental hazards of *geologic* origin, such as earthquakes and volcanic eruptions. Both can occur suddenly, causing widespread death and destruction. The response of Caribbean people to these environmental threats has been on the whole to remain hopeful. Indeed, powerful earthquakes and volcanic eruptions are sporadic occurrences; there are sometimes centuries-long intervals between destructive episodes. Nevertheless, the possibility of disaster is ever present as volcanic activity and earthquakes are difficult to predict accurately; to ignore the threat is to be deliberately careless about our own lives and livelihoods.

Plate tectonics

The theory of **plate tectonics** shows us that both earthquakes and volcanoes are related in their origins. It is a better attempt to explain the movement of land masses than was the theory of *continental drift* (Box 5.8). The theory of plate tectonics states that the Earth's crust is composed of several large slabs or plates of rigid crustal materials and some smaller ones, which are in continuous movement. Both oceans and land masses may be 'carried' on a plate. The Caribbean Plate (see Fig. 1.2) is one of the smaller plates. Where one plate meets another, at a plate margin or boundary, several kinds of **tectonic activities** (movement or displacement of rocks) may result.

The plates move relative to each other because of convection currents in the *mantle* (Fig. 5.18). There are three kinds of plate margins, based on the nature of contact between the plates.

- *Divergent margins*. Sea-floor spreading was first detected at these margins, leading to the development of the theory of plate tectonics. In the Atlantic Ocean new crust upwells as *magma* from the mantle, and then flows west and east, pushing older rocks before it. The Mid-Atlantic Ridge running the entire

BOX 5.8 Continental drift

Ever since maps were first made, people have hypothesized that the continents have drifted around over time. Early ideas about this were suggested by the shape of South America and Africa, which appear to be able to fit together. Historical and fossil evidence also suggested that some places had enjoyed an altogether different climate than the present one. This could imply either climate change or continental drift. Stronger evidence came in the form of similar, and in some cases identical geological formations, in West Africa and north-eastern Brazil.

These observations were also made in different parts of the globe, suggesting movements of land masses on a worldwide scale. It was hypothesized that there was only one landmass, Pangea, from which the continents broke off and have been moving ever since. However strong the circumstantial evidence was, it could not explain how and why until *sea floor spreading* was discovered. Scientists discovered that the rocks in the centre of the oceans were the youngest and on each side they got progressively older towards the continents. They found that new rocks were welling up from the mantle of the Earth, as magma, and solidifying into rocks on the surface, and these rocks were then pushed to either side by new upwelling magma (Fig. 5.19). They theorized that if new crust was being formed at certain places on the earth's surface then there must be places where it was being consumed. The theory of plate tectonics provided the answers to some of these puzzles.

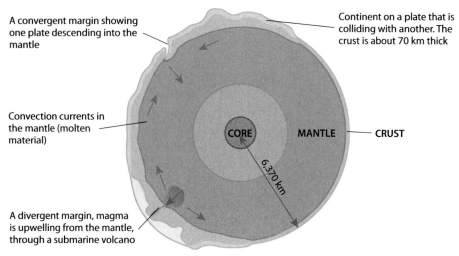

A convergent margin showing one plate descending into the mantle

Continent on a plate that is colliding with another. The crust is about 70 km thick

Convection currents in the mantle (molten material)

CORE · MANTLE · CRUST

6,370 km

A divergent margin, magma is upwelling from the mantle, through a submarine volcano

Fig. 5.18 The structure of the Earth

length of the Atlantic Ocean from the northern to the southern hemisphere is a line of submarine volcanoes and fissures marking the site of a divergent margin. Volcanic and earthquake activity are characteristic of such margins and they have been found in all oceans (Fig. 5.19). The rocks are continually being pushed by the upwelling magma, resulting in earthquakes.

● **Convergent margins.** These represent sites where crust is being consumed or pushed back down into the mantle. Along these margins plates collide and one plate rides over the other, forcing it downwards into a *subduction zone*. The descending plate is crushed as it grinds together with the other plate that is pushing over it. This friction generates tremendous heat, enough to melt the crustal rocks, and so as the plate descends into the mantle the rock material becomes molten. The many holes, crevices and cracks in the surface rocks allow some of this magma to flow back up to the surface to form volcanoes. Along

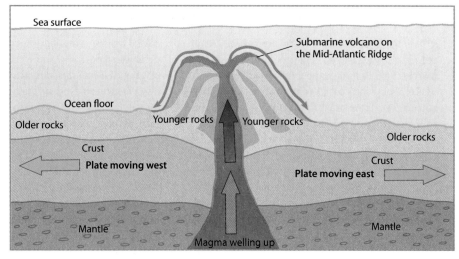

Sea surface

Submarine volcano on the Mid-Atlantic Ridge

Ocean floor

Older rocks

Younger rocks · Younger rocks

Older rocks

Crust

Plate moving west

Crust

Plate moving east

Mantle

Mantle

Magma welling up

Fig. 5.19 A divergent plate margin

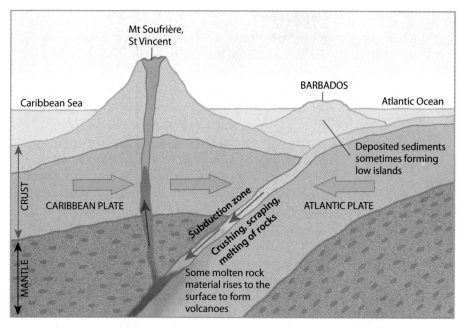

Fig. 5.20 A convergent plate margin: cross-section across the eastern Caribbean

convergent margins the tremendous pressures generated by rocks exerting great force against each other inevitably results in earthquakes as the rocks move suddenly to accommodate the stress. The constant grinding and scraping of rocks against each other also results in the deposition of a great deal of sediments in the area. Sometimes these form islands that are flat and low lying, but this is nevertheless part of *mountain-building activity*. Fig. 5.20 shows a cross-section through the Lesser Antilles, where there is a convergent margin.

● *Transform margins.* Where plates slide past each other pressures build up in the rocks in each plate and earthquake activity results when the rocks move suddenly to relieve the stress (Fig. 5.21).

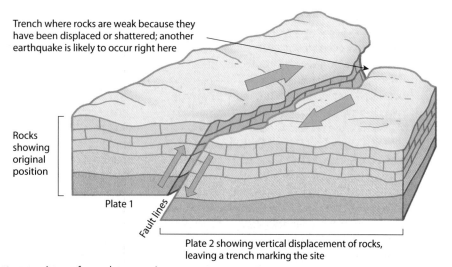

Fig. 5.21 A transform plate margin

Earthquakes

All the plate margins described above generate earthquakes. An earthquake is a vibration or tremor that occurs in the crust when there is a release of energy by rocks. This happens when there is a steady build-up of pressure in the rocks (through plates riding over each other at convergent margins, sliding past each other at transform margins or being pushed away by upwelling magma at divergent margins). When the rocks cannot accommodate the stresses any longer, they move and release energy. This energy may cause extreme displacement of rocks, which shift or move – land may sink (Fig. 5.21), or be pushed up, or move sideways – with adverse consequences for the population, particularly in built-up areas. And this dislocation may occur on ocean floors as well, where if there is a major shift in the rocks, a *tsunami* develops – a mighty wall of water travelling at great speeds that can inundate large sections of the coast, often with little warning (as occurred in the Indian Ocean in December 2004).

An earthquake leaves a fracture or *fault* in rocks – a line of weakness where future earthquakes are likely to recur. There are major faults at plate margins and in the Caribbean the convergent and transform margins are the sites of numerous fault lines indicating weakness in the rocks and areas of crustal instability (Box 5.9).

BOX 5.9 The Caribbean Plate

Although the Caribbean Plate is one of the smaller plates covering the globe, it is extremely complex and still not fully understood.

- The transform boundary in the northern Caribbean was once a convergent margin with active volcanoes. Today the islands of the Greater Antilles have only extinct volcanoes but the change from convergent to transform indicates dynamic processes that are not easily evident to researchers.
- There is a small divergent margin growing in the Cayman Trench area, complicating the already complex geology of the region.
- The boundaries between the Nazca, Cocos and Caribbean Plate are as yet not clearly defined.
- The convergent margin along the Lesser Antilles is still posing questions to geologists. It is a double island arc with mountainous, volcanic islands in the inner arc (Martinique, Montserrat, Dominica) and flat, low-lying, limestone islands in the outer arc (Barbados, Anguilla). The centre of active vulcanicity seems to be shifting southwards so that Saba is thought to be now extinct and Kick em Jenny, a submarine volcano just north of Grenada, is increasingly active.

The Caribbean Plate is a highly active tectonic 'hotspot'.

- The presence of deep ocean trenches off Cayman, Puerto Rico and Hispaniola indicate major plate boundaries with the potential for earthquakes of 7.5 and higher on the *Richter Scale*, capable of generating tsunamis.
- The meeting of convergent and transform margins at the southern margin is responsible for the extreme faulting and unstable nature of rocks in Trinidad and northern Venezuela bringing petroleum, natural gas and pitch-bearing rocks to the surface. (Trinidad is on the South American Plate and Tobago on the Caribbean Plate.)
- There are about 17 active volcanoes in the Eastern Caribbean, all connected at a subterranean level along the plate margin. Eruptions in one volcano can trigger eruptions in other islands. On May 7th 1902 Mt Soufrière in St Vincent erupted followed by Mt Pelée in Martinique causing the combined loss of 30,000 lives.
- The western edge of the Caribbean Plate in the Pacific Ocean off the west coast of Central America is even more active than the eastern margin. The convergent margin in the west records higher subduction rates (plates descending into the mantle) than along the Lesser Antilles and consequently earthquakes are much stronger. In 1972 an earthquake totally destroyed Managua, the capital of Nicaragua, and an equally destructive earthquake shook Guatemala in 1976. The potential for very strong earthquakes is high in the Central American Region and the shocks may affect the Greater Antilles. Volcanoes are more numerous than in the Lesser Antilles and there have been more violent eruptions as well.

In addition to tsunamis, earthquakes and faulting can result in *landslides, rock slides* and *mudslides* that may cause much more damage than the earthquake itself. In the aftermath of an earthquake, *aftershocks* can be dangerous, in that already weakened buildings are likely to collapse. Most of the deaths caused by an earthquake result from falling masonry and buildings. Threats to life also occur when gas and electricity lines and water mains are disrupted, so that there is also the danger of uncontrolled fires and the spread of disease. To reduce vulnerability to these threats there should be some serious consideration given to ways of improving earthquake mitigation and even prediction (Box 5.7, Box 5.10).

Volcanoes

Volcanoes are found on divergent and convergent plate margins. In the Caribbean the two convergent margins are the sites of both active and dormant volcanoes. *Active volcanoes* have erupted within the last few hundred years and *dormant volcanoes* have not erupted for hundreds of years. Compared to volcanoes on divergent margins (e.g. Hawaii), where lava continuously and quietly erupts, volcanoes on

---

BOX 5.10 Predicting earthquakes and mitigating their effects

The *Richter Scale* records the total amount of energy released by an earthquake. An earthquake measuring 5.0 on the Richter Scale is ten times as strong as one measuring 4.0. Those measuring 6.0 and above are major earthquakes resulting in strong shaking and wave-like motions of the ground. The convergent margin of the Lesser Antilles can generate earthquakes of 7.0 and higher, with a probability of once in every 20 years.

Since falling masonry and other built structures constitute the main hazard during an earthquake, mitigation efforts need to focus on the materials used in construction and the strict enforcement of building codes, as well as an evaluation of the geology of the site. These are long-term strategies that are born out of a commitment to public safety and civic responsibility and which rest on a strong geographical awareness about the environmental threats that Caribbean people face. If people are aware, for example, of how an earthquake affects a building, they may be more wary of building tall structures on reclaimed land or on poorly consolidated rock or they may be more demanding about building codes and inspections. During an earthquake the lower part of a building moves forward with the ground movement but the upper part remains still. As the lower part rebounds the top half now begins the forward movement. Buildings can be literally torn in two, especially if they do not have strong lateral bracing.

Some headway has been made in predicting earthquakes. Funding for research in this and other areas of environmental hazards tend to handicap Caribbean nations. Long-term record keeping and measuring the build-up of stress in faulted rocks leads to the development of a database that helps prediction efforts. In China observations such as the water level in deep wells, the unusual behaviour of animals and the presence of radioactive gases have been used to predict some earthquakes. However, it is not a precise science – it is impossible to tell where the *focus* of an earthquake would be (its point of origin deep in the crust or the mantle) and so it is difficult to predict the *epicentre* (the spot directly above the focus on the surface). Educated guesswork then usually influences decisions about which areas to evacuate when some scientific data is at hand foretelling the pre-conditions for an earthquake. However, that is a more comfortable scenario than one where there are no attempts at prediction.

Since the earthquake of 26 December 2004 and the resulting tsunami in Indonesia and South East Asia, there have been increasing calls for an efficient Early Warning System to alert people in a wide perimeter around epicentres of any earthquake event about the possibility of there being aftershocks or tsunamis. Although geologists are on the whole doubtful that such a destructive tsunami is likely to affect the Caribbean, the best course of action is to emphasize the importance of early warning systems and national drills and simulations conducted by disaster preparedness organizations.

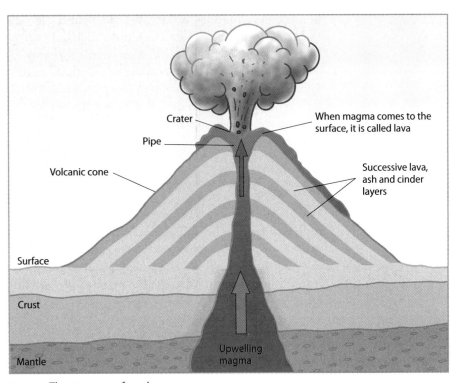

Fig. 5.22 The structure of a volcano

convergent margins erupt with great force. This is related to the type of magma that develops at each margin. At convergent margins the molten magma is thick and viscous so that when left in the *pipe* of the *volcanic cone* after an eruption, the new emerging magma for another eruption has to forcibly eject the old plug of *lava*. This is what happened when Mt Pelée erupted in 1902. Sometimes part of the volcano itself is blown apart in such an eruption, or the top or *crater* sinks to form a large *caldera* (Fig. 5.22).

When a volcano erupts with great force, the lava and surrounding rocks are blown to bits, producing *ash* and *cinders*. Larger fragments falling back to earth, *volcanic bombs*, can also be dangerous. The molten lava that pours out and flows down the sides of the volcano is several hundred degrees Centigrade, so that all life forms, buildings and other structures are wiped out. The 1995 eruption in Montserrat's Soufrière Hills (Fig. 5.23) was accompanied by *pyroclastic flows*, huge clouds of ash and cinders mixed with poisonous gases, reducing visibility to zero. Plymouth, the capital, was destroyed but remarkably only 20 persons were killed. The continuing eruption forced the evacuation of thousands and the south of the island is still regarded as unsafe. Society and culture in Montserrat is still trying to recover. In the 1902 eruption of Mt Pelée, clouds of poisonous gases, *nuées ardentés* and pyroclastic flows destroyed the town and 20,000 residents of St Pierre. This was probably the deadliest eruption of the twentieth century and was related to the eruption of Mt Soufrière nearby in St Vincent, where 2000 lives were lost.

Fig. 5.23 The 1995 eruption in Montserrat's Soufrière Hills

Summary

Environmental disasters such as severe soil erosion, drought, coral reef destruction, hurricanes, earthquakes and volcanoes result because of a number of factors. Economic activity that overly exploits land and sea resources destroys our means of maintaining our livelihoods. Inequality in incomes in Caribbean societies leads to use of land of marginal fertility. A lack of understanding of how drought-prone areas should be utilized as well as an unwillingness to be serious about implementing measures to limit the amount of destruction that a hurricane, earthquake or volcanic eruption could bring are among the reasons why Caribbean countries are vulnerable to environmental disasters. Perhaps the more fundamental reason is a lack of geographical awareness among Caribbean people, so that they continue to engage in practices detrimental to the environment and their own livelihoods.

5.4   IMPACTS ON CARIBBEAN SOCIETY AND CULTURE

Earthquake activity brings death and destruction in its wake. An earthquake occurs every day along the plate margins but may only register 2 or 3 on the Richter Scale and be difficult to detect without instrumentation. Stronger earthquakes do occur, as in 1997, when an earthquake registering 6.1 struck Tobago, and in 2004 one of a magnitude of 6.3 struck Dominica. Compared to the western margin of the Caribbean Plate though, there has been less severe destruction and loss of lives. The 1972 Managua earthquake (registering 6.2) killed 8000 people and the 1976 Guatemala earthquake (registering 7.5) killed 23,000.

Mt Pelée and Mt Soufrière opened the twentieth century with devastating eruptions. At the close of the century the eruptions in the Soufrière Hills of Montserrat led to evacuation, migration, death and the destruction of livelihoods. It was and is a continuing national trauma. Before that Montserrat had not seen an eruption for centuries, but Mt Soufrière in St Vincent has been continuously active and a new dome of lava forming an island has grown within the lake in the crater. Kick em Jenny, the submarine volcano in the south of the Grenadines, has recorded increasing activity, with lava outpourings that add to the height of the volcano. There is currently a zone around the volcano where shipping is prohibited.

There is, then, a continuing threat of environmental disaster in the Caribbean but prediction is difficult. The Eastern Caribbean is particularly at risk of earthquakes and volcanic eruptions (as well as hurricanes) and the rest of the Caribbean is liable to suffer earthquakes (and hurricanes). No Caribbean country has the necessary resources and personnel to be able to predict and monitor such events or to develop and implement mitigation plans single-handedly. They all rely on regional bodies and specialist organizations for funding and assistance. Being vulnerable and having to rely on outside agencies does not seem to have led to an increased level of geographic awareness of these threats, and mitigation efforts to date leave much to be desired. Perhaps this can be attributed to an attitude of complacency among countries where a destructive event has not yet occurred.

Even in countries where a destructive event *has* happened, people still farm the fertile, volcanic slopes and construct modern multi-storey buildings in the capital city on reclaimed lands. Perhaps there is a certain ambivalence to abandoning volcanic areas, because the soils are very fertile and the landscapes are spectacular, often bringing in considerable income from tourism. Proper **risk management** procedures can ensure a reasonable level of safety, but where the only consideration of risk is just a reliance on luck, then Caribbean people in coastal and built environments are extremely vulnerable to environmental disasters.

Some countries (those in the Greater Antilles, Guyana, Barbados and Trinidad and Tobago) are not at risk of a volcanic eruption so there may not be an adequate push to develop disaster preparedness initiatives. Caribbean countries, though, are too close together to be unaffected by each other's tragedies. Ash from exploding volcanoes affects jet engines and may fall in another country, with adverse effects for agriculture. Respiratory diseases are common in areas (even far-away areas) affected by ash fall. Large-scale destruction of one country's economy may start migrations that strain the welcome and economies of those countries that try to assist *only when a disaster happens.*

The impact of the eruption in Montserrat, where the capital and airport had to be closed, and where more than half the people were evacuated, some of them to Antigua, shows that without proper planning Caribbean governments were not readily able to assist. Even Montserrat's status as a British colony did not help very much in providing a level of comfort to the displaced people. If we are to learn lessons from the Montserrat experience, one of them would be that in small island states where the capital city is the hub of administrative, political, financial, economic, social and cultural life, an earthquake, volcanic eruption or hurricane that destroys the capital city paralyses the ability of that country to recover for years to come.

The poor are extremely vulnerable to environmental disasters, which they may survive but be unable to recover from. Squatters who live in rickety structures on hillsides around the capital cities are especially at risk. In the 1976 earthquake in Guatemala most deaths were caused when the hillsides collapsed, killing thousands of urban squatters. The poor and other marginalized members of society are usually unable to afford insurance, so that when the premiums go up (as happens in areas of repeated disasters), these persons are left destitute and dependent on the state.

In any event, environmental threats that we are unprepared for, and which consequently become environmental disasters, drain away attention, funding and other resources from developmental plans that were already earmarked for social improvement. The possibility of continuing major environmental disasters in the Caribbean in the near future should alert us to the necessity for meaningful planning (Box 5.7). Hazard mitigation and disaster preparedness focus on all areas of our contact and relationships with the land, not just the impact of a specific disaster. To be able to plan meaningfully then we should have a well-developed awareness of the environment.

Summary

Environmental disasters such as hurricanes, earthquakes and volcanic eruptions take a terrible toll on Caribbean societies. The on-going eruption in Montserrat has almost destroyed that society and it may be many decades before some semblance of normality returns. Hurricanes are an annual occurrence and meteorologists forecast many more major hurricanes per season than before. Lower-category hurricanes bring storm surges that erode coastlines and destroy boats and small craft as well as the infrastructure for marinas, hotels and fishing operations. Major hurricanes bring social and cultural life to a halt as preparations before and mopping up after can be extensive and expensive. On almost all occasions human life and property are at risk. Earthquakes are sudden and the whole region is vulnerable because of our tectonically active location. Generally speaking, the costs to the society are not only economic but psychological too, as there is often a reluctance to 'start over' as the trauma associated with a disaster may cause apathy. Human resources, too, may drain away as people migrate because hurricane-hit economies or volcanically destroyed landscapes take a long while to recharge.

WRAP UP

The Caribbean region is prone to a number of environmental hazards, some of which, like soil erosion, drought and coral reef destruction, can be overcome by sensible use of resources, data gathering, and proper management and monitoring. Some threats, however, are difficult to predict and control, such as hurricanes, earthquakes and volcanic eruptions. Increasing our geographical awareness of these threats is one way that will help us to develop more enlightened perspectives on the environment, which should not only protect the environment but significantly reduce our vulnerability as well.

This chapter has shown that increasing geographic awareness of environmental threats and disasters highlights the interesting point that these issues are not only geographical or geological but stem from social and cultural practices as well. Paradoxically, there is little emphasis put on meaningful development of mitigation strategies and long-term disaster planning, and even the threats we can control, such as soil erosion, are not priority issues in development planning. The poor, especially, suffer from a lack of attention to environmental threats.

PRACTICE TESTS

Structured response

1. (a) Explain what is meant by drought being a 'creeping hazard'. (2 marks)
   (b) Describe TWO mitigating strategies to address the problem of drought. (4 marks)
2. (a) Describe TWO cultural practices which lead to accelerated soil erosion. (4 marks)
   (b) Explain ONE way in which soil erosion is related to drought. (2 marks)
3. (a) Explain what is meant by the term 'mitigation strategy'. (2 marks)
   (b) Describe ONE long-term and ONE short-term mitigation strategy to address soil erosion. (4 marks)
4. (a) Describe TWO ways in which the natural physical environment influences settlement patterns in the Lesser Antilles. (4 marks)
   (b) Identify ONE way by which Caribbean people have altered the natural physical environment for the benefit of society and culture. (2 marks)
5. (a) Outline the theory of plate tectonics. (3 marks)
   (b) Explain why there are no volcanoes on the island of Barbados. (3 marks)
6. (a) Describe ONE advantage of volcanic activity. (2 marks)
   (b) Describe TWO ways in which society and culture in Montserrat have been adversely affected by volcanic activity. (2 marks)
7. (a) Distinguish between an environmental hazard and an environmental disaster. (2 marks)
   (b) Distinguish between environmental degradation and pollution. (2 marks)
8. Explain why hurricanes lose their strength over land. (4 marks)
9. For an identified hurricane (name and year), describe its effects on ONE named Caribbean country. (4 marks)
10. Explain THREE strategies that Caribbean people can take to minimize the threat from earthquake activity. (6 marks)

Essay questions (20 marks)

1. Explain what is meant by 'perspectives on land'. Show how aboriginal perspectives on land vary from that of mainstream Caribbean society.
2. (a) Describe the occurrence of earthquakes in the Caribbean. (10 marks)
   (b) Show how Caribbean people have increased their chances of experiencing an environmental disaster from earthquakes. (10 marks)

3. Describe the ways in which coral reefs have contributed to social and cultural life in the Caribbean.
4. Explain why the Caribbean is described as being at risk of drought.

Challenge essay questions (30 marks)

1. Discuss the point of view that poverty greatly increases the problem of soil erosion in Caribbean countries.
2. Using ONE Caribbean country as an example, examine the extent to which it has developed a comprehensive mitigation strategy for dealing with environmental hazards.
3. Account for the situation today in the Caribbean where the majority of people live in risky environments.
4. To what extent is knowledge of the theory of plate tectonics important for Caribbean people in all walks of life?

RESEARCH TOPICS

In a country where there has been a recent earthquake, volcanic or hurricane disaster, you could follow one of these ideas for developing a research project.

- Interview survivors to find out the strategies they used in coming to terms with the disaster.
- Interview (or use questionnaires) to find out how the disaster impacted on the economy in a small area.
- Interview people who experienced the disaster, as well as various authorities, to determine how the authorities 'managed' the different phases of the event.

Alternatively, you may wish to study accounts of two environmental disasters to compare and contrast their effects on Caribbean culture and society – perhaps Hurricane Ivan in Grenada and Jamaica or volcanic eruptions in St Vincent and Montserrat.

Other research areas pertinent to 'developing geographical awareness' are:

- studying the nature of pollution in an area and its impact on culture and society
- examining farming practices in an area to determine whether these practices contribute to soil erosion; or, to what extent farming practices are influenced by poverty
- compiling statistics on drought in an identified country in different years and studying the impact on culture and society

- making a case study of a coral reef, using documentary evidence and interviews with key informants on the nature of the threat, mitigation strategies and results
- analysing the perceptions of people about how they can safeguard life and property in the event of a disaster; to what extent are they well-informed?

REFERENCES

Bryant, D., Burke, L., McManus, J., & Spalding, M. (1998). *Reefs at risk: a map-based indicator of threats to the world's coral reefs*. Washington, DC: World Resources Institute.

Jay, M., & Morad, M. (2002). Cultural outlooks and the global quest for sustainable environmental management. *Geography*, 87(4), pp. 331–335.

Machel, H. (1999). *Geology of Barbados: a brief account of the island's origin and its major geological features*. Barbados: Barbados Museum and Historical Society.

Morgan, J. (2003). Teaching social geographies: representing society and space. *Geography*, 88(2), pp. 124–134.

Nagle, G. (1998). *Hazards*. Walton-on-Thames, UK: Thomas Nelson.

Prosser, R. (1992). *Natural systems and human responses*. Walton-on-Thames, UK: Thomas Nelson.

Sealey, N. (1992). *Caribbean world: a complete geography*. Cambridge, UK: Cambridge University Press.

Waugh, D. (1995). *Geography: an integrated approach*. Walton-on-Thames, UK: Thomas Nelson.

6 ANALYSING SOCIAL INSTITUTIONS

The family, education, religion and the justice system are social institutions which we as social beings have created and continue to re-create daily. Social institutions shape and direct our lives, our interactions and our thoughts, yet for the most part we are not consciously aware of them. This chapter intends to bring the taken-for-granted nature of social institutions to light. Each institution has a history and each has evolved in some way over time, showing evidence of both continuity and change. Each social institution is studied according to how it has evolved, how it impacts on Caribbean people and how they in turn are having an impact on it.

EXPECTED LEARNING OBJECTIVES

On completing this chapter, you will be able to
1 explain what is meant by social institutions and social organizations
2 describe the role that social institutions and social organizations play in society and culture
3 compare different sociological perspectives on social institutions
4 describe the history and evolution of selected social institutions in the Caribbean
5 analyse how the family, education, religion and the justice system impact on individuals, groups and other social institutions in Caribbean society and culture.

6.1 SOCIAL INSTITUTIONS

Social institutions have evolved to solve the problems of living in society. People who live together as a society need to agree upon certain arrangements if they are to minimize conflicts. Whilst people may have different ideas about how to rear children or educate them, for the purposes of the 'common good' there must be some agreement, at least in a general way, about how these tasks should be addressed. The social institutions of education, the **family**, **religion** and the justice system are all based on *organizing ideas* about how these key areas of social life should be ordered.

Social institutions embody all the ideas and **beliefs** of members of a society about how they think their lives should be organized. Any study of social institutions, then, must examine these ideas and beliefs, some of which are dominant and some of which are peripheral or marginal. The *dominant ideas and beliefs* are usually those of the ruling class or the rich and powerful, and tend to be the ones that others also find legitimate. The ideas and beliefs of minorities, the poor, radical groups, and others who are in some way against the mainstream, are also part of the social institutions of a country. However, their ideas and beliefs are not felt to be legitimate by the majority of people in a society and so may be suppressed or only associated with marginalized communities. Institutional ideas and beliefs, both dominant and peripheral, compete with each other over time, bringing about social change.

ACTIVITY 6.1

Think of TWO suitable examples in Caribbean society and culture where groups or individuals going against mainstream ideas and beliefs are 'punished' in different ways by members of society.

ACTIVITY 6.2

If churches are some of the social organizations associated with the social institution of religion, give examples of the social organizations associated with the social institutions of education and the economy.

For example, a dominant idea in the social institution of education is that it is best done in schools, but nowadays there are some people who are *home schooling* their children. They usually come under severe criticism from those holding mainstream views. The social institution of education, like that of the family or religion or the justice system, is made up of many ideas and beliefs about how best to accomplish the tasks of living in society. If someone goes against the mainstream, that person usually suffers some 'punishment' handed down by society – censure, discrimination, ridicule or ostracism. Parents who prefer to school their children at home face continued opposition from other parents, who invariably try to show them that what they are doing is wrong.

How does something as insubstantial as an *idea* or a set of *beliefs* become a basic building block for society? Whether it is rearing the young (family), learning knowledge and skills (education), valuing the next life (religion), or devising the **rights**, duties and obligations of citizens (the justice system), these are all based on ideas and beliefs. Each institution becomes tangible through the *organizations* that members create to fulfil these ideas and beliefs. So in the social institution of religion, members have created various churches, faiths, **sects** and **cults** to translate their ideas about a superior being into tangible forms such as **rituals**, sacred objects, creeds and **dogma**. Non-believers are also a part of the institution because they are denying 'the idea'; they form an opposing or peripheral group. Non-mainstream religions too are part of the social institution of religion, also posing alternative ideas, so that within the institution of religion there are tensions and conflicts between those holding dominant ideas and beliefs and those holding subordinate ideas and beliefs. The ideas and beliefs forming a social institution then become concrete in the society through **social organizations** that reflect these ideas and how they are held.

Socialization is the process through which the cherished ideas and beliefs of one generation become the cherished ideas of the next. Members are born into a society where they are socialized into accepting the social institutions that organize that society. Only if they are born into peripheral groups suffering some disadvantage will the institution seem oppressive. For example, members of the Rastafarian community who have experienced persecution in the past and today are more likely than, say, Methodists to feel that the institutional ideas and beliefs in Jamaican society about religion are oppressive. Even if an institution may be working to someone's disadvantage, as when thousands of students fail every year to obtain full examination credentials on leaving school, members may be so thoroughly socialized into accepting the present system that they do not question how education is organized. Thus, once the dominant ideas about education become concretized in the society through social organizations and the socialization process, it becomes difficult to change them. If change becomes imminent there is always a struggle between those who hold the ideas that have been dominant and those who hold the ideas that are now *becoming* dominant. For example, in our society primary education has always been offered to the masses but secondary education remained accessible only to a few, namely the more affluent classes. The move to offer secondary education to poorer citizens was opposed by those who felt that 'higher' education was a 'privilege' and not a **right**.

Within each social institution there are norms, values, statuses and roles. In the family as a social institution, **value** is placed on nurturing and caring for the young. From that value, **norms** arise – yardsticks and standards that have evolved about how we should act – and so there is a norm in the family about having loving relationships. These norms are carried out through our behaviour; in families parents are motivated by love to assume overall responsibility to feed, clothe, shelter and keep children from harm.

The **status** (or assigned position or location) of 'mother', 'father' or 'grandparent' confers certain **roles** (expectations of behaviour) that each should perform according to the institutional ideas of the family, and these are in keeping with the dominant ideas about values, norms and behaviour in that society. For example, motherhood is a cherished status and there are quite stringent demands made of mothers to conform to a particular role: namely, to always put their children first, to love and cherish them, and to attend to their wants and needs. 'Playing a role' is not a straightforward thing – a person's behaviour associated with a particular status (for example, mother, wife) is largely circumscribed by the institutional beliefs about how such a person should act. If, for example, a mother leaves her children for whatever reason, she will be going against the cherished ideas and beliefs associated with her status and role and thus the norms of behaviour that mothers adopt. She will therefore be criticized and perhaps ostracized. Although the act of leaving may have been necessary, she too will probably suffer personal guilt and remorse in not being able to fulfil such an important role. Rebellion, resistance and adopting a different point of view also come about when people find the institutional ideas that govern their lives irksome, and this tension creates the possibility of change in social institutions.

Social institutions, then, are the fundamental building blocks of any society. They vary from society to society and over time and are built on the ideals that people in that society have about the best ways of accomplishing the tasks of living together collectively. For example, the social institution of the family exists in all societies but different ideas and beliefs may be cherished from one society to another. In Islamic societies, authority, power and final responsibility lie with men. In many white American families today there is more emphasis on both the male and female sharing responsibilities, and in the Caribbean, among the poorer socio-economic groups, women who are heads of households are the main decision-makers. Institutional ideas and beliefs also vary over time. The Hindu family in the Caribbean has traditionally been **patriarchal** but today there is a growing number of Hindu professional women who opt to live alone or seek more equal status within marriage than their mothers had.

ACTIVITY 6.3

1. Match each term in Column A of Table 6.1 with its meaning in Column B.

2. Describe ONE dominant idea or belief and ONE alternative or peripheral idea or belief in the social institution of education in your country.

Table 6.1

Column A		Column B	
1	Social institution	A	A label identifying one's social position or location
2	Social organization	B	Concrete, structured patterns in social life based on ideas and beliefs
3	Status	C	The process by which one learns the rules of society
4	Norms	D	Accepted standards for behaviour in a society
5	Socialization	E	Cherished beliefs and values influencing social life
6	Role	F	A set of behaviours expected of one's status

Summary

Social institutions are said to be the building blocks of the society. The foundations of a society rest on the most valued ideas and beliefs it has about how life should be organized. Ideas and beliefs about how to bring up the young and teach them what they should know form the basis of the institution of education in a country. These ideas and beliefs comprising the institution of education become translated into concrete forms, structures, processes and entities called social organizations, such as the Ministry of Education, schools, parent–teacher organizations, and others. So it is too with religion and the **economy**. In each social institution there are competing ideas and beliefs, and usually those of the more powerful groups are translated into the kinds of social organizations that develop. With the passing of one dominant group, over time the social institutions undergo change and therefore the social organizations to which they give rise also change. However, while change occurs there always persist older dominant ideas and beliefs, so that a social institution is really a site of contest where older and contemporary ideas and beliefs, and those of marginalized groups, continually compete for **legitimacy** in the society.

6.2   THE SOCIAL INSTITUTION OF THE FAMILY

The social institution of the family is found in all societies and represents the cherished ideas and beliefs that people have about rearing children and socializing them into the norms of their society. It encompasses courtship, mating, marriage, child rearing and family life. The social institutions of education and religion interact closely with the family, as both are involved in inculcating certain values in members, but especially in young members, as they are expected to carry on the **traditions** of the society.

Historical context

In studying the evolution of the social institution of the family in the Caribbean we are in fact analysing the dominant and subordinate ideas about families over time. For example:

- The ways that Caribs or Tainos used to nurture the younger members of their society have all but disappeared from mainstream ideas about family today (for example, the **rite** of initiation of young Carib boys into the status of warrior).
- African peoples during the period of slavery preserved family life through an extended network of support, but it was not necessarily based on marriage. Family life centred around the mother (**matrifocal** relationships; see Box 6.1) and the extended **kin** (family connections).
- Europeans brought the dominant idea of the **nuclear family** to the Caribbean – two parents who were legally married with children of that union living together as a household. Their ideas became entrenched in the society through colonial rule yet the majority of the people lived in matrifocal families and continued to create them.
- Indians brought the **extended family** in the form of the **joint household** – different generations occupying one family compound. Theirs is a strongly patriarchal (Box 6.1) family structure with an emphasis on early marriage.

ACTIVITY 6.4

Conduct independent research on ONE of the groups mentioned here and describe at least one example of how its family forms or family practices differ from those in the mainstream.

BOX 6.1 Matrifocal families

Matrifocal families are those where the mother or a maternal figure is the centre (or focus) of the family. The caring and nurturing element provided by the mother is the hub around which the family's activities take place. Many Caribbean families are matrifocal in that whether the union is described as 'common law' or 'visiting', or the family as 'single parent' or even 'nuclear', the mother figure is the person who organizes the family's affairs.

She is the main cook and housekeeper and for the most part works outside the home. Her income, supplemented by that of the other adults in the home, goes towards buying food, household items, school books and 'helping out' other members from time to time. Even though a husband or intimate male companion is present, he tends not to be as deeply involved in the daily activities that take care of the needs of family members. He may, for instance, buy major household items, pay the rent or mortgage, and be a source of authority, but he does not really know the name of the school teacher or when the child has a school function; in fact he may only occasionally attend parent–teacher meetings, go to the grocery or shop for clothes.

In the Caribbean the central place of the mother or grandmother in the family goes on long after a child grows up, marries and moves away from home. She is a confidante and can help to manipulate situations because she is respected and has a certain amount of power within the family (for example, she can give advice and even strong direction in marital disputes, she assists with financial problems, she provides encouragement on a daily basis, and she takes care of her children's children). Members of the family visit regularly and these visits usually coincide with meals – food is a central theme around which the mother figure becomes the key to the whole family.

Matrifocal families are sometimes confused with *matriarchal* families. Some matrifocal families may in fact have matriarchal elements. **Matriarchy** means 'rule of the mother'. It occurs when women are the heads of their families and descent and inheritance are reckoned in the female line. In the Caribbean, issues of descent and inheritance are more likely to be through the father but there are many Caribbean households where a male figure is absent or so marginal to the family that the mother takes care of all the business of the family. However, as a general rule the man is the dominant figure in the family, whether he is there all the time or only some of the time.

As a source of contrast, Indian families are typically described as 'patriarchal'. *Patriarchy* means 'rule by the father' and descent and inheritance are reckoned in the male line. Men lead a privileged existence, resulting in the oppression of women. That being said, within the daily round of the family's affairs, matrifocal elements occur – around nurturing, caring, listening and giving advice. However, when the male members of the family grow up and impose their authority, decision-making may not take the mother's wishes or views into consideration. She becomes a respected but powerless figure.

● All the other smaller groups in the Caribbean today – the Maya, the Amerindian peoples of Guyana, the Javanese, the Chinese, the Syrian–Lebanese communities – have family forms and ways of organizing the family that sometimes differ from the prevailing mainstream institutional ideas about family.

The myth of the nuclear family

The institutional ideas about the family in the contemporary Caribbean reflect a bias towards accepting the *co-residential nuclear family* as the ideal to which we should aspire. During colonial rule **ethnocentric** scholars interpreted the diversity of Caribbean family forms as 'inferior' models of families. The many different kinds of unions – single parents, unwed couples, visiting arrangements, several partners – and the prevalence of matrifocal households were described as 'disorganized families' or 'unstable unions'. From there, the scholars of the colonial era went on to describe Caribbean males as irresponsible and females as promiscuous. Missionaries and colonial authorities thought that the salvation of the Caribbean family lay in enforcing marriage (Barrow, 1996).

The bias towards the nuclear family is at the heart of the negative portrayal of Caribbean families. Accepting the nuclear unit as the norm also meant that there was acceptance of the gender **stereotypes** where men were cast as 'breadwinners' and 'authority figures' and women as 'homemakers' and 'caregivers'. Any other arrangement – for example, a visiting union (see below) – was therefore portrayed as 'disorganized', 'loose', 'unstable' and 'irregular', because the conventional stereotypes could not be applied.

Caribbean family forms

Whilst marriage and nuclear families are more widespread today, Caribbean family forms continue to be extremely diverse – single parents, common-law and visiting relationships, one man with two or more families, children with different fathers residing with their mother as a household, and households headed by grandmothers. Many theories have been suggested to explain why these family forms persist in the Caribbean, when the institutional beliefs are biased towards the nuclear family.

- *African retentions.* Matrifocal households are typical of West Africa, where **polygamy** is commonly practised and a husband accommodates his wives in separate households. The view that Caribbean family forms are based largely on African **cultural retentions** is continually debated. However, this view acknowledges that slavery must have impacted on the traditional African family forms and altered them in some way.
- *Slavery.* Others believe that cultural retentions such as family life could not have survived slavery. The unions and practices that the enslaved were forced to adopt on the plantations influenced the family forms of today. Marriage was rare, cohabitation was irregular and life was unpredictable, so that stable families could not develop. Children remained with their mothers and European laws and **sanctions** discouraged marriage between the races or between enslaved persons.
- *Economic thesis.* Since slavery ended more than 150 years ago, some scholars believe that another theory may be more relevant. The fact that the variety in family forms is found mainly among the poorer classes suggests an economic argument. Their research shows that poor, unemployed or under-employed women are willing to get involved in sexual relationships for very practical reasons such as financial help, especially if they are mothers. Poor, unemployed or under-employed men can only occasionally provide that kind of support. Thus, women tend not to look for one enduring relationship that may become burdensome but seek several successive relationships, which will help to provide the means for the household to survive. The emphasis here on children, and not a stable relationship with a man, is because a mother regards her children not as liabilities but as a possible support network for her in her old age. Critics of the economic thesis point out that today there are extra-marital affairs, single parenthood, premarital maternity, visiting and common-law relationships, and 'outside' children, *at all levels of society*. And even when the **standard of living** rose and there were improvements in the living and working condition of lower socio-economic groups, there was no appreciable increase in marriage or nuclear households (Box 6.2).

BOX 6.2 Theorizing Caribbean family life

The economic argument that poverty is the root cause for the variety of Caribbean family forms assumes that wealthy persons establish mainly nuclear families, one household and monogamous relationships. The reality is that high-status men historically have always maintained 'outside' relationships with women of lower social standing and reared second and even third families, the children of which may benefit from their wealthy fathers' connections in obtaining increased opportunities for study and better-paying jobs. The economic argument is also put to the test because the increasing incomes of Caribbean families have not resulted in major changes in mating and marriage patterns.

R. T. Smith (2004) discusses the complexity of Caribbean family patterns and suggests that while African retentions and the experience of plantation life must have impacted on African Caribbean family forms, the persistence of

such forms today requires a more sensitive interpretation of family life. He too discounts the economic arguments as being the root cause. He feels that the persistence of **gender inequality**, which has not changed over the centuries in any substantial way, may have more explanatory power. He looks at studies describing 'masculinities' in the Caribbean and suggests that what gives men a feeling of power and control is not necessarily marriage and a monogamous household but a life outside of marriage. Thus, men may have outside families and relationships as well as deep commitments to activities and pastimes that take them out of the home for long periods – work, sports, relaxing with friends, playing cards, drinking in bars. This is an interesting analysis and it forces us to examine **gender socialization** in the Caribbean, the processes by which we socialize boys and girls into their respective social roles.

ACTIVITY 6.5

Examine each of the arguments above and suggest an explanation about the origins and variety of Caribbean family forms that seems credible to you.

Caribbean family life

The emphasis on family forms has not been meaningful in understanding Caribbean families so research has now shifted focus to examine how Caribbean families function and what the experience is like of living in such a family (Box 6.3). Caribbean family forms are 'normal' for those living in them. They carry out the same functions as the family anywhere provides for its members – love and belonging, reproduction, food and shelter, socialization and economic support. In addition, for Caribbean people the extensive *network of kin* constitutes 'the family', not the household. The focus on the *composition of the household* (based on the nuclear family as the norm) resulted in Caribbean families being labelled as 'disorganized' and 'irregular'.

The practices of *ritual godparenthood* and *fictive kinship* show the importance of kin in different types of Caribbean family, especially Christian families. Godparents, for example, are chosen to provide another source of support for a child. The family of the godparent (if not already relatives) become as close as kin, thereby extending the network of relatives. In Trinidad a woman may use the term '*my maco mère*' to describe her child's godmother, and the godfather is referred to as '*compère*' – both terms are derived from the French-based **patois**. This extended network can become so large that distinctions are jokingly made between who is 'family' and who are just 'relatives'.

Cooperation, support and caring for family members are normal parts of family life, whether it is lending help in building a house, or taking care of elderly relatives at home. The practice of *child shifting* – leaving a child with another (usually older) relative whilst the parent migrates for work or even moves to a different household – reflects the idea that the extended family is expected to shoulder responsibilities. This emphasis on family responsibility is also seen in land ownership. Individual

BOX 6.3 The sociology of the family

There are three major ways of understanding the social institution of the family in sociology. They are based on different assumptions of what is important and should be valued. Two of the perspectives are *macrosociological* in that they analyse the whole social system in general. The *microsociological* perspective focuses on the daily interaction of people in face-to-face contexts.

- **Functionalism**. This macrosociological perspective looks at the institution of the family in terms of the functions it should play for social stability. Any deviation from what may be thought to be 'normal' is considered a deviant pattern. Caribbean families have been misrepresented by ethnocentric scholars working from a functionalist perspective using the nuclear model as a point of reference for comparison. They have tended to confuse the *functions* of the family with family *forms*. Today we know that families are characterized by variety and they all carry out similar functions.
- **Marxism**. This macrosociological perspective focuses on the *economic* conditions of the family to explain family forms and functions. The nuclear family, they say, fulfils the demands of **capitalism** – two parents isolated from

supporting kin, oppressed by a system where their labour is sold to bring in money which is never enough to climb out of poverty. The variety of Caribbean family forms they see as rooted in the resilience of females in the face of poverty. Marxists also point to how women are exploited in capitalism *and* in the nuclear family. They get mostly low-paying work and their economic contribution to the household is subordinate to the man's. The exploitation the man experiences on the labour market is transferred to his relations at home.

- **The interpretive perspective**. In this microsociological perspective emphasis is put on family life and relationships. The other perspectives do not necessarily see dynamism in the family but interpretive sociologists point to changes in a family over time – the *family cycle*. They are able to show that unions involving a young man and woman go through several phases over time where the needs of the family, and even its composition, change. A family with babies differs somewhat from those with older children and those where the children have left the 'nest'. A family may also be nuclear at one time and extended at another, as when other kin or friends are accommodated, sometimes for years.

ACTIVITY 6.6

Conduct a small survey (choose a wide cross-section of persons) to investigate whether people have biases towards a particular family form and analyse the reasons they offer for their preference.

ownership of land, while important, does not detract from the significance of *family land*. No one member can claim family land and it can be used by various family members according to their needs. This arrangement requires cooperation and the feeling of caring and responsibility for one another, and is quite alien to European notions, which regard 'the family' as 'the household' and value private rather than communal property.

Impact of the family on Caribbean society and culture

The impact of the institution of the family on society and culture can be studied through its effects on individuals, groups and other institutions. The impact of the institutional ideas of family varies both between families and within them. Family child–rearing practices and norms depend on how the members of the family interact and what their notion of 'family' is.

Individuals

While a particular group is said to have a dominant set of ideas and beliefs about family, different individuals in that family will experience these ideas and beliefs differently. This can be illustrated by the example of Indian families, which traditionally have a *patriarchal* structure (for example, in Guyana, Suriname and Trinidad). The men are respected and obeyed, and family and gender relations are based on this 'family hierarchy'. The experience of a girl in such a family is far different from that of the eldest son, who is the heir and is groomed to take over as head of the family. Such a girl in the Caribbean will most likely be educated, even up to the tertiary level, but the relationships in which she lives demand reverence for her father, deference to her brothers and a code of conduct based on obedience and purity. This *authoritarian* structure is sometimes strained and the family can be traumatized when girls find themselves at odds with the family's wishes. This is most likely to happen in issues of courtship, marriage and family life.

Groups

The institutional idea of 'kin' and how it impacts different groups is discussed below, as well as the way institutional ideas about family affect women as a group.

- *African families*. Kin in the extended African family includes uncles, aunts, grandparents, and others related by blood, marriage or fictive kinship ties. These ties extend to people in the **diaspora** who send money back home or sponsor family members to become new migrants in the **metropole**. The idea of kin has a favourable impact on Caribbean people when they are helped but it can be burdensome when someone is expected to help an endless succession of relatives as a matter of course.

- *Muslim families*. In Islam the issues of kinship and the extended family include the practice of polygamy – the custom of having different wives. Within the Caribbean this is not widespread, even in countries with a large Muslim population, because of the dominance of an urban, western bias towards the nuclear model. Even so, polygamous families do occur, increasing the complexity of the notion of kin and the extended family in Caribbean society and culture. Such families come under a great deal of scrutiny by others and they may deliberately restrict their social interaction to avoid the curiosity and criticism of those in the mainstream. In other words, the dominant ideas and beliefs that privilege a nuclear family marginalize those groups who do not follow such norms.

- *Women*. Caribbean women find themselves accommodating to institutional ideas which have locked them into certain roles that have worked to their disadvantage relative to men. They are seen primarily as mothers – the major caregiver and nurturer and the 'natural' person to be the homemaker. Men seldom share this burden equally. For the most part women also work outside the home and then come home to the 'second shift' – domestic chores, taking care of children, supervising schoolwork and becoming up to date with what is going on with everyone. These institutional ideas and how they play out in individual homes are responsible for *gender socialization* – how young girls and boys in families understand the different roles played by men and women and learn to perpetuate them.

Institutions

Ideas about the social institution of the family have an impact on the institution of the family itself, in that dominant and alternative ideas of the family struggle with each other for legitimacy. In addition, the institution of the family has an impact on *other institutions* in society.

- **The family**. The nuclear family has long been privileged as the ideal family and has been at odds with diverse, uniquely Caribbean family forms. Today the institutional ideas of the family are more accepting of different families, even within the traditional nuclear family. For example, one parent with a biological child or children is understood today as a nuclear family. This 'single-parent' arrangement used to be frowned upon and was thought of as the 'breakdown' of the family. Today it tends to be more accepted, along with the 'adoptive' nuclear family (where a man or woman, or both as husband and wife, adopt a child or children). Interestingly, the emphasis on biological relationships becomes problematic in the case of '*in vitro*' families (when the egg or sperm, or both, come from an outside donor), and with 'surrogate parents' (when another woman bears the child for the family). Since the idea of the nuclear family has now expanded, other family forms seem to be more accepted (and even relatively new ones, such as 'same sex families', and 'reconstituted families' – when a man with children marries a woman with children). Thus, terms like 'illegitimate' are no longer valid because the bias favouring marriage is gradually being eroded in the institutional realm, showing that institutional ideas and beliefs undergo change over time.

- **Education**. The social institution of the family impacts on education in many ways. For example, educators continually call for 'parental involvement' because they know that a child's academic success is based largely on the support received at home. But research evidence shows that parents of lower socio-economic status are reluctant to interact with teachers, or visit the school, or supervise homework. Whilst there may be many reasons for this, including the demands of working-class jobs, an inadequate academic foundation, and being intimidated by the attitudes of teachers, it nevertheless remains true that family background is an important factor in educational performance. Thus, the social institution of the family has an impact on the social institution of education.

ACTIVITY 6.7

Describe ONE way in which the social institution of the family impacts the social institution of religion in your country.

Summary

The social institution of the family is the collection of ideas and beliefs that governs the rearing of children and the socialization of young members into society. These ideas and beliefs – dominant and otherwise – are inherited from previous generations and undergo some change over time. They are translated into more tangible forms known as social organizations. Dominant and alternative ideas and beliefs have an impact on the society at the level of individuals, groups and institutions.

6.3   THE SOCIAL INSTITUTION OF EDUCATION

Education is concerned with socializing members of society into the norms, values, knowledge and skills that a society deems important. In its socializing function, education is similar to the family or religion. Education can be formal or informal. In the family one learns many things about living and surviving in the society into

BOX 6.4 The sociology of education

As with the sociology of the family, there are three major ways of understanding the social institution of education in sociology.

- **Functionalist** views of education see it as performing a function or role in the social system so that it enhances social solidarity or integration of the society, and maintains order, for the benefit of all. Functionalist ideas in the social institution of education then emphasize the teaching of *skills* and *knowledge* so that the society can become more efficient and individuals can access social mobility. Functionalism is also concerned that young members of the society learn the *values* and *norms* of the society in which they were born and so a vital part of education is *socialization*. In this perspective, teachers, parents and students *all* have important complementary roles to play if the institution of education is to function effectively.

- **Marxist** sociologists, on the other hand, point to the *inequities* in the educational system and say that it is skewed so that the children of the elites and the talented will succeed. This results in *social reproduction* rather than *social mobility*. Thus, every year thousands fail in the educational system, severely curtailing their chances of attaining the 'good life'. These thousands tend to be the children of the poor. Thus, schools operate generally to maintain the status quo. The provision of school

meals, book grants and bus services to schoolchildren are some measures taken to address the persistent low performance by children of low socio-economic status. While Marxists will agitate for such measures, they also say that they do not address the root causes of *poverty* in the society.

- **Interpretive** sociologists are more interested in the *micro-processes of interaction* that go on in classrooms, corridors, playgrounds, the staff room, and between supervisory staff of the Ministry of Education, teachers and principals. They examine how people create and re-create schooling in certain stable images that are difficult to dislodge, even when they acknowledge that such images are unhelpful. For example, the idea of being 'bright' dominates school life, either explicitly or implicitly. Many decisions are based on who is believed to be 'bright' – by parents, teachers, and students themselves. Interpretive sociologists show that students use these assessments of themselves and others to negotiate their behaviours in school and out of school and examine how it affects their *self-esteem* and aspirations. For example, students who understand that they are not high achievers go to great lengths to preserve their self-esteem by deliberately not studying for a test, by never volunteering to answer questions and by maintaining minimal eye contact with the teacher.

which one was born; that is called *informal education* or *primary socialization*. In its formal aspects education refers to the transmission of knowledge and skills in social organizations such as schools, known as *secondary socialization* (Box 6.4).

Historical context

Under slavery, formal education was largely for the children of the Europeans. While the Spanish were not averse to giving religious instruction to the enslaved, generally speaking their education was discouraged. The planters felt that it would increase their capacity to think about their predicament and thereby stir up unrest. The 1834 Emancipation Act ensured through the *Negro Education Grant* that *elementary schools* would be built throughout the British Caribbean. After **emancipation** the **elites** felt that education would help the ex-slaves to make the transition to a free society. Only the 'elements' were encouraged, however. Reading, writing, arithmetic and a little geography were offered, the Bible was the main text and the curriculum was steeped in English values, songs, poems, stories and customs. *Elementary* (rather than *primary*) education meant that education was not expected to go further. To do otherwise, the planters felt, would disrupt the social order (that is, the system of **social stratification**).

There were, however, a few secondary schools where fees were charged. They were based on English grammar schools and a classical curriculum. Some Caribbean scholars (mostly males) were able to attend British universities such as Oxford, Cambridge and London. They returned as the eminent lawyers, doctors, writers, teachers and scholars who became involved in our efforts at **decolonization.** They moved into labour politics and then on to the formation of political parties. By the 1960s and 1970s most of the former British colonies had become independent, showing that the planters were right – that secondary and further education were likely to foster dissatisfaction and the desire to end oppression.

What were some of the institutional ideas about education from the nineteenth through the twentieth century in Caribbean society and culture?

- Education was a means to **social mobility** for the labouring poor, with parents seeking to 'get education' for their children so that they would be eligible for 'respectable' jobs (not manual labour) and increase their wealth and prestige.
- The elites sought to block the former enslaved and their descendants from accessing secondary education. While elementary education was provided free by the state and for a fee by denominational bodies, it was widely available. Not so secondary education. The general population felt obstructed in their quest for social mobility for their children.
- The secondary curriculum was steeped in European values and customs. African, Indian or Amerindian history and culture were not regarded as legitimate topics for Caribbean children. There was the strong feeling that only deeper understanding of western culture could help us to develop into a modern nation.
- Another idea was that only children who are 'bright' and show aptitude for academic work should be educated at the secondary level and beyond. There was keen competition to enter secondary schools, and even when more schools were built, the transition from primary to secondary schooling was accompanied by *high-stakes examinations* such as the *Common Entrance* (a qualifying examination for secondary education in Jamaica, Trinidad and Tobago and other Caribbean countries).
- As more schools were built, the issue changed from securing a place at the secondary level to accessing a 'good' school. A persistent idea is that 'a better quality of education' is available at the top-ranked secondary schools, usually the higher-achieving, denominational schools. Needless to say, the 'brightest' students are selected by virtue of examination success and the comparison is always made with state secondary schools, seen by many as low achieving and having many kinds of discipline problems.

These dominant ideas in education are translated into the social organizations that frame our education system – for example, schools, examinations, streaming. These customary practices and traditions are derived from the institutional ideas and beliefs about education. For example, students are 'sorted' and 'allocated' to secondary schools based on *selection mechanisms* such as *national examinations*. These examinations are thought to be fair and to give every student an equal chance at accessing the school of his or her choice. In schools students are further *streamed* according to ability. These practices are taken for granted but we should be aware that they stem from the institutional ideas that have become entrenched in the ways we have of organizing education. Ministries of education, examination boards, schools' internal examinations, scholarships, private lessons, placement of students, university matriculation requirements, choosing subjects, what counts as a full certificate – these are all examples of the social organization of education.

The social institution of education is also shaped to a lesser extent by the ideas about education that are less dominant. For example:

- The dominant idea about educating students with *disabilities* is to house such students separately, where they can get attention suited to their needs. The view that mainstreaming such students helps them to better integrate into society is less popular. Hence, in our education system, procedures, mechanisms and the special help they need for mainstreaming are usually absent.
- *Home schooling* is undertaken by families where there is a stay-at-home parent (usually the mother) who teaches her children using the curriculum of the public schools. Such families tend to feel that schools are dangerous places for their children, where they learn much that is undesirable – violence, obscene language, sexual practices, and values that do not privilege the spiritual and moral in everyday life. Some also feel that learning in school is too artificial, producing students who hate learning and are unable to think critically.

ACTIVITY 6.8

Identify ONE idea or belief about education in your country that you can see being implemented in the social organization of education.

The purposes of education

In the aftermath of slavery, the purpose of education (as the colonial authorities saw it) was to inculcate English values and customs so that governing the newly freed people would be easier. But to the former enslaved, education represented a means of social mobility. Without wealth or prestige, their only means of securing the independence of their children from a life of drudgery was through education. This would open up jobs in teaching and in the civil service. This very **instrumental** purpose of education is still with us – to get a 'good' job.

During the twentieth century, the purposes of the social institution of education became more complex. Now that it was mandatory for all children to be educated, there was the institutional idea that since they would not all eventually contribute to the society in equal measure, their education had to be differentiated in some way. This led to practices that selected, sorted and allocated students so that the 'bright' ones followed a different path from the others in seeking to obtain educational qualifications. Tertiary education, especially university education, was viewed in ways similar to how secondary education had been viewed a century earlier. Only the academic elite were expected to go on to universities and thus to jobs guaranteeing them higher socio-economic status as the **intelligentsia** (professional and intellectual) class. The social institution of education thus performs a *differentiating* function on children, categorizing them according to academic ability and placing them in different types of schools. Education, then, organizes the opportunities and life chances of young people.

Another purpose that came to be associated with education was the idea that it could contribute to ***social cohesion*** and harmony – enabling people to come together. This idea is very similar to those of the nineteenth-century colonial authorities. If members of society experience a common curriculum, especially in a culturally plural society, then the likelihood is that they will be socialized into a set of national ideals and values, helping to integrate the society. Achieving social cohesion, harmony, social stability or integration is an enduring purpose of education today.

The idea that education could contribute to **economic development** by inculcating skills and knowledge envisages the production of an educated workforce. A link was thus eventually made between education and national development ('development' or 'economic development' could be achieved by schooling people) – it was a means to an end. Thus many schools were built that were based on this theory of people as **human capital** – that the people of a country should be regarded as a resource just like land or capital, and could be 'upgraded' (through education) to make a meaningful contribution to economic development.

In the last decade of the twentieth century very different purposes were being considered by international bodies such as the United Nations, **postmodern** thinkers in education, and various groups in the society who were committed to helping the poor, the oppressed, the disabled, and others whom the education system had failed. The thinking changed from a human capital perspective to one concerned with how people could be given the *opportunities* to develop themselves and thus become *both the means and ends of development* (a *human development* perspective, see Box 6.5).

Stemming from this human development perspective, the major purpose envisaged by official policy of the various territorial governments for the social institution of education now is ***Education for All*** (the slow learner, the out-of-school learner, the academic failure, the disabled, even the teacher as learner). This is an altogether different idea of what education should be about and it is competing in the institutional realm with the more traditional ideas, those which stem from human capital assumptions and are less inclusive.

ACTIVITY 6.9

Reflect on the social institution of education in your country and identify practices and procedures that aim to develop an inclusive education system.

The impact of education on Caribbean society and culture

Individuals

Education is expected to confer social mobility on individuals. Many thousands of Caribbean students have moved through primary, secondary and tertiary education to secure professional occupations – teachers, lawyers, doctors, engineers, researchers – and others, such as positions in business and private enterprise. Those with lower qualifications have been able to access technical, industrial and clerical jobs. For all these individuals the dominant ideas in the institution of education have 'worked'; they were able to overcome the obstacles (the curriculum, examinations, distractions, family poverty) and secure credentials in order to obtain a suitable job – one where there is job security, the possibility of promotion, and the job is considered 'respectable'.

For many hundreds of thousands of Caribbean people, though, the institution of education has not been enabling. The extreme importance and status placed on

BOX 6.5 Human development and education

This is referred to as a 'postmodern' view of development. Postmodernism is a new wave of thinking that is based on 'deconstructing' previously taken-for-granted notions or perspectives that may have used theories to explain the experiences of people generally. They view these theories as *grand narratives* which subordinate the genuine experiences people have in the haste to portray what is 'normal' or 'typical'.

The **human development paradigm** sees a role for education that is quite unlike the institutional ideas that have historically been dominant in the Caribbean as the social institution of education. Some of its major positions are:

- *A belief in inclusion.* No one should be denied education at any level for any reason, including past failure. This assumes that *education is a right* that all people need to fulfil their potential. Older people and those outside the formal school system are as important as those within the system. Past practices are being transformed into more flexible *delivery modes;* for example, the traditional sixth form programme is now broken down into units taken in different years, and in distance-learning and face-to-face scenarios to accommodate out-of-school learners.
- *The content of the curriculum.* The focus on ethnocentric ideas and organization of knowledge has been balanced with more *indigenous* subject matter such as Caribbean Studies, and Caribbean history re-written from a Caribbean perspective, and the introduction of non-traditional subjects at examination level in secondary schools – Religion, Functional French, Functional Spanish and Communication Studies, all with a Caribbean focus.
- *The pedagogy of the curriculum.* It has been recognized that knowledge is culturally produced so that merely learning it involves learning other people's ideas about what everyone should know. Human development principles ask that the curriculum be *constructed* in interaction with students who bring *their* impressions and experiences of the subject matter to be interrogated by the knowledge from texts and experts. Together with the teacher the students discuss what they know of the subject matter and how that knowledge complements or even contradicts the knowledge in textbooks. This view acknowledges that the learner is powerful and not a passive sponge absorbing content; teaching and learning should be built around what the learner brings to the situation. In order to do this effectively, teachers need to know their learners very well. This means that the *social distance* between teacher and learner has to be scaled down in order to bring more meaningful relationships to the classroom. 'Social distance' implies the traditional boundaries between teachers and students that prevent them from getting to know each other, which tend to be maintained in the interests of 'discipline'. However, in this paradigm the teacher is also a learner.

these credentials have engendered feelings of low self-esteem in those who have failed to acquire them. These individuals are aware, too, that it will hardly be possible to realize their aspirations. Education, then, can demoralize those individuals who fail to achieve. *Under-achievement* may occur for many reasons, namely family poverty, family trauma, teenage pregnancies, drug use, indifferent teaching, learning disabilities, lack of learning readiness, negative experiences of schooling, lack of support, and disillusionment with schooling and disinterest.

Even so, the prevailing dominant ideas often lay the blame for under-achievement on the student, and very little is put in place to re-orient the student who has left school without credentials into ways of getting back on the educational track. Thus, on the whole the institution of education is very competitive, rewarding academic ability and those with the necessary social and cultural resources to meet its challenges. For the individual who fails to achieve, however, there are few options that can begin to lay the foundation for a life that he or she would want.

Groups

Education impacts on the various socio-economic groups differently. Theorists say that schools have a *middle-class bias* and are set up to reward children who have the necessary **cultural capital** to succeed in the academic world. For example, middle-class children are able to 'switch' competently between forms of the local language and the standard, such as between the patois or dialect and Standard English. This ease of switching is attributed to their many and varied experiences, including travel, educational toys, home computers, and involvement in varied extra-curricular activities, where they interact with different groups and in different contexts. They thus bring considerable linguistic competence to their schooling (their cultural capital). Lower-income students tend to be more competent in non-standard forms of the language and have fewer opportunities to use formal language. Thus, written language expressed in the standard for school and examination success is more likely to elude them. The school does not deal specifically with *how* the *first language* of students interferes with their capability in the standard form. The social institution of education therefore confers more challenges on children of lower socio-economic groups than on those of the middle classes.

Institutions

A long historic feature of the social institution of education in the Caribbean is its interaction with the social institution of *religion*. Denominational groups made the first serious attempts to provide education and parents tend to have a preference for religious schools. This has led most of them to become high-demand schools where only the very talented are accepted; thus they are also elite schools. The preference for religion in education does not necessarily mean that parents want their children to be inducted into the denomination of the school. Parents recognize the importance of socialization as well, and they feel that the values taught in a religious school will help their children to become better persons. This preference for religious schools has an impact on state schools, where religion is not emphasized, and this situation forms part of the institutional environment of education in Caribbean countries. State schools therefore tend to be seen as less legitimate than denominational schools in the business of socializing (educating) children.

The dilemma for the state is that it is concerned with **equity** for all and not primarily with promoting religious values. It thus has an obligation to provide for the education of *all* children and cannot select a religious perspective per se (especially in multi-religious contexts) or only focus on the needs of the most talented children. State schools then tend to be of all kinds – high achieving as well as low achieving – because they cater for all.

Summary

The ideas and beliefs that are dominant in the social institution of education lead to the purposes that the social organizations in education try to fulfil. Some purposes have become less dominant over time. In the aftermath of emancipation schooling was for social stability, and while that is still important, socializing the young into the knowledge, skills and values needed by the society, especially for national

---

ACTIVITY 6.10

Identify forms of cultural capital that middle- and higher-income students possess (other than standard language proficiency) which helps them to excel in school.

ACTIVITY 6.11

To what extent are denominational schools in your country held in higher regard than state schools?

development (human capital), has become a major purpose. This is a dominant idea today and struggles with postmodern notions of education for human development. All these ideas and purposes have an impact on individuals, groups and other social institutions in Caribbean society and culture.

6.4 THE SOCIAL INSTITUTION OF RELIGION

Religion is a social institution found in all societies. However, there are wide variations in the institutional ideas and beliefs from place to place and over time. The common idea and belief across most religions is that there are *sacred* elements (a god or a pantheon of gods, symbols, artefacts or scriptures/texts), which should govern our lives, as opposed to the *profane* things of this world – the ordinary. Not all religions believe in a *supernatural* body – Buddhism, Confucianism and Taoism revere great teachers. Religious beliefs generally prescribe ideal behaviours and there is usually some form of collective worship involving rituals and ceremonies, all of which are believed to impact in some way on an *afterlife*. The institution of religion, in societies that are not **theocracies**, has to contend and compete with *secular* values – practices and behaviours which seek to promote non-religious ideas. For example, in a theocracy like Iran education is based on principles from the Koran whilst in a secular state education could be based on values that promote democracy, cooperation and empathy. These may be similar to what religious schools teach, but in secular state schools they are not attributed to the beliefs and practices of any particular religion. This shows that non-religious ideas need not be *anti*-religious.

Sociology studies how the institution of religion is related to social life (Box 6.6), especially how behaviour is shaped through the social organization of religion. We see these forms of organizations in the rituals of attending Sunday services and Sunday schools, in participating in ceremonies such as baptisms, and those for the dead, in listening to church services on radio, television and in outdoor meetings, in being members of church groups, in undergoing special *rites* such as going on a pilgrimage or fasting, and a host of other customary and traditional ways of demonstrating commitment to religious beliefs. One major example of the social organization of religion (or the social organization of education) in the Caribbean is *denominational schooling* (see p. 182).

Historical context

The ideas of the elites and the ruling classes dominate the social institution of religion but there are also less dominant ideas in alternative and minority religions. The history of the social institution of religion in the Caribbean, like the history of the family or education, is largely a story about the struggle between the dominant ideas of the Europeans and those of the colonized peoples. Both change and continuity are evident in this brief, historical description of the social institution of religion in the Caribbean.

Through **syncretism** and **hybridization** the subjugated Caribbean peoples, mainly Amerindians and Africans, re-created the social institution of religion (see Chapter 3). The act of conversion is an interpretive one and subject peoples, whilst adopting the religion of the European, hybridized many of its forms and practices

BOX 6.6 The sociology of religion

Religion is the social institution that attempts to answer some of the 'unanswerable' questions that members of a society ask about the nature of being, death, the meaning of life, coping with distressing circumstances, the possibilities of a life after death, and a relationship with a supernatural being or life force. All societies have developed religion as a social institution in some way and offer varying explanations for some or all of these questions. Sociologists analyse the role that religion plays in society (how it impacts on members and other social institutions) as well as how the society impacts on religion.

- *Functionalist perspectives*. The emphasis in this perspective is on how religion functions in a society to preserve *order* and *social cohesion*. It is an optimistic view that sees participation in religious activities and submerging oneself in the values, attitudes and beliefs of the particular religion, particularly if it is a mainstream religion, as engendering unity and social solidarity. Functionalism sees religion as helping members to feel a sense of belonging, to provide support and guidance, and to create a community of believers through ritual and practices that reinforce commitment to the group. In so doing, members commit to the status quo and the preservation of society.

- *Marxist perspectives*. On the other hand, Marxism shows the 'dark side' of religious commitment. Marxists feel that religion prevents people from really experiencing the inequities, discrimination and oppression that are inherent in how society treats with the lower social classes, women and other disadvantaged groups. The solace, comfort and afterlife orientation that religion offers keeps people from resisting the miseries of this life. Religion becomes a 'drug' or an 'opiate' to help them endure their problems stoically and look for a reward in the next life. This works efficiently to entrench the elite class and perpetuate their dominance in the society. Religion is an illusion.

- *Interpretive perspectives*. In this micro-sociological perspective, religion is understood as a subjective experience. Emphasis is on understanding how an individual or a group constructs their ideas of god, and their relationship with god and/or a church, how they choose what to believe and what not to believe, how they relate to other religions, and how belief or non-belief affects their daily lives and actions. For example, while there may be a drop in church attendance generally, many non-church-goers speak of their personal belief in a supernatural force or forces and feel strongly that weddings, for example, should take place in a religious setting. They may even buy religious/spiritual books, tapes and music. Thus, there are many individuals who interpret and create their own personal forms of religion and spiritual life, adding variety to the social institution of religion.

ACTIVITY 6.12

For Antigua, Jamaica and Barbados conduct independent research to find out what the major religious denominations are. Organize the information in a table showing percentages of the population in different religions. What are the major patterns evident?

with their own traditions and creations. This began under slavery and has continued to the present day.

Caribbean people did accept membership into one of the major religions of Europe, or one of the smaller *Protestant* or *Nonconformist* denominations, who came later as missionaries (Box 6.7), so that varieties of Christianity are deeply **entrenched**. Each country has a different heritage of ideas about religion – for example, in countries where the Spanish and French were dominant the *Roman Catholic Church* has the greatest following (the Hispanic Caribbean, Trinidad, Grenada, St Lucia, St Vincent, Martinique, Guadeloupe, Dominica and Belize). In other countries a combination of Protestant religions are dominant, the pattern differing in each territory.

Religion is influenced by the stratified nature of the society. The upper classes (namely, Europeans, coloureds and some Africans) attended mainstream European churches and continue to do so. 'Dual membership' – formal allegiance to one of the European religions whilst participating in the rituals and ceremonies of a syncretic or Afro-Christian form such as Pocomania – was more likely among the poorer groups. Today religion continues to be a social class issue – there are some

BOX 6.7 Varieties of Christianity

The first European religion that was brought to the New World was *Roman Catholicism*. Not only Spain but virtually all of Europe was Roman Catholic in the fifteenth century. However, events in England during the reign of Henry VIII (1491–1547) prompted a breakaway movement and the founding of the *Anglican Church* (the *Church of England* or *Established Church*) with the monarch as the head. This is the dominant religion in England today. Continuing criticism of the Roman Catholic Church in England and other European countries prompted a movement known as the *Reformation* and many other *Protestant* churches came into being. A Protestant is someone who rejects the authority of the Roman Catholic Church. Anglicanism is a Protestant religion.

In England these other groups were known as *Dissenters* as they did not approve of the monarch being head of the Church or the beliefs and practices of the Established Church. These *Nonconformist* religions preferred a simpler, less hierarchical structure to their church and were called 'chapelgoers' because of this. Some nonconformist denominations are Presbyterianism, Methodism, Calvinism, the Baptists, Quakers, Moravians, Episcopalians, Unitarians, and others. All these religions are Protestant religions, meaning that they reject Roman Catholicism.

religions (Orisha, Shango, Spiritual Baptists – see Chapter 3) where few members belong to the elite class.

In the aftermath of emancipation there was a full flowering of syncretic religions that first had their genesis under slavery – *Myal, Revivalism, Pocomania, Santeria* and others, as well as more distinctive African forms such as *Shango* and *Vodun* (see Chapter 3). Grassroots religions were strong but their practice made the colonial authorities uneasy. The loud bellringing and preaching of the **Spiritual** (or **Shaker**) **Baptists** were believed to be ways of invoking *obeah* (the occult), long outlawed in the colonies because of its association with slave resistance. Laws were passed forbidding Spiritual Baptist ceremonies in Trinidad, and in St Vincent the Anti-Shaker Ordinance of 1912 allowed the authorities to invade and break up Shaker ceremonies and imprison its members. The institution of religion, then, has always held strong resistant elements that were opposed to **colonialism**. Under the outer guise of a Christian religion, Africans resisted European mainstream beliefs and world views by celebrating life and death with drumming, singing, chanting, shouting and invoking the spirit world. They took religion out of the churches into places they considered sacred near rivers, in the forests and by the sea. The theme of resistance was so strong that the Spiritual Baptists never dwindled in membership; today in Trinidad and Tobago 30 March is a national holiday – *Spiritual Baptist Liberation Day*.

Resistance also created another distinctive world view in the form of a grassroots religion, **Rastafarianism**, formed in the 1930s in Jamaica. Its roots lay in Myal and Revivalism traditions and in the philosophy of **Marcus Garvey** of a black god and a return to Africa (Chevannes, 1994). It is a **millenarian movement** as Rastafaris believe that *Jah* will personally reign on Earth, in Ethiopia, in the 'end times', and save them, his chosen people, bringing an end to their pain and suffering. Rastafarianism has since spread throughout the world and calls for introspection about our absorption into mainstream capitalist values, the white man's world (Babylon). Today the followers of syncretic faiths and African religions tend to be predominantly those of the lower socio-economic classes, showing the tendency of the poorer sectors of the community to find meaning, comfort and solace in religions that are alternatives to those of the upper classes.

In the nineteenth century the influx of indentured labour brought many thousands of **Hindus** to Trinidad, Guyana and Suriname. In Trinidad the Hindus belong to different organizational sects such as the *Sanatan Dharma*, the *Arya Samaj*, the *Kabir Panth Associations*, and others, all of whom own schools today. Many Hindus converted to Presbyterianism owing to the efforts of the **Canadian Mission**, who went as missionaries into the sugar estates in the nineteenth century and founded primary and secondary schools as well as a teachers' college. They offered a route to social mobility and a profession based on becoming Christian. One of the institutional ideas here is that Christianity could be an asset in 'bettering yourself', especially if your parents were illiterate immigrant workers speaking a foreign language. Later on, by the 1930s there was opposition from Hindu and Muslim organizations, which criticized the Canadian Mission for taking advantage of a natural desire to achieve social mobility by 'forcing' people to adopt Christianity.

Muslims, in much smaller numbers than Hindus, were also imported from India as indentured labourers. While some were converted by the Canadian Mission, they have maintained a vibrant presence largely through the founding of primary and secondary schools. Today, this traditional Indian Muslim community is being widened to include African converts, forming black Muslim groups. The Muslim community in Trinidad is fractured into several organizations, all of whom, like the Hindus, own and manage schools – the *Anjuman Sunnat-ul-Jamaat* (*ASJA*), the *Trinidad Muslim League* (*TML*), the *Tackveeact ul Islamic Association* (*TIA*) and the *Jamaat-al-Muslimeen* (a black Muslim group, responsible for the 1990 uprising). As a result of the militancy of the black Muslims and other fundamentalist Islamic groups, the Muslim community now receives national attention in Trinidad and Tobago out of all proportion to its numbers (5.8 per cent of the population).

Coming from the US in the latter years of the twentieth century, a surge of religious ideas have had an impact on the institution of religion in the Caribbean. Evangelical, Fundamentalist and Pentecostal faiths have been around for over a hundred years but today they are drawing more and more converts from Roman Catholicism and from mainstream Protestant or Nonconformist churches. **Fundamentalists**, a branch of evangelicals who base their beliefs on a literal interpretation of the Bible, believe that the 'end times' are at hand. Faiths such as the *Assemblies of God*, the *Church of God* and *Church of the Open Bible* therefore emphasize saving souls and being 'born again'. Members participate actively in services and outreach activities and commit to traditional moral codes. Because they tend to be small congregations, there is intense personal contact (engendering solidarity) as they condemn the behaviours of an increasingly secular world.

The **Pentecostals** believe that the Holy Spirit intervenes in emotional prayer sessions to bring about healing and communicates through prophesy and 'talking in tongues'. Fundamentalists, though, are wary of a way of arriving at truth that does not derive from a literal Bible statement. Fundamentalism tends to be attractive to the lower classes because its morally certain position acts as a buffer against the uncertainties of daily living. And Pentecostals too come from the same social class – their religious experience is a deep emotional catharsis insulating them from daily hardship and struggle. Whilst conversion to Fundamentalist and Pentecostal faiths represented resistance to colonialism in the rejection of mainstream Christian

ACTIVITY 6.13

List some of the purposes
of the social institution of
religion in society today.

churches, all of which have some connection with Britain, today these religions tend to uphold the status quo. Their rejection of the secular world and emphasis on personal morality and salvation call for an inward focus, though some do speak out and try to change public morals and values.

Impact of religion on Caribbean society and culture

The previous sections have already provided many examples of how the social institution of religion developed and impacted various groups and other social institutions in the Caribbean. This section adds to that by discussing some other ways in which religion has an impact on individuals, groups and institutions today.

Individuals

Religion can be a source of oppression to individual women. A woman in a mainstream religion, such as Roman Catholicism, plays a conservative role where religious laws affect her reproductive health (birth control, abortion). Even in resistance movements, such as the Rastafari, a woman is relegated to traditional roles. And in Islam, whether by custom or Koranic law, individual women find that their dress, behaviours and aspirations are prescribed. This may be more true in black Muslim communities or fundamental Islamic sects than in the typical Indian Muslim family in the Caribbean, which generally has more relaxed views than those involved in the resurgence of Islam worldwide.

Groups

Religion can help a group to maintain solidarity and keep its traditions alive in the face of **globalizing** western culture. The Garifuna of Belize continue some of their West African traditions such as the Dugu ceremony or Feasting of the Dead, where they commune with ancestral spirits. This and other practices distinguish them and preserve their cultural uniqueness in a society that is increasingly permeable to North American based media, 'televangelism' and other fundamentalist groups such as the *Mennonites*.

Institutions

What people think is right, fair or just (that is, the justice system) is shaped to a large extent by their religious beliefs. In an Islamic society capital punishment may be relevant for more than just unlawful killing. However, in Caribbean societies, where capital punishment is only sometimes enforced, Islamic groups may feel that what they believe is right cannot be imposed in this context, only in places where Koranic law prevails. Similar dilemmas occur with other groups whose religious beliefs are at odds with mainstream ideas about what is fair and right; for example, Jehovah's Witnesses refuse blood transfusions even when it may save lives. The central tenet of the ***Baha'i*** faith is that human beings belong to one race and one religion and they are working towards unification in one global society. As a result Baha'is find it extremely complicated to function in a *nation*-state. For example, they cannot use their calendar based on 19 months of 19 days, or work for nine of the eleven holy days of the year, or find a way of bringing about one world government. Thus, what people perceive to be right, just and fair (the justice system) is influenced by their religious background.

Another institutional effect of religion is its potential to generate conflict. Peaceful co-existence amongst the plurality of religions found in Caribbean countries is constantly threatened by those institutional ideas that do not tolerate other religions, or recognize only Christian denominations, or privilege the religion of the elites or dominant groups. There is also within-group diversity where fundamentalist sects and distinct groups (for example, the Charismatic Movement in the Roman Catholic faith) seek a 'purer' religious life. This diversity and its potential for conflict have prompted the institution of religion to look for some common ground on which the various denominations can communicate. Inter-religious organizations such as the Caribbean Council of Churches have been formed to mediate conflicts and there has been a definite press towards **ecumenism.** Even countries that have not been religiously diverse in the past are now becoming so (for example, Barbados), with the latter-day migrations of Indians from India and Guyanese Indians. These developments represent change in the institution of religion.

Summary

Religion has been deeply intertwined in the lives of Caribbean people from the times of our early ancestors, through slavery (when religion was discouraged), to the present day, where a variety of religions flourish. We see 'living history' today in how the religions continue to be socially stratified. We also see changes to the social institution of religion, with more aggressive religious groups gaining converts, but at the same time there is a growing **secularization** of the society. These aspects of continuity and change impact Caribbean people at the level of individuals, groups and social institutions.

6.5 THE SOCIAL INSTITUTION OF THE JUSTICE SYSTEM

The social institution known as the justice system refers to the ideas and beliefs in a society about *protecting and preserving the rights and obligations of citizens.* Stemming from those ideas and beliefs in the institutional realm are more tangible practices and procedures known as the 'social organization of justice', namely the political, legal and judicial framework in a country.

The *political framework* is based on the idea that citizens entrust power to their representatives to make decisions that defend and uphold their rights, freedoms and interests. The *legal framework* develops a system of laws that are fair to all parties. Enshrined in the **constitution** of a country are the basic rights and freedoms of citizens, the political principles on which the nation-state is built, as well as the powers and rights of governing bodies. The **judiciary** implement the laws by ruling on conflicts over rights, fairness and justice. (In a world without conflict there would be no need for the justice system, or the idea of rights; see Box 6.8). Ideas and beliefs about who is a citizen, and what is fair to whom, have changed over time. And although the constitution of a country guarantees our basic rights today, other ideas and beliefs that also comprise the justice system continue to entrench inequities, discrimination and injustice. So, as in all other social institutions, there are dominant, alternative and dissenting ideas and beliefs.

BOX 6.8 The idea of rights

The notion that all human beings have basic rights by virtue of being human has only recently become enshrined in international and national laws. The history of the Caribbean shows us all too well that Europeans did not regard others as having the same rights as they did, and other groups (Coloureds, Indians, Africans) did not regard each other as equals. The necessity and urgency of guaranteeing and protecting people's human rights came to international attention during and after the second world war. This war caused destruction and mayhem on a global scale and was based on the attempted genocide of the Jews. The United Nations (UN) was created out of world opinion to try to prevent human rights atrocities occurring on such a scale ever again. The 1948 *Universal Declaration of Human Rights (UDHR)* has guided the principle of ensuring justice for individuals and groups by guaranteeing them certain basic rights ever since.

Most Caribbean countries have patterned their constitutions at independence on recognizing the basic human rights described in the UDHR. These include the right to protection from violence, to freedom of belief and assembly, to vote and run for public office, and to be equal before the law. There are also *economic and social (or welfare) rights* such as equality for certain vulnerable groups (women, children and minorities), full access to employment opportunities for all groups, guaranteed safety at the workplace, freedom to participate in trade unions and collective bargaining, eligibility for social assistance, and the enjoyment of an adequate standard of living, health care and education. The justice system has accepted these as rights that must be preserved. Protecting these rights is seen as just and fair.

The protection of human rights is also an issue of social stability. History shows us that when people are treated unjustly and unfairly, the usual consequence is resistance, violence and social and economic dislocation. Caribbean history is one of centuries of oppression, **genocide**, rebellions, revolutions and resistance at all levels. Guaranteeing previously oppressed groups their basic human rights is one way to maintain peace and stability. However, it is one thing to enshrine human rights in the constitution, quite another to protect and preserve these rights in daily social interaction. Where conflicts occur it is the responsibility of the political directorate and its legal arm – the judiciary – to uphold the constitution. If this does not happen, escalating crime, civil unrest and disturbances are likely to occur. One way of understanding the increasing incidence of crime in Caribbean countries is to investigate the extent to which criminal groups enjoy a similar level of human, social and economic rights as other citizens.

The historical context

The justice system in the Caribbean evolved out of a history of colonialism, resistance and independence. The Europeans came as *conquerors* and this shaped the dominant ideas about rights in the society. As *captives,* the native peoples were treated so harshly that the Spanish priests Montesinos and Las Casas sought help from the Crown for their protection. In 1512 the Laws of Burgos allowed for the **encomienda** system but also made provisions for the indigenes to be fairly treated and converted to Christianity.

These rights were virtually ignored by the Spanish colonists, largely because they were far away from the seat of the empire in Spain, and the political and judicial systems in the colonies were based on the dominant idea of the native as an enslaved person. Rather it was the Spanish monarchs, the Dominican friars and certain intellectuals in Spain who held alternative views of the indigenous inhabitants as persons *with* rights. Thus, laws may exist but if the people in power do not believe that those laws are in their own interests, then they are not likely to be enforced.

Similarly, under slavery African people did not have any rights; they were 'chattel' or property, and Europeans, by virtue of being white, were responsible for them and held all power over them. In the Spanish colonies the *Siete Partidas* and in the French colonies the *Code Noir* each laid down laws relating to the enslaved population, but these were mainly concerned with the conditions of being a slave, and the punishments that were to be meted out for different crimes, including trying to escape. There were provisions made for housing, clothing and feeding the slaves but this was largely left up to the good judgement of the owners. In the British colonies the Assemblies, made up of the planter class, enacted laws to control, subdue and coerce the slaves. Whether or not legal codes existed, the rights of the enslaved were not protected because, again, the dominant ideas of the period saw the African as an inferior being to the European. What was regarded as 'justice' or 'fairness' did not extend to the African population. In fact, the judicial system sought to uphold the rights and privileges of the planter class.

In this case the political, legal and judicial systems were in close agreement. The very social fabric depended on this solidarity. The prosperity of the planters and the sugar-producing colonies were heavily dependent on enslaved labour. There would be strong sanctions against any person or group attempting to introduce alternative ideas about freedom, or even education, for Africans. The system of social stratification reflected rigid distinctions between blacks, coloureds and whites, reinforcing the dominant ideas and beliefs on which the political, legal and judicial systems depended.

However, there were always alternative ideas and resistance movements that could threaten the stability of the colonies. Religious groups, particularly nonconformist missionaries, sought to woo the planters into giving the Africans some religious instruction and the rudiments of reading and writing. They were largely unsuccessful during slavery but afterwards, while still a rigidly stratified colonial society, the Baptists (in particular in Jamaica and Guyana) led protests for better living and working conditions. Along with the Quakers, Moravians and Methodists, they were bent on restoring some of their *human* rights to the African population, rights that apparently did not come with them being declared 'free'. The ideas that led to emancipation and became enshrined as law had not appreciably modified the political or judicial systems in the colonies because the planter class still saw the Africans as inferior beings.

The watchwords of the *French Revolution* (1789) – *liberty, equality* and *fraternity* – spread throughout the Caribbean, particularly the francophone Caribbean, providing another set of alternative ideas in the justice system. In St Domingue (Haiti) the Free Coloureds and slaves mobilized to fight for freedom, resulting in the 1791 *Haitian Revolution* (see Box 4.8) and the establishment of the first independent country in the Caribbean, the Black Republic of Haiti (1804). Political upheaval in France provided the background of confusion as well as the powerful ideas about freedom that disrupted the tight link between the political, legal and judicial systems in Haiti at the time. A succession of black and mulatto leaders in Haiti enacted laws guaranteeing the freedom and equality of all citizens regardless of colour, race or condition. The justice system was now grounded in overturning prejudices based on white supremacy, but it still, ironically enough, tended to privilege the coloureds (*gens du coleur*) over the black masses. The militaristic footing on which the society was organized after 1804, to preserve the revolution, also contributed to a number of dictators. The rights of the Haitian people, despite being enshrined in law, were ignored by the political elite, who controlled the judiciary. The social institution of the justice system came to be dominated by fear and intimidation – very similar to the Caribbean under slavery and colonialism.

BOX 6.9 Injustice

Today in the Caribbean the justice system is based on a country's constitution and the political regimes through which the people are represented, and through which their rights are actually preserved. For the most part these are **democratic** organizations and practices. However, the political elites tend to wield tight control of the legal and judicial systems, so much so that lower socio-economic groups and other ethnic groups feel excluded.

For example, in the justice system of multiracial Caribbean countries, particularly Guyana, Suriname and Trinidad, political parties for the most part are based on racial affiliation. The supporters of the party in power and their detractors are locked in a perpetual debate about the wisdom of either one forming a government. This conflict cannot be resolved because it is based on **discriminatory** ideas about race. The political party in power tends to choose from among its own ranks to fill important posts and thus decisions about what is fair, right and just are sometimes made (or perceived to be made) based on racial characteristics. In other Caribbean countries where there may not be racial tensions, schisms may be no less deep.

Skin colour, social class and traditional political allegiance are points of reference in awarding jobs, rewards and responsibilities.

Commentators on this state of affairs in the Caribbean have tried to show that whilst we have inherited political, legal and judicial systems from Britain, we do not necessarily 'work' them as democratic systems. From the adjustments made to **constituency** boundaries, the drawing up of electoral lists, the planning of political campaigns, to procedures for elections and voting, there are major elements of fraud and irregular practices. Thus, we have inherited or adopted a centuries-old justice system from abroad, but how we administer justice differs from the rhetoric of the system. The administration of justice may depart from what is fair, right and just to what is good for the party in power, the supporters of the party, and perhaps business interests. The many complaints from individuals about their experiences in the political, legal and judicial systems usually centre on unfair treatment; for example, a harsher justice meted out to the poor and the powerless in the society.

In the rest of the Caribbean emancipation occurred after 1834. The coloureds and blacks gradually won some representation in the colonial assemblies, though the dominant ideas continued to privilege the British elites. At independence, most Caribbean countries adopted some variant of the *Westminster Model* of government. To attain political freedom we sought to remove ourselves from British control, but as independent countries our political, legal and judicial systems are based on British custom and practice. While that is not necessarily a negative comment, the debate about whether the *Caribbean Court of Justice* can deliver as fair and as just decisions as the (British) Privy Council shows the continuing ambivalence with which we regard European versus local creations. Some believe that whilst we have adopted the outer trappings of the British system of justice, we 'work' it in the interests of political parties and certain ethnic groups (Box 6.9).

The evolution of the justice system in the Caribbean shows a strong ideal towards ensuring basic human rights for the mass of the people – freedom of expression, of assembly, to own and protect private property, to have a fair trial, to vote and run for public office, to be guaranteed a basic level of social and economic welfare. Yet Caribbean societies continue to be stratified according to race, colour and ethnicity in ways that are very reminiscent of colonial society. Social stratification implies that those in the lower socio-economic groups, and who outnumber people in other income brackets, are not benefiting from the rights and freedoms enshrined in the constitution, compared with other groups. There are therefore entrenched inequities in the social institution of the justice system that the transition from emancipation to independence has not been able to address meaningfully (Box 6.10).

BOX 6.10 The sociology of the justice system

There are three main sociological perspectives on the justice system.

- *Functionalism* is the sociological perspective that dominates social life, in that most people, without even knowing it, subscribe to its ideas and beliefs. This happens through socialization as our values, norms and behaviours become prescribed for us when growing up. Our values, norms and behaviours eventually form a 'world view', or an understanding of what is real or what is valuable, and we use these ideas and beliefs to judge and assess others. Functionalists understand the justice system as important in preserving *social order* or *social stability*. Thus, being fair and equitable in our dealings with each other should ensure that discontent is minimized in the society. The problem with this view is that it tries to 'tack on' fair and just practices to a system with entrenched inequities. Poverty is a good example. One way of addressing this problem is to provide 'safety nets' for the poor – free health care, school books, meals and transport for schoolchildren. However, these legal entitlements cannot change the face of poverty. Political power continues to reside with the elites and the poor are the ones most often incarcerated by the judicial system.

- *Marxism* begins with the view that the economy (another social institution) is the reason for entrenched inequities. *Capitalism* stratifies the population according to who owns *the means of production* and who only have their labour to sell. The *surplus value* that capitalists acquire widens the social and economic gap between the groups. Marxists see society as organized into the **superstructure** (the social institutions) and the **substructure** (the economy). Those who wield power in the social institution of the economy are also the groups whose ideas, beliefs and interests are dominant in the superstructure. This Marxists refer to as the *social relations of production* because there tends to be differentiation in every social institution between the poor and the wealthy, whether it is religion, health, education, the family, or the justice system. For example, wealthy people or those with power in the society, and their relatives, seldom receive the full brunt of the law when caught wrongdoing. They are able to pay for the most expensive legal help and sometimes the police are intimidated by their rich and powerful captives to the point where they may be given special privileges. Not so the poor. In this view, then, the poor have rights equal to those of the rich for equity before the justice system, but that seldom occurs because the poor are for the most part without power in capitalist societies.

- **Interpretive sociology** studies microlevel processes of human interaction. It emphasizes the perspectives of people as they act out on a daily basis what ideas and beliefs they have about the justice system in which they live. If they are victims of a crime they may not call the authorities if they believe that the police are reluctant to venture into their neighbourhood. There is a recognition that their rights are being denied them because of where they live (and this most often means poor neighbourhoods). Similarly, females who are victims of sexual abuse often cannot face the criminal justice system because of the judgemental, insensitive, and sometimes sceptical attitudes of the officials they meet. If the justice system is 'gendered' in this way, then clearly the rights of these women are not being preserved and protected. Interpretive studies of the justice system then focus on how people are experiencing living in a society as citizens but not enjoying the same rights as others, and what strategies they use to cope with, or overcome, the inequities.

Impact of the justice system on Caribbean society and culture

We have inherited dominant ideas from European systems of justice and merged them with our own ideas of rights earned through resistance and opposition, as well as our understanding of the cultural diversity found amongst Caribbean people. Our constitutions therefore reflect the ideals we have for justice. However, these ideas impact us in different ways, according to our social location.

Individuals

The law actually protects an individual's right to have several wives as his religious custom, though he may only register one such marriage legally. This is an example of the way the law accommodates itself to cultural differences. It becomes **customary law** and individuals find that the justice system impacts them differently according to whether they follow **statute laws** or customary laws. (Statutes are enacted through legislation.)

Individuals may also find that their rights to wear the *hijab* or dreadlocks to school are upheld by the legal system though not necessarily by the educational institution they attend. At the same time, the law does not uphold a female's right to exercise personal choice about having an abortion – it is an illegal act. Thus while your right to religious dress and hairstyle is upheld, if you are a female, your right to make certain decisions about your own body is pre-empted by the law. In this case, the law sees itself as the guardian of the rights of the unborn.

Groups

In our constitutions, our fundamental law, young people are subject to certain restrictions based on age. Below the age of 18 a person is a minor and the responsibility of someone, and cannot vote or drive. There are also laws and conventions, for example, ***The Convention on the Rights of the Child***, that protect the rights of minors. These restrictions and special provisions for protection are based on dominant ideas in the justice system: before the age of 18 young persons are not mature and responsible enough to make good decisions about citizenship and personal well-being. So, to be fair and just these rights have to be denied until they come of age.

The system of compulsory retirement at age 65 years is another way in which age is used to legally discriminate between different groups. This time, however, it is not that retirement is considered to be just and fair for the elderly but that young, newly qualified persons need to be able to find jobs. That can only happen if an age ceiling is put on employment. Increasingly there are calls to discontinue this practice, because experienced and mature people, who have much to contribute, are being shunted out of their jobs, not because of failing health, but because they have attained a certain number of years. This is ***ageism***, discriminatory practices based on age, and deeply entrenched in the dominant ideas of the social institution of justice.

ACTIVITY 6.14

Suggest ONE way of ensuring more jobs for young people, other than the compulsory retirement of older people.

Institutions

Today domestic crimes such as abuse, violence and harassment, even among close family members, are accepted in court as valid claims for justice. This has come about because of the need to protect and preserve the rights of women in families dominated by patriarchy. However, we are tending to find a pattern where the legal and judicial frameworks devised to assist women in abusive relationships are now being manipulated against men. In the ***Family Court*** it tends to be the norm that women are routinely awarded child custody and child support laws are strictly enforced, even when the father is unable to pay, resulting in jail time. There is an unwillingness now to go against women's allegations lest one be seen as not 'politically correct'. In its attempts to ensure fairness between the genders in the family, the justice system has to some extent succeeding in perpetuating stereotypes and myths of both women and men.

Caribbean countries have become signatories to international conventions, declarations and treaties, such as The Convention on the Rights of the Child (1989) and The Convention on the Elimination of All Forms of Discrimination Against Women (1979). And so we have had to enact national legislation to prohibit atrocities and discriminatory practices, and to allow international bodies to scrutinize and criticize our level of compliance. The reports of international organizations, such as the Human Rights Committee and Amnesty International, publicly state a country's track record in upholding basic human rights and the civil and economic rights of its citizens. The social institution of justice, then, is enmeshed in international principles of what is right, fair and just, and this brings us closer to norms being observed across the world about the state's responsibilities to its citizens. Thus, whilst discriminatory practices and exclusion continue to be strongly entrenched in Caribbean societies, there are competing ideas about what is just, right and fair. The political, legal and judicial systems are increasingly being called upon to adjudicate in conflicts between these competing ideas about 'rights'.

Summary

The social institution of the justice system in the Caribbean evolved out of a history of oppression, the rights of members of society being won through violence, legal battles and the dismantling of colonialism. However, the development of fairness and justice in the political, legal and judicial systems has been influenced by the socially stratified nature of the society that has served to entrench discriminatory practices. Today these dominant ideas are competing against powerful global commitments calling for safety nets for the poor, a more inclusive education system, and a reduction in all forms of discrimination. The social institution of the justice system, then, is now the arena where dominant ideas that have long been entrenched by the powerful political elite and their supporters struggle with alternative ideas that are being pushed by international human rights organizations and their local adherents.

WRAP UP

Social institutions in the Caribbean, such as the family, education, religion and the justice system, are really strongly entrenched ideas we have as a society about how to rear children and teach them, how to think about our relationship to the divine and how to develop fair and just systems. All these institutions have undergone changes over time as the society developed from colonial to independent countries. While the dominant ideas within each social institution became concrete as social organizations, there continue to be marginal and less popular ideas that challenge the status quo.

PRACTICE TESTS

Structured response

1 (a) Distinguish between a social institution and a social organization. (2 marks)
   (b) Identify ONE social organization and show how it is related to a social institution. (2 marks)
2 (a) List THREE social organizations related to the institution of the family. (3 marks)
   (b) Describe ONE of the major functions of the family that is found in all societies. (2 marks)
3 (a) Describe TWO ways in which the social institution of the family interacts with the social institution of education. (4 marks)
   (b) Account for ONE example of continuity in the institution of the family. (2 marks)
4 Describe TWO ways in which the social institution of religion impacts the social institution of education. (6 marks)
5 (a) Explain what is meant by 'religion'. (3 marks)
   (b) Describe ONE characteristic of religion in Caribbean societies. (3 marks)
6 (a) Using examples, explain how a social institution prescribes the behaviour of members of society. (4 marks)
   (b) Suggest ONE reason that might account for members going against the behaviours prescribed by society. (2 marks)
7 (a) Identify TWO ways in which members of a religion may be discriminated against because of the practices and beliefs of their religion. (2 marks)
   (b) Suggest reasons for the TWO examples of discrimination mentioned above. (2 marks)
8 (a) Describe what is meant by the 'justice system' in a country. (2 marks)
   (b) Account for TWO influences on the development of the justice system in the Caribbean. (4 marks)
9 (a) Define the term 'social stratification'. (2 marks)
   (b) Explain how social stratification impacts on the justice system in the Caribbean. (4 marks)
10 Describe ONE way in which the justice system impacts on each of the following in Caribbean society and culture. (6 marks)
   (a) Individuals
   (b) Groups
   (c) Institutions

Essay questions (20 marks)

1 Outline the ways in which changes in the social institution of education have impacted Caribbean people over time.
2 Explain the influence of patriarchy on Caribbean families.
3 Describe the Rastafarian religion, showing how it has impacted Caribbean society and culture.
4 Illustrate how the social institution of the justice system interacts with other social institutions in Caribbean society and culture.

Challenge essay questions (30 marks)

1 Compare and contrast the justice system during colonialism and in the present era in the Caribbean.
2 Examine the argument that in Caribbean society and culture the nuclear family is the ideal type of family, especially in terms of bringing up children.
3 'While the social institution of education in the Caribbean contributes to social mobility, it has not been able to help the poor to improve their lives.' Discuss.
4 To what extent is religion in Caribbean society and culture influenced by social stratification?

RESEARCH TOPICS

Issue: Investigating the impact of a social institution on Caribbean people

You will have to name the specific institution you are studying. For example, you might choose the institution of the family and want to examine the issue of family form or family composition for Caribbean people. What are their beliefs and practices? Do they have biases that may help us to better understand the social institution of the family?

Research methodology

A survey employing a questionnaire (to about 40 persons) would be a suitable methodology. Administering a questionnaire to many persons helps you to present your findings in a range of formats – tables, graphs, percentages. Family type and form may be a sensitive issue to some people, so you need to word your questions carefully. What is important is how people feel and how they label their family type. If this does not conform to your definitions, you will have to be silent about it, and raise it in your discussion of findings.

Possible questions

1 How would you describe your family type:
   - Nuclear, single parent, extended, sibling, re-constituted?
   - If your family is of another type, please describe it.
2 How has your family composition changed over the last ten years?
3 How is your family composition likely to change in the next ten years?
4 What kinds of family types did your parents or guardians have?
5 What kind of family type would you like to have? Why?

These questions will yield data for constructing graphs as well as qualitative data on beliefs about changes and continuity in the family, historical information on the family, and perhaps biased beliefs as to an ideal family form.

REFERENCES AND FURTHER READING

Barrow, C. (1996). *Family in the Caribbean: themes and perspectives*. Kingston, Jamaica: Ian Randle.

Chevannes, B. (1994). *Rastafari: Roots and Ideology*. Mona, Jamaica: Syracuse University Press.

Distance Education Centre (DEC) (1997). *Introduction to Sociology: SY14G, Social Sciences Study Guide*. Barbados: University of the West Indies.

Smith, R. T. (2004). The Caribbean family: continuity and transformation. In B. Bereton (Ed.), *General history of the Caribbean, Vol. 5: The Caribbean in the twentieth century*. Paris: UNESCO and London: Macmillan Caribbean.

Taylor, S. (Ed.) (1999). *Sociology: issues and debates*. London: Macmillan.

7 INTERACTING WITH THE WIDER WORLD

Since the arrival of Columbus the Caribbean region has been involved in interactions with Europe and later on with the US and Canada – referred to collectively as 'the West' or 'metropolitan' countries. This interaction was an early form of globalization, which knitted the economy, culture and society of the Caribbean and Western Europe into a close relationship. However, it was also a relationship between dominant metropolitan and peripheral Caribbean countries. In this chapter we will explore the nature of the influences of western societies on the Caribbean and the latter's influences on them within a context of the imperialism and colonialism of the past, and the neocolonial and postcolonial relationships of today.

EXPECTED LEARNING OUTCOMES

On completing this chapter, you will be able to
1 explain how imperial and colonial policies influenced Caribbean society and culture
2 describe neocolonial and postcolonial aspects of Caribbean society and culture
3 assess how the identity of Caribbean people has been influenced by colonialism
4 discuss the influence of the consumption patterns, creative expression, politics, sport and tourism of extra-regional countries on the Caribbean
5 analyse the impact of the Caribbean on extra-regional societies using examples drawn from politics, economics, creative expression, religion and the culinary arts.

7.1 IMPERIALISM AND COLONIALISM

The *Age of Imperialism* began with the coming of the Europeans who conquered lands and peoples and established colonies. Spain, Britain, France, Belgium, Germany and the Netherlands carved vast empires in the Caribbean, in North, Central and South America, and in Africa, Asia, Australia and the Pacific. These **imperial** powers ruled their subject peoples through a combination of military might, fear and *deliberate psychological conditioning* promoting the European as the superior person or culture.

Conquered territories eventually became settled colonies under European rule. During **colonialism**, European attitudes, ways of life, dress, language, arts and political systems became **hegemonic** in Caribbean societies. This means that these values were not only imposed but that there was a fairly widespread acceptance that they were indeed true – that the European was the superior power. The European country (the 'mother country') exerted power in that it was the **metropole** (the political and cultural centre of the colony, the hub) and the colony represented the **periphery** of this European country. The colony became *a part of* Europe (it was not allowed to have its own *national* identity), but only a peripheral part of Europe.

With the exception of Haiti, all other Caribbean countries were subject to centuries of cultural conditioning into *Eurocentric* attitudes and values. In his study of colonialism, Memmi (1991) analyses relationships between the *colonizer* and the *colonized*. He shows that the colonizer established economic patterns in which the colonizer alone profited and that this relationship was based on **racism** – the colonized could never become the equal of the colonizer or have a voice in determining the terms of trade. Memmi also says that the colonizer was often a minor bureaucrat in his home country but was transformed in the colony, by virtue of his race and official position, into a superior being bearing a superior culture. To maintain hegemony in the colony the colonizer had to ruthlessly control, repress and suppress any showing of creativity or self-sufficiency amongst the colonized. Interestingly, Memmi suggests that the colonizer knew that he was exercising unlawful power over others, and that he grew to hate the colonized, because he could not let up on the repression, only intensify it.

In the school curriculum the history and culture of the colonizer were privileged and recounted with pride by both colonized and colonizer. That of the colonized faded into the 'other'. **Otherness** is a term used to describe the experience of any group that feels marginalized. Some of the colonized became like the colonizer because that was the only option that seemed to make any sense. In so doing they were rewarded in limited ways – minor and middle positions in the civil service and professional jobs (the opportunity to pursue teaching, medicine or law). In turn they suppressed their own people by emulating and promoting a position where the European way was the 'right' way. Colonialism was a period during which European culture was promoted and the culture of the Amerindian, African or Indian was treated as 'the other'.

Neocolonial and postcolonial societies

While most Caribbean countries are independent today, many question the extent to which political independence and nationhood have really transformed the colonizer–colonized relationship. The dominant attitudes, cultural norms, mode of dress, educational, political, religious and judicial systems, and trading patterns all show an orientation towards the metropole, *not the periphery*. The legacy of the colonizer is still hegemonic. Indigenous efforts have had to struggle to gain legitimacy (for example, **syncretic** and African religions such as Rastafarianism) or have been virtually ignored (for example, initiatives to introduce 'other' languages, such as Yoruba, Swahili or Hindi, of relevance to Caribbean people).

In addition, the economic structures of today greatly threaten what 'independence' means. **Multinational companies (MNCs)**, with their headquarters in the metropole, and without any serious allegiance to the Caribbean, take the bulk of their profits out of the region. The World Trade Organization (WTO) declares what is accepted practice in standards and trade regulations based largely on agreements that favour western interests. The dominance of the West in industrial, manufacturing and information and communications technologies (**ICTs**) means that the Caribbean has to import these goods and services, leading to an imbalance in trading relationships. These relationships today between the ex-colonizer and the ex-colonized are described as **neocolonialism.** The West continues to wield cultural hegemony, intensified by the effects of the foreign mass media. The West also wields economic hegemony through the policies of the MNCs, the WTO and their dominance in ICTs. These relationships embroil independent Caribbean nations in a state of dependency very similar to that of the colonial era.

More subtle is a mindset towards modernization that again privileges the metropole. There is tension or conflict among Caribbean people about where the future of the Caribbean lies. A resistant few feel that we should create our own ideas about what it means to be 'developed' and not import 'templates' (fixed solutions) and technology without first screening them to determine if they are relevant to us. Others feel that the global impact of ICTs has already locked us into a world system, so that while it may be worthwhile to desire a more indigenous way of developing that does not reflect the values and customs of the metropole, it has to be based on the products and technologies of the West. (These people then would prefer some degree of symbiosis and not just slavish dependence on western ideas and technologies.) The rest wonder what the debate is about – they see life in the twenty-first century as being lived as if we are a part of the West. In the Caribbean, the more affluent, the technologically inclined, and those who value western lifestyles will be using the same technologies as are used in the US, watching the same news and cable programmes, being fans of the same R&B or hip-hop artistes, and probably also dressing in the same way. They will be living out the idea of development that is being lived in the 'first world' or **metropolitan countries**. In so doing they come close to *becoming the colonizer*, according to Memmi's analysis (adopting a superior stance to the 'other').

Postcolonial society is a term used to describe how these neocolonial relationships of continued dominance and subjugation affect people in the ex-colonies. The postcolonial stance actively condemns the attitude and activities of metropolitan countries in sustaining relationships with the newly independent countries that position them as **subaltern** populations ('other', inferior, dependent). These studies examine how Eurocentric ideas, philosophies and ways of life are perpetuated in the ex-colonies as well as how they are resisted or re-created into symbiotic forms (Box 7.1).

Summary

The Caribbean region was brought forcibly into interactions with the 'Wider World' in 1492. Since then it has been locked into colonial relationships with different imperial powers. It is important to understand that the colonial subjugation suffered for centuries, and the installation of dependent economies by the 'mother country', did not substantially decrease or disappear in the era of independence or even in the decades afterwards. The imperial powers gave up political ownership and exploited the structures of trade and commerce that they had set up to maintain economic power. So for all of the past 500 years of its history the 'Wider World' has had a major hold on Caribbean society and culture. Political and economic power were supported all along by psychological conditioning that the ways of the colonizer were better. Today there continues to be a nagging tension in how Caribbean people prefer to see themselves – in the image of a western person, identifying with an ethnic group such as Africanist organizations, or creating a **hybrid identity** where western

ACTIVITY 7.1

Identify any radio or television stations in the Caribbean dedicated solely to indigenous programming.

1. What is the philosophy behind such an enterprise?

2. Describe the nature and type of its programmes.

3. Assess its success relative to other radio and television stations.

4. Given the nature of our neocolonial relationships, what would you suggest as enabling programming for local television and radio?

BOX 7.1 Postcolonial societies

In postcolonial society the West continues to be hegemonic, and for the most part the subaltern populations help to perpetuate this dominance by choosing to *conform* in valuing the social, cultural and economic products of the West. *Resistance* is another response, seen in efforts to bring indigenous and local issues, ideas and culture onto centre stage so that Caribbean people do not continue to see their own affairs as *peripheral*. Other ways of accommodating this tension about what is valued between the metropole and subaltern populations include *creative* strategies such as **hybridization**, symbiosis or **creolization** (Chapter 3). Creative strategies try to integrate aspects of what is well appreciated from western culture with indigenous input. The issue of western dominance and subjugation in the postcolonial society is being played out in all areas of social life.

For example, while cable television, cinema and videos are overwhelmingly of first-world origin and deepen our embeddedness in western ways, radio in the Caribbean is now somewhat of a resistant force. From being the main purveyor of western music and values, radio has re-invented itself to provide talk shows and call-in programmes emphasizing topical and local events. Today it is a medium for the dissemination of local culture – drama, music, a voice

for isolated communities, and even niche audiences (youth, the middle aged, ethnic communities, religious groups – all have their dedicated stations). This focus is *resistant* because there is a definite effort to address what Du Bois (1903) calls our 'double consciousness' – the experience of living both inside and outside of the West. It is a postcolonial strategy to *re-centre* the balance of the relationships we experience as 'core–periphery' by emphasizing the periphery.

Similarly, postcolonial scholars study local television in the Caribbean as an experiment in creative *symbiosis*. Sustaining an indigenous television industry devoted solely to local productions is difficult because of the high-demand, superior and cheaper products of the West. As a result local television stations tend to tune in to the foreign mass media part of the time (namely cable stations for movies), and in their own programming emphasize local news, investigative reports, political debates, talent shows, sporting events, and locally produced soap operas and comedies. However, this 'mix' or symbiosis still has a tendency to privilege western themes. For example, the way the news is delivered is patterned on foreign network news productions and local soap operas are based on foreign templates but with our own unique twists.

values and beliefs are melded with Caribbean traditions, or other combinations and stances. The postcolonial societies of the Caribbean, then, continue to struggle with the mental attitudes that revere western countries, even more so since they are the leaders in the new technologies, and downplay the possibilities that could arise from indigenous or local attempts at creating alternative products and lifestyles.

7.2   INFLUENCE OF EXTRA-REGIONAL COUNTRIES ON THE CARIBBEAN

In this section aspects of Caribbean society and culture are examined to assess the influences of extra-regional countries. The past colonial condition and the present neocolonial relationships form the basis of the analysis. Postcolonial theory shows how the dominance of the West is perpetuated, resisted or creatively integrated into Caribbean society and culture by interactions between metropole and periphery and by mechanisms of **socialization**.

Consumption patterns

Europe, and more recently the US, have profoundly influenced consumption patterns in the Caribbean. Colonial policy deliberately fostered a skewed economic

BOX 7.2 Historical trade and consumption patterns

The Caribbean has an outward focus where trade and consumption are concerned. A high percentage of the goods and services consumed in the Caribbean originate in western countries, particularly the US. Historically this pattern began with the **mercantilist** laws known as the *Navigation Acts*. The only goods that could be imported into the colonies had to come from Britain, or from a port controlled by Britain, on ships using a British crew. The colonies could not engage in manufacture because they acted as a source of raw materials for the **industrial revolution** in Britain and as a market for British manufactured goods. The mindset that Caribbean people seem to have of valuing and appreciating foreign manufactured goods initially stemmed from these mercantilist or trade laws that deliberately prohibited industrial development in the colonies.

Independence did not significantly alter these patterns. New Caribbean nations began manufacturing 'from scratch' but did not have all the necessary resources. As a result they continued to import manufactured goods from Britain. This situation was worsened by the fact that under colonialism productive lands went into cash-crop production for export, with little emphasis on food production. Agriculture itself tended to be avoided because of its association with manual labour and servitude. Consequently, there was a high food import bill in the ex-colonies for wheat flour and flour-based products, tinned peas, beans and vegetables, potatoes, pork and beef products, salted fish, milk, butter and cheese. So consumption patterns that demanded foreign manufactured goods and food products created a large foreign exchange problem for new Caribbean governments.

In the 1970s and 1980s in many Caribbean countries certain items were placed on a quota system and could only be imported with special licences, whilst others were placed on a 'negative list' – they could not be imported at all. **Tariffs** drove up prices, contributing to spiralling inflation. A *black market* flourished, where restricted items could be bought illegally, including foreign exchange. There were chronic shortages of basic food items and of other goods; red tape and bureaucracy tied up the process of importing goods and services.

These measures were resistant strategies designed to develop a local capacity in manufacturing. Local manufacture and local spending were deliberately encouraged by campaigns such as 'buy local' and 'discover Jamaica'. Caribbean governments protected local industry by imposing high tariffs on textile imports from other Caribbean countries. However, because of a lack of manufacturing experience, local goods were relatively expensive and badly made. They could not compete effectively with foreign mass-produced items without the help of tariffs and **monopolies**. The consumer, who was forced to buy the inferior alternative, came to associate 'local' with cheap and shoddy and a tradition developed of shopping abroad.

Over time, many Caribbean manufacturing firms have gone out of business as **trade liberalization** policies have increasingly opened the region to a flood of cheap foreign goods and services. The CARICOM Single Market and Economy (CSME) is another resistant strategy designed to nurture and facilitate growth in local industries and trade and make a greater impact on western countries *as a combined force*. It will be some time before this strategy can be assessed.

relationship by prohibiting manufacturing and encouraging *dependency* (Box 7.2). Today most of the goods and services consumed in the Caribbean originate in the West. Although there have been resistant and creative strategies designed to reduce dependency, subaltern populations continue to regard western products as hegemonic. According to postcolonial theory, consumption patterns therefore reflect a mindset privileging western values. We can analyse this mindset in the following ways.

- The value in assessing what is foreign – music, clothes, technology and ideas – as somehow 'better' than local alternatives. Some critics speak of this as a kind of self-hate imposed by the colonized on the colonizer, whereby the cultural forms and products of the West are believed to have more legitimacy than local forms.

ACTIVITY 7.2

Reflect on your own attitudes to buying the goods and services of extra-regional countries. To what extent is there a preference for these products? To what extent do you use resistant, creative and conformist strategies for different consumption items?

- The extreme importance associated with 'being modern'. This value encourages us to keep up to date with the latest innovations, fashions, movies, music and personalities that are 'happening' right now in the western world, as a matter of course. People see the West as the pacesetter and we have no other option but to buy into the latest forms, models, products and gadgets.
- Building **social capital**. Brand names and designer labels are popular among youth as it confers on them the approval and envy of their peers. For those who can only manage less recognized (cheaper) brands, there is ridicule and derision. The young person who dresses exactly like his or her counterpart in the West, particularly the US which, because of geography, is always a huge presence in the Caribbean, is saying that the Caribbean does not offer any alternative fashion statement that can compete with this level of hype, glamour and attitude.
- The universal feeling that the US is a 'must-see' destination, or even an 'only see'. Many Caribbean people visit the US over and over again and feel no interest whatsoever in visiting other countries. There is an indefinable feeling of being at the 'centre of the world'. It is even said that to have a US visa, even a holiday visa, is a prestigious status symbol.

Creative expression

While Caribbean creative expressions are unique in themselves, they show strong influences of extra-regional countries, namely those of the European colonizers. This influence, though, is masked by the creativity of Caribbean people, who have adapted the cultural forms of the colonizer into distinctive hybrid products of their own. The era after independence saw the most determined efforts to supplant or adapt the legacy of Europe with Caribbean cultural expressions. While there is this on-going creolizing, adapting and re-inventing, the US is exerting a strong influence, in particular by targeting youth through music, fast foods, fashions and festivals.

Festivals

Western countries directly influence Caribbean society and culture in the mainstream Christian observances of *Christmas* and *Easter*. They are celebrated in a similar fashion owing to the foreign mass media showcasing images of what commodities, decorations and gifts are in vogue. Christmas is especially commercialized and much of what we buy originates in the West. However, the more specifically Roman Catholic holy days such as *Corpus Christi, Good Friday, Ash Wednesday, All Souls' Day* (or *All Saints'* observed by Anglicans) are not major observances in either the US or Britain, nor are they in any way commercialized. They show long-established Caribbean traditions: for example, the Corpus Christi and Good Friday processions in the streets, being anointed with ashes at the beginning of Lent, and the 'lighting up' of the graves of the ancestors on 1 and 2 November. The West, too, has had little impact on the religious festivals of the Garifuna, Amerindian, Orisha, Muslim and Hindu groups. Thus, it is those religious holy days that are widely celebrated in the West, and which we also have, that tend to reflect a high degree of commercialization.

   Secular festivals and celebrations such as *Valentine's Day, Old Year's Night* (now more widely known as *New Year's Eve* because of the penetration of foreign media), *Mother's*

Fig. 7.1 Carnival in Port of Spain, Trinidad

ACTIVITY 7.3

Compile a list of festivals and other observances in your territory. Identify those which are overwhelmingly influenced by extra-regional countries, and those which have more local cultural significance. Suggest reasons for this division.

Day, Father's Day and *Halloween* are greatly influenced by the US. Fireworks, party hats and noisemakers are now typical of a New Year's Eve celebration in the Caribbean, which was not the case say a decade ago, and the traditional midnight song, 'Auld lang syne', is a Scottish ballad. Gifts, cards and email greetings for Valentine's Day, Mother's Day and Father's Day are virtually identical in the US and Caribbean, and to a large extent these novelty items and products originate in the US. The marketing and distribution networks of western countries, greatly enhanced by e-shopping and the cable media, influence what we purchase and how we celebrate these events – and this applies to all socio-economic groups. To some extent local entrepreneurs are creating cards, artefacts and novelty items to rival the foreign products and this is a symbiotic or creative response to domination. Halloween has been resisted by the lower socio-economic classes in Caribbean society, whilst the more wealthy groups, possibly with closer ties to North America (real or imagined), take part in 'trick o' treat' rituals in their neighbourhoods.

On the whole we see the influence of extra-regional countries on Caribbean festivals when there is a significant commercial aspect to the celebration. Even Carnival, that most typical Caribbean festival, shows evidence of extra-regional influence as it becomes increasingly commercialized (Box 7.3).

Music

Caribbean music is known for its resistant themes, undoubtedly springing from the region's history of oppression – colonialism, bonded labour and **social stratification**. No wonder then that the most successful musical forms generated by the British Caribbean – namely reggae, calypso and the steelband (Box 7.4) – originated in the tenement yards of Jamaica and among the shanty towns and urban poor in Trinidad.

BOX 7.3 Influences on Carnival

While Carnival is today synonymous with the Caribbean, Caribbean carnivals vary across the region in terms of the time of the year they are celebrated, whether they are nationwide celebrations with maximum popular participation, and whether they originated within the historic processes and events of Caribbean society and culture. Some of these features throw light on the extent to which extra-Caribbean countries influence the festival of carnival in the Caribbean.

Some say that carnival is a European phenomenon associated with Roman Catholicism (it precedes Lent – *carne vale*, a farewell to the flesh), though others trace its origins to the pagan festivals of Ancient Rome and Venice. Carnivals timed as pre-Lenten celebrations thus have a Christian origin. However, how these festivals were celebrated reflected the resistance of the oppressed people – they parodied and satirized European attitudes, dress and mannerisms under the guise of a celebration, so that the tradition of critique, social commentary and resistance was strongly entrenched in the celebration. Carnival, for example, in Dominica and Trinidad and Tobago is observed as a pre-Lenten celebration first associated with French Roman Catholic influence. However, there is some opposition to the idea of carnival having European roots. Afro-centrist ideas demonstrate evidence of *parallel* – not just parodic – celebrations rooted in African Caribbean slave culture and before that in specifically African rituals.

Carnival in Antigua and Barbuda and Barbados (Kadooment) is celebrated to commemorate Emancipation, which took place for most territories on 1 August 1834. Whether as a carnival or not, most of the other Caribbean territories celebrate Emancipation with a public holiday on 1 August either as Emancipation Day, August Monday or August Holiday. The themes of resistance and anti-white sentiments were also a part of these celebrations. In both Antigua and Barbuda and Barbados, which are major tourist destinations, the traditional August Monday and carnival celebrations have taken on a more elaborate portrayal, deliberately courting American and European tourists. Thus, the carnival celebrations in Caribbean islands where tourism is a great income earner have been influenced by extra-regional countries – in what events are staged, where they are located, how they are packaged to be of interest to the tourist, and the extent to which the festival

has been commercialized (admission for shows, selling the rights to reproduce certain events to the foreign media, the production of videos and CDs and other memorabilia).

In the elaborate rituals of carnival celebrations in Trinidad and Tobago, where there is mass participation on an unprecedented scale, there is still evidence of the influence of extra-regional countries, as the following examples show.

- *Technology*. Computer programs help to create images of costumes, foreign materials are sourced to build those costumes (whether fabric, wire, feathers, beads or sequins) and the latest developments in sound technology are evident in music recordings and live entertainment. Of late, the King and Queen of the Bands' portrayals require elaborate pyrotechnics and special engineering effects that depend heavily on imported gadgets and even expertise.
- *Development of ideas*. The *mas bands* are inspired by themes that range from sci-fi Hollywood representations and Broadway productions to abstract portrayals of globalization, capitalism, oppression, ecological awareness and gender issues. (There is a growing presence of gay/homosexual groups portraying *sections* in bands, and they are usually from abroad, though having a Caribbean heritage.)
- *Built structures*. We see large floats being presented on the road (with air-conditioned rooms), reminiscent of the traditional carnivals in New Orleans and Italy. This goes against the commonly accepted local understanding that being in a *mas* band means that you are an active participant, and even if you are King of the Band you are able *to carry* your own costume.
- *Music that is exported*. The traditional calypso, which is primarily about social commentary and difficult for the extra-regional visitor to understand because it portrays specific local events and controversies, is sidelined in favour of the *new wave, jump* and *wine soca* ditties.

To a certain extent extra-regional countries are influencing the way that the Trinidad and Tobago carnival is packaged and presented because it is now a multi-million-dollar earner and relies on the foreign tourist to make it a commercial success. No longer is it a national celebration only; major allowances are made for visitors from foreign countries and these subtly influence the festival.

BOX 7.4 The steelband – extra-regional influence

From the 1880s up to the 1930s in Trinidad *tamboo-bamboo bands* accompanied carnival revellers since the authorities had banned drums. In these bands music was produced by beating bamboo cuttings of varying widths and lengths with wooden sticks. Experimentation added an assortment of different kinds of disused tins and pans, 'tuned' to produce different musical notes. By the 1940s empty oil drums had become the preferred instrument – the top of the drum was pounded into a concave shape and different notes were tuned on its surface (Fig. 7.2). Whole drums (or 'pans') were used for the bass, and they were cut to different lengths to produce different octaves.

Britain and the second world war had an impact on the evolution of the steelband movement. The colonial authorities banned carnival celebrations during the war years but constant experimentation was going on in the backyards of Port of Spain to produce a versatile pan instrument. On the days of the various Allied victories in Europe, South East Asia and Japan, the steelbands paraded through the streets, winning the approval of the people, and when peace was restored the steelband and carnival became synonymous. The names chosen for the bands reflected Caribbean people's identification with the war and with Hollywood images depicting stories told against the backdrop of war. Major steelbands were *Tokyo, Red Army, Invaders, Desperadoes, Renegades, Tripoli* and *Casablanca*. In keeping with the themes of war, resistance and heroism, the steelbandsman was a grassroots 'soldier', a rough and tough character who defended his (there were few or no women playing pan at this time) band with fists and knives. The meetings of Red Army and Tokyo at any road junction on carnival days were infamous for the blood, injury and mayhem that ensued. The 'captain' or leader of the band was a community strongman who demanded unquestioned loyalty. His devotion to the band was supreme, often transcending his own domestic responsibilities, and like Rudolph Charles and 'Thunderbolt' Williams of Desperadoes, they were powerful folk heroes.

Today many of those same steelbands are still top contenders for the annual Panorama competition, and the typical *mas* played by the steelbands on carnival days continues to be either the fancy sailor or some other military costume (Fig. 7.3), reminiscent of the beginnings of the steelband movement in the war years. However, those playing pan today come from all ethnic and socio-economic groups, both men and women play (as do schoolchildren), and students and pan enthusiasts come from the US and

Fig. 7.2 The face of a steelpan

Europe annually to play with a steelband for the carnival season. There is pan on the curriculum of music schools in western countries and many of these countries have school steelbands. The seriousness with which western countries have grasped the steelband and the innovations they are making in sound technology, together with the fact that they enter steelbands at the annual pan-jazz festival in Trinidad and Tobago, is driving a deeper national and government interest in the instrument. More competitions are sponsored, school steelbands are being encouraged, and there are developmental plans for the national steelband association, PanTrinbago.

Today the steelband is known as an 'orchestra'. This term was a slightly later development, dating from the mid-1940s and given 'respectability' by the visit of the *Trinidad All Steel Percussion Orchestra (TASPO)* to the 1951 Festival of Britain in London. The orchestra is modelled on the classical European philharmonic orchestra, where there may be as many as 100 players, in different sections. The steelpan is a percussion instrument tuned to produce different sounds, similar to the different instruments of a conventional orchestra, so that in any large steelband there will be pans grouped in sections – tenors (soprano), double seconds, cello pans (baritone), double tenors (alto), guitar pans, four pans, double second (tenor), triple cello (baritone), tenor bass, six bass, nine bass and quadrophonic pans. The music is arranged and scored, and for formal concerts there may be a conductor. All kinds of music are played – calypso, soca, reggae, jazz, rhythm and blues, and even classical symphonies. One difference worth noting is that many pan players are poor, sometimes unemployed persons, who never learned to read music and so they learn their parts by ear.

BOX 7.5 The story of reggae

Today reggae is known worldwide; there are reggae concerts, festivals and bands in such far-flung places as Japan and South Africa. This genre of music came out of Jamaica and although there are many variations of the form, they continue to be known generally as reggae music. The story of reggae is bound up with the history of recorded music in Jamaica. The first kind of music to be recorded in Jamaica was the *mento* in the 1950s. The roots of mento lay in folk music, the drums of *pocomania*, and *junkanoo* rhythms. The style of music that was exported from the US at this time provided fertile ground for what was to become typical of the Jamaican music scene – constant experimentation and innovation relying on mass appeal to carry the development forward. This happened in the 1960s on the eve of independence, when an exuberant dance music known as *ska*, influenced by American pop music, began to be recorded and made its way to metropolitan centres, where there were significant Jamaican communities. Millie Small's hit, 'My Boy Lollipop', made ska known internationally.

By the late 1960s ska was a spent force, overtaken first by rock-steady and then reggae. *Rock steady* was slower than ska, influenced by the new *soul* music of the US, and it emphasized vocals. Like ska, it was associated with a particular dance style. Reggae soon became the dominant and long-lived music genre of Jamaica, capable of fusing and mutating into many related forms, especially with the adoption of the electric guitar and synthesizers. Reggae was even slower than rock steady, with more emphasis given to the bass and to 'conscious' lyrics – haunting melodies evoking stories and experiences of oppression, longings and yearnings, intertwined with Rastafarian religious themes focusing on Africa as redemption. Bob Marley (Fig. 7.4) was the best exponent of this form of reggae, which came to be known as *Roots Reggae*; 'No Woman No Cry' was one of his international hits with which a wide cross-section of humanity could identify. It is this deep connection that the world has made with Jamaica and reggae that tends to brand all the music coming out of Jamaica since then as 'reggae'. This strand of reggae continues to be created and is related to the *nyahbingi* sound of Rastafarian

Reggae music has always been associated with resistance and with the Rastafari (though not all Rastafari identify with the music). One reason for the universal appeal of reggae music is its message of resistance, defiance, overcoming, and hope in a better tomorrow – a message with which all persons who are oppressed in some way can identify. **Calypso** too had grassroots origins. Calypsonians sought to expose inequities such as racism and political oppression and voiced alternative opinions to that of the establishment about colonial politics and the Roman Catholic Church – an institution seen as 'colonial' and a source of oppression, particularly by resistance groups among the lower socio-economic groups. Their compositions combined biting wit, satire and humour to poke fun at important personages. They portrayed themselves as outspoken critics, unafraid and fearless of the colonial authorities – the *Roaring Lion*, the *Mighty Sniper*, *Attila the Hun* and *Growling Tiger*. The calypso was a means whereby the poor and powerless could resist and ridicule the highest authorities.

Fig. 7.3 A 'fancy sailor' in a steelband mas band.

Reggae and its various forms (roots reggae, dancehall, ragamuffin – see Box 7.5) and calypso and its various forms (soca, ringbang, chutney soca, rapso, raggasoca) evolved in response to the demand from younger generations for musical forms and styles that identified with world youth culture and music. This meant popular music created in extra-regional centres ceremonies where hand drums and chanting are emphasized.

In Jamaica the owners of sound systems and their DJs (disk jockeys) were central to the culture of innovation and experimentation with the music from as early as the 1950s, when many people did not own radios. Sound systems are turntables with powerful amplifiers and 'speaker boxes' suitable for holding 'block parties' in urban centres. The DJ or 'selector' was the driving force in winning the loyalty of the crowd to novel ways of pushing the music even further by singing and *rapping* over it, known as 'toasting'. For example, *dub music* emerged out of the practice of leaving one side of a 45 record free of the lead vocals (the 'version'), giving the dubmasters room to fill in with their toasting and mixing dexterity. This rap reached the US and flowered into *hip hop*, showing the strong influences of US and Jamaican music on each other. Dub and reggae continued strongly for most of the 1970s and early 1980s. More sophisticated mixing devices took the dub in new directions. Now in the studio DJs and others could take out and put in different elements of the music and manipulate sounds with electronic effects.

Dancehall was born out of this dominance of the DJ in Jamaican music and seemed to be a reaction to the spiritual and 'conscious' themes of reggae as its lyrics became increasingly bawdy. It was a youthful sound that had strong connections to American hip hop; indeed, dancehall, rap and American hip hop seemed to intertwine, constantly influencing each other. The music mutated drastically into *ragga*, with its heavy reliance on computerized and digital sounds. The lyrics moved from being strongly suggestive to 'raw', glorifying sexual conquests, portraying women as sexual objects, denigrating homosexuals, and preaching violence. Buju Banton, for example, advocated the killing of gay men and Bounty Killer celebrated gangsterism. Today the excesses of dancehall and ragga have been neutralized by the conversion of some of its leading exponents to Rastafarianism and more 'conscious' lyrics – namely, Capleton, Buju Banton and Sizzla. More spiritual lyrics are now combined with the energy and verve of the dancehall performance and the style is known as *culture*.

Fig. 7.4 Bob Marley

such as North America and Europe. Aspirations of reggae and calypso artistes in the 1960s and 1970s did not necessarily involve having hits in metropolitan centres, but since the massive 'breakthroughs' of the likes of Bob Marley, Third World, Shabba Ranks and others, reggae, dancehall and other forms of Jamaican music are now major contenders on the US, British, European and even Asian music charts and awards. Bob Marley's *Exodus* album was voted by *Time* Magazine as the Album of the Century. This extraordinary extra-regional success has been very profitable to the artistes and recording labels and has been responsible for changes in the music, a search for constant experimentation and mutations, as today's artistes look to an international audience for their measure of success. Music is a 'commodity' and the very success of reggae in western countries is impacting on its transformations in many ways, not the least of which is that its production, promotion and dissemination are being handled largely by capitalist interests in the western world.

The success of reggae in extra-regional countries has also impacted on the aspirations of soca artistes. Traditional calypsonians continue to sing their social commentaries and humorous renditions on love,

ACTIVITY 7.6

1. Outline some of the ways that reggae has been adopted and adapted by extra-regional audiences.

2. Choose ONE of the following – the *son* music of Cuba or *zouk* music of the French Caribbean, Dominica and St Lucia – and briefly research the influence of extra-regional countries on the development of this musical form.

marriage, courtship, infidelity and sexual prowess. While these enduring themes are still heard in calypso tents and at live concerts, they are seldom recorded because there is not a large enough market. Soca music, with its driving beat and reliance on the intense involvement of listeners, is more in demand, especially at Carnival. The desire to make a 'breakthrough' on the international front involves soca artistes in constant experimentation.

Every year new forms and sounds spring up: *sampling* (copying a few bars of already produced popular music); incorporating rhythm and blues, reggae and rock melodies and styles; the use of synthesized rhythms as well as hip hop and rap vocal styles; and *riding a rhythm* – where four to eight bars of music are repeated for an entire song, and many different songs (lyrics and melodies) use this same rhythm. The dilemma for soca artistes is to satisfy the demands of the home crowd and at the same time to present soca in a more 'palatable' form to extra-regional audiences. Arrow of Montserrat, with 'Feeling Hot, Hot, Hot', and more recently Kevin Little of St Vincent and Rupee of Barbados, have been successful in bridging hard-core soca with a more melodious sound, more attuned to the tastes of a non-Caribbean audience. Soca has some similarities with the punta rock of Belize yet in some ways is utterly different (Box 7.6).

BOX 7.6 Punta rock, Belize

Punta rock has the distinction of being the only music created in Central America and is usually associated with Belize. Both Pen Cayetano of Belize and the Honduran group Góbana are credited with starting this new genre, which includes elements of salsa, reggae, rap and soca, as well as the traditional musical form from which it was born, namely the *punta* of the Garinagu (Garifuna) people. The latter are found not only in Belize but also in Guatemala, Honduras and Nicaragua on the Caribbean coastlands. The punta mainly used two drums, with a range of percussion instruments – rattles, woodblocks, bottles, maracas (or sisira) and sometimes conch or turtle shells. It was performed mainly at family gatherings, wakes and other religious or cultural events and sung in the Garifuna language. Punta is distinguished from other musical genres by the *duple-metre ostinato* played on the *segunda* or bass drum and improvisations in rhythm on the *primero* (the tenor drum) (Greene, 2004). The songs are mainly of the 'call-and-response' kind so typical of African cultures across the Caribbean, with intense drumming.

Migration to metropolitan centres has been on-going in Belize throughout the twentieth century so that there was some concern over the loss of the Garifuna language and customs, especially on the part of Garifuna youth. The creation of punta rock in the 1980s served to rejuvenate interest in the traditions of the Garifuna and the popularity of the music swept throughout Central America, so much so that the metropolitan centres are now the engines of growth in recording, promoting and distributing this 'new' musical genre.

Punta rock held on to the Garifuna drums and other indigenous percussion instruments, such as different sized turtle shells, and increased the pace of the punta by adding the electric guitar, acoustic drums, and lead and bass guitars. The early songs were in the Garifuna language, celebrating their history and culture – for example, 'Uwala Uwala Busiganu' (Don't be ashamed of your culture) – and Dangriga became the centre of this sound. Today, with its widespread popularity in Central America and among Belizeans and other Central Americans in metropolitan centres, lyrics are also now in Spanish and English. While punta was the traditional dance music of the Garifuna people, punta rock is more widespread in its appeal, with faster rhythms and more provocative dancing.

Typical punta rock style is evident in the following releases:

- 'In Mi Country' – Pen Cayetano
- 'Sopa de Caracol' – Chico Ramos (writer, Belize), performed by Banda Blanca (Honduras)
- 'Til da Mawnin'!' – Andy Palacio, Stonetree Records

Theatre arts

Drama, dance and stagecraft comprise the wide array of cultural forms and expressions that are described as 'theatre arts'. In the Caribbean, theatre arts include cultural forms presented in the open air or any suitable 'space' – traditional dances, limbo, stick fights, folk singing, chanting, drumming and story-telling, and the rituals associated with wakes, wedding ceremonies, Carnival and *Jonkunnu*. These performances combine drama and dance in a staged setting, whether formal or informal, planned or spontaneous.

While theatre arts of the folk variety were always a part of Caribbean cultural life, they were relegated largely to the village or community setting in the colonial era, taking to the streets only during festivals and celebrations. Plays, dramatic performances, pantomimes and musical productions modelled on British or American theatre were the legitimate, colonial version of authentic theatre or 'high culture'. The independence era, with its themes of **decolonization**, liberation and nationhood, saw the conscious incorporation of the wide variety of Caribbean cultural forms into indigenous theatre productions. Local plays and comedies were written and produced; there were re-enactments of historical events using stick-fighting, story-telling, folk songs and dances; and there were also creative, choreographed dance productions staged by the newly established local dance companies, such as the National Dance Theatre Company of Jamaica.

Even though there was this push to embrace Caribbean art forms and ideas in theatre, the influence of extra-regional countries was very evident in how Caribbean theatre developed. Language was a major issue as there were some who felt that the native **patois** and dialects were much too difficult for others to comprehend and that the art form would not develop because of this; others felt that to be authentic and truly expressive of Caribbean life Standard English had to be abandoned. The relationship with extra-regional countries, too, was a common theme in productions within indigenous theatre. These themes were inevitable in an era of decolonization – conflicts and tensions over issues of identity, discrimination based on race, colour and class, as well as the interrelationships being forged between the diverse groups brought by the British. The writings of **Rex Nettleford** of Jamaica and **Derek Walcott**, Nobel Laureate from St Lucia, among many others, show the preoccupation of Caribbean people with this quest for identity. They interrogate in different ways how the white man's world and the legacy of colonialism could prove comfortable to a people who only have fragments of their own past and culture upon which to build an identity.

Theatre arts, then, are not only a form of entertainment but a serious attempt to confront Caribbean people with the issues and problems of their society and culture. This can be done through humour, tragedy, musical productions, dance, and even arts-in-education programmes for schools. Through the theatre people have an opportunity to experience life in all its many facets – as a participant (for there are many productions where the audience is involved), as one who empathizes with certain characters and situations, and as food for thought.

Caribbean theatre arts have grown into a creative adaptation of western styles and genres largely by incorporating Caribbean languages, local musical rhythms, the oral tradition, call-and-response episodes, folklore characters (for example, the *moko jumbies*), ritual drama such as *mas* or street theatre, and the use of *picong* (repartee that is stinging in its wittiness) and *double entendre* (saying one thing apparently innocently but meaning another, usually of a sexual nature).

ACTIVITY 7.5

Choose one Caribbean playwright, poet, dramatist or writer. Read what critics and reviewers have said about his or her works and identify any extra-regional influences on these works.

However, the West still plays a pivotal role in the growth and development of the poets, playwrights, actors, dramatists, writers and novelists whose works are often produced for the theatre. Many of our famous writers and playwrights felt compelled to leave the Caribbean in order to live among and work and perform for people for whom the arts were important. In the Caribbean, weaned on theatre that was an imitation of Europe's, people did not initially think it was much more than amusement, for it did not explain their lives meaningfully. Even today it is the worldwide acclaim and prestigious awards given to writers and playwrights such as Derek Walcott (Box 7.7), Vidia Naipaul, Earl Lovelace and Jamaica Kincaid (Figs. 7.5–8) that has helped to spread their reputation here in the Caribbean.

BOX 7.7 Derek Walcott and theatre arts

Derek Walcott was born in St Lucia on 23 January 1930 and won the Nobel Prize for Literature in 1992. His most highly acclaimed works are:

- **Poetry collections**: *In a Green Night* (1964), *Sea Grapes* (1976), *Another Life* (1973) and *Omeros* (1989)
- **Plays**: *Ti-jean and his Brothers* (1958), *Dream on Monkey Mountain* (1970), *The Joker of Seville* (1974) and *Odyssey* (1993).

Walcott can be described as a postcolonial playwright as his works focus on the conflict in Caribbean society and culture between what has been inherited by blood and memory and what has been inherited through colonialism and imperialism. As with other Caribbean postcolonial writers, there is a preoccupation with trying to describe Caribbean life and culture – teetering as it does between the values and aesthetics of the metropole and the periphery. People in the **diaspora** experience complex identities as they actually live in the metropole, bringing the contrasts, conflicts and accommodations between a western lifestyle and a Caribbean lifestyle directly and urgently into their own everyday lives. And people in the Caribbean of mixed heritage (including Walcott himself, who says that they are 'poisoned by the blood of both') teeter between the metropole and 'fractured peripheries' (belonging to different Caribbean ethnicities). It is this mixture of identities and how it plays out in each person's social location that brings Walcott's work out of a simple metropole–periphery model to show the hybridity of identities, both in the metropole and in the periphery among Caribbean people.

Walcott uses Standard English, West Indian dialects and patois in his works. He incorporates aspects of Caribbean folk culture into his theatre productions – story-telling, singing, dancing, calypso, the *mas* and street theatre – and at the same time excels in his use of traditional western

literary devices such as metaphor and poetry. This mixture of western and Caribbean heritage comes sharply to the fore in his great epic poem *Omeros* (Greek for Homer), where he rewrites the *Iliad*, the ancient work of the Greek poet Homer, and in his play the *Odyssey*, again rewriting another of Homer's epics. These ambitious works bring the ancient Greek legends, torments and conflicts right into the Caribbean present to address issues of rootlessness, banishment and exile relevant to Caribbean people of African, Amerindian, Indian and European descent.

Fig. 7.5 Derek Walcott

The influence of extra-regional countries, then, is significant in Walcott's work, even returning to the great classics of western literature to creolize and adapt them to a Caribbean present. He uses the English language superbly and does not seem to feel the tension that other writers report about using the language of the colonizer. At the same time he is adept at incorporating picong, sexual innuendos, fables, jokes and playful puns typical of Caribbean language. Walcott's work brings a certain perspective to bear on the usual questions that the theatre arts present to Caribbean audiences, and is an attempt at a positive resolution of these tensions and identity conflicts, not by choosing any model or specific identity, but by understanding the range of traditions that have been bequeathed to us.

Fig. 7.6 Vidia Naipaul

Fig. 7.7 Earl Lovelace

Fig. 7.8 Jamaica Kincaid

Culinary practices

Culinary arts in the Caribbean show a high degree of creative adaptations of the food traditions of Europe, Africa, India, China and the pre-Columbian peoples. From the time of contact in the fifteenth century there has been on–going experimenting across different traditions. Though fusion is at the heart of culinary practices in the Caribbean, making it difficult to pinpoint the particular influence of Spain or Britain, we can still discern colonial influences of the past and some neocolonial trends of today.

For example, a staple across the Caribbean is **saltfish** or salted cod. In Jamaica *ackee and saltfish* is one of the national dishes, as is *roast breadfruit and saltfish* in St Vincent, and *duckanoo and saltfish* in Antigua. This staple has its origin in the importing of salted and smoked fish from the British colony in Canada to feed the slaves. In addition, animal parts that were not considered fit for human consumption became typical foods for the enslaved. Today, salted, smoked and pickled meats are highly popular across the Caribbean – *smoked herring, pigtail, black pudding, pig foot or chicken foot souse*. Not only is the pig foot prized in making souse, but also *pigskin* and *pigface,* or sometimes only the *snout*. In Barbados, *pig's ears* are an important ingredient in souse. And we also use *fish heads, goat belly, ox-tail* and *cow heel* – animal parts that are not highly prized, if they are used at all, in western cooking. Once deemed fit only for slave consumption, these foods have undergone centuries of blending with different flavours and spices to produce the favourite foods of Caribbean people in all walks of life. There are similar traditions in the American South, where the influence of slavery is seen in the widespread fondness for *chitterlings* (the intestines of young pigs, cleaned and boiled, then dipped in batter and fried).

While certain foods are typical across the Caribbean, there are differences from one territory to another based on how the foods are prepared or served, and this may also have colonial origins. Rice and peas (or peas and rice) is a Caribbean staple. However the *red beans and rice* of Jamaica is very different from the *riz et pois*, the national dish of Haiti, or the *pigeon peas and rice* or *black-eyed peas and rice* in the southern Caribbean (Box 7.8). The French influence is still alive in Haiti, Martinique, Guadeloupe and Dominica, especially in their expertise in blending sauces and the use of *bouquet garni* (herb mixtures) to obtain a perfect balance of flavours. The specialities of *rouille* and *bouillabaisse* (Box 7.8) also speak of French influence.

BOX 7.8 Caribbean recipes

Haiti – Riz et pois

For Haitian rice and peas, small red kidney beans are used. The beans are first boiled in water and when almost finished they are taken out and sautéed separately in oil and a variety of seasonings such as chives, thyme, cilantro and garlic. The beans and seasonings are then returned to the cooking liquid, to which rice has been added, with some more water and the two are cooked together.

Southern Caribbean – Black-eyed peas and rice

The black-eyed peas are soaked for an hour and then boiled with salt, black pepper, garlic and a pinch of sugar. When the peas are half-way boiled, rice is then added, along with chive, mint, thyme, onions and pepper. Tomato is the last of the seasonings to be added, just before the rice is finished. Coconut milk, too, is added just before the rice is fully boiled.

Trinidad – Alloo choka

This is a traditional Indian food (*alloo* is a Hindi word meaning potato and *choka* is a general term meaning 'mixed up'). The potatoes are washed, peeled and cut in small pieces. In an iron pot, a clove of garlic and hot pepper are burned in oil. They are removed from the oil and the potato pieces, salt and onion are added and it is covered for a while. When uncovered, pieces of tomato are added and the mixture is stirred constantly as it is fried.

In all the above the emphasis is on timing and seasoning.

FRENCH CARIBBEAN

Bouillabaisse

Bouillabaisse is fish stew or thick soup using tomatoes, olive oil, garlic, fish and shellfish, chilli, orange, herbs, fennel and saffron. This stew is unique, possibly because of the wondrous flavouring imparted by the combination of saffron, fennel seeds and orange zest.

Rouille

This is traditionally served with bouillabaisse. It is a type of mayonnaise with an abundance of chilli pepper and garlic. This mayonnaise is spread on little pieces of toasted French bread, which are dipped in gruyère cheese and then placed in the soup bowls, before the soup is poured over it.

It is debatable whether the British influence is as alive in the cooking traditions of Jamaica, Barbados, Guyana or Trinidad and Tobago. Caribbean cooking is famous for its hot and spicy dishes – *curries, jerk pork, escovitch fish, chutney, pepperpot* – influenced by the Caribs and their use of hot peppers and by the African and Indian cooking traditions. Pepper sauce and a variety of herbs and spices, which not only season meats but vegetables, rice and peas as well, make Caribbean cuisine truly distinctive and a far cry from traditional British cooking. Perhaps the food item most directly linked to the British is the English or Irish potato, which was imported during the colonial era and has remained as another staple in the Caribbean diet – but cooked in far different ways, for example, as *alloo choka* (Box 7.8).

However, there are certain traditions associated with the British that have been creolized and are now accepted as typical Caribbean ways of life. Note how Caribbean people have taken the British habit of drinking *tea* and speak of it as anything from coffee and cocoa to Ovaltine or Milo. The idea we have retained about 'tea' being so hegemonic certainly reflects the British preoccupation with it. In traditional British cooking, sauces and gravies are used liberally but they are usually made independently of the main dish and poured on afterwards. Caribbean people have retained the love for gravy but have made it an integral part of the cooking process, soaking and cooking meats in marinades, seasonings, herbs, spices and peppers. The British influence lingers, too, whenever we have porridge for breakfast, but in the Caribbean oats and wheat have given way to a taste for cornmeal, maize being an indigenous food widely used across the region.

The West is also looming as important in Caribbean social and cultural life through the labour-saving gadgets, appliances and pre-cooked products of western countries that are influencing Caribbean culinary practices. Caribbean homemakers have relentlessly adapted and changed traditional recipes to fit the limited time at their disposal. No longer is a ham cooked from 'scratch' – that is, put in a pan to boil outside in the yard for hours on end, as was done a generation ago; now they come pre-cooked or with precise instructions for baking. Cakes are no longer beaten by hand; in fact pre-mixed cake in a box is a common grocery item. *Home-baked* bread and coconut bake lose out to the store-bought varieties and many of the traditional dishes are no longer cooked regularly in Caribbean homes but reserved for Sundays and special occasions.

Pre-cooked foods and fast foods supplement the diet of busy Caribbean people who have developed an appreciation for the convenience afforded by the food technologies of the West. The *junk food* phenomenon has earned the loyalty not only of young people but others as well. Fast-food chains from the US are well represented in many Caribbean countries. This is not to say that home cooking is dying out; Caribbean people still want their foods cooked in authentic ways but they have also embraced the convenience-foods culture, which means that it is now the norm that two or three meals a week (or more) may be of the fast-food variety. While this is a western trend that may impact negatively on the health and well-being of Caribbean people, the tendency of the latter to experiment, blend and creolize may still have a positive influence on American fare.

ACTIVITY 7.6

1. Beyond the fact of convenience, explain why American fast foods are so popular in the Caribbean.

2. In your opinion, to what extent do young people prefer junk foods over indigenous foods?

Political influences

In the 1960s and 1970s Caribbean countries were achieving their independence from Britain and the model of government that was installed was the ***Westminster system***. In fact this happened throughout the British Empire and today these independent, former British colonies, with similar systems of government, make up the **Commonwealth**.

The Westminster system is a form of **parliamentary government** where the head of government (or *prime minister*) depends on the parliamentary body for his or her position. What this means is that there is no clear **separation of powers** between the *executive* (head of government, cabinets, committees) and the **legislature** (the representatives of the **electorate** who comprise the law-making arm of government). There is also a head of state with only ceremonial powers. In the Caribbean there are many **constitutional monarchies** where the British monarch is officially the head of state and represented by a *governor general*, as in Belize, Barbados and Jamaica. Trinidad and Tobago, Guyana and Dominica have a **republican** form of parliamentary government where a *president* is head of state, but it is still largely a ceremonial post.

One way of understanding the Westminster system is to compare it with a different form of government, such as the *presidential system* in the US, where the president and the cabinet (comprising secretaries of state and advisers) comprise the executive arm of government. The president is both the chief executive *and* the symbolic head and is elected separately from the legislature. In the parliamentary democracies of the

Caribbean the prime minister is not elected by the population at large (only by his or her constituents) but automatically assumes that office as the *political leader* of the party winning the most seats in parliament. The US president appoints the cabinet from a pool of experts who are usually not part of the legislature. Thus, the people who are in the executive are not also part of the legislature, as happens under the Westminster system. There is a clear separation of powers.

In the era of decolonization the Westminster form of government was imposed on the British Caribbean without much input from the people. Two **houses of parliament** were installed – the *Lower House* consisting of elected members (named the 'House of Representatives' in Trinidad and Tobago, Jamaica and Antigua and Barbuda, and the 'House of Assembly' in Barbados and St Lucia), and the *Senate* or *Upper House*, comprising appointed members chosen from the winning party, the opposition, and independent individuals. (Dominica and St Vincent have a slightly different system with only one House, the Assembly.) Members win their seats by following the **rule of law** and observing the *electoral processes* associated with installing a government – political parties put forward eligible candidates for each **constituency**, they campaign by taking their party's stance on various issues to the electorate, they 'face the polls' (that is, they allow the electorate to vote or not vote for them without intimidation), and if elected they accept their seats in parliament to represent their constituents.

It is remarkable that in the transition from colonialism to independence (which was a rushed affair in many cases) Caribbean people were able to move so smoothly from anti-democratic colonial rule to the rule of law. Taking the whole of Latin America and even the Hispanic Caribbean into consideration, the former British territories were able to form stable governments with few deviations. The much-reported election fraud of the Burnham years in Guyana, the 1970s (Black Power) and 1990s (Black Muslim) political uprisings in Trinidad and Tobago, and the takeover of Grenada by Maurice Bishop (and his overthrow and the subsequent invasion by US troops; see Box 7.9) are perhaps the most serious incidents in the British Caribbean where the rule of law was compromised. However, after more than 30 years of independence, there are increasing criticisms of the Westminster system, which is said to seriously disadvantage certain sectors of the society. Caribbean society differs from British society; politics developed along ethnic and partisan lines, with prime ministers and political parties holding on to power for years on end, thus excluding other groups. The main issue is that the executive and the legislature are not separate. This compromises ***democracy*** because the prime minister becomes all powerful, and it elevates one political party to receive all rewards and honours (Box 7.10).

There have been recent calls for *constitutional reform* arising from the imposition by the British of a model of government that they thought was appropriate to the colonies – namely *their* model. They regarded the colony as a unit, largely because they had decreed it to be so. However, it was they who had imported labourers from different lands and followed a policy of divide and rule, so that at independence the different ethnic groups were left to work out their relationships with one another. The ways they sought to do this often followed lines of ethnic or partisan politics. Once a party got into power it consolidated its position by excluding other groups. This has been the trend in most Caribbean countries from independence until the present day.

ACTIVITY 7.7

1. After researching the issue, list examples of Caribbean prime ministers and political parties that have remained in power for decades.

2. Suggest why Caribbean people as voters tend to be 'diehard' supporters of one particular political party.

3. Suggest one approach to power sharing that can be introduced in Caribbean countries to redress some of the problems of the Westminster system.

BOX 7.9 Operation Urgent Fury

Fig. 7.10 Maurice Bishop and Fidel Castro

Fig. 7.11 Ché Guevara

Fig. 7.9 Eric Gairy

*E*ric Gairy was Chief Minister in Grenada before independence and prime minister from 1967 to 1979. His administration was toppled by a *coup d'état* in 1979 led by *Maurice Bishop* of the NJM or *New Jewel Movement* (Joint Endeavour for Welfare, Education and Liberation) with little popular resistance. The Gairy years were plagued by poverty, financial mismanagement and corruption. The *Mongoose Gang* was a group of thugs who terrorized his opponents, making him into a virtual dictator, though increasingly eccentric and preoccupied with UFOs.

The revolutionary government of Maurice Bishop was based on principles derived from the *Black Power Movement* sweeping the US and the Caribbean in the 1970s, and the socialist ideas of *Fidel Castro* (of Cuba) and *Ché Guevara.* Close relationships were established with Cuba, Grenada benefiting from the influx of expertise in health, construction and agriculture, and the development of cooperatives and investment in agro-industries. The economy was open to investment from abroad and private enterprise. A number of grassroots councils encouraged people to participate in politics. However, internal discord between Bishop, a moderate within his own movement, and *Bernard Coard,* an extreme Leninist, and Bishop's inability to deal with this challenge to his authority, led to strife and infighting. In October 1983 Coard and his supporters overthrew the government; Bishop and two of his ministers were executed and others arrested.

The prospect of an extreme communist government being established in Grenada led US President Ronald Reagan to approve *Operation Urgent Fury* – the invasion of Grenada by US Marines, establishing US rule of the island, expelling Cubans, and arresting a wide cross-section of Grenadians, including members of the government. It is remarkable that Grenadian and Cuban troops were able to fend off the US Marines until that force grew to some 5000. The leaders of the coup were tried and sentenced to death. In 1991 their death sentences were commuted to life imprisonment.

Any study of the influences of extra-regional countries on the politics of the Caribbean must acknowledge the US as the *superpower* in the region. Since the Caribbean is strategically placed to allow access to US territory, the region is closely monitored for any anti-US sentiments. Castro's long-standing communist regime in Cuba, virtually on Miami's doorstep, makes the US highly paranoid about any communist rhetoric elsewhere in the Caribbean. Hence, the US denounced the Bishop regime, withdrew much-needed aid, entered into talks with Gairy, but could not do much more until internal upheaval gave the excuse to mount an invasion and restore the rule of law (that is, the electoral process). For strategic and geopolitical reasons at the time (this was before the Berlin Wall came down and the Cold War ended), the US needed Caribbean countries to be essentially conservative outposts bound to the US through a web of influence – aid programmes, loans and trade agreements.

BOX 7.10 The Westminster system in the Caribbean

Although elections in the Caribbean seem to be free and fair, political commentators maintain that elections are just one aspect of democracy. They point out that political processes and institutions as developed in the Caribbean tend to promote only the ruling party and opportunities for alternative opinions are slim. True *participation* of all social classes and ethnic groups is not encouraged. The exercise of a citizen's right to vote every five years is seen as the most minimal form of participating in a democracy and from time to time the electorate shows its disillusionment with politicians by low voter turnout. This skewed understanding of democracy results from the phenomenal powers bestowed on the prime minister under the Westminster system of government. For example:

- The prime minister has the power of appointment to the cabinet and government ministries, to state boards, and to various strategic committees and companies.
- The prime minister can dissolve parliament at will.
- The prime minister and cabinet can propose a bill and, as members of the legislature, they also vote on it. Thus there is this close tie between the executive and the legislature.
- Other members of parliament belonging to the ruling party are constrained to vote along party lines. There is usually some form of debate involving the opposition but it tends to be a ritual; the legislation is almost always passed. There is not much room for independent opinion and dissent, either within the ruling party or from the opposition.

Stemming from these wide-ranging powers of the prime minister, the Caribbean experience has been that:

- A sitting prime minister can remove opposition members and supporters from key areas or appointments and replace them with his or her own supporters and party favourites.
- Any party that is relegated to the opposition knows that its members will not be allowed any key appointments and its opportunities in politics will be severely curtailed. This has been described as the *winner-takes-all* phenomenon of the Westminster system.
- This phenomenon reverberates on how political campaigning is done. Platform politics becomes an all-out, dog-eat-dog ruthless fight, largely based on character assassination, where the lines between political parties are drawn by hate and ethnic identification.
- If a party is based on ethnic identity or commitment to a particular **ideology** or tradition, and it does not win an election, then it knows that it will almost never do so because of the powers of the party in power to exclude it. If such a group represents a significant number of citizens, they will feel a sense of marginalization and frustration.

The way the Westminster system works in the Caribbean, therefore, is that the people vote every five years but have few other opportunities to participate on issues affecting the country. Parliamentarians themselves are constrained to follow the lead of their prime minister, and the close association between the executive and the legislature means that the latter largely carries out the wishes of the former.

However, the postcolonial reality is that all groups (not only dominant ones, but subaltern groups too) are organizing and mobilizing so that they have voice and representation. The British idea that Caribbean society was one nation has influenced our politics up to now, but today in each country – more so in the heterogeneous societies and cultures of Guyana and Trinidad and Tobago (and in Suriname where the Dutch also left different ethnic groups to fend for themselves) – people think of themselves as relating to the state in different ways. For example, people who think of themselves as Indo-Trinidadians may have quite different feelings to those who consider themselves to be Indians, or just Trinidadians. And that is just among one ethnic group.

The dismantling of colonialism is continuing to take place as the political system established by the British for the Caribbean is now under attack from different groups within Caribbean society. In the postcolonial societies and cultures of the Caribbean, previously excluded groups are calling for constitutional reform, often advocating some form of **power-sharing** (Activity 7.7). However, the ways that Caribbean people will work out their political systems are likely to be some variant of the Westminster model, rather than, say, adopting the US model, as it may be less stressful than adopting something radically new.

Migration

In Caribbean society and culture migration has been a traditional practice and regarded positively. Today large numbers of Caribbean migrants and their children live and work in metropolitan countries. It is a normal practice for Caribbean people to send home remittances to assist family members. These remittances also constitute a valuable source of foreign exchange for the home country, as they have done for decades. The phenomenon of migration has also helped Caribbean countries by lessening the pressure for jobs and social services locally (Richardson, 2004). However, migration is a negative approach to development and decolonization. While the Caribbean cannot remove itself from the global economy and would not want to deny its nationals job opportunities in metropolitan countries, these traditions make us vulnerable to the policies of extra-regional countries.

Over time Britain, Canada and the US have moved to curb immigration from the Caribbean and even stipulated their preference for highly educated and skilled persons. At the same time they have been forced to accept poor and unskilled or semi-skilled migrants on a seasonal basis because their own residents are unwilling to work at strenuous or low-status jobs. The labour shortage in farm work has given poor farmers and unemployed youth in the Caribbean and elsewhere an opportunity to earn an income in metropolitan countries. Caribbean people also migrate on a seasonal basis to perform domestic work, child care and taking care of the elderly. While Caribbean countries have benefited from the temporary or permanent migration of their people, there have also been negative influences:

- the 'brain drain' effect through the emigration of skilled people, most of whom were trained by Caribbean institutions (e.g. nurses, teachers, technicians)
- the experience of racism in the metropolitan country and being treated as second-class citizens as far as wages, benefits and grievances are concerned
- the injustices felt by seasonal workers, who are largely segregated from resident communities on large farms or orchards and who hold down jobs that residents think are too menial for them (Box 7.11)
- the 'mindset' that better opportunities lie with extra-regional countries.

The migration experience today (particularly seasonal migration), while seemingly beneficial, continues the syndrome of *dependency* on extra-regional countries. Moreover, a great deal of the poverty and underdevelopment being felt in Caribbean countries today can be attributed to the trade liberalization policies that we have had to adopt in our **globalizing** economy. The opening up of markets by the reduction in trade restrictions of all kinds has enabled cheaper products, including foodstuffs, to find markets in the Caribbean, thus displacing local products. Agricultural workers in poor communities have not been able to match these prices and have become further impoverished. It is these persons who are then recruited as seasonal farm labour in the developed world.

BOX 7.11 Caribbean migrant farm labour

The sugar cane fields of southern Florida and the extensive orchards of the Niagara Peninsula in Canada see an annual migration of Caribbean workers to hand-pick fruit, harvest cane manually, and work in tobacco factories and canneries. The field labour is hard, back-breaking work, from sunup to sundown, without overtime pay. While many come back year after year and do not seem to mind the deprivations, they are housed in substandard structures, receive the minimum of medical and other treatment, live apart from the general population, and are speedily returned to the Caribbean if there are any disputes or disagreements about the work or their contracts.

Their recruitment in the Caribbean is based on agreements between the governments of the Caribbean and the receiving nations. Their air fares are paid for by the farmers and the contract may be from six weeks to eight months, depending on whether they are contracted for fruit picking or factory work. They are returned promptly to the Caribbean once their contracts expire. They are paid a lowly wage by Canadian or American standards, but it represents a substantial sum in Caribbean currency. However, they tend to spend much of it on the eve of their departure in September, buying different kinds of small appliances and gadgets, clothes and gifts.

Although these migrant labour schemes involve thousands of Caribbean workers, mainly from Jamaica, and smaller numbers from the Eastern Caribbean, they are not covered by health and safety legislation nor can they bargain collectively. They cannot move from one farm to another looking for better conditions either. There is a social distance between the workers and the farmers and townspeople, emphasized by race and colour. In short, it is an exploitative system similar to those previously imposed by Europeans under the plantation system. The farmers counter these charges by saying that they too have to be competitive in a system of trade liberalization and so the cheaper their production costs the more likely they are to stay in business.

Sport

Cricket

Cricket has dominated sport in the British Caribbean, as it has in most of the countries once belonging to the British Empire – namely, the West Indies, Australia, New Zealand, Pakistan, Sri Lanka, India, Bangladesh, Zimbabwe and South Africa. Those countries field the major teams today, contesting international test matches and one-day events. While a direct import from Britain in the nineteenth century, the West Indies has embraced the game and made several innovations, transforming it from being a staid 'Englishman's game' into something dominated by flamboyant personalities, complicated Caribbeanized 'strokes', rituals involving spectators, and music.

In the aftermath of slavery, cricket became a means whereby the white planter class could continue to demonstrate moral and racial superiority over their black and coloured subjects. Played first only among whites in **elite** clubs, the popularity of the game spread as the colonized tried to emulate a sporting tradition where 'gentlemanly' traits were courted more than physical prowess and expertise. Cricket as played by the British was a languid game conducted politely among equals: it did not matter if you lost but it was important that you did so gracefully; the batsman was expected to 'walk' when he was out, even if this was not detected by the umpire; and it was not winning that was important but celebrating British culture and sportsmanship.

Even though local cricket clubs were stratified according to race and colour, colonial people of all hues sought to transform the game into something more

BOX 7.12 Cricket today

Whilst cricket was introduced into the Caribbean in the nineteenth century by the British, who dominated the sport for a long time, today the influence of extra-regional countries is again being felt. Cricket today has been transformed from the Victorian ideals that Englishmen once held about the game. It is now a major sport in a number of countries, the salaries and awards are lucrative, various players from one country routinely play in other countries at the county level, and the frequency with which test matches are carded means that styles become familiar and homogenized. It is hardly possible nowadays to discern a cricketing style distinctive to one country or region. Today all the teams have fast bowlers and spin bowlers and powerful batsmen who learn the best aspects of style and skill from each other.

In the twenty-first century the game of cricket has been influenced by:

- technologies such as the 'third umpire' – cameras that record the play and provide evidence to make a more informed judgement about whether someone is out, if the umpire is not sure
- a departure from the ideals of good sportsmanship of yesteryear, with allegations of match fixing, bribery and corruption across the different teams; hostility among players degenerating into racial slurs and name calling; and infighting and indiscipline, as has happened regularly in the West Indies team in their relations with each other and with the West Indies Cricket Board
- becoming highly commercialized and a valued commodity of the mass media, especially the sports media, which buy rights of transmission and exclude others
- efforts to make the game more profitable and attractive to the consumer and player, with many more one-day internationals, higher prize money incentives drawing the best players and keen competition, a 'season' that is now virtually year round as a cricketer may play in two or three test series for the year as well as at the county level, and innovations such as the Stanford 20/20 variant of the game, which was short-lived
- the personal endorsement contracts of players, which sometimes conflict with the interests of the team as a whole.

representative of Caribbean society and culture. When the West Indies cricket team soundly beat England at Lord's cricket ground in 1950 the victory was especially important because the colonized had beaten the colonizer at his own game *in the mother country*. That was one of the strongest teams the West Indies ever fielded, including batsmen Frank Worrell, Everton Weekes and Clyde Walcott (the Three Ws) and two top-class spinners, Alf Valentine and Sonny Ramadhin. From that time onwards teams from around the Commonwealth have repeatedly triumphed over the mother country in cricket supremacy. What was to be a colonizing mission, the introduction of cricket to the colonies, turned out to be another medium for the phenomenon of creolization. For example:

- 'Cutting' was a batting stroke invented in the Caribbean, demanding great skill, flair and style, likened by James (1963) to the works of art of Michelangelo, deliberately equating Caribbean cricket with great western art forms – a postcolonial stance of resistance to the norms of the colonizer.
- The portrayal of cricketers as gentlemen of moral superiority was resisted by Caribbean people, who introduced opposite values – employing fast bowling in such a way that it terrorized batsmen (Learie Constantine in 1929 against England, and later on Wes Hall), and ferocious batsmen 'possessing the murderous hitting power of Weekes, Walcott, or Lloyd' (St Pierre, 1973, p. 14).

● Composing calypsos about cricket confirmed the importance of cricket in Caribbean society and culture, particularly among the grassroots (an unintended consequence). The 1950 West Indies victory exploded into a 'jump-up', Carnival style, with Lord Beginner composing on the spot 'Cricket, lovely cricket', about 'those two little pals of mine, Ramadhin and Valentine', as Lord Kitchener led joyous West Indian spectators around the grounds and down the road, something which stunned the English public.

Today an international cricket match played in the Caribbean is the scene of loud music (reggae and soca) in between each 'over' (a set of six balls bowled to the batsman from one end of the pitch; the next 'over' is bowled from the other end), dancing, food, revelry and colourful individuals with their signature horns and conch shells who add to the applause and excitement. No longer do cricketers wear only white; all teams now wear colourful uniforms splashed with the logos of the companies they endorse.

ACTIVITY 7.8

1. Explain why cricket remains very popular in the Caribbean even though it is a protracted game steeped in traditions that date back to the nineteenth century.

2. Name FOUR West Indies cricketers who have been knighted.

The internationalization of cricket among the members of the Commonwealth has increased its commercial potential. While there are many formal and informal cricketing clubs and matches organized at the village, district and national level in each Caribbean country, the emphasis in cricket culture lies in the ebb and flow of the fortunes of the West Indies cricket team. Professional cricketers are well paid and today play all through the year. Thus, having begun as an instrument to entrench British colonialism, cricket was itself transformed into a Caribbean institution, and today is undergoing still more changes through its internationalization and commercialization to the point where profitability becomes the major rationale (Box 7.12).

Basketball

Basketball is rising in popularity in the Caribbean, largely owing to the dominance of the American mass media, and it is particularly popular among the region's youth. The phenomenal success and multi-million-dollar contracts that young black men have earned in this sport in the US have captivated the attention of Caribbean youth. The Caribbean heritage of Patrick Ewing, Shaquille O'Neal, Tim Duncan and others has also deepened interest in the game. Unlike cricket, a basketball game lasts for about 40 minutes and so there is no room for boredom; it is fast paced from beginning to end.

Whilst being popular, basketball is very much a village and community sport, with local inter-club matches. There are regional basketball championships but relatively few high-profile international competitions. Local basketball players may look forward to the Olympics but most Caribbean countries cannot afford to send many teams to compete in different events, so sports fielding ten or more players tend to be sidelined. However, the astounding financial rewards of the game in the US continue to encourage Caribbean youth with the right skills to seek a sports scholarship to the US (see Chapter 10).

Soccer (English football)

Soccer or English football has taken the world by storm. It is perhaps the most popular game today, judging by the importance of the World Cup, which rivals the

Olympics in status and prestige. Unlike cricket, Caribbean countries have not been able to pool their respective talents to produce a West Indian football team. Only Haiti (1974) the *Reggae Boyz* of Jamaica (1997) and the *Soca Warriors* of Trinidad and Tobago (2006) have been able to make it to the World Cup finals. Collectively we might stand a chance of repeating that feat more regularly or have greater successes at that event. However, the region does see active inter-island and international competitions between many local clubs and there is a long tradition of secondary school football. As with basketball, many an aspiring Caribbean footballer has sought recognition through gaining a sports scholarship to the US, a country relatively new to soccer but with tremendous resources to develop the sport. Alternatively, the most talented players hope that they will be recruited directly by the prestigious and well-paying English or European football clubs at the heart of the action.

Tourism

Tourism is by its nature an industry that encourages dependency. Today it is largely the tastes and interests of the foreigner that dictate what type of tourism product will be promoted, and it is the finance and expertise of foreign companies that have developed the Caribbean tourist industry. Tourists in the Caribbean come mainly from North America and Europe. Hence any boom (or recession) in the economies of these countries directly impacts the Caribbean. Proximity is the main factor accounting for the large numbers of American visitors. Cuba was the preferred destination until the 1960s, when it became a communist state. Americans then chose Jamaica, the Bahamas and Antigua, where a traditional tourist package was available – sun, sea and sand. Barbados has always had an English clientele, possibly because its tourist industry developed during the colonial era and it was seen as an outpost of the empire that was very 'English'. Today, both European and American tourists are found all over the region.

Some Caribbean countries have developed as world-class tourist destinations: Jamaica, Barbados, Antigua and Barbuda, the Bahamas, the Virgin Islands and St Lucia are the most popular. These countries are better able to offer what the tourist wants – a warm location (there is a definite seasonal aspect to Caribbean tourism, with many visitors arriving in the colder months of the northern winter), stretches of pristine white sandy beaches, calm seas and varied types of accommodation (from luxury hotels and all-inclusive resorts, to cheaper hotels and apartments, as well as guest houses). As tourists have become more sophisticated and demanded a different experience, so the tourism product has changed. This has given other Caribbean countries a chance to develop tourist attractions of a different kind. For example:

● *Ecotourism*. Some Caribbean countries, such as Dominica, have resolved to develop tourism in keeping with environmentally sound principles and to resist the high-rise hotels associated with mass tourism. In Dominica, Belize, Guyana and Suriname, the rainforests, and their flora and fauna, cater for the 'nature lover' (especially those interested in birdwatching). Special reserves and sanctuaries, such as the Mountain Pine Ridge in Belize and coral reefs, are also popular with this group.

- *Adventure tourism.* In Guyana and Suriname the great rivers offer white-water rafting and canoeing and expeditions are mounted into the interior, for example to Kaieteur Falls in Guyana. Hunting is growing in importance, too, in Dominica, and mountain climbing in St Lucia.
- *Sports tourism.* This is usually associated with sea sports – surfing and kiteboarding, sailing, scuba diving, snorkelling, deep-sea big-game fishing, and powerboat racing. Specifically, there is the Grenada Yacht Club Race, the Spring Regatta of St Maarten, and the Blue Marlin Competition in Curaçao.
- *Health tourism.* Typically this was found where people came to bathe in mineral-charged waters thought to be beneficial for various ailments, especially in volcanic areas: for example, Bath, Jamaica, and in St Lucia, Dominica and Montserrat, where there are many hot springs. Today world-famous hotel chains have established spas and health resorts in the Caribbean to cater for those who want to detoxify, reduce stress and have a Caribbean vacation at the same time.
- *Enclave tourism.* The 'playground of the rich and famous' and 'fun in the sun' are promotional ideas of the Caribbean that encourage all sorts of hedonistic behaviour. The extreme antics of thousands of American college students enjoying Spring Break every year are well known. Usually all-inclusive hotels catering only to couples promote wild and carefree behaviour such as nudity and promiscuity as 'attractions'.
- *Festival tourism*. Some Caribbean festivals have in recent years been deliberately promoted to attract the extra-regional tourist. Examples include *carnivals* such as kadooment in Barbados, the *St Lucia Jazz Festival*, the *St Kitts Music Festival*, *Reggae Sunsplash* in Jamaica, the *World Creole Music Festival* of Dominica, and the *Maroon Festival* of Carriacou.
- *Cruiseship tourism.* Many Caribbean islands have constructed docking facilities for the major cruise ship lines – *Carnival, Royal Caribbean* and *Princess* – because each vessel carries upwards of two thousand tourists, a rich potential source of foreign exchange. Interestingly, these visitors are more attracted to the 'floating theme park' on which they are sailing and tend to spend little in the few hours during which they visit a Caribbean island.

To a large extent it is US and European interests – international hotel chains, the travel industry, financial and investment companies – that help to promote and develop these tourism products in the Caribbean. The big hotels and the more recently established all-inclusive resorts with extensive waterfront real estate are mostly owned and financed by foreign capital. Caribbean people have sought to cash in on the influx of tourists – as vendors at the ports of call of cruise ships, as taxi drivers, and as guides; by developing local businesses such as car rental companies, restaurants, and local art and craft shops; and by the strategic staging of cultural events. There have also been unfortunate ways of wresting money and other valuables from the tourist; as the numbers of tourists rise there tends to be an increase in crime (mainly theft), especially in areas of high unemployment.

Few Caribbean countries can say that nationals own any of their largest hotels or resorts. One of the few examples challenging this theme of foreign domination is Gordon 'Butch' Stewart of Jamaica, who created the 'Sandals' and 'Beaches' all-inclusive resorts and spas in Jamaica; these have since spread to Antigua, St Lucia,

ACTIVITY 7.9

1. How does the marketing strategy of the West, portraying the Caribbean as a mythic, exotic location, affect Caribbean people?

2. Suggest TWO measures that can be realistically put in place to enable Caribbean countries to reap greater benefits from tourism.

the Turks and Caicos, and the Bahamas. In addition, his involvement in the national airline of Jamaica helped to reduce the dominance of international carriers in the region. This, however, is a rare local success story. On the whole Caribbean tourism is controlled by foreign interests and events, and even by the world environmental lobby (Box 7.13). These issues are considered further in Chapter 8.

Summary

The influence of extra-regional countries on many aspects of society and culture in the Caribbean is still strong. However, this influence is masked or is undergoing change in different ways. For example, Caribbean people have adapted the cultural forms of the colonizer (plays, foods, the symphony orchestra, sports) into distinctive hybrid products of their own. Political systems such as the Westminster system of government have undergone changes and today previously excluded groups are calling for constitutional reform and experiments in power-sharing. The long-

---

BOX 7.13 Standardizing the tourist industry

Recently, extra-regional countries have been in the forefront of the international debate on **sustainable development**. The 1992 *United Nations Earth Summit* in Rio de Janeiro endorsed a set of principles to ensure sustainable development, known as *Agenda 21*. Since then environmentally friendly organizations have been working out how to apply these principles in different areas of society and culture.

Fig. 7.12 The Green Globe logo

Green Globe 21 is a set of standards devised specifically for the travel and tourism industry – for tourists, companies and communities involved in tourism. These standards are expected to be upheld worldwide and are meant to remedy the environmental problems that have accompanied the development of mass tourism markets. The goal is to establish conditions for sustainable tourism.

'Sustainable tourism' refers to practices that cause little harm to the environment, even while it is being exploited for economic purposes. Both the natural and social environment are recognized. For example, it is felt that building hotels and establishing tourist centres should not marginalize local people but empower them to contribute to the tourism industry and make a viable livelihood. The standards laid down by Green Globe 21 enable a company, a hotel or a lodge, for example, to be ranked in terms of energy and water consumption, waste production and disposal and how well it integrates local people into its policies and practices. Green Globe 21 addresses,

among others, issues such as pollution, deforestation, land degradation and biodiversity, as well as equity and social justice.

An operation such as a hotel or a tour company has to achieve a minimum level of sustainable performance before it receives the Green Globe logo without the tick (Fig. 7.12). To be fully certified (that is, to receive the logo with the tick), all of the prescribed standards must be met and an independent audit should be conducted. Companies and communities that display the Green Globe logo see it as a device for attracting those tourists who are environmentally conscious. The latter constitute an increasingly sophisticated group, who now demand not only sun, sea and sand, but that the materials used to build a facility blend into the environment, that the timber was cut in the least exploitative manner, that the workers are being paid a fair wage and that the local people are not obstructed, for example from accessing the beach.

Whilst the exploitative nature of the tourist industry stemmed largely from the practices of big business interests, which were mainly extra-regional in origin, environmentally friendly groups from those same countries are now contesting the adverse effects of mass tourism on the natural and social environment. The Caribbean is caught within this struggle because the nature of the tourist industry is one of heavy dependence on the extra-regional countries.

established farm workers programmes involving temporary stays of Caribbean migrants in the metropole are now being seen as a form of economic exploitation. As an important tourist destination, the Caribbean is inevitably subject to strong extra-regional influences, but even here there have been some moves to challenge this state of affairs.

7.3   CARIBBEAN INFLUENCES ON EXTRA-REGIONAL COUNTRIES

The previous section has underscored the unequal nature of the power relationships between the countries of the developed north and the Caribbean region, leading to the hegemony of the US, in particular, in the region. This section shows that even within such a relationship, there is scope for Caribbean society and culture to make an impact on extra-regional countries.

Political influences

Migration

Caribbean migrants in the metropolitan cities of the US, Canada and Europe take a close interest in the much-publicized debates there that focus on immigration policy. Citizens of the host country tend to be hostile to immigrants because they feel that they will accept lower wages and keep the price of labour down. In addition, there are usually racial and ethnic tensions between immigrants and members of the host nation. The US, Canadian and British governments are strongly attuned to how their citizens feel about migrants, especially in times of economic downturn, and there continues to be a powerful **lobby** to drastically restrict immigration, at the same time that a growing number of organizations are committed to defending migrants' rights. Politically, then, immigration and the laws governing migrants' status are highly charged issues.

Periodically these extra-regional countries engage in exercises to round up illegal aliens (or visitors who have overstayed their welcome), as well as non-citizen criminals who have completed their prison sentences, and send them back to their countries of origin. This policy of sending deportees back to the Caribbean with little warning has been sharply criticized by Caribbean governments, forcing the US in particular to recognize the sensitivity of the issue and to pledge cooperation with Caribbean security officials. Increasingly, the US is finding that cooperation with Caribbean governments is a better policy to adopt than taking an arrogant stance, especially when both are trying to address some common problems.

Caribbean people, though, are not yet sufficiently organized to be a force that directly impacts US politics. One exception is the Cuban population of South Florida, an anti-communist group dedicated to overthrowing the Castro regime. They have formed powerful associations, one of which is the ***Cuban American Foundation***, which relentlessly lobbies US politicians and policy-makers to maintain a hardline attitude to Cuba and to continue to enforce the **trade embargo**. One reason for their success is that the US government is also bent on removing the communist presence from its doorstep.

There are Caribbean people who have attained high office in the various arms of the US government and judiciary who are able to work 'from the inside' in influencing local policy. Many hold **dual citizenship** so they are both Americans and Caribbean citizens. It is interesting to note that a large number of Caribbean migrants are not averse to returning home, before or after retirement, and maintain close ties with their home territories. To this end they are very interested in efforts by Caribbean governments to recognize their diasporic communities, especially in the issue that comes up periodically – allowing Caribbean citizens abroad to vote in national elections. It is not unlikely, therefore, that these individuals with loyalties to both the US and the Caribbean are able to influence policy in ways favourable to the region whenever they can.

Political scientists point to the openness of the American political system (Payne, 2000) to show that issues pertaining to the Caribbean may well find a sympathetic hearing through one of many policy-making routes. Since the legislative, judicial and executive arms are separated in the American system of government, policy can be influenced by a host of lobbyists promoting different issues and causes. In addition, the Pentagon, the Central Intelligence Agency (CIA), the Treasury and the Department of Defense are all influenced by their own special interests and the lobbies that promote those interests. Moreover, a US state enjoys a great deal of autonomy in its relations with the federal government in Washington, and states try to protect their rights as much as possible. Thus, a state such as Florida, while not responsible for US foreign policy, can influence major issues to do with the Caribbean because of the high volume of trade it transacts with the Caribbean, and because so many Caribbean people live in Florida and are able to form pressure groups that get the attention of some office in the state policy apparatus.

ACTIVITY 7.10

Conduct independent research to examine how the Haitian 'boat people' and the Haitian lobby in the US are influencing politics in that country.

Narcotics

The Caribbean is a major link in the chain of international drug smuggling that stretches from the mountains of South America (Colombia, Bolivia and Venezuela) to the high-demand markets of the US. Both Trinidad and Tobago (closest to South America) and the Bahamas (closest to the US) are important transhipment links along this chain, but Haiti, the Dominican Republic, Jamaica, Anguilla, Antigua and Barbuda, as well as the Associated State of Puerto Rico, are also heavily involved. While a significant amount of drugs is imported into the US via air using drug mules, the bulk imports are conveyed by fast launches utilizing sea lanes in the unpatrolled waters of the Caribbean.

One of the strategies of US drug enforcement agencies is to prevent illegal drug shipments from reaching the US but they have found it extremely difficult to deal effectively with all the sovereign nations through which illegal drugs are smuggled. The **Shiprider Agreement** is one way of dealing with this problem but several Caribbean countries, including Barbados and Jamaica, have been reluctant to allow US security personnel to enter their territorial space in 'hot pursuit' of criminals engaged in drug trafficking. This response is forcing the US to realize that respecting the sovereign rights of even poor nations must be seen to be part of their overall strategy in winning the drugs war.

Increasingly the US is realizing that what affects the Caribbean affects the US (see Box 7.14). There is concern that Caribbean countries have neither the resources nor the expertise to monitor and control the drug smuggling operations that use their territories as a base. These **international criminal syndicates** or *cartels* have resources that far exceed those of many Caribbean nations. These monies can easily be used to destabilize a small, relatively poor country by bribing key personnel in its police, judicial and political agencies. Connected with drug smuggling are gun running – to protect the valuable cargo, and **money laundering** – opening bank accounts and setting up companies that enable drug lords to invest their money in apparently legal ways, protected by strict bank secrecy laws. These large sums of money may eventually find their way into big business and even into the coffers of US political campaigns.

From the point of view of a superpower like the US, the destabilizing of any Caribbean country means that there is a security problem in its 'backyard', which it will have to 'fix'. Thus, to maintain the status quo in the Caribbean and to be more effective against drug smugglers, the US is increasingly involved in initiatives that assist the Caribbean in establishing:

- drug surveillance and monitoring operations
- databases to improve the collection and exchange of intelligence information
- training for security officials in forensic accounting and banking to better detect and trace the movement of large sums of money across international borders.

Economic influences

Trade

BOX 7.14 Caribbean influences on US trade

The Caribbean is the tenth largest importer of US goods and services in the world. The businesses and firms engaged in supplying these exports to the Caribbean employ upwards of 400,000 persons in the US. The state of Florida does most of its trade with the Caribbean and this supports about 80,000 jobs (Payne, 2000). In this trade the US enjoys a healthy surplus, to the tune of several billion dollars. Thus, any threats to the economic stability of the Caribbean are of concern to the US.

In recent years the threat of terrorism has opened US eyes to the vulnerability of the Caribbean, where terrorists may be able to establish bases and destabilize the region. So in addition to *homeland security* (vigilance about its own borders), the US is also concerned about its lucrative market in the Caribbean and its supply of strategic raw materials. For example, Trinidad and Tobago is a major producer of methanol and ammonium sulphate and provides 40 per cent of US imports of liquefied natural gas (LNG). The petrochemical industrial complexes producing these strategic materials have minimal security measures in place (Bryan and Flynn, 2002).

Its vulnerability, small size and few resources, which made the US in the past either ignore the Caribbean or invade it with impunity, are today major issues forcing a change of attitude. There is more of an understanding now that a spirit of cooperation should be the new way of doing business with Caribbean countries because the security of the Caribbean directly impacts the security of the US. However, this does not necessarily mean that the Caribbean can oppose the US freely (for example, as on the Shiprider Agreement) because of the possible backlash, such as withdrawal of aid or closing off of markets.

Festivals

Trinidad-style carnivals and reggae and dancehall festivals are becoming an integral part of the culture and society of extra-regional countries. London's *Notting Hill Carnival* is the biggest open-air festival in Europe with more than two million visitors spending around UK£30 million. *Caribana* in Canada and Brooklyn's *Labour Day Parade* are the major open-air festivals in North America. About one million attend Caribana celebrations and two million gather annually for Labour Day in Brooklyn. Patrons spend millions of dollars, constituting an important source of income for these metropolitan centres. In addition, carnivals in Miami, Washington and Atlanta are growing. Even the small Caribbean community in Australia now organizes a 'Sydney Bacchanal', which most likely will grow as the others have grown, largely because these extra-regional societies do not already have the equivalent of a street festival combining music, dancing, theatre and creative costuming. Caribbean migrants are driving the development of carnivals wherever they settle, not only enhancing the cultural diversity of these cities but contributing to their economic life as well.

Cultural influences

Caribbean music

Whether it is reggae, soca, son, punta or zouk, Caribbean music affirms Caribbean people's sense of identity with their homelands. In a way it makes them feel more comfortable living in the diaspora. Caribbean migrants have tended to settle in the big cities of the developed world; it is these cities that are more likely to reflect a cosmopolitan outlook quite different from culture in the rural areas. Thus the impact of Caribbean music has been largely in urban areas, and mainly among the Caribbean diaspora. Only reggae has made a breakthrough further into the mainstream culture of the US, Canada and Europe (Box 7.15).

Rastafarianism

Together with reggae music, Rastafarianism has had a significant impact on urban cultural life in the big cities of North America and Europe. The distinctive dreadlocks and the colours of the Ethiopian flag (red, green and gold) are the most obvious symbols of the Rastafari. A great many persons who affect the hairstyle, colours and style of language of the Rastafari do not necessarily observe their religious and dietary practices. For many in the visual and performing arts, especially, the Rastafari is an image or a **role** that they feel they can identify with without becoming fully fledged 'Rastas'. For countless others, particularly men, it is just a hairstyle that is now in vogue.

How do true Rastafarian beliefs and lifestyle affect extra-regional countries? Through the lyrics of reggae music, especially Bob Marley's music, the message of the Rastafarian movement has spread into non-Caribbean cultures and societies. It was a message that received widespread acceptance, particularly among youth. Today more people worldwide are able to at least identify the term 'Jah', recognize a picture of Bob Marley, and know the connection with Ethiopia and Haile Selassie.

BOX 7.15 Why does Caribbean music not have a greater impact?

Caribbean recording stars, record producers and promoters, and cultural organizations recognize that they have not been able to penetrate the huge markets of extra-regional countries effectively. The markets for Caribbean music remain strongly tied to the people of the Caribbean diaspora. The North American and European markets will continue to be major markets for Caribbean artistes but only a tiny percentage of that market is being tapped at the moment. Those involved in music should now brainstorm ways of bringing Caribbean music to a wider audience in western countries.

One way is through securing a larger share of the radio listenership. How to get non-Caribbean people to tune into and become appreciative of Caribbean music? The obvious answer lies in promotions of different kinds – festivals, advertisements, music, foods, personalities, gifts, vouchers, competitions – to arouse interest. The potential exists for the expansion of the market share that Caribbean music now enjoys in extra-regional countries and this would increase the profitability of the industry for Caribbean artistes and countries.

So far neither governments nor private enterprise in the Caribbean have taken much of an interest in the marketing of cultural products. Yet they can both play a crucial role in expanding the market share that Caribbean artistes now command in foreign countries. One strategy may be for Caribbean governmental agencies or private entrepreneurs to acquire funds and negotiate with the major mass media networks to set up Caribbean radio stations on foreign soil geared to capturing a non-Caribbean audience. Traditionally, the Caribbean middle or moneyed classes have invested in retailing business and industry, whilst artistes have tended to be from the grassroots culture. Thus it is not a traditional partnership that is being advocated, but such an arrangement could provide the funding to establish an aggressive presence on the American market, for example.

The Caribbean music industry has grown up largely through the efforts of talented individuals who undertook to record, produce, market and distribute in small (sometimes one-man) companies. Caribbean music now competes with the multi-million-dollar productions of the major recording studios and cannot continue to do so effectively because of the obvious disadvantages. These big recording labels, too, have signed up the best of Caribbean talent and are now producing the reggae superstars. While this is very profitable for the individual artiste, no profits accrue to the Caribbean country. It is a whole uncharted area of possibilities that Caribbean governments and private enterprise have ignored as investments, yet non-traditional cultural products like music have the potential to contribute enormously as invisible exports to Caribbean countries.

Indeed, Caribbean Studies as a cultural studies programme is growing in popularity in universities abroad, and reggae and Rastafarianism are major components of such a programme. In fact it may be true to say that the examples of hybridization and syncretism that have emerged as Caribbean cultural expressions represent fascinating areas of study for non-Caribbean people.

Culinary practices

To people in extra-regional countries Caribbean cuisine represents one more type of ethnic food that any metropolitan centre offers. It has to compete with Italian, Indian, Chinese, Greek, Polynesian and a host of other ethnic foods. However, the Caribbean migrant communities support their restaurants and markets because, like music, to enjoy food from home is like having the best of both worlds. Curries, rice and peas, saltfish, jerk meats, coconut milk and highly seasoned foods are slowly being made known to non-Caribbean people. Usually they come to know it through their friends from the Caribbean. There are now successful Caribbean restaurants in some of the bigger cities and in certain areas Cuban or Haitian food may be popular, but the bulk of Americans, Canadians or Europeans have yet to be exposed to and acquire a taste for Caribbean cooking.

Summary

Within a relationship in which extra-regional countries continue to be hegemonic, the Caribbean is still able to wield some influence in the West. Immigration issues, as well as the international narcotics trade and terrorism, are forcing the US to be more vigilant about the Caribbean because of its strategic location. As the superpower in the region, the US must necessarily be proactive or else it will be vulnerable if unwelcome events do occur. Thus, it is finding that the Caribbean must be an important ally with whom it needs to cooperate. Caribbean carnivals are also important to extra-regional countries as they bring in millions of dollars. And Caribbean cultural and religious forms (music, Rastafarianism and culinary arts) have increasingly penetrated extra-regional markets and cultural life in metropolitan cities.

WRAP UP

The Caribbean has been embroiled in a relationship with western countries since the fifteenth century in which it has played a subaltern role. All aspects of society and culture under colonialism and afterwards have been influenced in significant ways. In the aftermath of independence Caribbean people have tried to resist this influence – novelists have written about it, scholars and ordinary people have investigated it, performances have been created using our indigenous cultural art forms, and our entrepreneurs have looked for creative ways to develop alternative products, be it tourism, culinary arts, music or sports. Postcolonial thinking has provided a way of examining this influence and our varied responses to it – resistance, conformity and creative strategies. The insights provided by postcolonial thought should help us to continue to examine these matters as the forces of globalization now bring the ex-colonizer and the ex-colonized together again in a neocolonial association.

PRACTICE TESTS

Structured response

1 Using TWO examples, show how colonialism has influenced consumption practices in Caribbean society and culture. (2 marks)

2 (a) Distinguish between imperialism and colonialism. (2 marks)

   (b) Distinguish between neocolonialism and postcolonialism. (2 marks)

3 Give TWO reasons to explain why Caribbean countries found it difficult to establish manufacturing industries when they became independent. (4 marks)

4 (a) Explain why 'social capital' for youth tends to be associated with sporting US designer labels. (2 marks)

   (b Suggest why reggae music has enjoyed such large-scale acceptance in extra-regional countries. (2 marks)

5 Identify ONE country traditionally associated with each of the following types of music: (a) son, (b) spouge, (c) ska, (d) zouk, (e) punta and (f) parang. (6 marks)

6 Describe TWO ways in which extra-regional countries have influenced Caribbean theatre arts. (4 marks)

7 Identify TWO ways in which slavery has influenced culinary practices in the Caribbean. (4 marks)

8 Outline TWO criticisms of the Westminster system of government in the Caribbean. (4 marks)

9 Describe ONE constitutional reform in Caribbean countries that may address criticisms of the Westminster model. (2 marks)

10 Explain TWO ways in which Caribbean migrant farm labour contributes to the economy of extra-regional countries. (4 marks)

Essay questions (20 marks)

1 Explain why the countries of the Caribbean, even though politically independent, are still seen as dependent on extra-regional countries.

2 Using examples, explain how Caribbean cultural expressions have been influenced by extra-regional countries.

3 Describe how cricket has been used by Caribbean people as a force of nationalism and development.

4 Outline ways in which the Caribbean mass media can be transformed into a means of resisting the dominance of western countries.

Challenge essay questions (30 marks)

1 Using Caribbean society and culture as an example, explain what is meant by a 'postcolonial society'.

2 Analyse the nature of the tendency among Caribbean people to prefer foreign goods and services.

3 Using ONE named Caribbean example as a case study, show how its tourist industry is influenced by extra-regional countries.

4 'It is largely self-interest that motivates the US to provide assistance to Caribbean countries.' Discuss.

RESEARCH TOPICS

Issue

A major research issue for Caribbean countries is the psychological implications of our colonial and neocolonial condition. One way of examining this issue is to try to interrogate the bases of the thinking that people usually employ in making decisions about what goods and services to buy, especially when there is a choice between a 'first-world' product and a local product. Here we will focus on music.

Research methodology

One convenient way of collecting data for this study is to gather three or four persons whom you think are articulate and reflective enough to take your project seriously. This is a focus group interview which you will have to tape and you will need to ask the participants to resist the tendency to speak while others are speaking. You are interested in getting clear feedback from the tape so these are considerations that as researcher you have to think about.

Questions to the group may include what type of music they like and what they are likely to buy. You may ask them to comment on what each other is saying so that you collect different views. You can directly introduce controversial themes, such as the claim that they may have a colonial mindset if there are strong preferences for music from extra-regional countries. The arguments they put forward are important for you to capture. You must also try to probe beneath answers such as 'because I like the music' to ascertain as far as you can what people mean when they say they like a particular form of music. The individual, too, may not be able to give exact reasons but this may be an interesting phenomenon for you to dwell on – the extent to which people are aware of why they like something or why they dislike something else. Remember the study is about people's thinking about the choices they make.

Finally, having collected the data you need to do more than present the views of the participants. You should comment on the main themes that you detect and where possible use insights from postcolonial theory about how people accommodate to the influences from extra-regional countries – do they demonstrate conformity, resistance or creative strategies?

REFERENCES

Bryan, A., & Flynn, S. (2002). Free trade, smart borders and homeland security: US–Caribbean co-operation in a new era of vulnerability. Working Series, Paper No. 8. Coral Gables, FL: University of Miami, Dante B. Fascell North–South Centre

Du Bois, W. E. B. (1903). *The souls of black folks*. Chicago, IL: A. C. McClurg & Co.; Cambridge, MA: Cambridge University Press, John Wilson and Son.

Greene, O., Jr. (2004). Ethnicity, modernity and retention in the Garifuna punta. *Black Music Research Journal*, 22(2), pp. 189–216.

James, C. L. R. (1963). *Beyond a boundary*. London: Hutchinson.

Memmi, A. (1991). *The colonizer and the colonized*. Boston, MA: Beacon Press.

Payne, A. (2000). Rethinking United States–Caribbean relations: towards a new mode of trans-territorial governance. *Review of International Studies, 26*, pp. 69–82.

Richardson, B. (2004). The migration experience. In B. Brereton (Ed.), *General history of the Caribbean, Volume 5: The Caribbean in the twentieth century*, pp. 434–464. Paris: UNESCO and London: Macmillan Caribbean.

St Pierre, M. (1973). West Indian cricket: a socio-historical appraisal, Part 1. *Caribbean Quarterly*, 19(2), pp. 7–27.

MODULE

2 CARIBBEAN DEVELOPMENT

The first module on Caribbean society and culture provided the context and background essential for a study of Caribbean development, the subject of this second module. This module introduces you to different conceptions of development and how they have changed over time, the factors that promote and hinder development, and how Caribbean people and institutions have shaped the region's development. It is important to realize that the colonial past and the neocolonial present influence almost every aspect of the process of development – the traditional imbalance of trade flows with developed countries, the foreign tastes and preferences for consumer goods, the penetration of the region by the foreign mass media, a western-oriented education system, the over-developed port and capital city and underdeveloped rural hinterlands, and the stratified nature of society and culture. These conditions form the backdrop against which Caribbean countries have been grappling with development efforts from the decolonization era to now.

GENERAL MODULE OBJECTIVES

On completing this module you will be able to demonstrate an understanding of
1 'development' as a contested concept
2 the dynamic interaction of politics, economics, culture, society, technology and the environment in the development process
3 the efforts of Caribbean people and institutions in promoting development.

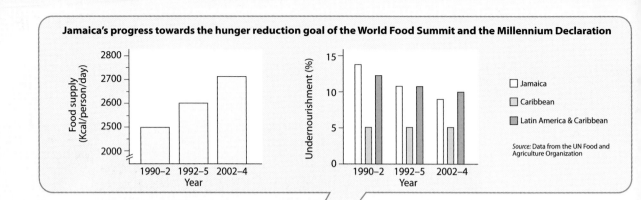

Jamaica's progress towards the hunger reduction goal of the World Food Summit and the Millennium Declaration

Jamaica
Caribbean
Latin America & Caribbean

Source: Data from the UN Food and Agriculture Organization

Sugar	2000	2001
Area cultivated (000 ha)	8.6	8.5
Production (000 tonnes)	58.4	49.8
As percentage of GDP	57.3	47.8
Exports (000 tonnes)	54.8	48.9
Export earnings (BDS$ million)	54.1	47.2
Production cost per tonne (BDS$)	1366.2	1549.0

Agricultural production in Barbados

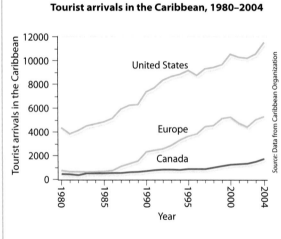

Tourist arrivals in the Caribbean, 1980–2004

Source: Data from Caribbean Organization

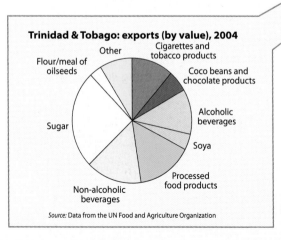

Trinidad & Tobago: exports (by value), 2004

Source: Data from the UN Food and Agriculture Organization

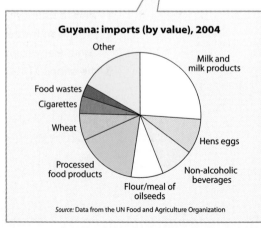

Guyana: imports (by value), 2004

Source: Data from the UN Food and Agriculture Organization

8 CONCEPTUALIZING DEVELOPMENT

'Development' refers to both a process and a desired end-state. This chapter explores the different conceptions of development that have had historical significance in the Caribbean, as well as the factors that promote and hinder development and how they interrelate. At least three different conceptualizations of development are discussed. These ideas show that there are varying ways in which development can be measured, leading to the use of different indicators. National development became an all-important goal in the aftermath of the second world war, when Europe had to be rebuilt and its overseas colonies began to seek independence. We have thus had several decades where different models of development have been tried in the Caribbean.

EXPECTED LEARNING OUTCOMES

On completing this chapter, you will be able to

1 analyse different conceptions of development
2 show the interrelatedness in different approaches to development – economic development, sustainable development and human development
3 examine different indicators of development
4 describe the factors that promote and hinder development
5 evaluate how development has been influenced by political, economic, social, cultural, environmental and technological factors.

8.1 CONCEPTIONS OF DEVELOPMENT

Three main ideas have imbued the concept of development, even long before countries determinedly began to focus on development in the aftermath of the second world war. It is important to separate out these ideas because they overlap in the models of development that we will study later and it is insightful to see which ideas are emphasized in the different models. It also helps to make sense of the ever-present discussions and arguments that take place around the concept of development.

● ***Development as the enactment of human values*** is a conceptualization that is saying that for anything to develop or become better, improvement has to be related to some **values** that are being enacted. For example, what would it take for *you to develop as an individual*? Certainly, placing a value on the acquisition of knowledge and skills might well be one aspect of this, and perhaps attention to your interrelationships with your fellow human beings, making sure that the contact is humane and enabling for both of you. And most people would place a high value on material possessions and the comforts of life. Hence, when improvement is being contemplated for anything, including societies, some set of values is going to be emphasized, depending on what model or approach to development has been chosen. For instance, an approach to development based on a model of economic growth emphasizes values that have to do with increasing the **standard of living** – the material wealth of people.

- *Development as increasing differentiation or complexity* is a conceptualization of development that states that for anything to develop it must become more complex and more differentiated – its component parts will interrelate with better and deeper linkages. It will therefore become more efficient and more integrated. A very good understanding about this comes from how societies are described – as *developing* and *developed*. A *developing country* is probably an agrarian society or has a high percentage of its labour force in agriculture. The industrial and manufacturing sector may be small and located only at the port city. A *developed country*, on the other hand, is one where much of the labour force is engaged in industry, manufacturing, business, commercial activities and other services. These activities generate much larger profits than agriculture. Agriculture, though, is much more efficient than in the developing country because of mechanization, needing only a small labour force. Agriculture has been 'developed' by increasing the use of machines, which need large tracts of land to operate efficiently. That leads to the closure of small farms and their amalgamation into huge concerns operating just like factories. Thus the transition from 'developing' to 'developed' reflects an increasing differentiation and complexity within the society and the various sectors of the economy.

- *Development as liberation or human freedom* is a conceptualization of development that has come from philosophers, educators, humanitarians, and even economists and political scientists. This states that for any people to be developed this must be accompanied by growth in their autonomy, in the options they can pursue, and in their sense of self-efficacy – that their actions are significant and can make a difference. Many people see development as liberty or human freedom being achieved through *education*. This is one of the reasons why education is so much a part of a country's developmental plans. An educated person has a range of knowledge and skills that he or she can call on to better understand the world, to reflect on why people act the way they do, and to critically appraise the best options and decisions that can be made to live a better life. The more education one has the more likely it is that one will be free of the encumbrances of life, namely poverty, a narrow outlook, and minimal aspirations. That is why many parents scrimp and save so that their children can have the opportunity to go on to secondary and post-secondary education. Even people who have had only some education intuitively know of its potential to **empower** and liberate. Education, then, is just one approach that might be taken in a development model to achieve a basic conceptualization of development – one concerned with liberation and human freedom. This idea of development tends to be prominent in the development discourse in the Caribbean and other postcolonial societies because those societies were forged under conditions of oppression and inequality. However, education seems to be central to all the models discussed above, though for different reasons.

Summary

The three persistent ideas or conceptualizations of development discussed above provide us with tools to examine the different models and approaches to development that have been tried in the Caribbean. They help to reduce the confusion in understanding development discourse as these ideas continually overlap in quite different development models or approaches to development. The three conceptions of development are (i) development as *the enactment of human values*, which is sometimes expressed in terms of an increase in the standard of living, (ii) development as *increasing differentiation or complexity* in the institutions of the country, and (iii) development as *liberation or human freedom*, an idea that is now receiving much more attention.

8.2

APPROACHES TO DEVELOPMENT

We are familiar with many everyday terms that in some way imply the development status of a country and implicitly or explicitly the particular emphasis deemed important. For example, look at Table 8.1.

Table 8.1 Development terms

TERMS USUALLY ASSOCIATED WITH EX-COLONIES	TERMS USUALLY ASSOCIATED WITH EUROPE, NORTH AMERICA, AUSTRALIA, AND THE STRONG ECONOMIES OF ASIA
Developing	Developed
Third World	First World
South	West, North
Agrarian societies	Industrialized societies
Less Developed Countries (LDCs)	More Developed Countries (MDCs)
Economically Less Developed Countries (ELDCs)	Economically More Developed Countries (EMDCs)

ACTIVITY 8.1

1. Conduct independent research to find out what NICs are? What other terms are sometimes used to distinguish between 'developing' and 'developed' countries?

2. Give examples of countries that may be difficult to classify as either developed or developing. Explain why they are difficult to classify?

The list in Table 8.1 suggests several ideas about development:

1. Countries like the Caribbean which are 'developing' are expected to attain the conditions and ways of life of the 'developed' countries – a 'stage' or evolutionary model of development.
2. The ranking of 'first' and 'third' worlds indicates the inferior status of developing countries.
3. A term such as 'the south' indicates a growing understanding that more neutral terms should be used, even though there is a problem of fit when Australia is grouped as being part of 'the north'.
4. 'Agrarian society' indicates a type of economy that cannot sustain development as experienced by 'industrialized societies'.
5. LDCs and MDCs are being replaced by EMDCs and ELDCs to show that development is a multi-faceted process, and even if a country's economy may not be as strong as another's, the whole society and culture cannot be categorized as 'less developed'.

The use of different terms and changes in the terms over time indicate that certain approaches to development that were once dominant are today being contested. However, all the terms are presently in use, indicating much confusion about what development really entails. One very durable conviction about development is **economic development**.

Economic development

Most of the terms in Table 8.1 emphasize a notion of development based on the economy. The specific goal of development in the decolonization era was economic development through **economic growth**. This refers to an 'increase in the value of goods and services produced by a country within a time period'. It was expected that the problems of poverty, inadequate schooling, technological backwardness and rural neglect would be automatically addressed once Caribbean countries were experiencing improvements in economic growth. It was believed that since more goods and services were being produced, more people would enjoy material benefits through increased income and the standard of living would rise.

A tradition began of devising indicators that could measure different aspects of development. These indicators were numerical measures that could be compared across different countries to determine 'development', but they usually succeeded only in measuring 'economic growth'. The specific indicators were:

- *Gross National Product (GNP)* is the value of *output* (goods and services) produced by a country plus any income derived from abroad. *GNP per capita* is obtained by dividing the GNP by the population. This indicates the average income of citizens in a country and is used to classify countries as high, middle and low income. While it is a good indicator of the economic strengths and weaknesses of countries, it cannot be said to indicate *economic development* (Box 8.1).
- *Gross Domestic Product (GDP)* is the total market value of the output (goods and services) of a country in a given year. *GDP per capita*, the GDP divided by the population, is also used for comparison purposes.
- *Population growth rate* is calculated by considering birth and death rates, as well as migration statistics, and is a key indicator of economic growth. Usually it means that if a country can keep its total population growth down, then its per capita income should rise.
- *Age dependency ratio* is the ratio of *dependents* – people younger than 15 and older than 65 – to the working-age population (those aged 15–64). This measure suggests that if there were more *economically active persons* than dependents then they would be better able to take care of their dependents. Hence, governments would not have to spend so much on social services and would be able to spend that money on infrastructure and development works.

Traditionally, emphasis was put on measures that focused on increasing *output* and increasing the per capita share of that output through increasing production and limiting population growth. These ideas formed the basis of economic policies in the 1960s, 1970s and 1980s in the Caribbean. They tended to be based on **ethnocentric**

BOX 8.1 Criticisms of economic growth indicators

An indicator is a quantitative assessment of how countries are ranked on some variable or category such as population growth or savings per capita. It is used for making comparisons across countries and regions. However, it is important for a country to know where it stands in relation to variables that measure aspects of its development. In order to plan effectively, the country must get a good sense of its performance to date, and this is where well-conceived indicators can be invaluable.

Although economic growth indicators are widely used to measure a country's development, they should be approached with caution, particularly when only one indicator is used. This often happens with *GNP per capita,* which is in common use by international bodies to categorize the income levels of countries and forms the basis of judgements about whether countries are rich, poor, developing or developed. GNP measures economic growth but not *all* aspects of growth. In addition, to use it to infer something of the development status of a country shows a limited understanding of the concept of development. For example:

- GNP per capita only captures the production statistics that go through official accounting procedures. It cannot report on the activities of the *informal economy*. This includes subsistence farming and barter activity, the black market and drug trade as well as domestic work and small businesses where people are paid in cash-only transactions.

- GNP per capita is recorded in US dollars, but in different countries one dollar is able to buy more than in another. Thus for purposes of comparison the raw GNP per capita statistics should be converted to another statistic – the *purchasing power parity (PPP)* which sheds more light on the development status of a particular country, and the effects of inflation, shortages and dislocation of the economy.

- GNP per capita for a country does not show how that income or wealth is distributed. The increased income may be concentrated in the hands of a few. Another indicator, the Gini Index (see p. 250), is used to show income inequality more specifically.

- GNP per capita does not take into account how natural resources are being depleted in the drive to increase output and raise productivity. Many countries which record increased economic growth have done so at the expense of the environment. Another statistical procedure known as *natural resource accounting* is used today to measure these costs to the environment.

approaches to development that portrayed it in a uniform way, modelled on the development experience of western societies (Box 8.2). However, much of the development efforts expended in those decades did not significantly address the problems being faced by citizens. Thus while production *has* increased in Caribbean countries, the ordinary citizen has not benefited meaningfully from such growth – the resources produced (goods, services, amenities) have not 'trickled down' to the mass of the population. Today there is more of a willingness to acknowledge that economic development is multi-faceted and that economic *growth* is only one aspect of it. Economic development as understood today emphasizes the **welfare** of people in a country and is very much concerned with *poverty reduction*.

ACTIVITY 8.2

Identify TWO ways in which conceptions of development in the Caribbean were derived from the ethnocentric ideas of developed countries.

Human development

Development thinkers sought to show that there was a preoccupation with economic development construed narrowly in terms of economic growth. Economic development is much more than this; it is concerned with human welfare but the economic growth idea tended to dominate thinking. This led to a search for a new way of describing development, resulting in the 1990s in the **Human Development Paradigm (HDP)**. This brought together ideas about economic development and **sustainable development** to show that they referred to the same thing and that

BOX 8.2 Ethnocentric models of development

The models that eventually had an impact on Caribbean development had their beginnings in theories from sociologists and economists in the western world that tended to emphasize 'progress' as economic development. There was a preoccupation in western thought about the steady progress of mankind and this *evolutionary perspective* influenced approaches to development.

Modernization theory

McClleland (1961) suggested that the 'achieving society' was one where citizens held values that promoted achievement and were open to economic and technological advancement. Inkeles and Smith (1974) devised a *modernity scale* to test whether members of a society held modern *values*. They felt that once modern institutions such as factories and schools were established, a modern set of values would become commonplace. For example, both schools and wage labour would help to develop values associated with punctuality, regularity, regard for extrinsic rewards such as certificates and wages, understanding the chain of command, the profit motive, individual effort and achievement, openness to change, mixing with diverse groups, technology, production and industry and a desire for acquiring status symbols.

These theorists were thinking of what it would take for a largely agrarian society to begin the process of development. Critics point to the extreme ethnocentrism of this view, which bases what must be considered 'development' on the experience of western countries. It also assumes that traditional values are incompatible with development. However, there are many scholars and others in the Caribbean who endorse this view and are firmly wedded to a western model of development. For

example, in the Caribbean our earliest thrust into national development planning advocated 'industrialization by invitation' – inviting foreign assembly-type factories to come and set up plants in exchange for tax holidays (see pp. 344–7).

Human capital theories

This involved indices that were more easily measured than modern values. Human capital theorists saw the people of a country as its most important resource in the development thrust. For the country to develop, the people had to be upgraded and improved – in short, treated as **human capital**. In enunciating the theory, Schultz (1961) began a movement that swept through the newly independent nations of the world. *Education* was seen to be the most important investment that would pay off in national development. If education was to be offered to as many citizens as possible, so the theory goes, then they would possess a high level of knowledge and skills that would ensure high labour productivity. They relied on indicators such as percentage of the national budget invested in primary, secondary and tertiary education, literacy levels, educational performance, school enrolment and labour productivity (measured mainly by GDP per capita). Again, this theory had elements of the modernization thesis in it, including the emphasis on a western education system that would produce citizens with the necessary knowledge and skills for a labour force mainly involved in industrial production. It was only after many schools had been built, leading to an increase in the educated unemployed, that development planners, economists and others sought to reconceptualize development in more holistic terms that did not place undue emphasis on economic growth.

a more holistic portrayal of development was obtained by putting human beings at the centre of the process – **human development**. All three may have different emphases but there cannot be one without the other: for example, for economic development to be sustainable it has to pay attention to human development, and planning for human development must necessarily rely on a sustainable programme of economic development.

The Human Development Paradigm has certain basic views:

● that people are the *means and ends of development*; people are thus central to the development process and we know when development has occurred by looking at the quality of their lives

- that development is largely about *broadening people's choices*; they have more options and opportunities to develop themselves along the lines that will bring them the greatest sense of well-being as well as income
- that *poverty* and *income inequality* are the major problems of human societies that prevent a better quality of life.

Given the above, the HDP envisages development as a process whereby a country works on eradicating the barriers to four key areas of development: *equity, productivity, empowerment* and *sustainability* (Box 8.3). These are called the 'pillars of the HDP' and build on each other, **equity** being the most important, as it begins the process. These ideas originated in the United Nations and related organizations and, unlike the modernization and human capital approaches, are not considered to be ethnocentric. This is because the HDP is concerned with general areas of human well-being; how a country decides to pursue the 'broadening of human choices', for example, will differ considerably from one country to another.

It may well be that one country sees universal primary education (UPE) and universal secondary education (USE) as the main routes towards this goal. Other countries, perhaps with greater resources, could increase access to tertiary education by ensuring that the state pays part of the tuition fees. In another country, investing in distance education may be more appropriate. On another front, increasing the minimum wage, opening up Crown Lands for leasing, or providing additional work-related training for youth may be what some people need to develop themselves. Hence, the HDP does not stipulate or prescribe *how* the development process should be undertaken. Each country sets its own developmental goals by addressing the four key areas in ways that it deems appropriate while adhering to an understanding of development as an *increasingly better quality of life for citizens* (see Box 8.4).

ACTIVITY 8.3

Analyse the Human Development Paradigm as an approach to development and show how the three conceptions of development described earlier are evident in the Human Development Paradigm.

Sustainable development

This is usually defined as 'development that meets the needs of the present without compromising the ability of future generations to meet their own needs'. It is often spoken about as if it is primarily an environmental issue. But for any degree of sustainable development to take place there must be commitment on the part of the people of the country, and that depends on the extent to which their human development needs (equity, productivity and empowerment) are being addressed (see Box 8.3). Again we come back to the scenario where the various approaches to development – economic, human and sustainable development – are similar but discussed in ways that lead people to think that they may be quite different things.

For example, if equity is severely compromised, so is the environment. In societies where there is *inequality in the distribution of income*, where many live in abject poverty, daily survival will be more of a priority than the well-being of future generations. We see this in Haiti, where the forests have been cut down for firewood, leading to massive soil erosion. Hence most of the measures designed to ensure sustainable development are directed at poverty reduction and reducing inequalities (which are also areas of concern in economic and human development).

BOX 8.3 The pillars of the human development paradigm

Equity

'Equity' refers to a commitment on the part of the government and people of a country to enable all social groups to access the opportunities that the country offers and to be fair to all groups as they grasp these opportunities. Thus the poor, those who live in rural or isolated areas, women, the handicapped, those of different religious or political views and other ethnic groups should all be equally able to access opportunities. What this means can be far ranging in terms of putting the necessary planning in place. For example:

- where schools are sited is a major consideration and a *school mapping exercise* should be undertaken to ensure that as many as possible benefit from the building of new schools
- *poverty* may be a reason why some cannot access educational opportunity, so subsidized transport, books and school meals may become a priority.

Other than education, the distribution of land may be a barrier to equity. A small percentage of the population may own a large percentage of the land. *Land redistribution schemes* are vitally necessary in some countries but entail a deep commitment to the cause of development as ensuring a better quality of life for all, because what is necessary to accomplish this may disrupt the status quo. Land may be taken from some and they will need to be compensated. Land may be given to others but with the understanding that they will pay over time. Other than education and land reform, there are many areas of social life where equity can be addressed.

Productivity

'Productivity' refers to more than an economic understanding of growth. It is based first of all on *equity*. The understanding is that if people have equal access to educational and job opportunities then it is quite likely that their productivity will be high. This is based on the notion that if one takes advantage of what opportunities there are and becomes qualified, so that one can access jobs based on qualifications, then there is a certain level of commitment to that job. This pillar is trying to address the problem of people being in a host of 'dead-end' jobs where they are

bored, or see no opportunity for advancement, or where the job involves routine tasks that do not challenge them. Productivity, then, is more than the quantitative output measured in GNP per capita or GDP. Productivity in the HDP is based on how much people like their jobs and are happy in them and the following factors influence this:

- job security
- opportunities for staff development and professional advancement
- structures that allow workers a voice in how the work is managed and organized
- a reduction in the stress related to the job
- the extent to which working in a particular place affords certain kinds of benefits (e.g. financial institutions giving workers softer loans, companies giving workers discounts on merchandise, government departments running advanced training courses tied to promotion).

Empowerment

'Empowerment' refers to the degree to which individuals feel a sense of *self-efficacy* – the knowledge that they are capable of doing things to improve their lives. Again it is based on *equity*, allowing persons to become productive citizens in whatever area they choose. If persons have benefited from the equalization of educational and economic opportunity and are developing themselves in their work, the chances are they will have a high regard for themselves (*self-esteem*). This enables them to make decisions that are in their best interests and perhaps broaden their range of interests.

Sustainability

This is the goal of the HDP, to attain sustainable development by following a process of development that puts people first – a philosophy of human development. According to the HDP, development initiatives cannot be sustained unless they are built solidly on concerns of equity, productivity and empowerment. If those three are put in place, then sustainability becomes a matter of course. The HDP therefore not only endorses sustainable development, it outlines a process by which it can be attained.

Where big business interests operating on a quantitative understanding of *output as productivity* destroy the forest resources, and are responsible for overfishing and for polluting the environment, sustainable development is threatened. The costs of a controlled afforestation programme, of using only nets of a certain size, and of disposing of waste safely all cut into profits. Such activities also jeopardize the livelihoods (and productivity) of poorer folk who depend on the resources of the forests, sea and land. To make such companies observe safer environmental measures, both the state and the citizenry must be empowered enough to challenge big business. Thus measures designed to ensure sustainable development may well be directed at empowering village groups, communities and grassroots organizations to raise issues pertaining to the operations of big business interests.

Sustainable development, then, depends on a host of conditions in the society that enable citizens to understand the importance of engaging in practices that do not harm the environment. It goes against the unbridled economic growth of the past and the understanding of 'development' as 'human progress'. It also takes the view that an increase in the *standard of living* is a consumption-oriented indicator that encourages overuse of a country's resources. Sustainable development, then, goes against the ideas of those who promote *economic growth* as 'development'. It is more concerned with the *quality of life* of citizens, not just a material improvement in their existence; the **Human Development Index** (Box 8.4) lists those indicators which are thought to give an accurate picture of **human welfare**. All these concerns are also concerns of economic development (Fig. 8.1).

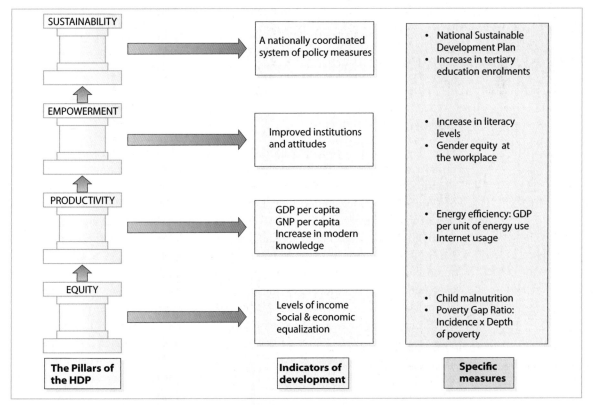

Fig. 8.1 Human development indicators

BOX 8.4 The Human Development Index (HDI)

The HDI has been developed by the United Nations Development Programme (UNDP). It uses a combination of *socio-economic measures* to give an indication of human welfare. Sustainable development (and economic development) is only possible where human welfare is being addressed positively. These measures are:

● *Longevity* (measured by life expectancy at birth). This gives an indication of the health resources of the country, access to those resources, levels of poverty in the society (which may impact on nutrition and pre- and post-natal care), whether people have access to safe drinking water, as well as whether wars and civil strife are an on-going problem. It may also indicate the levels of education that mothers have had because there is a general correlation between the health of a family and the education level obtained by the mother.

● *Knowledge* (measured by access to education, adult literacy and mean years of schooling attained). This indicates the extent to which members of a society are able to embrace opportunities related to further and continuing education in order to improve the quality of their lives, such as **ICTs**. Subsidizing education (as well as health) raises productivity levels. In some societies girls are restricted in their attempts to access further educational opportunities and this is seen as working against their welfare, preventing them from attaining their full potential.

● *GDP per capita* (an economic measure adjusted for *purchasing power parity* that reflects the difference in the cost of living between countries). This underscores the point that economic growth and economic development are major components of any development programme.

Increasingly the HDI is being adopted by international authorities as a better way of assessing development than using only economic growth indicators, as in the past. The HDI formed the basis of the *Millennium Development Goals (MDGs)* adopted by the UN in 2002 as guiding principles for countries to establish:

● Goal 1 – eradicate extreme poverty and hunger
● Goal 2 – achieve universal primary education
● Goal 3 – promote gender equality and empower women
● Goal 4 – reduce child mortality
● Goal 5 – improve maternal health
● Goal 6 – combat HIV/AIDS, malaria and other diseases
● Goal 7 – ensure environmental sustainability
● Goal 8 – develop a global partnership for development.

These goals suggest that the approaches to development should combine the basic ideas of economic, human and sustainable development.

Summary

How development is conceptualized shapes the approaches that a country adopts to improve the quality of life for its citizens. While *improvement* was thought to result from economic growth and progress, that emphasis is now believed to lead to environmental deterioration and increasingly wider income disparities between the rich and the poor. It is now recognized as a flawed idea about *economic development* but it is still held, for example, when we see numerical indicators such as GNP and GDP used to give an idea of the development status of a country. The importance given to *economic growth* approaches to development stemmed from our belief in the ethnocentric theories that conceptualized development as a uniform process that could happen in the Caribbean just as it did in western societies. These approaches minimized the problems faced by citizens in newly independent countries. Economic development as understood today emphasizes the *welfare* of people in a country and is very much concerned with poverty reduction. Approaches to development that emphasize human development or sustainable development are really only different aspects of an approach to economic development that values a holistic portrayal of development. All three ideas about development are interrelated and focus on the welfare and well-being of people.

8.3

FACTORS INFLUENCING DEVELOPMENT

In this section the conceptualizations and approaches to development discussed above are applied specifically to the Caribbean. Various factors that influence development are analysed using understandings about economic growth, economic development, sustainable development and the four pillars of the human development paradigm – equity, productivity, empowerment and sustainability. In addition, indicators of development are highlighted.

Political factors

Political **ideologies** and popular movements have from time to time challenged the status quo in the Caribbean. Political ideologies are systems of **beliefs** about governance and power that reflect the needs and aspirations of particular social groups. These beliefs are held so strongly that they become prescriptions for social life. **Capitalism**, **communism** and **socialism** (see Chapter 11) are ideologies. Capitalism is the dominant political ideology in the Caribbean. It emphasizes *market–led development* (minimum of restrictions by the state) and is also known as *free enterprise*.

There were no specific attempts at poverty reduction in the development efforts of the independence era; the emphasis was on increasing economic growth. Yet poverty was a major problem. Some Caribbean thinkers began to consider ways to reduce poverty and raise the quality of life of people by installing *alternative political ideologies* to that of capitalism. They were influenced by the dependency theorists of Latin America. *Dependency theory* is an approach to development that emphasizes *underdevelopment* – showing how the colonial condition encouraged dependency and poverty through the imbalance in trading relationships and a mindset that regarded the colonizer as the legitimate source of ideas. Furthermore, these conditions were being exacerbated by modern–day **neocolonial** trends. To focus on poverty reduction rather than economic growth would have political implications largely because the poor are powerless and the people who are usually in government represent the moneyed classes. To directly target the poor would entail radical measures.

The **Marxist-*type revolutions*** of Cuba (1959) and Grenada (1979), and the attempts to gradually establish similar principles in Guyana (1960s and 1970s) and Jamaica (1970s), were directed at increasing human development (Box 8.5). These measures aimed at *increasing equity*. In Cuba the country suffered under a brutal dictator, Fulgencio Batista, an ally of the US. The revolutionary forces were responding to demands from the Cuban people for jobs, health care and land reform. When Fidel Castro declared in 1962 that the revolution was *socialist*, the USSR became an ally, pumping millions into the economy, even before that the US had withdrawn all diplomatic personnel, technical assistance and aid, and instituted an *economic embargo* that lasted for decades.

The Cuban economy was centrally planned, with the state owning all productive enterprises and property. The population benefited by being able to buy goods and services that were previously priced out of their reach, and by having free health care and better housing. They were enjoying increasing levels of *equity* and poverty was reduced. However, *productivity* waned as the centrally planned and subsidized state enterprises became inefficient and corrupt. The Cuban economy was described as 'dependent socialism' as it relied heavily on aid, credit and trade from the Soviet Union. While in the beginning Cubans felt great enthusiasm for the revolution and became involved in the many local assemblies, they soon grew to realize that they were not expected to participate in a substantial way. There was no room for dissent. Thus, *empowerment* through opportunities to make changes in the course of their lives became less and less possible. As political repression worsened, even the initial gains of equity were severely compromised. The 1990s threw the Cuban economy into a tailspin as communism was dismantled in the USSR and Eastern Europe. Cuba was now alone, trying to survive without its safety net on the global market. In the meantime, the US intensified the embargo. Castro was forced to institute more *liberal* policies inclined towards opening up Cuba to tourism, making the dollar legal tender, encouraging self-employment, and diversifying into citrus, nickel and medical products.

Undoubtedly to the majority of Cubans in the 1960s and even the 1970s the revolution was necessary to free them from the repressive regime of Batista. One can say that there were major strides towards promoting human development (especially equity). The US, however, was violently opposed to communism; as the superpower in the region, only a few miles away, it played an important role in influencing the process of development in Cuba. Through invasion ('Bay of Pigs' in 1961) and economic sanctions the US tried to destabilize the country. Even though the Castro regime lasted for decades, the US policy of **destabilization** severely weakened the economy, causing internal dissension and harsh repression similar to that under the Batista regime. In addition, a viable, resilient economy that could function independently of the USSR was not established.

As commentators on the process of development, we can say that regardless of whether a political ideology is market-driven or state-driven, if development is the goal then each should be tempered with what is necessary to promote equity, productivity and empowerment. Perhaps because the socialist state was under constant attack and censure, it could not be more flexible, a stance that it now seems to be adopting. The capitalist states of the Caribbean have fared better because as part of the mainstream they had nothing to prove in terms of trying to justify alternative ideologies. They did establish a role for the state in a market-driven economy to ensure equity. In most Caribbean countries the state has firmly taken on the role of providing education and health care, but there are partnerships with private providers. States are also able to establish *pro-poor services* by taxing the private sector and can also intervene in the market directly by imposing controls on prices, again a measure to ensure equity for citizens. However, there is constant debate about how much a state should interfere in the workings of the market. Following a particular ideology, then (whether capitalist or socialist), does not seem to be as important as reconstructing that ideology to ensure development goals – the promotion of equity, productivity, empowerment and sustainability.

ACTIVITY 8.4

1. Suggest TWO reasons why either the state or the market should 'lead' in the process of economic development in your country.

2. Explain why the US was so committed to the destabilization of Cuba as a socialist state.

BOX 8.5 Jamaica and socialism

Michael Manley's first term as prime minister of Jamaica lasted from 1972 to 1980. He came to power at a time when Jamaica was experiencing a poverty crisis. The development measures that had been tried after independence were largely unsuccessful. The transition from **colonialism** to independence and a capitalist economy needed not only a transformation in the economic and political institutions but also in the social situation. There was a large gap in the material circumstances and welfare of the Jamaican people. The policies tried in the years after independence tended to follow the formula of 'industrialization by invitation'. This encouraged *foreign direct investment* but it could not increase production and output enough to make a material difference to the population.

Manley felt that the principles of *democratic socialism* would be beneficial to Jamaica's poor. His goal was to establish a **planned economy** to equalize opportunity, especially for the poor and dispossessed. Most of the large industries were **nationalized** and *welfare* was increased to the poorer sectors of the society. Unfortunately, he did not pay so much attention to *productivity*. The newly nationalized companies did not function efficiently because of mismanagement and retaliatory tactics on the part of those who had to leave but still controlled access to world markets. The bauxite companies, for example, reduced their imports. The US cut its flows of aid by about 75 per cent. With output down and expenditure up the external debt grew. This situation was exacerbated by external shocks

such as the OPEC oil crisis of the 1970s, when oil prices soared. During the Manley years productivity, measured by GDP, fell some 16 per cent, and unemployment and inflation increased. Severely strained for income, the programmes and policies put in place for the poor had to be abandoned.

Edward Seaga, the next prime minister, began dismantling the socialist policies and re-establishing the **free market** system and friendly relations with the US. Manley's later return to power saw him largely following these policies, thus attesting to a failed socialist experiment. Did Manley hinder the development of Jamaica by pursuing a political ideology that was in marked contrast to the rest of the Commonwealth Caribbean (except for Guyana at this time)? His goal was to reduce the levels of inequality in the society. The capitalist regimes before and after him did not pursue that goal as vigorously – neither did they increase productivity to the levels where significant growth was experienced. The problem does not seem to lie with socialism per se but with how the international community reacts. Unlike Cuba, Manley did not have the communist world to prop up the regime, most probably because he was not interested in building a full communist state. And the whole question of whether Caribbean people, poor or not, are in favour of socialism is still unresolved. The wealthy left Jamaica and Guyana in large numbers. In all three Commonwealth countries where it was tried (Grenada as well), it ended in failure. It raises the vexing question of how to provide for the poor and still be able to pay all the bills.

Social factors

The *distribution of wealth and resources* is a factor that can either promote or hinder development as it influences the *income generation* in the society. Using *levels of income* as an indicator shows how wealth is distributed among the various socio-economic groups, and the Gini Index (see p. 250) measures the *level of inequality* in the society. The primary importance of these indicators is to give a good idea of the levels of poverty and inequality in a country, as national development – whether economic, human or sustainable development – is more difficult to attain when poverty and inequality are **entrenched** and widespread.

Caribbean countries inherited a society characterized by **social stratification**, a legacy of the plantation economy. The **elites** (the descendants of the white ruling class and near whites) owned much of the land and capital. The middle group of coloureds and blacks owned some property and other assets such as educational credentials (human capital, in other words). Poorer groups lower down the social hierarchy had only their labour power to sell. This inequality in income distribution severely hindered development in many Caribbean countries, and the extent to which Caribbean societies have been able to reduce the levels of poverty and inequality has resulted in increasing human development and more sustainable forms of development.

Poverty

Household and family income surveys measure the ability of citizens to buy basic consumption items – food and non-food items such as education, housing and transportation. Using this measure, Haiti recorded the highest poverty levels (76 per cent) for the region. In Guyana about 35 per cent of the population lives in poverty, in Jamaica about 20 per cent, while Antigua and Barbuda (12 per cent) had the lowest incidence of poverty (World Bank, 2005).

Poverty seems to be more widespread in rural areas where agriculture provides the bulk of the income. In 2002 in St Lucia 16 per cent of the urban population lived in poverty compared to 30 per cent of the rural population. The situation is very similar throughout the Eastern Caribbean, where rural areas tend to be characterized by larger households and unstable incomes owing to both volatile market prices for agricultural goods and weather hazards. In addition, these households tend to have inadequate access to safe drinking water, sewage disposal, electricity supply, transport, education and health care (OECS Human Development Report, 2002).

Studies of poverty raise the issue that if we are serious about development then we must re-examine our understandings of the causes of poverty. The usual explanation for poverty revolves around the conditions of the poor – family poverty, few resources, debt, limited education. However, development theorists see it as a condition arising out of the social and economic weaknesses in the society. These weaknesses stem in the first instance from a lack of equity among social groups, which becomes entrenched over time; thus to alleviate poverty one must tackle the bases of inequality in the society (Box 8.6).

Inequality

The inequality survey using the **Gini Index** (where 0 indicates perfect equality and 100 perfect inequality) showed the highest inequality in Haiti (65). High inequality was also measured in St Vincent and the Grenadines (60), Antigua and Barbuda (50), the Dominican Republic (47) and Guyana (43.2). These statistics are amongst the highest levels of inequality in the world; compare them with, for example, Norway (25.8), India (32.5), Ghana (30.0) and the US (36.0) (UNDP, 2004). In some countries high poverty levels coincide with high levels of inequality (for example, Haiti, St Vincent and the Grenadines, and Guyana). However, a country may show a relatively low percentage of people living in poverty but the disparity in income between those people and the other socio-economic groups may also be high (as, for example, in Antigua and Barbuda). Thus, income inequality is a significant and continuing feature of the distribution of *wealth* in Caribbean countries and raises questions about the extent to which this hinders development.

When there is a large income gap between the different social groups, social stratification becomes entrenched and poorer groups suffer from social inequality and **social exclusion**. For instance, there will be few opportunities for them to access

Understanding poverty

One of the reasons why poverty remains a persistent problem for Caribbean governments is that the policies designed to reduce poverty have a particular view of the poor that is misguided and undermines the success of the initiatives. The interesting observation is that the wealthy, the well-to-do and government agencies all feel they know what poverty is like; consequently the measures they implement do not usually have the input of the very people to be helped.

Traditionally the poor are helped through national poverty alleviation schemes where funds are earmarked in the national budget for the social sector and disbursed to ministries dealing with social services and agencies that help the poor and the disabled on a daily basis (NGOs, charities and religious organizations). They give out payments as public assistance and social security as well as supporting organizations helping single-parent families and unwed mothers, and providing unemployed youth with casual labour opportunities. All of these levels of assistance are referred to as a 'safety net' for the poor.

Even in times of economic growth, when there are more funds available for these programmes, *the poor remain poor*. A basic misunderstanding about poverty lies in the perception that the poor do not have many material goods, so that if these are provided their distress will be alleviated to some extent. There seems to be a reluctance to understand that poverty is maintained by being *powerless*. If poor people were to be helped to organize themselves – which is what grassroots community groups try to do – they would be in a better position to make demands and be listened to. The tendency has been to help the poor through philanthropic gestures and through a desire to keep social tensions down.

Recently initiatives have been discussed that are *pro-poor*. A pro-poor economy is one where planning takes place within an enlightened and informed understanding of where the poor are, what activities they are engaged in, and what some of their greatest needs are. Hence, resources are channelled into, for example, rural economies, inner-city areas or places where women need help if they are to function effectively in the labour market – early childhood care and education centres, all-day clinics, small urban businesses, and work and study programmes. These are human development initiatives that broaden the choices of the poor and help them to empower themselves.

decent jobs, credit services, relevant training, or even proper health care and housing. The poorer the household, the more there is a tendency towards low educational attainment and erratic participation in what training is available. Social exclusion therefore exacerbates the conditions of poverty, making it virtually impossible for the poor to help themselves out of poverty. This has a negative impact on efforts to improve and increase both human development and sustainable development in the society (Thomas and Wint, 2002).

In countries where the income distribution is less unequal (for example, Barbados), some members of the poorer groups are able to access a higher level of educational provision, thus making them eligible for higher-paying jobs, and eventually enabling them to move out of poverty – **social mobility**. One indicator used to measure the extent to which members of a society are experiencing social mobility is the index of *social and economic equalization* (the degree to which all groups are experiencing similar levels of income, access to goods and services, and other opportunities). In Caribbean societies education has been the principal means whereby the poor could *change their class boundaries* and reduce the extent to which they experience social exclusion and social inequality. In a more 'open' society more citizens are involved in the economy in a productive way, thus contributing to income generation.

Therefore the distribution of wealth in a society directly influences the extent to which different groups can access the resources of the society. The wealthy have

ACTIVITY 8.5

What are THREE areas that would be of interest to you in reporting on the index of social and economic equalization for your country?

easy access to financial, educational and training resources, which allow them various options and choices that work to their advantage. If inequality is so great that poorer groups cannot access at least some of these resources, then the society would be denied the income that these groups would have generated if they had had the opportunity. Moreover, more public expenditure will have to be allocated towards social welfare. Thus, high levels of income inequality hinder economic as well as human and sustainable development.

Economic factors

The 'productive sector' refers to the economy of a country – the production of goods and services. While the concept of development has outgrown the strong emphasis on economic growth, it is nevertheless true that development cannot occur without a vibrant and buoyant economy or productive sector. Whether development occurs or not is directly related to the conditions and structures operating within and impacting on the productive sector. It can be thought of as the engine of growth that can have a positive effect on human development and sustainable development but only if this is a goal that the government and people think is worth pursuing. If not, there can be growth but without development.

The productive sector has traditionally been classified into the following types of economic activity:

- *primary* or extractive industries (fishing, forestry, farming, mining)
- *secondary* or manufacturing industries (the processing of raw materials in factories, e.g. agro-industries, bauxite smelting, bottling and canning)
- *tertiary* industries or services (e.g. teaching, insurance, retailing, transport, tourism).

Recently, another category has been added – *quaternary* – research and development activities and computer- and knowledge-based industries that do not need a specific location (also called 'footloose industries').

The colonial Caribbean was treated as a *primary producer* of raw materials – mainly agricultural commodities – which were exported to Europe for processing. Thus, the Caribbean does not have a strong tradition in manufacturing, or secondary industries. There is, however, a well-developed tertiary or services sector today, which holds a promise for the future, because reliance on agriculture has proven to be misguided in the past and manufacturing on a large scale is just not an option for most of the smaller territories. In addition, the possibilities of quaternary industries are now being explored in terms of the 'dot com' economy and e-shopping.

Some of the most important factors that impact the productive sector, and thus Caribbean development (in terms of boosting economic growth), are as follows:

- *Competitiveness.* To a large extent the agricultural commodities and manufactured goods produced by Caribbean countries are high-cost items, largely because labour is highly priced compared to other developing countries and some inputs need to be imported. These products will not sell easily on the world market unless they enjoy some *preferential* protection (Box 8.7; see also Box 9.5).

ACTIVITY 8.6

Using documented sources, sketch a pie chart showing the structure of the productive sector in your country (i.e. the percentage distribution of primary, secondary and tertiary industries). In your opinion, what is an ideal distribution for optimal economic development? Give reasons for your answer.

This is the name given to a series of agreements between the countries of the European Economic Community (EEC) and the ex-colonies of Africa, the Caribbean and the Pacific (the ACP countries). Lomé I came into being in 1973 and assisted the ex-colonies by ensuring aid, soft loans and preferential trade markets for traditional exports such as sugar, rum and bananas. These preferential terms of trade helped to sustain the Caribbean agricultural sector, which depended on the export of these commodities. Although the price for these commodities fell steadily on the world market, the ACP countries were guaranteed higher prices by this treaty. Caribbean farmers came to depend on these preferential rates so that little was done to improve agricultural efficiency, to diversify into promising alternative crops or to expand and intensify production. As a result, production processes were costly and inefficient and labour was expensive.

Lomé IV came into being in 1994. The European Union (EU) was a very different entity from the EEC of yesteryear and now included many countries without any ties to former colonies. It was increasingly being pressured by the World Trade Organization (WTO) to liberalize trade and dismantle all preferential agreements, and this it has been doing on a phased basis. The Caribbean has done little to prepare itself for the inevitable day when agricultural exports are expected to face world market prices on a competitive basis, without being 'propped up' by preferential rates. The present agreement between the EU and the ACP promises technical assistance for countries to upgrade their economic sector so that they become more competitive and viable (see also Box 9.5).

- **Demand.** The goods produced in the Caribbean (e. g. clothing, handicrafts, beverages, paper napkins, cosmetics, appliances) do not command a large market either inside or outside the region because others can also supply them. However, promising markets have opened up for Caribbean foods and preserves (e.g. jerk seasonings, confectionery, pepper sauce, ketchup, coconut milk) as well as alcohol and soft drinks in the Caribbean **diaspora** in places like New York, London and Toronto. Future growth may lie in creating similar unique and 'niche products' that others cannot supply.
- **Productivity.** Agriculture has low *labour productivity* because of the tradition of manual labour and preferential trade agreements. Labour productivity is an indicator of efficiency in agriculture. Operations that are highly automated show much higher *production rates per worker* but labour has to be well educated and technically skilled to perform in these environments (e.g. oil and petrochemicals, electricity production, micro-electrics, networked systems). Opportunities for post-secondary training in a wide range of skills will better equip labour to function in these settings.
- **Infrastructure.** Some Caribbean territories do not have fully functioning telephone systems, reliable and safe systems of public transport, regular water and electricity supply, reliable telecommunications services, and a quick turnaround at ports. In addition, ministries that control certain aspects of trade and industry have a tendency to tie up business in complicated bureaucratic procedures. Thus, the *institutional framework* within which the productive sector functions must recognize producers as partners.
- **Investment climate.** While *private domestic investment* and *foreign direct investment (FDI)* in the Caribbean has been high, the investment climate needs to be boosted to be more encouraging to investors. Two particular areas of concern are productivity and economic diversification. The price of labour is high in

the Caribbean compared to that in other developing countries so investors are not attracted unless we develop products that are competitive and unique. Such products would command higher prices because of their uniqueness (few competitors), and labour productivity would therefore increase (more value earned per worker). Local investors suggest that governments can play a big role in encouraging **entrepreneurship** in new areas by reducing risks for entrepreneurs. Subsidies or loans that can reduce the costs of experimentation or risk will go a long way in generating a good investment climate that should ultimately result in more competitive products.

- *Debt*. One of the factors that can severely hinder Caribbean countries in their quest for sustainable development is the level to which they are indebted to foreign loan agencies. In the OECS, for example, debt almost doubled between 1997 and 2003. Guyana and Jamaica have long-standing debt commitments, Belize saw a 100 per cent increase in its debt in 2003, and Dominica has recently experienced a debt crisis (World Bank, 2005). Paying huge sums of interest on these debt accumulations tends to nullify any growth in the economy. It is not easy to solve the debt problem because it is a function of the imbalance of trade, whereby we import so much more than we produce. The tendency to borrow for huge developmental projects such as airport construction, and to finance educational reform and the building of schools, where expensive cost overruns are incurred, as well as corruption and mismanagement, also increase our debt.

- *External shocks*. The debt problem is also made worse by 'external shocks' to the productive sector. In studying development in the Caribbean we need to keep in mind that our population is small, our economies are small and our markets are small, compared to the wider world. We are thus in a vulnerable position when adverse circumstances or shocks occur. All shocks involve us in huge expenses that increase our indebtedness. For example, after the impasse between the EU, the WTO and the banana producers of the Caribbean, Europe's preferential treatment of ACP bananas was discontinued. This was an extreme shock for countries like St Lucia and Dominica, where employment and incomes decreased appreciably in the latter half of the 1990s. Other kinds of shocks that seem to occur with increased frequency are natural hazards such as hurricanes (see Chapter 5). The tremendous dislocation of the economy in Grenada in 2004 after the passage of Hurricane Ivan, soon to be followed by Emily in 2005, accounts for the reduction in economic growth and the increase in poverty in that country.

- *Technology*. Current investment in knowledge about information and communication technologies (**ICTs**) in the region is inadequate and cannot effectively support the needs and expansion of businesses and industries that have to compete in a **globalizing** market. Technical expertise needs to be deepened and constantly upgraded in electronic communication, e-marketing and e-commerce, designing web pages to promote products, compiling digital databases, using the internet to respond to customers in a timely fashion and be attuned to their needs, as well as in the infrastructural areas of networking and connectivity. Local businesses need ICTs to boost their operations and foreign firms need to know that Caribbean labour is technically up to the challenge.

ACTIVITY 8.7

Study the indicators and information listed in Table 8.2 and then answer the following questions.

1. Look at the first column showing the imports of goods and services. Explain the difference in statistics for the US and Jamaica.

2. Look at column 4. Why is Norway such an anomaly among the other countries?

3. What does the information about high-technology exports in the third column suggest about the nature of Caribbean economies?

Table 8.2 Structure of trade for selected countries (2002)

COUNTRY	IMPORTS OF GOODS AND SERVICES (% OF GDP)[a]	EXPORTS OF GOODS AND SERVICES (% OF GDP)[b]	HIGH TECHNOLOGY EXPORTS (% OF MANUFACTURED EXPORTS)[c]	PRIMARY EXPORTS (% OF MERCHANDISE EXPORTS)[d]
Norway	27	41	22	74
United Kingdom	28	26	31	16
United States	14	10	32	14
St Kitts–Nevis	71	46	–	27
Trinidad & Tobago	43	47	3	54
Suriname	45	21	–	22
Antigua & Barbuda	68	60	–	–
Jamaica	60	39	–	27
Barbados	55	52	16	47

Source: UNDP (2004), pp. 19 2–193

[a] The value of the goods and services imported by a country are expressed as a percentage of the value of all the goods and services produced by that country. It is felt that imports should be kept down as much as possible because they have to be paid for, for the most part, using the foreign exchange that exports earn.

[b] The value of the goods and services exported by a country are expressed as a percentage of the value of all the goods and services produced by that country. As a general rule, countries try to export as much as possible to earn foreign exchange to pay for their imports and finance projects.

[c] High-technology items are shown as a percentage of the country's manufactured exports. These include digital devices, software, medical equipment and computers. These are expensive and should bring in much revenue.

[d] The value of the primary exports of a country are shown as a percentage of all the goods exported by that country. Primary products tend to earn lower revenues than manufactured goods.

The productive sector, then, can promote or hinder development through its impact on economic growth. More and more it seems that the traditional economies need to be boosted by innovations and efficiencies, including a search for niche products. Investors are likely to invest if the economy shows some signs of growth. And growth is needed to withstand the effects of any external shocks, which are inevitable for small, vulnerable island economies.

Cultural factors

How groups and individuals define their Caribbean cultural identity does not normally come up when development is being discussed. Yet how one understands and interprets Caribbean history and Caribbean future will certainly influence how development is seen and how one chooses to participate in it. Our ideas and assessments of Caribbean society and culture and what Caribbean development means are shaped by our **socialization** – at home, in school, and by the media. How we understand our cultural identity continues to be re-shaped daily by our experiences. It relates to how we assess ourselves in relation to others, the values we hold, our perspectives on the environment and on the past, and our aspirations for ourselves and our society. It will show up in our attitudes and behaviour.

Attitudes and behaviour are outward manifestations of our psychological orientations. The colonial experience is widely described as having been a type of psychological conditioning that privileged the values and achievements of the western world and denigrated the potential and achievements of the colonized. There are different views and interpretations of how Caribbean identity and experience should be defined and these have different implications for development.

Western model

One group takes the view that Caribbean society can be discussed in relation to the concepts about society and development found in the western world. Caribbean society is seen to be merely at an earlier stage in the modernization process but the concepts of growth and human progress are equally applicable to Caribbean societies as any other. The model of capitalism, and the values associated with growth, profit-making, efficiency and the accumulation of wealth are accepted ways to access the 'good life'. It is only through this model that the Caribbean can be smoothly connected within the world capitalist order and the various instruments and regulations of globalization.

For those who hold this view, development is essentially about the enactment of human values in which the emphasis is on *modernization* and a western lifestyle. These values are said to have universal applicability. If someone points to Caribbean societies today to show that these values are not working for us (for example, the large numbers living in poverty, declining productivity and a downturn in economic growth), the rejoinder will surely be that governments are not implementing policies in a rational way. They might point out that the poor remain poor because the tendency is to give them handouts and not enable them to help themselves (Box 8.6). The reduction in growth and productivity may be explained in terms of a low work ethic amongst Caribbean people and a tendency to only find fulfilment in fun, entertainment, music and celebrations. This way of defining Caribbean people's experience and identity has the effect of deepening our commitment to a westernized model, encouraging us to try to improve on how we adapt western values to our societies. The point is made that Caribbean people in the diaspora successfully learn productive work habits to increase their material comforts. Thus, to make a case for Caribbean *exceptionalism* (that it is different from the western model) is to jeopardize the development process.

Exploitation

A radically different definition of Caribbean people's identity and experience come from those who see Caribbean societies as unique, even among other New World societies. For example, the Caribbean did not have the huge indigenous populations that were found in Central and South America where *conquest* was the main objective. We are also considerably different from the white settler societies of North America and Canada where *settlement* was the main objective. Caribbean society from the beginning and throughout **colonialism** was based on *exploitation* and the large-scale import of labour to form a rigidly stratified social system.

If this is how our experience and identity have been defined, how do we go about development? The obvious place to start would be in developing more of our institutions in our own cultural context. For example, the institutions we have inherited were all created under conditions of oppression and inequality. To accept the institutions as they are without reflection and without reform is tantamount to substituting a *black elite* for the colonial masters, an elite who in turn keep their fellow citizens in subjugation. Even though we have been engaged in decades of school reform our education systems are plagued by inequities. The children of the rich and powerful in the society, whether black, white or coloured, excel in academic achievement. Basic problems of literacy are predominantly found among the poor. We have mainly British traditions in education and these encourage elitism, segregation by ability, and the presence of low-status and high-status schools (see Chapter 6). The social institution of education, then, according to this argument, perpetuates inequities and thus hinders the development process.

Similarly, in all our other institutions there is a heavy top-down model of management that has been clearly inherited from the colonial masters without much thought given to making the structures more egalitarian. The notion of 'participation' is given only token recognition, yet it is this very process of nurturing avenues and channels of equal communication to give people opportunities to participate that will go a long way to removing the structures that exclude them. Nurturing this kind of participation means helping people to *empower* themselves politically by sitting on village and community councils and taking part in the debates and issues that occur in the society in some organized way. Our inherited political forms do not encourage this mass level of participation as a continuing feature of political life. In fact, our governments are socialized into *ruling* and have only fledgling ideas about what *leading* entails – they can command but do not seem able to nurture an orientation where people grow by leading themselves. The latter comes about through being given opportunities for meaningful participation. This way of defining the Caribbean experience sees *improved institutions and attitudes* as the major focus of development efforts and relies on a development process *from below* (from the grassroots, from communities, and from schools developing themselves, as in school-based management).

Inherent in the view of development described above is the **enactment of values** such as equality and reform. That is so because our societies began in oppression. However, there are also other elements that pertain to the persistent ideas about development that we met earlier. For example, through reforms that result in a set of improved institutions there will be increasing *differentiation and complexity* in the society. This means that if communities, the grassroots, and organizations such as schools are encouraged to lead their own development they will have to develop new alliances and structures, rather than waiting for decisions to be handed down from a central authority such as a ministry, as happens under the present structure. More complex structures will result.

Culture sphere

Another definition of the Caribbean experience also sees it as unique in how it has become a 'culture sphere'. It examines the adaptations that people from different parts of the world have made in meeting and mixing with each other to develop the unique products and cultures evident in ethnic combinations and creations of foods, music, art, religion, dress, literature, the healing arts, and other expressions. This is essentially the **creolization** thesis, which says that these adaptations came about through necessity when people were thrown together in a context that called forth creativity and resilience, and that this little-understood process has become a continuing feature of Caribbean society. The region is therefore recognized as a culture sphere where **syncretism**, **hybridity**, adaptation and creolization processes have occurred to a greater extent than perhaps anywhere else in the world.

For people who uphold this view of Caribbean experience and identity, the important idea in development is to study and examine this defining feature of Caribbean life. There is no clear view as to how this creolization process happens so there is a continuing emphasis on seeking ways to harness the creative spirit generated by the meeting and mixing of Amerindian, European, African, Indian, Chinese, Portuguese, Javanese, Syrians, Lebanese and other cultures. For example, there are more and more works being published about the smaller ethnic communities of the Caribbean in an effort to better understand their contribution to development. There is also constant experimentation in cultural hybrids in music, art, literature, dance, drama, festivals and cuisine.

Development according to this way of thinking would give full flower to our *cultural industries* and seek avenues to create products that will showcase the expressions of Caribbean people and at the same time provide unique cultural products to market. Some people disagree with this view, saying that it reduces culture to a product and that it seeks validation from abroad. There are therefore disputes about how culture can be harnessed in concrete ways for development purposes. Even though the Caribbean is an acknowledged culture sphere and its music especially is enjoyed internationally, there is still a great need to create ways in which business, and research and development, can increase our market penetration abroad. The whole area of cultural industries is a potential gold mine that has scarcely been tapped.

This view of development would perhaps best coincide with what economic experts say the Caribbean needs right now to boost competitiveness and demand for its products – to create and develop unique products that will be able to command a niche market. It is only in this way that economic experts see the Caribbean thriving in a globalized world where trade is increasingly being liberalized. The focus on creativity and adaptation also has relevance, though, for improving many other aspects of the economy and society. It is just that development has not been conceived in terms of creativity before.

For example, such a mindset will:

- invigorate the performing arts and enable more artistes and other talented people to come forward and see the cultural sphere as something worthwhile, profitable, and important to them personally in terms of expression and creativity
- challenge educators, curriculum planners and parents to design a curriculum where liberation and empowerment are the main themes rather than just academic knowledge and acquiring credentials

- encourage the media to develop themselves so that their goals reflect regional development and Caribbean consciousness without necessarily sacrificing our need to know and be up to date with western ideas, technologies and popular culture
- encourage those who see the potential of cultural products, instruments and knowledge to become entrepreneurs, knowing that they will be backed by reasonable access to credit facilities and technical assistance as they develop their ideas
- mobilize the entire population to become computer literate and enhance the skills and expertise of those talented enough to adapt the technology for our needs and purposes and to develop software
- provide the impetus for the Caribbean integration movement to go forward strongly in merging the economic, fiscal, trade and monetary laws and regulations (among others) to improve our balance of trade with extra-regional countries.

The definition of Caribbean experience and identity in this view can be summed up in values that emphasize creativity and adaptation. This depends on the processes of creolization from which hybrid, syncretic and new forms and products may emerge. The idea of development as the *enactment of values* is central to this definition of the Caribbean experience, but as we have seen, the values being espoused are quite different from the values put forward by those who uphold capitalism and the modernization thesis. This definition of the Caribbean experience has some agreement with those who call for increasingly *differentiated* institutions as evidence of development because creativity is needed in transforming the colonial institutions we have inherited. Finally, the view of development as leading to *freedom* is very evident here because it is saying that the unique culture of the Caribbean can be harnessed, if we continue to try to understand it, to lead a development process that affirms what Caribbean people have to offer.

Thus, the definition of Caribbean experience and identity can be seen from at least three different perspectives. Each has a different stance on how development should proceed. This is not necessarily a factor that hinders development because each should not be taken as an ideology or a prescription. Rather we should distil from them important questions to inform how we chart the way forward.

Environmental factors

Natural disasters are one type of environmental factor that hinders development in the Caribbean, namely hurricanes and volcanic activity (see Chapter 5). Four or five hurricanes every year do at least some damage to the islands in the Greater and Lesser Antilles, as well as to Belize, and the volcanic eruptions in Montserrat almost destroyed that society and economy. In St Vincent volcanic eruption remains an ever-present threat. Earthquakes, while a continuing feature of life, are felt more strongly on the western edge of the Caribbean Plate.

Environmental hazards cannot be avoided, but as we saw in Chapter 5, the risks associated with loss of life and destruction of buildings and crops can be minimized. When an **environmental disaster** wreaks havoc, economic growth is reduced and human welfare is jeopardized as many may face dislocation, poverty and destitution. It makes good sense, therefore, since environmental hazards are a continuing feature of life in the Caribbean, that we should do as much as possible to minimize risks. However, Caribbean societies seem to face a stumbling block here, moving at a snail's pace in enacting legislation directed at disaster mitigation, or even devising and implementing basic environmental indicators.

While all groups may suffer some loss in the event of a natural disaster, the poor tend to suffer the most because they have scant resources (for example, surplus cash, insurance cover) with which to rebuild their lives. That the poor are the main casualties may be the reason why we hear about disaster preparedness and disaster management strategies but they do not seem to be realized in serious and purposeful ways. Such a scenario is typical until a particularly serious disaster strikes. It is only then that wealthier groups realize that widespread dislocation and destitution among the poor directly impacts their own business interests and that infrastructural damage makes recovery difficult. The factor hindering development in this instance is not the natural disaster in itself but the half-hearted attempts to *devise a rationally coordinated system of policy measures* to deal with the event.

Disasters caused by human activities also have a negative impact on development, in this case sustainability. Big business interests tend to pollute the environment and poor farmers, especially on hillslopes, engage in practices leading to **soil erosion**. Again these cannot be categorized only as environmental problems that could possibly be solved by legislation to enforce cleaner procedures in factories or land reclamation schemes. The modernization effects of large-scale capital enterprises such as industrial complexes and mining operations tend to be viewed favourably by the government and development planners in a country. To attract investment for such projects is no mean achievement. As a result, governments are slow to enforce regulations that penalize companies for any harm they cause to the environment. The idea of development as the *enactment of human values* can therefore be criticized, depending on which values are being privileged. In this case, values to do with productivity and output (economic growth) are privileged over environmental health (Box 8.8).

Both natural disasters and those encouraged by human actions hinder economic growth and reduce the sustainability of development efforts. The occasional nature of hurricanes seems to engage governments in a game of probability and an assumption that this year they will be spared. This is a careless and irrational attitude to adopt if all other efforts target development. Human-induced disasters, too, such as soil erosion, seem hardly to warrant prolonged attention by decision-makers. One may ask why, given the decades-long quest in the Caribbean for development, the environment can be so sidelined? The inevitable conclusion seems to be that the values dominating the development process did not initially include sustainability, and so efforts to insert it now run up against the power of big business interests and ignorance. The rather lackadaisical attempts to curb soil erosion and other human-induced disasters speak to a harsh reality that, although there is much talk about *human* development, people still tend to equate development with production and economic output.

ACTIVITY 8.9

Explain why the activities of small farmers in encouraging soil erosion cannot be solved by giving attention only to environmental factors.

BOX 8.8 Environmental indicators of development

The development debate began with attention being given to economic indicators such as GDP and GNP per capita. Today the Human Development Index uses economic indicators as only one aspect in assessing the human development of a country. It also places emphasis on education and longevity, which may be thought of as socio-economic indicators (as they are), but the trend now in discussing environmental indicators is to be holistic. For instance, we have to think about what contributes to environmental health? Certainly indicators that tell us about the income levels of a region and its population distribution will contribute to an understanding of resource use and the *carrying capacity* of the land. If, for example, the carrying capacity of the land is exceeded by whatever economic activity is being pursued, certain features of environmental degradation may result, measured by indicators of soil erosion, land quality and pollution. Thus, to reach more informed judgements about sustainability and environmental health, social and economic indicators need to be added to environmental indicators.

One of the most recent environmental indicators to be devised by the World Bank is called the 'wealth measure'. However, it is very different from an economic measure. It is a 'stock measure' in that it estimates the total wealth of the country (assets, human capital and natural capital) as a starting point. It works together with another indicator, 'genuine savings' (called a 'flow measure'), which adjusts the wealth balance sheet by estimating how much the country has added to its stock of resources (including production and investments in education) and/or lost wealth through pollution, land degradation, human sickness and increases in poverty. The final tally is an indicator of the sustainability of the development process.

Tourism

Tourism is the biggest industry in the world today and all Caribbean countries, whether long developed as tourist centres or 'off the beaten track', are looking to attract more income from tourism. The general idea is that tourism has the potential to increase economic growth and, through that, economic development. We have already seen, though, that increased growth as reflected in increased GNP per capita, for example, does not necessarily result in improvements in human welfare or poverty reduction. Unfortunately, the way tourism is presently organized in Caribbean countries tends to be hindering development rather than promoting it.

Chapter 7 pointed out that even in those Caribbean countries where tourism is most developed, it is largely controlled by *foreign* financiers and investors and world-famous hotel chains, and is dependent on international tour companies and cruise-ship companies to bring the tourists. Most of the profits thus seep away through all these channels, though where tourism is dominant (as in the Bahamas, Jamaica, Barbados, the US Virgin Islands, the Turks and Caicos and Antigua and Barbuda), the income remaining in the country is significant, and higher than that from other sectors of the economy. If ways can be devised to increase the proportion of the income from tourism that stays in the Caribbean, then tourism will be well poised to contribute to economic development.

The growth of tourism in the Caribbean has been rather ad hoc, with some countries more able to take advantage of airline routes and more able to offer a traditional tourist package of sun, sand and sea. As we have seen, the initiative has usually come from abroad, from companies with an international reputation in delivering some aspect of the tourist product. Local input built on these initiatives, but these individual private or government-sponsored projects scarcely thought of tourism as a planned, strategic development enterprise. Tourism grew as the traditional agricultural export sector collapsed. Its growth was thus accidental and hasty, in some cases leading to many of the challenges associated with tourism today – environmental damage, high-rise hotel complexes in the most scenic parts of the country, marginalization of local populations, inflation, the spread of sexually transmitted diseases as well as western values that threaten local ways of life.

The three problems or challenges facing Caribbean tourism are:

- that tourism should contribute more to human welfare
- that the dependency on foreign institutions should be lessened
- that the tourism industry should be put within a national and even regional development framework.

These issues tend to undermine the contributions that tourism is making – increased GNP, increased employment, greater promotion for Caribbean culture, more efficient utilities and enhanced infrastructure. Current thinking about tourism advocates the development of sustainable tourism and therefore in the Caribbean there is the need to deal with the challenges posed above.

Sustainable tourism

In 2004 the World Tourism Organization defined sustainable tourism in terms of its impacts on the host country. It advocates tourism policies, activities and programmes that are economically, socio-culturally and environmentally sustainable. This means that any segment of the tourist industry must be in the process of achieving or maintaining a balance between the environmental, social and economic aspects of its operations and ensuring that no harm or damage occurs. The linkages that are forged between these three areas should contribute to an on-going profitable concern of benefit to all.

Sustainable tourism advocates tourism that:

- has minimal negative impacts on the land and culture of the host nation
- generates income and employment, especially for local people
- helps tourists to be knowledgeable abut their destination and the need for conservation of the environment and having a low impact on the culture
- helps residents to better understand other cultures in dealing with foreigners who may have different expectations and outlooks
- helps residents to better appreciate their own environment and culture
- encourages tourists to observe environmentally sound behaviours such as minimizing energy consumption, waste, water use and the use of detergents
- monitors the 'carrying capacity' of the land and does not crowd or overrun scenic areas and fragile ecosystems with too many tourists at any one time.

In the case of Caribbean tourism, where the economic gains are not as large as they could be, where foreign domination persists, and where there is a need for planning involving all stakeholders, the principles of sustainable development can do much to address these issues.

A rationally coordinated system of policy measures

The ad hoc way in which Caribbean tourism grew, and continues to grow, must be addressed by pursuing an all-embracing goal that rationalizes the many policies, activities, programmes and projects planned and under way. The ideal of sustainable tourism (which is subsumed within sustainable development), if insisted upon at every level and segment of the industry's operations, would begin to have a positive impact on equity, productivity and empowerment because it would be targeting human development rather than economic growth.

One example of this is the recent initiative that supports pro-poor tourism – policies and programmes that have been planned with the understanding that the benefits that can accrue from tourism are much greater than we once believed. However, it needs the input and cooperation of a range of stakeholders, including the poor. Tourism is a business and businesses are interested in economic growth and profitability. Pro-poor tourism advocates the bringing together of stakeholders from business, environmental and social groups to chart a way forward that is sustainable and that makes business, environmental and social sense.

To achieve gains on this scale demands planning on the part of public sector authorities, tourism providers, community groups, environmental planners, local NGOs and investors. It calls for conscious and well-thought-out strategies to integrate the poor into the tourism development process in meaningful ways. It calls for a commitment beyond economic growth to ideas about sustainability, and that all should be involved for this to happen. This type of practice is based on encouraging and nurturing patterns of growth that put the poor at the centre. A few examples show what can be done:

- Reducing imports and keeping farming families out of poverty can be achieved by buying, as Sandals Jamaica does, large amounts of cantaloupes and watermelons and other fruits and vegetables from farmers that Sandals supported in the first place with the infrastructure to produce on such a scale.
- Projects that rely on tourists as a market can be set up with help from local and community investors, businesses and small manufacturing concerns. Projects of this kind reported from around the world include:
  - constructing a bottling plant using discarded bottles that are recycled by refashioning the glass into artistic cultural forms by local craftsmen and artistes
  - contracting local suppliers to create and make the furniture, curtains, draperies, bed linen, table napkins and other decorations for hotels
  - providing expertise from the hotel or tourism sector to local entrepreneurs setting up small business concerns or cultural shows and exhibitions that help to expand the range of experiences for the tourist
  - setting up training in hotel management and various aspects of the tourism industry for local citizens, allowing them flexible programmes of working in the industry while they study.

ACTIVITY 8.10

Keeping in mind your local context, its needs and challenges, suggest at least ONE pro-poor tourism strategy that may be helpful in human development.

For Caribbean countries to effectively address the challenges facing the tourist industry, sustainable tourism offers an opportunity to devise a rationally coordinated system of policy measures. It is a sign of advanced development when an industry as diverse as tourism can be planned and controlled to achieve objectives such as maximum optimal participation by all, especially the poor, and without harm to the environment. Human development is increased by attention to policy measures that put sustainable tourism as the overarching framework guiding the growth and expansion of the industry.

Summary

Development is a multi-faceted phenomenon. Whilst economic growth and productivity are important aspects of the process, the sections above have sought to show that political ideologies, social stratification and inequalities, the institutional environment in which business is conducted, and our culturally dominant ideas about what development looks like are all equally important. If these factors are taken into consideration when development is being discussed, then it is more likely that groups would not be marginalized in the process, that the environment would not be ignored, and that we would be on our way to developing rationally coordinated institutional systems to provide a framework for our development efforts. If we do not put such a system in place then development will continue to be focused on a particular project or reform and the opportunity to see how it could help or hinder the wider society will not arise; the emphasis will be on getting the project off the ground. Conceptualizing development properly, then, calls for a thorough examination of our social and cultural contexts, as well as our mindsets, and not only obviously economic factors.

WRAP UP

This chapter has analysed different conceptions of development – economic growth, economic development, human development and sustainable development. Apart from economic growth, all the others depend on processes that enhance the welfare of human beings and see improvements in equity, productivity and empowerment as gains leading to sustainable forms of development. The indicators of development have undergone a change over time so that today the Human Development Indices are more prominent than those indicating only economic growth. Finally, the chapter has evaluated the influence of political, economic, social, cultural, environmental and technological factors on development in the Caribbean.

Structured response

1 (a) Explain what is meant by 'economic development'. (2 marks)

   (b) How is economic development related to sustainable development? (2 marks)

2 Explain why economic growth does not reflect development. (4 marks)

3 (a) Identify TWO indicators of economic development. (2 marks)

   (b) Explain the importance of the TWO indicators listed above. (4 marks)

4 (a) Explain what is meant by 'political ideology'. (1 mark)

   (b) For any ONE identified political ideology, explain ONE way in which it influenced development in the Caribbean. (3 marks)

5 Describe TWO ways in which the distribution of wealth in a country can influence development. (4 marks)

6 Outline ONE example to show how ICTs can impact positively on development in the Caribbean. (2 marks)

7 (a) Explain what is meant by the 'productive sector'. (1 mark)

   (b) Describe TWO ways in which the productive sector can increase the human development of Caribbean people. (4 marks)

8 Describe ONE positive and ONE negative impact of tourism on development in the Caribbean. (4 marks)

9 Suggest TWO reasons why an agrarian society is not considered to be a 'developed' society. (4 marks)

10 Explain why poverty reduction is a major development goal. (2 marks)

Essay questions (20 marks)

1 Describe what is meant by sustainability in development.

2 What indicators can be used to assess the extent to which development is conscious of human development goals?

3 What factors impact negatively on Caribbean development?

4 How can the Caribbean increase its capabilities in information and communication technologies (ICTs)?

Challenge essay questions (30 marks)

1 Assess how differing definitions of the Caribbean experience can impact on development issues.

2 Evaluate the extent to which approaches to development in the Caribbean still focus largely on economic growth.

3 Discuss the pros and cons of foreign direct investment in the Caribbean.

4 'Caribbean governments are more concerned with maintaining their political power than creating the conditions necessary to increase human development.' Discuss this statement.

An investigation based on the analysis of published statistics or indicators can throw light on development processes in the Caribbean. This study will be based on secondary data and it might be useful if you could compare data from two countries. The following are possible lines of inquiry.

- **A study of land tenure and farming practices** in Haiti and another country as comparison. You will need data on size of farm holdings, labour productivity, percentage of the population engaged in farming, percentage of GNP from agriculture, and human development indices such as child mortality rates, literacy, access to clean water, etc. Studying the indices should give you evidence to make judgements about development in both countries. You should also point out the inadequacies of the indicators where possible.

- **Using the Gini index** for selected Caribbean countries to try to account for the patterns of inequalities and the differences in the patterns by analysing the historical and political development of each country.

- **Looking at the Human Development Index** for one or more Caribbean countries over time and trying to account for the variations or the lack of variations.

- **Gathering as many tourism-related statistics** as you can for your country and using them as a basis to make judgements about the linkages to different sectors of the society, pro-poor policies and sustainability practices.

REFERENCES

Inkeles, A., & Smith, D. (1974). *Becoming modern*. London: Heinemann Education.

McClelland, D. (1961). *The achieving society*. New York: The Free Press.

Schultz, T. (1961). Investment in human capital. *American Economic Review*, 51 (March), pp. 1–7.

OECS (2002). *Human Development Report*. St Lucia: OECS Secretariat.

World Bank (2005) *A time to choose: Caribbean development in the 21st century*. Caribbean Country Management Unit, Poverty Reduction and Economic Management Unit, Latin America and the Caribbean Region.

Thomas, M., & Wint, E. (2002). *Inequality and poverty in the Eastern Caribbean*. ECCB Seventh Annual Development Conference. Basseterre, St Kitts: Caribbean Development Bank.

Busta Says We Leavin'

One From 10 Leaves 0

Jamaica Opts Out

9 CONTEXTUALIZING DEVELOPMENT: GLOBALIZATION AND REGIONALISM

The two forces of globalization and regional integration dominate the context of development in the Caribbean today. There have always been conscious efforts at regional integration and we have experimented with different structures in the past. On the other hand, globalization is a process generally perceived as having its own dynamic, over which we have little control. Most of the time it is confused with the processes associated with internationalization. In Chapter 8 we learned that for development to be truly sustainable it should take into account human development and its emphasis on equity, productivity and empowerment. In this chapter, then, we examine the context of development shaped largely by popular conceptions of globalization, as well as the regional integration movement, which is opposed to many of the processes associated with globalization. The forces of globalization and integration bring home very clearly to us the challenges posed to small states; if we are not vigilant about defining what development means to us, others will impose their own version.

EXPECTED LEARNING OUTCOMES

On completing this chapter, you will be able to
1 define globalization
2 compare globalization and internationalization
3 present a critique of the work of organizations that attempt to facilitate globalization
4 assess the ways in which globalization affects development in the region
5 describe the evolution of the integration movement in the Caribbean
6 explain the ways in which the integration movement has influenced development in the region.

9.1 DEFINING GLOBALIZATION

A typical definition of **globalization** is that it is the process whereby 'flows of trade, finance and information between countries are broadened and deepened so that they function as one global market'. If trade, finance and information are being globalized, then what we will find, logically speaking, is that all countries in the world will have an increasing capability in trade, finance and information to act as partners in this 'one global market'. Thus, in theory a university from Singapore could set up a campus here in the Caribbean and have the same rights and privileges as a Caribbean university. It would be as if there were *no borders* – what could be set up in Singapore could be set up here, and vice versa.

Globalization is a process that has been going on for some time and perhaps meant something different two decades ago (Box 9.1). Today, with the rapid spate of inventions and developments associated with the microchip and microelectronics, **information and communications technologies (ICTs)** are driving the globalization process as never before. Digital technologies, the internet and cell phones truly operate as if the world had no borders (Box 9.2). This is the *logical meaning* of globalization – whether applied to trade, finance flows or communication – for some commodity to be equally available to all, anywhere, *as if the nation-state did not exist*.

There is much positive talk about globalization, but if it is taken to its logical limits it is not something that many countries or groups with special interests will find particularly desirable. What a truly globalized world is about is one where there is a 'level playing field', where, for instance, everybody can benefit from the trade in technology. This has been happening with cell phones. From the nomadic peoples of the Sahara to Caribbean people in shanty towns to fishermen going about their trade, almost everyone uses cell phones to communicate. This is an example of something that has been truly globalized and gives us a good understanding about what globalization as a process is really about. It is not that those groups of people are necessarily communicating globally, but that *the use of cell phones* is a global phenomenon touching all income groups.

However, this may not necessarily continue. The giant state-owned telephone companies in the region, as well as those that service more than one country, enjoyed a virtual **monopoly** in the service they provided for decades. The fact that ordinary citizens are now very much more aware about prices globally for the same

---

BOX 9.1 Stages of globalization

The increasing **internationalization** of the economic institutions of Europe and North America in the nineteenth and early twentieth centuries is heralded as the start of the first wave of globalization. The reduction in transport costs by improvements in shipping and railways led to labour becoming more mobile, and trade fed off this reduction in the costs of production and increased output. This era came to an end at the outbreak of the first world war in 1914.

It was not until the end of the second world war (1945) that economic institutions recovered enough to resume the process of internationalization. The work of the organizations set up in the aftermath of the war helped in this respect – the United Nations, the World Bank, the IMF and the General Agreement on Tariffs and Trade (GATT). Their combined efforts helped to stabilize currencies and increase trade and production, largely in industrialized countries. They kept a tight hold on the regulation of international monetary flows. This period came to an end

in the early 1970s when the OPEC countries hiked up the price of oil, throwing economies into disarray, the **Bretton Woods Institutions** (see p. 277) could no longer maintain their regulation of a fixed exchange system and the dollar declined.

Since the 1970s the world has entered a period in which there has been a gradual minimization of controls. The idea of **free trade** has spread, and international capital now moves about the globe as **transnational corporations (TNCs)** seek to establish themselves fully. The revolutions in communications technology drive the increasing integration of the economies of the developed and developing worlds. The fast pace with which this internationalization of systems has occurred has prompted much debate and discussion on the phenomenon of globalization, trying to understand whether internationalization is a stage before full globalization, whether they co-exist, or whether internationalization will prevent globalization from taking place.

BOX 9.2 Technology and globalization

The fast pace of the internationalization of communications systems, trading relationships, and flows of finance and capital across the globe has been facilitated in recent times by ICTs. These technologies allow people to communicate in 'real time' – there are no delays. Cell phone technology, e-mail and 'chat rooms' allow instant communication anywhere in the world. Business and industry have been quick to see the advantages of incorporating these modern communications technologies into their operations. Not only do they enable businesses to communicate with suppliers and customers in a timely way but computer technologies have now become an indispensable part of actual production. Whether it is the bottling of soft drinks, the manufacture of furniture or retailing, key areas of operations are computerized. Companies of all kinds have seen the need to incorporate these technologies into their businesses.

In the World Bank's *Report on Development in the Caribbean* (2005, p. 137), the example is given of a small group of businesses, known as *Unique Jamaica*, which was able to put ICTs to work for them in novel ways. This group of small hoteliers and tour operators needed to boost their productivity. They first revised their vision, basing it on attracting those interested in adventure and nature tourism.

They then designed tour packages around the themes of nature, culture and culinary arts. ICTs were incorporated into their marketing campaign because this was the most cost effective way to launch their plans and advertise their business. In addition, an interactive web-based booking engine helped them to generate business (see http://www.uniquejamaica.com).

However, businesses and industries that are slow to modify their operations or have inadequate infrastructure cannot take advantage of the savings and efficiencies from the global technology sector, and will not be competitive. For example, as the same report states (World Bank, 2005, p. 136), the Caribbean has been a disappointment to companies of the developed world and even regional companies seeking to *outsource* certain low-end areas of their operations. One area where this has been evident in several Caribbean countries is in the setting up of telemarketing call centres, which rely on low costs of connectivity to be competitive. In both Antigua and Jamaica investment in setting up these centres did not pay off for a variety of reasons, but mainly because of antiquated rules and regulations governing telecommunications, poor technological and communication infrastructure and inadequate skills.

services, about high-speed internet connections, and that international call centres are cheaper, means that they are making demands on the old monopolies, which also have to accommodate to the idea of new providers coming into the region. They have had to look at their operations in a critical light to see what services they can offer and what pricing they can use to neutralize the threats emanating largely from new technologies that enable competitors to set up business.

This is an example of how globalization, facilitated by the advances made in ICTs, has been able to go a long way in levelling the playing field for many where communication is concerned. However, it has necessitated changes in the way companies operate, so one may question the extent to which **capitalist** organizations can tolerate a truly global world. For example, the old monopolies of the telecommunications authorities have had to be dismantled and are no longer as profitable as before. Computers, too, are less expensive and more accessible to more income groups. All this is pointing to a dilemma for capitalist ventures – the technologies are now being mass produced and more people can afford them; *where is the money to be made?*

The process of globalization is not fully understood. The situation described above encourages us to speculate about how the process will proceed. If an increasing number of people use cell phones and other companies copy and create features that

ACTIVITY 9.1

How do you expect cell phone technologies to change in the next five years? How will those changes bring about different kinds of relationships between cell phone users, the telecommunications providers and other citizens?

may be similar to those of one particular make, what will happen next? Certainly inventiveness is going to proceed and increasingly sophisticated features will be designed, becoming more expensive. Already digital technology allows us to show the photographs we have taken with the cell phone on the computer. Recently watches were invented to network with cell phones and computers. The point is that amongst all today's happy cell phone users there are many who will be left behind in a new kind of **digital divide** – not only will the gadgets be priced out of their reach but they will be hard-pressed to understand all the applications and possibilities of the new technologies. A combination of natural creativity and the demands of capitalism will bring about a situation where the playing field will be upset. Does this mean globalization will have received a setback? We do not know; it is a process largely in the making.

What we do know is that *globalization as a process is eroding distinctions between one place and another.* This is mostly seen in relationships governing trade, finance, information and digital technologies. It seems to be removing the advantages that some groups once enjoyed (for example, the national or regional telephone companies) and levelling the playing field for others. We have also seen different responses. The large companies have had to rethink their operations to continue to make profits amidst competition. The cell phone companies themselves are spurred by their own success to make more complex products. It is perhaps through ICTs that the globalization process has made the first breakthrough to show what is really possible. Yet as we have seen there are determined efforts to reconfigure the playing field to return to a situation where there are new, sophisticated, elite, highly priced products and services. There are then *contradictions* built into the process of globalizing.

When people speak of globalization, this more nuanced view is not the conception that they have. They may use the definitions and the language – 'a world without borders', 'a global village' – but they do not realize the full implications. They are speaking metaphorically. They want limits. One more example will suffice. Today there is an explosion in the *knowledge industry*, with more people everywhere having access to educational materials, as well as cultural knowledge and that disseminated as popular culture. But are people in different places all *producing* their own knowledge? This is what globalization of the knowledge industry would mean – more people in all parts of the world being able *to produce and disseminate their own cultural knowledge.* On the contrary, more and more people are subject to the American mass media and it is this cultural knowledge purveyed worldwide that is described as the 'globalization of knowledge'. Even if one regarded the internet as a neutral space where anyone can post information, the fact is that the knowledge it disseminates more often than not reflects American views and perspectives. This suggests that much of the discussion about globalization and much of the work of international organizations linked with the globalization process is actually about something else.

Internationalization

The term 'internationalization' is a more accurate term to describe the present programmes and policies of institutions such as the World Bank or the International

Monetary Fund (IMF) concerning flows of capital, finance and trade. It is more accurate because, first, *it recognizes the nation-state*. It is a process conceived of as interactions between nations or countries. There is no conception in the way the World Bank does its work, for example, about doing away with borders. Secondly, the concept of internationalization does not conceive of all countries as equal. The work of the World Bank and the IMF is primarily directed at *developing countries*. What they present as development options to developing countries, or the threats and conditions they impose, are unthinkable in their relationships with developed countries.

The internationalization of flows in trade, capital and finance refers to the increasing interactions among the countries of the world as their markets become more integrated and the volume of trade between them increases. This is a far cry from globalization because there is no deepening and broadening of the linkages in the flows of trade, finance and capital to help countries operate *as if borders did not exist*. So we have a confused situation when we hear people talk about globalization and when we read much of what has been written about it. We need to remember these distinctions to make sense of the whole issue. Although accurate definitions of globalization are used, when explanations are called for it is more often the concept of internationalization that is being addressed. We also know from our previous discussion that capitalists and rich countries do not necessarily want globalization in the strict, logical sense of the definitions they continue to use. The following section, analysing the interconnections in trade, finance and capital markets, draws on the previous discussion.

Critiquing 'globalization': internationalization processes

This section analyses the processes and procedures that are internationalizing the flows of trade, finance, capital and other commodities between different countries, and which are loosely referred to as 'globalization'. We will find that there tends to be an emphasis on the economic dimensions, but the process whereby markets become internationalized impacts on (and is sometimes determined by) the social, cultural and political responses in a country. We will also find that development agencies such as the World Bank have bought into the internationalization idea as a development path to be recommended to developing countries. In fact, the failures associated with some of these recommendations have influenced developing countries to re-think their own paths to development. We also need to remember that the process of internationalization is taking place between actors on an unequal footing – superpowers, TNCs, industrialized countries, developing countries and very poor countries. There is no 'super-government' to administer the process and it is largely a situation whereby the richer countries seem to profit far more than others.

The processes of internationalization are as follows:

● *The expansion of free trade.* The expansion of **free trade** is also known as **trade liberalization** (Box 9.3). It requires that countries reduce or remove the **tariffs** they have placed on imports to protect their own industries. This is extremely problematic because if one country removes tariffs but other countries can produce the goods more cheaply, then the likelihood is that the first country's market will be flooded by the cheaper foreign products and it will not be able to sell its own products. And a country ignoring the call to lift trade restrictions will be left behind because others would be participating in larger and larger free trade areas.

- **Measures to tighten efficiency**. These measures are instituted to increase output and reduce the costs of production where necessary. This often means the mechanization or automation of some processes in agriculture and industry and the laying off of workers. Countries wishing to dismantle their own tariff and other barriers, so that they may have equal access to other countries' markets that have also been liberalized, need to put these measures in place so that they can become more *competitive*. Trade liberalization cannot be of advantage to a country if its production costs are high.

- **The persistence of tariffs**. In developed countries in particular some tariffs persist and they often resort to subsidizing the costs of production of selected products

---

BOX 9.3 Globalization and trade

The present internationalization of world systems of trade in goods and services, flows of capital and finance, and information, is based on an **ideology** of *free trade* and *open markets*. This theory of trade was first advocated by Adam Smith in the eighteenth century as a reaction to **mercantilism.** It basically said that once governments no longer intervened in the terms of trade, each country could specialize in the commodities that it could produce especially well (in which it had a *comparative advantage*). Productivity would then increase, leading to exports.

This may sound simple but what it is saying is that the *market* is the sole engine of growth. It is the market that we should allow to balance needs, supply and demand. Some people feel that this is a dangerous path to take as the question arises: 'whose markets will be the important markets?' This policy of free trade that is being employed to internationalize world trade has certain impacts:

- *Labour*. Trade both creates and destroys jobs. The focus on increasing trade among countries needs to differentiate the effects of increasing imports and increasing exports. If exports are increased, then it is likely that this is based on jobs in the country that produces these exports. However, when there are increases in imports this usually means that those items which could have been made locally are not. Jobs, then, are lost when a society imports more and more of its needs and wants.

There is nothing in the market to put a halt to these imports. Some regulatory mechanism has to be set up to prevent uncontrolled imports. Other countries with more competitive advantages will flood the markets of developing countries with cheap goods (for example, China today is able to flood both the developed and developing world with mass-produced goods). The result of these processes is a **balance of payments** problem and a loss of jobs in the importing countries.

- *Balance of trade*. Disguised and open *protectionist* policies are still very much in place in Europe and North America, showing that they recognize that free trade cannot be implemented without any barriers whatsoever. They still retain protectionist measures for those products where they are fearful that developing countries hold an advantage (textiles, artistic creations, canned and bottled foods). Heavy *subsidies* to farmers in Europe make it that much more difficult for developing countries to export to these markets. Additionally, the aid that they offer is much less than the subsidies they pour into their own economies. Free trade, although advocated as the means to globalize economies and societies, is not being practised. What is happening in reality is that different rules seem to apply to different countries. The present organization of trade relations is skewed so that poorer countries act as markets for the products of the developed world.

so that they will be competitive (Box 9.3). This is an issue about 'having your cake and eating it too' – being able to flood the markets of lower-income countries, most of whom have complied and removed tariffs, but maintaining your own so they cannot flood your markets.

- *Market integration*. Even with the uneven situation regarding **protectionism**, the markets of developing and developed countries have become increasingly integrated; the volume of trade in goods and services between them has greatly increased in the last few decades. The claim is sometimes made that the more 'open' an economy is to goods and services or financial and capital flows, the more likely it is that economic growth will be promoted. This is disputed by many.

- *Flows of capital*. Capital can be moved quickly to anywhere in the world, facilitated by the revolution in ICTs. *Foreign direct investment* is easier now in developing countries because of the liberalization of regulations governing the international movement of capital. However, there is no similar move to mobilize *labour* across borders; there are continued tight restrictions on immigration in most countries. In fact, developed countries have preferences for highly skilled and professional labour and have drained developing countries of some of their most educated talent. Clearly *selective* immigration is being encouraged rather than freedom of movement.

- *The dominance of transnational corporations (TNCs)*. These are large firms (also called **multinational companies**) which operate as internationally integrated production systems. While their headquarters may be in Europe, Japan or the US, their factories may be at several sites in developing countries. For example, they may be involved in primary production in one country where the resources are – say, forestry in Guyana. They may send the cut lumber to another developing country for manufacture into a range of products. Their reasons have to do with what is best for the firm – it may be that this country has a very stable government or currency situation or that its infrastructure is sound or that its labour force is cheap (for example, Costa Rica, India, the Philippines). While they represent a large amount of foreign direct investment which developing countries need, they generate minimal employment, being highly modernized, capital-intensive firms (Box 9.4).

- *Homogenization of institutions*. Certain organizations, called **multilateral organizations**, such as the World Bank and the IMF, lend money to assist in the internationalization of markets as a key factor in development. In addition, the World Trade Organization (WTO) oversees trade regulations. These organizations persuade and coerce individual governments to accept their advice relating to trade, finance and capital flows as measures to increase their productivity and competitiveness. As a result, the development processes recommended by these institutions are remarkably similar across countries. Their prescriptions have had a homogenizing influence on the development of institutions dealing with trade, industry, banking and governance in each country – for example, **structural adjustment policies** (see p. 278) that encourage cutting back on social reforms, reducing the workforce, and reducing salaries.

BOX 9.4 Transnational corporations

These multinational companies are some of the largest players in the internationalized world economy. Some are richer than nation-states. The top 500 corporations of the US make about 60 per cent of its GDP. It is said that the combined income of Ford and General Motors exceeds that of all of Sub-Saharan Africa. Some of the largest TNCs in the world include BP, Exxon, AT&T, Coca-Cola, Dell, Google, Halliburton, Honda, IBM, Macdonald's, Microsoft, Nestlé, Nike and Gap. More than half of all the TNCs are owned by just five nations: France, Germany, the Netherlands, Japan and the US.

Despite persistent criticisms from developing countries about the practices of TNCs, their home governments have not tried to regulate their operations effectively. This is what *free trade* is about – the removal of restrictions. In fact the TNCs receive a great deal of support from their home governments and multilateral organizations because they are the ultimate triumph of free trade, and the unencumbered movement of capital, finance and investment across borders.

Whatever their practices, developing countries tend to welcome the *foreign direct investment* (FDI) brought by TNCs and offer them incentives (such as tax holidays and reduced environmental checks) to establish branches. The TNCs use the *low-cost labour* of developing countries to produce a competitively priced product. They can leave anytime they choose and they do not employ enough persons for there

to be a solid justification for their presence. Some TNCs have been guilty of extremely serious human rights violations and other crimes in poor countries, while adhering to regulations in their home countries. Shell, Nike and Gap have been accused of exploiting workers. Other TNCs have been found guilty of tax evasion, money laundering, and hiding funds in offshore banks. There has also been some speculation that the TNCs play a political role in that they pursue the interests of developed countries at the far reaches of the globe. Moreover, the world decision-making bodies for development, monetary strategies and trade regulations are controlled by developed countries, which often act in favour of the TNCs (Box 9.5).

The UN report on foreign investment in Latin America and the Caribbean suggests that governments need to intervene to control the activities of these companies.

It was found that the benefits of FDI are not automatic and that they vary according to the strategies pursued by transnational corporations ... It was suggested that host countries in the region should define what they expect from FDI and what role it should play in their national productive development strategies, in order to give priority to the corporate strategies considered most relevant in this context. In other words, FDI policy is important and has consequences. (Economic Commission for Latin America and the Caribbean, 2005, p. 11)

ACTIVITY 9.2

Describe how you think it would be like to live in a truly globalized world, one where borders are increasingly not recognized.

Summary

The points raised above summarize the nature of the processes involved in the *internationalization* of markets and commodity flows between countries. These processes tend to be described as *globalizing* processes. The rhetoric is about globalization but the practices advocated maintain the distinctions between countries. Globalization is about abolishing the distinctions between nations. In the following sections we consider the main organizations that facilitate internationalization and globalization.

9.2 MULTILATERAL AGENCIES

A multilateral agency or institution is one where many members can participate on an equal footing. Each institution is dedicated to achieving certain goals and has devised procedures for all to follow in the pursuit of these goals. There must be agreement by all. Examples of multilateral organizations are the **World Bank**, the **IMF** and the **WTO** (formerly, the General Agreements on Tariffs and Trade, GATT). All three had their genesis in the aftermath of the second world war. They were formed by a special United Nations meeting at Bretton Woods in Hew Hampshire, in the US, in 1945, and are sometimes known as the 'Bretton Woods Institutions'. The ambitious goal was to seek ways to ensure the economic development of all countries so that the conditions that led to the Great Depression of the 1930s, and indirectly to the war that followed, would not happen again. These institutions were entrusted with managing the world system of trade and ensuring development amongst the world's trading partners. There was no reference to globalization in their early mandate.

The World Bank

Established in the aftermath of the second world war, this institution was named the *International Bank for Reconstruction and Development (IBRD)*. It is now more popularly known as the World Bank. Its headquarters are in Washington, DC, and there are some 184 member countries. By custom, the president chosen for the Bank has always been a US national. The Bank has largely been involved in providing finance for projects to promote development. It used to have an exclusive focus on *economic growth* but now that emphasis has changed to *poverty reduction*. This is in accordance with changing definitions of development to include **sustainable development** such as **human development** (see Chapter 8).

Loans are long term and go mainly to the developing countries of the world to promote equity and productivity in education, health, agriculture and industry. In return, the Bank may make the loan conditional on improvement in some aspect of social life that goes against principles of freedom, equity and human rights. In the past the Bank has made demands such as asking a government to begin the transition from a totalitarian state to a democratic one and insisting on safeguards to reduce corruption.

While the Bank has earned the respect of some countries, it has been severely criticized by others as a 'tool of western imperialism'. This stems from its unconditional endorsement of the internationalization of markets through trade liberalization policies as the path to economic development. These policies benefit the richer countries because they can more easily take advantage of the **free markets** of developing countries. The critics have often said that imposing a regime of free-market reform policies on developing countries suggests that the Bank experts assume that *all* developing countries are alike and that it will take the same remedy to get each on the road to economic development. This is not likely to be possible in countries suffering ethnic conflict, famine and war. It is also debatable whether changes in how the market is structured can be the basis for a comprehensive development programme.

The Bank has also been accused of having a US bias. Critics suggest that the policy of consistently pushing for the liberalization of trade and capital markets to promote imports and exports is largely to support growth and output in the US and other wealthy countries. In addition, the Bank has been extraordinarily supportive of TNCs involved in oil, gas and mining concerns, even in the face of environmental destruction. These firms (largely US-based) continue in their operations despite the fact that, as critics have pointed out – oil and gas production do not lead to a reduction in poverty.

The World Bank today is an instrument for the internationalization of trade and services. This is a limited objective compared to that of globalization. The Bank focuses its activities on developing countries and privileges developed countries' rights to establish firms and access the markets of those countries. As a result, it has helped to boost economic growth in some countries, but where human development is concerned, gains have been considerably less.

The International Monetary Fund (IMF)

Another Bretton Woods institution, the IMF, works closely with the World Bank and has the same membership. Its headquarters are also in Washington, DC, and by custom the president is usually European. The two organizations reinforce each other, a situation referred to as the *Washington Consensus*. The focus of the IMF is on fostering global monetary cooperation and ensuring financial stability worldwide. It extends loans and forms of technical assistance to expand trade, and to help countries promote exchange stability and manage their *balance of payments* problems. It helps them to control their debt and gives advice on the policies most likely to encourage stable exchange rates and economic growth. On a global level the IMF is responsible for overseeing the entire international monetary and financial system.

The IMF has been cast in the role of a first-world ogre preying on hapless poor countries and forcing them into a downward spiral of austerity and poverty. Again part of the problem may lie in its commitment to a uniform concept of development – prescribing the same policies for all developing countries. The standard solutions that the IMF suggests are austerity based. For example:

1 keep interest rates high to stabilize the currency
2 **devalue** the currency in order to boost exports (other countries will find the lower price attractive) and this will help to decrease imports, which become more expensive
3 reduce government spending, especially in 'non-productive' sectors such as health, education and social welfare, and increase taxes
4 sell public and state-owned corporations, especially utility companies, to private owners as they are a drain on the public purse (**privatization**).

These austerity-based measures are popularly known as 'structural adjustment policies' (SAPs). They had to be agreed to by the respective governments in developing countries before the IMF would render any assistance and so are also known as 'conditionalities'. Implementing these SAPs has resulted in widespread unemployment and increasing poverty. At the same time, the IMF as an institution has made huge profits in restructuring loans for debtor countries. The removal of subsidies on milk and other basic food items, and the laying off of workers through *downsizing,* hurt the poor in developing countries, particularly Africa. In addition, increasing **inflation** brought about by devaluation increased the prices of basic foodstuffs and other necessities, leading to increasing levels of poverty wherever these policies were implemented. Over time the SAPs developed such a negative reputation that the IMF thought it prudent to re-name the same group of policies as the 'Poverty Reduction Strategy'; this may seem somewhat ironic, considering that the major effect wherever the SAPs were introduced was to *increase* poverty.

Like the World Bank, the IMF was conceived more than fifty years ago. Both institutions are development institutions and their understanding of development has changed over time. They are about lending money and giving technical advice. Their track record has not been encouraging. Poverty is still widespread, though they have reported significant reductions, and while trade liberalization has opened up markets, giving an aura of modernization, many developing countries simply cannot compete under conditions of free trade. These organizations were never meant to facilitate globalization; their mandate was development. However, they have adopted a view of *development through globalization*, which they have attempted to enact in developing countries. The problem is, however, that it is only *internationalization* of flows that they have succeeded in establishing.

The World Trade Organization (WTO)

The WTO was formed as recently as 1995 with the demise of the General Agreement on Tariffs and Trade (GATT). Its headquarters are in Geneva (Switzerland) and it has about 148 members. It goes beyond regulating trade in goods, as the GATT did, to include services such as telecommunications and banking. It is a more modern organization than the World Bank and the IMF and its mandate clearly speaks of *globalization*, not internationalization. Its task is 'to remove all barriers or encumbrances of any kind to trade anywhere in the world'. Its activities are not restricted only to the developing world. It certainly has the potential to facilitate globalization, in the logical sense of that term.

The WTO is the only international body set up to oversee the rules of international trade and to arbitrate disputes arising from those rules. Its members make the rules and for a decision to be taken there has to be widespread agreement. The machinery set up to do this is more enlightened than that of the other two Bretton Woods institutions but criticisms have been mounting that the democratic procedures governing decision-making have been subverted. For example, the WTO has been accused of bias in favouring TNCs and developed nations (Box 9.5). The US, the European Union (EU) and Japan are said to exert undue pressure on developing countries in the decision-making process.

Recently, the Seattle (1999) and Cancún (2003) WTO meetings have been the target of criticism, demonstrations and encounters between protesters and the police. Talks have broken down totally as developing countries have refused to accept some of the decisions. Attempts to reach consensus have become more and more difficult. Here we can plainly see that, given a mandate of globalization, the richer countries of the world hesitate. They are more interested in the internationalization of trade and the negotiations governing those interactions than in implementing *fair trade*. The only form of 'free' trade they will sanction is one where they reap the greatest benefits. Thus, we see that large numbers of the public are aware of how the WTO has subverted its own goals and become an instrument of internationalization, like the World Bank and the IMF.

BOX 9.5 Free trade: the banana impasse

In 1996 a row erupted when the US accused the EU of giving bananas from *ACP* (African, Caribbean and Pacific) countries *preferential rates of entry*. This was causing hardship to Central American banana producers and companies, such as *Chiquita,* a US-owned company. The ensuing events were played out in the courts of the WTO but showed the powerful position of the US (which does not produce bananas) in swaying the rulings of the court.

The countries of the Caribbean have long relied on the preferential tariffs they were entitled to under the *Lomé Convention* (see Box 8.7). Caribbean bananas, with only 8 percent of the EU market, were allowed in according to a specially created 'two-tier tariff quota' under which Caribbean bananas paid the lower tariff, allowing them to be sold more cheaply than their competitors. When the US challenged this lower tariff on behalf of Chiquita Brands International (a US-based TNC), which controlled half the European banana market, it did so on the basis that this special arrangement violated the principles of free trade.

It did not matter that bananas were the mainstay of small farmers in the Windward Islands and that Chiquita was a powerful company that could not possibly be experiencing hardship over this small loss of market. The matter dragged on in the WTO for a while, with the US objecting to every suggestion of the EU to ease the burdens of the Caribbean farmers. The citizens of the EU even decided that they would be willing to pay *more* for fair trade bananas (those produced by small farmers on their own lands) than 'standard bananas' (those produced on large plantations owned by TNCs with headquarters outside the region). The US opposed every suggestion and instituted punitive tariffs against the EU.

Today the EU has abolished its trade and tariff preferences. The countries of the developing world struggle with events like these every day. Powerful lobbies manipulate the courts established to settle trade disputes and determine the economic future of lesser developed countries. While the internationalization of markets and free trade has been going on for some time now, developing countries are still asking for increased market access to developed countries' markets and the elimination of subsidies in developed countries.

The context of development

The press towards the internationalization of economic systems and the global reach of ICTs is transforming the context of development for Caribbean countries. Increasingly our supermarkets and department stores exhibit a wide range of goods from all parts of the world. They increase choice for the consumer, who benefits by choosing cheaper products that may not be locally produced. However, these imports have to be paid for with foreign exchange that we would normally derive from our exports. But exports have reduced significantly, due to the following factors:

- the removal of trade preferences (especially the case for the banana farmers of the Windward Islands)
- the underselling of local products by cheaper foreign goods and services (for example, furniture, canned and bottled food and drink, airline and travel options)
- the closure of both large and small firms who cannot compete with the technological efficiencies of foreign competitors (for example, car assembly plants, garment manufacture, and sugar cane processing).

This means that the context of development for Caribbean countries as a result of free trade practices is one of spiralling debt and decreasing productivity and output. Reliance on free trade **ideologies** is leading to unbalanced development (Box 9.6). Development efforts have to look for creative ways of penetrating this world market by establishing a demand for niche products and countering some of the negative effects that the developed countries seem to be inflicting on small, vulnerable economies, perhaps by deepening the regional integration movement.

ACTIVITY 9.3

To what extent is trade liberalization a reality in your country? In answering this question you may need to tap into the memories and experiences of older persons. Ask several people about access to goods and services today compared to 10 or 15 years ago.

BOX 9.6 Globalization as an ideology

An 'ideology' is a set of ideas, doctrines or beliefs that forms the basis about how someone or a group thinks of the political, economic, religious or some other system. People tend to have strong views about globalization, even when they do not understand it. They may feel that it is inevitable and brings about modernization and development. If they commit to such views, even in the face of evidence to the contrary, then this is an example of casting globalization as an ideology.

To have an ideological position on globalization means that there will be support for another ideology – *free trade*. A *free market* is thought to be the mechanism which can ensure development and progress for everyone. If people were able to exchange goods and services freely and choose freely what goods and services they want to produce then there would be benefits for all. This was Adam Smith's justification for free trade (Box 9.3). This system of **beliefs** is therefore saying that if there is any intervention in the market by the state then the rate of economic growth and prosperity will slow down. Such ideas have formed the major assumptions of some schools of thought in economic theory, mainly **neoliberal** economics. Basically, these theorists say that for development to occur based on increased output, restrictions on capital must be removed, as must laws that restrict employers, investors and TNCs. An unfettered market is the engine of growth.

However, these ideas have been repeatedly criticized. They are too simplistic in that they ignore the issue of *context*, because what works in one country may not do so in another, with different historical and cultural traditions. There has also been a wealth of empirical evidence attesting to the failure of economic policies based on these premises from all over the developing world. That the proponents of free trade are still calling for it in the simple, non-problematic way that suppresses differences between countries, underscores its ideological nature. For those who equate globalization with the economic policies of free trade, globalization is an ideology.

Summary

The Caribbean has been involved in a system of internationalization of trade, finance, capital and information flows that has increasingly integrated its economy and society with those of developed countries. There is some dispute as to whether this incomplete internationalizing of systems can be called 'globalization', which logically refers to the integration of markets and other aspects of social life as if the nation–state did not exist. The internet is possibly the best example of globalization. However, the multilateral institutions which assist in development projects in the developing world have embraced the ideology of free trade as the road to development through globalization. This has had mixed results, as globalization is itself not fully understood and developed countries use unfair trade practices in their interactions with developing countries.

9.3   REGIONAL INTEGRATION

It has long been apparent to Caribbean people that they form a natural regional entity. History and geography have contributed to this. Among New World groupings they are unique – they do not share the traditions of Hispanic America emanating from the Conquest and they are very different from the white settler communities of North America. That being said, history and geography also contribute to many of the divisions that continue to threaten regional integration even today (see Chapter 1).

As we saw in Chapter 1, the Caribbean is divided according to European languages and traditions. Any form of regional integration initiative encompassing the entire Caribbean was almost unthinkable until the relatively recent formation (in 1994) of the *Association of Caribbean States (ACS)*. Integration amongst the ACS functions as broad levels of cooperation. The English-speaking territories, recognizing their basic similarities, have long experimented with different forms of association: the *West Indies Federation, CARIFTA* and *CARICOM* were all efforts at regional integration, though only involving part of the region. On the subregional level, the *Organization of Eastern Caribbean States (OECS)* was another attempt at integration within the larger body of CARICOM. In addition, the existence of Antigua and Barbuda, St Kitts and Nevis, St Vincent and the Grenadines, and Trinidad and Tobago point to attempts at integration on a much smaller scale, the sub-national, even though some of these associations were imposed by the colonial authorities.

Regionalism and globalization

These are two opposing forces in the world today. As we have seen, globalization is a set of circumstances that have come together largely in ICTs to enable countries to function as if there were no national borders. Globalization is actively being pursued by world bodies that believe that it can be facilitated by free trade and a free market system. But nation-states see these policies of internationalization of trade, capital finance and information as a threat to their autonomy and identity. The latter is the second force – a *nativist* response by nation-states, or even ethnic groups. Not only is it difficult for nation-states to monitor and regulate e-commerce for tax purposes and to control piracy of music and other forms of intellectual property from the internet, or even the availability of pornography, but the autonomy of nations is also threatened under a free-market economy by larger and more efficient producers. The terms of trade and regulations governing trade are monitored by the WTO and are often skewed against small, vulnerable economies. Thus, small states in particular feel a need to come together in some way to fight their absorption and the loss of their identity.

Under systems of increasing internationalization nation-states have found it advantageous to integrate some part of their operations so that they can better deal with the threat posed by the free-market ideology (Box 9.7). In the Caribbean we tried a bold move for political integration on the **federation** model, which was not successful. We then began anew, with more modest goals, to establish a free trade area in the form of CARIFTA. This policy was aimed at using the free-market idea to reap benefits through functional cooperation across states and thus minimize the difficulties of being a small producer. Within the free trade area members could therefore trade with the minimum of taxes and tariffs. This limited amount of cooperation led Caribbean countries to seek deeper association, especially as the free market, as a strategy for development, was endorsed by world bodies. CARICOM thus came into being.

The regional integration movement, which has had a long existence in the Caribbean, is today being shaped by the perceived threat to nation-states' autonomy and economic survival from globalization. Ironically, the regional integration movement is using the same strategy as the global movement – *free trade* – to increase the volume of trade between members so as to boost output and productivity. At the same time, CARICOM is ensuring that as a collective body we can maintain competitive prices and limit the extent to which the region is flooded with cheaper

BOX 9.7 Development options for the Caribbean

The failure of *neoliberal economic theory* (Box 9.6) to bring about credible development (and therefore the failure of free trade and economic globalization, which were ideologies pushed on to developing countries) is forcing Caribbean thinkers, economists and policymakers to find another solution to the issue of development. This is extremely difficult because the Caribbean cannot withdraw from the present system of international structures and flows of trade, capital and finance. Yet to small developing countries it increasingly seems that free trade and economic globalization are solutions meant for developed countries. Thus we have to find another way.

Our previous strategy was to focus on *import substitution* – where foreign firms came in, imported parts and inputs from abroad and established assembly-type industries in the Caribbean. It avoided the need to have local investment capital, or to find markets or expertise, as these firms were already well placed. They provided employment and were supposed to build a capability in labour so that later local industries could be established to increase our growth and output. This policy had limited success. Today we have to look for another strategy.

What are our options?

- To put *human development* at the core of any development strategy. Emphasis on the market

marginalized the poor and other groups and what we need are more **empowering** strategies.

- What have we not done before? The masses of our people are poor. They have been traditionally excluded from *widespread participation* in the social institutions of the land. Can we consciously incorporate them by seeking equity in health, education, land distribution, employment and training? In other words, we need the political will to do so.

- To intensify *regional integration* along principles which promote the good of Caribbean people. It would be a contentious issue, as trade and tariff issues would come up and we would be likely to incur the wrath of the WTO, the IMF, the World Bank and the TNCs. In other words, we could experience the withdrawal of aid, tariff restrictions and the closure of markets for our products.

Our option(s) have to be a path we consciously choose, given our context as small, developing countries enmeshed in an historical association with the superpowers. The other models that we have been pursuing are context-free. But we cannot escape context, and thus the issue of regional integration must be factored in as an option that we can actively tap to set us on a better path to development.

products. Thus, the regional outlook is to protect the Caribbean from global forces of competition by integrating various aspects of our economies.

Regionalism, though, is just as complex as globalization and there are many contradictions within it. While most people agree that it is beneficial in the face of the global threat, the mechanisms and the levels of cooperation that are necessary are hampered by a number of factors. Some of these are examined in the following section, which looks at the evolution of the movement towards regional integration.

Evolution of the integration movement

The recognition that the peoples of the English–speaking Caribbean share a common identity, even within diversity, has prompted persistent efforts at regional integration. However, within the region there are strong feelings about the autonomy of each territory and a general reluctance to cooperate without strong advantages being evident for the home territory. This tension between the forces of regionalism and more parochial, national sentiments tend to be exacerbated by globalization. Development efforts in the Caribbean thus operate within a context characterized by this tension between regionalism and globalization.

The West Indies Federation (1958–62)

This was an early attempt at developing a *political union* among the various British colonies. Guyana, Belize, the Bahamas and the Virgin Islands did not participate. A 'federation' is a union of self-governing territories which are states or nations in their own right. The overarching authority for all the states is centralized in the federal government. The capital of the Federation was established in Port of Spain with the British Lord Hailes as Governor General and Sir Grantley Adams, Chief Minister of Barbados, as the Prime Minister. A Council of State (or Senate) as well as a Federal House of Representatives were established. From the beginning the Federation suffered from inadequate financing and over time there was growing alienation between the federal authorities and local governing bodies.

The Federation quickly ground to a halt as Jamaica and Trinidad and Tobago bickered over their own interests. Eric Williams, Prime Minister of Trinidad and Tobago at the time, was uncompromising in his refusal to accept unrestricted freedom of movement because he felt that the poor and dispossessed from other countries would flock to the twin-island state. Jamaica was not in favour of accepting a binding customs union and held a **referendum** in 1961 where the people voted against remaining in the Federation. Jamaica became independent soon after that. Williams's now rather infamous statement – '1 from 10 leaves 0' – also prompted the withdrawal of Trinidad and Tobago from the Federation. The 'agony of the eight' kept the idea of federation alive a little while longer among the Eastern Caribbean states, which have always been closer and more inclined towards cooperation. But they too eventually had to abandon the idea of federation.

Although the attempt at political union had ended, there were still other on-going efforts at integrating various aspects of Caribbean life. For example:

- The *University of the West Indies* was established as a three-campus regional-wide tertiary learning institution.
- The *Regional Shipping Service*, which was set up during the Federation to control the operation of the two ships donated in 1962 by the government of Canada (the *Federal Palm* and the *Federal Maple*) continued after the break-up of the Federation.
- The *Caribbean Meteorological Service* was established in 1963 and replaced in 1973 by the *Caribbean Meteorological Organization (CMO)*.
- Special arrangements were made for the islands of the Eastern Caribbean through the *West Indies Associated States (WISA) Council of Ministers* in 1966 and the *Eastern Caribbean Common Market (ECCM)* in 1968.

CARIFTA (1968)

Several years were to pass after the demise of the West Indies Federation before the idea of regional integration was raised again. By 1968 Jamaica, Trinidad and Tobago, Barbados and Guyana had achieved independence. Their political leaders were now motivated by the ideas of **decolonization**, nationalism, self-determination and, most of all, **economic development**. Given the plight of small states, newly independent from the control of the colonial power (but also from forms of assistance from it), they agreed to try a type of economic integration that focused only on trade by removing trade barriers or tariffs on intra-regional trade in goods produced within the region.

CARIFTA (the Caribbean Free Trade Area) was formed in 1968 with the following members: Anguilla, Antigua, Barbados, British Honduras (Belize joined in 1971), Dominica, Grenada, Guyana, Jamaica, St Kitts and Nevis, St Lucia, Montserrat, St Vincent and the Grenadines, and Trinidad and Tobago. Two of its major achievements were the establishment of the *Commonwealth Caribbean Regional Secretariat* in 1968 and the *Caribbean Development Bank* in 1969.

CARICOM (1973)

Less than a decade after CARIFTA was formed Caribbean leaders found it necessary to extend and deepen the links within the region by moving from a simple free trade area to a limited *common market*. This they felt would ensure a stronger path to development, especially in the face of greater competitiveness from global forces. The **Treaty of Chaguaramas** signed the Caribbean Community and Common Market (CARICOM) into existence. It established the bases of a common market where there was internal free trade, a common external tariff, and some provisions made for the eventual removal of restrictions on the movement of capital, services and labour within the region. For example, it was recognized that opening up the region to complete freedom of movement should come gradually.

Organization of Eastern Caribbean States (OECS)

In 1981 the **Treaty of Basseterre** formalized various aspects of economic cooperation among seven island states in the Eastern Caribbean – namely Antigua and Barbuda, Dominica, Grenada, Montserrat, St Kitts and Nevis, St Lucia, and St Vincent and the Grenadines. The bases of this cooperation were laid earlier through WISA and the ECCM. The citizens of these countries have always felt a sense of unity and identity, making them a distinctive subregion within the Caribbean. As much smaller states they are all especially vulnerable to natural disasters and external shocks to their economies. They went into independence in the knowledge that their economic survival depended on greater cooperation between them.

Today the OECS is a recognized subregional grouping within CARICOM where *the unit of the subregion* is used to promote the region, to pool resources and to rationalize development projects. For example, each country's national development plan is factored into the regional development strategy of the OECS and development aid is sourced and based on the needs of the subregion as a whole. The aim of the OECS is to work for full economic union with free movement of people, goods, services and capital. It has already achieved a single currency, a central bank, a single judicial system, and a joint civil aviation authority, as well as various initiatives in education, health and the environment.

Association of Caribbean States (ACS)

The ACS was established in 1994 among 25 nations of the Caribbean region (Box 9.8). Together they comprise a population of over 237 million people and form the world's fourth-largest trading bloc, after the EU, the North American Free Trade Association (NAFTA) and the Association of South East Asian Nations (ASEAN). The primary aim in setting up this wider Caribbean regional body was to promote economic cooperation and encourage a coordinated approach to issues of importance

Antigua and Barbuda	Dominica	Honduras	St Vincent and the
Bahamas	Dominican Republic	Jamaica	Grenadines
Barbados	El Salvador	Mexico	Suriname
Belize	Grenada	Nicaragua	Trinidad and Tobago
Colombia	Guatemala	Panama	Venezuela
Costa Rica	Guyana	St Kitts and Nevis	
Cuba	Haiti	St Lucia	

ACTIVITY 9.4

Puerto Rico and the US Virgin Islands are not members of the ACS. Suggest a reason for this and comment on how it impacts on development in the region.

to all of the countries of the region – trade, tourism, transportation, health, science and technology, education, culture and environmental protection. It is often the case that issues of crucial importance transcend national borders, and even those of regional entities such as CARICOM, and demand a wider network of cooperation. The secretariat of the organization is located in Port of Spain, Trinidad and Tobago.

Free Trade Area of the Americas (FTAA)

The FTAA is a proposed agreement to eliminate or reduce trade barriers among all the nation-states of the western hemisphere, with the exception of Cuba. It is strongly influenced by the WTO and the forces of internationalization of trade, finance and capital. To create a free trade area for the entire western hemisphere is a highly complicated exercise, the major area of difficulty being the great range in the development status of countries, especially those in Latin America and the Caribbean.

There are persistent negative reactions to the FTAA. The main arguments are:

- that such an undertaking is going to make social life subordinate to large corporations and promote capitalism and material wealth as dominant **values**
- that because of these values the environmental lobby will be ignored because to preserve the environment or even establish conservationist schemes requires investment
- that there will be a race to the bottom in terms of prices and costs of production, and those who cannot subsist on lowered costs will become economic casualties
- that there will be increasing inequality and poverty for those people and regions that cannot compete effectively.

ACTIVITY 9.5

Resistance against the FTAA has seen various Latin American countries coming together – for example, Venezuela and Bolivia, among others, who are also courting alliances with Cuba. Conduct independent research to find out how this movement is faring and what the response is from the US.

The on-going criticism and opposition directed at the FTAA is aimed at preventing it from coming into being as planned. Various critics have pointed out that it is based on a narrow interpretation of globalization, one that is driven by relatively few giant corporate bodies. They propose alternative interpretations of globalization in which grassroots people are not sidelined and they offer a picture of socially responsible and environmentally sustainable trade. For example, they state that trade and investment should not be ends in themselves, but rather the instruments for achieving just and sustainable development.

Summary

The English-speaking Caribbean has experimented with different forms of regional integration largely because of the threat of being overwhelmed, economically speaking, by world producers of goods and services. However, there is also a sense of common identity and a yearning to come together as a region – though that is constantly threatened by nationalist sentiments which arise from time to time. Some see CARICOM as important and fundamental to the survival and empowerment of Caribbean people in an age of globalization and internationalization, while others feel that the commitment towards regionalism among Caribbean people is only half-hearted. Thus, the regionalism movement is fraught with its own challenges even as it tries to better prepare the Caribbean to exist in an increasingly globalizing environment.

9.4

ACHIEVEMENTS AND CHALLENGES OF REGIONAL ORGANIZATIONS

The regional integration movement in the Caribbean has generated a number of organizations whose work is to carry out the mandate of functional cooperation. As the previous section has shown, regional integration must take into account the wider global context of the increasing internationalization of flows of trade, capital, finance and information. As we will see, regional organizations too are adopting the tenets of free trade ideology, although regionalism is opposed to globalization as a force that erodes the distinctions between countries. Thus, in both regionalism and globalization there are contradictory elements.

The Caribbean Community (CARICOM)

By 1973 there were substantial changes on the international front which prompted Caribbean leaders to seek deeper forms of integration. The preferential tariffs enjoyed under the Lomé Convention (see box 8.7), especially for sugar, were being threatened by Britain joining the European Common Market. In addition, the Bretton Woods system of keeping foreign exchange fixed collapsed in the early 1970s, opening the way to the internationalization of capital flows and the increasing penetration of TNCs in the region.

In such a global environment, CARICOM was intended to give Caribbean countries more diplomatic and bargaining weight in their relations with outside countries, as well as provide a specific path to development. Regionalism, then, was felt to give opportunities to Caribbean countries trying to make an impact on a globalizing world. For example, CARICOM established the *Regional Negotiating Machinery (CRNM)* that was to coordinate the Community's external negotiations. CARICOM thus entered into discussions with international bodies on the future of the Lomé Convention, the FTAA and relations between the ACP and the EU at the WTO. An outcome of this interaction between CARICOM and the global players was the perceived necessity to transform CARICOM itself into a more integrated economic unit and deliberately seek partners and alliances. Through initiatives brought by CARICOM, the ACS came into being in 1994, and not long afterwards (in 2001) the Revised Treaty of Chaguaramas was signed, bringing the CSME (CARICOM Single Market and Economy) into existence.

However, the promised increase in trade and economic development throughout the Caribbean has not materialized. Some countries with initially stronger economies, such as Trinidad and Tobago, have benefited from free trade but others have not seen an increase in intra-regional service trade or strong two-way cross-border capital flows helping to create indigenous Caribbean companies. This is one of the reasons prompting deeper integration of the economic system into a *single* market and a *single* economy. A single market cannot discriminate against other parts of itself.

Another major challenge for CARICOM is that regionalism is not a consistent and urgent desire on the part of Caribbean people. The driving force behind it has always been one or two visionaries or aggressive regionalists who have pushed the ideas and policies forward. As a group, Caribbean leaders tend to be apathetic about deepening the linkages between the countries of the region. That may stem from the nationalism that puts one's own country first and a reluctance to consider the broader picture.

On the whole CARICOM seems removed from the day-to-day lives of people in the various territories, perhaps because it is not seen as having much authority to enforce a decision. What authority it has seems to disappear as one goes closer to the context of each territory. For example, if Tobago or Nevis or Barbuda, as sub-national entities, want to consult with CARICOM, is this need recognized? This was brought home very clearly in 1994 as events unfolded in Haiti and President Aristide was ousted: CARICOM countries were powerless and divided. Haiti is a member of CARICOM but there was no clear policy or course of action that CARICOM leaders could take to come to the aid of one of its members.

ACTIVITY 9.6

Examine possible reasons why CARICOM does not have the machinery to enforce its decisions. How do you think CARICOM should organize to deal with situations such as the ousting of the Haitian president?

University of the West Indies (UWI)

The University College began in 1949 in Mona, Jamaica, and by the early 1960s campuses had been established at Cave Hill in Barbados and St Augustine in Trinidad and Tobago. The UWI was one of the earliest forms of regional integration and it has grown to become the premier tertiary institution of the English-speaking Caribbean. However, the internationalization of education systems poses threats to regional bodies and the UWI is no exception. The three campus countries have benefited from having a fully fledged university situated locally, which minimizes costs considerably for their citizens. The non-campus territories, however, have always smarted under this arrangement, especially as they contribute funds for the university's upkeep but have only small extra-mural departments established as distance-education centres. The asymmetrical relationship between the campus and non-campus territories has fuelled the fires of nationalism and led to different countries striving to establish their own universities.

The way that many have chosen is for their community colleges and teachers colleges to forge links with tertiary institutions such as the UWI to award associate degrees. Students can then go on to UWI or another university to complete the degree in two years. It is only a matter of time before each community college is able to put the necessary programmes and quality checks in place to award its own undergraduate degrees. This might come about most easily by collaborating with the UWI, so that local tutors can teach some of its programmes under the coordination of UWI lecturers who visit from time to time. Belize, for example, has established the University of Belize.

Ironically, two campus territories have also established their own universities – the University of Technology in Jamaica (UTEC) and the University of Trinidad and Tobago (UTT); both are technologically oriented. The UWI cannot meet the demand of all those who now aspire to post-secondary education. And it is not involved in all kinds of post-secondary subject areas, particularly technical–vocational and industrial arts and crafts. Thus, a demand has been growing which the UWI cannot fulfil; moreover, its entry requirements and the competition to access places can be high. This situation has played into the hands of those who wish to establish national universities, rivalling the regional institution of the UWI. Thus, ironically, one of the strongest forces for regional development in the Caribbean has actually contributed to the setting up of national universities.

The increasing internationalization of education systems is also driving this movement, at least at UTT. Most of its programmes are in technology and engineering and are offered through existing arrangements with foreign universities, such as the Southern Alberta Institute of Technology in Canada. The challenge for the UWI is to position itself such that these new universities are linked to it, strengthening tertiary education in the whole region. Although they may have sprung up in response to strong national demands, they can still be incorporated into a more balanced regional framework for tertiary education. A more serious threat comes from the proliferation in the region of foreign universities offering *distance-learning* programmes or other arrangements. Quality assurance is often difficult to ascertain in the way these programmes are run. For example, the UK's Brunel University/Henley College of Management offers business degree programmes through partnership with local schools, which will teach the programme; the students are then examined locally. The foreign university only certifies the student, and for this foreign credential students pay a lot of money. The UK's Sheffield University has similar arrangements throughout the region but lecturers from Sheffield do actually participate from time to time.

The UWI has produced many of our greatest leaders, in all fields and disciplines. For a small developing region our educational accomplishments have always tended to be world class, and the UWI has provided much of the impetus for this achievement. However, the strong regionalism that first set up the UWI and ensured its success is being broken down by equally strong global forces leading to the internationalization of education systems. This means that it is increasingly easy for foreign universities to set up some part of their operations here (even just the granting of certificates, as we saw above) and proceed to conduct business. Also, they may not even come here, but we can go there via distance-learning modes. Thus, the new technologies too are whittling away at UWI's pre-eminence in the region. For the UWI to take advantage of international developments it will have to offer programmes abroad, enter into collaborative arrangements with foreign universities, and strengthen its distance-learning provision. Ironically, this must mark a new phase in the existence of a *regional* institution.

ACTIVITY 9.7

How can the UWI enter into partnerships with national universities such as UTEC and UTT to form a 'more balanced' offering of tertiary education programmes?

Caribbean Examinations Council (CXC)

In 1972 for the first time the territories of the former British Caribbean were able to dispense with the centuries-old tradition of following British syllabuses and sitting examinations that were set and marked in Britain. The Oxford and Cambridge Examination Syndicates gradually gave way to syllabuses developed by Caribbean people and examinations set and marked in the Caribbean, with substantially more Caribbean content and attention to the local and regional context. Today there are 16 participating territories in CSEC (Caribbean Secondary Examinations) and CAPE (Caribbean Advanced Proficiency Examinations).

CXC has developed syllabuses covering a wide range of subjects that go beyond the traditional academic disciplines to include those of importance to social development and the labour market: for example, religion, music, art and design, Caribbean Studies, Communication Studies, environmental science, and technical–vocational curricula. They have emphasized more meaningful learning by establishing a tradition of *school-based assessments* which encourage student-led projects, independent learning and critical thinking and inquiry skills. *Formative assessments* tend to have more educational value than a system of terminal examinations where the final score is all that is taken into consideration in awarding certificates.

A present challenge being faced by both the CXC and educational institutions in the Caribbean is that coming from the internationalization of examination systems. For example, the *Scholastic Assessment Test (SAT)* has become increasingly popular as an alternative path to post-secondary education in the US. If an individual obtains a good score on this test he or she has access, and perhaps scholarships and half-scholarships, to universities abroad. This means that the sixth form as an institution is declining and that the CXC will be examining a decreasing clientele. The investment that the CXC has made in developing and maintaining the CAPE may not bring the expected returns unless they become very competitive in the region. For example, it is now seeking out the distance market – those in isolated communities, those who left school and now want to obtain certification, and those who are forced to stay at home (perhaps housewives, young mothers, the sick or handicapped) – whereby self-learning modules and internet connections can enable persons to access the tuition necessary for them to pass the examinations.

The challenge and the possible solutions are very much related to how systems are being internationalized. The CXC as a regional examinations syndicate is facing threats from students in the Caribbean now being able to access SATs, and even the tuition to help them, right here in the region. The institutions that the SATs make accessible do not need the CAPE qualification. The solution has been to become more competitive, to seek different markets rather than relying only on the captive market of sixth-form students. Thus, distance education is a strategy that casts the net wide – it includes prisoners, and all those who under normal circumstances would not be able to attend an institution to study. The means whereby this is to be done increasingly depends on ICTs (such as the internet). Thus, a private candidate can do a CAPE programme that is taught at a community college via distance learning.

What we are seeing here is that when we regionalize something, say examinations, at some point in time global forces will intervene in our arrangements. We need to be always vigilant and constantly assessing the trends about us. The SATs are an avenue

ACTIVITY 9.8

There has been a lot of disagreement in the region about the currency of a CAPE diploma. Brainstorm the possible advantages and disadvantages of choosing to do SATs rather than CAPE to access tertiary education.

to tertiary education in foreign countries, and also a way for foreign countries to select the best talent we have to offer. It is not often that young people seeking the best possible tertiary education think along these dimensions when assessing, say, a CAPE qualification against those like the SATs.

West Indies Cricket Board (WICB)

Cricket represents one of the earliest forms of Caribbean integration. It is the only sport that has consistently fielded a regional team and it is easy to see why the spirit of nationalism and Caribbean identity is bound up in cricket (see Chapter 7). The fortunes of the West Indies Cricket Team have made us proud in the past and as a region our cricketing heroes are from different countries – Sir Frank Worrell, Sir Garfield Sobers, Sir Vivian Roberts, Rohan Kanhai, Alvin Kallicharan, Malcolm Marshall, Curtley Ambrose, Brian Lara and many others. More recently, however, the cricket team has given some dismal performances and there has been much debate on the reasons for its deterioration. Arguments tend to focus on the captaincy, the lack of discipline amongst the players, the fact that there is no long-term policy of recruiting and training exceptionally talented children in the sport, and the administration of the WICB. While all the above are challenges, the WICB as overall manager of the sport is in a way responsible for all of them.

The most serious issue to date relates to the impact of corporate globalization on the sport. When the Irish company, Digicel, new to the Caribbean and a giant in the telecommunications industry, became the sponsor of the West Indies Cricket Team in 2004, they objected to the endorsements contracts that some West Indies players still held with Cable and Wireless. The latter was an English firm with a long presence in the Caribbean, and a previous sponsor of the team. This objection became a major contentious issue, with Digicel directing the WICB to drop certain key players if they did not relinquish their contract endorsements with Cable and Wireless. Digicel had committed US$20 million over five years to improve West Indies cricket and was thus in a position to give directives to the WICB, which had to comply.

In its defence the WICB said that Digicel had agreed to fund the development of cricket that not only focused on the West Indies team but also on youth cricket and the nurturing of cricketers from a very early age. That had been one of the problems of cricket in the past – a lack of emphasis on a long-term vision in recruitment and training. However, in seeking to remedy one of the problems another was created – the domination of the sport by a transnational corporation capable of infusing millions of dollars for its development. Whilst Cable and Wireless, another TNC, had occupied this position in the past, it did not appear to have had such a hold on the WICB. Possibly because there is now a rival in the region, their activities in sport have become an area of conflict.

Thus, global capital has now infiltrated the world of cricket in a way we have never witnessed before. What was a force for regional integration has now been put on a firm business footing, where individual endorsement contracts must be vetted by the sponsoring agency as a matter of course. The West Indies Players Association (WIPA) is now making demands for salaries and other conditions of work that we have not witnessed before. Perhaps Digicel is a modernizing influence bringing West Indies cricket into better alignment with how international sports are sponsored, organized and promoted.

ACTIVITY 9.9

What impact do you think the increasing internationalization of sports will have on West Indies cricket and the WICB?

Caribbean Tourism Organization (CTO)

The CTO is made up of government and private sector operatives in the tourism industry across the Caribbean. It collects and disseminates research and data on the development of the regional industry and there are chapters all over the world promoting Caribbean tourism. The achievements of the CTO are based largely on its efforts to mobilize government ministers, Caribbean leaders, tourism associations, NGOs, economists and environmentalists to convene forums such as tourism conferences where options and challenges are discussed, and to interact and negotiate with global tourism organizations and interests.

The CTO sees the following as some of its major challenges:

- There is now a high degree of *foreign ownership* of the various stages of the tourism product in the Caribbean. For example, international hotel chains and tour companies dominate all aspects of tourism (see Chapter 7). They advertise the product, organize package deals involving air transport, ground transfers and a stay at their hotels, as well as optional tours and sightseeing. These foreign hotel chains are described as 'vertically' and 'horizontally linked' so that they are able to cash in on all aspects of the tourism product.
- Foreign dominance is increasing with the advent of *ICTs* in the industry – the international chains maintain interactive websites to advertise and book all aspects of a holiday. Increasingly the tourist is a sophisticated person who wants to plan and choose *and pay for* these aspects beforehand. This cuts out the middleman in the Caribbean and much of the profits remain in foreign hands. The ability of our airlines and local hotels to deal with e-tickets and e-registration is not yet smooth and efficient and there are hundreds of small tourism providers (family-run hotels, guesthouses, local tours, restaurants) that are not e-ready.
- The *environmental situation* is such that large numbers of tourists are being accommodated on fragile ecosystems. There is a drive to minimize waste and to conserve energy, as well as to manage resources effectively, but there is a continual dilemma of balancing the growing tourism industry with environmental concerns.

ACTIVITY 9.10

Identify ONE strategy that the CTO could promote in helping small tourist businesses in the Caribbean to remain profitable.

The CTO is also in an ambivalent position, just like any organization which is 'Caribbean', in attempting to speak for and develop policy for a number of countries which are all autonomous entities and which may or may not agree. Thus, while the CTO may show that a regional airline or one travel document would considerably boost tourism in the region, this comes up against insular fears and protective measures that continually support the status quo.

CARICOM Single Market and Economy (CSME)

In 1989 CARICOM decided on an integrated development strategy and altered the Treaty of Chaguaramas to accommodate this new vision for regional integration (see p. 288). This strategy – the **Grand Anse Declaration** – laid out a framework to deepen economic integration by going beyond a *common market* towards a *single market and economy*. It also made provisions to widen the community to incorporate Haiti and Suriname, which are today full members, and committed itself to strengthen trading links with non-traditional partners.

The CSME is designed to represent a single economic space where people, goods, services and capital can move freely. One of its greatest advantages is that it will encourage intra-regional trade and allow CARICOM states to negotiate as a single entity, thus affording them a better opportunity to influence policies concerning global trade. This will require the harmonization and coordination of social, economic and trade policies by participating members. However, there has to be a guarantee that goods and services are of an acceptable standard. The **Caribbean Regional Organization on Standards and Quality (CROSQ)** was established to set guidelines and regional standards for members in the manufacture and trade of goods. The CSME also made necessary the **Caribbean Court of Justice** to provide the legal basis for its operations.

A major challenge for the CSME, however, is that its members (especially the smaller states) are uncertain about whether their existing businesses and workforce can survive the increased competition when those that are more successful enter the local market. Many states feel that the economically stronger countries, such as Jamaica, Trinidad and Tobago and Barbados, will effectively put smaller firms in the other territories out of business. While the CSME is putting in place a protocol to assist states experiencing hardship in the transition to a single market, there is still a great deal of fear. This situation seems identical to the globalization scenario discussed earlier, in which the developing countries of the world (including the Caribbean) feel vulnerable to the actions of the developed countries under a regime of free trade. Here in CARICOM the CSME replicates those pressures in a microcosm. It raises some fundamental questions about the context of development – the CSME is a regional strategy reacting to the internationalization of trade, finance, capital and information flows in a free global market. It opposes the effects of unbridled free trade on the small economies of the Caribbean. Yet it finds itself resorting to that same strategy within the CARICOM region in order to mount a good defence against the free traders of the world!

Another major challenge for the CSME is that it requires very deep levels of cooperation and commitment on the part of many actors in one country, and that is sometimes an insurmountable barrier. For the CSME to be fully operational all regional governments have to agree on certain policies and take them to their various parliaments, where they have to be inserted into the domestic laws and regulations. At each point and level of these procedures changes are called for and major disagreements often result in a breakdown in talks. These agreements affect a wide variety of procedures that all need to be standardized – customs and excise, consumer protection, banking and securities, intellectual property, standards and technical regulations, labelling of food and drugs, workers' rights, trade union regulations and labour laws

The creation of the CSME is the most ambitious project undertaken by the regional integration movement yet. Europe is the only other region that has sought to institute a process of integration similar to that of CARICOM. There the decisions made by regional bodies were respected and entered into law, which then had to be ratified by national law. Here the decisions taken by CARICOM bodies still largely rely on inter-governmental cooperation and harmonization exercises that try to avoid national rivalries and fears. Thus, the successful implementing of one economy in the region is going to severely test the willingness of each country to put regional interests first.

ACTIVITY 9.11

Access at least ONE of the blog sites devoted to discussion of the CSME. Organize the arguments that the bloggers offer for and against the CSME.

(A blogging site is a place for serious discussion of a specific issue on the internet. It is an example of globalization because the people engaging in the discussion may be from anywhere in the region or the world but are giving informed opinions based on how they are being affected. The discussion tends to be of a high quality although strong opinions may be expressed. It is said that this may be the newest form of the mass media.)

Regional Security System (RSS)

In October 1982, five Eastern Caribbean states – Barbados, Antigua and Barbuda, Dominica, St Lucia, and St Vincent and the Grenadines – signed a memorandum of understanding creating a Regional Security System (RSS). It came at a time when Grenada was under the control of the socialist policies of the Bishop government (see Box 7.9). There was some uneasiness, too, among the US security forces about Bishop's intentions in the region. The RSS relied on US and British intelligence expertise in forming and designing the security system.

The RSS sought to put in place mechanisms for the peaceful settlement of disputes and agreement on common threats such as drugs, arms trafficking, disaster cooperation and terrorism. The regional communications information and intelligence system needed to be upgraded. Since then the US and RSS member states have taken part in several exercises simulating the takeover of an airport by armed forces and planning and executing a strategy to re-take the facility. While there has been an upgrading of personnel and security measures, the RSS faces several challenges:

- Funds are limited to carry out the original intentions of maintaining databases on intelligence issues, extending the training to more of the armed forces, and monitoring the region by better equipping the coastguard service.
- Some of the territories do not agree with the extent of US involvement in developing the system and carrying out manoeuvres locally.
- All CARICOM member states are not involved. If it is a security system for the Caribbean, policing *part* of the Caribbean will not solve the security issues. While it may be a first attempt at cooperation in this regard, it certainly needs to bring in not only all CARICOM countries, but other Caribbean countries facing similar risks and security issues.

The RSS and other forms of cooperation show the continued difficulty Caribbean countries face in trying to develop and maintain regionally integrated organizations. While most people seem convinced by now that trade is an issue of such great importance that we need a CSME to seek our collective interests, security issues do not seem to be high on the agenda. The continuing interest of the US in the security of the region (securing its own backyard) will continue to be an issue in the Caribbean because some countries may not approve of US activities in the region. The US, on the other hand, will not be likely to listen to us seriously because we do not have an organization that deals with these issues and represents the region.

ACTIVITY 9.12

How does geography impact on the development of an effective RSS in the Caribbean?

Summary

Regional organizations such as the UWI, the CXC, the WICB and the CTO, among others discussed above, have grown over time to represent the Caribbean as a distinctive region. They have deepened the processes of regionalism and encouraged a commitment to that process. However, today these organizations are threatened. Both external and national initiatives are putting regional educational organizations in jeopardy by removing some of their clientele and offering new and different curricula. To offset this threat Caribbean regional organizations now have to become increasingly internationalized. Cricket is dominated by a transnational corporation that is tending to internationalize and commercialize West Indian cricket in ways that have become normal with other sports globally, such as basketball and soccer. What we are seeing is an interpenetration of our regional organizations by internationalizing forces. This demands that we read the signals right and try to maintain some form of regionalism even as we are forced to recognize that international forces are impacting on and shaping our traditional regional organizations.

WRAP UP

All the organizations which have been discussed in the later sections of this chapter echo the themes of the first section – regionalism and globalization. The UWI, CARICOM, the CSME and others were established out of a sense and passion for regionalism. This emanates from a view of the region as a resource that can be tapped to position it against global forces that are tending to neutralize it as a region. This sense of regionalism goes so far as to enact the tactics of the global world to strengthen the region. Thus, free trade ideology apparently working in favour only of developed countries was deliberately instituted in the Caribbean once the area was hedged around with a common external tariff. This has not only been tried here but in North America and Mexico (NAFTA), the EU, and in other trading blocs. Globalization is forcing and deepening regional movements. Regionalism, though, could be fracturing owing to nationalist pressures and the internationalization of systems that manage to stake a claim in the region. Both forces and their inherent contradictions represent the context of development today in the Caribbean.

PRACTICE TESTS

Structured response

1 (a) Define the term 'globalization'. (2 marks)
   (b) Explain ONE process by which globalization happens. (2 marks)
2 Distinguish between the terms 'globalization' and 'internationalization'. (4 marks)
3 (a) Explain what is meant by regionalism. (2 marks)
   (b) Describe how globalization is related to regionalism. (2 marks)
4 (a) What does CSME mean? (1 mark)
   (b) Describe ONE difficulty associated with the CSME. (3 marks)
5 Describe ONE achievement of CARICOM and ONE challenge it faces. (4 marks)
6 (a) Identify ONE example of hemispheric cooperation in which the Caribbean is involved. (1 mark)
   (b) Identify ONE example of sub-national cooperation in CARICOM. (1 mark)
7 Identify TWO differences between a free trade area and a common market. (4 marks)
8 Explain TWO reasons why the West Indies Federation failed. (4 marks)
9 Suggest ONE way in which globalization assists development and ONE way in which it hinders development. (4 marks)
10 Explain what is meant by the ideology of free trade. (2 marks)

Essay questions (20 marks)

1 Describe the evolution of the integration movement in the Caribbean.
2 Explain how globalization is being assisted by information and communication technologies (ICTs).
3 What are the pros and cons of sourcing World Bank aid for development purposes?
4 Identify some of the major transnational corporations (TNCs) located in the Caribbean and explain how they influence development.

Challenge essay questions (30 marks)

1 Assess the extent to which what is being called globalization is really the internationalization of systems.
2 Examine the criticisms levelled at the Bretton Woods Institutions on the issue of sustainable development.
3 Analyse the contradictions inherent in the regional integration movement in the Caribbean.
4 Discuss the extent to which the CSME is adequate in providing for the development needs of the region.

RESEARCH TOPICS

The topics in this chapter can be developed in different ways. One example that takes into account both globalization and regionalism is the issue of foreign dominance of the productive sector. You may want to investigate whether trade liberalization and openness of the economy is really occurring, and to what extent, in your country. Possible lines to pursue include the following.

● Make a list of the major industries and businesses in your country and categorize them according to ownership (foreign or local, if foreign whether it is a TNC or not), state or private, primary, secondary or tertiary. Some industries and establishments may be partly state owned.

● If you are meticulous about collecting the statistics and representing them graphically you may be able to come to some interesting conclusions about whether there is foreign dominance or not. Remember, though, that foreign dominance is not only a matter of quantity (numbers of businesses owned by foreigners) but rather whether the output is significantly larger than that of local companies in the same business, whether exports are higher, and whether employment is greater. (Another thing to keep in mind, though, is that while output and exports may be higher, foreign companies may employ less labour.)

● Such an inquiry broken down into primary, secondary and tertiary industries will give a good sense of what the structure of the productive sector in your country is like, and from this information you can go on to make inferences about the effects that trading patterns seem to be having on the economy. (Remember that trading patterns can be influenced by both globalization and regionalism.)

● Note if there are quaternary industries.

● What are the implications of such an issue for the regional movement?

REFERENCES AND FURTHER READING

Dunn, H. (ed.) (1995). *Globalization, communications and Caribbean identity*. Kingston, Jamaica: Ian Randle Publications.

Economic Commission for Latin America and the Caribbean (2005). *Foreign investment in Latin America and the Caribbean, 2004*. Santiago, Chile: United Nations.

Girvan, N. (Ed.) (1995). *Rethinking development*. Kingston, Jamaica: Consortium Graduate School in Social Sciences.

West Indian Commission (1992). *A time for action: report of the West Indian Commission*. Mona, Jamaica: UWI Press.

World Bank (2005). *A time to choose: Caribbean development in the 21st century*. Caribbean Country Management Unit, Poverty Reduction and Economic Management Unit, Latin America and the Caribbean Region.

World Health Organization (1997). *Health and environment in sustainable development: five years after the Earth Summit*. Geneva: WHO.

10 PROMOTING DEVELOPMENT: SPORT AND THE MASS MEDIA

While both sport and the mass media have very wide popular appeal, they are not usually regarded as playing a role in national or regional development. Traditionally, sport appealed to ideas of physical prowess, winning fame and glory, and achieving health and fitness. And the mass media served as a means for the widespread dissemination of information and for entertainment. However, the greater potential of both is now coming to the fore, especially because the emphasis in conceptualizing development is now on *human development*. In this conception, sport and the mass media can contribute significantly to how people experience equity, productivity, empowerment and sustainability. In this chapter we explore and critically evaluate the importance of sport and the mass media in contributing to development in the region.

EXPECTED LEARNING OUTCOMES

On completing this chapter, you will be able to
1 distinguish between leisure, sport, recreation, play and physical education
2 define the mass media
3 describe the contribution of sport and the mass media to development in the Caribbean
4 critically analyse the impact of sport and the mass media on human development
5 discuss the relationships between sport, the mass media and society.

10.1 SPORTS, LEISURE AND RECREATION

Before we can engage in a discussion of how **sports** may contribute to development in the region, we need to clarify what we mean by sports, especially in relation to similar terms that tend to be used interchangeably. The following discussion clarifies these terms and raises important issues to consider in a study of development.

Sport has grown with the increase in leisure time in modern societies. **Leisure** is that time that a person has to do with as he or she pleases, that time that is not devoted to work, doing chores, running errands, or fulfilling family and other obligations. One's leisure time can be spent with the family but the understanding here is that it is spent doing 'fun' or relaxing things. Many individuals today enjoy a great deal of leisure time as a result of automation (in business, industry, agriculture, and in the home), the five-day work week, paid mandatory holidays, and widely available child-minding services and early childhood education centres.

The different forms and avenues that leisure takes are usually associated with fun and relaxation that help to *re-create* (or renew) the individual. Forms of **recreation**, then, are activities that people engage in during their leisure time. For recreation, one might read a book, travel, play a game, watch television, work in the garden, take aerobics classes, 'hang out' with friends, party, or become involved in sport. Of course, professional athletes are not engaged in forms of recreation when they play their sport.

But amateur sportspersons, even those who follow a strict training regimen to meet the criteria to join clubs and for competitions, are using their leisure time to engage in recreation, albeit in a more focused and demanding way than most people.

'Sport' refers to physical activities that have a history and precise rules about how a game is played; it may also refer to more casual activities such as aerobics, or even walking. The goals of someone who participates in sport are usually to improve physical fitness and all-round well-being, as well as to improve proficiency in the particular activity. For some being a sportsperson means participating in keen competition at the club level (amateur or professional), and for a small minority sport represents the achievement of excellence at the Olympics or at the global level. This understanding of sport encompasses the activities of the whole population and is better than the narrow definitions of yesteryear, which were limited to competitive games and focused on the talents and exploits of super-athletes. This is in keeping with the thrust to promote sport as an avenue for **human development**, which must thus be relevant to everyone.

Sport contrasts with 'play', which is a spontaneous activity that children engage in where they make up the rules; or there may be no rules or even no objective other than immediate enjoyment. Both sports and play are forms of recreation pursued in leisure time. However, in schools sports may come under the umbrella of 'physical education', where they are not considered to be leisure activities or recreation but have specific curriculum objectives: for example, health and fitness, movement for coordination, poise and grace, and teamwork for nurturing values such as cooperation and good sportsmanship. And in early childhood and primary education play is believed to have positive educational outcomes, such as problem solving and developing a broad range of other learning and social skills, so that it becomes an integral part of the curriculum.

In the following discussion on sport and its potential for human development, then, there are at least two distinct levels we should keep in mind. First there is the world of professional or competitive sports much publicized by the **mass media** (the world of the **elite** athletes), where sport can be characterized as 'entertainment'. Secondly, there is that offered in schools or engaged in for recreational purposes, where people who are not athletes participate in sport as a form of 'physical activity', usually for intrinsic rewards, such as enjoyment, health and fitness and maintaining social relationships. These sports may or may not be played on a competitive basis.

We should also keep in mind the tendency to restrict any discussion about sport to youth and the able-bodied. For example, the names of ministries of government that have responsibility for sport also tend to be tied to youth development. While that link is very important in promoting the human development potential of youth, other groups also need their potential to be recognized and promoted. Sports should therefore be conceived of as activities that include everyone. The elderly and the disabled also have leisure time, more so perhaps than other people. The Paralympics is an attempt to recognize and promote sporting activities among the disabled.

Finally, the foregoing section raises the interesting question of how aware we are of how we use our increasing leisure time in effective recreational activities. There is an assumption running through the entire discussion about sport, play, leisure and recreation that these activities serve to *balance* the time and energy spent on other type of activities that may be stressful, urgent, and have to do with making a living.

ACTIVITY 10.1

Reflect on how you spend your time each day: for example, work/study, chores, errands, domestic duties, family obligations, clubs, sport, being with friends, watching television, listening to music, sleeping, or any other.

1. Compute how much of your time in a week is spent as 'leisure'.

2. To what extent do you engage in recreational activities that are fun and relaxing in your leisure time?

3. To what extent is sport part of your recreational activities?

4. How similar is your profile about leisure, recreation and sport to that of your friends?

SUMMARY

Sport has been sidelined in the national dialogue about development simply because it has not been recognized as an activity that includes everyone in the society. The perceptions of sport have traditionally tended to confine it to the world of professional athletes and competitive events. Even in schools that view tends to be dominant. Today, as discussions about development are increasingly based on human development and a more inclusive idea of development, these narrow ideas about the contribution of sport to national development are being questioned. In the view of human development, sport, leisure and recreation are all related and represent an avenue for people in a country to increase **equity**, productivity and **empowerment** in their lives.

10.2

SPORT AND DEVELOPMENT

Many people speak about sport in glowing terms, praising its contribution to the good of the individual and society. In this section some of the ways that sport can contribute to development are described and critically evaluated.

Generation of income

One way that professional sports and organized amateur sporting associations can contribute to development in the region is by marketing their activities to generate increased income. This increases productive activity in the economy and enables a particular sport to be self-sufficient. As it is, almost every sport in the Caribbean has to rely on some form of assistance from outside its club or association. If there is a recognized potential for drawing many spectators, particularly from both regional and international countries, a sporting body will usually be able to acquire government and corporate assistance to mount a particular competition or tournament. Less popular sports receive less funding.

However, the increased leisure time that people have is a resource that can be tapped if attractive enough package deals (airline, hotel and tickets to games) are made available. Even if a sport is not as popular as, say, cricket or football, the leisure that people have, in the Caribbean and elsewhere, provides an opportunity that can be factored into its marketing strategies. **Sports tourism** has shown that it has considerable potential to generate increased income for Caribbean countries. The test matches and one-day internationals in cricket are the best examples in the region of how a sport can draw spectators from different countries and generate income. Events like the Cricket World Cup 2007, which are high-profile international competitions, are likely to greatly increase revenues and have prompted new venues to be built and old ones refurbished. As a result, today games are played in venues beyond the traditional cricketing grounds of Bourda (Guyana), Queen's Park Oval (Trinidad and Tobago), Kensington Oval (Barbados), the Antigua Recreation Ground and Sabina Park (Jamaica). Arnos Vale Sporting Grounds (St Vincent), Queen's Park (Grenada), Warner Park (St Kitts–Nevis) and Beausejour Stadium (St Lucia) are among the additional venues enabling more Caribbean people to see the West Indies team live. This means higher gate receipts and more profits for the West Indies Cricket Board (WICB).

Sport, income and the mass media

To a large extent the profitability of sport is dependent on its links with **information and communications technologies (ICTs)**. The mass media dominate how professional sporting activities are portrayed and in fact influence how successful those activities are. The mass media publicize events across the region and amongst the various media houses there is competition to buy the rights to record and broadcast live and taped broadcasts of matches. For cricket, these rights are often worth millions of dollars, which go to the WICB. These monies can be re-invested to develop the sport further through increased salaries for players, better prize monies and incentives, buying the services of higher-quality coaches and technical expertise, staging more sporting events, and training amateurs and young enthusiasts through clinics and sporting camps.

The mass media, especially cable television, have been able through increasingly sophisticated technical innovations to market the game in ways that the consumer finds exciting and informative. The commentaries, replays (often in slow motion), entertaining graphics, shot selection, and the many camera angles give the home viewer a comprehensive and detailed portrayal of the game that a spectator does not normally have. The popularity of home viewing (or sports bars with gigantic screens) therefore competes with the income that the live staging of games could generate. Negotiations between the mass media company buying the rights to air the match and the WICB sometimes result in agreements to show the match as a delayed telecast, or in real time only if the live event is sold out. Recently, large screens mounted in sporting arenas have given spectators a detailed perspective of the live performance similar to what they would have enjoyed at home. Thus, the mass media have promoted the popularity of certain sports by marketing them as a form of 'packaged reality' to an audience of millions. Inadvertently, this threatens the income-generating power of staging the *live event* for the WICB, as well as for those persons who depend on the event itself for an income – food and drink vendors, retailers of items with sporting logos and products endorsed by sporting heroes, transport workers and those providing support services (for example, those who maintain the sporting facilities).

Sport, income and employment

The growth of sport for entertainment (elite athletes, high-profile teams) as well as for physical activity (as recreation) has contributed to the generation of both income and employment in the region. For example, professional players receive large salaries and additional income from endorsement contracts, which are taxed by their respective countries, and so too are the profits of the WICB. Less directly attributable to sport are the taxes levied on the annual profits of media houses and other companies, such as those retailing sports goods, amongst other merchandise.

Coaches and those involved in sports management – from technical experts, nutritionists, personal trainers and instructors to medical personnel and other support staff – represent growing areas of employment. This is likely to continue to grow as the idea of sport as physical activity or recreation, important for everyone, is promoted. More specialized areas are coming into being – sports medicine, sports psychology and exercise psychology – contributing to a new set of workers in the sports sector. In addition, the building and maintenance of sports stadiums and other infrastructure and facilities provide employment for construction workers and others; the production of sports goods and equipment involves manufacturing, marketing and retailing; the administration of sport and sporting facilities requires managers and clerical workers; and advertising and sports journalism have spawned journals, magazines and websites devoted to sports news and issues generating a database of particular sports and sports icons.

However, compared to North America and Europe sport in the Caribbean still has much unrealized potential in generating income. Cricket is the only exception. The fact that there is one regional cricket team means that it has *regional* support. This is not the case with other sports. And cricket is played on a well-travelled international circuit. While many criticize the overarching role that a foreign company plays in West Indies cricket (Digicel – see Chapter 9), the fact remains that such a company is better able to afford the millions to invest in the sport than national governments or other local bodies.

Sport, whether played for entertainment on a competitive basis or for recreation, needs *sponsorship* and an infusion of investment capital. National teams aspiring to compete at the Olympics or other competitions (Box 10.1) find it difficult to send a fully equipped team abroad. Moreover, in most Caribbean countries there are increasing numbers of athletes, especially in cricket and football, willing to play in domestic clubs on a semi-professional basis, thus deepening the community's involvement in sport and broadening opportunities for many. However, a sports club needs considerable financial outlay: players, coaches and officials have to be paid some level of salary, as do those responsible for maintenance of the grounds and other facilities, and the club also has to pay for the athletes' meals, transport, uniforms and equipment as they travel to participate in competitions.

In competing for the scarce resources of governments or corporate sponsors, some sports are repeatedly sidelined (car racing, golf, swimming and tennis, sometimes described as 'elite sports'). Nevertheless, even the more popular sports such as football, netball and basketball hardly attract multinational investment capital in Caribbean countries. In fact, many sports are struggling just to remain in play – to be able to schedule annual competitions for various teams and to provide expertise and other forms of assistance to those teams so that they can compete effectively in the round of matches and fixtures. Thus, they can hardly generate income. The funding issue must be tackled, perhaps in novel ways because sources of assistance from governments and local companies have proven to be inadequate in uplifting sport to a level where it can generate income and contribute to its own development.

The question of sports teams and associations being able to generate income by organizing on a business footing is a possible developmental strategy, as well as sourcing multinational sponsorship. The latter, however, depends to a large extent on already being a successful team, with sporting stars capable of giving the multinational company advertising advantages. Thus, although the potential is there for sport to generate income to further its own development, for the time being such potential is not being fully realized.

ACTIVITY 10.2

'A Caribbean football team would stand a better chance of attracting international corporate investment and be a stronger candidate for World Cup success than the practice of fielding individual national teams'. Examine the implications of this statement.

ACTIVITY 10.3

1. Investigate to what extent local institutions such as business and government finance or support sport in your country, and which sports tend to benefit.

2. What might be considered 'creative' ways to attract more funding for sport?

BOX 10.1 Competitive sporting opportunities

For Caribbean athletes desirous of competing at the highest levels, as well as those committed to achieving excellence in a specific sport, there are opportunities to meet, compete with and learn from their colleagues internationally. However, funding remains a problem. Other than governments and corporate sponsors, the sporting association or club to which an athlete belongs finds that it has to enlist the help of NGOs, families and even friends in meeting the costs of sending athletes to attend sporting events abroad. These events, though, are important in the development of athletes and sports in general. For young athletes they provide opportunities for keen competition and for assessing their achievements against the very best athletes regionally and internationally. The following are some of the more popular events in which Caribbean athletes participate.

- *CARIFTA Games.* Held in a different Caribbean country each year around Easter, these games are important for the development of young athletes. They offer competitions in two categories – under 17 years and under 20 years. The games began in 1972 as an important step for young athletes in testing their skill and proficiency and as a training ground for those who would go on to become professional elites in their sport.
- *Commonwealth Games.* Held once every four years, these games are open to all the countries of the **Commonwealth**. One of the goals of the Commonwealth Games Federation is to encourage the development of sport and physical recreation throughout the Commonwealth. A recent addition (2000), the *Commonwealth Youth Games*, is open to athletes under 18 years, and presents another opportunity for our young athletes to meet international competitors.
- *Central American and Caribbean Junior and Senior Championships (CAC Games).* These games are held every other year and give Caribbean athletes an opportunity to compete with their counterparts from Central America. The Junior Championships have sections for athletes under 17 years and those under 20 years.
- *IAAF World Youth Championships (International Association of Athletics Federation).* This takes place every two years for athletes between 15 and 17 years of age and is an international meet usually dependent on performance at the CARIFTA Games or the CAC Junior Championships. The IAAF is the world governing body for the CAC games.
- *Pan-American Junior Championships.* This is held every two years for track and field athletes aged 19 years and under.

Participation in these regional and international competitions must necessarily be an important goal for athletes wishing to strive for excellence in their sport. At such meetings standards of performance are set against which athletes need to measure their performance. Thus, they represent important steps in the careers of Caribbean athletes, but the various sporting bodies in the Caribbean cannot afford to give many of their top athletes such an opportunity.

Sport as physical activity

The focus on highly competitive sports for recreation or entertainment obscures the importance of sport as physical activity for the mass of the population. For this to happen more of the citizenry needs to be won over to a lifestyle based on health and fitness. If the demand for sporting facilities and services grows, the income generated should be substantial. Today the price of gym membership and fees for fitness clubs tend to be prohibitive, largely because so few people have lifestyles where sport is a major form of recreation. A policy of promoting sport as physical activity for recreation should have health and fitness benefits for the population, as well as generating increased income from all the facilities, services and events that are patronized by the public.

Health and fitness

The health benefits of keeping physically active are widely known. Lower rates of heart disease, stroke, obesity and osteoporosis are some of the benefits of being physically active. Physical movement leads to the strengthening of bones, muscles and the cardio-vascular system. These in turn contribute to greater endurance and physical fitness, enabling the athlete or individual to improve performance. To be able to consistently improve fitness and strength, however, a dietary regimen and lifestyle that enhances good health and well-being must be followed. Thus, sports professionals and those who engage in sport for recreation tend to be vigilant about what they eat, abstain from alcohol and smoking as well as from other drugs, and try to organize their lives so that they get enough sleep. If health benefits are the well-documented outcomes of physical exercise, then we must consider why schools are not more aggressive in promoting physical fitness and sport in the curriculum (Box 10.2). We also need to examine the milieu in which young people are growing up and which influences their participation in sport, exercise and healthy lifestyles (Box 10.3).

Health and fitness, though, is a holistic condition that depends not only on physical well-being but also involves the mental and emotional state of the individual. On-going research seems to suggest that an exercise programme or involvement in sport helps individuals to achieve lower rates of anxiety and lowers stress levels, perhaps by altering their biochemistry (Scrignar, 1991). Emotional distress is often associated with feelings of inadequacy and low self-esteem. The achievement a person experiences in even a modest exercise programme, or in playing a sport, seems to result in a feeling of having control over one's life and a sense of mastery over circumstances.

BOX 10.2 Sports and physical education in schools

Psychologists such as Howard Gardner (1983) have put forward theories about human development that suggest that movement is an 'intelligence' similar to linguistic or mathematical intelligence. What he and his colleagues propose is that we do not have general intelligence but are intelligent in different areas. Some of those areas include logical-mathematical intelligence, spatial intelligence, interpersonal intelligence, intra-personal intelligence and bodily *kinesthetic intelligence* (or movement). Thus, people have 'multiple intelligences' and our education should involve training in each of them to help us to realize our true potential. One criticism of conventional schooling is that it focuses on logical-mathematical knowledge (abstract reasoning, critical thinking, making deductions) and linguistic intelligence (reading, writing, speaking and listening) as the most important knowledge for students to have. Music (musical intelligence), physical education (bodily kinesthetic intelligence) or social skills (interpersonal intelligence) become relegated to extra-curricular activities.

Gardner says that sports and physical education help individuals to use their bodies in a skilled way for self-expression and to achieve goals. To be able to dance, take part in dramatic productions, play basketball, exercise, or practise mind–body coordination (as in sports or yoga) are examples of displaying bodily or kinesthetic intelligence (as well as social skills). And this is a necessary part of the development of human beings. That schools are not more aggressive in promoting this intelligence suggests that educators, parents and students themselves rank the intelligences necessary for academic success as mainly linguistic and logico-mathematical knowledge and see the others as having minimal importance. However, if human development is to be an achievable goal of Caribbean countries, then *all* children should have a full programme of physical activity.

BOX 10.3 Youth and sports

Many studies show that youth participation in sports helps to decrease their involvement in drugs, gangs and smoking, and reduces the incidence of dropping out of school or becoming pregnant. However, whilst there is more interest and information in sports, health and fitness than ever before, there seems to be declining participation on the part of youth, as well as other groups. In fact, there is an increase in child obesity, which seems to signal that declining participation in sports is having a destructive effect on youth (Deckelbaum and Williams, 2001). Fraser (2003, p. 338) says that in 'the recent Adolescent Health and Fitness Study in Barbados, 18% of the children were already overweight, and many girls were becoming "couch potatoes". A shocking 20% of girls, compared to 8% of boys, reported no regular physical activity'.

Various theories have been put forward to try to account for the lack of interest that young people (particularly girls) are showing towards getting involved in sports and exercise programmes. They include the following:

- Many prefer to be spectators, and this is attributed to the sports programmes in schools (particularly high schools) which encourage early specialization in a particular sport, trying to find a suitable school team for competitions. If a student is not as talented as others, say in netball, and does not make the team, the opportunities for continued exposure to the sport dwindles to that of being a spectator. There are few examples of vigorous sports programmes in schools for *all* children. Whether it is conscious or not, school sports are bent on producing the *youth sports elite*.

- Students, both in high schools and in primary schools (where there is an increase in organized sports for young children) point out that once sport is organized in teams, coached and supervised by adults, it becomes more like work and less like play. The spontaneous, fun-oriented aspect vanishes and the regimen imposed by adults becomes a source of stress. (In the US this is one reason advanced for the popularity of *extreme sports* – bunjee jumping, skateboarding – which depend on individual effort with the minimum of adult supervision.)

High school students involved in early sport specialization are often honing their talents towards a particular end. Being able to access a prestigious sports scholarship and a university education is an increasingly popular goal for Caribbean students (see p. 311). Others are bent on achieving recognition and representing the country at international meets and even the Olympics. Still others seek the upward mobility that comes with being recruited into foreign professional football clubs. Coaches, parents and teachers tend to collaborate to help these students realize their dreams.

ACTIVITY 10.4

Recently, the apparent mismatch between sport and its sponsorship by tobacco companies has arisen as a hotly debated issue. Outline the main ideas in this debate. Do you believe that tobacco companies that are also sports sponsors jeopardize the goal of health and fitness for a country?

Sport and exercise are also recommended for the aged and the disabled. Exercise diminishes the need for costly medical attention for the aged. Medical experts say that the circulatory system and the muscles can be trained even after the age of 70. Perceptions that the aged should retire gracefully from life play a large part in preventing them from living full and active lives. They too are likely to accept the limitations that society tends to impose on them. For similar reasons the **Special Olympics** were introduced to popularize the idea that persons with disabilities can improve their health, fitness and self-esteem, as well as social skills, by active participation in sporting events. The needs of the disabled are usually not a priority with governments, so that it is left largely to volunteer organizations to provide opportunities for their continued development. It takes a lot of the time, energy and finance for volunteers and supporters to mount qualifying rounds for the Special Olympics. And in some countries that is just not possible.

In a very real way, then, sport and physical exercise have an important role to play in improving the health and fitness of all the people of a country and are therefore central to any development goals that a country might have. However, this ideal is compromised by an education system that pays token attention to *holistic* development. Schools tend to focus on academic success or even sporting success, minimizing the opportunities for *all* students to be involved in a meaningful programme of physical activity. The elderly and those suffering from intellectual disabilities also tend to be sidelined in this area of their development. For sport to make an important contribution to national and regional development it must move beyond its present emphasis on competition and performance enhancement to also include 'sport as physical activity' for everyone.

Caribbean identity

Success at sport, particularly competitive sports, is popularly seen as a means towards achieving a common feeling of Caribbean **identity**. Cricket has been able to do this as most Caribbean countries identify with the West Indies Cricket Team. A large part of the success of cricket in building a Caribbean identity is due to the fact that it can draw on players from *all* Caribbean countries. More recently, football has energized supporters as the most important means whereby the Caribbean could earn recognition as a sporting presence on the world scene, even though it may be only a national team achieving such honours.

The successes and failures of the West Indies Cricket Team, the controversies associated with it, the selection of players and its heroes are all issues that concern and interest Caribbean people across the region, as well as those in the **diaspora**. There is no single bond that unites Caribbean people so much as cricket. C. L. R. James (1963), in *Beyond a Boundary*, suggests that cricket occupies a unique place in our psyche. It cannot be understood just as a game, it is too closely associated with British rule and **colonialism**. James sees the Caribbean person as having made a commitment to things British, subconsciously or not. Thus cricket, that very British institution, was not abandoned but rather embraced and West Indianized, making it into something fiery and 'better' than the British version. Besting the British at their own beloved sport has been an important part of our **decolonization** process and, as James implies, a performance through which we have been able to find ourselves and develop our capabilities.

Where other sports are concerned – football, track and field events and swimming – the success of Caribbean athletes representing their individual countries in international competitions has been a source of pride for all Caribbean people. For example, the long and successful history of Jamaica in track and field, second only to the US in the amount of medals won, is an astounding feat, given our scarce resources in promoting sport. Football or soccer is widely popular all over the region, and the qualifying matches for the World Cup present a unique opportunity to see the many classes and social groups in Caribbean society feeling a sense of common identity as they cheer on their national football teams (Box 10.4).

Beyond the specific cases of cricket and football, sport in general has been credited with the potential for nation-building, an important part of developing a national identity. One of the reasons for incorporating sports programmes into the curriculum in schools, for example, is to promote unity among diverse peoples. However, schools vary in their ability to provide instruction and experience in the different types of sports. Some schools do not have playgrounds, whilst others have funding enabling them to buy a school bus to transport their athletes. We have already noted the marginalization of those who display little sporting prowess and

ACTIVITY 10.5

The glory days of West Indies cricket seem to be mainly in the past yet Caribbean people remain as interested and involved as ever before. To what do you attribute this loyalty?

BOX 10.4 Sports: presence on the world scene

Many people have commented on the power of sports, especially football, to foster a sense of almost national hysteria when qualifying matches are near, particularly those for the World Cup. Although cricket is much loved and has a long tradition in the Caribbean, the kind of hype and national jubilation or depression that follows an international match involving the national football team seem quite unique to football. Commentators have also remarked on the apparent feeling of oneness among the various ethnicities in a country as they prepare to cheer on their national football team and cite the ability of sports to integrate the country.

When Trinidad and Tobago qualified for the World Cup finals in Germany in 2006, several football fans tried to explain why there is this obsession with football and its apparent power to unite the public. Here are some of their replies:

- There is a tremendous love for the sport but the opportunities to witness live first class soccer only come to the Caribbean when an international competition is at hand; local club teams do not display the level of skill and performance that an international meet provides. So there will always be enthusiasm, excitement and sell-out matches when this happens.

- Rallying around any national team is a normal occurrence. However, support for the national football team even involves persons who are usually uninterested in sports. This is because football is possibly the most popular sport in the world and any participation by the national team in international matches means that the Caribbean is staking a claim for international attention.

- This could be put another way. It is about respect. All nationals want their country to be acknowledged as a presence on the world scene. Football more than any other sport (even cricket) has the potential to bring a Caribbean country into the spotlight with the whole world as an audience. There is then this striving for respect, to be accepted with world acclaim, overcoming the constraints of small size, few resources, and a history mired in bondage and oppression.

The anxiety and national hysteria that attends a qualifying round of the World Cup in the Caribbean, then, has to do with this hankering about being recognized as a presence on the world scene. Any unity of class, colour and creed that one notices at these times are temporary lapses in the ordinary state of affairs, because whether the team wins or loses, **social stratification** remains unaffected.

ACTIVITY 10.6

Reflect on the role sports play in development in your country. If any of your sports teams is victorious at any regional or international competitions, to what extent does that contribute to nation-building?

how they tend to be excluded from sport or exercise programmes. In addition, it is mainly the well-to-do who can afford the extra tuition, coaching clinics and the costs of competing abroad for their children who show sporting talent. Sport can do little to bridge the gap between the haves and the have-nots and cannot be a force for nation-building if socio-economic groups remain apart in the schools they attend and if they have access to different types of infrastructure – swimming pools, clinics, available transport and training facilities.

Discipline and morale

One of the benefits of playing a sport is the appreciation the participant develops for a disciplined approach to the game, as well as the cooperation or teamwork necessary for success in many sports. Serious athletes learn to pit themselves against their last best performance in their bid to achieve excellence. It is said that within sport a person can achieve high moral character by observing the spirit of fair play, honesty and endurance that the sport demands. In committing to excellence in performance, in preparing for competition, in winning or losing, an athlete's main concern is how he or she plays the game. An athlete knows that the highest form of discipline and morale comes from the journey and not necessarily from the finish. Sports, then, have long been promoted as having character-building potential for individuals, depending on how they approach and play the game.

The **Olympic Games** is undoubtedly the most prestigious international sporting event for most athletes and for the general public. The participants are the best in the world in their field. Its status comes not only from the high quality of the competitors, but also from the respect accorded its ancient beginnings and lofty ideals (Box 10.5). The Olympic movement is based on the understanding that sport (through the experiences of preparation and competition) can lead to healthier and happier individuals and a more peaceful world. It is thus not only about sport itself but the contribution of sport to peace. It therefore does not recognize discrimination amongst nations or groups and regards all human beings as interconnected.

These are indeed lofty ideals, and sportspersons, coaches, officials, teachers and players' associations, as well as the general public, recognize the intrinsic worth of having such ideals. If a serious commitment is made to upholding the Olympic tradition, then sport would make a definite contribution to development. It would provide an avenue to display humanitarian attitudes, fairness and justice and nurture

BOX 10.5 The Olympic Games: then and now

The Ancient Olympic Games of Greece, originating somewhere around 776 BC, honoured the god Zeus, and were therefore a religious event. Like today, the Games were the most important athletic event of the times. The winners were treated to similar accolades that sports superstars enjoy nowadays. Sums of money were bestowed upon the victors, statutes of them were erected in their home cities, and songs and poems were created in their honour. During the Games a truce was to be observed and a cessation of all hostilities.

Also very similar to what obtains today, historical records show that cheating and bribery were common occurrences amongst rival athletes and the truce was often violated. The Games tended to be dominated by nationalistic fervour, nations feeling triumphant and having a sense of superiority when their athletes won. In ancient Greece the city-states viewed the competitions almost as if they were waging war against each other. Over the centuries in which the Olympics were in existence its religious and athletic ideals were repeatedly dishonoured. In 393 BC the Roman Emperor Theodosius abolished the Games, citing them as a form of pagan practice.

In 1894, through the tireless efforts of Baron Pierre de Coubertin (a French educator), the **International Olympic Committee (IOC)** was formed and the modern Olympic Games came into being. A little known fact is that the IOC Charter envisages sport and the Olympics as a vehicle for promoting **values** which must be taught. This more recent Olympic tradition is an educational one, seeing sports as a medium through which participants learn to co-exist harmoniously with each other, especially at international competitions where fair play and good will predominate. The IOC Charter is a charter for world peace. The present arrangements and organization of the Games, then, do not necessarily reflect the traditions and ideals of the ancient Games. The emphasis on ethical principles, unity and peace are the foundation on which the modern Games are based.

Ironically, the present Olympics have seen no end of cheating, doping, boycotting, acts of sabotage and terrorism, as well as political interference and improper conduct of coaches, judges and even IOC members. The *commercialization* of the Games is often cited as the major reason why there is so much dishonesty at an event founded on principles of ethics and fair play. One aspect of commercialization refers to the valuable prizes that athletes vie for. The glory of winning an Olympic gold medal is also accompanied by the possibility of lucrative endorsement contracts for multinational business interests and promises of houses, large sums of money and national awards from the athletes' home countries. A second aspect of commercialization refers to how the media select, package and promote the athletes they decide should be world-class superstars. Athletes are *commodified* in this way and become highly prized on the market.

The media also influence the Games themselves. Their broadcasting fees contribute enormously to meeting the costs of staging the Games and the IOC tends to accommodate American television networks in the scheduling of events. The sheer size of the television viewing audience for an Olympic event makes a fortune for the mass media in terms of advertising and the broadcast rights they sell to other companies.

a more peaceful society. However lofty these ideals are, the fact that the Olympics are held in such high esteem means that people recognize the spirit that imbues this sporting tradition and feel that it should continue to inspire. Since the Games were restarted in 1896 they have been held every four years (except during the two world wars), attesting to a general desire to hold on to something that speaks to an enlightened view of the individual and the promise of a better world.

It is a matter of continued concern, then, that at every Olympics in recent times there has been evidence of banned drug use by athletes and their coaches to achieve higher standards of performance. The dilemma here is that the ideals of the Olympics are not being echoed by present-day values, which applaud winning as everything and any other place as not worthy of mention. Winning at all costs encourages dishonest practices such as taking illegal drugs and engaging in tactics to destabilize a fellow competitor or gain an unfair advantage. Commentators seem to think that the increasing commercialization of sport in the US, Canada and Europe especially, turns on the large salaries and lucrative endorsement contracts that athletes earn. The foreign mass media glorify athletes and report on their luxurious lifestyles, and this continued hype encourages aspiring world record holders to use any means necessary to win, because to win means a chance of becoming eligible for all these rewards.

The irony of our sports-crazy world is that the notion of sport being purveyed is one that has been created, packaged and disseminated by the mass media. Many Caribbean people watch NBA basketball on television. The camera angles, the music, the interjections by the commentators, the audience reactions, the replays and the clips on individual athletes are all carefully designed to portray these athletes as larger than life, as superheroes. The portrayal of violence in North American ice hockey is particularly gruesome and alarming, in that so many people seem to enjoy it. The orchestrated television version of games and the coverage of violence in sport are all calculated to appeal to the sports spectator's desire for fast-paced action, confrontation, aggression, hostility, a war of words or even fights, which perk up interest in the game.

While sports in the Caribbean are not as commercialized as in North America and Europe, the fact remains that the foreign mass media hold great sway over Caribbean audiences, who regularly tune in to basketball and other games. The icons of the American sports world are everywhere in the Caribbean, not only on television but on posters, billboards, caps, T-shirts and magazines. Today sport in the Caribbean is conceived largely as *competitive* sports and as a means of promoting the Caribbean on the world scene, a source of national or regional pride. That pride comes from winning and from world recognition of Caribbean athletes. The notion of sport for character building and for health and fitness seems to have lost out against the more popular image of sport as entertainment.

The emphasis on winning and the commercialization of sport largely through the mass media thus pose a dilemma to the school of thought that promotes sport as having the potential to nurture character-building qualities such as discipline, honesty and fair play, as well as toleration and peaceful co-existence. In this dilemma we witness one of the major problems of development – the pull or lure of riches transcending moral principles. An emphasis on material wealth, fame and glory promotes an attitude of winning at all costs. This mires the Olympics and other championships in controversy after controversy over doping scandals and incidents of cheating. All this plays directly to the media, which get considerable commercial

ACTIVITY 10.7

Describe ONE way by which sport as a vehicle to promote discipline and morale among Caribbean people can be achieved.

mileage out of reporting these incidents as they unfold. Sport as a means of contributing to the moral development of Caribbean persons, then, is being jeopardized by the increasing importance of the foreign media in influencing how sport is portrayed.

Educational opportunities

Demonstrating excellence in a particular sport can help Caribbean students to access higher education. On qualifying, they can attain social mobility, earn more income and use their expertise in improving conditions in whatever line of work they find themselves when they return home. The US *sports scholarship* has emerged in recent years as an alternative path for accessing a university education, not only for poorer students but also for those who associate the scholarship and US universities with more prestige than the local alternatives. To this end the most talented secondary school students in sport routinely take the SATs to be eligible for US universities (see p. 290) and compete as far as possible in meets where scouts from US universities may be present. Thousands of Caribbean students are now studying at universities abroad, whether on a full or partial sports scholarship. The US has many avenues through which our students can access funding – grants for under-represented minorities, grants offered by Caribbean people in the diaspora for those students resident in the US and of Caribbean heritage, and at certain universities grants offered by their international alumni for disadvantaged students from the Caribbean. Local organizations, too, are beginning to offer sports scholarships. For example, the Caribbean Tourism Organization now provides scholarships and study grants for those athletes wishing to study tourism hospitality and languages locally.

ACTIVITY 10.8

Outline some of the ways in which a foreign sports scholarship impacts negatively on Caribbean development.

A sports scholarship offers a route to a professional career in a particular sport or a career in other disciplines studied at the university. The educational opportunities that are accessed through this means can result in development for the Caribbean. If the athlete returns to the Caribbean, he or she adds to the cadre of professional talent, either in sport or other areas. People achieving tertiary education are able to earn a fairly high standard of living in the Caribbean. They are also able to contribute to the national good through their expertise in different fields. Even if the athlete continues to live and train abroad (taking advantage of superior training facilities and expertise) but still competes for the Caribbean, his or her success also means fame and glory for the Caribbean, but this does not necessarily help to develop sport locally.

Undoubtedly the sports scholarship exposes an athlete to training and professional expertise as well as a level of competition that will hardly be found in a small Caribbean country. However, apart from the individual advantage of social mobility and the indirect benefits that may accrue to the country through the growth of an expert and professional class, sport itself may not necessarily profit from the educational opportunities a sports scholarship affords young athletes.

In quite another way sport can contribute to educational opportunities for youth. An active sports programme designed for students and out-of-school youth can set up alternative paths, especially for 'at-risk' youth, which help them to stay in school, refrain from unhealthy practices and even learn marketable skills within a sports programme (Box 10.6). As an avenue for out-of-school youth to access educational opportunities, sport thus has the potential to contribute to national development by reducing costly risky behaviours.

BOX 10.6 Sports and 'at-risk' youth

In the World Bank (2003) report on Caribbean youth development, the following statements are made:

- Sexual and physical abuse is high in the Caribbean and socially accepted in many Caribbean countries.
- The onset of sexual initiation in the Caribbean is the highest in the world (with the exception of Africa, where early sexual experiences take place within marriage).
- The region has the highest incidence of HIV/AIDS outside of Africa.
- The incidence of rage among young people is extremely high.
- Youth unemployment is especially elevated in some Caribbean countries.
- In contrast to the United States, which has high levels of youth violence, the proportion of Caribbean adolescent males who carry firearms is extremely high.
- Although data on drug use are scanty, anecdotal evidence suggests a widespread social acceptance of alcohol and marijuana in some Caribbean countries, among both in-school and out-of-school youth. (World Bank, 2003, pp. xiv, xv)

The report states that while youth were not *responsible* for these problems they were deeply enmeshed in them, causing many to be involved in risky behaviours (those that tend to result in negative outcomes). Responsibility for these problems lies in the **family**, where many young people may be physically abused, especially through corporal punishment from an early age, and where parental guidance is not as strong as it should be. In addition, the education system continues to privilege high academic success and does not have adequate programmes designed for children who are intelligent in other areas. Many drop out of secondary schools or if they continue, are alienated within the system. Dropping out of school, poverty and few options are suggested as possible reasons why youth become involved with drugs and crime as well as early sexual encounters.

Some progress is being made to offer at-risk youth educational opportunities involving sports as a means to overcome negative outcomes. In St Kitts–Nevis, *Project Strong* has achieved international and regional recognition for its combination of physical activity, computer training and other skills linked to an apprenticeship scheme for out-of-school youth involved in risky behaviours. The project has spread to other Caribbean countries, where the emphasis on a core sports programme to nurture positive attitudes, discipline and morale seems to be more successful in building confidence and self-esteem than specialized, separate academic or sports programmes. The *Healthy Lifestyle Project*, originating in Jamaica and spreading across the Caribbean, targeted female youth to become involved in netball as a means for experiencing self-esteem, appreciating healthy living, and for learning leadership skills. Today it welcomes males and has grown to accommodate all kinds of sports.

Although these programmes help to build the human development potential of individuals, they also help in national development as the costs of risky behaviours are expensive to the country. The World Bank report puts it this way:

- *A single cohort of adolescent mothers is estimated to cost society, in terms of foregone benefits from alternative uses of resources, more than US$2 million in St. Kitts and Nevis.* (This means that in any year a substantial percentage of the monies to pay for developmental projects has to be diverted to state services to address the needs of young mothers and their children.)
- *School leavers in Guyana forego hundreds of thousands of dollars in net earnings over their lifetimes, costing the state thousands of dollars in lost income.* (Paying for a student's education is expensive. A nation does this with the expectation that education would equip an individual with skills to contribute to the country. If a student drops out of school he or she is wasting the money spent by the state on education and personally denying himself or herself the earnings that could have been made over a lifetime.)
- *Youth crime and violence in St. Lucia generates more than US$3 million in lost benefits to society and US$7.7 million in lost benefits to private individuals annually.* (The financial costs that the society has to pay for arrests, prosecution and detention could be used for developmental purposes. Private costs to individuals include installing security systems in their homes and cars and upgrading security generally – improved locks, burglar-proofing and guard dogs. In addition, there are other costs such as stolen or destroyed private property, the psychological costs experienced by the victims, and the fall-off in tourist flows). (World Bank, 2003, p. xv)

There is great potential, then, in developing sports and related programmes for out-of-school youth to reduce the incidence of risky behaviours. Such programmes, by impacting positively on youth and their choices, also save the country substantial financial costs.

Summary

Sport can increasingly make a contribution to development in the Caribbean through generating income, encouraging health and fitness, promoting a sense of Caribbean identity and nurturing important character traits such as discipline, honesty and perseverance. More recently, for those winning sports scholarships, sport has become an avenue to illustrious careers as sports professionals, or professionals of other kinds. However, the contribution of sport to development remains minimal in the Caribbean because on its own it cannot accomplish the goals of a healthy nation or high morale. The dominance of the foreign mass media, which seem addicted to sport, undermines the ways that sport can contribute to Caribbean development. In addition, if the society suffers from a great deal of inequity, sport can hardly bring about a more equitable state of affairs. Sport as entertainment may be able to help individuals to achieve success, but sport as physical fitness, organized for national and regional development, can do much more. The problem is that this focus on sport as physical fitness, or sport for all, is not pursued seriously.

10.3

THE MASS MEDIA

We have seen above that the mass media exert great influence on sport and its developmental potential. However, they also play other roles that are of importance in considering the issue of development in Caribbean countries. These are considered in this section.

The mass media are so much a taken-for-granted part of Caribbean society and culture that their role in development is seldom analysed. To better understand their role today we should be aware of when they came into being in the region and for what purpose. The idea of a 'mass' media points to the notion that the masses (the 'common folk') should have the same access to information as the elites in the society. This would level the playing field and all citizens would have the same information as a basis for action. Such ideas gained increasing popularity in the era of decolonization leading up to independence (Box 10.7).

Media of communication

'Media' is a shorthand way of referring to 'media of communication'. A medium of communication between two or more persons or in small groups having face-to-face contact may take the form of gestures, signals and language (oral and written). 'Mass media', on the other hand, refers to forms of communication organized to reach large audiences and includes radio, television, newspapers and the internet. A medium of communication such as newspapers becomes a part of the mass media when it publishes information for the public. *Publishing* refers to the act of putting information out for public viewing. Traditionally, publishing was associated only with the *print media* (books, newspapers, magazines) but today one can publish on the internet as well as publish music or computer software. By the same token, we should be able to say that radio and television 'publish' the news but the term 'broadcast' is more often used. They are referred to as the *broadcast media,* though the term *electronic media* is also appropriate.

BOX 10.7 The 'mass' media: for the common folk?

In the decades before independence, newspapers, pamphlets and other print media were used to popularize ideas about equity and stir up support for the trade union movement, black consciousness, and ultimately the struggle for independence. Local politicians realized that for democracy to be a success, the participation of the people was necessary, and so they had to have access to *information*. Newspapers, later radio, and after that television, were all harnessed to provide information to the masses. This was seen to be 'development' because people now had information about politics, and other matters affecting their lives, which they could use to make decisions in the national interest.

Another view opposed this understanding of the mass media and development, suggesting that it was a sanitized version of what really happens with the mass media. What is showcased as 'the news' (then and now) is a simplified version of events. In fact, what is included and what is discarded is very much someone's opinion about what others should know (and not know). To a large extent this criticism is aimed at big business today, which either owns media houses or supports the media with profitable advertising contracts. Business interests, then, control the media, who in turn manipulate the news that is beamed to 'the people'.

This critical view of the mass media says that they mislead the public. For example, newspapers continue to maintain their stance as bearers of truth for the common folk, images from the early days of the mass media, through the names they adopt. In the list below, see if you can identify the country associated with each newspaper:

- *The Gleaner* – to find out all things, even those hidden, to make sense of things
- *The Nation* – all-encompassing, for everyone; patriotic values
- *The Advocate* – having a special position or supporter for the people
- *The Chronicle* – recording the truth impartially for purposes of transparency
- *The Herald* – good news
- *The Voice* and *The Express* – a forum for 'freedom of speech'

Thus, in thinking about the mass media and development we must be conscious of whose interests are being secured. The above discussion suggests that big business controls the news although newspapers carry names that indicate their purpose to be one of hard-hitting investigative reporting that has the interests of poor people in mind.

Fig. 10.1 shows the many terms used to classify the mass media today. Technological advances have transformed various media into multiple ways of delivery so that one form may now fall under overlapping labels. For example, the internet and the World Wide Web are increasingly used for broadcasting and analysing news. Not only are there conventional newspapers publishing *on-line editions* but there is also the new phenomenon of **blogging** (see p. 293). A 'blog' is a webpage that may be devoted to discussion of some topical issue, often breaking news. Contributors may come from all over the world; they may be a select group of experts or just interested persons. The discussion is often of high quality and alternative opinions and experiences may be expressed contrary to those being portrayed in the 'mainstream' media. Very differently to how newspapers treat the news, bloggers persist with a story, analysing all its aspects and consequences. Thus, the internet and the World Wide Web are an integral part of the 'news media', the 'electronic media' and the 'digital media' (computerized images and text). There is even internet radio, making it part of the 'broadcast media' as well. It is also interesting to note that small personal items of electronic media such as webcams and cellular phones can network into computers and beam images that may find their way into the news. Whilst all forms of media of communication are growing and developing in different ways, our region is increasingly immersed in the

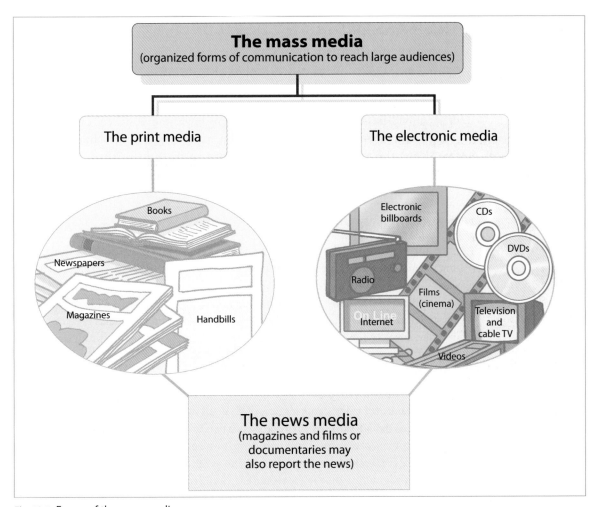

Fig. 10.1 Forms of the mass media

electronic and digital media – radio, television, video, film (cinema), CDs, DVDs and ICTs – and their increasingly sophisticated ways of coming together as *multimedia*.

Summary

The various forms of the traditional mass media – newspapers, television, radio and magazines – had specific audiences and material that tended to keep them distinct in the types of information they pervaded. Today all that has changed with ICTs where internet and computer technologies now network with radio, television, newspapers and other print media, as well as with electronic media such as DVDs and cell phones, to transmit any type of information globally. The pervasiveness of the mass media, and in particular the foreign mass media, in the Caribbean inevitably impacts on how we are conceptualizing development. As a result, we should be aware that actively debating and discussing the role and function of the mass media in our context is a development issue.

10.4

THE MASS MEDIA AND DEVELOPMENT

The **human development paradigm** (Chapter 8) promotes an idea of development not just as economic progress but as increasing the levels of **equity**, productivity, empowerment and sustainability experienced by people. If the mass media, as a major social institution, are contributing to development in the Caribbean, then there should be some evidence that they are impacting positively on the equity, productivity, empowerment and sustainability experienced by Caribbean people. In this section the role and functions of the mass media are examined to determine whether, or how, they may be contributing to human development.

Provision of information

A major function of the mass media is to provide and disseminate information to citizens. In studying the relationship of the mass media to development, we must consider what information is transmitted and how that could contribute to development. Television, radio, newspapers and the internet provide a wealth of information from politics, natural disasters, fashion, entertainment and cooking to the weather, astrology, economic and financial trends and exercise and health options.

Advertisements

Much of the information transmitted by the mass media is in the form of advertisements for goods and services. These ads are paid for by the businesses that choose a particular form of media to advertise their products. Advertisers bring in a lot of money so that their interests tend to be promoted where programming is concerned. For example, advertisers may not wish to buy advertising space during a television programme on the environment, preferring an American 'sit com', as they believe that more people would be watching the foreign show. Without advertisers willing to buy the airtime, local productions that have educational content will disappear and we will lose access to valuable information.

News

Newspapers, and television stations dedicated only to news coverage (such as Fox News and CNN), are the main ways in which news is disseminated, but radio stations, news magazines and internet sites also broadcast the news. 'News' is defined as any happening in which people may be interested. This is important to remember in considering whether the information given as news contributes to national development. For example, sometimes the mass media are accused of *creating* the news – inventing or speculating about developing stories in a manner calculated to keep the public interested. The obvious reason why they would do this is to keep people buying newspapers and tuning in to radio and television stations. The media industry is a business and the news itself can be sold many times over if it is protracted and packaged in different ways. We have witnessed this where a 'lead story' several days old is revitalized by having one or more experts come on the air to discuss the case. At this point we have to ask ourselves if it is still news, this unfolding 'footage' produced by the television station's news crew. And we do have to consider whether

---

ACTIVITY 10.9

If you read newspapers regularly or listen to news and talk shows on the radio or television, what issues or events would you say you are more informed about? Reflect on whether, or how, that information has had any impact on your human development.

ACTIVITY 10.10

In what other ways is the information (content, opinions) disseminated by the mass media influenced by advertisers?

ACTIVITY 10.11

'News is really someone's version of what is important.'

1. Make a list of the topics/events that seem to be 'newsworthy' in your country.

2. Consider what gets reported and what seems to be ignored or sidelined.

3. Is there any basis for the statement made above?

BOX 10.8 Who defines the news?

If we are concerned about human development we must ask certain questions about the news. For example, whose interests are continually reported on? Which groups do not get to air their concerns and grievances? Let us take newspapers. In Grenada, Dominica and Belize there are no daily newspapers, only weeklies. In other territories there are one or more dailies, a few weeklies, and sometimes the 'evening news' or those published twice a week. There are even hard-hitting, openly critical newspapers targeting government officials and policies. The *Outlet* of Antigua and Barbuda ran from 1969 to 2004, but today the *Star* of St Lucia ('bringing the truth to light') and the *Mirror* of Trinidad and Tobago serve the same function. These newspapers do not necessarily favour the opposition but are inclined to give prominence to individuals and groups who are normally sidelined by the national daily newspapers.

For example, while crime may feature prominently in the widely circulated dailies and Sunday newspapers, it is a particular position about crime that is aired. The photographs, reports, editorials, and articles focus on spiralling crime statistics, the details of criminal acts, the resources of the protective services and who may or may not be responsible (who is to blame). These opinions may range from inadequate parenting, the lack of good male role models, the failure of the education system, the incompetence of the police, the foreign mass media and the connections between officials and drug lords. Critics say that this is a middle-of-the road, even middle-class, view of the news.

Those newspapers which offer an alternative view are really about giving the public additional information that they need to understand an issue. However, they are often labelled as scurrilous and scandalous and can only stay in circulation as long as they attract advertisers. While some newspapers affect a 'tabloid' style, there are those which are mainly concerned with airing information that does not normally get published. For example, in the war against crime, certain places in a country are regarded as breeding crime, such as West Kingston in Jamaica and Laventille in Trinidad and Tobago. One will rarely see a newspaper that regularly gives a voice to people in these areas – to hear about job opportunities, their conditions of life, *their* take on the crime situation – because their views are often not the views portrayed in the mainstream media. They will more likely point back to those pointing at them to ask why they are not being employed, why their schools are not being improved, how are they supposed to live when public transport, ambulances, postal workers, delivery trucks and other taken-for-granted services do not venture into their area? They will also ask why their area and their people are vilified in the press when law-abiding citizens live there, young children, old people and enterprising adults desirous of making something of their lives.

These criticisms suggest that the mainstream media showcase a *consensus* approach to the news – the views and opinions of the powerful or elite groups. The mass media tend to bring in experts, specialists and professionals to discuss issues. This suggests that the opinions and experiences of those who live in the troubled areas are not as valid. These people may not be as fluent or articulate as the professional, and moreover they may resort to argumentative and confrontational stances that do not have a place in polite debate. The 'news' that an **underclass** may generate is not really considered newsworthy in the broadcast media.

by the same token there may be groups and events which do not make the news at all (Box 10.8), as well as those (often very serious) matters that get covered for a short period and are then dropped, even though they remain serious.

A free press

Many people equate the growth of the mass media with a free press, seeing a free press as a positive sign that democracy is being enhanced. This can be traced to the decolonization era when the mass media were supposed to assist in the process of popularizing the cause of freedom (Box 10.7). If democracy is being enhanced by a free press, then certainly that would be evidence that human development is taking place. A free press suggests equity and that everyone has a right to express their views, so long as they do not commit acts of slander or libel (Box 10.9). This would mean that even marginal groups would have a voice in national affairs.

BOX 10.9 Libel and slander

In the mass media statements about people are published. The onus is on the publishing house to be certain that those statements do not defame the character of anyone in the mind of the public.

- **Defamation** of character refers to a lowering of the estimation of that person in the eyes of the public. If a statement is defamatory then that person could bring a case of libel against the publisher.
- **Libel** refers to defamatory statements which are published in some permanent form (newspaper, television tapes, internet sites).

- **Slander**, on the other hand, refers to defamatory statements made while speaking.

Because of the libel laws, the mass media have to exercise responsibility and good judgement in deciding to publish statements which may threaten a person's good reputation. For many journalists this threatens the freedom of the press. However, if the statements are found to be true (or reasonable) by a court of law then the libel case can be thrown out.

The issue of whether we do have a free press in the Caribbean is a contentious one. The debate about this issue turns on *who owns the media*. In the decades after independence, governments slowly gave up their tight control of radio and television broadcasting because cable television and the foreign media were making it unprofitable to continue to run public broadcasting networks devoted to local news and events. In some Caribbean countries today governments still own at least one radio or television station or have majority shares, but to a large extent the local media houses are privately owned. Some business interests own both newspapers and radio and television stations so that there is a concentration of media ownership among private enterprise. Whether owned by the government, public corporations or private investors, in recent years the Commonwealth Press Union and the International Press Institute have recognized a gradual improvement in press freedom in the Commonwealth Caribbean. However, both Caribbean journalists and these international *watchdog* associations cite several issues that have compromised the freedom of the press in the region in the recent past (Box 10.10).

A major continuing issue that journalists have with their governments concerns the laws governing *libel*. There have been repeated calls to liberalize these laws. Journalists believe that the fear of unwittingly libelling someone causes them to be very circumspect in their language. And they must also be aware that laws still exist prohibiting certain information from being made public. For example, in Belize financial disclosure statements submitted by public officials cannot be questioned; if that happens, in the print media or otherwise, the offending journalists can be fined or jailed. This encourages self-censorship amongst journalists. What do journalists want?

- Freedom of the press enshrined in the constitution and not just freedom of expression, as is the case now in most Caribbean countries.
- Laws that protect them from any libellous content in the news items they use that have been sent to them by other news or wire services.
- Laws that protect them in criticizing public institutions and government officials.
- Ensuring that laws guaranteeing their freedom of movement throughout CARICOM are observed.

ACTIVITY 10.12

Today the Barbados 1996 Defamation Act is considered a model piece of legislation that other Caribbean governments should follow.

1. Find out what are the basic provisions of this Act.

2. Suggest why other Caribbean governments are 'dragging their feet' in implementing similar legislation.

BOX 10.10 Harassment of the press

Trinidad and Tobago

During Basdeo Panday's term in office as prime minister, the press endured a relentless campaign of harassment:

- In 1996 Panday called for the removal of *Guardian* editor Jones P. Madeira from office for alleged 'bias'. In an editorial, Madeira had asked the prime minister to prove his allegations that the PNM (People's National Movement, the opposition) was planning to destabilize the government. Madeira was asked by his bosses, a business cartel, to resign.
- In 1997 Ken Gordon brought a charge of slander against the prime minister for calling him a 'pseudo racist' in front of a large political gathering. Gordon was head of the media house Caribbean Communications Network (CCN). It was widely believed that that attack came about because of Gordon's opposition to the government's Green Paper on Media Reform – that it was too controlling of journalists. Gordon won the suit and the appeal in court, though the settlement was reduced. You can read up on the arguments advanced for and against the charge at http://www.privy-council.org.uk/files/other/5.rtf
- In 1998 the work permit for Barbadian journalist Julian Rogers was not renewed and there was widespread speculation that it was because he incurred the displeasure of the prime minister by airing on the call-in television programme, 'Morning Edition', content that opposed the government.

Antigua and Barbuda

The Bird family dominated politics in Antigua and Barbuda for three decades: Vere Bird, founder of the Antigua Labour Party (ALP) was prime minister from 1981 to 1994, when he was succeeded by his son, Lester Bird. There have been many attempts to control the media:

- In 2001 virtually all the media were in the control of the Bird family. However, *Observer Radio*, the first independent radio station, began to broadcast after years of trying to obtain a licence. In 1996 they had been shut down the day after they began broadcasting. (This is very similar to events in Trinidad and Tobago in 2005 when a new local television station – Cable News Channel (CNC) – was prevented from broadcasting four hours before they were due to go on air by the Telecommunications Authority of Trinidad and Tobago (TATT) stating that they were in breach of regulations.)
- In 2002 the Barbadian journalist Julius Gittens, host of a news programme, 'The Big Issues', was hastily expelled from the country ostensibly because he did not pay for his work permit. Even though a receipt was produced he was told that he could not be re-instated because there was a new rule where only two non-nationals could work in any media house. Many believe it was because discussions on the show called for inquiries into government misconduct.
- In 2002 the *Observer* recorded an interview with a 14-year-old girl alleging that she had had sexual relations with the prime minister and was a drug courier for him. This video tape was apparently leaked to the public and Prime Minister Lester Bird sued the *Observer* for libel. The *Observer* was next threatened with closure for not paying millions of dollars in back taxes. A government position paper on the issue can be viewed on the internet at http://www.antigua-barbuda.com/business_politics/pdf/government_statement_videotape_affair.pdf

Press freedom is seen in different ways, depending on one's position. From the perspective of mass media workers the press in the Caribbean is not free. It would be free if (as in the US) the press had fewer restrictions to contend with in reporting on the actions of people in public life. From the perspective of governments, on the other hand, the press is 'too free'. From the perspective of poorer groups in the society the press tends to be dominated by the views and perspectives of big business and middle–class attitudes. From the perspective of international watchdog sites, the press in the Caribbean enjoys a great deal of freedom because all newspapers and other media publish some forms of criticism of public officials and government policies (Box 10.11).

BOX 10.11 Investigative reporting

Investigative reporting is regarded as the pinnacle of journalistic practice. The example is often cited of the two reporters in the US (and an informant, Deep Throat) who played a central role in unravelling the Watergate scandal in the early 1970s, which eventually toppled the presidency of Richard Nixon. Investigative reporting is seen as the hallmark of a free press. Reporters are free to pursue a story and follow leads from individuals, protecting their sources, and, in a systematic way, going after those persons involved in crime or a cover-up so that the media actually are involved in detecting and solving crimes.

Journalists in the Caribbean find that they are unable to do in-depth investigative reporting. Much of their news coverage is actually a response to something that is happening (a press conference, a budget speech) to which they have been invited, or an event or incident (murder, robbery, fire, strike) which they are called upon to report

in a routine way. While journalists cite the libel laws as the main reason for their caution in reporting crimes, they also mention that building up evidence and exposing, for example corruption, in the media is a far cry from getting a conviction in a court of law. The latter operates on the 'presumption of innocence' and the long and protracted court battles often end in victory for the defendants.

Journalists also point to the political culture where people are unwilling to give up information that may incriminate members of their own party. In a highly politicized culture, generations of one family are sometimes loyal to one political party, come what may. In addition, the private and business interests who may own the media play a role in what is investigated and what is not. Reflect on any examples of investigative journalism that you know about in your territory – to what extent does that kind of reporting occur?

Behaviour change

The mass media are considered to be a force in the development process because they provide citizens with information that helps them to be knowledgeable about a variety of areas important for them to lead a full and healthy life. If this is what the mass media are supposed to be doing we should be vigilant in examining what type of information they provide. Is it information that helps the population to keep healthy, or to better understand political and economic trends, or to improve their quality of life? In fact, we may well wonder to what extent the actual provision of information helps to change behaviours.

Caribbean people get information from a variety of media. The foreign mass media, such as cable and direct television and the internet, compete with local television and radio stations as well as local newspapers. As a result Caribbean people should be well informed about news, sport, politics, health, economic trends and other topical issues such as fashion, music and cinema. This information can be used in a variety of ways to make better choices and enhance living conditions in the Caribbean. For example, a documentary on global warming might show what can be done to conserve energy use. An individual viewer may be struck by the relevance of such information to the Caribbean, to the link with hurricane formation, and decide to reduce energy consumption on a daily basis. This would be an example of the mass media helping to change behaviours to those that are more environmentally friendly. A viewer acting on the information demonstrates empowerment – a sense of *self-efficacy*, that he or she can make a difference.

However, the mass media did not change that person's **beliefs**, **values** and attitudes. And another person looking at the same documentary might not have been similarly moved. While we may never know what causes someone to act on information received, we do know that the advertising industry seems to believe that

ACTIVITY 10.13

As a Caribbean person interested in promoting your country's development, what would you like to see (and in what proportions and at what times) aired as television programming? Compare your choices with those of another person, noting the arguments put forward.

repeated messages, subtle or otherwise, encourage people to buy. If that is so then we should be seeing the mass media using the same strategies to change behaviours when they broadcast programmes designed to give information about enhancing citizens' quality of life. To what extent do we see attractive presentations, using powerful images and graphics and a variety of formats, some of them entertaining, addressing issues such as drug and other forms of substance abuse, HIV/AIDS, teenage pregnancies, family life and low self-esteem?

It may be argued that television and radio are businesses. They might air these programmes if they were produced by concerned authorities and were of high quality. What would be important is whether an advertiser would pay for the airtime. The basic point here is that the mass media, powerful as they are in influencing the public, are commercial enterprises that for the most part do not necessarily see their role and function as nurturing the human development capacity of citizens. To assume that the information-providing function of the media is all that is required to have a positive impact on behaviour is therefore misleading.

Entertainment

Another major function of the mass media is entertainment, and indeed a good deal of programming in the electronic media is devoted to entertainment. You yourself may have arranged a schedule for the mass media in Activity 10.13 that highlights entertainment. The mass media entertain through the music played, the movies, soap operas, music videos and talk shows aired, the celebrity interviews, and the feature stories about topics as varied as cooking, fashion, natural wonders, tourist destinations, technological breakthroughs and home decorating. Some of these, and documentaries, are referred to as 'edutainment' – informative and entertaining at the same time. To what extent does entertainment on the mass media contribute to development?

Enjoyment

To be able to listen to music for enjoyment, and to look to the media for fun, laughter and relaxation are important avenues for releasing stress and are part of a balanced existence. In this sense the mass media can be a source of recreation. The many comedies and attractively packaged shows – be they suspense thrillers, scary movies, football games, talk shows (Box 10.12), concerts, cartoons or game shows – have the capacity to rivet our attention. In so doing we forget about day-to-day problems and worries. The ability to engage with characters in an unreal world for a few hours and to emerge entertained and with a feeling of well-being must be beneficial to the viewer (however strange it sounds!).

Entertainment, then, plays an important role in development. Perhaps its importance has been undervalued as the lighter side of life has often been subordinated to work – either in school or on the job market. However, because of its great success in entertainment the mass media may be a superior way of delivering messages that are educative to the society. Messages about lifestyle, health and fitness, environmental awareness, appropriate dress and behaviour, as well as consumer education or even issues to do with national consciousness, can all be delivered to a more receptive

BOX 10.12 Radio entertainment

Since the beginning of the twenty-first century there has been a great increase in the number of talk shows on radio. While television, especially with the many foreign cable stations, drew a large audience away from radio, radio sought to make a comeback by focusing on local issues and events in a call-in talk-show format. Some radio stations focus only on talk shows. To what extent does the content of these shows contribute to human development?

It is perhaps the case that some people are better informed by listening to or participating in such shows. They tend to vary in quality and some may be more informative than others. For example, there are shows where people call in to complain about their treatment by government departments or public utility companies. Their complaints are aired and taken up by the host, who undertakes to get a response on the matter. This certainly helps citizens to feel that whether they live in an isolated rural area or even if they are elderly and home-bound, there is an agency that can help them resolve their problems. This ensures a sense of equity.

However, many of the shows which seem to be largely about entertainment are of uncertain value. The host is typically some charismatic personality, or perhaps just forceful, and the show revolves around his or her opinions and reflections. People call in to praise or enrage the host. The dialogue is intemperate, to say the least, and the caller may be castigated and vilified. Frequently such shows are anchored in a certain political perspective – supporters of a particular political party. It is clear that many of these talk-show hosts have little training in journalism, sometimes they are just 'radio personalities'. To what extent does the entertainment afforded by these programmes enhance human development? Certainly people get a chance to air their opinions. But what happens after that? Those who agree with the host and his or her position merely entrench their views. Those with an alternative opinion give the others the opportunity to rant and rave. To some extent, then, the mass media seem to be reinforcing bias and **stereotypes** (the roots of prejudice) as there is no serious analysis of what contributors say.

On a general note, perhaps it is instructive to be a spectator when people say they are debating an issue. On the air or in person there is more than a tendency to merely wait through someone's contribution that might oppose one's view (or even impatiently interrupt) with the intent of airing one's own opinion, which of course is the right one. What might be the reasons why we are reluctant to admit, far more to consider, alternative views? Sociologists have suggested that how we are **socialized** makes us prone to engage in behaviours showing that we are superior to others, that our opinions make more sense, that other people are troublemakers, and that the other political party cannot be trusted. This characteristic way of dealing with the world stems, sociologists say, from when we were growing up: our families did not celebrate human differences and show that other people had a point of view (or a religion) they considered valid. We have been socialized into an 'Us and Them' view of the world.

audience if they are infused with what makes entertainment successful – comedy, memorable characters, drama, setting, props, and local cultural content such as music, dance and artefacts.

Forum for cultural expression

The mass media provide a place where the talents of musicians, singers, actors, novelists, artists and story-tellers or commentators can be showcased. The forum or platform that the mass media provide for entertainers makes it possible for the entertainment industry to grow and for individual artistes to gain fame and increased income. We can say that without the mass media it would be very difficult for performers to become known. Thus, the mass media are important in promoting artistes. Through *copyright agreements* some musicians, short-story writers, video producers, artists, photographers and song writers are able to earn **royalties**. The boost that entertainers get from being showcased on the mass media helps to develop cultural industries – music recordings, local television serials, dramatic presentations – that are widely disseminated not only in the region but among the Caribbean diaspora as well.

ACTIVITY 10.14

Generally speaking, the mass media provide a forum for cultural expression. Analyse the cultural content that is being showcased on the mass media (you may choose to focus on only one form of media) in your home territory by devising categories and estimating how much programming on a daily (or weekly) basis falls into each category.

1. What conclusions can you draw about the types of programmes that are emphasized?

2. What types of local cultural expression are emphasized?

National identity

It would be extremely difficult for a country that was in charge of its own destiny, an independent country, to build a sense of national consciousness and loyalty if it did not have the services of the mass media. A major goal of newly independent countries is to organize government-owned, public broadcasting services. (In fact, when there are *coup* attempts, a priority area for the rebels is to get control of the mass media.) A nationally owned mass media allows important information to be disseminated to keep the public well informed about the government's activities and issues of national importance. It also allows local culture and national heroes to be celebrated, thereby building a sense of belonging and a collective destiny. This is especially important in independent countries with significant numbers of people belonging to different ethnic and racial groups.

In the era following independence Caribbean governments took an active part in owning radio and television stations and in screening the content aired. Technology eventually put an end to much of these efforts at *censorship*. The coming of cable and direct television and the internet, made possible by satellite technology, also made it easier to set up local radio and television stations. Today there are more local radio and television stations in most Caribbean countries than ever before. Because of the competition amongst them some have reinvented themselves to target a different audience and thus their aims and objectives have changed. For example, local radio and television stations may aim specifically for entertainment, or for serious debate and analysis, or to promote local music and culture, or to the needs of those ethnic groups that have been under-represented before (sometimes in a different language). This diversity within the mass media makes it a force for equity and empowerment.

Today we have moved from a position of **monopoly** media (where the government owned all or a large part of the mass media) to another kind of monopoly – now, big business interests dominate as owners. While this can threaten equity, in that a pro-business slant may predominate, there are also a number of private groups which seek the interests of ordinary citizens. One important example is *community radio*. Certain areas of a country, perhaps isolated areas, have sought to bind their communities together by organizing local radio networks to publish community news, events and debate about the larger society. In Trinidad and Tobago, Tobago has its own radio station, *Radio Tambrin* (beaming from 1998), giving greater coverage of Tobago's affairs than the mainstream media. Similarly, *Radio Toco* serves the information needs of this remote, mountainous, north-eastern corner of Trinidad, which used to receive only a weak radio signal. UNESCO provided funds to establish Radio Toco and other community radio initiatives in the Caribbean, such as that in Bluefields and in Port Antonio, Jamaica, as part of their thrust to help empower rural residents. The relative ease with which investors can now obtain broadcast licences suggests that the local mass media in each Caribbean country are well poised to meet the information and entertainment needs of their citizens and be instrumental in nation-building (Box 10.13).

Just as the mass media can be a potentially integrative force for the country of Belize (Box 10.13), we can make a similar case for CARICOM and the regional integration movement. The Caribbean stretches from Central to South America and incorporates islands in between which are diverse in geography, history and cultural life. The mass media have a country focus so that Caribbean people do not

BOX 10.13 Belize – the mass media and national identity

Belize is a large country (23,000 square km, around 9000 square miles) by Caribbean standards. It has a small, scattered and ethnically diverse population (300,000 in 2005). Large numbers of Belizean migrants live in the **metropole** and many migrants from Guatemala and other Central American countries have moved into Belize, further strengthening a Spanish presence that began with the Mexicans migrating to Belize following the Caste Wars of 1854. An unsettled border dispute with Guatemala means that Belize lives with the ever-present threat of invasion. These factors have contributed to prolonging the process of reaching a fully developed sense of national identity. The mass media can in this context either facilitate nation-building or be a divisive force.

Belize does not have any daily newspapers but several weeklies, some of which, like the *Reporter* and the *Amandala* (two independent newspapers), have daily on-line editions. The *Guardian* is the official organ of the United Democratic Party, which won the 2008 election, and the *Belize Times* is the newspaper of the Peoples United Party. There are two main television stations, *Channel 5 Belize*, which covers a larger area of the country than *Channel 7 Belize*. However, they both only relay news in the week, not on the weekends, and they mainly transmit US cable programming. There are many radio stations but only one (*Love FM*) is nationwide in coverage, transmitting in English, Spanish and some Creole. The other radio stations are restricted in coverage. Other local radio stations exist in different parts of the country, as well as a number of US evangelical stations.

The print and electronic media focus on the largest population centres of Belize City and Belmopan, the capital. In these areas there is a concentration of jobs, government departments, facilities, educational institutions and entertainment. Governments, political parties and the mass media target the people and businesses found there. Consequently, the other regions of Belize, particularly the south, are poorly served by the mass media. This kind of inequity in the communications network of a country puts rural people, the Maya in particular, at a disadvantage and is a contributing factor to rural underdevelopment. It exacerbates the problems of developing countries because the imbalance in opportunity and information contributes to rural–urban migration – the towns grow and the countryside becomes underpopulated.

Two proposals have been put forward in an attempt to strengthen the communication links within the country and thus to build a feeling of national solidarity, important in developing a national identity. One is community radio and the other is regional newspapers. They both need advertising dollars to survive, however. Whilst government departments pay quite a lot to advertise vacancies, notices, and other forms of public information, their advertising tends to centre in the urban areas. However, regional newspapers or radio can well survive if some of this advertising comes their way, and at the same time this will be helping to knit the country together. At present people in the interior do not have up-to-date and accurate information about the workings of government departments, or about their entitlements under health benefits and recent reforms, for example.

necessarily know much about what is going on in another Caribbean country. The regional news providers that do exist, the *Caribbean News Agency Radio* (Canaradio) of the Caribbean Media Corporation, and the *Caribbean Broadcasting Union* (CBU), have not been able to compete with the foreign news media and have more or less turned to sport, particularly cricket coverage. Thus, a potent force for Caribbean integration, a fully functioning regional mass media, is yet to emerge.

Cultural imperialism

It is well known that Caribbean countries are overrun by the US mass media, especially by cable television programming. The images, lifestyles, fashions, stories, stereotypes and news disseminated and portrayed by the US media have become part and parcel of the knowledge and daily experiences of Caribbean people. The **cultural imperialism** thesis says that the foreign mass media export cultural products to the countries of the developing world, where they are gladly embraced, leading to the adoption of foreign **norms**, values and ways of life. It is a simple theory that says that if we are bombarded with images from the US all the time we will eventually become conditioned to those images and begin to regard them as normal. In so doing we are quite likely giving up on some aspects of our Caribbean culture.

There is a lot of debate about whether this happens in the way described above. Certainly there is much evidence that young people, especially, buy into the idea of US designer wear and music, and that the US is a desirable destination. But to what extent was this *caused* by the mass media? Migration is still a strong cultural norm and almost all families have relatives living in the US, so that there is a long history of Caribbean people regarding the US in a favourable light. The liking for US music and films is not limited to youth but permeates the whole society. In addition, the dependence we now have on the computer and computer software makes technology a way of life, and the US is the leader in computer technologies. So, while US images and lifestyles are everywhere evident on the mass media in the Caribbean today, our history, traditions and development as an information society predispose us to be receptive to those messages.

The increase in the number of cable television stations and increasing access to the internet in recent years have certainly intensified the impact of foreign cultural images and lifestyles on Caribbean people. The information and entertainment packaged by the foreign mass media, according to the cultural imperialism thesis, will tend to shape what we know, and what we don't know, as well as promote the concerns of the US as our concerns. Hence, the search for Bin Laden, the threat of terrorism, and the stereotypes painted of Arab and Muslim people become normal to us because of our constant exposure to US television. After a while we do not even question why Arab people are almost always portrayed in a negative light, why we are not treated to their side of the story, their triumphs. We come to accept that we are on the US side (without much conscious thought) and seemingly do so out of our own free will. The cultural imperialism thesis, then, says that the constant exposure to US culture and perspectives brings about these pro-US sentiments.

Cultural imperialism refers to the **enculturation** of one society by another, and in the twenty-first century the US mass media are seen as a force that intensifies that process in the Caribbean. It is not only the pervasive presence of US images and representations of US lifestyles that contribute to this, but the actual structure of the US mass media. For instance:

- The large US media conglomerates (ABC, CNN, NBC and Fox News) are able to produce the news or television features more cheaply and effectively than small media houses in the Caribbean, so they dominate Caribbean media.
- This structure of the mass media means that there is an over-abundance of US views, news and perspectives. This raises the question of whether we have a 'free press', as the majority of our news is produced by the US.
- The idea of a free press becomes more doubtful when we consider that among the US conglomerates there is a concentration of media power, with one conglomerate owning a fleet of television stations, newspapers and movie production studios.
- The competition amongst these media houses reverberates on the Caribbean in the form of programming. They vie with each other to provide exciting, spectacular, sensational news coverage and highly rated shows. What we receive and think is real may be distortions and stories slanted in particular ways.

In these ways Caribbean life has become saturated with images and messages from abroad. We live in a media-saturated environment. The cultural imperialism thesis is saying that given this set of circumstances US culture is becoming dominant in the Caribbean. Those who oppose this view say that while a Caribbean person may wear US designer labels, listen to hip-hop, watch MTV, and be an avid filmgoer, that does not make him or her less Caribbean.

The threat of cultural imperialism largely stemming from mass media imperialism should be forcing a reaction from Caribbean governments and mass media organizations that is not evident as yet. A major need is clearly for an educational initiative to demystify the barrage of US cultural images via media literacy in our school curricula. Either through direct and systematic analysis of American news and other programming, or through watchdog sites that report inaccuracies, oversimplifications and prejudicial views, both in schools and in the broadcast media, some effort must be made to help citizens understand their media-saturated environment. A second major need is for regional consultation on the role of the media in Caribbean society, leading to a policy paper that envisions a programme for the development of the media. This programme should have national and regional development as goals that are as important as economic viability. Hence, programming would encompass the building of equity, productivity and empowerment in sustainable ways among Caribbean people.

Summary

The mass media have great potential to play a leading role in the development process in the Caribbean because almost everybody is tuned in and turned on. Caribbean governments, institutions and other groups should understand how closely people are attuned to the mass media and actively seek to harness them for change and transformation. The mass media today are largely being used for entertainment but the ingredients that go towards packaging successful entertainment should be incorporated into the airing of more serious national issues, such as health and well-being, civic education, political awareness and even media literacy. The potential of the local mass media for development, though, is obstructed by the dominance of the US mass media, which many see as agents of cultural imperialism.

WRAP UP

In this chapter the contribution of sport and the mass media to development in the Caribbean has been explored. They have been examined in relation to how they are impacting on the human development potential of citizens. A major component of human development is equity and both sport and the mass media have been analysed to establish whether they are equalizing opportunities for many and contributing to a fair and a just society. To a large extent more people are involved and interested in sport than hitherto, but it is structured to promote a view of sport as entertainment, greatly aided by the mass media, whereas a view of sport as recreation or physical activity would do much more for human development. The Caribbean mass media have tremendous potential for leading the development thrust because they reach almost everyone, but they too have a view of themselves as mainly for entertainment and are obstructed in developing more effective programming by the pervasive presence of the foreign mass media.

Structured response

1 (a) Distinguish between sport and recreation. (2 marks)
   (b) Describe ONE way in which sport can contribute to development. (2 marks)
2 Describe THREE ways in which participating in sport can be beneficial to an individual. (3 marks)
3 Suggest TWO goals for a sports programme in schools. (2 marks)
4 Outline TWO ways in which sport can increase equity in the society. (4 marks)
5 (a) Explain what is meant by 'sports tourism'. (1 mark)
   (b) Suggest TWO reasons to explain why sports tourism is not well developed in the Caribbean. (4 marks)
6 Describe THREE ways in which sports are influenced by the mass media in the Caribbean. (6 marks)
7 (a) Define the mass media. (2 marks)
   (b) Explain how blogging is transforming the mass media? (2 marks)
8 Describe THREE ways that the mass media can contribute to human development in the Caribbean. (6 marks)
9 (a) Distinguish between libel and slander. (2 marks)
   (b) Give TWO reasons to show that a free press exists in the Commonwealth Caribbean. (4 marks)
10 Describe THREE ways in which the mass media can be used to help develop a sense of national identity in Caribbean countries. (6 marks)

Essay questions (20 marks)

1 Discuss the possible reasons why sport as entertainment is a more popular view than sport as physical activity among Caribbean people.
2 Explain why cricket is the only sport in the Caribbean to have a regional team and suggest what implications this may have for other sports.
3 Examine how the mass media's role to provide information can lead to the development of the society.
4 Describe how you and other Caribbean people may be influenced by the foreign mass media.

Challenge essay questions (30 marks)

1 'If sports are supposed to be ensuring equity, why are women's sports still treated as inferior to men's?' Assess the claims being made in this question.
2 Examine TWO key issues that should be included in any national plan to develop sport in the Caribbean.

3 Explain, with examples, what becoming a 'wise consumer' of mass media means.
4 To what extent do Caribbean countries enjoy freedom of the press? Discuss this issue using examples from at least two Caribbean countries.

A possible research inquiry could be built around analysing the type of media messages found in a particular form of the mass media to determine its influences on development. Your specific concern could be cultural imperialism. You might choose, for example, several cable television channels and list the types of programmes they air at the peak hours of viewing. You will also have to examine the content that is being aired in relation to your research questions about development. Steps that you might follow include the following:

- Formulate a brief questionnaire which you may hand out to your classmates, family and neighbours. Ask about favourite cable stations, favourite programmes, and what times tend to be their peak viewing times. You may also ask about why these were their favourite programmes.
- Using the information, decide which were the most popular programmes and select those for the study.
- You undertake to watch these programmes over a period of time (you may switch between those that are on at the same time). To be able to record and assess what you are viewing, you need some sort of checklist or rating scale for each programme (see Table 10.1).
- For example, you could rate each programme according to criteria you devise that are important in development. In other words, what do you think television programming should provide in terms of information, values, enjoyment, etc. that contribute in some positive way to the development of the society.

Table 10.1 is just one suggestion of how you might rate programmes. You can present your data in the form of a table where you combine all your information. Remember the numbers are just rankings and cannot be treated as if they had a value, so you cannot add them together, for instance, or create pie charts, as that would demand numerical values. So one way of presenting the data you produced by watching these programmes and rating them is to tabulate them, as in Table 10.2.

Table 10.2 says that having watched programme X over a week or the movie slot at a certain time in that week, this is how I assessed each programme on each of

Table 10.1 A possible rating scale for evaluating television programmes

CABLE NETWORK: TIME: 8:00 – 9:00 P.M.	SHOW:			
CRITERIA	**POOR (1)**	**MEDIOCRE (2)**	**GOOD (3)**	**EXCELLENT (4)**
1. Moral: emphasis on good, fair, just (positive values, e.g. law and order)				
2. Entertainment: absorbing, relaxing, providing balance, reflection				
3. Equity: stories which uphold the equal value of human beings				
4. Empowerment: ideas, stories that highlight 'overcoming', self-efficacy				
5. Critical: programmes which encourage a critical stance to mainstream ideas				

the criteria. These data then have to be interpreted to see if these programmes are on the whole contributing to the development of the viewers. You should be cautioned that this study relies on *your* perceptions and tastes to a great extent and that is why you asked respondents of the questionnaire to state why these were their favourite programmes. You will have their views to consider as you interpret the findings.

You can also use the questionnaire data to produce pie charts or other kinds of statistical graphs showing numbers (or percentages): for example, those liking a particular show and/or the reasons given.

REFERENCES AND FURTHER READING

Beckles, H. (1997). *A spirit of dominance: cricket and nationalism in the West Indies.* Kingston, Jamaica: Ian Randle Publications.

Decklebaum, R., & Williams, C. (2001). Child obesity: the health issue. *Obesity Research*, vol. 9 Supplement, pp. 239–243.

Dunn, H. (Ed.) (1995). *Globalization, communications and Caribbean identity.* Kingston, Jamaica: Ian Randle Publications.

Fraser, H. (2003). Obesity: diagnosis and prescription for action in the English-speaking Caribbean. *Pan American Journal of Public Health*, 13 (5), pp. 336–340.

Gardner, H. (1983). *Frames of mind: the theory of multiple intelligences.* New York: Basic Books.

Table 10.2 Summarizing data on television programmes

PROGRAMMES	MORAL VALUE	ENTERTAINMENT	EQUITY	EMPOWERMENT	CRITICISM
The Bold and the Beautiful	2	4	1	2	1
NBC News	3	3	4	4	3
Hardball					
Movie					

Ince, B. (1998). *Black meteors: the Caribbean in international athletics*. Kingston, Jamaica: Ian Randle Publications.

James, C. L. R. (1963). *Beyond a boundary*. London: Hutchinson.

Scrignar, B. (1991). *Stress strategies: the treatment of anxiety disorders*. Gretna, LA: Wellness Institute.

World Bank. (2003). *Caribbean youth development: issues and policy directions*. A World Bank Country Study. Washington, DC: IBRD.

World Health Organization. (1997). *Health and environment in sustainable development five years after the Earth Summit*. Geneva: WHO.

11 THEORIZING CARIBBEAN DEVELOPMENT

In this chapter we examine certain bodies of thought or intellectual traditions. They are usually referred to as ideologies that have shaped Caribbean development. An ideology is a set of strong beliefs about how social life can be improved. They tell us what is considered acceptable or not acceptable in how we think about certain questions – white superiority, male domination, capitalism, industrialism, native societies, and so on. Some ideologies are contested – for example, capitalism versus Marxism – and so offer alternative ideas for development. Some ideologies are mainstream and others marginal – for example, European traditions as opposed to those of indigenous peoples. When a group commits to an ideology and begins to write, act and analyse social life according to its ideas, an intellectual tradition is formed. This has implications for development because a view or ideological position is being put forward to stimulate thought about the right way of doing things.

EXPECTED LEARNING OUTCOMES

On completing this chapter, you will be able to
1 explain what is meant by an 'ideology'
2 describe the values underlying the following ideologies: pan-Africanism, négritude, Marxism, feminism, capitalism, Indo-Caribbean and indigenous perspectives
3 identify the key thinkers in each of these intellectual traditions
4 analyse the impact of each of these ideologies on Caribbean development.

11.1 IDEOLOGY

An **ideology** is a frame or lens through which certain problems or issues in social life are viewed and interpreted. To have an ideological position is to have a set of **values** which justify thinking and acting in a certain way. This is sometimes called a 'world view'. Ideologies are important because they address problems and issues and therefore focus on improvement or development. They also signal to us what other groups think is important and therefore give us an insight into how others may be perceiving disadvantage. **Pan-Africanism,** for example, takes the position that survivals of Africa in the **diaspora** should be studied and active links made to Africa as the motherland. The *back to Africa* movement is a value position for black people in thinking about development. Ball and Dagger (2004) give the following definition of 'ideology':

> . . . an ideology is a fairly coherent and comprehensive set of ideas that explains and evaluates social conditions, helps people understand their place in society, and provides a program for social and political action. (p. 4)

The ideologies studied in this chapter have given rise to social movements trying to right some wrong in society. As a result, their programmes for action recommend political change. Whether it is **Marxism** or neo-Marxism, Indo-Caribbean or **feminist** thought, for any ideology to develop fully into an intellectual tradition that has developmental potential and recommends political change, it must relate to the Caribbean context and treat with those conditions that shaped our society – primarily our experience of **colonialism**, exploitation, **ethnocentrism** and nationalism.

It is important to recognize that ideologies relate to certain practices and ways of thinking that some people had even when they did not know of a label to describe their ideas. The term 'pan-Africanism' is one that is applied with hindsight. The various movements in the late nineteenth century whereby Africans in the New World sought to learn more about Africa and call for the repatriation of Africans were not labelled as the ideology of pan-Africanism. At the time they were expressing certain ideas about development that other people took up and formulated in their own way. Later these ideas were deemed important to a larger body of people and became organized as a systematic ideological position.

When ideologies move from certain practices that some people have had about how they negotiate the world to being given a name and a description, they become idealized. They take on strong overtones about what is acceptable or not, what is good and right, what is possible and what is not. In this form they can be discussed and debated and their implications for development explored with greater ease than when they were the personal convictions of a few. Thus, pan-African ideas existed long before they became a coherent body of thought associated with 'founding fathers' and various 'movements'.

All ideologies claim that they are putting forward a path to 'freedom', even if they are opposed to each other. They all claim liberation from some inhibiting condition. For example, **capitalism** sees freedom as reducing the control of business by governments and other bodies that try to restrict the market. Marxism sees freedom in a society where business and industry come under complete control and so the workers are free from being exploited. A pan-Africanist wants to liberate black people whilst Indo-Caribbean thought sees Indians in the Caribbean as being in an inferior position in a dominant Afro-Caribbean society. Indigenous peoples see their survival in retaining the culture of their ancestors and feminists see a male-dominated society as hindering the interests of women. Thus, each ideology puts forward a 'grand theory' of how we should understand the world, but as **postmodernists** say, no one theory can fully explain the world. In fact, an ideological stance does not accept other world views, only those that are congruent in some way with its main **beliefs**. We should also keep in mind that some ideologies offer ways of understanding the world which tend to be *utopian* (an unreachable ideal).

ACTIVITY 11.1

1. Define the term 'ideology', giving THREE characteristics.

2. Explain how the study of intellectual traditions contributes to an understanding of Caribbean development?

Summary

An ideology is a set of ideas that explains and evaluates social conditions, helping people to understand how they are implicated in social life and what they can do via social and political action to improve their lot. When an ideology begins to have followers and adherents a movement is formed: writers, thinkers and activists communicate these ideas to a wider public so as to create the conditions for a better society, in their estimation. In so doing, intellectual traditions are born. In the Caribbean ideologies are at the centre of the pan-African movement, **négritude**, capitalism, Marxism, feminism, and Indo-Caribbean and indigenous perspectives, which are all considered in the rest of this chapter.

11.2

BLACK NATIONALISM: PAN-AFRICANISM

This movement began in the eighteenth century in sporadic acts by African people in North America trying to get back to Africa. It showed their conviction that they were in the wrong place, a place to which they had been brought illegally, and they now wanted to go home. The ideas that eventually developed into pan-Africanism were spearheaded in the early twentieth century by people in the African diaspora, notably from the Caribbean and North America. Over time the emphasis on certain ideas changed but the foundation values continued.

In 1900 **Henry Sylvester Williams**, a lawyer from Trinidad, educated in England and the US, convened the first pan-African conference in London. At that conference gathered a collection of like-minded people of African origin, mainly from the Caribbean, the US and Britain. Over the years they continued the tradition of organizing pan-African conferences and founded newspapers and organizations to promote their thinking about a better world for African people. Although their ideas about pan-Africanism were similar, they disagreed on how to achieve their objectives. Their main objectives were:

- to promote the view that black people wherever they lived had a bond which united them
- to raise the consciousness of African people (and others) about the humanity, culture, civilization and history of Africa
- to free Africa from the political and economic control of Europeans
- to seek justice for black people
- to promote black pride, black consciousness and black nationalism
- to repatriate Africans back to Africa, their motherland
- to seek the unification of the entire African continent under African rule.

Many Caribbean people, including the Jamaican **Marcus Mosiah Garvey** (Box 11.1), Nevisian **Cyril Briggs** and Jamaican **Claude McKay** (Box 11.3), and Trinidadians **George Padmore** (Box 11.4) and **C. L. R. James** (Box 11.8), as well as African-Americans such as **W. Du Bois** (Box 11.2), were involved in establishing the movement in the early twentieth century. By the 1940s the leadership had passed from Caribbean and African-Americans to African scholars and patriots. Chief among them were **Kwame Nkrumah** (Box 11.5) and **Jomo Kenyatta,** who went on to become heads of state in Ghana and Kenya respectively.

BOX 11.1 Marcus Mosiah Garvey

Marcus Garvey was born in 1887 in St Ann's, Jamaica, and had to leave school at an early age to work. He became involved in printing, the newspaper business and politics. As early as 1914 he started the *Universal Negro Improvement Association (UNIA)* in Jamaica because his ideas were always about improving the lot of the poor, black people. When he migrated to the US he founded a chapter of the UNIA which grew so rapidly that it became the headquarters of the movement. He tirelessly formed other organizations such as the *African Communities League (ACL)* and the *Universal African Black Cross Nurses* to address the social and economic needs of the black underclass. His *Black Star Line* was an ambitious project of transporting people and goods to Africa and was a symbol of black commercial success.

Through his newspapers – the *Negro World*, the *Blackman* and the *New Jamaican* – he attempted to raise the consciousness of African people and to preach about the freedom of African countries which were under colonial rule, and the unification of Africa, in a similar way to the US. His ideas and message came at a time when in both the US and the Caribbean there was economic hardship, hitting the poor in particular. His public appearances were dramatic, colourful affairs accompanied by marches, with the UNIA membership in uniform, bands, and slogans proclaiming the beauty of the black race, the brotherhood of all black people, and that black people should see God in their own image. This kind of effrontery was unheard of in the US in the 1920s and 1930s and it was quickly embraced by those marginalized in a white-dominated, capitalist society.

In the 1930s in Jamaica it was also adopted by the *Rastafarian* brethren, who translated his words to mean the existence of a black god. The rhetorical and symbolical statements made by Garvey, that a king will come out of Africa, and the prominence he gave in his newspapers

Fig. 11.1 Marcus Garvey riding in the UNIA parade through Harlem in 1922

to Haile Selassie's coronation, convinced the Rastafarian movement to proclaim Haile Selassie as 'King of Kings and Lord of Lords'. His advocacy of repatriation to Africa was taken up wholeheartedly by the Rastafarian community. However much he used imagery from the Bible, Garvey was not interested in a religious interpretation of the return to Africa. His pan-African ideas were mainly about improving the social and economic circumstances of black people.

Garvey, a national hero of Jamaica, lives on in the reggae music made famous by Bob Marley, and in the inspiration that his tremendous work gave to budding politicians, trade union leaders, the civil rights movement of the US, black power advocates, and the **decolonization** movement in the Caribbean and Africa, based on black nationalism.

BOX 11.2 W. E. B. Du Bois

William Du Bois was born in 1868 in Massachusetts in the US. He was gifted with academic ability and managed through the contributions of family, friends and scholarships to be educated at some of the premier educational institutions in the land. He is reputed to have been the first black person to graduate with a PhD from Harvard. All his scholarly efforts, though, were bound up in trying to understand the plight of black people. His first-hand experience of **racism** made him determined to study and analyse the living and working conditions of black Americans. His book published in 1903, *The Souls of Black Folks,* as well as his other publications, are still used by historians and sociologists today.

Du Bois was a founder member of the *National Association for the Advancement of Colored People (NAACP)*, an inter-racial organization formed in 1909, and editor for over 25 years of its official magazine, *The Crisis*. He wrote stinging criticisms of the social and economic system of the day that allowed racism and the marginalization of black people to be a normal part of life. His goal was to awaken white and black people to the injustice being heaped upon black Americans. His was one of the first voices to be raised in protest for black Americans. He did not approve of Garvey's grassroots organization, with its mass popular appeal, largely because it was so different from his own intellectual style. However, Garvey's UNIA and the NAACP were the two leading black associations of the day, and today the NAACP and *The Crisis* live on.

A trip to Africa convinced Du Bois that his fight for black Americans could not be done in a vacuum. He had to embrace a wider conception of the problem affecting the race as a whole. For Africans to be free, they should be free everywhere. With that realization he really began to follow the basic ideology of the pan-African movement as espoused by Garvey, Padmore and later Nkrumah. He attended the first pan-African conference in 1900 convened by Henry Sylvester Williams and was the main organizer of many of the conferences thereafter, including the famous one of 1945.

Fig. 11.2 W. E. B. Du Bois

Another trip, to Russia in 1927, served to convince Du Bois that the problem of poverty could not be addressed within the capitalist system. He studied the works of Marx and Engels and became converted to **communism** as an ideology that held much promise in opposing the current oppressive system in which blacks lived and worked. Communism was opposed to colonialism and so was pan-Africanism. He became less and less convinced that the civil rights movement in the US being led by Dr Martin Luther King and others was going about the business of 'black redemption' in the right way, and many in turn shunned him because of his communist leanings, which were considered 'un-American'. Some of the pan-African conferences he chaired specifically explored how Marxism and pan-Africanism could work together.

Like Garvey, *Cyril Briggs*, a native of Nevis, was born in 1887. He later moved to the US where he formed a black, radical organization called the *African Blood Brotherhood (ABB)* in 1919. Like Garvey, Briggs was also involved in the newspaper business. The *Crusader* was the paper of the ABB where he wrote about black nationalism, national independence for African colonies, and **economic development** for Africans. The social context in the big American cities was one of entrenched poverty for black workers and racial segregation. He advocated that African groups arm themselves for self-defence. There were even ABB groups within UNIA chapters, showing that Briggs supported Garvey's work, and he took part in the conferences organized by Garvey in New York in 1920 and 1921.

However, Briggs came to see that the pan-African philosophy of black nationalism would not be able to succeed within the capitalist system in the US. He observed that capitalism was the fundamental cause of the poverty and oppression faced by black people. In this respect he differed from Garvey, who felt that, with support and initiative, Africans could establish an economic system to rival that of the whites. The ABB eventually became an arm of the Communist Party in the US. At this point we see a

palpable difference from Garvey: Briggs was now outlining ideas based on **class** rather than race, and this meant that both white and black workers were seen as being oppressed.

Briggs, an ardent supporter of pan-Africanism, also became the first black leader of the US Communist Party. This shows how the initial ideas of Garvey were found to be workable within another kind of ideology altogether – communism. There were many pan-Africanists who followed this lead by realizing that working for the emancipation of the black **underclass** could not come about within a capitalist system of economic and social relations.

Claude McKay (1890–1948), the celebrated Jamaican writer of *Banana Bottom*, was also an associate of Briggs, a member of the ABB and a committed communist. He had travelled to Russia in 1922, where he addressed the Third Communist International in Moscow. He was an activist in the US, where he edited newspapers and wrote about the plight of black Americans. He also wrote poetry and was a prolific author. He was given the title 'Father of The Harlem Renaissance'. The Harlem Renaissance was a period in the US when black artists were being recognized for their abilities and Claude McKay's works were recognized as being a major influence on these artists.

Malcolm Nurse was born in Trinidad in 1901. He attended university in the US, where he joined the Communist Party and used the name George Padmore in covert operations. In 1929, Padmore went to Russia to study communism first hand and became the secretary of the *International Trade Union Committee of Negro Workers (ITUC–NW)*. The main aim of this committee was to undermine colonial control in Africa and he sought to do this through the *Negro Worker*, a newspaper he founded as an organ of the communist negro movement to agitate and mobilize the black working class. The Russian leadership used pan-Africanists such as W. E. B. Du Bois and Padmore to spread communist ideas in Africa, North America and the Caribbean. But whereas

the pan-Africanists were interested in overthrowing the colonial authorities, the Russians were more interested in converting the millions of Africans to communism. Padmore's attraction to communism was based on it being blind to race – all workers were equal, according to the ideology.

However, by 1933 the Russian leader Josef Stalin found it necessary to cut down on his anti-colonial activities because of the rise of a **fascist** threat in Europe. Adolf Hitler in Germany and Benito Mussolini in Italy (both opposed to communism) posed an immediate threat to the USSR. The ITUC–NW and the *League Against Imperialism and for Colonial Independence (LAI)* were disbanded because Stalin felt that such a decision would make European

BOX 11.5 Africa and the pan-African movement

Kwame Nkrumah (1908–1972) followed a path similar to those of Cyril Briggs and George Padmore. Like them he emigrated to the US to study and became active in the social and political issues of the time. He was from the Gold Coast in West Africa, a region ruled by Britain which today is known as Ghana. In 1944 he went to London where he met Padmore and C. L. R. James, both Trinidadians and committed pan-Africanists. He was later to say of Padmore that he knew when he met him he had met a kindred spirit. In fact, the young Nkrumah became a protégé of Padmore's. They were all instrumental in staging the pan-African Conference held in Manchester in 1945 presided over by W. E. B. Du Bois, where Africans began to take the lead in advancing the objectives of pan-Africanism.

Nkrumah, under the guidance of Padmore, returned to Ghana and campaigned for independence. After many conflicts with the British authorities, including a stint in prison, Nkrumah achieved prime ministerial status of the first black African country to win its independence from Britain. However, he worked tirelessly for the freedom

Fig. 11.4 Kwame Nkrumah at a Commonwealth Conference in 1964

of other African countries as well. Pan-Africanists believed that the independence of Ghana would only be complete when all African countries were free. To this end, Padmore was given responsibility within the Ghanaian government to establish a pan-African secretariat to work for African independence from the European imperial powers, and after that to work for the political unity of all Africa. This work was begun through a series of conferences to initiate dialogue, but the various countries (black, Arab, and white South Africa) were more interested in winning national independence and becoming countries in their own right, rather than being a part of a united Africa.

The fact that a Caribbean national was instrumental in beginning the process of bringing colonialism to an end in Africa was not lost on Caribbean people. The example of a Caribbean national working high up in the Ghanaian government to further the cause of pan-Africanism was a motivating force for pan-Africanists working for Caribbean independence.

powers more likely to help him in the case of a fascist offensive. Padmore resigned from the party in disgust and turned his attention to other ways of bringing an end to colonialism in Africa.

Fig. 11.3 George Padmore arriving at the White House in 1956

Pan-Africanism in the United States

Marcus Garvey (Box 11.1) was undoubtedly the greatest single influence on the pan-African movement, which evolved later into different strands, all acknowledging in some way his call for the 'redemption of African people'. His successful mobilizing skills resulted in the spread of the pan-African movement through the organization he founded known as the Universal Negro Improvement Association (UNIA). There were chapters in the US, Canada, the Caribbean, Europe and Africa, rallying African people on a scale that was unsurpassed. He was a fiery, charismatic figure who dressed in military uniforms with helmet and plumes and his supporting organizations, such as the Black Cross Nurses, also wore uniforms. He sought to provide meals, education and jobs for black people as well as inform them about black pride through the *Negro World* newspaper, which was read by thousands of people on both sides of the Atlantic. He was remarkably successful in establishing a number of organizations that sought to give African-Americans health and social services denied them by American society.

Garvey criss-crossed the Atlantic between the Caribbean, the US and Europe, and his fame and popularity grew. Although his was a grassroots organization, the other pan-Africanists at the time, notably W. E. B. Du Bois (with whom he had differences, and who was an outstanding academic), had to give credit to Garvey's uncompromising stand that he was equal to any white man. He was an inspiration as well for later generations of pan-Africanists and he had a direct impact on the Rastafarian movement (see Chapter 6), where his ideas live on. Garvey died in 1940.

By the 1960s the struggle for the uplifting of African peoples was taken up by *Martin Luther King* and the **civil rights movement**. They sought to liberate black people from their marginalized role in white America by peaceful protest. Their main aim was a fully integrated society. The movement encountered opposition from white racists who did not want integration and the nation was engulfed in demonstrations, riots and increased racial tensions. *Malcolm X* and the *Nation of Islam* under *Elijah Mohammed* preached a more radical message than King. They stood for *black separatism* from white America and built schools to educate black children. Malcolm X had Caribbean roots (his mother was Grenadian) and both his parents were members of Garvey's UNIA. Garveyism was at the core of this movement, but it also had an Islamic base and believed in armed insurrection. As *Black Muslims* they formed a revolutionary arm within the philosophies that sprang from pan-Africanism, and which Malcolm X called *Black Power*. *Louis Farrakhan*, who later took over the leadership of the Nation of Islam, was also of Caribbean heritage, his mother being from St Kitts. Today this organization is under constant surveillance by the American government for its militant stance.

There were also the *Black Panthers*. One of their leaders was a Trinidadian, *Stokely Carmichael* (Box 11.6), who originally belonged to the civil rights movement but broke with King's policy of peaceful non-violence to embrace the more militant route of black power, as preached by Malcolm X. They viewed the struggle as a war and vowed to use any means necessary to ensure that African-Americans be allowed to form their own institutions, to enjoy the same **rights** as other citizens, and to establish their own communities and schools.

BOX 11.6 Stokely Carmichael and Black Power

Stokely Carmichael (or Kwame Toure) was born in Trinidad in 1941. His family migrated to the US and he went to Howard University, where he became the chairman of the *Student Nonviolent Coordinating Committee (SNCC)*, one of the main organizations of the American civil rights movement. The members were of all races and sought to project racism into the national arena by sitting down in cafeterias in areas reserved for whites, and also in stores. They were harassed and abused by whites and the police. Many went to jail, but they did not resist. They engaged in the famous (or infamous) *Freedom Rides,* where volunteers boarded buses bound for the Deep South, where segregation was the order of the day everywhere, including bus stations. On one of those rides Carmichael was arrested when he entered a waiting room reserved for whites. The rides were marked by violence and mass arrests as the action drew the attention of the nation.

Carmichael began to invoke black power in his speeches and joined the Black Panthers, a Marxist organization. They wanted the means of production owned by the whites to be based in the community, housing and land to be made into cooperatives owned by the people, and an education system to teach people about themselves, their culture and their identity. As the Black Panthers moved more and more towards a black militant organization ready to use violence to support their cause of revolution (to establish economic, social and political equality of blacks), the civil rights movement distanced itself. The Federal Bureau of Investigation (FBI) under J. Edgar Hoover saw the Black Panthers as the single most important threat to the stability of the country. The Black Panthers eventually became a spent force as the FBI infiltrated the organization, made mass arrests and assassinated key members.

Fig. 11.5 Stokely Carmichael

Carmichael had had differences with the Panthers. His understanding of black power was based on the thinking of Malcolm X that did not allow coalitions with white people, whilst the Panthers as Marxists allowed white radicals. In 1967 he had visited Africa and later became convinced that black liberation could not come about without closer links with Africa. He settled in Guinea, where under the influence of the now exiled Ghanaian leader, Nkrumah, he deepened his efforts to spread pan-Africanism. He changed his name to Kwame Toure (after Nkrumah and Guinean leader Ahmed Sekou Toure). He helped to form the *All-African People's Revolutionary Party (AAPRP)* in 1972, calling for the unification of Africa. Carmichael died in Guinea in 1998; in his lifetime he had been a civil rights activist, a black power revolutionary and a pan-Africanist.

Pan-Africanism in the British Caribbean

Pan–Africanism, in all its various forms, impacted the Caribbean. In the interwar years (1918–1939) there was growing discontent with colonial control and worsening economic conditions. The newspapers of Marcus Garvey found their way to all Caribbean countries (even though they were banned in some, including Trinidad). Cuba had about 50 UNIA chapters, Trinidad 30 and Jamaica 10. In the British Caribbean in the 1930s there were widespread strikes, riots and the growth of trade unions. The dispossessed were attracted to the rhetoric of black **empowerment** that they read about in Garvey's newspapers. According to Chevannes (1995):

> *. . . by trying to unite blacks across continents under the inspiration of a single destiny tied to the decolonization of the African motherland, Garvey's movement, more than any other, made Africa into a powerful symbol of unity. (pp. 91–92)*

To the lower classes, then, the struggle for bread merged into one desiring the downfall of colonialism, a growing consciousness of unity, and black nationalism.

The first **Rastafarians**, too, were very much influenced by Garvey, who combined the strong political message of black nationalism based on the Holy Bible with a prophecy that 'princes shall come out of Ethiopia'. They regarded him as a second John the Baptist, especially when **Haile Selassie** was proclaimed emperor of Ethiopia, as he seemed to have predicted. They were inclined to take his 'back to Africa' call literally. The Rastafari more than any other group put into practice the teachings of Garvey that idealized and symbolized Africa.

In this period there was a surge of nationalist sentiments. It coincided with the end of the first world war and the return of Caribbean soldiers who had fought for the British. They had had a chance to understand politics on a much wider stage than at home and experienced racial discrimination within the ranks of the British armed forces. The rhetoric of the pan-African movement served to mobilize nationalist sentiments and deepen the **decolonization** movement. Caribbean people were intensely interested in Africa, perhaps more so than today. Martin (2004) says:

> *[Thus] Henry Sylvester Williams could have two Caribbean employees in his Cape Town law practice from 1903–1905; Caribbean workers in Kano, Northern Nigeria, could organize a branch of Marcus Garvey's Universal Negro Improvement Association (UNIA) around 1920; and a Vincentian, J. G. Gumbs, could be chairman of South Africa's Industrial and Commercial Workers Union in the 1920s (the executive committee often contained three or four Caribbean members). This cross-fertilization of experience is richly demonstrated in the case of Jamaican, A. S. W. Shackleford, who emigrated to Nigeria as a railway employee, headed Marcus Garvey's UNIA in Lagos and became an important businessman in Ghana and Nigeria. (p. 228)*

Italy's attempts to invade and annex Ethiopia in 1935, leading to the fall of the capital, Addis Ababa, and the exile of Emperor Haile Selassie, caused widespread concern and anger in the Caribbean. It was a naked act of aggression on one of the few remaining independent states in Africa. A minor border dispute with Italian-held Somalia was all the excuse Benito Mussolini, the Italian dictator, needed to invade. Mussolini's intent was to build a large empire similar to those of Britain, France, Spain, Portugal, Germany and Belgium in Africa (Fig. 11.6). By annexing Ethiopia he would be able to link the two Italian-held territories of Eritrea and Somalia into a large Italian African empire. This act of war against a personage that the Rastafarians considered a god deepened their hostility to the white man's world (or 'Babylon'). The worship of the Ethiopian monarch was also a thorn in the flesh of the British, who saw it as denial of their authority, and they relentlessly persecuted the Rastafarians. These incidents angered Caribbean people, not only Rastafarians. In Trinidad dock-workers refused to unload Italian ships and in other Caribbean countries young men tried to enlist in the Ethiopian army.

Pan-African sentiments again swept the Caribbean in the late 1960s and 1970s when the region was caught up in the message of Malcolm X and Stokely Carmichael about black power. It again coincided with a period of economic downturn. The

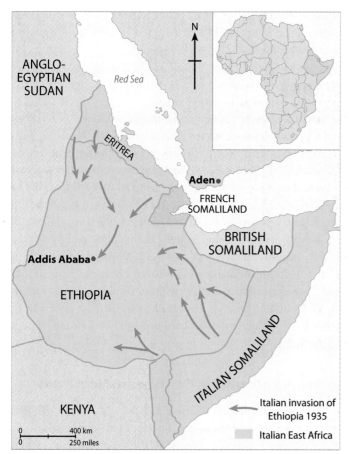

Fig. 11.6 The location of the Italo-Ethiopian war

'industrialization by invitation' policy (see p. 344) of the newly independent Caribbean countries was not delivering on its promises and there was widespread unemployment. The economy was largely controlled by foreign-owned, **multinational companies**. Black power analysts felt that the black **intelligentsia** and governments had failed the people. The British colonial overlords, they said, had merely been replaced by a black **elite** who feathered their nests and did little for the poor. They felt that Caribbean governments had to be more sensitive to the economic empowerment of black people and less involved with **ethnocentric** ideas. Moreover, governments should enable the people to better appreciate their African heritage and their links to the continent of Africa – a whole experience of history, culture and thought, and an economic goldmine yet untapped – that was ignored in education and social life.

The movement had lasting consequences for the Caribbean. *Walter Rodney* (see Box 11.9) a Guyanese historian, black power activist and pan-African scholar who taught at the Mona campus of the University of the West Indies (UWI), was prevented by the authorities from returning to Jamaica in 1968. Students on the Mona campus led a mass protest, three persons were killed and the unrest spread to the other campuses. At about that time Caribbean students at the George Williams University in Montreal rioted, protesting **racism**. In support, UWI students also demonstrated against Canadian organizations here in the Caribbean, such as banks. At the St Augustine campus they picketed the gates, refusing entry to the Canadian Governor General and the Prime Minister. The unrest spread and in Trinidad the *National Joint Action Committee (NJAC)*, an organization seeking the empowerment of black people and made up mostly of university students, lecturers and black power advocates, became the body around which a revolution developed. Later they were joined by the Indian sugar workers, the unemployed and trade unionists. The mass movement culminated in 1970 in the mutiny of the army and a state of emergency.

There were similar incidents throughout the Caribbean and in Grenada the unrest led eventually to the 1979 takeover of the government by the New Jewel Movement (NJM). In Cuba the heightened interest in the struggle of black people resulted in Cuba giving assistance to liberation groups in Africa fighting for their independence, notably in Angola against the Portuguese. In all these cases the emphasis was on the ideas of Garvey and pan-Africanism – more empowerment to African people, better economic conditions and less emphasis on foreign customs (ways of dress, doing away with 'slave names' and adopting African names, recognition of local and indigenous languages, and the brotherhood of African peoples).

Pan-Africanism in Africa

By the 1940s more Africans had become involved in the pan-African movement, notably Nkrumah from Ghana, Kenyatta from Kenya, and later Nyerere from Tanzania. Garvey's ideas were still prominent in the focus of the movement on the removal of the European colonial powers. Later, in what was called **Continental Pan-Africanism**, there was an emphasis on uniting the countries of Africa, mostly in forms of economic cooperation such as the Organization of African Unity (OAU). Today, Africa's massive problems of poverty, AIDS, civil wars and growing numbers of refugees are being tackled through a vision largely outlined by pan-Africanist ideas for development. For example, trade blocs fostering economic cooperation should be instrumental in reducing dependency on western countries by mapping out an inward-looking strategy of development. In a manner similar to the evolution of the European Union (EU), trade blocs are expected to ultimately give way to forms of political union, doing away with the European-drawn borders which established the present map of Africa.

Pan-Africanism in the Francophone Caribbean: Négritude

A unique brand of pan-Africanism emerged in the 1960s in the French colonies of the Caribbean and Africa – *négritude*. It called for all people of African origin to celebrate their blackness. It did not recognize geographical or regional distinctions. Its main thinkers were the Martiniquans Aimé Césaire (Fig. 11.7) and Frantz Fanon (Fig. 11.8), Léon Damas of French Guiana and Léopold Senghor (Fig. 11.9), who later became head of state in Senegal. The movement began in Paris, where members published a journal providing a forum to express sentiments about the French policy of total cultural assimilation of its colonies, the sidelining of African culture, and the near impossibility of gaining independence.

Négritude tended to focus on black consciousness and black pride because, as these activists saw it, living in a context where only French culture and civilization were promoted threatened the core of a black identity. In both Martinique and Guadeloupe small Marxist groups sought to mobilize the people to overthrow the French, but with little success. **Aimé Césaire** resigned from the French Communist Party on the grounds that the race struggle was different from the class struggle. In the intellectual movement of pan-Africanism there was a definite urge to move away from traditional European ideologies such as capitalism, and from the earliest days there were experiments with communism. However, there was still dissatisfaction, because this too is largely a European ideology.

Frantz Fanon represents the more radical arm of négritude. He was a student of Césaire and worked in France and Algeria as a psychologist, experiencing first hand the cruelty and barbarity of the French police in their treatment of Algerians fighting for their independence. It was a long and bloody war documented by Fanon in his

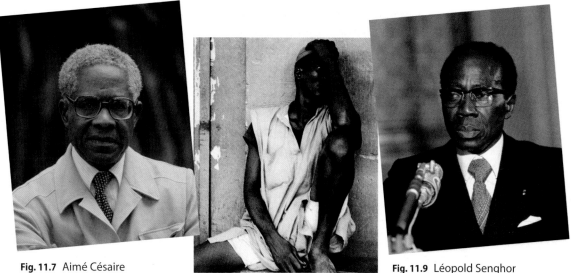

Fig. 11.7 Aimé Césaire

Fig. 11.9 Léopold Senghor

Fig. 11.8 Frantz Fanon's famous book,
The Wretched of the Earth

ACTIVITY 11.2

1. Explain why 'pan-Africanism' is considered to be an ideology.

2. Conduct independent research on Edward Blyden, a native of St Thomas who became a Liberian citizen and an ardent pan-Africanist.

3. What evidence can you offer to show that the ideas of pan-Africanism are still important today?

book *The Wretched of the Earth,* published in 1961. In a later publication, *Black Skin, White Masks,* he sought to explore the alienation of black people from their cultural roots. Fanon saw no other course but the violent overthrow of colonial governments. At the time such sentiments lent support to the growing black power movement in the US.

Léopold Senghor, writer and poet, was president of Senegal from 1960 to 1980. He sought to celebrate blackness in his works by describing the traditions and values of African culture as distinctly different from the European. For example, Africans, he claimed, were more intuitive, more emotional and more spiritual, whilst Europeans relied on cold and clinical reason. He too experimented with socialist ideology as outlined by Marx but felt that since communal life had long existed in Africa, an African type of **socialism** was more relevant. Fanon criticized Senghor's portrayal of black people, saying that it narrowed the individual and left no room for Africans who are analytical and abstract thinkers. In fact, it stereotyped Africans.

The French Caribbean has absorbed the philosophy of négritude and it is given full flower in poetry, art and literature today.

Summary

In the Caribbean the pan-African movement influenced the decolonization process through the growth of trade unions and political organizations promoting black consciousness and the unity of African people. Its main tenets stemmed from the ideological outlook of Marcus Garvey and were mainly responsible for the formation of several related movements and ideologies – the civil rights movement, black power, négritude, Black Muslims, the Rastafari religion, and the Continental Pan-African strategy. All these different ideologies held broadly similar views but differed on how to realize their goals. For many, this meant embracing Marxism as an economic antidote to the capitalism of the oppressors. For others it meant armed struggle. For still others the goals of black consciousness and black pride were to be discovered in the arts – literature, poetry, drama – which today are increasingly popular media for the dissemination of black thought.

11.3 ECONOMIC PERSPECTIVES
Industrialization by invitation

Any discussion of the economic strategy known as 'industrialization by invitation', popularly adopted by Caribbean governments in the 1960s, must mention *Sir William Arthur Lewis* (Fig. 11.10). He was born in St Lucia in 1915 of Antiguan parents and became a distinguished economist, lecturing at universities internationally and spearheading economic reforms in developing countries. He also became vice-chancellor of the University of the West Indies (UWI) and was instrumental in establishing the Caribbean Development Bank in Barbados. For his work, which threw light on the economic problems of ex-colonial countries and the strategies to improve **economic growth**, he was knighted in 1963 and awarded the Nobel Prize in 1979. He did not use the term 'industrialization by invitation' though; that was applied with hindsight by economists critical of the policy.

In Puerto Rico around the 1930s and 1940s, *Operation Bootstrap* was established. Its goals were to propel Puerto Rico from being an agrarian society and exporter of primary products to an industrialized nation. The policy sought to use cheap available labour as an incentive to multinational companies to come in and establish industries. Those companies taking up the offer would also receive tax-free concessions. The result was that Puerto Rico became industrialized and large numbers of agricultural workers left poorly paying jobs in the rural areas to join the ranks of factory workers earning wages. It met with mixed success as the rural areas became underpopulated and neglected and urban populations and poverty grew, stimulating migration to the US.

This policy of deliberately *inviting* foreign direct investment interested Lewis, who eventually put forward his ideas about how it could work in the context of the small ex-colonies of the British West Indies. Our economies were mainly agricultural and we needed to stimulate industrial growth and trade in manufactured goods to diversify the economic base. We had *monocrop economies*. While that term is usually applied to our dependence on sugar or bananas, it also characterizes our dependence on tourism or the oil industry. These are also referred to as the 'offshore sector', or that part of the economy organized for export to earn foreign currency. Lewis proposed a strategy to invite foreign investment as an interim measure to stimulate growth, not only in industry but also in agriculture, and therefore to reduce our dependency on the export sector.

Lewis reasoned that what we had in great abundance was unskilled labour in agriculture and amongst the unemployed. We did not have much capital. One way of stimulating industrial growth (and increasing exports) in the short term was to invite foreign **multinational corporations (MNCs)** with millions of dollars at their disposal to set up their operations here. They would earn large profits by employing the cheap surplus labour from agriculture. They would also benefit from tax holidays for the first five or ten years of their operations, and other concessions such as subsidies. In agriculture the price of labour would rise (higher wages) because the excess had been absorbed into industry.

The products of the MNCs would be marketed through the excellent distribution networks that they themselves already owned (for example, shipping fleets) and sold in the markets that they already commanded. By using the MNCs in this way, Caribbean countries would not have to bother with owning or leasing sea and air transport to export the finished products, at least in the short term. Neither would they have to rely on the goodwill of other countries to allow their products in without punitive **tariffs**. The MNCs, with their tremendous resources, had already penetrated markets in the developed and the developing world. In Lewis's opinion no Caribbean country had the capital, infrastructure or market share penetration to make a successful attempt at industrialization. Thus, the strategy of inviting foreign investors to set up shop and boost the export of manufactured goods could neutralize all these negative factors.

Fig. 11.10 Statue commemorating Sir William Arthur Lewis and his Nobel Prize for economics

It is too simplistic to describe Lewis's strategy as just 'industrialization by invitation'. It was never meant to be only about industrialization but was an attempt to deal with the situation of a large surplus labour force and what to do to jump-start economic diversification. In this scheme the rural areas would become more prosperous, benefiting from better wages in agriculture and the higher wages paid by the multinationals. Lewis also envisaged that as wages went up in agriculture, technical innovations would become possible to increase productivity. There was the possibility of local initiatives in agriculture contributing to manufacturing in the form of agro-processing – the bottling and canning of fruits, preserves, confectionery and drinks – as well as to service industries, as in hotels, restaurants, or the export of food products, flowers and so on. The *backward and forward linkages* that people would be able to develop would create a locally based industry that was integrally linked to agriculture (and increasingly independent of foreign capital). All the time we would see the active involvement of the rural areas in this strategy.

Lewis's strategy was based on capitalist ideology and saw the MNCs as a transitional phase to enable Caribbean nations to emerge from the depressed condition they had inherited from colonialism. They would learn managerial and technical skills and the plan was that the state could set up industries based on these skills once the MNCs left, or develop a partnership with them to continue production for export. At the same time, vibrant local initiatives would spring up, feeding off the higher wages in agriculture and the linkages that local people were creating between agriculture and industry.

The strategy eventually failed, which led critics to say that the ideas were wrong. Caribbean governments *invited* the MNCs but did not *control* them. Governments provided sites or industrial estates with warehouses and infrastructure (water, roads, electricity and telephone service) for the MNCs, which also benefited from the tax breaks and duty-free concessions. When that initial period was over they closed up shop and moved on. In addition, theirs were mainly capital-intensive industries which did not significantly lessen the numbers of unemployed and the numbers in agriculture. Virtually no provision was made for training citizens to organize and run similar plants, such as the assembly of motor vehicles and small appliances.

This model was strongly criticized, especially by Caribbean thinkers who used a **plantation model** to describe the problems and issues in Caribbean economy and society. *Lloyd Best* and the *New World Group* (a movement of intellectuals and radical thinkers established in the early 1960s with members from the Caribbean, the US, Canada and the UK) believed that any economic strategy for the Caribbean had to recognize the **dependency model** of economic thought. This model sees the Caribbean as a **plantation society** – one that is still enmeshed in colonial structures such as terms of trade that favour the **metropole** and where local technology, capital, entrepreneurship and markets are only minimally developed, making the society dependent on the metropole. In such a context Best and his colleagues said that what was needed to address the problems of Caribbean societies was independent thought – inward thinking and creativity – not dependence on foreign capital, expertise, technology and markets. Foreign companies were likely to keep Caribbean countries as plantation societies. They would hardly encourage the development of local industries, change the mindset that preferred foreign goods or develop rural infrastructure if they did not profit from these moves.

While the 'industrialization by invitation' policy did not result in significant economic growth in the Caribbean, the critique by Best and the New World Group did not deny that Lewis had made a fundamental contribution to economic thought. His focus on the problem of a large labour supply in developing countries and how to mobilize a country from this state to one of export-led growth was a breakthrough. Economists in developing countries today, where surplus labour is a major problem, find Lewis's transitional and interim strategies about using the MNCs immensely practical, provided that the MNCs can become more attuned to the development needs of the particular country. MNCs are still being seen as an important means to economic development. In fact, the phases that Lewis envisaged, and the scheme in all its complexity, were never fully implemented. In today's world of **globalization**, where MNCs drive global industries, Lewis's ideas are more relevant than ever to Caribbean governments.

ACTIVITY 11.3

1. Both Lewis and Best put forward ideologies of industrial development. Consider the history of economic development in your country; which model seems to be more important at the moment, and why?

2. If you were to follow Best's idea about independent thinking when applied to development issues, what strategies do you think might be useful in your country in deepening economic development?

The policy of industrialization by invitation was based on the ideology of capitalism, focusing on foreign capital as a trigger to spur on economic growth. It failed because capitalist forces tend to be solely interested in profits and some meaningful negotiations should have taken place to ensure that the benefits as originally envisaged had a chance of being realized. Lloyd Best and the New World Group pointed out the need to control our own resources and to move away from traditional economic models that make us dependent on foreigners and perpetuate the legacy of colonialism in how the Caribbean economy is structured. Both ideological positions have some merit, as today MNCs are more prevalent than ever but this time they 'now routinely offer scholarships, engage in more community work than previously, contribute to educational development and generally take a stakeholder approach in the countries in which they operate' (Tewarie and Hosein, 2004, p. 336).

Marxism and Neo-Marxism

Karl Marx (1818–1883) put forward a theory about how societies develop over time and its underlying concepts proved to have great power in explaining Caribbean life, with Marxist and neo-Marxist thinkers forming a radical tradition in Caribbean intellectual life. Marxist ideas have been embraced by many Caribbean thinkers of different ideologies. These theorists sought alternative explanations to capitalism in investigating the plight of the black underclass experiencing racism, colonialism and the persistence of colonial structures. From writers and novelists to pan-Africanists, dependency theorists, and economists such as those in the New World Group, they have adopted Marxist and neo-Marxist positions in contributing to the debate on development.

Marx's theory saw society as *evolving through various stages* where the economy and the *relationships of different groups* within the economy defined the type of society that evolved. For example, the very earliest societies were *communitarian*, based on equal distribution of work, where everyone owned the property of the clan, and there were few distinctions between members. This was an *egalitarian* society. Over time more powerful groups subjugated others as slaves, and a system of **social stratification** developed. As the economy developed it became necessary to have workers who had some kind of freedom to move, to make decisions, and to develop a variety of skills. This could not come about easily under slavery. The **feudal** system then developed, in which powerful nobles and aristocrats were able to protect the villagers on their lands in return for labour, produce and loyalty. In each case Marx was able to show that the societies underwent change when *contradictions* or *tensions* developed in the economy, bringing about changes in the social relations between groups.

For example, feudal society in Europe saw members of the aristocracy owning vast estates on which serfs lived and worked. There were marked social distinctions and inequities but this system of social organization remained stable for centuries in Europe, until the coming of the **Industrial Revolution**. During the seventeenth and eighteenth centuries an enterprising class of traders, merchants and industrialists grew up, who made vast amounts of money in shipping, banking and manufacturing. They lured thousands of the serfs into the newly expanding towns where they were paid wages for factory work. The new class of capitalists was able to buy the estates of the nobles, who had become increasingly impoverished. Because they now owned land they became eligible to enter parliament and make laws favouring investment, business, and the development of a middle class. Tensions and contradictions developed in how society and the economy were changing, leading to the decline of the nobles. The economic base shifted to business, manufacturing and heavy industry, such as iron and steel. Society became reorganized into workers (those with their labour to sell) and capitalists (those who owned the **means of production**, for example, land, capital, factories, banks and businesses).

Marx lived in England during the nineteenth century and was able to observe the capitalist phase of his theory at first hand. He saw how for capitalism to grow and thrive the workers had to be *exploited* by their bosses. For example, workers were not paid on a par with profits earned but at the very lowest level. The owners of business and industry maintained a common front to keep wages down. Low wages meant high profits. Thus, capitalists made large profits which sustained a high standard of living and a lifestyle very different from that of the workers. However, Marx pointed out that this state of affairs had inherent contradictions. The capitalist needed workers in order to be a capitalist and to make profits; the worker needed capitalists to provide a job and wages. But it was not a harmonious relationship – the capitalist was committed to extracting maximum labour for the lowest wages and the workers struggled for better wages and working conditions.

It was inevitable, given this state of affairs where the rich grew richer and the poor increasingly poorer, that collective action would come about in the form of **trade unions** agitating for better conditions and wages, holding out the power of labour to strike. However, the poor cannot maintain strike action for long, whereas capitalists (if they have a mind to) can prolong a strike so that workers are actually glad to return even if their demands are not met. The stage is set for a series of economic crises in capitalist societies and there will come a time, according to Marx, when the **proletariat** (workers) will seek to overthrow the **bourgeoisie** (capitalists) and bring an end to that form of society.

This next stage Marx described as **socialism**, where the goal is to bring about a *classless society*. This can only come about when all members of society share in the means of production. For this to happen all people need to understand their class position. For example, capitalists must understand that their position implies oppression of others, and any system where oppression occurs cannot last because of its inherent contradictions. Workers too need to understand that under a capitalist system they are oppressed, and so low wages or unfair treatment should not to be taken as normal. According to Marx, only when people can see through this **false consciousness** in which they have been **socialized** will they recognize the need for socialism.

The socialist stage of Marx's theory of human and social development is a transition to communism. Socialism is the period when institutions are being put in place for everyone to own the wealth of the land and to have an equal voice in government. When this has been achieved, there would be no need even for a state. According to Marx the state 'withers away' because a state is really a machinery to get things done, to ensure that no group is exploiting another, to protect people, and so on. Communism is thus an ideal (some say utopia) towards which socialist states are working – a situation in which the people, now enlightened and able to see clearly the nature of oppression, alienation and illusion, are free to form a democratic society.

ACTIVITY 11.4

1. Suggest several reasons why the terms 'socialism' and 'communism' tend to be used interchangeably.

2. Summarize the dissatisfaction that Caribbean thinkers have had with capitalism as an economic system.

Marx therefore criticized capitalism but saw it as a necessary stage during which mankind will grow to better understand oppression and see the need to build a society based on communal values. It is no wonder, then, that the intellectual traditions in the Caribbean are so intertwined with Marxism. From the end of the nineteenth century Caribbean thinkers saw freedom from racial and class oppression in a Marxist understanding of society more than any other. Pan-Africanists such as Cyril Briggs and Claude McKay (Box 11.3), George Padmore (Box 11.4), and C. L. R. James (Box 11.8), as well as black power advocates such as Stokely Carmichael (Box 11.6), and négritude activists such as Fanon and Césaire all at one time in their careers preferred a Marxist or neo-Marxist (Box 11.7) vision for Caribbean society. Later on the *dependencia* theorists and some members of the New World Group focused on underdevelopment within a neo-Marxist framework: for example, George Beckford and Walter Rodney (Box 11.9). Those who have gone beyond thought to bring Marxist principles to bear in governing Caribbean countries include Fidel Castro in Cuba (1959, through revolution, see Chapter 8), Maurice Bishop in Grenada (1979, through a *coup d'état*, see Box 7.7), Michael Manley in Jamaica (1970s, through legislation, see Box 8.5), and Cheddi Jagan in Guyana (through the democratic election of a socialist party, in 1953, 1957 and 1961, each time overthrown by British or American intervention).

BOX 11.7 Neo-Marxism

Many persons used Marx's ideas to devise theories of their own about the relationship between changes in the economy and changes in society. V. I. Lenin and Leon Trotsky are two Russian thinkers who merged their ideas with that of Marx in bringing the Soviet state (the USSR) into being. Mao Zedong of China also fused his understanding of the Chinese people and their culture in the creation of a socialist state. Marxist thinkers who greatly elaborated the role of the superstructure in influencing social life are called *neo-Marxists*. While Marx did discuss the **superstructure** (those social institutions such as politics, religion, the family, education and the **mass media** where the dominant ideas and beliefs reflect those of the elite groups in the economy – see Chapter 6), his emphasis tended to be on the economy or **substructure**.

For example, neo-Marxists showed that through its control of the mass media, the police and politics, the capitalist class is able to increase and consolidate its dominance in the society. These institutions and organizations of the superstructure enable the capitalists to not only hold economic power but political and cultural power as well. For example, their religion is the dominant religion, their children are found in the elite schools, and they fund many of the politicians who aspire to power. This control does not necessarily come out of force and

coercion. Much of it comes about in the world of ideas. (Remember that the superstructure is made up of ideas and beliefs and the dominant ones fashion how our various social institutions work.) The ideas and beliefs of the dominant class become *normalized* through the mass media and through the efforts of leading figures in the society – members of the clergy, politicians, educators, spokespersons for the business community, and so on. It is not uncommon for poor people to hold the ideas and beliefs of the elites as legitimate. For example, they may believe that the system of schooling is okay as many people do well; that their children are failing may be attributed to wrong attitudes. To criticize the system, how it works (that is, its main ideas), is regarded as 'rocking the boat' or disrupting the status quo. Marxists and neo-Marxists refer to this as 'false consciousness'.

For people to overcome this condition a new set of ideologies have to replace those of the dominant groups. In Box 11.8 we see how C. L. R. James described the Haitian Revolution in terms of a new set of ideas in the superstructure replacing those of the colonial regime. Other neo-Marxist thinkers about Caribbean development include the *dependencia* theorists and the New World Group, including Walter Rodney (Box 11.9).

BOX 11.8 C. L. R. James

C. L. R. James (1901–1989) is considered to be one of the foremost intellectuals of the twentieth century, and not only by Caribbean persons. He was born in Trinidad where he began to write novels and study the game of cricket as an art form, a colonization tool, and a means of decolonization. He then left for England, where he continued his literary career and studied the works of Marx, Lenin and Trotsky. He became a *Trotskyist* and from then on became part of the *radical tradition* influencing Caribbean life. He wrote extensively on Marxism, lectured, and engaged Trotsky himself in debate. Like all Caribbean thinkers who have been attracted to Marxism, he was concerned about linking the struggles of the oppressed in the colonies with the oppression of the proletariat in capitalist countries. He journeyed to the US where he studied racism and the condition of the American blacks. He even mobilized blacks in a sharecropper's strike in the American South.

In his speeches and writings in the 1930s James put forward the view that the American blacks constituted the most revolutionary force in the US. This was difficult

Fig. 11.11 C. L. R. James

for others at the time to see. Conventional opinion among radical white organizations, economic support groups and even the socialist movement was that the American blacks needed the advocacy of mainstream groups to assist them in their bid for freedom. James saw the black struggle as having a vitality of its own, rather than being dependent on other organizations such as the labour movement or Marxist groups to lead it. Two decades later his ideas came into being with the civil rights movement and black power. (Garvey had had similar ideas about black people owning their own institutions but did not conceive the issue as a working-class revolution.)

James was also closely associated with George Padmore (see Box 11.4) in the pan-African movement. In London James edited both the Trotskyite newspaper and the pan-African newspaper of Padmore. They both found that the peculiar racial struggle of black people in the Caribbean could not find an exact equal or answer in the ways Marxism was being interpreted by theorists at the time. This led them both to eventually seek independent thought on the struggle of black people for liberation.

Caribbean perspectives on British capitalism

Caribbean perspectives on British capitalism focus on the historical experience of the Caribbean in tracing the origins of our social and economic problems today. Many Caribbean writers who have studied British capitalism write from a Marxist or neo–Marxist perspective. Even those who are not specifically Marxist call for a re-orientation of thinking, to debunk an economic system which continues to support an elite class and large masses in poverty today. It is no wonder, whether Marxist or not, that the critics of British capitalism have been described as the 'radical school' in Caribbean intellectual thought. In much of this thinking, 'British capitalism', important in the colonial era, is seen as merely being replaced by the influence of global capitalism on Caribbean countries.

James, though, never gave up on the power of a Marxist analysis of society. His search for a revolutionary path to liberate African people led him to a thorough study of the **Haitian Revolution** of 1791, producing the *Black Jacobins* in 1938. In this book for the first time a *neo-Marxist* explanation of the events in San Domingo (the French colony that became Haiti) was put forward. He likened the enslaved population in San Domingo to the proletariat working in the 'factory' that was the plantation and its manufacturing processes, producing goods for export. For example, he says:

> The slaves worked on the land, and, like revolutionary peasants everywhere, they aimed at the extermination of their oppressors. But working and living together in gangs of hundreds on the huge sugar-factories which covered North Plain, they were closer to a modern proletariat than any group of workers in existence at the time, and the rising was, therefore, a thoroughly prepared and organized mass movement. (James, 1963, pp. 85–86)

Previously, the Haitian Revolution had been explained in terms of a spontaneous reaction to the brutality of the French planter class. Now James was saying that as workers under factory-like conditions they had developed a sense of class consciousness, and the events of the French Revolution (1789) served to draw the veil from their eyes, revealing the false consciousness under which they had been operating. In James's opinion the Haitian Revolution was a fully fledged workers revolution overthrowing the capitalist class and establishing a socialist state. (The watchwords of the French Revolution were *liberty, equality* and *fraternity* – many times more relevant to the Haitian masses than the French peasantry.) James was of this opinion because the revolution continued year after year from 1791 to 1804, organized and successful against a number of European armies, and throwing up leaders (Toussaint L'Ouverture, Dessalines and Christophe) to carry on the fight. It was not a mere spontaneous rebellion but, in neo-Marxist terms, the dominant ideas in the superstructure had been replaced by a different ideology, one based on the watchwords of liberty, equality and fraternity for black people. This was the basis for the proletarian revolution, after which the Haitian leaders sought to distribute land to the landless and pay a fixed wage – socialist policies.

This kind of analysis influenced the radical tradition in Caribbean intellectual life. For example, Eric Williams (a student of James) later analysed British capitalism in the Caribbean by focusing on the role of the substructure (the economy) in destroying slavery (Box 11.10). He was able to show that the new arrangements or contradictions in the economy brought about superstructural ideas, forcing the British to abolish slavery. The New World Group of the 1970s and the *dependencia* theorists (including Walter Rodney – see Box 11.9) also explored neo-Marxist explanations and analyses of Caribbean life.

Dr Walter Rodney of Guyana, historian and political analyst, and a committed Marxist, wrote the now famous book, *How Europe Underdeveloped Africa,* to examine how capitalism, under colonialism, sought to keep colonies in an economically backward state (Box 11.9). **Dr Eric Williams**, the first prime minister of Trinidad and Tobago, analysed the reasons for the abolition of slavery in relation to the demands of British capitalism rather that the traditional explanations, which spoke of a humanitarian attitude on the part of the British public and parliamentarians such as William Wilberforce. While Williams was not a Marxist he used the analytical tools of Marxism to investigate capitalism and slavery (Box 11.10), and this thesis continues to be debated by international scholars even today. Both Williams and Rodney came under the influence of C. L. R. James, as members of his discussion groups and as his students in London. Some of the theorists belonging to the New World Group, such as George Beckford, who wrote *Persistent Poverty*, were also Marxist in orientation.

BOX 11.9 Walter Rodney, capitalism and underdevelopment

In his short life (1942–1980) Walter Rodney maintained a consistent activist stance in criticizing the government of his native Guyana, the government of Jamaica where he was lecturing, and the system of capitalism in Africa, where he lived for a time, lecturing, writing, researching and mobilizing the masses. Wherever he lived he sought to show how capitalism was built on a premise of underdevelopment for the colony. This directly impacted the poor. Rodney regarded himself as Guyanese, Caribbean, as well as African, and was an advocate of pan-Africanism and black power. His stirring speeches and the following he drew frightened pro-capitalist governments so that he was banned from Jamaica, and in running for election in Guyana he was assassinated.

Rodney's best known work, *How Europe Underdeveloped Africa*, is a critique of capitalism under colonial conditions. He lived and worked in Tanzania between 1968 and 1974 and took an active part in the liberation struggles going on in Africa. He developed a following or school of thought around the idea put forward by C. L. R. James two generations before in relation to the Haitian Revolution, that self-emancipation of the working class was necessary, and entirely possible. Rodney found that the post-colonial leadership, the black elites (in the Caribbean and Africa), could not be depended on to improve the living and working conditions of the impoverished masses; they were the servants of international capitalism.

He saw capitalism in colonial territories as being a 'double negative'. For example:

- In the colonies, capital from Europe was invested mainly in agriculture and large profits were derived, using cheap manual labour. This went to Britain to develop more industries and better infrastructure. The value of what colonial labour had contributed to the accumulation of such profits was never paid to the colony, even in the form of social services. The colonial relationship compounded the exploitative nature of capitalism.

Normally, a capitalist would re-invest his profits locally to expand the business, and even though workers were poorly paid they would benefit from better roads and services, and would perhaps learn different skills.

- The British did not see the importance of establishing industries locally. In fact, they actively sought to prevent any industry developing that would threaten the volume of industrial exports from Britain. This led to the peculiar situation where the colonies exported raw sugar to Britain and imported refined sugar from Britain.

British capitalism was mainly responsible for the lack of available capital in the colonies, although economic activity had been going on for a long time; for the lack of industries, because this would have threatened British exports; and therefore for the lack of a diversified economy, which could have grown from the backward and forward linkages between agriculture and industry or between industries. Thus, the opportunity for developing competencies in a whole range of skills, which is what happens with workers under capitalism, did not have a chance to take place. The ultimate aim of British capitalism seems to have been to develop skills and industrial strength in the metropole and to keep the colony as a source of cheap manual labour engaged in the extraction of raw materials or agriculture for export to Britain (that is, in an underdeveloped state).

Rodney felt that workers had to fully understand the *social relations of production* under capitalism to come to the realization that it was not in their best interests. He worked with several African countries in seeking a socialist path of development to bring about more egalitarian structures and relationships. His was an example of neo-Marxist thought – that workers needed to appreciate not only their class oppression in the capitalist, colonial scheme of things but even more important was the racist ideology or system of ideas that sought to maintain white capitalist domination even when colonialism was no more.

Other Caribbean thinkers developed perspectives on British capitalism that were not necessarily Marxist. Lloyd Best, for example, showed that development in the Caribbean was obstructed by the historical capitalist structures of the plantation system; even today we have only succeeded in creating a *modified plantation economy*. This stance influenced his main criticism of Arthur Lewis's strategy for industrialization (see above); it called for an increase in the activity of foreign capital in the Caribbean yet we continue to be enmeshed in foreign, colonialist and capitalist structures. According to Best, what we need to combat the legacy of British capitalism as independent

BOX 11.10 Eric Williams, capitalism and slavery

In 1944 Eric Williams published *Capitalism and Slavery*, in which he gave a new perspective on African slavery and its abolition. He showed that the Caribbean slave plantation was an early form of capitalist enterprise and that the *surplus value* generated drove the engine of the Industrial Revolution and what was to become the advanced capitalist society of Britain. In commenting on this, Beckles (1997) says that the sugar plantations

> ... produced crops with capital and credit from Europe, imported food and building materials from mainland colonies, and exported their commodities globally. Facilitated by a transcontinental complex of brokers, agents, and financiers, the West Indian planter held the known world with his gaze and made 'good' with the extensive array of goods produced. Using their economic success to maximum effect, they lobbied and bought their way into metropolitan Parliaments and Imperial Courts in an effort to protect and promote the world they had made. (p. 778)

All this capitalist wealth was built squarely on slavery – Britain's exploitation of the people and resources of Africa and the Caribbean. Without the **slave trade**, slavery and the plantation system, Britain would not have become such a big industrial power.

Williams then went on to give a Marxist explanation of why slavery was abolished. Traditional explanations tended to focus on British efforts, such as that of the humanitarians, the Quakers, and those politicians who spoke for mercy and charity for the enslaved people of the Caribbean. This was the moral argument that had been given for years about why Britain had abolished slavery. Williams, however, showed that when capitalism had reached an advanced stage of technological, industrial and scientific applications, it no longer needed the labour-intensive input of the enslaved from overseas plantations. In fact, capitalists now found that slavery was an expensive and outmoded system that prevented the introduction of modern technologies

Fig. 11.12 Eric Williams as prime minister of Trinidad and Tobago, seated between Milton Obote of Uganda and Indira Ghandi of India

to increase efficiency. Thus, the capitalist machinery that was the sugar plantation came into being to provide excess capital and wealth for newly industrializing Britain and was destroyed by Britain when it did not need such a system any more. Williams was thus saying that in Britain abolition was an ideology connected less with humanitarian goals than with the 'freeing up' of labour, trade and capital for the transition into advanced global capitalism. Britain by now had a worldwide empire and did not need to prop up expensive and backward slave regimes.

While James was concerned with the removal of slavery through a proletariat revolution (as in Haiti, Box 11.8), Williams was concerned with how the changing emphases of capitalism (shown up in the substructure or economic base of the society) resulted in changes in the superstructure (the transition from slavery to a free society).

countries today is a focus on the *non-plantation* aspects of the economy: for example, that part of the economy that is not primarily bound up with export, cash crops, foreign capital, and MNCs. We need to develop the subsistence economy and the food economy, and create new alliances and new technologies to support indigenous industrialization. Best is of the opinion that there is still scope for local theorizing and local entrepreneurship in alleviating our problems. For this reason he does not uphold Marxism (an imported ideology), and feels we can develop our own economic ideologies that support economic independence, which has been elusive to date.

Summary

There is a rich debate in Caribbean intellectual thought that centres on the economy and how it can be purged of its colonial or plantation-like features. The policy of 'industrialization by invitation' was based on the ideology of capitalism but saw foreign capital as a trigger to spur on economic growth, including rural development. It failed because foreign direct investment could not be influenced to put in train measures that would help Caribbean economies to become resilient. Other ideologies sought a re-thinking of British capitalism and how it had impacted the Caribbean. They called for indigenous-based solutions to our problems, and to continue a tradition of interrogating underdevelopment to help us to better understand development. The promise of Marxism influenced many Caribbean thinkers, who were drawn to its egalitarian nature, especially as Caribbean societies suffered from racial, economic and political oppression.

11.4 CARIBBEAN FEMINIST PERSPECTIVES

Long before feminism became an ideology (or group of ideologies), there were feminists. Individual women concerned with the inequities being suffered by women as a group, as well as other disadvantaged groups, were willing to take leadership roles to address the issue. In the US women were involved in the anti-slavery and **suffragette** movements. In the nineteenth century in both the UK and the US there were efforts to capture different feminist agendas through associations, conferences, public meetings and pamphlets. The Caribbean also had a remarkable group of women, our early feminists (Fig.11.13 and Box 11.11).

The intellectual tradition of feminism is based on the perceived need for *equality of the sexes*. Contrary to popular opinion, feminism is not about *rule* by women; it is very much concerned with men and the relationships between men and women. Feminists, then, may be both women and men as they study the issue of **gender inequality**, whether at the workplace, in politics, in leadership positions or in the **family**. Feminist writers show that in almost every sphere of social life men are the

Fig. 11.13 Women protestors in Martinique in the 1930s

BOX 11.11 Early Caribbean feminists

A remarkable Caribbean woman was *Mary Seacole* (1829–1881), who was born in Jamaica as a free person of colour in a slave society. She learned the healing arts from her mother and became a nurse by teaching herself and learning from doctors. She had a tremendous desire to help others and became very expert in nursing. She was of the belief that through this strength she could overcome racism and the limitations imposed on women. The activities of Florence Nightingale in the Crimean War made the news all over the world and Mary decided to journey to England to volunteer her skills. Ms Nightingale would have nothing to do with her. The intrepid Mary made her

Fig. 11.14 Mary Seacole

Fig. 11.15 Amy Ashwood Garvey

own way to the Crimea and set up a hospital closer to the front than the Nightingale nurses and went on to earn the respect of all who knew her. She would not have heard of the word 'feminist', or even thought of gender equality as something imaginable for all women, but she was able to chart a course through racist and gender ideologies and triumph over them by living life on equal terms with others.

Similarly, *Elma François* (1897–1944) was born in St Vincent in humble circumstances. Working in a sugar factory as a young woman, she tried to organize the workers to bargain for better conditions, and was fired. These were times of economic depression and widespread hardship, particularly among the poor. Like Mary Seacole, she was concerned about human suffering and seemed equally fearless. She migrated to Trinidad where she became an ardent pan-Africanist and a union activist, campaigned ceaselessly on the highways and byways to expose the inequities and oppression of colonialism, challenged the power of the Roman Catholic Church, and became a communist and a founding member of the *Negro Welfare Cultural and Social Association (NWCSA).* This organization promoted political activism and had

women's bureaus, it formed two national trade unions, and its membership supported Butler in the nationwide strikes of 1937. Elma was arrested for her role in the unrest and tried for sedition. She opted to defend herself in court and was found not guilty. Like Mary Seacole, Elma was not willing to recognize that racial, ethnic or gender ideology could keep her from doing her life's work.

While these two women were spectacular in how they resisted the structures in their lives, there were also others imbued with a spirit of resistance and committed to working for the liberation of black people. Pan-Africanism was a forum for much of this activism. *Catherine McKenzie* of Jamaica was outspoken on the subject of equal rights for women. So was *Amy Ashwood Garvey*, the first wife of Marcus Garvey, who in London was closely associated with the suffragette movement. *Una Marson*, a Jamaican living in London in the 1930s became active in the pan-African movement, journeying to Africa and obtaining a post at the League of Nations in Geneva (Reddock, 2004). Garveyism and pan-Africanism inspired many women leading the struggle to end colonialism in the Caribbean and in their quest for equality and liberation they were our early feminists.

primary decision-makers and exert influence and power over others, leading to an imbalance in power between the sexes. This imbalance leads to inequitable access to resources and to the oppression of women by men, a condition that feminists say arises from **patriarchy** (Box 11.12).

Internationally, feminists first focused on Women's Studies and 'women's liberation' in order to equalize the **status** of women and men and thus release women from subordinate positions. In the Caribbean this was represented by the ***Women in Development (WID)*** programme of the UWI and the University of Guyana to integrate women into the development process through income-generating projects and increasing access to educational opportunities.

Later feminists focused on ***Gender Studies***: that is, the study of 'the social relationships between men and women', historically and in contemporary life. For example, the nature of gender **roles** is studied (what does 'masculine' and 'feminine' mean), and how it leads to the *sexual division of labour* (woman as homemaker and caretaker and man as breadwinner). The creation of gender **identities** is part of this study (how persons commit to a certain image of self that is male or female) and this to a large extent brings the process of **gender socialization** under examination to interrogate how gender **stereotypes**, gender bias and gender ideologies develop. Interrogating these concepts within Gender Studies led to a more holistic approach in ***Gender and Development Studies***. The ***WAND (Women and Development)*** Project of the UWI was concerned with how to incorporate a gender system as we have it into national, political, economic, social and cultural life so that both men and women can contribute and benefit equally (Box 11.13).

Feminism is an ideology (or group of ideologies) that seeks to end the oppression of women by men. The different ways the issue is conceived lead to different emphases, as seen below.

BOX 11.12 Patriarchy

This is a central concept of feminism. It is the condition in social life that feminists are attempting to change. The term 'patriarchy' refers to the organization of society where *gender ideologies* that promote men's interests as superior to women's are dominant. They see it as a historical condition that must be changed if *gender equality* is to be achieved. A patriarchal *gender system* subordinates women and therefore also the traditional womanly spheres – pregnancy, child rearing, child minding and domestic or housework. At the same time, such a system blocks the aspirations of women who may want to venture into traditional male centres of power.

While that is the core understanding of patriarchy, feminists go on to show that men as a uniform group and women as a uniform group do not exist in social life. The patriarchs that dominate the society also dominate men of lower socio-economic groups, men of a different race or **ethnicity**, and men with different sexual preferences. The men who control social, economic and political life block the aspirations and paths of men who are different. They have the power to hire and fire. They also try to exert power in keeping their womenfolk from consorting with 'other' men. Where homosexuals are concerned, there may be violence and murder (*homophobia*) because this goes against *machismo* and understanding of maleness in patriarchy. This is a deeper interpretation of patriarchy; that it is a gender system that inflicts violence and oppression – men oppress women, and wealthy and powerful men oppress men who differ or who are perceived as a threat. Poor women in particular are at risk; they are oppressed by their menfolk, who are more often than not themselves experiencing oppression from the capitalist class.

One interest of feminists is how women collude or cooperate in promoting patriarchy. They say that to the extent that women see themselves as sexual objects they are supporting the exploitation of women by men. To the extent that women do not examine the gender ideologies that limit and restrict them only to certain careers, that prohibit them from running for political office or church leadership, that make laws which control their own bodies (contraception, abortion), they are silently allowing patriarchy to prevail.

BOX 11.13 Defining gender

- *Gender*: the social construction of meanings and the relationships that define masculinity and femininity which tend to be based on one's biological sex. A boy is supposed to display masculine behaviours such as 'taking charge'. 'Boy' refers to a biological or sex category. 'Masculine' refers to ideas and ideologies in society about how boys should behave (a gender category).
- *Gender bias*: unfair treatment based on one's gender. There are certain types of jobs where women are not expected to be successful, which are considered 'unfeminine' (e.g. engineering, welding, politics).
- *Gender equality*: when males and females enjoy rights and opportunities that do not depend on whether they were born male or female.
- *Gender identity*: how a person defines and expresses what they believe their gender to be. Boys will almost never wear a dress unless they are in special circumstances – as a costume or playing a prank. Men who wear dresses are identifying with a different construction of masculinity than mainstream ideas.
- *Gender ideologies*: strong beliefs or ideas about the roles that males and females should play and how they should behave. These ideologies may or may not be stereotypes. The gender ideologies of feminists and homosexuals tend to differ from those of the mainstream.
- *Gender roles*: how a person understands how they are expected to behave, given their gender identity. A woman may more likely take up the homemaker role in a house than a man, but it can probably be done just as well by either one. A role is a set of expected behaviours usually assigned by society and one may or may not choose to play the role as society ordains (of course, there are consequences).
- *Gender socialization*: the process whereby members of society induct new members into the appropriate roles and behaviours that they should take up to conform to society's expectations of masculinity and femininity.
- *Gender stereotypes*: gendered behaviours that are expected of males or females who, if they do not conform seem 'odd' and attract negative comments. Thus, it is expected that a man will do the plumbing and repair the roof while a woman will cook (stereotyped gendered behaviours).
- *Gender system*: the characteristic set of gender relations that are dominant in a particular society. These relations will stem from the dominant gender ideologies in that society.

Liberal feminism

This is one of the earliest ideologies developed by feminists – that the sexes were equal and should both enjoy political, social and economic equality. This movement began with the struggles of the suffragettes to win the right to vote and eventually expanded to include the removal of all legal and institutional barriers that prevent women from enjoying the same rights and opportunities as men. The liberal feminist movement is criticized as being too benign – it does not interrogate the root causes of inequities but feels that legislation and education can bring about gender equality.

Radical feminism

This ideology sees the root cause of the inequity being suffered by women as their *oppression* by men. Society, they say, is organized along a male system of power and privilege (patriarchy) that encourages **sexism** – a form of discrimination where one sex, women, is believed to be inferior to the other. Radical feminists tend to stress the differences between men and women while liberal feminists stress sameness or equality. It is the recognition of this difference as something to be respected that radical feminists are seeking. For example, they feel that traits such as nurturing, caring, helping, teaching, facilitating, mothering, empathizing, listening, and others considered to be largely 'feminine' virtues, should be accorded appreciation and not dismissed as inferior to being aggressive, loud, firm, strict, controlled, forceful, aloof, impersonal, and others considered to be largely 'masculine' virtues. They therefore call for an interrogation of gender roles and identities and of subtle forms of sexism to deepen our understanding of patriarchy and its beliefs. On the whole, radical feminists see their work as bringing about a cultural change that debunks stereotypes of women (and also, necessarily, of men).

Marxist feminists

Marxist feminists believe that the relationships between men and women as set up by capitalism encourage the oppression of women. The economic system (the 'substructure') and the legal system, politics, religion, education and the family (the 'superstructure') are all dominated by a patriarchal system of beliefs. In a capitalist system the traditional work of women (reproduction, caring, nurturing, home-making) is devalued and subordinated to men's work outside the home (production in business and industry). Marxist feminists argue that domestic work (the 'second shift') should be seen as paid work as women also work outside the home. The patriarchal beliefs that see men's work as more important considerably oppress women who work both inside and outside the home, and who at the same time have the responsibility for the spiritual, moral and emotional life of the family.

Caribbean feminism

Caribbean feminists are not in full agreement with the liberal, radical and Marxist feminists abroad. They see the concerns and issues of women in the Caribbean as differing from those of white, western, middle-class women. For example, 'woman' tends to be a uniform concept in white, western scholarship. However, women in the Caribbean are fractured into different social groups based on race, ethnicity and social class, and because of this membership suffer different levels of oppression. Intersections of gender, race and class, then, comprise a prism in which to study feminist issues in the Caribbean.

History

One of the main concerns of Caribbean feminists is to produce a realistically *engendered* history of the region, one that opposes the traditional focus on male-dominated activities in history – war, government, diplomacy, economy and religion. Brereton (1999), as a historian concerned with feminist issues, has sought to uncover the parallel lives of women in Caribbean history through unconventional sources – diaries, journals, memoirs, autobiographies, narratives, letters and archived documents. These flesh out traditional accounts by showing how historical events impacted on (and were influenced by) a group that has been silenced by men's writing of history. Some of her sources include:

- *autobiographies and memoirs* of Mary Prince (Bermuda/Antigua, 1831) and Yseult Guppy Bridges (Trinidad, 1980)

- *diaries and journals* of Eliza Roberts (Jamaica, 1805) and Maria Nugent (Jamaica, 1801–1805)
- *letters* of Elizabeth Fenwick (Barbados, 1814–1821) and Eliza Elleston (Duchess of Chandos, Jamaica, 1770–1880).

No study of male/female relationships in the Caribbean would be satisfactory without reference to the historical experiences of colonialism, slavery, **indentureship** and independence. Slavery in particular has been the focus of feminist inquiry to throw light on contemporary relationships within the Afro-Caribbean family. For example, contrary to traditional historical accounts, it is now fairly certain, especially in the era after the abolition of the slave trade (1807, in the British territories), that slave families as nuclear units did exist. This contributes to the debate outlined in Chapter 6 about whether the African family in the Caribbean is an African retention or was shaped by plantation slavery, or whether it was a response to poverty. These three theses in various ways attempted to explain the prevalence of non-nuclear types of family arrangements among African-Caribbean people today. The more gendered understanding of the enslaved that now comes about from feminist historians shows that the **nuclear family** is very much a part of this mix and not an anomaly.

Beckles (1997), studying enslaved women in Barbados, was able to show that they continually rebelled and resisted their condition, yet their lives have gone unreported. Leaving women out of the historical picture skews what we know of as history.

> *Slavery degraded women and womanhood, forcing aspects of resistance in specific forms and with women at times offering loyalty in return for protection and privileges, at other times running away, committing murders, supporting revolutionary action. Armed rebellion was rarer. The more ordinary day-to-day anti-slavery activities were the norm, actions to weaken the slave system and hasten its collapse. (Stubbs, 1999, p. 119)*

Caribbean feminists, through a study of history, say that the issues concerning white, western women differed considerably from those of the gender system in the Caribbean. For example, in the white, western world men were the traditional breadwinners and women were tied to domestic roles, with little support from a family network. Their pursuit of careers or work outside the home was criticized because of their role as mothers. Caribbean women, however, especially from the lower classes, were more often the consistent breadwinners as well as the dominant adults in the home. They had help from a wide network of family and friends. However, being powerful in the home did not translate into being powerful in the public domain. A continuing trend in Caribbean feminist study has therefore been the issue of power.

Power

Feminists find that the gendered relations existing between men and women are organized in subtle and not so subtle ways to maintain patriarchy or male dominance. One of their aims, then, is to explore and lay bare how power exists within gendered relationships. They feel that theories to date which attempt to explain the formation of gender identities and gendered behaviours as 'benign socialization' (Barriteau, 2003, p. 4) leave out the domain of power within gender relations. 'Benign' descriptions of gender socialization are those that tend to make the process seem neutral and harmless. Feminists want to call attention to *how* gender ideologies are passed on within a gender system where males hold more power than females. It is not an unbiased process and feminists want to expose the gender stereotypes and bias that are passed on because of this very imbalance in power.

For example, Box 11.14 describes a study by Robinson (2003) in which she examines how citizenship in the Caribbean has been built on an image of males as the ideal citizens, and even when it is stated in the **constitution** that there is gender equality the laws are based on men's lives. Thus, the gender ideology that says that men are the more powerful and dominant of the species has imbued the creation of Caribbean constitutions and its laws perpetuate this imbalance in power. Box 11.15 continues the theme of analysing the relations of power between the sexes by studying the now famous thesis of ***male marginalization***. Feminists criticize the theory, based on the power men continue to wield in the society; they do not see any marginalization taking place.

Fractured gender identities

The neat polarity between male and female evident in early feminist writings from the West was not meaningful for the Caribbean, where each gender was fractured into racial affiliations (African, Indian, white, Chinese, Amerindian, Mixed, and so on), ethnic and religious groupings (Christian, Hindu, Rastafarian), urban/rural populations, social class divisions and age categories. Caribbean feminists are interested in studying how all these intersections of age, race, class, ethnicity, geographical location and historical experience come together to create and perpetuate gender ideologies, gender identity and gender socialization within and between different groups.

One example of this interest is shown in the study of the Indian group in Trinidad and how they relate to the longer-established African group, both being of equal numbers. Both groups have different gender systems and ideologies. The Indian community is overtly and historically patriarchal, with women playing a subservient role to men. The African group is **matrifocal**, with women enjoying much autonomy. This is not to say that patriarchy is not present. In fact, the prevailing

---

BOX 11.14 Gendered citizens

As a feminist lawyer, Tracy Robinson (2003) was interested in how the issue of gender equality was represented in Caribbean constitutions and legal systems. Although the various constitutions stipulated that women were equal citizens before the law, she was able to show that the notion of 'citizenship' was derived from a model that was more relevant to men than women. This raised the interesting question of whether women were lesser citizens than men.

She used as an example the case of Guyana, which makes it clear in its constitution that all women and men are to enjoy equal rights. This was tested in the courts in 1982 when a Guyanese woman could not get the court to rule in her favour that her foreign-born husband was a 'dependent' and therefore could live in Guyana. However, the foreign-born wife of a Guyanese man *could* be deemed a 'dependent' and live in Guyana. The law was based on a notion of a woman as being dependent on her husband but not the other way round. The power of the patriarchal system of gender relations that dominated the law-makers and judges could not admit that a man should claim such subordinate status as a 'dependent'. It meant that Guyanese men and women were not equal citizens.

BOX 11.15 Male marginalization

In 1994 Professor Errol Miller said that owing to patriarchy the racism and **classism** existing between men led to the owners of business and industry (white and brown men) sponsoring the rise of females in the society. He based this on the closure of male teaching colleges in Jamaica in the nineteenth century, which effectively cut poor black men off from attaining a professional career. He could see no reason for this other than the attempt by the colonial elite to obstruct black men from achieving social mobility. He went on to say that there were similar processes at work in Caribbean societies and others, cutting men off from achieving a better standing in the community, and that women were benefiting from this – women from all groups and social classes.

> Black women in Jamaica did not become teachers because they demanded such opportunity . . . They did not actively seek to replace men as teachers. The women who would benefit and the colleges for female teachers that would grow as a result of the decision had done nothing to cause this outcome. They were the only innocents in the matter. Unknowingly, the black woman was being recruited by the ruling minority as an ally against the black man. (Miller, 1994, pp. 94–95)

Caribbean feminists have been quick to contradict Miller's thesis by showing that even if more females are enrolled in educational organizations and obtain higher qualifications and better jobs, that does not mean they go on to hold positions of power and leadership. The issue, as feminists see it, is one of power. Patriarchal gender ideologies continue to be dominant whether women are more successful now than before. And women, whether they are successful or not, have to deal with patriarchal domination at home and in the workplace. The system of patriarchy does not wither away because more women are accessing social mobility. As Box 11.14 shows, the gender system is so enmeshed in patriarchy that even the question of who is a citizen is a gendered issue. Feminists go on to say that only those who hold the ideology of male dominance dear will interpret the success of women as the marginalization of men. This is a *binary* or *polar* view that sets the genders up as opposites, with one being necessarily dominant and the other subservient.

Barriteau (2003) has a different view about why some men seem to be marginalized and suggests that

> . . . it is time to analyze the content of the gender identities that boys and men acquire as part of the larger gender ideologies circulating in gender systems in our society. These gender ideologies are embedded in relations of dominance. They are relations of power that play out between women and men, but also, significantly, between men and men. (p. 340)

In effect, Barriteau is saying that patriarchy may be ultimately most destructive to men as it stipulates ideologies of manhood that prevent them from exerting effort for success or forming meaningful relationships, or expressing themselves in a variety of ways.

ideologies about the superiority of men are found in the African community and are widespread in the power relations between men and women, but they are not as explicit as in the Indian community. For urban, Christian Indians, and for all groups, whether Muslim or Hindu, the traditional, explicit patriarchal structure has gradually been eroded as education, in particular, has levelled the playing field between males and females. What feminists note is that in this 'mix' of cultures, where ethnic groups still live a somewhat polarized existence and vote differently, Indian females have been adopting gender ideologies modelled by the African group. This has exacerbated the culture of competition between Indian and African masculinities, with the former seeking to resist forms of **creolization** in a bid to control the sexuality of Indian women. **Interculturation** could be the process whereby the gender ideologies of African women are gradually being adopted by Indian women.

Rampersad (1998) suggests that the struggles of the Indian woman against patriarchy could be more successful if she played more of a role in breaking down the ethnic polarity that exists between Indians and Africans. Here gender and ethnicity interweave. If the Indian woman becomes more involved in politics, in literature, in

ACTIVITY 11.6

1. Feminism tends to have a negative image. Suggest why that may be so.

2. Examine the situation in your country in relation to what Miller has said about male marginalization. To what extent do you believe that this phenomenon exists?

3. Outline what a study of patriarchy in your country might reveal.

drama, and the arts, from which she is conspicuously absent, then she will be moving that much closer to being as active and involved in social life as African and other women. Under the patriarchal system practised by Indians, women were almost never allowed into the public sphere. While education has removed many barriers, there is still a dearth of Indian women in public life. Feminists suggest, then, that the more Indian women are integrated into *all* aspects of life in the society, the more resources they will have to resist the structures that have traditionally kept them subordinated. Others argue that the traditional values to which Hinduism and Islam appeal will continue to construct the Indian woman in a conservative mould.

Summary

Caribbean feminists are in the forefront of the intellectual movement contributing to an understanding of patriarchy. The fractured nature of identities in the Caribbean gives us a unique insight into the complexities of patriarchy as a system of male oppression. Not only does patriarchy oppress males considered to be the 'other' (those who are poor, of another race or sexual orientation) and females of different socio-economic brackets and ethnic groupings differently, but there are intersections of race and class: for example, poor Indian females and poor African females are each affected in different ways. Finally, there is scope and space for women to reduce the power of patriarchy if they can transcend traditional **caste** and class lines and form alliances with other women and men who are similarly oppressed.

11.5   INDO-CARIBBEAN THOUGHT

This section looks at the body of writing and scholarship produced by Indians in the Caribbean, and others who have studied Indo-Caribbean thought (Box 11.16), to isolate its main concerns. Guyana, Trinidad and Suriname have the largest concentrations of Indians in the region. In Guyana and Trinidad there are two major ethnic groups, the Indians and Africans, whilst in Suriname there are significant numbers of at least four ethnic groups – the Hindustanis or East Indians, the Creoles or Africans, the Javanese or Indonesians, and the Bush Negroes or Maroons (see Fig. 4.9).

Identity issues

A dominant theme among Indians is the struggle to make sense of strong ethnic loyalties in a context where there are calls for a national identity. Unlike the African group,

Indians have retained many of their cultural norms and practices, many pertaining to the religions of Islam and Hinduism. Whilst most Indians today accept western dress (other than when they go to the temple or mosque), **religion** still prescribes a code of conduct, **rituals**, food preparation, and the authority of the *pundit* or the *imam* in domestic affairs. More importantly, custom and religion come together to reinforce **endogamy** – the practice of choosing prospective wives or husbands from the group (caste, class or clan). Thus, Hindus are expected to marry Hindus (of like standing or caste) so that the traditions and ethnic ideologies get passed on from one generation to another; similarly, Muslims marry Muslims. However, in the context of the Caribbean and the imbalance of females to males during indentureship, society and culture could not be recreated exactly as in India. The caste requirement had to be abandoned and Hindus and Muslims also intermarried. Although relationships and marriages across ethnic lines, between Indians and Africans, continue to be rare, there is a significant 'mixed' population in Trinidad, more so than Guyana.

As a result, the ethnic loyalties of Indians to their ancestral country remain strong. Some Indo-Caribbean writers say that these ties are 'imagined' – they reside in customs, traditions and beliefs about India, not many having been to India; to fifth- and sixth-generation Trinidadians and Guyanese, India is remote. Ties to India are really a commitment to maintaining a way of life in the Caribbean that continues the ancestral traditions. It is seldom acknowledged that these ties are tenuous, and so in the struggle over identity there are painful questions – if ethnic loyalty to India and 'things Indian' is dwindling amongst the younger generations, what does being 'Indian' mean in Trinidad or Guyana? If creolization and interculturation have been going on for some 150 years, what is Indian culture? For example, Desmangles et al. (2003) say:

> Hinduism in Trinidad . . . cannot be said to be an Asian religion that has been transplanted. Through the years, it has evolved differently in the Caribbean than its counterpart in South Asia. It developed new myths, as well as rituals and festivals (such as the annual Holi Pagwa) that bear few resemblances to those of India; they are original to the region. (p. 272)

Are ethnic loyalties necessarily at odds with a national identity? Given the above questions, how should Indians work out their commitment to a Caribbean nation when they have always been treated as transients?

Indians were brought to the Caribbean in the nineteenth century and entered an already established society. Africans had been there for three hundred years or more and the society was organized around European values and norms. In the aftermath of **emancipation**, Africans could have worked on the plantations if they were paid well enough, but Europeans did not intend to support a free peasantry that was paid a fair wage. Hence, the indentured scheme was designed to resurrect a cheap and exploited labour supply dependent on Europeans. The Africans looked on the Indians as scab labour and the Indians felt utterly alien in a foreign land. Moreover, they were kept on the estates, away from the towns where Africans predominated, and they were penalized by vagrancy laws from travelling. Their low wages meant that they were constantly indebted to the European master. They kept out of education as they were mistrustful of it. Europeans, then, did not give the Africans and Indians a chance to unite, exploiting their natural distrust in order to maintain a pool of lowly

BOX 11.16 Indo-Caribbean writing

Well-established Indo-Trinidadian writers such as *V. S. and Shiva Naipaul, Samuel Selvon* and *Ismith Khan*, and Indo-Guyanese writers *Clem Seecharan* and *David Dabydeen*, equally well-established, have together explored the major themes that concern Indo-Caribbean people. Most if not all have written about the Caribbean while in the diaspora – the metropolitan centres of Britain and Canada. Collectively they have explored what it is like to grow up in traditional Indian families, inter-family dynamics (especially in an extended family dominated by men), inter-ethnic relations with other groups in the society (whites, Africans, Portuguese), the legacy and traditions of India and how they are creolized in the Caribbean setting, the dilemmas of being Indian in a 'foreign' land, the theme of transience, and how migration to the UK or Canada does not solve these issues but doubles the tensions. Their language, the tone and rhythms and the humour reflect their Caribbean heritage even while their characters wrestle with problems of identity, placelessness and a sense of hopelessness.

Recently, Indo-Caribbean female writers have been seeking to redress the situation of male writers portraying their lives. They desire to speak of the 'spaces' that occur under patriarchy, which they have seized to realize more of their potential through subtle and subterranean manipulation of circumstances. Many do this by way of autobiographical fiction – and they explore hitherto taboo subjects such as sexuality and lesbianism as well as mixed-race heritage – enabling them to bring multiple perspectives and identities to bear on Caribbean life. On the other hand, they also explore in full-length novels situations that are familiar to a Caribbean audience, such as political tyranny and the dark side of the tourist industry. Some of these writers include:

> *Ramabai Espinet:* The Swinging Bridge, Nuclear Seasons – Poems
> *Shani Mootoo:* Out on Main Street, Cereus Blooms at Night
> *Oonya Kempadoo:* Tide Running, Buxton Spice
> *Narmala Shewcharan:* Tomorrow is Another Day
> *Lakshami Persaud:* Raise the Lanterns High, Butterfly in the Wind

paid labour wholly under their control. It helped with social stability, too, to have the large numbers of Africans and Indians, both exploited groups, distrusting each other. Indo-Caribbean writers today analyse the continued polarity amongst the races and discuss why, once colonialism had ended, the African and Indian population did not sink their differences to make a success of independence (Box 11.16).

Citizenship issues

Instead a national discourse took place in the newly independent Caribbean countries of Trinidad and Tobago and Guyana, which sought to weigh the claims of both groups to citizenship. No group felt, on independence, that they were equal as citizens. Africans felt that their long history of settlement and suffering gave them a prior claim as the authentic citizens of these lands. Indians attested to their own work in building the agricultural sector and rescuing the colony in the aftermath of emancipation. The situation was exacerbated by a feeling amongst Africans that they should have been granted land on emancipation, as happened at the end of the indentured period. On the whole, in both territories this group felt a sense of superiority over the new Asian immigrants because they had had access to education, Christianity and British civilization.

This discourse led only in the direction of increasing polarization between the two ethnic groups, who later both sought to form political parties and governments where one ethnicity dominated. The *Westminster system* (see Chapter 7) allowed one

ACTIVITY 11.7

1. Describe what kind of power-sharing strategies Guyana and Trinidad might adopt to reduce exclusion and marginalization of ethnic groups.

2. Do you agree that a strong ethnic identity in a country with several ethnic groups prevents the development of a national identity?

party to obtain all the rewards and perquisites that a government in office could enjoy (appointment to powerful boards, controlling funds and tenders, and developing a system of patronage). Having lost an election, the opposition parties knew that their members would be marginalized and sidelined in the contest for work and rewards. Hence, elections were keenly contested, with many charges of fraud, especially in Guyana where, with a majority Indian population, Forbes Burnham and the PNC (the People's National Congress – an Afro-Guyanese party) were repeatedly returned to power. Thus, who is a *genuine* citizen and who has rights to the national 'cake' become contested issues when ethnic relations are polarized.

Indo-Caribbean social scientists and others have made a study of cultural pluralism and ethnic relations in the southern Caribbean to illuminate the issue of contested citizenship. Premdas (1998), in his study of Guyana, showed that in the lead-up to independence there was a 'moment' when the African and Indian community came together in one party under the leadership of Burnham *and* Cheddi Jagan. However, personal conflicts, habitual ethnic loyalties and Jagan's announcement of his communist beliefs led to external intervention, the ascendancy of the PNC under Burnham and the increasing exclusion of Indians from all positions of power and influence. Open ethnic violence (approaching civil war in its extent) ensued during 1963 and 1964, as well as violent incidents in the following years as elections continued to be rigged and people were traumatized by a campaign of terror.

Premdas (1998) observed that whilst politicians exploited inter-ethnic rivalries freely to promote their own ends, there was a point beyond which there is only hate, when it becomes difficult to pull back and the country disintegrates. Those who are disenfranchised descend into poverty or migrate. Various sectors of the economy collapse and the group in power increasingly becomes the target of its own members, who suffer in the deteriorating conditions. Repression and terror now have to be employed against them. The troubles in Guyana led to an examination of the question: what makes a society cohere?

Although the situation in Trinidad has not descended into open ethnic violence, the political parties seem to be treading a similar road. The solutions offered point to some strategy of **power-sharing**, which is very difficult to take root in a climate of racial animosity. Even now, after more than 30 years of independence, when Indians outnumber Africans in both Trinidad and Guyana, their citizenship is still contested. Both in *their* minds and in the minds of the African group, the tensions arising from their strong ethnic affiliation as Indians are difficult to reconcile with a national identity.

Summary

Indo-Caribbean thought is bound up with investigating ideologies of ethnic identity in a Caribbean context. There are continued efforts to interrogate what it means to be 'Indian' as opposed to 'African' in Caribbean society. Some feel that a creole-centred Caribbean identity is as alien to them as an Afro-centred identity. Their efforts, though, to present an authentic Indo-Caribbean identity are complicated by the fact that some creolization has already taken place. Birbalsingh (2004) cautions against an ideology that promotes national identity over ethnicity: for example, the thinking that says if you declare yourself Guyanese rather than Indo-Guyanese or Afro-Guyanese, this solves the problem. He says: 'This is a piece of dangerous, if well meaning nonsense that needs to be smartly scotched; it is mere wishful thinking that seeks to erase fundamental feelings and attitudes entrenched in Guyanese history' (pp. 56–57). For both Guyanese and Trinidadians the issue continues to be worked out; how one bears one's ethnicity may in the final analysis be open to individual choice.

11.6 INDIGENOUS PERSPECTIVES

Descendants of the early peoples of the Caribbean Basin are found today in significant numbers in Guyana, Belize, Dominica and Suriname (see Boxes 3.4 and 3.5) and in smaller numbers in Trinidad and St Vincent and the Grenadines. Their stories and myths, as well as their activist stance in seeking to protect their rights, tell us something about their perspectives. There are about 3000 Carib Indians in Dominica, which has a total population of 70,000 people. The Carib Territory was established in 1903 as a 3700-acre (1480 ha) homeland for the Caribs and today it is still owned as communal lands.

The Amerindians of Guyana (numbering about 40,000) are scattered throughout the interior of the country in at least 65 reserved areas. The entire Guyanese population numbers about 800,000. There are nine tribal groupings among the Amerindians (see Box 3.2) and they live in different regions (Fig. 11.16), many of them still waiting to have official confirmation of their land titles.

In Belize, where there are about 280,000 people, 48.7 per cent are Mestizos (mixture of European and Amerindian), 24.9 per cent are Afro-Creole, 10.6 are Maya, 6.1 per cent are Garifuna (mixture of Africans and Caribs from St Vincent) and 9.7 per cent represent other groups such as the Menonnites, Indians, Syrians and recent Central American immigrants. There is a continuum among the Amerindians as a group – those who strongly identify with their Amerindian heritage at one end and those who prefer to identify with the other ethnic group or groups to which they belong at the other. To a large extent, then, the **Garifuna** and the **Maya** (Mopan, Kekchi and Yucatec) represent the most important Amerindian groups in Belize, and it is to these groups we look to learn about indigenous perspectives (Box 11.17).

Deconstructing myths

The indigenous peoples of the Caribbean are seeking to change a powerful myth that Europeans created about them: that they are extinct or that the small surviving populations are not 'pure' Amerindians. Whilst millions of indigenous peoples suffered genocide at the hands of the

Fig. 11.16 Amerindian groups in Guyana

BOX 11.17 Belize: indigenous perspectives

In Belize, the different ethnic groups are found in different parts of the country. The Mestizos are located in the north and west; the Creoles in the Belize district; the Mayan groups such as the Kekchi, Mopan and Yucatec live in the north and the Toledo district; and the Garifuna in the south around the towns of Stann Creek, Dangriga and Toledo (Fig. 11.17).

The Garifuna and the Maya suffer similar kinds of injustices to those of other indigenes, namely the Amerindians of Guyana, and have resorted to similar strategies to fight for recognition and redress. First, they have formed advocacy groups as a focus for their cause and to win support – for example, the *National Garifuna Council (NGC)* and the *Toledo Maya Cultural Council (TMCC)* – and they are represented on the **Caribbean Organization of Indigenous Peoples (COIP)**. Secondly, they have formed alliances with groups that seek to promote the rights of indigenous peoples. An Inuit group from Canada (also an indigenous group) has helped to form an organization known as the *Belize Indigenous Training Institute (BITI)*, which offers training programmes to Maya and Garifuna people in order that they may take advantage of social and economic opportunities in the society.

Since the Maya lay claim to over 200,000 ha (500,000 acres) of Belize as their ancestral lands they have been constantly at loggerheads with the government, because the latter is only prepared to grant around 31,000 ha (77,000 acres) on nine separate reserves. The Maya complain that these boundaries were drawn without consulting them and fragment their land. Events came to a head, however, when the government granted logging rights to over 200,000 ha (500,000 acres) of land, including a great deal of territory claimed by the Maya, to two MNCs in Toledo district. The TMCC challenged this in the courts, claiming that the government's action was unconstitutional. Claims like these have become more numerous over the years and have been largely ignored by the government.

To increase the level of advocacy Mayan groups then sought to work through their international allies to have this and similar cases heard as a violation of human rights. The **Inter-American Commission on Human Rights (IACHR)** researched the case and determined that the government had indeed violated the rights of the Maya and recommended that their right to traditionally occupied communal property be recognized. The government has been slow to respond to

Fig. 11.17 The Amerindian population of Belize

the report and some concessions have been made but they continue to issue leases to timber and other companies to extract resources from Mayan ancestral territory.

The Garifuna people have different concerns from the Maya, though both are interested in the same thing – preserving their cultural heritage. A case in point is their language, which is formally taught only in a few places. Since few written records of the language exist and many Garifuna do not speak it in the urban areas and in the diaspora, it remains a language spoken only by a dwindling group. Garifuna culture on the whole is threatened by migration to the US and Canada as well as by the education system, which has failed to incorporate aspects of its language and culture into the curriculum. (See Box 12.1 for a view opposing the claims of Amerindian groups.)

Europeans, indigenes today are saying that it was in the interests of the Europeans to construct a myth that the original peoples had more or less disappeared. On the basis of this myth a case was made for slavery. Later on this same myth gave European capitalists the freedom to move into ancestral territory and set up mining and timber industries as if there were no previous owner. This myth was deepened when those of mixed heritage were treated as if their Amerindian roots did not exist. Thus, there may be many more thousands of Amerindians in the Caribbean than are accounted for in censuses. And for some Amerindians today there is a reluctance to self-identify because of the stereotypes that are painted about native populations – lazy, dirty, subnormal, backward, and the like.

History texts have also played a part in portraying the indigenous inhabitants as passive and submissive (except for the Caribs who were labelled as 'cannibals' – another myth justifying the intent to exterminate them). Accounts of the early history of Guyana showing the Amerindians making strategic decisions to resist the Spanish are not found in textbooks. The Amerindians allied with the Dutch, who provided guns, other weapons and training in manoeuvres and tactics. The Dutch were interlopers on the Spanish Main and the Amerindians' fate seemed to be death or capture by the Spanish – hence their alliance, which even allowed the Amerindians to launch attacks on Spanish monasteries and settlements. This aspect of Caribbean history, in which the Amerindians sought to actively defend themselves, is absent from the traditional historical record. It opposes the stereotype of the Amerindians as friendly, docile and unsophisticated.

In 2005 a controversial issue developed between the film company Disney and the indigenous peoples of Dominica. The sequel to *Pirates of the Caribbean*, starring Johnny Depp, to be filmed in Dominica, sought to portray Dominica's Carib Indians as cannibals. The Carib Chief Charles Williams held talks with Disney personnel, who refused to edit the script and insisted on continuing to portray the myth of cannibalism that Europeans had created. The Caribs of Dominica received support from other indigenous groups around the world who, by publicizing the issue, hoped to bring to world attention how indigenes are invariably ignored by mainstream society and capitalist interests.

Marginalization

Indigenous peoples in the Caribbean tend to be the most marginalized in the society – socially, economically and politically. For example, Amerindians in Guyana point to a simple but telling observation: while Guyanese speak of being Afro-Guyanese and Indo-Guyanese, the Amerindians are considered to be a separate group, located far in the interior, thought to be 'primitive' and referred to as just 'Amerindians'. Although they are the original inhabitants of this land, their strong ethnic ties to their ancestral heritage is viewed as something that makes them not authentic Guyanese. Here we see a bias in cases of national identity, conferring 'true' citizenship on those groups who were instrumental in the nationalist and independence movements. The attitude towards the Amerindians, then, is that they are inferior in some way and not true Guyanese.

Not surprisingly, Amerindians tend to be economically marginalized. Most of them live in poverty, battling disease, isolation and a lack of amenities. They tend to marry early and have large families. There is a high incidence of alcoholism. Few have opportunities to pursue secondary education because that involves travel to the coast or regional centres, where a child's living expenses may be too high for the family to afford. In addition, there is a high drop-out rate as the young Amerindian students experience ostracism and discrimination from the coastal and urban cultures. The 'coastlanders' tend to feel that Amerindians are spendthrift and unable to manage money, hence their impoverished condition. The Amerindians, on the other hand, tend to focus on values that emphasize family life and communal ties rather than a savings ethic. With little in terms of capital accumulation, they have little power to influence the state. This becomes important as they struggle to have their rights recognized.

Land rights

In Dominica, Guyana and Belize (Box 11.17), the right of the original peoples to their lands has become a politically sensitive issue. This has forced the Caribs, Mayas and other groups into an activist and confrontational stance. When the Carib Chief in Dominica tried to oust non-Carib men who were consorting with Carib women from the Carib Territory this provoked a national debate, and the feeling was that no 'state within a state' could exist in the Commonwealth of Dominica. Although the Caribs had a right to their territory, they had to conform to the laws of the national government.

In Guyana the traditional rights of Amerindians to their ancestral lands tended to be ignored by the government. In 1997 the Wai Wai, Wapishana and Makushi peoples were increasingly concerned that mining and timber companies were infiltrating their lands but their repeated pleas to the government went unheeded. They formed the *Touchau's Amerindian Council* of Region 9 to defend their homeland from the activities of mining and forestry companies. The callous response from the government was that such a council amounted to treason and they were threatened with immediate legal action.

In Guyana the Amerindians have been engaged in a protracted struggle to have their claims to their ancestral lands formalized and recognized by the government. The Amerindian Act, which gave guidelines for land titling, was inadequate for the task. There were numerous complaints that the long delays in recognizing claims allowed miners and loggers to freely enter ancestral lands and exploit their resources. There was also the claim that land titles tended to be distributed just before a general election. Amerindians, comprising about 8 per cent of the population, are seen as having potential influence in helping one of the two dominant political parties into power. The Act was redrafted in 2006 and can be downloaded from http://www.fpcn-global.org/downloads/reports/AmerindianAct.LegalNote.20060518.pdf.

Also in 2006 Guyana, responding to international criticism about the inequalities suffered by the Amerindian peoples, submitted a report (overdue by 26 years) to the UN Committee on the Elimination of Racial Discrimination (CERD). These developments are positive achievements won mainly by the Amerindian peoples and their supporters.

Activism

Continued marginalization and the lack of respect shown for their way of life have encouraged Amerindians to take a more activist stance in dealing with the wider community. They have been organizing into pressure groups so that they can take issues to other organizations that may be able to help. The **Amerindian Peoples Association (APA)**, representative of most of the tribal groups in Guyana, works closely with the **Rainforest Foundation** of the US, which provides assistance to develop self-sufficiency among the Amerindians. An important development occurred in 1999 when the **Amerindian Legal Services Center (ALSC)** was set up. This body now helps to bring some of the land rights cases to court and occasionally to the international courts.

In November 2005 the aboriginal populations all over the world mobilized to send representatives to the prestigious **Summit of the Americas** in Argentina. They worked on a declaration of rights to present to world leaders at the Summit, pressing for greater recognition for claims and rights, and for equity in job opportunities. They feel that the present emphasis on the Free Trade Area of the Americas (FTAA) is giving too much focus to MNCs and capitalist concerns and ignoring values such as spirituality, which form part of the indigenous peoples' world view.

Summary

The perspectives of indigenous populations in the Caribbean show that they are primarily interested in preserving their rights and, by extension, the values they hold dear. While they have been ignored and sidelined in the past, there is now a militant and activist stance as well as research and scholarship into their history, culture and languages. They are supported too by world bodies advocating more recognition and restoration of the land rights of indigenous peoples. If this is the case, then we are likely to see in the near future changes to our history texts and school curricula, and at the same time increased confrontation as governments try to mediate between the interests of mining and forestry companies (capitalist projects that boost the economy) and the claim of indigenous groups to extensive ancestral lands.

WRAP UP

The intellectual traditions of the Caribbean have been described as ideologies that have served to inspire people of the region to improve some condition of social life that they felt was oppressive. These included racial ideologies (pan-Africanism and négritude) promoting black consciousness, economic ideologies that contrasted Marxism and capitalism, ethnic ideologies that explored the issue of belongingness among Indo-Caribbean peoples and the issue of threats to heritage among indigenous groups, and feminist ideologies that explained the oppression of women in a patriarchal system of gender relations. These ideologies translated not only into written works but also into the lives of great men and women, as well as the organizations and newspapers they founded. In cases such as the indigenous groups of the Caribbean, where the many languages remain unknown to mainstream Caribbean society, their ideologies can be determined by their art, their cultural traditions, and by the actions they are taking to preserve their heritage.

PRACTICE TESTS

Structured response

1 Distinguish between pan-Africanism and négritude. (4 marks)
2 Explain what is meant by an 'ideology'. (2 marks)
3 Identify THREE ways in which pan-Africanism has influenced Rastafarianism. (6 marks)
4 Describe ONE way in which pan-Africanism has influenced political movements in the Caribbean. (4 marks)
5 Explain why Eric Williams's thesis about capitalism and slavery is a Marxist argument. (4 marks)
6 Distinguish between Marxist and neo-Marxist analyses. (4 marks)
7 Suggest why many pan-Africanists adopted the ideology of Marxism. (2 marks)
8 Distinguish between socialism and communism. (2 marks)
9 Distinguish between 'gender studies' and 'feminist thought'. (2 marks)
10 Describe ONE example showing how patriarchy is oppressive to both men *and* women. (6 marks)

Essay questions (20 marks)

1 Using ONE ideology as an example, show how it has influenced development in the Caribbean.
2 Outline the activities and intellectual thought of ONE Caribbean person whose ideological stance influenced development in the Caribbean.
3 Describe the main ideas, strategies and objectives of Caribbean feminists.
4 Explain how capitalism under colonial rule impacted development in the Caribbean.

Challenge essay questions (30 marks)

1 Examine the arguments which say that the strong ethnic loyalties of Indo-Caribbean people hinder the development of a strong national identity.
2 To what extent are Indo-Caribbean women 'doubly oppressed' in Caribbean society?
3 Develop a reasoned position about what the future holds for the indigenous people of the Caribbean?
4 Using examples, outline the main ideas that should inform any initiative designed to meaningfully address an ethnic problem in the Caribbean.

RESEARCH TOPICS

'Gender relations' is an issue where the data surround you. However, because it is so familiar a part of social life, it is not so easy to collect data. Participants tend to take it so much for granted that they cannot separate it out from their lives and talk about it meaningfully. If you are thinking about studying gender relations you should keep this in mind in how you structure your questions. It is a good idea to use questions which prompt people to speak at some length (so you can capture their ideas) rather than 'True/False', 'Yes/ No', or forced-choice items.

If you wanted to examine some aspect of patriarchy or gender oppression you might try the following among your classmates or any group of your peers, both male and female.

- Give each person a list of about ten characteristics that people tend to stereotype as 'masculine' or 'feminine'. Ask them to say which ones they believe are typical of men and women and which are not easy to classify. Make sure at the end you know which response is from a male and which from a female. You also have to think hard about the ten characteristics you will eventually choose. You don't want to put too many that are clearly one or the other, according to prevailing stereotypes. You want to use those that if a person finally says this *is* a male characteristic, it will tell you something about what that person thinks a male is like. For example, 'kind', 'dependable', 'determined' are some that may elicit a variety of answers. You may want to *pre-test* your list on friends first and discard some of your original items.

- In each case, once the person has completed the exercise, ask them about their reasons for making the selection that they did. Note the reasons; they may be in the form of stereotypes, they may indicate whether the person believes in the inherent superiority of one of the genders or vice versa, they may cite previous knowledge that they know males or females like that, they may show a lot of ignorance about what it is like to be a person of the opposite gender, and so on.

- You can represent the first set of data in two bar graphs where the vertical axis represents how many were included in the study (e.g. 20 persons). The horizontal axis will be divided into ten sections for each of the characteristics.

- One graph could be named 'Perceptions of Femininity' and the other 'Perceptions of Masculinity'. Analyse these images.
- You will need to do qualitative data analysis (see Chapter 13) to show what the other data you have collected mean. For example, which were the characteristics that persons could not classify? Were they the same ones all the time? Could you interpret something from this? Did your results show no clear stereotypes? Can you account for this?
- Bring in the second set of data, where persons spoke about why they made certain choices – that should give you some in-depth understanding about how the genders think of each other.

REFERENCES

Ball, T., & Dagger, R. (2003). *Political ideologies and the democratic ideal*. New York: Pearson Longman.

Barriteau, E. (Ed.) (2003). *Confronting power, theorizing gender: interdisciplinary perspectives in the Caribbean*. Kingston, Jamaica: UWI Press.

Beckles, H. (1997). Capitalism, slavery and Caribbean modernity. *Callaloo*, 20(4), pp. 777–789.

Birbalsingh, F. (Ed.) (2004). *Guyana and the Caribbean: reviews, essays and interviews*. Chichester, UK: Dido Press.

Brereton, B. (1999). Qualitative research in history: personal documents authored by women as sources for Caribbean history. Presentation at the Qualitative Research Symposium, School of Education, University of the West Indies, St Augustine, 4 Nov. 1999.

Chevannes, B. (1995). *Rastafari: roots and ideology*. Syracuse, NY: Syracuse University Press.

Desmangles, L., Glazier, S., & Murphy, J. (2003). Religion in the Caribbean. In R. Hillman, & T. D'Agostino (Eds), *Understanding the contemporary Caribbean*, pp. 263–304.

Kingston, Jamaica: Ian Randle and Boulder, CO: Lynne Rienner Publishers.

James, C. L. R. (1963). *The Black Jacobins: Toussaint L'Ouverture and the San Domingo revolution* (revised 2nd ed.). New York: Vintage Books.

Martin, T. (2004). African and Indian consciousness. In B. Brereton (Ed.), *General history of the Caribbean, Volume 5: The Caribbean in the twentieth century*, pp. 224–281. Paris: UNESCO and London: Macmillan Caribbean.

Miller, E. (1994). *Marginalization of the black male: insights from the development of the teaching profession*. Mona, Jamaica: UWI, Canoe Press.

Premdas, R. (Ed.) (1998). *Identity, ethnicity and culture in the Caribbean*. St Augustine, Trinidad: UWI, School of Continuing Studies.

Rampersad, S. (1998). *Jahaaji Behen? Feminist literary theory and the Indian presence in the Caribbean*. Warwick, UK: University of Warwick, Centre for Caribbean Studies.

Reddock, R. (2004). *Reflections on gender and democracy in the Anglophone Caribbean: historical and contemporary considerations*. Amsterdam/Dakar: SEPHIS and CODESRIA.

Robinson, T. (2003). Beyond the bill of rights: sexing the citizen. In E. Barriteau (Ed.), *Confronting power, theorizing gender: interdisciplinary perspectives in the Caribbean*, pp. 231–261. Kingston, Jamaica: UWI Press.

Stubbs, J. (1999). Gender in Caribbean history. In B. Higman (Ed.), *General history of the Caribbean, Volume 6: Methodology and historiography of the Caribbean*, pp. 95–135. Paris: UNESCO and London: Macmillan Caribbean.

Tewarie, B., & Hosein, R. (2003). Arthur Lewis and Lloyd Best on development strategy in Trinidad and Tobago. In S. Ryan (Ed.), *Independent thought and Caribbean freedom: essays in honour of Lloyd Best*, pp. 309–352. St Augustine: UWI, Sir Arthur Lewis Institute of Social and Economic Studies.

12 HUMANIZING DEVELOPMENT: SOCIAL JUSTICE

Today in the Caribbean social justice is a major concern and is seen as a necessary part of the development process. The traditional ideas about development – that it was mainly concerned with economic growth – have been gradually giving way to more humanistic conceptions. Social justice refers to the ideal that all groups in the society should be treated fairly. Any breaches of social justice are acts of discrimination. However, there are different interpretations about how a society should establish fair treatment for its citizens. In this chapter we examine several conceptions of social justice – that fairness is a natural right, that society has a duty to ensure equitable levels of human welfare, and that socially just practices operate to the mutual advantage of groups. We also examine prejudice and discrimination based on age (ageism), gender (sexism) and ethnicity – namely, religion (creedism), race (racism) and social class (classism). In all these cases it will be shown that a breach of social justice has a negative impact on development.

EXPECTED LEARNING OUTCOMES

On completing this chapter, you will be able to

1 explain the relationship between social justice, human rights, equity, equality and discrimination
2 analyse contrasting conceptions of social justice such as natural rights, welfare and mutual advantage
3 examine cases of social injustice on the grounds of age, gender and ethnicity (race, class and religion)
4 explain how breaches of social justice impact development in the Caribbean.

12.1 DEFINING SOCIAL JUSTICE

Listed below are several statements about **social justice** that we can examine to determine what people mean by the term and then we can come up with our own definition.

Social justice is about:

A. preventing human rights abuses
B. obtaining equality for different groups
C. overcoming the barriers that prevent some people from enjoying a better quality of life
D. maximizing everybody's welfare
E. ensuring that different groups in the society meet their obligations and responsibilities so that the whole society benefits.

The ideas that seem to imbue these notions of social justice are:

- **Fairness**. This is conceived of as equal treatment for all social groups. For example, groups that have been marginalized could be brought into the mainstream by having more political power, as indigenous groups have been in Guyana through representation at the various levels of district administration. Statements A, B, C, D and E are all based on a notion of fairness or **equity** as *equal treatment* amongst groups. Although only A states it explicitly, there is the understanding that groups must be treated fairly because all persons are equal, and as such they have **rights** that must be recognized.

- **Welfare**. Some groups may need special measures to take advantage of the opportunities that are provided under *fair* treatment. For example, to fully participate in the political process indigenous groups may need better access to secondary and tertiary education (e.g. scholarships) and economic opportunities that raise them out of poverty. Statements B, C and D refer to this when they mention previously marginalized or obstructed groups needing assistance in 'maximizing everybody's welfare' (**welfare** refers to standards of living). Statement E also refers to it in that there is the expectation that the welfare of all will be increased, if the society extends help to those that need it most.

- **Responsibilities**. To live in society, to contribute to and benefit from it, is the essence of social justice. This refers to an idea of social justice where all groups should be acting out of a sense of reciprocal transactions with the country and other groups. For example, suppose the indigenous peoples were given 'handouts' over a long period of time without making any significant contribution to the country; that would be an unjust situation. They would not merit such continued assistance. Only Statement E states explicitly that citizens are engaged in a situation of mutual *responsibilities* for the rights they enjoy.

- **Rights**. Running through the statements is the idea that people have some basic *rights* that all share, and to deny one group the ability to exercise those rights is a human rights violation. However, Statement E states that social justice has to be based on *merit* (not only on a right to something), that the group in question is seen to be fulfilling its obligations and responsibilities.

Social justice, then, hinges on several ideas we all share – that everybody is equal and although we are organized in different social groups (based on gender, religion, age, social class, and so on) we should all be treated fairly. Ideas of equality (same treatment) and equity (fair treatment) between persons mean essentially that each person has rights – for example, the right to life, to express oneself, and to worship freely. These human (or natural) rights are what we use to judge whether a person or group is being denied social justice.

Conceptions of social justice

A study of social justice highlights the different conceptions people have about why there should be fairness or equity between the different groups in society. The ideas expressed in the statements in the section above represent three different conceptions of social justice which we now examine in greater detail.

ACTIVITY 12.1

1. Using the discussion here, compose a short definition of social justice.

2. Explain the relationship between social justice and 'humanizing development'.

Natural rights

All human beings are equal and therefore all human beings are entitled to the basic human rights enjoyed by others. The basis for making this claim often rests on a supernatural authority such as 'God-given rights'. Another basis for making the claim about natural rights lies in an appeal to the moral positions that most groups have, which appear to value human life, liberty and the dignity of people. Thus, human rights or natural rights occur as divinely ordained sanctions and as moral **beliefs** and **norms**.

However, these are not the only rights that people are entitled to, according to the *UN Declaration of Human Rights*. This document goes much further than 'natural' or 'human' rights to 'entitlements' that people should have to be able to live in a just society. They are more about social living than basic human rights and it seems to have become the responsibility of governments and international organizations to ensure that they are enforced. These 'rights' are really high-priority areas that seem to be necessary for all people to enjoy similar benefits. For example, the following are included in the UN Declaration of Human Rights for all member states to follow:

- *Civil and political rights*: the right to freedom of expression, to assemble and form associations, to participate in the political process and to run for public office
- *Economic and social rights*: the right to education and health care, to fair wages, to join trade unions, to safe conditions at the workplace, and to an adequate **standard of living** (these are sometimes referred to as 'welfare rights')
- *Ethnic rights:* the rights of minorities, and any religious, linguistic, political or cultural group, to the same treatment as other groups in the society. Such rights protect **ethnic groups** from murder, torture and genocide, as well as from unfair practices in employment and access to education.

To uphold all of these rights/entitlements inevitably brings conflicts and tensions, as it may seem that some people are entitled to more than others. Box 12.1 discusses the argument that by giving the indigenous peoples – for example, the Maya of Belize – their historic claim to vast tracts of land (which is their right), a situation results where other ethnic groups claim unfair treatment.

BOX 12.1 Being right versus being fair

In the section on 'indigenous perspectives' in Chapter 11 we discussed the historic claims of the Maya to large areas of Belize and the fact that they had only been granted a fraction of this claim. To the indigenous groups this is unfair and against their natural rights as indigenous peoples. Various human rights organizations have taken up this struggle in international courts seeking social justice for the Maya.

To the other ethnic groups in Belize these claims are unfair. Granting the full claim of the Maya would greatly reduce the economic landscape of Belize, on which *all* citizens depend. The Maya would have this land for their exclusive use. Afro-Creoles in Belize, in particular, point to other dangers inherent in such action. They refer to national development in a multi-ethnic society where it is important that one group is not seen to be reaping more rewards than others and being 'a state within a state'. Recognizing the indigenous right of the Maya in this regard would be unfair to other Belizean citizens. In any case, there is a body of opinion in Belize saying that some Mayan groups in Belize are not indigenous to Belize, having come into the area in the early nineteenth century from neighbouring countries.

To a large extent these expanded natural or human rights are enshrined in the **constitutions** of most Caribbean countries in a general way. Caribbean governments are also committed in that they have signed international agreements to protect rights in law. These agreements include the ***Convention on the Elimination of all Forms of Discrimination Against Women,*** the ***Convention on the Rights of the Child*** and the ***Rome Statute*** which establishes membership in the ***International Criminal Court***. Only some of these international agreements, though, have moved into law in individual Caribbean countries. For example, laws to protect women in the home and the workplace, and a family court to judge disputes, are now more evident in the legal systems of Caribbean countries than, say, laws treating with unsafe drinking water or the right of citizens to a safe and secure environment. This is largely because Caribbean governments often do not have the resources to provide clean water to all groups and communities in the different regions, or to monitor and evaluate the potential for **environmental hazards** and **disasters**. Those who live in areas with an irregular water supply or one of uncertain quality, as well as those who live in areas prone to flood, experience social injustice through the inability of a country to fully address certain conditions of social life, leading to disadvantage and marginalization.

When social justice issues are regarded as human rights, it presupposes that all persons should be treated equally. To uphold these rights, though, depends on the legal system or international **sanctions** by policing bodies such as Amnesty International. As we saw above, there are many areas of social injustice where a country may have signed an international convention that agreed to secure the rights of indigenous persons, or people with disabilities, or minority communities, and so on, but laws to concretize the agreement have not yet been made. Social justice as a human or natural right, then, is largely left up to the legal system and international bodies to oversee and enforce.

Nothing much is said about individual citizens and their obligation to ensure that the human rights of others are observed. **Values** such as respect for persons, tolerance, and affirming the worth of everyone are largely left up to the **socialization** processes taught in the home, school and church. Whether or not these values are taught and whether they are internalized remain important questions in building a society where human rights are preserved. From the point of view, then, of social justice as a human right, we see that it is an ideal to which we subscribe in an abstract way because it will improve the quality of life for all. However, it becomes difficult to guarantee if there are no laws to protect certain categories of persons and if in the society itself there are not well-thought-out ways of dealing with the problem of human difference at the individual level.

ACTIVITY 12.2

Find out what declarations and conventions concerning human rights your country has signed. Which of these have become formalized as a body of laws?

Welfare

Conceptions of social justice based on ideas about welfare deliberately focus on the distribution of resources in a society that leads to well-being and satisfaction. This idea of social justice sees the need for marginalized and disadvantaged groups to experience more of the material rewards of the society and for the gap between them and the well-to-do to be closed. This more often than not relates to social and economic conditions: for example, wages, equality of job opportunity, conditions of work, training for those without credentials, a more humane education system, housing, social security and unemployment relief.

Obviously, this means not treating people equally but *treating unequals unequally*. The poorer groups are given more subsidies, resources and opportunities to upgrade their standard of living. Welfare is a notion of 'being fair' that does not emphasize equality or sameness. However, the question of what is 'fair' is continually asked. For example, do Caribbean governments have the necessary resources to supply the poor with free health care, an unemployment relief programme, discounted food items, transport costs and clothing? Even if it is accepted that a government would not be able to supply all of these *social security measures*, the issue remains about whether it is fair to tax other groups more heavily to pay for subsidies and whether the funds could have been expended in developmental efforts such as job creation to help the poor and others as well.

Welfare is an example of **distributive justice** – that the material wealth of a society should be shared around. While it might be based on the *right* of human beings to social justice, it tends to focus on the *needs* of specific groups. It acts out of an understanding that there is a **social contract** outlining the relationship between a state and its people. Citizens give up certain dimensions of their power (their ability to be violent, to 'take the law into their own hands') in order that most of their needs be met by a government, which they themselves elect. Members of government accept this power and in turn are mindful of their responsibilities to citizens, to provide the conditions for an equitable standard of living.

Those who criticize welfare policies as 'handouts' that are too burdensome on taxpayers tend to see only a narrow picture. Improving a family's economic circumstance goes a long way towards improving the nutrition and health of that **family**. Access to education for the entire school-age population also goes a long way in reducing the levels of ignorance in the society, of increasing those who understand the political process and democracy, and those who can make informed choices about their future. Poverty and lack of education left unchecked conspire to keep persons out of the political process, increase the likelihood of unemployment, and thus create a marginalized group in the society.

Welfare, then, is a form of social justice based on the inherent right of persons to equal treatment, but more specifically it is based on the needs of certain groups, which mandate that they be helped to reduce the inequities in the society. Critics of the welfare model, however, say that it is very expensive and leads to dependency, and to varying degrees it is unfair to other groups which have to be taxed to support these measures.

Mutual advantage

This view of what is socially just is also based on the idea of the social contract between the state and its citizens. However, it does not approve of welfare provisions for the poor unless the poor are prepared to reciprocate by taking advantage of welfare and growing out of poverty. This would be mutually beneficial to the state and its citizens. It is a view of social justice that is based on *merit,* rather than *need* or *rights*. What is 'fair' in this view is the mutual arrangements between state and citizens that reinforce the strengths of each party. Thus, an unemployed person on welfare should commit to finding a job, undertaking training or accepting temporary employment – in other words, to actively showing that being unemployed is not

ACTIVITY 12.3

Investigate the concept known as 'affirmative action'.

1. Are there any examples of affirmative action in your country?

2. Explain how affirmative action is related to the discussion above on welfare.

where she or he wants to be. This is another example of distributive justice, but this time it means that only those who deserve it should receive the rewards of the society – their 'just desserts'.

This conception of social justice, then, criticizes the welfare model. The mutual advantage model is saying that welfare can lead to dependency and in so doing is not 'fair' to anyone. The state would be committed to expending enormous funds as 'handouts' and those citizens on welfare would enjoy a life where they did not have to work or contribute to the society. However, critics of this model say that it is highly generalized and speaks of groups as if they had the same power, the same circumstances, and the same levels of equality. It lumps all people on welfare together as if they were one uniform group.

Much of the language of the mutual advantage advocates stresses *self-reliance* as a cardinal virtue that must be nurtured in a fair and just state. By stating that a system of mutual obligation where welfare is concerned should go a long way towards nurturing self-reliance, these advocates are in fact being unfair to poor people. The latter may well be inclined towards developing self-reliance, but family circumstances, low levels of education and few employable skills constrain their choices or even their awareness about what courses exist and what is a good option to take. In addition, their self-confidence about looking for work and doing well in interviews may not be on a par with those of citizens who are affluent, skilled and knowledgeable. Thus, to say that they have to be self-reliant rather than dependent, and that if they do not show this quality their allowances would be removed, is unfair. It assumes that indigenous peoples, poor rural and urban folk, and disabled people all have a similar set of values and circumstances so that blanket judgements can be made.

The mutual advantage model of social justice accepts that all citizens are inherently equal and those who are not experiencing an equitable level of socio-economic well-being should be helped to do so. In return, however, they should resolve to grasp the opportunities provided and move off the need for welfare. Since those of the poorer socio-economic groups are less likely to want to invest in long-term training for rewards several years hence, they are not likely to be helped by this model. This way of thinking about social justice values the goals and norms of mainstream society, such as a capitalist system of social and economic relations.

Summary

While issues of social justice are very topical in the society today, different ways of understanding social justice tend to emphasize human rights, human needs or merit. Each view of social justice advocates different strategies for minimizing inequities in the society. The most serious disagreement, however, is between those who see welfare as the major avenue for establishing fairness in the society and those who criticize welfare without controls, saying that it is the reciprocal relations *between* groups which ensure fairness.

ACTIVITY 12.4

Briefly describe the concept of social justice based on (1) natural or human rights, (2) welfare and (3) mutual advantage.

12.2 SOCIAL INJUSTICE

Caribbean societies have evolved out of a set of historical circumstances – conquest, slavery, **colonialism** and the plantation system – that have **entrenched** social injustice and left a legacy of **social stratification** and unfair practices based on class, religion, race and colour prejudices. These are not our only forms of social injustice. Women, **minority groups** such as indigenous peoples, the disabled and the elderly, all suffer from some form of inequity as well.

When a group does not experience fairness or equity, a state of disadvantage or marginalization is taking place. Those who study inequities focus on the existence of **prejudice**, **discrimination** and **stereotypes** in the society. 'Prejudice' and 'stereotypes' refer to attitudes we have whilst 'discrimination' refers to acts or behaviours that are unfair in some way. As we see below, prejudice may or may not result in discrimination and vice versa – they can occur independently of each other.

Prejudices and stereotypes

A 'prejudice' is an *attitude* based on the *belief* that another social group is inferior (or superior) in some way. The belief is based on a **pre-judgement** about others, which is a tendency to think of others and decide about them in advance of a situation, without much knowledge of the people or the specific situation. For example, if one harbours racial prejudices against a whole group of people and a conflict situation occurs between some members of this group and another, then one is likely to believe everything bad about the group one is prejudiced against. This is a pre-judgement, knowing very little about the persons and situation where the conflict took place and already formulating a version of events. Pre-judgements may be both positive and negative. For example, there is the tendency to think of the rich and famous as also being intelligent. This belief or pre-judgement encourages an attitude towards the rich that is largely positive and optimistic, when there is no basis for such thinking in the first place. Usually, however, the problems in society arise from prejudices which are based on negative or pejorative stereotypes.

A 'stereotype' is a fairly rigid set of ideas about a group of people that typifies them as belonging to certain categories or having certain well-defined traits: for example, that black people have no head for business, that Indians hoard money, and that the Chinese are inveterate gamblers. Prejudices and stereotypes intertwine and support each other. Usually the build-up of a prejudice is due to some stereotyping along the way.

A prejudice or pre-judgement may develop as a result of our socialization through the agencies of the family, the peer group, the church, the school and the **mass media**. Usually it is 'caught' rather than explicitly taught, as when we internalize and take as 'true' the dominant emotions, feelings, judgements and orientations that our friends and family have for certain groups. For example, when we are growing up we hear from family members or members of our church about how other faiths worship Mary rather than Jesus Christ, where pastors live an affluent life off tithes, or where idols are worshipped and strange practices occur, as when the Spiritual Baptists go on the 'mourning grounds'. In such cases, and others having to do with race for example, our attitudes to groups are born out of pre-judgements – ideas about others that are based on flimsy evidence, hearsay, and the cues we get from our family and friends about them. These are the stereotypes we borrow from our people and upon which we build prejudiced ways of thinking about others.

BOX 12.2 The roots of prejudice

Prejudices and stereotypes are examples of things that we have learned from others, usually our family and friends and also from the mass media. These 'learnings' tend to be very stable and resistant to change. Even when we encounter evidence to the contrary we tend to prefer our original perspectives. For example, we might meet a house-husband who was content with his life; after thinking about it for a while we might well conclude that he is odd and the majority of men would not tolerate a life that was only deemed suitable for women. In other words, we prefer to retain a notion of some homogeneous body of men who hold certain beliefs strongly. This is a prejudiced way of thinking – we have no way of knowing all these persons and their feelings on the issue.

One reason put forward to explain the strength with which we hold prejudices and stereotypes is the way in which we learn – either at home, in school, or via the media and other agencies. If you reflect on the curriculum in school, for example, you will notice that there is hardly any in-depth study of highly controversial issues necessitating an interrogation of different views and arbitrating between them to come up with a fair assessment. In school, what is taught is largely textbook knowledge which has been simplified and clarified and reduced in such a way that it can be learned quickly. As a result students have very little experience in pondering social life and learning skills to negotiate complexity.

The learned behaviour of simplifying and sanitizing topics does not stand students in good stead when they have to observe, listen to and participate in scenarios where prejudice, stereotypes and discrimination arise. As a result, students tend to depend on how they have learned – the branding of an entire group of people with certain labels, and for those who are different, just saying that they are different – because dealing with complexity has largely been avoided in their education.

To take fully on board the task of wondering why someone is different and if there are others like that, and whether this would necessitate a change in one's world view, is something that many people find much too difficult to begin to contemplate. People thus shy away from this kind of critical thinking and to a large extent this is responsible for the stability of most prejudices and stereotypes.

It is ironic that we tend to hold our prejudices very dear even though they are based on flimsy evidence. The usual test of a prejudice or a stereotype happens when we meet someone who clearly does not fit the traits we have already assigned to him or her. We find the person to be 'normal', someone who could even be our friend. The way we have of dealing with this situation is to think of the person as 'different', 'exceptional', 'not like the others'. In that way we can approve of the person *and continue to hold our prejudices* for his/her referent group. It begins to seem that approving of 'others' is not something that we really wish to do; it seems more likely that we actually want to hold prejudiced attitudes about 'others' (Box 12.2).

'The Other'

Sociologists and psychologists have studied the nature of prejudice and focus on how our socialization leads us to construct *our* way of life, *our* groups and *our* people as 'normal' and acceptable whilst those of another religion, race, ethnicity, income bracket, and even another nationality are regarded as 'the Other'. We see this in the Caribbean in how we regard another Caribbean territory. We attribute some very scathing judgements to our CARICOM neighbours, the outcome of which is that we feel superior to them. We see this too when we speak of other people as 'having an accent', when in truth and fact everybody has an 'accent'. And when we have a disagreement with another (even a person belonging to our circle of friends and family), it is invariably the case that we were wronged and that it is the *other* person's fault. In all these cases there is a central tendency to value ourselves and anything to do with the 'I' as superior to the 'Other'.

ACTIVITY 12.5

The point is sometimes made that stereotypes actually help us to negotiate life. Explain what you understand by this statement.

Thus, to explain prejudice and the development of stereotypes there seems to be a common urge to judge others in terms of our own reference points, lifestyle, beliefs and values. To judge others using solely your own standards and values is to have an **ethnocentric** point of view. If this is a characteristic trait of the different groups in society, then the incidence of prejudice and stereotyped thinking is likely to remain high unless measures are taken to address our ways of thinking about the 'other'.

Discrimination

'Discrimination' refers to acts or behaviours that treat others unfairly. Such acts may arise from a prejudice or a negative attitude towards others. For example, if you believe that young black men are lazy and prone to engage in violence (in other words, a stereotype), as an employer you may not hire them and prefer another age, race or gender group. This would be an act of discrimination as it is an unfair practice based on a belief that cannot be justified in relation to your applicants, who are new to you. On the other hand, you may hold such prejudices but hire members of the group because you think it politically prudent to do so. Or you may have no prejudices towards the group yet feel that the clientele you serve would prefer to deal with others, in which case you do not hire young black men. This is a case of discrimination but without holding a prejudice.

Additionally, the institutions of society may discriminate even though the members may not hold any prejudice. For example, in some countries, while women can be part of the armed forces, they are not allowed to face actual combat. This arises from prejudices about women that pre-judge them as the 'gentler sex' and as 'reproducers' of the human race and in need of 'protection'. In the armed forces, these attitudes are **institutionalized**. For a woman desirous of serving her country, in a job for which she has been trained, these restrictions are discriminatory.

Acts of discrimination increase levels of inequity in the society. Ethnic discrimination is very prevalent in Caribbean societies; for example, where employment is concerned, skin colour is still associated with qualities having to do with such seemingly unrelated character traits as diligence, courtesy and intelligence. White or near-white groups tend to be awarded jobs, contracts and prestigious positions based on a belief that their skin colour confers on them superior traits. This is **racism** and is an act of discrimination against others who cannot access such rewards. Acts of discrimination against older persons (**ageism**), women (**sexism**), the disabled (ableism), religions (**creedism**), socio-economic class (**classism**) and other attributes (for example, rural residents) exacerbate social injustice in a society. These acts are based on attitudes of prejudice and stereotyping which result largely from how we privilege the 'I' in relation to the 'Other'. Social injustice heightens conflict in the society and severely impacts development. In the following sections certain prejudices and related discriminatory acts are examined in the context of Caribbean society and its developmental goals.

Summary

The inequalities and inequities faced by certain groups in the society usually stem from other more powerful groups deliberately putting them at a disadvantage because of their differences. The problem of human difference is one that bedevils mankind, as can be seen today on the world stage – a lack of understanding of others, a refusal to empathize with others, and a continuing belief that one's own perspective is the right one. This solid belief that what one thinks and what one's group believes are the correct ways to understand something lead to the development of prejudices and stereotypes about others, which for the most part result in discriminatory acts against them. Social injustice, then, is an outcome of setting up obstacles for less powerful groups because they are different in some way from the dominant groups in the society.

12.3

AGEISM

'Ageism' is an attitude towards mainly older people (Box 12.3) that treats them as objects of not much worth. It is therefore a prejudice and is built up through a number of stereotypes we have acquired about older people through our socialization and our habit of always locating ourselves as separate from the 'other'. Logically we should not be having prejudicial attitudes or engaging in discriminatory acts towards older persons because aging is an automatic process and all of us, if we survive, will reach old age one day. So, logically, why do we think negative things about older persons when sooner or later we will be old? Perhaps it is because we think that *we* will be different, that we will age differently? If this is so, then we are judging a whole group of people based on the idea that we will not be like that when we age – judging others according to the 'I'. It may well be, though, that to younger people the thought of being old is just embarrassing and they associate it with negative stereotypes. Whatever the reason, there are a number of stereotypes associated with growing old that we need to interrogate.

It is important for us to realize that there are *differences* among those described as 'older'. Demographic standards refer to 'old age' as between 65 and 75 years. 'Old, old age' refers to those between 75 and 85 years, and the 'oldest old' are older than 85 years. The majority of persons aged 65 to 80 are able bodied enough to take care of themselves. Most of them will probably have a major or minor chronic illness (arthritis, heart problems and deafness are the most common) but can hardly as a group be labelled sick, infirm or frail. Many persons at 65 and over are still active members of the workforce. The oldest old are more likely to need some help in getting about, yet only a few are institutionalized. When they have multiple illnesses at this age they are indeed more likely to be sick, frail and infirm. Where 'mental deterioration' is concerned, however, older people normally retain all their faculties even as they grow older. They may slow down, especially if they have to learn something new such as computer skills, but they may also be slow to learn because they are less motivated than others. It is a fallacy to believe that old age equates with losing one's mental faculties or with mental illness. Whilst Alzheimer's is a serious disease that may afflict any category of older person, for the majority of old people there is only some loss of long-term memory. Perhaps among all the stereotypes

ACTIVITY 12.6

The list below summarizes four stereotypes that are commonly felt about older people.

- 'Older people are usually sick, frail or infirm'.
- 'Older people's mental faculties decline with age'.
- 'Because of physical and mental deterioration, older people cannot support themselves and are dependent on others'.
- 'Older people suffer from depression'.

List about ten persons you know who are considered to be 'older' (perhaps, 60 years and over). In what ways do these persons reflect the stereotypes listed above? What conclusions can you draw about stereotypes from this exercise?

BOX 12.3 Ageism across groups

While ageism is usually associated with the elderly, and they feel its effects consistently, other age groups also suffer from age-related prejudices, stereotypes and discrimination. For example, young children are considered a most vulnerable minority group as they tend to be regarded as the property of their parents or guardians. This may work out well if they receive protection and security. But the very fact that parenthood tends to be portrayed in a positive light make the plight of children who live in abusive homes all the more difficult to detect. Children are dependent on their caregivers, yet because they are very young and dependent and virtually powerless they are routinely beaten and neglected. These acts of age discrimination hinge on the age range of children. Abusers may not attempt such actions with older children. Ageism in this context is based on prejudicial attitudes and stereotypes that portray children not as individuals in their own right but as 'property' which can be treated according to the wishes of the owner.

Adolescents suffer from many negative stereotypes which they resent because it lumps them into a uniform group, not recognizing variation and individuality. They are characterized as obsessed with sexuality, loud and anti-establishment music, the use of alcohol and drugs, the maintenance of a bizarre dress code, and being easily susceptible to crime. The mass media and the advertising media build these images and consistently target this group, as adolescents seem able to tap into their parents' pockets very efficiently. The mass media also portray youths in crime and school crime in sensational ways. These negative stereotypes affect adolescents, especially in how they devise ways to resist and react to the low levels of respect for them in the society. In fact, youths could assess situations where they are being stereotyped as 'bad' – for example, how security personnel interact with them and how they are closely monitored in stores and shops.

At the same time there are prevailing prejudices associated with youth that paint it in a positive light. Youth is seen as beautiful, agile, flexible, creative, happy, carefree, friendly, upbeat, and so on. These stereotypes actually work against youth because they are not seen as individual people with problems, and especially in the transition from childhood to adulthood they need help, care and guidance. These are not likely to be forthcoming from those who think youth is a positive stage of being. Similarly, positive stereotypes of older persons as wise and kind may be very wrong. A person is hardly likely to show wisdom and kindness at 65 if she or he did not show those qualities before. Thus, stereotypes do not help us to understand others but they seem very resistant to change (Box 12.2).

listed in Activity 12.6, the one that has the greatest ring of truth is the problem of depression. It is a common problem of old age, yet a little-known fact is that it is also a common problem among the younger age groups.

If we examine these stereotypes we realize that all have some kernel of truth but they are unfair in how they apply certain traits or dispositions to a whole group of people whose members are extremely diverse. For example, from those who study aging (*gerontologists*) we learn that males and females age differently and have different characteristics. Women tend to outlive men by five to eight years (Shrestha, 2000) so they are more likely to experience widowhood, they are more likely to be ill, and the most recent research tells us that they feel more pain than men. Those who study pain are only now admitting that they have been treating pain as if it were gender neutral; studies now show that women feel more pain throughout their lifetime and experience it in more body areas and with greater frequency than men. Other than gender, there are age differences in aging among the aged! Those aged 60–70 years live very different lives compared to the oldest old. The span of 25 years between 65-year-olds and 90-year-olds represents almost a 'generation gap'. Thus, the older age groups in society are very diverse but stereotypes portray them as uniform, and this dehumanizes them, making them into an 'object' apart from mainstream society.

Ageist stereotypes and prejudices operate to produce behaviours or acts that are discriminatory. The person guilty of discrimination may not be engaging in it as a conscious act but rather out of a socialization response to a minority group that is habitually devalued. A minority group in society is one without much power and resources. Those in the mainstream or dominant culture regard members of minority groups as inferior. A minority group could be the indigenous population in Guyana. While they number several thousands, it is not numbers that determine the status of being a 'minority' but the fact that the group is *marginalized*, that it is very different from the dominant groups, and that it cannot do much to change its position. The aged, then, are a minority group in the unenviable position of being seen as the opposite to youth – some of the prevailing prejudices and stereotypes about youth portray them as synonymous with beauty, vigour, happiness and endless possibilities (Box 12.3).

Ageist behaviours

Examples of discriminatory practices against the older age groups include the following:

- *Social activities*. Older people are excluded from social activities, restricting their recreational possibilities. Many older folks are home-bound because of the few opportunities for them to go out and socialize. Going to church assumes a big role but researchers say that that is only so if the person was already a regular churchgoer.
- *Media stereotypes*. In the mass media older persons are either absent or stereotyped as 'the wicked stepmother or mother-in-law', 'the grouchy old man', the 'old maid', the 'nosey neighbour'. There are few important, dynamic roles played by older women on television and cinema, though there seems to be a variety of roles for older men.
- *Jokes*. Older persons are made the butt of jokes – aspersions about their hearing, seeing and memory functions, and their involvement in sexual activities, are seen as improper and scandalous. Researchers say that sexual activity among older people is made to seem odd, even 'dirty', because it is embarrassing for others to think that their parents and grandparents may be involved in such activities.
- *Health care*. Medical research has not focused on geriatric problems as much as those to do with other age groups. This becomes a national problem as the numbers in the older age groups keep rising with increased longevity and better standards of living. Medical facilities and expertise, then, are at present inadequate to cater for this growing population. This neglect is due to the prejudice that older people may be more 'expendable' than others.
- *Employment*. At the workplace, there is a reluctance to hire older workers as there is the attitude that they are harder to fit in, especially in a young staff, that they may be technologically slow, and that they do not have innovative ideas. Perhaps the greatest act of discrimination that is enshrined in law is compulsory retirement, usually at 65 years. This is an arbitrary number and one wonders how it was chosen. The rationale is that younger workers need to find jobs and so older workers have to leave at some point. If you are in paid employment, retirement happens whether or not you want to continue working (Box 12.4).

BOX 12.4 Constructing dependence

Stereotypes and prejudices that portray older persons as dependants, depriving younger persons of resources, stem from the nature of modern urban and industrial life. In agrarian societies or in rural areas today older persons lead busy and productive lives and often occupy a privileged place in the family structure and in the village or community. They work as farmers, gardeners and fishermen, and as craftsmen and artisans, and sell in the market. At home they are usually the ones to see about cooking, cleaning and taking care of the very young. Through story-telling they teach younger members about morals and the history and folklore of their country.

This kind of involvement in the life of the family, in being engaged in work, in making one's own decisions, in playing an important role in children's lives, is less likely to be found in an urban environment where retirement laws send the older people home. Urban areas have less potential in terms of keeping the older person busy and productive. Many become homebound, seeing to domestic chores to help the family but suffering from the lack of an active life with a wide range of social contacts. Urban environments also tend to be more unsafe and family members may put restrictions on their older relative to curtail too much independence.

A set of circumstances, then, in urban areas conspires to construct old age as a dependent state and reinforce the widespread prejudices associated with this group. Having been deprived of work the older person now becomes dependent on welfare and pensions. At work, employers often use a strategy of ending older workers' contracts and hiring younger workers at reduced pay. There are few training programmes that actively target older workers to help them overcome resistance to new computerized technologies at the workplace; sometimes they themselves leave because they are intimidated by the new learning involved.

Through all these changes necessitated by transformations in the economy and social life old age has been reconstructed. Modernization brought a devaluing of the role of the elderly in social life. The notion that paid employment now defines being a productive member of society made those persons who were not playing an active part in the labour market seem irrelevant. With few opportunities to engage them meaningfully after retirement, the elderly have had no choice but to become dependent on others. Stereotypes portraying the aged as a dependent and needy group on which much resources are spent describe a condition largely brought on by modern economic life.

- **Language**. Medical language tends to portray the older person as a stereotype. For example, in medical literature and practice, a 50-year-old may be described as 'elderly', which implies to some extent 'sickly and frail'. In certain scenarios you may find older people described as if they are owned and somebody's responsibility: for example, 'our seniors', 'our loved ones'. This kind of paternalistic language is not used for the younger adult population but stereotypes about the aged influence us to treat them as if they were children.

Ageism and development

Age discrimination is a form of social injustice and affects the development of Caribbean countries. For example, ageism perpetuates the 'generation gap' and reduces the possibility of healthy, mutually respectful relations between the generations. The older generation has much to contribute in homes, workplaces and public life based on their accumulated knowledge, experience and wisdom. In effect, though, the majority are sidelined, made to retire, and not seen as a resource to tap. What compounds this problem is that the aged tend to take on and accept as real the prejudices that mainstream society has about them. They begin to behave like spectators to life, acting out a self-fulfilling prophecy. On the other hand, if they resist these stereotypes they may come into conflict with their own families, those who 'take care' of them.

For a whole group of people in the society to feel unfulfilled and marginalized means that in such a society equity and productivity, as well as the sustainability of the development effort, is thwarted. It is not only a question of economic productivity being diminished because society does not want their labour, but ageist practices entrench unfairness and this can easily be extended to other groups with 'minority' status – women, ethnic groups such as Rastafarians, and the poor. Over time, social injustice encourages the rise of resistance and conflict as groups suffering inequities begin to seek ways of living that actualize their potential. In the Caribbean, older people as a political force is not yet a reality but in countries such as the US the *Gray Panthers* are a watchdog association determined to make a fuss and bring legal action against those dealing unfairly with older persons. Similarly, their *Association of Retired Persons* is a powerful **lobby** advocating better medical, insurance and care options for the elderly.

The concept of development as **human development** is not being advanced in societies where there are entrenched inequities. Human development requires that people are put at centre stage for the development effort and that development means broadening choices and options for everyone. Ageist attitudes, however, seem to be narrowing the choices of older people and forcing them into a path of literally 'preparing to die'. Inevitably, though, as more people enter these age groups, resistant actions will begin and the society will have to deal with conflict as this minority group makes a bid to change several entrenched social customs and practices. In fact, in the English-speaking Caribbean the numbers in the aged groups are increasing so much that it is predicted that by 2025 the oldest old will make up 8 per cent of the population. Cuba and Barbados are leading this demographic trend. Tomorrow's elderly are less likely to conform to ageist stereotypes perhaps because more of them will have benefited from education and more of them, being women, will have benefited from increasingly equitable opportunities in adult life. And, not unimportantly, they will represent a large constituency that politicians will want to capture. However, they will also be pitted against those groups who feel that social justice means distributing resources equally and that the elderly are already receiving more than adequate resources whilst many younger groups (for example, children) are living in poverty. The stage is thus set for increased conflict in social life.

Summary

Prejudices and stereotypes about aging are commonplace in the society. Younger members of the society are socialized into such prejudices and stereotypes via their friends, families and the media, and accept and participate in discriminatory acts against the aged without thinking much about it. In fact, in social life there is more than a tendency to treat the aged either as if they were invisible or as if they were children. In other countries there has been an awareness of this issue and deliberate attempts are made to integrate older persons into social activities and to recognize their limited financial circumstances by offering senior meals at reduced prices in restaurants and the like. The Caribbean is slow to come on board in recognizing this persisting problem of social injustice.

12.4   SEXISM

'Sexism' refers to prejudices, stereotypes and acts of discrimination against people based on their sex and not on individual merits or failures. Sexist practices are directed at both men and women. For example, the assumption that a man is the breadwinner in a house or even the head of the household is sexist when the only criterion used to conclude that is that he is a man. It is sometimes difficult to identify sexism in daily life because it is so much a part of our **gender socialization**. In Chapter 11 we looked at **feminist** perspectives in the Caribbean and at how gender **ideologies** developed through our socialization into the prejudices and stereotypes common under the gender system known as **patriarchy**. Feminist thought is mainly concerned with ways of reducing social injustice through developing a gender-just society. In this chapter we extend the study of patriarchy by focusing on examples of sexual discrimination resulting from sexist prejudices and stereotypes. While the big issues in studying sexism tend to emphasize sexual discrimination as experienced by women, men are also victims of sexist beliefs and attitudes, and men too suffer acts of sexual discrimination, particularly at the hands of other men (Box 12.5). Just as ageism results in a breach of social justice, so too is sexism unjust, with negative implications for Caribbean development.

BOX 12.5 Sexism among males

We witness sexist beliefs and practices among boys and men when a judgement is made about an individual based on whether he is or is not being 'manly' enough – referring to some universal conception about what a man should be like. This has nothing to do with the person himself but with a set of behaviours that men seem to think defines them and their activities. When a judgement is being made about a particular male it is therefore made in relation to a whole sex group known as men – and this is sexist.

For example, the extent to which a man joins in and participates with other men in 'masculine' activities such as sport or talking about sport adds to or subtracts from the assessment being made of him. A man who is not very interested in sport will have a difficult time in maintaining his place in a group of male friends. He will be on the periphery and often the butt of jokes. This is sexist because in this case he is being judged against some yardstick that says explicitly what are considered to be 'manly' behaviours. And these behaviours do not recognize *different* masculinities but tend to be rigidly uniform. For example, men wear a limited number of colours and colour combinations to demonstrate quite clearly how they differ from females. Only a few are engaged in such 'marginal' male pastimes as ballet and poetry. And to embark on a career move to be a secretary or a nurse means that a man will have experienced several heart-to-heart chats with those seeking his interest. In each case these are forms of sexist discrimination perpetrated by men on 'other' men.

In a recent study of gender and school achievement in the Caribbean, researchers found that boys in secondary schools tended to have certain 'rules' about studying at school. If other members of the group were studying for a test, then it was easier to settle down to study. If, however, the group was just talking and laughing or deciding to play a game it became very problematic for an individual to go against this male camaraderie and opt to study. If he did, he would get several good-natured remarks thrown his way at first, but if he persisted in such 'odd' behaviour, over time he would definitely cease to be a core member of that group. And the transition would not be amicable because it would be recognized that he was renouncing certain of the agreed beliefs and attitudes that males who are 'true males' should have. The fear of being labelled 'other' by one's own male friends controls to a great extent the behaviour of men and boys. And this 'otherness' has largely to do with judgements about how close the behaviours of boys and men come to those of girls and women.

There is, then, an extreme distaste on the part of men for tolerating seemingly 'feminine' tastes or traits in other men. This is the issue that causes the charge or accusation that some men actually hate women. Box 12.6 explores different theories about why boys and men avoid feminine behaviour and try to prohibit it in other males.

Sexist beliefs and attitudes

Patriarchy gives rise to several fairly stable sexist beliefs and attitudes (or prejudices and stereotypes) that threaten social justice. For example, to justify the belief that one sex (the male) is superior to the other (female), biological, religious and historical evidence is commonly offered. The male is clearly shown to have certain characteristics of physical strength and endurance, which most women cannot demonstrate, and this is why sports, for example, are segregated. It would be an unfair competition to pit men, clinically proven to be stronger, against women in the sporting arena.

Based on this 'evidence' from multiple sources, it seemed logical to conclude that men and women are fundamentally different and this difference should be reflected in their social **roles** and behaviours. For example, the 'weaker sex' should be confined to the home environs and not have to deal with the pressures of going out into the world to make a living. She should be dependent on her husband to take care of her. In return, as the child-bearer she should be the homemaker – providing a nurturing and stable home environment for rearing children and catering to the needs of her husband. These appear to be 'natural' roles ordained by the Creator and reflected in biology. One of the criticisms of this sort of thinking is that it is sexist – reducing all men and women to *essentialist* categories, where if you are male or female then that suggests what you should be doing and what you should be concerned about. This thinking is also unjust as it does not entertain at all the idea of equality of the sexes.

Sexism is also evident in how each group thinks of the other. There is the tendency among men today to conclude that 'women are taking over the world', as they witness women entering all fields of endeavour and winning legal battles to regulate men's obligations to family. Women, on the other hand, are more than likely to say that patriarchy somehow survives even as they move up the socio-economic ladder and that they encounter discrimination at home and in the workplace. They conclude that it is still 'a man's world'. These beliefs and stereotypes are sexist and unjust because in each case they are attributed to an entire sex group, only recognizing the sex category and nothing else as important. (The statement that 'highly educated women in higher socio-economic groups are more independent of men' is not a sexist statement. Although the focus is on women, the statement is not saying that their sex allows them to do this, but that their accomplishments enable them in certain ways.)

Resentment tends to lead to stereotyping and acts of discrimination have become more pronounced as the feminist movement has gathered steam over the last thirty or so years. It has led to the 'war of the sexes' and charges of **misogyny** and **misandry** (Box 12.6). However, sexism occurs in different ways and is not always immediately evident. *Hostile sexism* describes the traditional kinds of prejudices under patriarchy where women are stereotyped in negative ways – clinging, manipulating, emotional, dependent. *Benevolent sexism,* on the other hand, also under patriarchy, sees women as needing protection and care, unable to make important life decisions, and so men should not be as exacting with them. The whole issue of sexism and social justice seems to turn on whether we consider males and females to be equal, whether they are different, or whether they could be different *and* equal.

You will probably find in your discussions that the idea of *generalization* keeps cropping up. The urge to impose order on social life leads us into holding several prejudices and stereotypes which simplify and generalize how people are by just

BOX 12.6 Misogyny

Misogyny is a term used to describe men's hatred of women. While there are discriminatory practices in most religions that tend to exclude women from higher office, or from congregating with men, or there are special provisions of dress for female worshippers, some say that these are merely sexist. Others say that they reflect deeper misogynist attitudes and beliefs and that we are reluctant to admit that a great deal of the sexist beliefs and practices we witness are actually related to some men's hatred of women.

These persons say that the term 'hatred' is very strong and we may shy away from it, but that one way we can better understand the issue is to think of racism and who is a bigot. A bigot, a person who hates or is prejudiced against a member of another race, does not necessarily advertise this, except perhaps to close friends and family. It does not have to result in violence but rather hatred could reside in refusing to acknowledge 'the other' as fully and equally human and be compassionate about them. Thus, the jokes made about women, the tendency to talk loudly over a woman speaking, forcing women in different ways to take on all the housework and domestic chores, treating women as 'objects' (for example, sex objects), and even 'womanizing', are seeing women as not being on equal terms with men. They are the 'other' that should be treated differently. Misogynists, like racists, can have friends belonging to the 'other group' (a misogynist may even marry someone he believes is 'different' to how he sees women on the whole), and this, they say, 'proves' that they are not racists or misogynists. Thus, hatred of women is not at all easy to discern in our society because it tends to be masked in myriad ways by activities that *seem* to admire women – for example, pornography, philandering, protecting women, making decisions for them, and so on. This is a *feminist view*.

The belief that some men hate women is further developed by feminists in relation to how men tend to treat with homosexual men. A man-to-man relationship cannot be tolerated because in such a relationship a man is taking the place of an inferior being, a woman, and acting like a woman. This is repugnant behaviour for a man and 'straight' men are driven to harass and even physically assault men engaged in such demeaning behaviours (homophobia).

A *postmodern view* of this relationship between the genders sees it differently. Men may feel that the absolutely essential and highest quality of being a 'man' is a sexual relationship with a woman. Under patriarchy this often translates into possession of a woman and seeing the female as a 'sex object' to be dominated. This defines a 'man' and it is this 'manliness' (macho behaviours, aggression, sports consciousness, leadership qualities) which they believe makes them attractive to women. Anything that threatens this ideal of manhood, then, must be stamped out, because it is not real, it is 'queer'. It undermines all that they hold sacred, their very conception of self; so homosexuals, by trying to possess another man as if he were a woman, are threatening this dominant model of masculinity. In other words, homosexuals cannot be allowed to just be themselves because homosexuals are actually saying that 'this is another kind of masculinity, different from the others, but just as valid'. 'Straight' men see this as interfering with and devaluing their own ideal of manhood. This cannot be tolerated, and so under patriarchy *homophobia* results – fear and hatred of homosexuals – resulting in taunting, violence and sometimes murder.

'Misandry' is the situation where women hate men. Both men and women agree that it is not at all common but men in particular say that since the strengthening of the feminist movement, extreme views urge hatred for men. This, they say, has resulted in many feminists becoming committed lesbians. This time men charge women with being sexist because the reasons associated with hatred for men all seem to hinge on being a man, and not certain categories of men with typical kinds of behaviours, for example, abusers.

not recognizing, for example, that a range of masculinities and femininities exist. While motherhood is a biological role that women undertake, it does not necessarily mean that all home-related obligations become theirs. A mother can also be a highly successful career-oriented person if her partner undertakes a more nurturing role. We saw earlier that one of the roots of prejudice lay in our reluctance to deal with complexity (Box 12.2) and a desire to try to fit everybody into pre-ordained categories. When men and women do not fit easily into these 'boxes', society employs a range of coercive strategies – humour, taunts, ostracism, forms of sexual harassment and physical violence – to urge conformity to gender roles.

Sexual discrimination

At the workplace

Sexual discrimination is any unfair action motivated by whether a person is a man or woman. Thus, to promote men because they are men is an act of sexual discrimination. The labour market is an area where women typically feel the effects of sexual discrimination and experience social injustice. The lowest-paying jobs in the society are reserved for women, perhaps because employers feel that they are less likely to instigate actions for better wages and conditions of work. Clerks, secretaries, receptionists, store attendants, and those employed in retail and fast-food outlets tend to be overwhelmingly female and lowly paid. While there are not many opportunities to work one's way up in such establishments, the few men present are the ones usually selected for supervisory or lower management positions. In jobs where many women are present, employers tend to feel that a man should be in charge. Not only in lowly paid jobs but also in education, at all levels, women predominate, but the school principal or the university professor tends to be male – a phenomenon referred to as the 'educational harem'.

Men dominate the highest-paying jobs. Women who rise to high levels in the corporate structure seldom make it to the very top. They are obstructed in their careers by the sexist attitudes of those making the selection, which proclaim women to be inferior, as well as women's own internalization of sexist attitudes. For example, women tend not to bid for the highest positions because they feel it may be unseemly and construed as unfeminine for a woman to command authority over large numbers of men. This phenomenon has been called the 'glass ceiling' and limits women's opportunities.

In addition, a most blatant source of inequality is that men are often paid more for their services than women in the same job. This is a burning issue, particularly amongst professional groups of lawyers, doctors, economists and business executives, where salaries are large, but to be underpaid because you are a woman is still dehumanizing. Fig. 12.1 demonstrates in the case of Trinidad and Tobago that in many occupational areas women earn substantially less than men in the same jobs. This is entrenched sexual discrimination. Employers counter this by saying that they are not as sure that women will remain in employment because they are the ones likely to interrupt their careers for pregnancy and child-rearing.

Sexual harassment

Forms of sexual discrimination where individual women are targeted for unwelcome sexual advances, promised job promotions for sexual favours, subject to inappropriate touching or other physical contact, made to listen to sexist jokes about women or called names portraying women as sex objects, and stalking are all examples of sexual harassment. Both women and men could be harassers but in the overwhelming majority of cases the harasser is a man and the victim a woman. It is a form of sexual discrimination because it is perpetrated on a woman just because she *is* a woman. In recent years, more prevalent in the US and other developed

Table 12.1 Women's average income as a percentage of men's in occupational groups, Trinidad and Tobago, 1998–2000

OCCUPATIONAL GROUP	1998	1999	2000
Legislators, senior office managers	52.9	52.3	52.8
Professionals	75.6	80.6	73.5
Technicians and associate professionals	76.7	79.7	84.1
Clerks	86.6	85.9	87.8
Service workers (including Defence Force) and shop sales workers	50.2	53.5	57.7
Agricultural, forestry and fishery workers	52.9	67.3	68.7
Craft and related workers	50.0	47.3	55.2
Plant and machine operators and assemblers	54.9	64.8	64.9
Elementary occupations	61.9	64.1	64.4

Source: Ministry of Planning and Development, Central Statistical Office, *Labour Force Reports* (1998–2001).

countries (Box 12.7) than in Caribbean countries, women have been making claims that they are being sexually harassed, particularly at the workplace. As yet in the Commonwealth Caribbean, only Belize has a comprehensive body of statute laws to address this issue specifically, including compensation for victims (Robinson, 1999). Legal authorities are still grappling with how to define and conceptualize sexual harassment as an offence. They teeter between the lobby that sees it as an issue of sexual discrimination that threatens social justice and equality, and the feminist lobby which prefers to view the issue as one of violence to women. In the meantime, sexual harassment continues in schools, public places and in homes. It may be assessed as 'harmless' or women put up with it in order to safeguard their jobs. Under patriarchy, where women are the 'second sex' and largely felt to be inferior to men, this harassment has been a 'normal' part of the process of gender socialization for both boys and girls.

In conducting research on sexual harassment abroad, Thomas and Kitzinger (1997) found that how females say they would react if they become a victim is quite different to how victims actually react. The guidelines about how to react when faced by sexual harassment are fairly consistent and include confronting the harasser and/or making a formal complaint. However, researchers find that victims try to pretend that the situation is not happening, ignore the innuendos, or endure in silence, hoping it will just end. They may also try to avoid persons and situations where or with whom such encounters arise. This is very similar to Caribbean women's response to catcalls, sexist jokes, leering and uncalled-for endearments. Feminists are of the opinion that the reluctance of females to confront or report their harassers stems from their acceptance of the 'fact' that men oppress women, that it has always been so and is not likely to change, and for many who have learned 'to live with it' it is not perceived as a serious problem.

BOX 12.7 Anita Hill vs Clarence Thomas

In 1991 President George Bush nominated Clarence Thomas to fill a vacancy in the US Supreme Court. Thomas was an African-American federal judge, with a conservative bias in his rulings. In the US, nominees for such high public

Fig. 12.1 Anita Hill

office usually have to undergo questioning before certain committees, such as the Senate Judiciary Committee. Thomas was questioned on issues the public had raised, including his conservative stand on Affirmative Action, his lack of experience as a federal judge and his views on abortion. The committee's deliberations were inconclusive and so the hearings moved to the Senate to be put to a vote.

Enter Anita Hill, law professor, with accusations that Thomas had sexually harassed her when they had both worked at the Equal Employment Commission. She alleged that he had repeatedly asked her out on dates even after being refused many times. He had mentioned sexually explicit subjects in their conversation, such as pornography, and used his hands to show comparisons of men's sexual organs and women's breasts. There was instant uproar and a media frenzy erupted. The testimony of Anita Hill was televised around the world and in a moment the relatively staid Senate Judiciary Committee hearing was brought to everyone's attention. Hill faced a battery of inquisitors, who were mostly white males and who had initially decided not to bring these charges before the court, deeming them trivial.

Eventually Clarence Thomas was confirmed as a judge of the US Supreme Court. The allegations of sexual harassment boiled down to whether or not Hill was believed. Thomas denied every allegation. The members of the committee who questioned

Fig. 12.2 Clarence Thomas

Hill seemed to believe that if her allegations were true then she should have left the job and not continued to work with Thomas. Feminists were outraged at this lack of sensitivity about women's lives – why should she leave her job, she had done nothing wrong, and her education and ambitions had landed her in a job she wanted. It was clear that a committee of men debating a charge of sexual harassment (which to them was a non-issue) worked against Hill.

In the Caribbean, as in the US and other countries, this became an important watershed case. For the first time men and women were debating their experiences, and while men were aghast at the kinds of 'normal' behaviours that now seemed to be illegal, women felt some degree of relief that at least the work environment might now be less sexist than before. Anita Hill's accusations brought the whole issue of sexual harassment at the workplace to the attention of men and women in the Caribbean. It also highlighted gender issues in a different way – the people who judged the matter were 90 per cent male. This fact energized feminists the world over to work for more women to enter the political arena.

Domestic violence

Domestic violence entails a wide range of abuse: for example, inflicting physical, sexual and psychological trauma on another person in the family or household, or someone with whom one has a close relationship. It also includes withholding economic support and wielding power over a person who becomes afraid for his or her personal safety or for that of loved ones. It is a form of sexual discrimination because to a large extent it is perpetrated by men on women. However, children and the elderly at home can become victims as well.

There are many easily identified immediate causes for spousal abuse and other forms of domestic violence. Abuse tends to occur in homes where a man is addicted to drugs or alcohol, where frustration levels may build up due to unemployment, poverty, or family disputes, and where there is a suspicion of infidelity. These are the immediate triggers that may unleash a protracted scenario of escalating violence in the home. However, the root cause is the acceptance by the male partner that women are subordinate and that his wife or partner is his property. He can only maintain these ideas and behaviours, though, if women are powerless. And many women *are* to a large extent powerless in their relationships. They rely on their abuser (and this may occur in homes of all socio-economic brackets) for financial support, especially

---

BOX 12.8 Violence against women in the Caribbean

Many reports on violence against women in the Caribbean have been prepared to inform the work being done internationally by the United Nations Conferences on Women. The *Fourth World Conference on Women* was held in 1995 in Beijing, China and from that a *Platform for Action* was agreed upon that focused on the **empowerment** of women in all spheres of social life, especially power-sharing in homes, workplaces and public life. In 2000 *Beijing +5*, which was a review process of that Platform for Action, again called for reports from all member countries to assess each region's progress towards achieving gender equality. Many women's groups, NGOs and government agencies, as well as CARICOM initiatives, have been involved in these international working groups in compiling statistics and analysing the trends in violence against women. They have raised awareness of the problem of violence against women in the Caribbean and have been the main advocates for gender-based law reform. Amongst the many organizations involved are:

- the Centre for Gender and Development Studies, UWI (CGDS)
- the United Nations Development Fund for Women (UNIFEM)
- the Caribbean Association for Feminist Research and Action (CAFRA)
- the Association of Women's Organizations of Jamaica (AWOJA)
- Men Against Violence Against Women (MAVAW)

However, even with all this public exposure of the issue, violence against women continues to be the most serious problem faced by women and children in the Caribbean.

Bailey (1999), in the *National Report on Gender Violence against Women in Jamaica*, lists several myths that serve to maintain high levels of domestic violence in the society. For example, there is the prevailing belief that females provoke rape by wearing tight or otherwise suggestive clothing, that women tend to enjoy rough treatment, and that the perpetrators of these crimes are not normal (most likely being drug addicts or mentally unstable, or even from lower socio-economic groups). Bailey dispels these myths by showing that the rape of very young children and the elderly demonstrates that it is not a crime of passion or lust but one of violence. The mass media, dance hall music and the pornography industry to a large extent portray women as sex objects to whom unspeakable things could be done. And rapists and those who commit incest have no set of well-defined characteristics – they can come from any group of men, including those with no previous history of violence, drug or alcohol abuse; in other words, they may be apparently law-abiding men with what look like normal families.

The violence against women continues largely because under patriarchy women are regarded as men's property. Thus, for a long time police officers have been reluctant to intervene in domestic disputes because they were deemed to be 'family business'. At the same time, many cases of violence went under-reported because of the shame and embarrassment the women felt on having to make public disclosure. Even when reports are made, the police say that victims frequently withdraw their accusations as they depend on the perpetrator for economic support. Violence against women is an ingrained social habit in the Caribbean, and whilst hotlines, women's bureaus, shelters, safe houses and counselling are now widely available, a major victory in the struggle against domestic violence would be to recruit men in greater numbers to address not only the symptom but the causes as well.

when children are involved (Box 12.8). Men's power, too, prevails when a woman decides that this is a 'home problem' and chooses to live with the violence.

The use of power, aggression and violence in the home are tactics that are used by men to keep women (as well as children and the elderly) under control. UNIFEM (2002) details some examples of the kinds of behaviours that constitute domestic violence taken from CAFRA (2000). Note that once *intimidation* is used to coerce someone to do something against their will, that is an act of violence. For example, *isolation* is a psychological tactic to weaken the will of the wife or partner. She may be forbidden to leave the house or prevented from visiting family, friends and her church (her support network). Psychological tactics continue as she is subject to different forms of *degradation* – sexual abuse, verbal abuse, belittled in front of others, expected to do the most menial chores, and having to ask for money. The situation at home may deteriorate to the point where every move has to be weighed and second

---

BOX 12.9 Rape

Rape is one form of sexual violence and is both a domestic abuse issue and part of the larger societal picture of a violent society and violence against women. Whilst men are sometimes the victims of rape, particularly by other men, the majority of rape victims are women and the majority of rapists are men. In the Caribbean, rape is a crime that seems difficult to control. In the Bahamas, where rape, including spousal rape, is illegal, there were 111 rapes reported in 2003 and between 2003 and 2005, 26 tourists were raped (Lush, 2005).

It is difficult to get a full picture of the incidence of rape in the society as many believe it to be under-reported. Rape victims tend to be intimidated by the public and insensitive nature of the process of reporting a rape, being medically examined, identifying the rapist, and participating in lengthy court proceedings. Stereotypes about rape add to the torment of the victim. It used to be thought of as a sexual crime and many victims were blamed as inciting desire through wearing suggestive clothing or displaying themselves in a way that might arouse a man. Research, however, shows that it is more accurately described as a *violent* act because the rapist is primarily motivated by the urge to dominate and control. Forcible sex is the rapist's way of expressing hostility and the need for power. Thus rapists are not usually people who are deprived of sexual intercourse; many of them are married or in steady relationships.

Even though rape is now considered a violent crime, court appearances continue to be a harrowing experience for the victim. This arises from the difficulty of proving that the act happened and the intense grilling of the victim that is necessary to prove that it did or did not happen. There are two major issues. In cases where two adults are involved, the court wants to know that the act was done *without the consent of the complainant*. To prove that the act happened against her will is very difficult and often boils down to his word against hers. This becomes a typical defence strategy for a rapist – that they were having 'consensual sex' – and is often invoked in 'date rape' and where the victim and rapist know each other. The other issue concerns *corroboration* of the story. The court cannot convict on the victim's word alone; there must be a witness or circumstances that corroborate her story. Since many rapes occur without witnesses, the victim has to be able to provide corroborating evidence. The judge and jury can perhaps infer that the act did happen if the victim appeared to be distressed or disoriented immediately after the incident, when seeking help or when telling someone. The court also has to be convinced that such witnesses appearing for the complainant are truly independent. There is also much discussion about whether the victim was truly distressed or merely misleading others. Complications arise, for example, if the complainant initially gave her consent and then changed her mind. In such a case the court has to decide whether the alleged rapist honestly believed that the initial consent was still operating.

Rape within marriage (*spousal rape*) was not considered to be a crime until recently. Other than the difficulty of proving that a criminal act did occur, it was widely believed that such an act could not logically take place between married partners as marriage implied 'permission' to have sexual intercourse and a wife was expected to attend to the needs of her husband. It is only with the relatively recent advocacy and lobby of women against violence to women that the crime of rape within marriage has been recognized. However, it is more likely to be proven in cases where the partners are separated or there is a restraining order in effect.

guessed, especially when the abuser starts *enforcing trivial demands*. For example, he may insist on certain minor things as if they were a matter of life and death, such as making demands that the woman change her appearance (hairstyle, dress, make-up) immediately, or bring all his meals to him with perfect table settings. The abuser controls the woman and others in the house by *threats* to kill and maim, to pursue and capture if anyone leaves, or to cut off all finances. These psychological forms of abuse tend to lead to sexual and physical violence (Box 12.9).

It is difficult to know how much violence goes on in families, or the extent and nature of spousal, child and elder abuse, although today more than ever people are making reports, if not to the police, to hotlines, help-desks and shelters. In 1999 Morrison and Biehl found that in Latin America and the Caribbean 'between 30 and 50 per cent of adult women with partners are victims of psychological abuse each year, while 10 to 35 per cent suffer physical violence' (p. 5). In 2005, the group known as Help & Shelter carried out a study in Guyana which found that the incidence of domestic violence was on the rise and there were increases in the number of serious injuries and murders. Domestic violence is now recognized as a little-understood social problem that has links to violence in the wider society. It is not only a family problem or typical of dysfunctional families. Sexist violence against women in families is reflective of the larger picture of discrimination and abuse of women *and children* in society as a whole. For example, in Jamaica in 2004 UNICEF reported that 70 per cent of all sexual crimes reported involved children and 119 children were murdered in that year.

Caribbean societies were founded on **genocide** and exploitation and continued under the barbarous systems of slavery and **indentureship**. Independence has not brought a lessening of the conditions that tend to exacerbate violence – social stratification, poverty, marginalization and patriarchy. While all groups suffer under these forms of social injustice, women and children are the most vulnerable.

Sexism and development

Sidelining and marginalizing women through sexist prejudices and stereotypes, as well as through acts of sexual discrimination, have far-reaching effects for Caribbean societies. Each case of sexism, whether it is in the job market or a case of rape, is an example of social injustice and a human rights issue. In addition, by implicating women sexism also involves others closely dependent on women – children and the elderly. Thus, when women are treated as the 'second sex' and suffer injustices, these are also passed on to others, and in the case of children, affect the future generation. For example, denying women equal pay for equal work and restricting women's access to the higher-paying jobs means that whole families are affected, because in the Caribbean female-headed households are prevalent. Many young, single mothers are employed in services and lowly paid work because they are females. This captive group of women is thus being exploited by sexist labour market practices, with the result that they cannot climb out of poverty. Levels of social and economic equalization, one of the indicators of development, would be even more difficult to achieve because of this breach of social justice.

The incidence of sexual harassment, sexual violence, spousal abuse and child abuse in homes is likely to adversely affect generations of Caribbean people.

Psychological research shows consistently that victims of child abuse usually grow up to be aggressive and likely to be abusers themselves. Those who have not been abused but who observe their mothers and other relatives being violently abused are likely to grow up with problems of relating meaningfully to others. As adults, these persons know few other strategies to cope with conflict or frustration. The high levels of violence in Caribbean societies are likely to continue to increase if family violence is not addressed as a national and regional issue. This is hardly raised in present-day discussions about fighting crime and yet the quality of life for all citizens would be severely compromised, subverting development goals, if this situation is not addressed.

Whether women are being sexually discriminated against in the labour market or whether they are being abused at home, there are economic costs for the country. Abused women and children cannot be productive workers or students. This means that a mother who works infrequently because of abuse will earn less, impacting negatively on the health and well-being of herself and her family. Her buying power will also be reduced and thus her contribution to economic life. Additionally, the enormous investments that Caribbean governments are making in education can to a great extent be nullified if children are apathetic, hungry and living in fear. Thus, breaches of social justice through employment discrimination or domestic abuse negatively affect the development of a country by reducing productivity and reducing the capacity of citizens to take advantage of opportunities.

Domestic violence is also expensive for the government. More and more resources are now being directed towards efforts to prevent abuse, to plan and carry out intervention programmes for abusers and victims, to devise better laws to address the problems of victims and at the same time make the perpetrators accountable, and to provide the police with specialized units to deal with sexual violence and sexual crimes. Less attention is being paid to the tremendous costs associated with hospital and rehabilitative care and therapy and counselling for survivors of domestic abuse.

If one calculates the impact on ill health of domestic violence, the results are sobering: the World Bank estimated that rape and domestic violence cause 9 million disability-adjusted life years (DALYs) to be lost annually in the world, more than the total for all type of cancers affecting women, and more than double the total DALYs lost by women in motor vehicle accidents. (Buvinic et al., 1999, p. 16)

Summary

Sexism, then, oppresses women and keeps them in a subordinate role to men. While individual women may achieve much more than some men, in society as a whole the prevailing sexist prejudices and stereotypes continue to portray women as inferior beings, as the 'other', dominated by men. The highest offices in politics, religion, business, industry, medicine, law and other spheres tend to be the almost exclusive preserve of men. This is a breach of social justice, in that one whole group of humankind is being obstructed from achieving equality. But sexism is more than the phenomenon of social injustice suffered by women; it plays a crucial role in socializing the next generation and has the potential, if not addressed, to perpetuate the social and family violence we are experiencing today.

12.5

RACISM, CLASSISM AND CREEDISM

Discrimination also occurs when groups are targeted because of their culture. Someone's race, social class or religion indicates their ethnic or cultural identification. This section discusses prejudices, stereotypes and acts of discrimination based on racism, creedism and classism. In all cases these beliefs, attitudes and actions threaten social justice and development in Caribbean societies.

'Racism' is the negative (or positive) value placed on a group of people who belong to a particular race or have a certain skin colour because they are believed to be inferior (or superior). Hitler had the racist idea that people of Aryan stock in Germany were the superior race and that the Jews were inferior; this led to genocide – millions of Jews were killed in Europe between 1935 and 1945. 'Creedism' refers to any form of prejudice, stereotype or act of discrimination based on **religion**. Again such beliefs and actions are based on the idea that a particular religion is inferior (or superior) in some way. In the colonial Caribbean, grassroots religions such as the Shouter Baptists, Myal and Revivalism were felt by the majority of the population to be inferior to the established religions. 'Classism' refers to the negative (or positive) ways that persons of a particular socio-economic group are portrayed. For example, those of high socio-economic standing tend to be regarded as articulate, beautiful and having good 'breeding'. Those of a poorer or working-class background tend to be seen as rough, loud and needy. Caribbean societies were created under conditions of rigid social stratification and today, whilst the barriers are no longer 'rigid', they are quite stable, perpetuating class segregation and the potential for classist prejudices and behaviours.

In Activity 12.9 you must be careful to state a prejudice as an attitude to others that comes about through pre-judgements, flimsy evidence, or an unwillingness to see the 'other' as people equal to any other group. A prejudice is often related to a stereotype, a rigid set of behaviours ascribed to a group. For example, Chinese people, to a prejudiced way of thinking, think of little else but money. This is a prejudice; it is an attitude someone adopts towards all Chinese people in his or her mind. It is based on the stereotype of the Chinese shopkeeper, or the grocery, laundry, bakery or restaurant owner. While many Chinese people are engaged in these activities (and that is where the stereotype has some 'truth' in it) and they seem to have a flair and talent for these activities, we must recognize it as a stereotype. An equal number of Chinese people may be involved in very different activities – teaching, painting, music, the professions – but their existence does not chip away at the stereotype because we tend to say that those individuals may just be 'different'. If we stop to think of the Chinese in China we will realize that our stereotypes of Chinese people cannot be maintained. In China, *all* Chinese will be involved in different activities. This may lead us to think that immigrant Chinese in a strange land developed ways of surviving based on memories, talent and networking with others to create a niche that they held on to. And it is this we associate with them today. By assigning certain characteristics to the Chinese people in this way, portraying them as very different to mainstream groups, we are setting up a situation where we can think of them as different enough to be 'the other'. When that happens, racial discrimination can quite easily follow, as when we mimic their language, and make jokes about their

ACTIVITY 12.9

1. Identify ONE example of (a) racial prejudice, (b) religious prejudice and (c) class prejudice in Caribbean societies.

2. Show how in each case the *prejudice* you have identified is related to *stereotypes* of a racial, religious and social class group.

ACTIVITY 12.10

Brainstorm a number of circumstances or scenarios that would help to break down the stereotypes that any identified group in your society experiences.

BOX 12.10 Sino-Jamaicans

The term 'Sino' means 'Chinese'. Several waves of immigration brought Chinese labourers and small traders to Jamaica in the late nineteenth and early twentieth centuries. Today, although they make up only 0.2 per cent of the population, they have been remarkably successful in business. On arrival they faced a situation where they were an extremely different racial and cultural group within the dominant Afro-Jamaican population. As a *minority* they encountered strong negative prejudices and stereotypes. They set themselves up in the retailing end of the grocery trade and were branded with the name 'Chin', and said to be dishonest and clannish. Even so, they began a process of interaction with the Jamaican public who were their customers. Because there was a shortage of Chinese women, many Chinese men in the early days cohabited with Afro-Jamaican women and a mixed race of Jamaican Chinese (or Sino-Jamaicans) was born. Most of the Chinese converted to the Roman Catholic faith.

They prospered and their grocery and other businesses spread across the island. A set of conditions came together in 1918, 1938 and 1965 that sharpened the racial tensions between the groups and resulted in the burning and looting of Chinese shops and injury to persons. In each instance there was economic hardship that hardened attitudes to the Chinese, who as 'aliens' in Jamaica were doing much better than 'natives'. There was also the popularity of Marcus Garvey and pan-Africanism (see Box 11.1), which nurtured black racial pride. Several Afro-Jamaican groups began a campaign to vilify the Chinese, calling for them to go back to China, and for the government to close down their shops

and take note that the Chinese were responsible for the increase in opium and alcohol sales and gambling (Bryan, 1996).

In **plural societies** different ethnic groups live in daily contact whilst harbouring some prejudices and stereotypes about each other. These are apparently 'facts of life', given our socialization regarding those who are different, as 'the other'. Prejudices and stereotypes do not usually, however, erupt into extreme and violent cases of racial discrimination unless there are trigger factors – such as increasing poverty – which encourage persons to look for scapegoats. It would not have been difficult to place the Chinese in that role because of the initial prejudices regarding them.

While the Jamaican Chinese population has to a large extent been **creolized**, they too have prejudices and stereotypes about the dominant group. Minorities also harbour negative attitudes and beliefs (but they have *fears* as well) regarding the dominant group. The Chinese focused on forming their own institutions, and bringing in their relatives from China as workers. Even though they consorted with Afro-Jamaican women they valued racial purity and sought brides and bridegrooms in China. This is a situation where racism was evident from the beginning, and where racism continues, but to a large extent it has gone underground. It shows that groups are not just 'oppressors' or 'victims' but often the oppressor class has quite close relationships with those who are oppressed and the latter can find creative ways to resist and prosper even under conditions of oppression.

names and their stature, the shape of their eyes, and so on. These are all acts of racial discrimination, and while we may assess these behaviours as only of minor importance, we still need to acknowledge that they are born of a prejudice that says 'they are not equal to us' (Box 12.10).

Institutional discrimination

Racism and classism

In the previous section we explored how racial prejudices based on stereotypes could fuel acts of racial discrimination. In society the prejudices and stereotypes of the dominant groups become entrenched in the social institutions of the land. This results in institutionalized forms of discrimination that serve to marginalize and exclude those groups without power in the society. For example, the educational system rewards those who belong to the middle and higher social classes, those of the established or other mainstream religions, and the race/colour groups associated with higher social status.

Thus, the children of the poor, even when the state pours resources into education, receive an education not fitted to their needs and interests. It fits the needs and interests of those students who are excelling. The fact that this basic model of schooling is institutionalized as the curriculum means that the poor as a social class group (or their representatives) do not have the power to change the model to something more meaningful. What follows is *institutionalized classism* as the secondary school system is segregated into schools where the children of the more affluent social groups excel and those where the children of the poor fail in large numbers. It is also a system of *institutionalized racism* because the poor tend to be overwhelmingly black and, in some countries, Indian. It does not matter that black children are found at all levels, what matters is that they are concentrated in the failing schools, while children of other races — white, Chinese, Syrian–Lebanese, and also Indian — are concentrated in the excelling schools. In such a system there is little equity and social justice, yet the present model continues because it works for the dominant groups.

Class and racial discrimination become further entrenched in the society when the students leave school and face the labour market. Schools (or examinations) serve to sort and allocate students to different types of institutions with different curriculum orientations. Academic success at secondary school usually means a route into university and other forms of tertiary education, and eventually professional careers. Success in technical and technological subjects usually means further study too, usually in community colleges, and careers in business or technology. For those who fail, the lowest-paid jobs in the labour market may come their way, jobs that have little security or benefits or pension plans. Added to these segregated labour market prospects, the future for a young, poor, black person is further limited by the hiring and firing policies of employers, who may be of a different race/colour or ethnic group.

It is well known that employers perform a '**gatekeeping**' function in the system of social stratification. They have the power to employ deserving persons, who are qualified, who might be poor, and who need to earn a living and live a better life. However, employers tend to judge prospective employees on **ascriptive** criteria (race, colour, social class, physical appearance) that they were born with rather than **achieved status** (qualifications, credentials, experience). In so doing they tend to give the better jobs to those persons belonging to their own network of friends, family and connections. This is an example of discrimination based on race/colour or social class because the applicant is being judged on criteria he or she cannot change and about which the employer has prejudices and stereotypes. This scenario perpetuates poverty and conflict in the society as the obstructed groups recognize this gatekeeping function of the employer class. These tactics result in social reproduction – those who are poor stay poor and therefore do not get the opportunity to challenge the traditional **elites** for power in the society.

Ultimately such education and employment policies adversely affect development in Caribbean countries because a socially stratified society is maintained, with little prospect of bringing about social and economic equalization. Groups that are victims of racial and social class discrimination in the labour market eventually become an **underclass**, turning to crime, drugs and prostitution; for some, extreme poverty and homelessness result. In time the entire society becomes victim to a spiralling crime rate and the quality of life deteriorates for all. Institutional discrimination, then, based on racism and classism, sabotages efforts towards social justice and subverts the development process.

Creedism

Although there are a multitude of religions and **cults** in the Caribbean, the issue of creedism does not normally arise as a major social justice problem compared with ageism, sexism, racism and classism. All countries subscribe to freedom of religion as a basic human right. On a personal level, though, amongst individuals there will be examples of religious prejudices and stereotypes because of our socialization into believing that whatever group we belong to is the superior group. There are incidents where Jehovah's Witnesses are referred to as 'Jehovah's Wickedness', Evangelical and Pentecost sects as 'small church', and Hindus as 'idol worshippers'. The attitude that the whole range of African-influenced religions – namely Spiritual Baptists, Orisha, Pocomania and Shango – are nothing more than cults practicing *obeah* or 'black magic' is a persistent prejudice and stereotype. Nevertheless, these only become social justice issues when they prevent or obstruct the faithful in some way – for example, from achieving social and economic equalization – or interfere with productivity or adversely affect the quality of life of members.

At the institutional level of social life, however, we can detect examples of religious intolerance and attempt to assess its impact on social justice. Where denominational schooling is concerned, many institutions of learning, while not overtly prohibiting members of other religions from entering, make little provision for these students to deepen their own religious life. In the past and today some of these schools, during the Religious Instruction period, have attempted to provide alternative instruction for the benefit of such groups of students. But this has been limited to instruction in the major denominations and has not been relevant to all individual students' needs. The whole ethos of a denominational school, formally and informally, is to teach and practise their religion and to proselytize. Thus, in denominational schools on the whole, religion is the most important aspect of school life and the spiritual life of young persons of other faiths is neglected.

Largely because Caribbean societies are multi-religious, and tolerance is a human right, many contentious issues have arisen in *state* schools. In the past instruction in the dominant religion was given because in the British tradition education has always been linked with religion. However, since state schools are for all citizens, that became problematic, especially in multi-ethnic and multi-religious societies. The issue is not as contentious all across the Caribbean. While Dominica is mainly Roman Catholic and Barbados is mainly Anglican, in Trinidad religion is a major divisive factor, with large numbers of Hindus, Muslims, Roman Catholics, Anglicans and smaller numbers of all faiths. The present practice is to favour **ecumenical** or inter-faith services and prayers and to follow a policy of not emphasizing any specific religion. Where freedom of religion is everybody's right, state schools are struggling to find ways to fulfil their obligation to deliver an all-round education to all students without seeming to favour one denomination or excluding others.

ACTIVITY 12.11

1. What has been your experience of religious instruction in primary and secondary schools?

2. Do you believe that a denominational school should only take care of the spiritual needs of students who belong to that religion?

3. Is the practice of having denominational schools an example of religious discrimination?

In the Caribbean the European traditions in religion largely dominate and in the past there were efforts to stamp out African and Christian **syncretic** religions that seemed to threaten national security. Creedism, when it has occurred in the Caribbean at the institutional level, has not usually been concerned with **dogma** or beliefs, but seems to have been motivated more by political and other considerations. The plight of the Shouter or Spiritual Baptists is a case in point and Box 12.11 shows that it was mainly the lack of success of the British authorities in curbing what seemed to be resistance to a British way of life that led to extreme acts of religious discrimination against this group. Today, however, charges of creedism are becoming increasingly evident as ethnic groups, particularly in multi-racial and multi-religious societies, make a bid for more national recognition of their customs and practices. This can be seen as a reaction to centuries of creedism practised by the European traditions in religion, in which Christianity was thought to be superior to the other religions in the land. The removal of the Trinity Cross as Trinidad & Tobago's highest national award was largely a response to the objections of Hindu groups who viewed it as a Christian symbol.

BOX 12.11 The Spiritual Baptists

Binding the head with a white cloth, ringing a bell at intervals during meetings, holding lighted candles in the hands, turbulent shaking of the body and limbs, shouting and the expression of guttural sounds, writing with chalk marks on the floor in addition to other practices were prohibited. Leader Archie, who had a church in Cocorite, St. James, often had two watchmen at the door to herald the arrival of police. On seeing the police, the watchmen would shout loudly, 'Sampson, Sampson, the Philistines are upon you!' (Stephens, 1999, pp. 28–29)

In 1917 the ***Shouters Prohibition Ordinance*** was passed in Trinidad and Tobago and became law. It was quite simply an act of religious discrimination which led to the persecution of members of this faith caught engaging in worship. They were beaten, arrested, fined and jailed and their houses of worship destroyed. The Shouter/Spiritual Baptist religion of the Southern Caribbean (namely Grenada, Barbados, St Vincent and Trinidad and Tobago) is a Christian-based religion giving primary devotion to the Holy Spirit, but at the same time it has adopted African traditional forms of worship such as emotional singing, chanting, drumming and dancing. It is also African in being a complete and comprehensive belief system that guides the practitioner through all aspects of life.

It is also a form of resistance that has survived the institution of slavery and enduring persecution during colonialism. It was allegedly banned because it was too noisy, but various historians have suggested that it was banned because it was a vibrant, grassroots movement that seemed to be playing a role in empowering the underclass in a public and brazen fashion, complete with shouting, shaking and bell-ringing. Their distinctive dress was also seen as evidence of resistance and provocation. This example of creedism we cannot attribute directly to prejudices about beliefs and rituals, though they existed, but to larger questions that showed that the British were not 'comfortable' with the public displays of worship (even on street corners) of this group, who largely comprised poor African people without power in the system. However bizarre the beliefs and practices seemed to British authorities, they would not have sought to ban the religion unless they felt threatened in some way. Creedism in this instance stemmed from the association of religion with race, class and politics.

Fig. 12.3 Shouter Baptists in Tobago

creedism has occurred in the past, when political concerns erupted, and today we see creedism again coming to the fore, with politics, race and religion coinciding.

Today all over the world we are witnessing a **nativist** challenge to traditional authority. Previously marginalized groups – the disabled, the elderly, women, indigenous peoples – are becoming more vocal and resisting the values and norms in modern life that are tending to minimize what they stand for. Some people believe that nativism today is a reaction or a complement to the process of **globalization** that is tending to unify the world under some common values and symbols. This resurgence of religion is a political factor today, as seen in the increasingly militant stand of Hinduism, Islam and Roman Catholicism, and can be explained in relation to nativism, which is essentially protecting and asserting one's identity.

Thus, as we have seen, creedism occurred in the past as blatant forms of religious discrimination against non-Christian or syncretic religions, especially where such religions seemed threatening to the political authorities. In contemporary life, aspects of creedism can be identified in how religious organizations, particularly denominational schools catering to the public, treat with other religions. It may not be a case of actively targeting members of other religions for discrimination but more a sin of omission in seeing to the welfare of all. However, charges of creedism are more likely to be heard about in the future as members of all religions try to establish themselves as identifiable national groups that have a right to be recognized as contributing to the development of the country. This is a political context where religion may be what is talked about but the debate also rests on the race and class of members.

> **ACTIVITY 12.12**
>
> Conduct independent research on the following issues:
>
> 1. Examine any incident in the recent past, in your country or another Caribbean country, where students were refused entry to a school because of religious wear or practices.
>
> 2. Compare this incident and how it was resolved with how the matter of the *hijab* has been treated in France.

Summary

Racism, classism and creedism have been discussed in this section as forms of prejudice and discrimination based on ethnicity that resulted in breaches of social justice. It is easier, however, to identify practices that show racism and classism as on-going forms of social control that have adversely affected how certain groups experience social and economic equalization than it is to do this for creedism. It seems that only in the individual personal sphere are members of a religion discriminated against because of their beliefs. At the institutional level, what tends to happen is that religious groups may be discriminated against more because they belong to a particular racial, ethnic or social class group than to specific aspects of creed or dogma.

WRAP UP

In this chapter we have examined the concept of social justice according to natural or human rights, welfare or need, and merit or mutual advantage. These three criteria have been used to assess the extent to which equality and fairness occur in Caribbean society among different groups. The groups studied belong to different categories of age, sex, race, social class and religion. In each case levels of social inequality show that the development needs of the region have been threatened by unfair practices based on prejudices, stereotypes and discrimination. In many cases we have been able to see that discrimination against a group of people led to a situation where they became marginalized – with little chance of acquiring social and economic parity with other groups, and suffering loss of productivity and a decrease in the quality of their lives.

PRACTICE TESTS

Structured response

1 Distinguish between 'prejudice' and 'stereotypes' using examples. (4 marks).

2 (a) Explain what is meant by 'discrimination'. (2 marks)
   (b) Show how prejudices and stereotypes are related to discrimination. (2 marks)

3 (a) Define the term 'social justice'. (2 marks)
   (b) Describe how discrimination impacts social justice. (2 marks)

4 (a) Explain what is meant by achieving 'equity' in the society. (2 marks)
   (b) Describe ONE way in which equity could be threatened. (2 marks)

5 Explain what is meant by social justice conceptualized according to
   (a) natural or human rights
   (b) welfare
   (c) mutual advantage. (6 marks)

6 Outline ONE situation where there is conflict between natural rights and welfare rights. (4 marks)

7 Explain how the idea of a 'social contract' works in TWO different ways to ensure social justice for citizens. (6 marks)

8 Describe TWO ways in which poverty leads to social injustice. (4 marks)

9 (a) Define 'ageism'. (1 mark)
   (b) Explain TWO ways in which ageism leads to social injustice. (4 marks)

10 Describe THREE ways in which women are discriminated against, leading to a breach of social justice. (6 marks)

Essay questions (20 marks)

1 Using religion as an example, describe TWO theories which attempt to explain why prejudice and stereotypes persist in how we relate to different religious groups in Caribbean society.

2 To what extent are stereotypes necessary in how people understand and negotiate the world? Use examples drawn from Caribbean society and culture.

3 Explain what is meant by 'classism'. Using examples from Caribbean social life, show how classism impacts on social justice.

4 Discuss the argument that the aged represent a minority group in Caribbean society.

Challenge essay questions (30 marks)

1 Assess the argument that sexist practices stem largely from gender socialization of males and females in the Caribbean.

2 Suggest why feminists prefer to categorize incidents of sexual harassment as acts of violence against women rather than examples of discrimination.

3 Discuss the view that racism tends to occur in the Caribbean in combination with classism.

4 Using examples drawn from the Caribbean, examine the argument that discrimination represents a violation of social justice.

RESEARCH TOPICS

An interesting study to investigate issues of social justice can be constructed around the prejudices, stereotypes and acts of discrimination relating to ageism. A number of elderly persons can be interviewed about their experiences of growing older and how others have related to them. It could be divided into areas such as work, home and family life, and socializing. The researcher could also draw conclusions about whether the older person agrees with the stereotypes about older persons or whether there has been a spirit of resistance.

Alternatively, the study could be constructed around younger persons who are asked questions about growing old, and their attitudes to mandatory retirement at 65 years, and to the prospect of older persons playing a more active role in social life (for example entering politics, starting new careers and forming social clubs, even marching and demonstrating against forms of social injustice). However, the researcher must phrase the questions in such a way that the respondent is not tempted to only say what may be politically correct. For example:

- 'At what age would you like to retire? Why? What do you think of the mandatory retirement age in force right now?'
- 'Do you think that once people retire they tend to get sick and die?'
- 'Most people have a horror of growing old, why do you think that is so?'
- 'There seems to be a tendency in the society to think negative things about old people. Why do you think that this is so?'

These questions are not directly on target but try to get the respondent to focus on the issues in a personal way that is likely to yield genuine attitudes and beliefs. This strategy tends to be used in researching topics where the respondent is not likely to have thought about the issue in depth before, and so there could be a tendency to adopt whatever cues they may be getting from the interviewer.

REFERENCES AND FURTHER READING

Bailey, B. (1999). *National reports on the situation of gender violence against women: report on Jamaica.* Inter-Agency Campaign on Violence Against Women and Girls. UNDP Regional Project RLA/97/014.

Bryan, P. (1996). The creolization of the Chinese community in Jamaica. In R. Reddock (Ed.), *Ethnic minorities in Caribbean society*, pp. 173–272. St Augustine, Trinidad: UWI, Institute for Social and Economic Research.

Buvinic, M., Morrison, A., & Shifter, M. (1999). *Violence in Latin America and the Caribbean: technical study.* Sustainable Development Department, Inter-American Development Bank.

Caribbean Association for Feminist Research and Action (CAFRA) (2000). *Training manual for frontline social workers and police officers.* IDB Regional Training programme.

Help & Shelter (2005). *Rapid assessment: awareness and attitudes to domestic violence and child abuse in Guyana.* Georgetown, Guyana: UNIFEM and Community/Police Outreach of the Domestic Violence Prevention Initiative.

Lush, T. (2005). In the Bahamas rapes often go unnoticed. *The St Petersburg Times*, online. 10 October 2005.

Morrison, A., & Biehl, M. (Eds) (1999). *Too close to home: domestic violence in the Americas.* Washington, DC: Inter-American Development Bank.

Pan American Health Organization and Merck Institute of Aging and Health (no date). The state of aging and health in Latin America and the Caribbean. Accessed 26 November 2005: http://www.redtiempos.org/ult_not/LAC_Eng.pdf

Pinder, M. (2005). Domestic violence should be considered crime against the state. *The Bahama Journal*, 22 November 2005. Accessed at http:www.jones.bahamas.com

Quamina-Aiyejina, L., & Brathwaite, J. (2005). *Gender-based violence in the Commonwealth Caribbean: an annotated bibliography.* Mona, Jamaica: Centre for Gender and Development Studies and Barbados: UNIFEM.

Robinson, T. (1999). Naming and describing it: the first steps toward the development of laws relating to sexual harassment in the Caribbean. *Caribbean Law Bulletin*, 4, (1–2), pp. 50–66.

Sanders, R. (2003). Crime in the Caribbean: an overwhelming phenomenon. *The Round Table*, 370, pp. 377–390.

Shrestha, L. (2000). Population aging in developing countries. *Health Affairs*, 19 (3), pp. 204–212.

Stephens, P. (1999). *The Spiritual Baptist faith: African New World religious history, identity and testimony.* London: Karnak House.

Thomas, A., & Kitzinger, C. (Eds) (1997). *Sexual harassment: contemporary feminist perspectives.* Buckingham, UK: Open University Press.

Trinidad and Tobago Ministry of Planning and Development. Central Statistical Office. Accessed at http://cso.gov.tt/statistics/pdf/Table5_1998–2000.pdf

UNIFEM. (2002). *Anti-domestic violence advocacy resource manual.* Georgetown, Guyana: Help & Shelter.

MODULE

3 RESEARCHING SOCIAL LIFE

The act of conducting *re-search* involves re-thinking and re-assessing traditional ideas and stereotypical knowledge. It is a search for the 'truth' or deeper understanding. As a result it falls within those critical thinking skills that all persons should master, particularly young people, who are being called upon to 'change the world'. A commitment to research and a good grasp of what research involves helps today's students to develop a critical and analytical stance to all knowledge. Caribbean societies need this sort of commitment, as historically it has been a region where ethnocentric ideas have been imposed and where local theorizing and local knowledge have been downplayed.

In this module, which consists of only one chapter, the foundations of good research are described. It does not focus unduly on a particular approach to research, nor on particular methods. Rather, the chapter emphasizes that the most important aspect of research is the problem itself, and all decisions (whether relating to the approach or to the methods to be used) must be appropriate to the problem.

GENERAL MODULE OBJECTIVES

On completing this module you will be able to
1 conceptualize an inquiry into a research problem
2 appreciate the difference between quantitative and qualitative research
3 develop a working knowledge of how to conduct systematic research
4 appreciate the ethical issues and dilemmas involved in systematic research.

13 RESEARCHING SOCIAL LIFE

This chapter introduces you to how to conduct well-thought-out research into social issues and problems. A 'social' issue or problem may refer to almost any aspect of life in society – economic, religious, family, gender, crime, health, education, and so on. Research or investigations into social life where human beings are involved differ substantially from laboratory research in the natural or physical sciences on animals, plants, human tissue, and inorganic materials, where the emphasis is on conducting experiments. However, within the social sciences there are competing assumptions about what is 'good' research. All research, though, must follow ethical guidelines so that no harm or disrespect is done to persons and the inquiry itself is conducted in a trustworthy manner. This chapter guides you through the different phases and stages associated with inquiry in the social sciences, where the goal is not just to increase knowledge but to increase knowledge that people can use to improve their lives. The goal is human development.

EXPECTED LEARNING OUTCOMES

On completing this chapter, you will be able to
1 understand that the nature and purpose of research varies with the assumptions of the researcher
2 identify a research issue or problem that affects human development
3 assess the ethical considerations that arise at each stage of an inquiry
4 conduct an investigation into an identified issue or problem using appropriate methods
5 make informed decisions and recommendations based on the outcomes of the inquiry.

13.1 WHAT IS RESEARCH?

Social scientists conduct research in different ways. You yourself have done 'research' informally in everyday life and for school projects. Cast your mind back to any time you wanted to find out information about someone or some event or issue. What methods of inquiry did you use? Did you ask someone whom you thought knew more about the person or issue than you did? Well that could be thought of as interviewing an expert! Did you decide to make the observations yourself? Then you needed to have some information to know when and where to station yourself and you had to make decisions about whether you wanted the 'subjects' to see you or not. Research, then, could be conducted obtrusively or unobtrusively. Members of your family might at some time be engaged in research about what to do and where to go for an upcoming holiday, or where and what model appliance to buy, which mutual funds to invest in, and sometimes, if moving house, which neighbourhood is more suitable. Research in the library for a school project might only involve reading documents. These are all everyday examples of 'research'.

ACTIVITY 13.1

Answer the following questions based on the example of market research discussed in the text.

1. If the researchers wanted to find out about light bulbs, what decisions might they make about whom to choose as participants in the research?

2. Suppose the researchers wanted to expand their study and try different supermarkets, to get the opinions of a larger cross-section of people, should they change their approach in any way? Explain your answer.

3. In what ways can these studies be considered relevant to human development?

However, research where the outcomes are about improving **human development** must be attempted in more systematic ways than those used in informal research efforts. If you ever met some people inside a supermarket asking your opinions of a certain product you knew that they were conducting some form of research. In this case it would be called *market research* and they were trying to find out (that is, collect information) from different people about how they assess the product (what are their experiences and thoughts having used the product). Thus, research is about (a) finding out some information (not just any information but specific questions you want answered), (b) from a group of people (and it is important who you choose and how you choose them), and (c) maintaining an ethical stance in collecting, analysing and reporting the information. While these three characteristics answer the question 'What is research?', it is important to realize that different researchers will carry out their inquiries in different ways (see 'Conceptions of research', below).

It may seem obvious, but the market researchers already mentioned made decisions about where and when to carry out their study. They did not stop people on the street nor did they go to a toy store. They chose a supermarket where the product was sold. To get maximum responses they probably chose a time when the supermarket would be full of people, because not everyone would be using the product or even know about it. If the product was baby's milk they probably made a decision to be stereotypical in their thinking and chose to ask only women who seemed to be of a certain age. They would be friendly and courteous and engage the customer in a quick discussion about the product, using the same list of questions for every person questioned. Using this strategy, the researchers would have felt that they would (a) get relevant information by (b) identifying members of the 'target population' who used the product and (c) that they would get the information without hindering shoppers, or being a nuisance, or asking questions of an unduly personal nature (in other words, they conducted the research in an *ethical* manner).

Reliability

Research is often described as 'systematic inquiry that is valid and reliable'. The market researchers had a *systematic* approach in that they had a ready set of questions (the **interview protocol**) that did not vary as they interacted with different consumers, who were chosen according to certain criteria. Great efforts were probably made to ensure that the **instrument** used, the interview protocol, was reliable. 'Reliability' in research refers to the degree to which an instrument is interpreted in the same way by all the subjects being interviewed. In other words, the questions asked and the terms used should not be ambiguous or have multiple meanings. In some contexts, for example, the mothers may interpret the term 'formula' correctly whereas in other cases they may be more familiar with 'making tea for the baby' or 'making a bottle for the baby'. The reliability of an instrument therefore depends on the consistency with which the questions are interpreted in a variety of places and over time.

Validity

Systematic inquiry must also be valid. Research is 'valid' when the questions asked and the methods used are likely to produce relevant answers to the questions posed by the researcher. The questions must be about what is being studied. While this may seem rather obvious it is quite easy for a researcher to investigate issues that are only tangential to the research study. In the case of baby milk, the researchers are likely to inquire about whether the availability, size and nutritive value of the product are acceptable, whether the baby seemed to like the product, if there were any allergic or other reactions, and how it rates against similar brands. They are interested in the consumers' assessment of the product. Questions that are not likely to add to the validity of the study would include:

● 'How often do you come to this supermarket?' (They may visit the supermarket but not necessarily buy baby milk on every occasion. They may also visit other supermarkets.)
● 'Will you continue to buy this product?' (While this may seem to be directly on target, the likelihood is that people may just say 'yes' because if they say 'no' they think they will have to give a reason and then the market researcher may reply and they will get caught up in a dialogue that they don't need when shopping.)
● 'Is the price acceptable?' (Now market analysts have a good sense of what other similar products cost and make strategic decisions about competitive pricing. They cannot rely too much on what consumers say in this regard because they know the majority would always say that it could be cheaper. Such a question would not contribute any significant knowledge to the research.)

Questions that only focus on the consumers' assessment of the product would make for a valid research instrument, whether as a *questionnaire* or an interview protocol. (Both questionnaires and interview protocols are instruments that *measure* responses.) Validity, then, is a characteristic of research that says that the data collected should be faithful to what the researchers are interested in finding out. If questions are used which yield data that is superficial, unhelpful (for example, if the questions listed above were used) and off-target, then the research will have serious problems of validity.

The nature of research, then, is that it must be systematic and employ procedures that ensure reliability and validity. This is because research aims to find out information and this information could be wrong or misleading if the procedures used are not carefully thought out. So, when someone says they are going to the library to 'research a topic' this is just a popular way in which the term is used. That person is indeed going to find out something about some topic, but the skills they need tend to be only the ability to read, comprehend and analyse the material. On the other hand, conceptualizing a research project in a systematic way involves:

● *identifying a problem* that impacts human development
● *formulating research questions or hypotheses* by devising a set of questions or concerns that focus on what the researchers want to be informed about
● *conducting a literature review* to inform themselves about as many aspects of the topic as possible, usually by reading books, journal articles and newspapers
● *choosing a suitable data collection strategy* (or strategies) in relation to their concerns

● *analysing the data collected* using their original questions, concerns or concepts as a guide

● *interpreting* what they have found and considering the possible implications.

This way of conceptualizing the research process is popular among researchers and represents one conception of how research could be conducted. Fig. 13.1 shows this process diagrammatically. However, it must be remembered that research can be conceived differently, depending on what the researcher wants to find out. Other ways of conceptualizing research will have different ways of ensuring that the process is systematic, and therefore reliability and validity will have different meanings (see 'Conceptions of research', below).

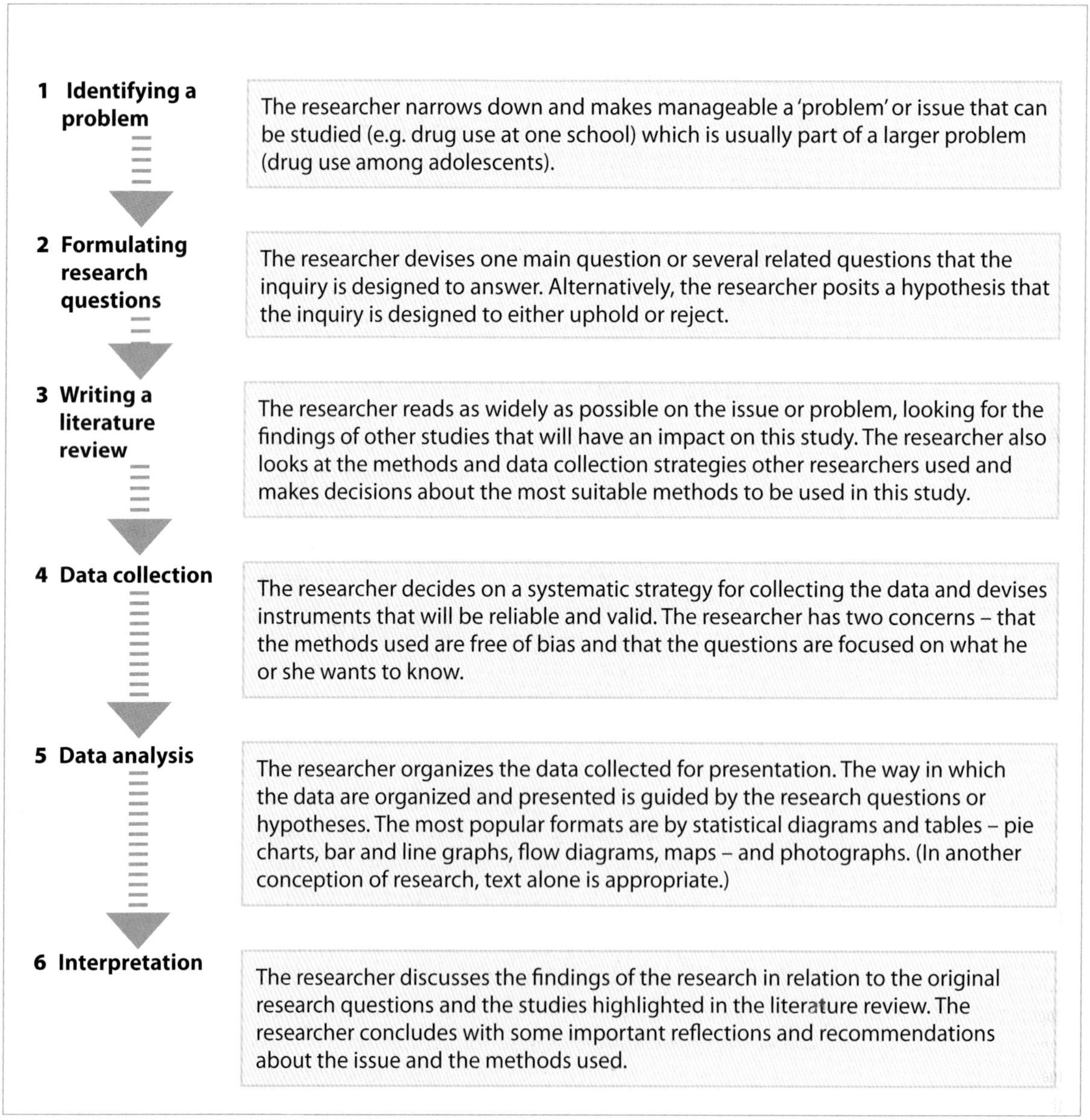

1 Identifying a problem

The researcher narrows down and makes manageable a 'problem' or issue that can be studied (e.g. drug use at one school) which is usually part of a larger problem (drug use among adolescents).

2 Formulating research questions

The researcher devises one main question or several related questions that the inquiry is designed to answer. Alternatively, the researcher posits a hypothesis that the inquiry is designed to either uphold or reject.

3 Writing a literature review

The researcher reads as widely as possible on the issue or problem, looking for the findings of other studies that will have an impact on this study. The researcher also looks at the methods and data collection strategies other researchers used and makes decisions about the most suitable methods to be used in this study.

4 Data collection

The researcher decides on a systematic strategy for collecting the data and devises instruments that will be reliable and valid. The researcher has two concerns – that the methods used are free of bias and that the questions are focused on what he or she wants to know.

5 Data analysis

The researcher organizes the data collected for presentation. The way in which the data are organized and presented is guided by the research questions or hypotheses. The most popular formats are by statistical diagrams and tables – pie charts, bar and line graphs, flow diagrams, maps – and photographs. (In another conception of research, text alone is appropriate.)

6 Interpretation

The researcher discusses the findings of the research in relation to the original research questions and the studies highlighted in the literature review. The researcher concludes with some important reflections and recommendations about the issue and the methods used.

Fig 13.1 The conventional idea about research: stages in the research process

ACTIVITY 13.2

Which of the reasons listed here (there can be more than one) do you think were important in conducting the market research described in the section above?

Why conduct research?

Whatever the conception of research, the reason why research is conducted is to gather information about some phenomenon. However, the reasons why this information is needed tend to vary. These reasons point to the *purposes* of the research. In the conception of research typical of the format in Fig. 13.1, the reasons or purposes why research is conducted tend to be:

(a) to generate new knowledge
(b) to solve a problem
(c) to be able to predict an event or outcome
(d) to test a theory.

Let us consider the research project discussed in Chapter 1 (p. 24). There it was suggested that any form of the mass media could be selected in order to describe and analyse how it presented 'the Caribbean'. Of the four reasons given above, the most likely reason to have prompted this study would be the desire to test a theory we already have about the issue. This is the purpose of this research project. It may be that we felt that Caribbean countries were marginal to the 'news', that some countries were repeatedly ignored, and that some were only represented when violence and mayhem occurred. We could survey the news, for example, only in newspapers, over a period (a week, a month) and collect data which would throw some light on our theory. However, there are some ways in which research is conceptualized where the reasons for conducting the inquiry vary considerably from the four reasons listed above.

For example, in Activity 13.3 the researchers are primarily interested in gaining a deeper understanding of the link between religion and family life. They are less likely to be testing a theory or generating new knowledge. In fact, the four reasons for conducting research listed above tend to be typical of mainstream research conducted according to the **scientific method**. The study on religion and family values represents an alternative conception of research, where the purpose of the research is usually to seek deeper understanding of some complex phenomenon where there are no straightforward answers.

ACTIVITY 13.3

Imagine you were conducting a study about 'religion and family values' as a significant and important issue in Caribbean society and culture, and you asked people their opinion of how religion impacts on family values now as opposed to years ago.

1. Of the four reasons for conducting research listed here, which one(s) do you believe are appropriate in this case of 'religion and family values'?

2. If none of the four seems appropriate enough, suggest other reasons why people may undertake research of this kind.

Conceptions of research

There are three major views or perspectives about research, just as in other areas of social life there are mainstream, alternative and radical perspectives. The conception of research portrayed in Fig.13.1 and the description of market research above illustrate the mainstream perspective, but a problem arises when people begin to believe that is the only way that research should be undertaken. The conception of research chosen must necessarily relate to exactly what the researcher wants to find out. In the following pages we describe three of the major ways in which research can be conceptualized.

Mainstream ideas about research

Conventional ideas about research are based on the scientific method (see Fig. 2.2), which describes how scientists conduct inquiries in the natural or physical sciences.

Chapter 2 provided some useful information on how the knowledge generated by research in the natural sciences is regarded as somehow more 'solid' than knowledge in the social sciences because it has been produced by the scientific method. Many social scientists respect the scientific method and have attempted to study social life using similar principles. As a result, in mainstream social science research investigators try in many ways to preserve 'objectivity', to reduce 'bias' and to conduct the research process in a linear way, moving through one step at a time.

For example, they use the same questions for all respondents and do not become familiar with the 'subjects' (those interviewed or participating in the research). Because they assume reality lies outside a person (a fundamental tenet of science), they try to keep their feelings and emotions (as well as that of the subjects) out of the research and stick to facts, which can be verified. For example, the data they collect are *empirical* (collected in the field) and thus of a *sensory* nature (they can be seen, felt, tasted, smelled and/or heard). The aim of research in the natural and physical sciences is to study many instances of a phenomenon (for example, sickle cell anaemia in different parts of the world) so that researchers can generalize their findings to the entire population (all sickle cell anaemia patients). Thus, in this conception of research in the social sciences there is an emphasis on studying many persons in an attempt to generalize findings. A *sample* must be chosen that is 'representative' of the entire population for whom a generalization will be made. A lot of thought therefore goes into choosing an appropriate sample. Since the research involves large numbers of persons, the data generated usually have to be statistically analysed and presented in the form of graphs and tables, giving rise to the term *quantitative research*.

Box 13.1 presents a brief description of an actual study conceived in this way. One characteristic of this form of research in the social sciences is that the researcher is seen as an expert who comes from outside the context to study a problem or phenomenon. The people at the site or sites are questioned, observed and/or interviewed, documents are analysed and statistics collected. However, the researchers stick closely to their questionnaires and interview protocols (their instruments) and do not deviate, neither do they become friendly with any of the 'subjects' lest they introduce bias into the study and jeopardize its objectivity. They feel that the 'insider' information these informants have would be biased and be based on their value positions.

This conception of research ignores the psychological world of the people at the site. The language used tries to keep distance between the researcher and the researched. They are referred to as 'subjects', indicating that they are passive sources of information. Ethics in this form of research is aimed at preserving a value-free or objective set of conditions, similar to how a scientist in a laboratory studies microbes. The researchers, though, are careful to approach the subjects in a respectful manner. While it is the most widely acceptable form of research today, its usefulness in addressing the problems of human development has been seriously challenged by other conceptions of research.

Summary

One conducts research mainly to find out information to treat with a problem or issue that is of concern at the moment. It may be done through informal and library

ACTIVITY 13.4

Read about the study described in Box 13.1 and answer the following questions.

1. Identify ways in which this study was influenced by the scientific method (Fig. 2.2).

2. How did the researchers try to reduce bias in the study?

3. Why did the researchers expect their findings to be generalizable to all schools in St Jude even though they had only received questionnaires from 100 students in each school?

BOX 13.1 Mainstream research

The aim of this study was to investigate the nature and causes of school indiscipline and violence in St Jude parish in a Caribbean country. The school system was plagued with differing levels of indiscipline and lawlessness, and St Jude being the parish with the highest population densities, the largest number of schools, and an increasing incidence of violence and serious breaches of the school rules, was singled out for the study. There were ten secondary schools in St Jude and one researcher was sent to each school to collect data. The research team had discussed the problem beforehand and created a *hypothesis* that they expected the inquiry to uphold or reject:

> *Students coming from low-income families or families experiencing major problems are more likely to be involved in indiscipline*

They next created a questionnaire that they were going to use at all ten sites. It was pilot tested on a small number of students before the investigation began to assess its reliability and validity. This instrument was to be administered to students and they were asked to be as truthful as possible since it was anonymous. The questionnaire had 20 questions, of the *forced-choice* type, for example:

> *(11) How often in the last month were you a victim of bullying?*
> *(a) 0–5 times (b) 6–10 times (c) 11–15 times (d) 16–20 times*

> *(12) How often have you been involved in fights in school?*
> *(a) 0–5 times (b) 6–10 times (c) 11–15 times (d) 16–20 times*

> *(13) How often have your parents/guardians been called in because you were involved in a violent incident?*
> *(a) 0–5 times (b) 6–10 times (c) 11–15 times (d) 16–20 times*

Since each school had about 1000 or more students, that would have generated about 10,000 questionnaires to be analysed. The researchers therefore had to choose a sample that they expected to be *representative* of the whole population. From a list of names in each class they used *a table of random numbers* to select 100 students in each school. They collected what data they could on these students' home situations from the form teachers and guidance officers (though they were bound by confidentiality and could only give general information) and other school records. They estimated the socio-economic situation of the family from the occupations stated for the breadwinner of the family.

When data collection was complete the researchers had about 1000 questionnaires to analyse. They keyed the data into a computer program for statistical analysis. For example, for question 11 they would just key in '(b)' if that is what a student had indicated. The printout would show for question 11 not only how many students had been a victim of bullying but how many times that had occurred in the last month. Data for each question could be represented in tables, pie charts and bar graphs. They could then correlate or match delinquent students with their family data to see if their hypothesis was upheld or rejected. After presenting the data, the researchers would discuss their findings, consider the implications and suggest recommendations.

approaches or it may be conceptualized in a more systematic manner. Systematic research in the social sciences has long been modelled on the scientific method, even though social issues are difficult to examine thoroughly through the 'objective' procedures of this mainstream form of research. The goals of mainstream research have focused on generating new knowledge, solving a problem, predicting an event or outcome, or testing a theory. This is the dominant idea about 'what is research' but it is being increasingly challenged by alternative conceptions about the nature of research.

13.2 ALTERNATIVE IDEAS ABOUT RESEARCH

Box 13.2 presents a study on school indiscipline conceptualized according to ideas about research that do *not* regard the researcher as an expert in the context being studied and sees a more active role for the 'subjects', who are now called 'participants'.

Their argument is that all research is about knowledge production and researchers have to regard the people at the site as having valid and 'insider' knowledge of the phenomenon being studied. Tapping into and using their knowledge base will help to make the research a more useful undertaking than one where the researcher keeps the researched at arms' length. In this conception of research the researcher acknowledges that he or she has to rely on the people in the context, on their cultural knowledge and 'know-how' in deciding what kinds of data are important and what may be the best ways of going about data collection. The researcher works with the participants to make sense of the data because he or she understands that how the participants see or experience the problem or issue is important in whether this investigation will be helpful or not.

Such a study is conducted to deepen understanding of a phenomenon and you may have suggested 'understanding' as one of the answers to Activity 13.3. 'Understanding' by itself, though, is seldom advanced as a reason for conducting mainstream research. Mainstream researchers tend to focus on (a) producing 'new knowledge', (b) solving a problem, (c) prediction, or (d) testing a theory. This shows the influence of the scientific method on their conception of research. (Box 13.1, for example, describes a study looking for the 'causes' of indiscipline, or at least the factors associated with it – it is a 'why?' study.) Researchers working with an alternative conception of research, however, do not feel that there is any 'new knowledge' to be unearthed about social

BOX 13.2 Alternative forms of research

The study was an investigation of the incidence of violence and lawlessness in the secondary schools in St Jude parish. The researchers decided to focus on only two schools and study them in an in-depth way. Their main research question was:

How does indiscipline affect students at School X?

In each school they conducted:

- long, conversational interviews with five delinquent students and two law-abiding students, the principal, a dean of discipline and two teachers
- observations of classrooms, corridors and playgrounds
- document analysis of the records and achievement profiles of each student interviewed, as well as diaries that they asked the students to keep.

The long conversational interviews are a means of gathering maximum data from a participant where he or she speaks at length on their perspective. The researchers must necessarily be in the school for a long time to gather data and so they become friendly with staff and students and such bonds help to facilitate the flow of information that might not have surfaced in a formal interview using a structured format. This investigation then sees the people at

the site as having the information that the researcher needs to carry out the study and that their perspectives must be taken into account or else the study would lack authenticity. However, people do not just give up their views so easily and thus a questionnaire would not have been appropriate. People have to be given the opportunity to express their views in a non-threatening and relaxed environment.

Sampling is not a serious issue as there is the feeling that any teacher, student or principal would have a wealth of knowledge that could illumine the issue, because they all experience it in various ways. Consequently, this kind of research is not interested in making generalizations, as is characteristic of the scientific method and conventional forms of research. The main objective is to seek *understanding* of a phenomenon. When the report is written up it becomes an in-depth description and analysis of student indiscipline and its effects *at two schools* in St Jude parish. No case is made that the findings should be generalizable to the other eight secondary schools. However, if members of those other schools read the report and find similarities based on their own experiences, then the measures and recommendations that the report suggests may be of use to them.

life. They feel that the people at the site already have the knowledge, which they may hold as beliefs, attitudes, myths, assumptions, ideas and so on, and it is this knowledge which has to be drawn out and reported. This strategy of data collection results in a large volume of text material and is termed **qualitative research**.

Maintaining an ethical stance in this mode of research differs somewhat from that in mainstream research. The researcher is interested in *subjective knowledge* – what people think they know, their beliefs and feelings – and so the stance of the researcher is to approach these people not as an expert but to court their approval in gaining access, to win their confidence in speaking about their lives and experiences, and to liaise with them in the development of an understanding of the problem or issue. However, just like in mainstream research, procedures must be put in place to ensure that the inquiry is systematic – that it is rigorous and thorough. These are ethical issues too because the research process must be seen to be truthful and honest.

As in mainstream research, *reliability* and *validity* are the main criteria used to ensure that the inquiry is systematic. However, each is conceived differently; the emphasis is not on reducing bias but authentically portraying the views of the participants. 'Validity' refers to how *credible* and *dependable* the research procedures are – for example, that the researcher stayed at the site for a long time, that the interviews were in-depth and that the findings were discussed with the people at the site. This suggests that what was observed and reported was 'on target' and not off the focus of the research. 'Reliability' is obtained by using *different methods* (some combination of observations, interviews and document analysis) to study the same phenomenon so that how participants truly feel is brought out. Reliability is a measure of how consistently each person interviewed interprets what is being asked.

Reporting the research may not vary significantly from how mainstream research is presented. Even though there is considerably more input from the participants, the researcher eventually writes up the report and interprets the findings. In the final analysis this conception of research is about an expert researcher using the knowledge of the people in the context to be able to conduct research that is more sensitive to the context than research in the conventional mode.

Radical ideas of research

A more radical approach to research is conducted by 'action researchers'. People who advocate **action research** do not see the value of having researchers come from outside a context to investigate social life, whether the researchers depend heavily on people at the site or not. This is because no one can understand the culture and ways of life of people in the context as well as its members. If researchers do not understand this fully then their investigation may only be partially useful and there is little point in conducting such a study. This form of research is more explicitly concerned with human development than the other two approaches we have studied. One of the reasons for 'why conduct research?' they would answer is to empower people, leading to sustainable development. This 'purpose' of action research is not explicit in the other approaches to research. It is by nature *collaborative*, people getting together as researchers to understand their context better and to improve it. It cannot be meaningfully done by one researcher.

People investigate themselves (Box 13.3). They may get training in research techniques but the point remains that they do not see themselves as 'the researched'. They see themselves as people with a problem that they are actively involved in solving. They may only allow a 'researcher' in if he or she is prepared to develop a social connection with members, to experience the research process together as equals. The researcher is of value only if he or she is prepared to be immersed in the context and be deeply engaged with the people there. Action research is undertaken by people who understand that they have the power to investigate and improve their own lives. Whatever reforms they create would tend to be sustainable because they will have grown out of the collective deliberations of the people to whom improvement would be important. This approach to research is *site based* (for

---

BOX 13.3 Action research

Five members of the Lower Sixth in a secondary school in St Jude parish decided to embark on an action research project focused on improving the levels of lawlessness and indiscipline in the school. They brainstormed the project, choosing their informants, establishing a time line, discussing alliances they had to seek, and the challenges and difficulties that might lie ahead.

- They selected 25 students from across the school, some of whom they knew to be in the habit of breaking school rules, and they included themselves. They had to enlist the help of the school's administration in obtaining permission from the parents of those students who were selected. They received permission for about ten students.
- Their main research question was '*What can be done to improve discipline at School X*'?
- A multi-method data collection strategy was planned – interviews with each student and one researcher; focus-group interviews with three students and a researcher; an exercise based on several school scenarios where an opinion was called for on a discipline problem and a justification of the measures needed to curb indiscipline – this was carried out between one researcher and one student at a time. Researchers committed to keeping a journal describing their ideas and beliefs about indiscipline and how those changed over the time of the study.
- All this information was recorded. The researchers (and the ten students) studied the data, discussed the possible alternatives for a plan of action and used their own knowledge of the context to assess what could or could not work.
- They came up with a five-point plan (see below) which was submitted to the administration. The data to support

these measures were presented in statistical diagrams such as tables and graphs as well as text; for example the verbatim language of the participants in a research report. They made the following recommendations:

- To increase the extra- and co-curricular activities of the school and to vary the kinds of activities offered.
- To give equal focus to non-competitive and recreational sports and not only emphasize those sports that involved the school in competitions.
- To give more students responsibilities in school functions.
- To 'twin' the school with another so that they could visit and assist each other and they could make new friends.
- To vary the teaching and learning methods used and to incorporate the new information technologies.

- As is the case with action research, this is only one phase of the project that could be written up as a research report. *Getting ready to implement the proposals* is another phase requiring active involvement of the administration and commitment on the part of the principal, teachers and students to work together. The next phase is to *implement the proposals* followed by *evaluating* what has been done and trying to remedy any problems that may arise.

Action research should not be looked on as merely a problem-solving exercise. The aim is to educate and liberate. Student researchers working together learn ways of collaborating and interrogating their own lives to devise well-researched strategies to improve their own context. It is a 'bottom-up' approach to research that empowers researchers.

example, one school) rather than system based (for example, many or all schools), and in the process everyone learns more about their role, that of others, and how they are involved in the problem or issue. It is educative and it is concerned with human development.

Summary

There is no one way of doing research although the scientific method dominates how research is conducted in the social sciences. All approaches to research, however, must observe ethical relations with the people involved and in the stance taken towards the inquiry – the research process must be systematic, ensuring reliability and validity. The reason why research approaches differ is because they answer different questions. Mainstream research tends to answer the question 'why?'; it looks to explain events. Alternative conceptions of research seek understanding and ask 'how?' or 'what?' questions, whilst action research is purpose-driven and looks for 'what can be done?'.

13.3   BEGINNING A RESEARCH PROJECT

Any kind of research project must begin by *identifying a topic* that has some worthwhile aspect to it. From a general topic the researcher is expected to develop a narrower focus and isolate a *problem* or *issue* that impacts the human development of Caribbean people in some way. A 'research problem' can be interpreted as a possible dysfunction or some difficult situation in social life such as 'social problems' (drug addiction, crime, homelessness), or it can be interpreted as an 'issue'. The latter refers to some general questions about which there is continuing controversy in the society; for example, the relationship between social class and academic achievement, whether males are being marginalized in society, or the challenges and benefits of tourism.

In Chapter 3, language was suggested as a topical issue in Caribbean society and culture. Many people have strong opinions and judgements about the appropriateness of using the creole in a variety of contexts. Such a topic could be developed by the researcher into a specific problem; for example, whether in social life people rank each other according to use of the creole as against forms of the standard language. Where human development is concerned, such a study could point out threats to equity as people may not be judged fairly based on their use of language. The first step, then, for a researcher is to identify a topic that is worthy of study and formulate a problem.

The problem selected must also be of interest to the researcher or else the inquiry is likely to end prematurely or be done half-heartedly. Research is time consuming and absorbing, especially as you reflect on its various stages, the participants, and the analysis that is developing. It sometimes does not go as planned and so the researcher has to be flexible in considering new lines of analysis for the data. Thus, choosing a topic that is interesting helps to keep the researcher on course.

To conclude a successful research project, the researcher must be mindful from the start that it should be conceptualized in a manageable way. Take the language project mentioned above. If a researcher is working alone and has four months to

Fig. 13.2 Thinking about the research constraints

pursue the research and he or she is doing other things as well, such as attending classes, then some decisions have to be made about data collection and selection of informants to make the process manageable, but at the same time ensure its validity and reliability. For example, questionnaire data might be too limited for such a study, though questionnaires are relatively easy to analyse. Because of the nature of the problem, interviews would probably yield more in-depth information. However, interviews generate pages and pages of data which are time consuming to analyse. Considering all this, at the outset a researcher may decide to interview two teachers, four students and two adults outside the school situation. If for some reason the researcher finds that this is not working out successfully, the selection could be changed to focus only on students. What is important is that at the beginning of a project the researcher, especially if he or she is working alone, begins to think about how to manage the project effectively and what constraints will have to be addressed in order to conduct the research successfully (Fig. 13.2).

ACTIVITY 13.7

Identify a topic for research that you would like to develop into a problem for a fully fledged research project. At the end of each chapter in this book specific ideas are offered for you to work with in identifying and developing research problems. They could be altered according to your interests, resources and time available. You can work with your chosen topic in the various sections below to develop your project fully. To help you, one topic is identified here and taken through the various stages as an example of how you can develop your own.

Research Topic: Students' perceptions of the world of work

At this stage this is a 'working' title (it is only a topic). For the inquiry to develop further the researcher needs to focus on a specific problem or issue coming out of this general issue. In the section below 'Focusing the Inquiry' a problem or issue will be identified based on this topic.

Finding information

One of the reasons for choosing a particular topic is that you know there will be some sources of information that you can tap to provide adequate, relevant and objective or trustworthy data. (Note that in the quantitative approach to research, 'objectivity' is prized, while in qualitative approaches the 'trustworthiness' of subjective data is important to the study.) If, for example, you thought of a topic such as 'Toxic waste disposal in the Rio Cobre Valley', then you must already be aware that there is adequate information available in environmental reports. Such a study could rely entirely on documentary or secondary sources. If this information was not available and you were still interested in pursuing the topic, then you would have to collect *field data* (observations of the site and from experts) and narrow the study to one area, possibly where there was a threat to the environment (where a factory or a dump site was located). Thus, one of the decisions a researcher must make at the beginning of a study is to assess whether adequate information exists that he or she can access.

For a study such as 'Students' perceptions of the world of work', the possible sources of information a researcher will know about before the project starts will be (a) people (students, teachers, principals) and (b) documents (timetable, course outlines for each subject, and records of special planned programmes, such as Career Days, speakers from outside, visits to workplaces and so on).

Perhaps you would have preferred to know exactly how the researcher was going to conduct the study in order to be accurate about the sources of information in Activity 13.8. For example, 'Banana production in Dominica' could be a study done solely using statistics of production figures and newspaper and internet data about causes, consequences and alternatives. However, the researcher could have conceived the study as relying solely on interviews with small banana farmers in Dominica or in combination with statistical, documentary and internet sources. Thus, some idea of how the study is to be conducted will help the researcher to identify the best sources of information for the study.

At the outset, then, a researcher must investigate sources of information about the topic (Table 13.1) and these sources must be accessible. If for example in the study 'The oral tradition in St Vincent in the twentieth century' much of the information lies in very old persons, experts, scattered throughout the country, the researcher may not be able to identify many of them or be able to reach them. Additionally, written accounts of various historical periods may exist as archived data in museums but may be written in a different language – French – in which the researcher may not be fluent. Whatever the data source, the researcher must be convinced that the selected data are:

ACTIVITY 13.8

Identify the possible sources of information for the research topics identified below:

(a) The issue of censorship in the mass media of Barbados

(b) The oral tradition in St Vincent in the twentieth century

(c) The rise of crime and the tourist industry in St Lucia

(d) Banana production in Dominica

Table 13.1 Sources of information

SOURCES OF INFORMATION	EXAMPLES
Print resources	Books, periodicals, journals, newspapers, statistical digests, atlases, diaries, yearbooks, minutes
People	Experts, witnesses, oral histories, participants
Archived materials	In libraries, museums or private collections as print, video, audio or artefacts
Mass media	Radio, television, magazines, newspapers, the internet, film/cinema/video, DVDs, CDs

- adequate – that is, the data should address the dimensions that the researcher wants to study
- relevant to the issue – that the data are not off-focus or dated
- trustworthy and/or objective – whether in quantitative or qualitative approaches researchers want to be assured that the data they obtain are truthful and honest.

Focusing the inquiry

Students' perceptions of the world of work

Although we have identified a research topic that impacts on human development and we have thought about possible sources of data for the study, we cannot begin to collect data until we have focused the inquiry in such a way that it isolates a specific problem or issue. Two researchers can take this topic and develop two different research projects based on the problem they each select. For example, Researcher 1 could be interested in how the school is shaping students' perceptions towards the world of work. What messages are sent by the school (via the curriculum, teachers, career programmes, advice and counselling) that influence how students perceive the workplace? Additionally, the researcher could also find out those perceptions that are quite independent of the school. Researcher 1 could focus and state the problem as follows:

Students' perceptions of the world of work: how is the school preparing them?

ACTIVITY 13.9

Think of how you can focus your identified research topic to indicate the specific problem or issue you are interested in researching.

Researcher 2, on the other hand, may be interested in finding out what careers students wish to pursue and how they visualize themselves attaining those careers in the present organization of the world of work. The researcher may use a ranking of careers (for example, high, medium or low status and high, medium or low income) and assess students' career aspirations in that light. The researcher may then come to some conclusions about whether the careers identified are useful to a developing country, whether the students want to stay in the Caribbean after qualification and, in their own estimation, whether they are likely to achieve these aspirations. In such a case the research topic could be focused *and clearly stated* to read:

Students' perceptions of the world of work: aspirations of youth and the needs of the society

Focusing the inquiry also leads to the development of research objectives, hypotheses, research questions and ways of stating the problem. These are all devices that help the researcher to get a clearer idea of the inquiry. They also are examples of how research can be made systematic.

Clarifying the problem

Research objectives

Research objectives are used to summarize what the study is expected to achieve. In developing research objectives for your study you should keep in mind that they should be relevant and directly linked to the research problem, they must be informed by the sources you have selected and they must be clearly written. For example, for our research topic and problem '*Students' perceptions of the world of work: how is the school preparing them?*', the following could be research objectives:

- to identify students' perceptions of the world of work
- to explore to what extent the school is adequately preparing students to function effectively in the world of work
- to use the findings to make recommendations about the relationship between school curricula and the world of work.

These are the basic 'issues' that this study wants to find out about and represent the most important components of the problem that the inquiry intends to achieve. When you are thinking about the research objectives for your study, think about what are the essential sub-components of the problem that you have identified. Another example, for a study which identifies the research topic and problem as '*Students' perceptions of the world of work: aspirations of youth and the needs of the society*', could have the following research objectives:

- to identify the range of students' career aspirations
- to assess whether students are likely to achieve these aspirations
- to use the findings to make recommendations about the relationship between student career aspirations and the development needs of the country.

These three objectives represent the key issues for the researcher undertaking this inquiry. It is important to be clear about your research objectives because they are then used to compose your hypotheses or research questions and the ways in which you state the problem. They are all part of the process of focusing the inquiry.

Research questions

These are the central questions that the research is attempting to answer. They are derived from the research objectives. Research questions identify the problem and the relationships that the researcher would like to know more about. They are narrowly focused on the relationships between the concepts and/or variables under study. For example, in the study '*Students' perceptions of the world of work: how is the school preparing them?*', the study is focusing on the relationships between how students perceive work and how that is related to their experiences of schooling. 'Students' perceptions' and 'the school' are both variables. A *variable* is the term given to an entity, a factor or a characteristic that is likely to change. The term is more commonly used in mainstream research which is strongly influenced by the scientific method. Other research approaches tend to use the term 'concepts' and in this study it is equally appropriate to refer to the relationship between the concepts 'students' perceptions', 'the world of work' and 'schooling'. (The term 'variable', which is used in scientific research, as in chemistry, perhaps sounds too impersonal for social science research and so alternative approaches prefer to use 'concepts'.)

A research question, then, states a relationship between two (or more) concepts (or variables) that the researcher wants to investigate. If you look back at the research objectives for this particular study you will see how closely they are tied to the following research questions:

1. What are *students' perceptions* of the *world of work*?
2. How does *the school* prepare students for the *world of work*?

Note that the two concepts are emphasized in each question and each question is seeking to find out more about the relationship between the two (that is, the relationship between students' perceptions and the world of work in the first, and between the school and the world of work in the second). Note also that you do not have to have three research questions just because there were three research objectives. The information needed to realize research objective no. 3 (*to use the findings to make recommendations about the relationship between school curricula and the world of work*) comes out of the two research questions.

For the study '*Students' perceptions of the world of work: aspirations of youth and the needs of the society'*, possible research questions might be:

1. What kind of career aspirations do students have?
2. Why do students choose these careers?
3. What factors do students think will influence whether they achieve their aspirations or not?
4. What are the development needs of the country?

In this study the world of work does not appear explicitly in the research questions yet questions 1 to 3 are designed to elicit beliefs, facts and ideas students have about the world of work. The research questions explore the relationship between student career aspirations and the reasons why they choose such careers and the factors that may help or hinder them. Information on the 'needs of the society' (question 4) could be obtained from development plans, employment reports and other documentary evidence. The third research objective (*to use the findings to make recommendations about the relationship between student career aspirations and the development needs of the country*) is achieved when the researcher reflects on the information from students and compares it with the country's development prospects.

Research questions are central to the inquiry because they directly influence data collection. The researcher takes each research question and generates sub-questions to include in interviews, questionnaires and other forms of data collection. The systematic nature of the research process is indicated by the close link between research objectives, research questions and data collection measures.

ACTIVITY 13.10

Read the description of a research inquiry in Fig. 13.3. Given the description of the study, what could be three relevant research questions?

RESEARCH TOPIC:	Censorship in the mass media of Barbados.
RESEARCH/ISSUE PROBLEM:	Censorship in the mass media of Barbados: whose idea of censorship?
RESEARCH OBJECTIVES:	(i) To explore the nature of censorship in the mass media
	(ii) To determine the process by which material is reviewed for censorship

In this study the researcher's sources of information will be people (experts such as media personnel, members of censorship boards, and advocates against censorship) as well as documents (reports, newspaper articles).

Fig. 13.3 A research enquiry on the mass media in Barbados

Hypotheses

A hypothesis is an expectation or prediction about the relationship between two variables in a research study. You do not have to have both research questions *and* hypotheses in your study. Usually a hypothesis is required for studies based on mainstream research and the scientific method where experimental research is important. Examples of hypotheses in experimental research include: 'Temperatures will decrease with increasing altitude' and 'Bacteria X causes the disease Y'. Variables such as temperature or altitude are quantified and the incidence of a disease can also be quantified. In social life 'variables' may be complex phenomena such as 'censorship', 'gender' or 'aspirations', which are multi-dimensional; experiments to determine cause and effect are well nigh impossible. Thus, hypotheses tend to be found in studies in the natural and physical sciences, which quantify variables and rely on statistical data analysis.

However, the scientific method has been embraced by mainstream social scientists so that it is quite common to find social science research where both research questions *and* hypotheses are posed. In such cases the hypothesis narrows the research question so that it is very clear what information is being sought. But there can never be a case where one variable or concept is said to have 'caused' an effect simply because in social life there are so many variables affecting people. For some of the studies described above, where research questions were developed, hypotheses can also be developed. For example:

- 'Censorship in the mass media in Barbados is mainly influenced by the Church.'
- 'Students' career aspirations bear little relation to the developmental needs of the country.'
- 'The school curriculum does not effectively promote knowledge about the world of work.'

Notice how a hypothesis in the social sciences uses different terminology from one in the natural sciences: 'is mainly influenced', 'bear little relation to' and 'does not effectively promote'. In social life and in trying to explain human behaviour it is almost impossible to say that *this* causes *that*, because human beings and the circumstances of their lives are so diverse. Thus in social science research, all the hypothesis does is to narrow the research questions further. Hypotheses can either be upheld or rejected by the outcomes of the research. Alternative and radical approaches to research prefer to use research questions alone as they are more flexible and can accommodate the variety and multi-layered realities of people much better than a hypothesis.

The statement of the problem

This is a concise description of the nature of the problem you are undertaking to investigate and what you deem important about it; for example, the emphasis you will be bringing to bear. It is not a re-statement of the topic or a re-statement of the research problem itself but at least a short paragraph fleshing out the problem in some depth, giving some idea of the context of the research, and why this problem is worthy of our attention (its purpose, its educational value, its perceived impact on human development). Following are some examples of different studies and how they articulate the statement of the problem.

Students' perceptions of the world of work: how is the school preparing them?

This study seeks to investigate how Springfield High School is preparing 4th and 5th formers for the world of work. Informal chats with students reveal that they know very little about choosing careers nor do they have informed plans about further study. This researcher feels that the school may have too heavy an emphasis on academic work which, ironically, is supposed to be preparing students for the workplace, but the realities and competencies about how to choose and develop a career are sadly lacking. This study therefore aims to assess the school's curricula, looking for examples of career development and how the school prepares or does not prepare students for the workplace.

This statement of the problem says explicitly what the situation seems to be to the researcher and where the emphasis of the research lies. It does not mean that if contrary or different information crops up it would be excluded.

Censorship in the mass media of Barbados: whose idea of censorship?

This study undertakes an exploration of the processes of censorship in the mass media in Barbados to illustrate that what gets censored is largely content of a sexually explicit nature. The researcher is of the opinion that the members of various churches who sit on the censorship boards heavily influence these decisions and that a cross-section of the Barbadian public might not necessarily agree with these decisions. It is intriguing that extreme violence continues to pervade cinema, television and DVDs, showing that the moral position of the censors tends to be biased. Censorship is highly subjective and infringes the rights of others. To continue to build the human development capacity of citizens these processes should tap a wider group of persons of different affiliations.

Again, this is an explicit statement of how the research problem appears to the researcher and what emphasis is employed in investigating the issue. In no way does this influence the outcome of the research, which may be quite contrary to what the researcher originally thought. If this happens, it becomes a fruitful area of discussion within the study.

The following example is a problem statement that is *not* clear on several issues and thus does not have the potential to guide the researcher carefully in conducting the inquiry.

The rise of crime and the tourist industry in St Lucia: skewed development

This study investigates the tourist industry in St Lucia to show that there is a direct correlation between its growth and a rise in crime statistics. The researcher considers several factors that may have impacted on this situation, particularly the uneven nature of development, where tourism is the only major alternative to the traditional sector yet it does not have the capacity to absorb much of the unemployed. In a modernizing economy where hundreds of youth are marginalized, the luxury and wealth associated with tourists provide a startling contrast to the lifestyle of the under- and un-employed.

Towards the end of this statement of the problem the researcher is suggesting that the wealth associated with tourism lures poor, unemployed persons to commit crimes. This is something that the research will not be able to show conclusively because in research on human subjects cause and effect is difficult to demonstrate with certainty. The best we can do is to show a correlation and then try to account for it. The inquiry would be more convincing if it analysed the nature of crimes committed over the time tourism was increasing to determine whether much of it was tourist related. Only then could the researcher speculate that the tourists' apparent wealth made them an obvious target for out-of-work youth who committed these crimes. The research itself would have to survey the job opportunities available to be able to make this claim.

Sometimes you will see research reports where the 'statement of the problem' is followed by a 'problem statement'. This is a shorter and more succinct statement of the problem, such as:

> It has been reported that the rise in crime in St Lucia recently has been linked to development initiatives such as the growth in the tourist industry. This study seeks to investigate how the rise in crime in St Lucia may be related to the increase in tourism in that island.

It is a matter of choice whether you wish to summarize the statement of the problem with a problem statement, but they are not the same thing. (In some research report formats the statement of the problem and/or the problem statement is followed by a separate 'Purpose of the Research'. For example: 'This study seeks to investigate how the rise in crime in St Lucia may be related to the increase in tourism in that island' is the purpose of the research. However, the simpler format is to combine the statement of the problem/problem statement and the purpose of the research, as above.)

Writing the literature review

Reading relevant source material is a fundamental aspect of research. You will use what you have read about the research problem to construct the literature review – the summary of information derived from books, journals, newspapers and other print sources. However, it is not a summary of *all* existing information but only the information that is *relevant* to the research questions of the study. Your research questions, then, are a guide as to what to read and how to select information to include in the review. An adequate literature review has the following characteristics:

- It summarizes important information on the problem.
- It reports on studies done on the same or related topics.
- It locates the present study in relation to others studying the same or related problems.
- It identifies the strengths of the studies read and 'gaps' that this study should be able to address.
- It emphasizes the methods used by other studies, comments on them, and compares them with the methods of the present study.
- It pinpoints any challenges previous researchers experienced in investigating this issue and how the researcher intends to address those challenges.
- It criticizes the existing literature by comparing studies and indicating where they agree or contradict each other.
- It reflects on what has already been done and what others have said, and gives personal opinions and insights.

The literature review in Box 13.4 integrates many of these characteristics.

BOX 13.4 A literature review

Topic: Gender and Schooling
Research problem/Issue: Male marginalization

Research objectives

1. To explore how males and females learn masculinities and femininities at school

2. To determine how the learned behaviour of masculinities and femininities impacts on school performance

Research questions

1. How do males and females experience schooling?
2. What are males' and females' perceptions of each other?

Literature review

Research on gender theorizing has gone through many emphases over time. It began with studies explaining gender differences such as the academic achievement of males and females in terms of sex role theory – meaning that the roles and statuses individuals adopt are due to their sex or biological make up (Parsons and Bales, 1956). Academic achievement then had to do with biology. This emphasis on biology then shifted to the role of cultural factors in shaping gender identities (Parry 1996, Evans, 1999), which tended to focus on essentialist categories about masculinity and femininity. Being different was considered to be a matter of gender socialization not genes and in different cultures what was expected of males and females would differ because of cultural differences in gender socialization. However, the relatively new development of brain-based learning showing that there were indeed capabilities and responses that were different and biologically in-built in males and females threatened to set back gender theorizing to its biological roots (Moir & Jessel, 1991, Gurian, 2001). Today, there is a certain amount of acceptance that the sexes are not equal, they are different, and it is this difference that needs to be studied in all its dimensions (Mac anGhaill, 1996, Bailey, 2000, Warrington and Younger, 2001). This study attempts to add to the knowledge base about the differences in academic performance between boys and girls and the theoretical position that has emerged in the Caribbean – that of male marginalization.

Summarizes, reports on different ways to conceive the issue

All the traditions have treated with the phenomenon of male marginalization and to a large extent their findings are inconclusive. Some theorists, especially feminists, doubt that male marginalization exists as portrayed (Barriteau, 2003); some believe that boys are victimized or sidelined in schools, especially co-educational institutions (Sommers, 2000); and, some that schooling is feminized or not adapted to the inherent characteristics of maleness (Parry, 1997). More interpretive and critical frameworks move away from generalizing the issue of underperformance in school as a problem for all boys by pointing out that it happens with some boys and some girls (Gilbert & Gilbert, 2001, Weaver-Hightower, 2005). Critical theorists in particular point to the intersection of race and class in this phenomenon, again showing that it is not a generalized problem among boys (Ferguson, 2000). Feminist perspectives have tended to focus on girls as oppressed by the gender system of patriarchy with only some realization that boys too are disadvantaged by patriarchy (American Association of University Women, 1995).

Conflicts in the studies

Researcher's own opinion

'Gaps' occur in the theory of male marginalization

Criticizing, comparing studies, showing the strengths of different positions

Once the debate moves away from studying only one gender and its perceived disadvantaged position in the school system, we realize that both boys and girls are involved in a gendered curriculum and power relationships that they negotiate in different ways. Today in an attempt to study how boys and girls are different more work is being done on the development of masculinities and femininities, seeing such characteristics as a continuum, meaning that femininity or masculinity are diverse and complex in themselves and we can no longer speak of them as having essential qualities (Martino, 1999 and Nilan, 2000). This study about the development of gendered identities in the secondary school reflects the most recent ways that researchers are studying the issue of how boys and girls experience schooling. The methodologies include in-depth conversational interviews where students are encouraged to speak freely about schooling and their perceptions of each other. In this way researchers can study how boys and girls are learning to develop their masculinities and femininities, how they are similar and different, and how masculinities and femininities impact on learning. It addresses the challenge of regarding 'masculinity' or 'femininity' as a fixed entity – a major flaw in previous works.

Locates the present study in a body of work

overcoming a 'challenge' in previous work

Summary

Much thought is needed in the preliminary phases of planning a research project because the study as a whole is tightly integrated around the problem stated. Identifying the problem and stating it clearly is central to the success of a research project. Based on how the problem is stated, the researcher generates specific research objectives, questions and/or hypotheses and the issues these raise are further explored in the literature review. These issues will need to be investigated through research methods and procedures that are likely to yield the information required. The findings of the study are then analysed according to the issues raised in the original research questions. Any new information that the study generates, together with findings that are supported by previous studies, are then discussed, looking for related implications and recommendations. The research project, then, is tightly integrated, specific, and focused.

13.4 COLLECTING DATA

From the very beginning of the inquiry the researcher has to be thinking about how to collect the data. However, it is only after the research questions have been developed and fine-tuned that the researcher is really sure about exactly what information is needed, its depth and emphasis. Thus, the final decision about how the data should be collected depends on how the researcher interprets the research questions. Fig. 13.4 illustrates the specific decisions a researcher has to make and how they are closely tied to how the problem is conceptualized.

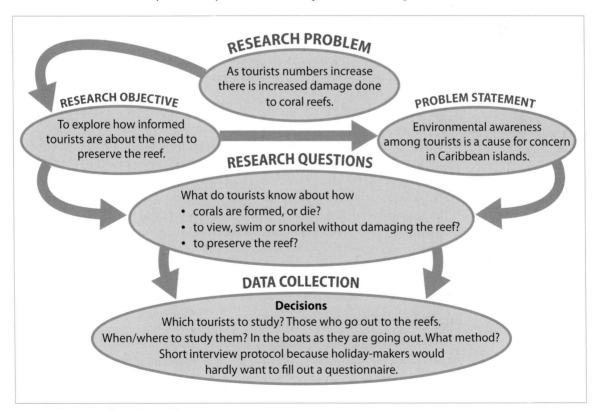

Fig. 13.4 Decisions about data collection

The most important decisions a researcher has to make about data collection are:

- how to select the people who (or the sites which) can help to answer the research questions
- what kind of information is required (facts, observational data, beliefs, attitudes)
- how many people or sites to study
- how the data can be collected in an ethical manner.

Sampling

Deciding on which people or sites to select for the study involves the researcher in sampling. A *sample* is a subset of a *target population*. In Fig. 13.4, the target population (the people from whom the researchers want information) are the tourists who board glass-bottomed boats to go out to the reefs. However, they cannot get information from all the tourists because there may be too many, the numbers of researchers may be few and time may be short. In this case they select a sample that is *representative* of the target population. If the sample is representative then the findings of the study can be applied to the entire target group.

Random sampling

Random sampling is the means whereby a researcher selects a representative sample. There are two kinds of sampling procedures – *probability* and *non-probability*. Random sampling is an example of probability sampling and is characteristic of research that follows the scientific method. If random sampling was being applied in the case of the tourists, researchers would have ready a list of random numbers and observe and identify tourists by a number as they came on board. If the numbers on the list ended in 8, 16, 1, 5, 10, 2, and 20, they would seek an interview with those seven persons on this trip.

In a random sample every member of the target population has an equal chance of being chosen for the study. There is no *researcher bias* in the selection of informants. Thus, the likelihood is that they will have come from a cross-section of tourists who will normally visit the reefs and not from some specialist population – all being marine biologists, for example. (Even if that happens, carrying out the study over a period of time on different boats will nullify the effect of any specialist population.) If the sample is chosen randomly then researchers feel that whatever the findings, they are likely to be a true reflection of the state of affairs. And most importantly, the findings of such a study could be *generalized* to all tourists who are visiting that island and the reefs (the target population). Random sampling, then, allows researchers to generalize their findings.

Stratified random sampling

This is based on random sampling but divides the sample into subsets based on certain categories that are important to the study. Suppose researchers were studying how secondary school students manage their money (pocket money, allowances, gifts, money earned doing chores or odd jobs), they might want to specify older students, who possibly might have more money to spend, and equal numbers of girls and boys. This could be done without introducing researcher bias. For example, lists of fourth- and fifth-form students could be organized by gender. Then by applying a list of randomly generated numbers the researcher could select the desired number of students – say 20 males and 20 females from that master list. This would be an example of a random sample stratified by age and gender and it would be generalizable to the whole fourth- and fifth-form target population.

Systematic sampling

In certain situations researchers may want to use random sampling but because of the nature of the context they cannot do so. Suppose market researchers stood in a grocery store near some food item they were researching and wanted to randomly sample users of the product. They would not be able to use a table of randomly generated numbers. Such a table might yield 25, 9, 50, 12 and so on. By the time the twenty-fifth person approached the shelves the ninth and twelfth would have long gone (though researchers could devise ways to make this work). If the researchers wanted to be able to generalize their findings to the target population of the buying public for that good they might decide to use systematic sampling.

This allows the researcher to select any *nth person* to form the sample. Depending on the context a researcher might decide that $n = 5$ or $n = 8$ and only request information from every fifth or eighth person who comes along. This form of sampling is very popular among mainstream researchers although it does not ensure that *every* member of the target population has an equal probability of being chosen. Some persons will never be chosen; if $n = 5$ then only the fifth, tenth and fifteenth persons (and so on) will be eligible for the sample. However, researchers feel that systematic sampling still has a random character to it that allows them to generalize to the target population with confidence. One condition that might increase their confidence in the generalizability of findings is if the sample is very large, say about 1000 persons. Then they could feel certain that although they were using systematic sampling the likelihood was that they were getting a good cross-section of their target population because the sample was so large.

Purposive sampling

Probabilistic sampling measures are typical of mainstream research in the social sciences and experimental studies in the natural and physical sciences. These studies tend to rely on large samples because the generalizability of the findings is considered to be important. Consequently, they do not seek in-depth data but a 'snapshot' look at the population under study – a quick summary of the state of affairs now. Since sample size is large the data tend to be quantified so that they can be reduced and presented in the form of statistical diagrams. Non-probabilistic sampling is utilized in alternative research approaches and action research, where it is not important to generalize findings to the target population. These studies are designed to seek deeper understanding of a context rather than generate new knowledge, test a theory, or solve a problem. In such studies researchers deliberately seek subjective data because they need to know more about the social and cultural life of members. Unlike in mainstream research, researcher bias is not a major consideration and so a sample could be chosen in different ways. One typical way is by purposive sampling.

Suppose researchers were interested in studying how the elderly persons in an area were experiencing social life. The kind of information they would want would be the experiences of these people, their reflections on their lives, their fears, beliefs, habits and practices. This is in-depth, subjective data and each person generates a great deal of data that the researcher has to manage. Hence, sample size cannot be large. Depending on the time frame and the researcher's resources, it may be that only ten persons could be sampled. However, just ten persons *could* generate data for a whole book, and often that is the case because the researcher remains in the context for a long time.

The researcher can begin in a tentative way by studying one such person. A second person may be selected based on information from the first person, or from information the researcher gets otherwise. Based on data from the first two persons the researcher may start developing a line of analysis and so looks for a third person who might help to deepen this analysis. For example, in speaking to the first two elderly persons the researcher may begin to see differences between them based on their family circumstances. He or she may be interested in exposing as a myth the belief that being at home with a family is comforting to the elderly by demonstrating the extent to which they are treated as children and even abused. Purposive sampling tends to be used in qualitative studies where in-depth understanding is sought. There is no attempt to generalize findings because the purpose of the study is to better understand the lives of the elderly persons studied.

Convenience sampling

This is perhaps the most popular method of sampling that is used in small-scale studies. For convenience or economy the researcher selects the people or sites nearby to study. This may be your classmates, a group of farmers living close to you, traffic congestion near where you live, pollution along a river valley in your area, and so on. This is a non-probabilistic sample and the findings cannot be applied to anyone or any site not included in the study.

Decisions about data collection, then, depend on many factors – namely the research problem, the research objectives, the statement of the problem, and the research questions or hypotheses. Taken together these give a clear indication of what type of data are being sought. This helps the researcher to decide on a sampling strategy, which inevitably leads to the study being labelled as either quantitative or qualitative. These labels should not mask the fact that the quantitative study is based on a mainstream approach to research and the qualitative study is influenced by alternative approaches and action research perspectives. Sometimes researchers use a mixture of methods (which allows them to present data in statistics as well as text).

Methods of data collection

In social science research there are certain typical ways in which data are collected. In mainstream research that seeks a 'snapshot' of a state of affairs the most widely used methods are **surveys**. Survey data are obtained through questionnaires, structured interviews and observations using research instruments (see below) devised by the researcher. Other approaches to research may use the interview or observations but they do not place as great an emphasis on the instrument as in survey data collection methods. In these approaches *the researcher* is regarded as the 'instrument' as he or she has to rely on intuition, experience and evidence to know which questions to ask and how to probe and prompt the participant.

Alternative and radical approaches to research seek in-depth information. This can be obtained through semi-structured, conversational and focus-group interviews. A focus-group interview is conducted by the researcher with three or four members of the sample and has a different dynamic to a one-on-one interview. Or the researcher may be or become a participant-observer and live at the site or become a member of the group being studied. He or she will use as many methods as possible to deepen understanding of the context – largely informal interviews and constant observations. Researchers may also collect data by asking members of the sample to keep diaries or write narratives of their experiences and they will also keep a journal of the research process.

Research techniques/instruments

Research based on the scientific method once dominated the world of the social sciences and many of the terms and concepts from research in the natural and physical sciences were adopted, though the meanings underwent changes as social science research developed alternative and radical approaches (see the discussion above on p. 417 with reference to 'reliability' and 'validity'). Scientific experiments *measured* changes in, for example, temperature, density, leaf fall, chemical reactions, and so on. Scientists relied on instruments they either built or designed on paper to measure these changes. In mainstream social science research the 'instruments' used for data collection are the *questionnaire* (it *measures* attitudes, perceptions, opinions), the *interview* protocol or schedule (a list of questions created by the researcher to 'measure' responses on the problem), and the checklist (a table where observations are recorded). If researchers are interested in collecting survey data, they would use a conventional questionnaire (Box 13.5) or a structured interview protocol (Box 13.6) and/or an observational checklist (Box 13.7, Fig. 13.6). However, researchers interested in collecting in-depth data may choose the semi-structured, conversational or focus-group interview, but any instrument devised will have to be simple as it changes with each person or context studied. Today computer technologies have the potential to expand the range of possibilities in data collection; for example, electronic questionnaires, interviews and chat sites (Box 13.8).

Summary

In collecting data, the researcher has to be clear about the type of research that is being conducted. If the purpose of the research is to generalize findings, test a theory or generate new knowledge, then sampling procedures must be organized so that generalizability is a consideration. If understanding a phenomenon is being sought, then sampling can be purposive. Similarly, in interacting with participants the type of research being conducted dictates the instruments, techniques and approaches used for data collection. If the research project relies on survey data then conventional questionnaires and structured interviews and observations may be sufficient. If, on the other hand, in-depth understandings of people's feelings and perspectives are needed then a range of subjective data collection strategies may be used – focus-group interviews, conversational interviews, journals, narratives and autobiographies.

BOX 13.5 Questionnaires

A questionnaire is both a *technique* and an *instrument* of data collection mainly used in survey research. The instrument (the actual questionnaire) is given out for others to complete or it can be administered over the telephone. Questionnaires yield data that are easily analysed because the responses are usually one-word answers, numbers, or short statements. However, they give a 'static' picture of the participants or the context because they are a one-off means of collecting data – used once without much knowledge of the *respondents* (those answering the questionnaire), without knowing if they are telling the truth or if their perceptions change from time to time. Researchers feel that the advantage of simplicity of data analysis offsets these disadvantages. If most of the questions are of the *forced-choice* type then such data are easily analysed, for example:

1. *To what age group do you belong?*
   (a) 20–25 years (b) 26–30 years
   (c) 31–35 years (d) 36+years

6. *What is the most important reason why you migrated from the rural to the urban area?*
   (a) employment (b) transport
   (c) education (d) other

All the researcher will have to do is to tally all the numbers of people giving (a) (b) (c) or (d) as their response to each question and then analyse the patterns emerging. However, as you can see the amount of information each question yields is limited. This could seriously jeopardize an inquiry

because the choices that the researcher set for the questions may be off-target. This is why many questionnaires have a few questions towards the end that are *open-ended* where the respondent can give more information. Open-ended questions tend to be few in mainstream research because to a large extent the responses cannot be reduced to numbers and statistically analysed. For example,

12. *How do you compare city life with that of the rural area?*

13. *What development initiatives do you think should be undertaken for both rural and urban areas?*

The researchers will have to use techniques similar to qualitative research data analysis to analyse open-ended questions (see p. 446).

In creating questionnaires the researcher has to make sure that most of the questions are central to the inquiry, with only some background data on each respondent if it is necessary. The layout of the questionnaire should be attractive and provide no challenges for the respondent (see opposite). There should not be too many questions and so the researcher has to think hard to ensure that all questions are relevant. For example, if 'age' amongst adults is not an important consideration in your research (for example, information on effects of river pollution in an area), then it can be left out; similarly you may not need to know someone's address or occupation. The less personal information requested, the greater the likelihood that the

BOX 13.6 Interviews

The interview is a technique of data collection that is popular in survey research. The instrument used in data collection is the *interview protocol* or *schedule* – a list of the questions the researcher wants to ask in the order that would be used for all respondents. In mainstream research approaches where survey data are collected, *structured interviews* are used for data collection. In structured interviews the researcher does not deviate from the list of questions, or the order, but it is more flexible than a questionnaire as the respondent can give some added information. The interview is so structured because of the ease of data analysis – although the respondents are allowed

some freedom in responding they are not allowed to speak at length – just enough for the interviewer to understand the point they are making. Thus, in data analysis the researcher does not have a great volume of data to analyse.

Research studies that call for more in-depth data use the technique of a *semi-structured, conversational* or *focus-group interview*. In the semi-structured interview the researcher has an interview protocol to follow but allows the respondent to comment freely as the interview progresses and to deviate from the list if necessary. Conversational interviews do not have a written protocol; the researcher generally knows what he or she wants to find out but questionnaire will be completed. If you are doing a study on income you will have to find secondary data to fill in information that you cannot ethically ask on a questionnaire (e.g. 'What is your salary?') since most people are uncomfortable answering such questions. Even making it a forced-choice item does not make it acceptable to people.

An example of an acceptable layout and format for a questionnaire is shown in Fig. 13.5.

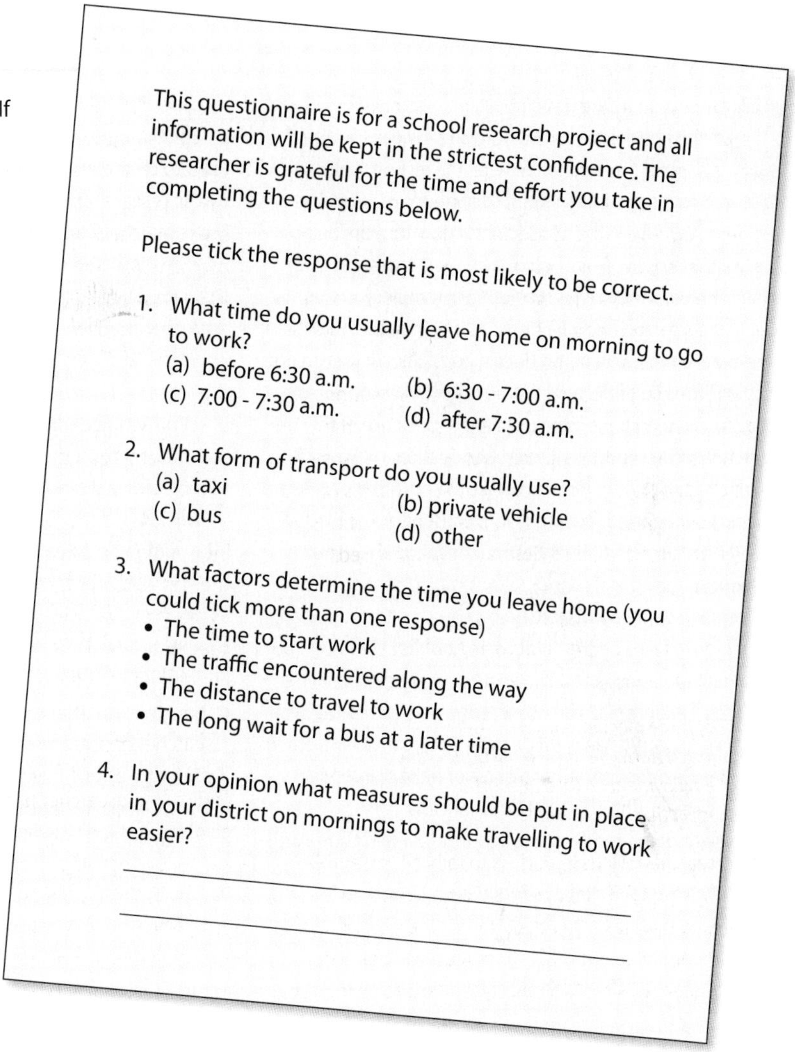

This questionnaire is for a school research project and all information will be kept in the strictest confidence. The researcher is grateful for the time and effort you take in completing the questions below.

Please tick the response that is most likely to be correct.

1. What time do you usually leave home on morning to go to work?
    (a) before 6:30 a.m.
    (b) 6:30 - 7:00 a.m.
    (c) 7:00 - 7:30 a.m.
    (d) after 7:30 a.m.

2. What form of transport do you usually use?
    (a) taxi
    (b) private vehicle
    (c) bus
    (d) other

3. What factors determine the time you leave home (you could tick more than one response)
    • The time to start work
    • The traffic encountered along the way
    • The distance to travel to work
    • The long wait for a bus at a later time

4. In your opinion what measures should be put in place in your district on mornings to make travelling to work easier?

_____

_____

Fig. 13.5 An example of a questionnaire

the emphasis is on getting at the perspectives of the respondent. To reach that kind of in-depth knowledge of a person the researcher has to conduct long and sometimes multiple interviews with the same person and allow them to do most of the talking. A focus-group interview is a technique where three or four respondents are brought together for a discussion of issues under the lead of the researcher. He or she might have a tentative protocol but the trend of the discussion in the group determines how the interview proceeds. The point of a focus-group interview is to unearth the perspectives of the respondents as they respond to and comment on a discussion *among their peers*, which may yield data that might not emerge in an interview between one member and the researcher.

In-depth data collection techniques generate a large amount of data that is mostly text. Qualitative data analysis methods are used to make sense of the data but it is a time-consuming exercise. That is why studies which focus on in-depth knowledge of a context only select a few respondents, whilst mainstream research collecting survey data requires a large sample. The latter is influenced by the scientific method, where generalization is important. In in-depth research sampling is less important as the specific context itself is being studied.

BOX 13.7 Observations

Observational data give important information about a social context and provide a means for the researcher to corroborate what the respondents say in questionnaires and interviews. Observations may be done in an *overt* way, where the respondents know they are being observed, or *covertly*. While both may have disadvantages, in certain situations they can be useful. For example, you may think that if a person knew he or she was being observed, the chances are that person might not act normally. If it was on one occasion that is possible, but for on-going studies the persons being studied tend to become used to the presence of the researcher and act naturally. Covert observation (or 'spying') has ethical implications. Would you like to know that people are studying your behaviour without your consent or knowledge? However, a blanket judgement cannot be made against this technique as the ethical considerations vary with each scenario. For example, suppose you were doing a study on pollution and you wanted to focus on the habits of the public in littering. You might want to station yourself in an area where there are litter bins to see if people really do use them and what they do with their trash. You could justify this technique by convincing others that there was a possibility that a questionnaire or interview might not yield truthful data in this instance.

Survey research tends to use instruments to observe and record social life whilst alternative approaches seldom do so. For example, a *checklist* is the most common instrument used to record instances of certain behaviours observed by the researcher in survey research. Note that in Fig. 13.6 the researcher limits the kind of observations made to what is stipulated on the checklist. Over time, looking at the data for each student the researcher can analyse the data quantitatively and come to some conclusions about how boys and girls behave in classrooms at that school. If the research is carried out in many schools representative of schools in general in the country, then according to the scientific method the findings can be generalized to all schools in the district or country.

However, if the researcher wants in-depth observational information on a few students he or she may observe them in classrooms, corridors and playgrounds and record as much as possible using field notes. If an observation checklist is used it is less rigid that that shown in Fig. 13.6 and the researcher adds or removes categories according to how the situation is developing. In survey research the researcher ends up with numerical data – how many times a student was observed behaving a certain way over, say, a month – while in-depth approaches end up with field notes and descriptions to be analysed by qualitative methods.

BOX 13.8 Electronic mail

Email greatly enhances the possibilities of tapping a larger sample than a lone researcher could manage given the usual time and travel constraints. However, it will only be useful for some studies because it means that all the respondents must have a computer or are at least be computer literate. They constitute a technologically savvy sample. Thus, it will be useful for a study, for example, on how the internet and/or email can help or hinder secondary school students in their school work because this sample will be knowledgeable about this. It will be less useful in a study about how television impacts students' academic work, as most people have a television but not all have home computers or access to one. If you are thinking of collecting data via email, you have to be certain that those who do not have access to computers or are not computer literate (those you are excluding) do not have important information that you need for your research.

If the majority of your class or a group you interact with all have email addresses and are willing to participate in a study you can email them your questions via bulk mail. It is also useful for open-ended responses as the text you receive is already in a typed format that you can 'cut and paste' continuously as you analyse the data. However, you must note that it would not be an anonymous questionnaire

A researcher is investigating how gender differences are manifested in a co-ed classroom and wants to do this by collecting survey data. The researcher devises an observational checklist that he or she will use every five minutes to record observations of the classroom throughout the day. Ten students have been selected (five boys and five girls) to be observed using a checklist (below) for each student.

Schedule of Observations

Date: 20/2/07   Gender: [M]   [F] ✔

Name: Jane Douglas

Form: 4C

Timetabled Subject: English (3rd period)

What is the student doing at these times?

Behaviours/time	10:05	10:10	10:15	10:20	10:25	10:30	10:35	10:40	10:45
Listening to the teacher – on task	✔	✔	✔						
Writing – on task								✔	✔
Interacting with the teacher – on task				✔	✔				
Participating in different ways – on task						✔			
Talking to class mates – off task							✔		
Walking around – off task									
Being disruptive									
Ignoring the teacher									
Ignoring the task in other ways e.g. not doing anything, doing other work									

Fig. 13.6 An observational checklist

you are administering. This strategy will yield survey data but if you wish you can choose to use the email to seek knowledge at greater depth by interacting with only a few persons and requiring them to give detailed accounts, feedback and descriptions. And you may engage them further by questioning or asking for clarification on what they have already submitted so that in effect you have a second round of interviews.

It may be possible to use the email to access business and industry if they have websites showing email contacts, as well as groups and organizations such as NGOs, and humanitarian, environmental and cultural associations.

Using email may enable you to access activists more easily than more traditional techniques (for example, leaders of environmental awareness groups or those advocates lobbying for some changes in social life which could be relevant to your research). Sometimes there will be no response, so your initial contact must state clearly what your research is about, who you are and exactly what information you are requesting, and how you will use this information. Needless to say, there are some areas you should not ask about – financial affairs being the main one.

13.5   ANALYSING THE DATA

Data analysis involves two processes. The first requires that the researcher thinks hard about what data have been collected, reading or examining the information several times. The researcher thinks about this information in relation to the research questions and how it can be organized to show its relevance to them. He or she experiments with classifying and categorizing the responses from the respondents in various ways. The second step is to present the range of data collected in a research report and this varies according to the approach to research adopted.

Mainstream social science research places more emphasis on the collection of survey data than other approaches and tends to use a large sample. Since much of the information collected can be quantified, this approach to research normally uses *quantitative methods of data analysis* where the data are organized and presented in the form of tables and statistical diagrams. The latter include all type of *graphs* – pie charts, horizontal and vertical bar graphs, population pyramids, and line graphs – as well as flow diagrams and maps showing quantitative data (see Box 13.11). In alternative and radical approaches to research the data are mainly in the form of *text* (from interviews, observations, diaries and field notes). Data analysis consists of reading the information, organizing chunks of it into categories or themes that seem to relate to the research questions and looking for recurring or new themes (see Box 13.12 and Fig. 13.7). This is described as *qualitative data analysis*.

Both these approaches present the data for the reader differently. For example, in quantitative studies there is scope for the data to be presented in an array of diagrams and tables, sometimes described as the 'Presentation of Findings', where there is little text or discussion of issues. In such studies the following section is described as 'Interpretation of Findings', where the researcher indicates what the findings mean for example, in relation to the research questions and the research problem. This is continued in a further section entitled 'Discussion', where the implications of the findings and a wider range of issues are discussed, including the comparison of the findings with those studies cited in the literature review. However, in a qualitative study, once the researcher begins to present the data (in descriptive and analytic statements, through the verbatim words of the participants, in vignettes, narratives or stories), data interpretation also occurs – in this mode 'presentation' cannot occur without 'interpretation'. As a result, discussion and implications are also tied up with the stories and portrayals that the researcher is seeking to present. The organization of a qualitative research report, then, differs significantly from a quantitative study where the findings are concerned.

Ethics is an ever-present aspect of research, even in data analysis. It does not only concern people and how they are treated but also involves the researcher's commitment to rigour and systematic procedures throughout the research process. An ethical stance in data analysis requires that the researcher lets the data speak for themselves and resists the temptation to impose his or her own assumptions in trying to understand the data (Box 13.9).

BOX 13.9 Ethics and the research process

Maintaining an ethical stance throughout the research process acknowledges that there is a commitment to:

1. treating the respondents or participants as human beings and deserving of respect
2. conducting the research in a truthful and trustworthy manner.

Being sensitive to the needs and the context of persons includes how the researcher:

- gains access to the site (proper channels must be followed in getting permission to study members of an organization – a school, workplace, a group)
- treats with minors (if students and children are involved in the study, permission must be sought from parents and guardians)
- introduces the study (the participants should be given enough information about the study, so that they can make up their mind about participating)
- collects data:
  - whatever measures are used, the researcher should keep in mind that the information is confidential and if it is to be disclosed then that should be discussed with participants
  - in collecting data the researcher must always treat participants with politeness and respect so that if they do not wish to answer a particular question then that wish is respected
  - permission should be sought from the interviewees if the session is to be audio-taped

- there should be strong justification for unobtrusive measures
- leaves the site (in some cases, especially where the research was conducted in an organization, the researcher should give members who participated some indication of the findings of the study or a copy of it).

Conducting research in a truthful and trustworthy manner means that the researcher should:

- ensure that there is linkage between the research problem, the research objectives, the statement of the problem and the research questions (this makes the study focused and is a systematic way of outlining the problem)
- select appropriate studies to report on and analyse for the literature review (this is an effort to present the most relevant studies and their findings and the context in which the present research is to be located)
- reduce bias as much as possible in collecting data, especially in alternative approaches where subjective data are important and the researcher is the 'instrument of data collection'
- design instruments according to principles of validity and reliability
- analyse the data using multiple sources to corroborate evidence and keep a paper trail of decisions made and analytic procedures used to support the analysis
- present findings without attempting to change or alter data from the participants
- report the findings truthfully and maintain confidentiality when reporting.

Summary

Data analysis varies according to the type of research project carried out. Mainstream research based largely on survey data is analysed using a range of quantitative techniques and presented as statistical graphs, diagrams and tables. These show trends and patterns in the data which are interpreted and discussed in subsequent sections of the research report. Alternative and radical approaches to research, relying mainly on interview and observational data (mostly text), are analysed by examining the statements or behaviours of persons and looking for trends, patterns, areas of emphasis or things that are ignored. When data analysis is presented in a qualitative-type study, interpretation and discussion come immediately into play so there are no separate sections relating to findings, interpretation and discussion as in the reporting of mainstream research. In both types of research, ethical considerations at the stage of data analysis require the researcher to be true to the data and not concoct or manufacture relationships that are not present.

13.6

WRAPPING UP THE STUDY
Conclusion

After the data have been presented, interpreted and discussed, the researchers conclude, summarizing the main findings and their implications, and stating how those findings relate to the studies already done on this problem. For example, the findings may disagree with or support previous work or extend the knowledge gained by these earlier studies. The study may also suggest lines for further research by other researchers to deepen our knowledge of this phenomenon. At this point the researcher or researchers could mention some factors considered to be limitations of the study – for example, if the sample was small or only a convenience sample, or if a significant population was left out that might have impacted differently on the findings (those of a certain age, socio-economic group, or occupation), or if data collection took place in a short period of time, where time may have mattered to the outcome of the study. For example, in a study of traffic congestion conducted during the month of September there could have been quite different findings if the data collection period had extended to Christmas. The conclusion ends with some recommendations that the researcher believes are appropriate and could have a significant impact on the problem, but the recommendations must be related to what the study revealed about the problem.

References

An important aspect of scholarly work is the list of references at the end of the study. This serves several purposes. It gives readers as much information as possible on various texts and articles consulted and cited so that they will be able to source the same material if they wish. The materials read by the researcher inform readers whether the study is based on wide or limited reading on the topic and whether a variety of references was used. This could be just for information purposes but it is also important in evaluating the study, always remembering that some topics may be difficult to source in a variety of media, for example, pollution around dump sites in the Caribbean, the incidence of diabetes in ethnic communities in the Caribbean, and so on. The most important reason, however, for citing the works used is to acknowledge the authors and their ideas and thus avoid the charge of *plagiarism* – using someone else's work (their ideas or their actual words) without acknowledging the source.

Various styles are used in scholarly works to organize the reference list, one common one being that of the American Psychological Association (the APA system; see Box 13.10). There is sometimes confusion as to whether 'references' or 'bibliography' is the correct term for this list. Normally 'bibliography' refers to works that were consulted as background and extended or further reading, while the list of 'references' includes only those texts or sources which are specifically mentioned in the paper. The APA also gives guidelines on quoting and citing other persons' works within the text.

BOX 13.10 Conventions of the APA style

Referring to works in-text

- If you are citing a work by summarizing it or making a reference to it without actually quoting it, give the author and date of publication within the sentence, in brackets, e.g. (Johnson, 2007).
- If you are quoting the author's words the page number is added, e.g. (Johnson, 2007, p. 2). If the work is an electronic source where page numbers may not be given, refer to the paragraph, e.g. (Johnson, 2007, ¶ 2). The symbol ¶ is used for 'paragraph'.
- If there are three or more authors, include all their names and the date of publication, e.g. (Grey, Baylor, Messiah and Jones, 2006) the first time the work is cited and subsequently use (Grey et al., 2006).

The reference list

The list of references is placed after the text but before any appendixes and has the following style characteristics:

- It is arranged alphabetically.
- The authors' surnames are placed first, followed by the date of publication.
- The place of publication is placed before the publisher.
- Italics are used for the names of books and journals.
- For electronic works as much information as possible should be provided (e.g. author's name, date of publication, date of retrieval, title of the document, and the web address or URL – uniform resource locator).

The following examples show the punctuation and styles used for different types of work.

- ***Book – one author:*** Fay, B. (1996). *Contemporary philosophy of social science.* Oxford, UK: Blackwell.
- ***Organization as author:*** Caribbean Examinations Council. (1999). *Social studies syllabus effective for teaching from September 2000 and for examinations from May/June 2002.* St. Michael, Barbados: Author.
- ***Three authors:*** Dynneson, T. L., Gross, R. E., & Berson, M. J. (2003). *Designing effective instruction for secondary social studies* (3rd. ed.). Upper Saddle River, NJ: Merrill Prentice Hall.
- ***Journal article:*** Garratt, D., & Piper, H. (2003). Citizenship education and the monarchy: examining the contradictions. *British Journal of Educational Studies,* 51(2), 128–148.
- ***Edited book:*** Farganis, J. (Ed.). (2000). *Readings in social theory: The classic tradition to post-modernism* (3rd. ed.). Boston, MA: McGraw Hill.
- ***Internet source:*** Collins-Kreiner, N. (2005). Maps and meaning: Reading the map of the holy land. *The Qualitative Report, 10*(2), 257–275. Retrieved (January 3rd 2007), from http://www.nova.edu/ssss/QR/QR10–2/collins-kreiner.pdf

Appendix

The final section of a research study is the appendix, though not all studies will have one. Additional information that is pertinent to the study is included in the appendix. In a study of river pollution, a map of the parts of the river studied is directly relevant to the substance of the research topic and should be included in the text. A map showing the location of the entire river within the region or country is also relevant, but less so, and could be safely included in the appendix. Such a map provides background or context for the study. It is often the case that data are included in appendices that are considered too detailed for the main text. Appendices are usually labelled by a letter, as 'Appendix A', 'Appendix B', and so on.

BOX 13.11 An example of a mainstream or quantitative study

Introduction

The influence of television on youth, particularly cable television and the foreign mass media, has been widely reported in the press and various scholarly studies. They portray television as a major force in youth socialization, predisposing them to violence, aggression and anti-social behaviours. This study conducted locally is an attempt to compare the habits and attitudes of a small cross-section of Caribbean youth with what is reported in this international literature. The purpose of this study is to assess the general orientation of youth to the media and to determine whether this orientation is helpful in the human development of Caribbean youth.

Research Topic/Problem
Television and its influences on youth
Research Objectives
1. To examine youth's television viewing habits and their attitudes to television programming.
2. To explore the nature of television programming that would help in the human development potential of youth
Problem Statement
Youth is seemingly susceptible to the violence and aggression portrayed on television. This study investigates the habits and attitudes of youth to television programmes in the Happy Valley community.
Research Questions
1. How often do youth look at television?
2. What are their favourite television programmes?
3. Why do they watch these shows?
4. What are their views on television programming?

Literature review

The international literature shows that more youth in the world watch television than listen to the radio, read newspapers or use the internet. For youth, then, it is the dominant form of the mass media. Gigli (2004) says that 'average daily use of television among school age children around the world with access ranges from between 1.5 hours to more than 4 hours' (p. 2). For small developing nations, then, what is actually purveyed on television screens becomes extremely important as they constitute a major socialization agency for our young people.

Commentary by Caribbean health professionals deplores the ways in which violence is constantly showcased on television – both in local news programming and in the entertainment fare provided by cable television (Brown, 2005). In a society where violence is a major part of daily life and entertainment, organizations such as PAHO fear that our youth will be influenced to become violent, aggressive and anti-social. In the Caribbean mental health experts extend this concern to a constant feeling of fear, especially of youth in inner city areas, and a lack of sensitivity displayed by the media to victims of violence (Robinson, 2005).

There are relatively few studies on how youth actually assess their television viewing and the programmes they tend to watch. Is it because they have few choices or they actually like to watch violence and anti-social themes? UNICEF (2004) has undertaken focus group interviews with youth across the globe in an effort to gather data on this issue and it is interesting that while the rest of the population feel that the media showcases youth more than others, youth feels that the media stereotype them and portray them negatively.

The present study is located within this body of international research data and presents survey data of a cross-section of youth in a Caribbean community. It adds to the growing body of work on youth and its challenges and possibilities in the Caribbean, as few studies have yet been undertaken specifically on youth and television with an emphasis on their assessment of the medium. While survey data provide only a 'snapshot' this study could be extended by researchers in the future to conduct qualitative studies to unearth more in-depth perspectives.

Data collection

30 students (15 girls and 15 boys) were chosen by stratified random sample from the Happy Valley Community School from forms 1 to 5. They were approached individually and asked whether they would like to participate in the study. All agreed. The researcher then obtained permission from their parents and the school's principal to conduct the study. A five-item questionnaire was administered to all students on one day after school. Three items were of the forced-choice type and two were open-ended. (The instrument is included opposite.)

Data analysis

(a) Presentation of findings

Figure 1 opposite shows that most students in the sample watched on average 1 to 2 hours of television every day. And a significant number watched 3 to 4 hours daily.

This questionnaire is designed to elicit data on youth and television viewing. There are no right and wrong answers – all information is welcome. Your responses will be treated in the strictest confidence and the questionnaire is anonymous.

M ☐   F ☐

1. How many hours of television do you estimate that you watch every day?
    (a) 30 minutes   (b) 1-2 hours   (c) 3-4 hours   (d) more than 5 hours

2. Which day of the week do you watch more television than other days?
    (a) Fridays   (b) Saturdays   (c) Sundays   (d) no particular day

3. Rank your 4 favourite television programmes by preference.
    (a) _____   (c) _____
    (b) _____   (d) _____

4 Give ONE reason why you like to watch EACH programme:
    (a) _____
    (b) _____
    (c) _____
    (d)_____

5. What kinds of programming would you like to see more of on television and give your reasons?
    (a) _____
    (b) _____
    (c) _____
    (d) _____

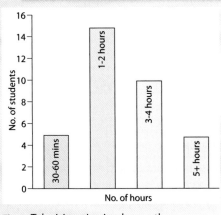

Fig. 1 Television viewing by youth

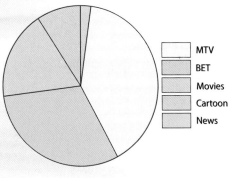

Fig. 2 Pie graph showing television programming preferences

(continues overleaf)

BOX 13.11 continued

Figure 2 shows that most students watch music videos, black entertainment programmes and movies. Only some are interested in cartoons and foreign news. There was no mention of documentaries, local television programming, travel, soap operas, sports, business or technology.

Table 1 below tabulates the reasons that students offer about their television viewing preferences. Table 2 below illustrates what characteristics students would like to see in new television programming.

(b) Data interpretation

The data show that the youth at Happy Valley community demonstrate similar television viewing habits to those internationally. Figure 1 indicates that most youth watch 1–2 hours of television daily and some many more hours than that. Only a minority of students watched less than one hour of television a week. Their major interests were music videos and black entertainment programmes (Figure 2); surprisingly movies were not so highly regarded, perhaps because many are re-runs and follow similar or even identical themes. Table 1 illustrates that youth seem to appreciate the emphasis on youth culture in music videos and other kinds of programming in black entertainment on the US cable networks. It is possible that they see scope to imitate or try certain fashions shown on these programmes and use this medium to be informed about youth culture, especially about music worldwide, and especially in the US. At the same time, some of them saw elements that focused on the kinds of knowledge that could be obtained from watching these types of programmes; that it was not only for entertainment but for information as well, especially for those for whom music is a hobby. Table 2 indicates that youth are not necessarily 'tied' to the types of programmes they watch now but could assess their worth and identify 'gaps' that are at present inhibiting the development of young people.

(c) Discussion of Findings

Since television is a daily phenomenon in the lives of youth, we must agree with Gigli (2004) that it performs a major socialization function. While youth seem to be uncritical of the violence portrayed in music videos, movies and even cartoons, it is quite possible that they are not aware about how it may contribute to mental health problems, as was suggested by Brown (2005). Thus, it is heartening to see that

Table 1 Characteristics of good programming

NUMBER OF STUDENTS	TELEVISION PROGRAMMES	REASONS FOR VIEWING
9	Music videos	Highly entertaining, visual content, youth culture
8	Music videos	Information on music, singers, entertainment industry, trends over time
7	BET	Entertaining, sexuality content, fashion, styles
3	Movies	Action movies, fighting, weapons technology
1	Movies	The storyline, interesting characters, morals
1	Cartoons	Relaxation, funny
1	Cartoons	Everything in adult movies can be found in cartoons

Table 2 Television of the future

NUMBER OF STUDENTS	WHAT TELEVISION PROGRAMMES SHOULD BE LIKE
13	More realistic shows about ordinary people's lives
10	More 'serious' issues but presented in a less 'talking down' manner
5	More on youth in different parts of the world
1	More on youth in news, not just sensational bits but about their achievements and challenges
1	More on youth programmes where youth are not only showcased but youth are involved with the directors, producers and creative personnel

given a choice they would not be so wrapped up in the kinds of programmes they are criticized for watching and look for those that are more uplifting for youth. However, youth do not design and create media; that is done by metropolitan countries and disseminated worldwide, endeavouring to incorporate all youth into similar lifestyles and attitudes based on the US model. While the students in this study did not criticize the dominant US focus in television programming, they did call for a more enlightened view of youth on television, meaning that the present programmes tend to be what adults think youth want to see. This study, then, supports the view that more youth should be involved in developing programmes for youth in whatever ways they may be able to contribute.

Conclusion

This community of students in the Caribbean demonstrates similar television viewing habits and attitudes to youth

worldwide. It therefore supports studies done on this problem before. However, it goes further by suggesting that youth have certain viewing preferences because they have to choose from programming that seems to be similarly flawed. As a result they choose those programmes that seem to be created for youth but the ideas about youth are from an adult's perspective. While youth have been able to penetrate this state of affairs they do not seem to be as concerned about the lack of Caribbean content in television programming.

This study is limited by the small sample size and so the results cannot be generalized to a wider body of students but certainly it presents ideas that could be built on by a larger-scale study. One finding that other researchers may want to pursue is the lack of criticism about the dominance of the US media in the Caribbean and the dearth of locally produced programmes.

BOX 13.12 A qualitative study

Qualitative studies tend to use only a few participants so that it is possible for you to conduct such a study with the minimum of inconvenience. You would not have to construct and administer questionnaires to a large sample for example. However, when it comes to analysing the data it could get tedious as you can collect a lot of data through conversational interviews. The study outlined below may encourage you to try what is still an alternative approach to research. Although the whole study is outlined, emphasis is placed on data analysis procedures in qualitative research.

Research Problem
The apparent loss of cultural knowledge in Caribbean society today about herbs and other plants. (Here you may choose any topic that you are interested in – music, dance, languages, culinary practices, technologies and so on.)

Research Objectives
To explore the knowledge that older people have about herbs and plants and assess how that knowledge is used today.

Problem Statement
The cultural knowledge that older persons possess is in danger of dying out with them. This study seeks to investigate whether

the cultural knowledge that older persons possess about herbs and plants proves useful in everyday life.

Research Questions
1. *What knowledge do older persons possess about herbs and other plants?*
2. *Do they use that knowledge in any way?*
3. *What factors hinder or encourage the use of this cultural knowledge?*

Literature review
This may be a difficult area to source previous studies. In such a case you look for general themes – for example, studies about cultural erasure, cultural loss, modernization, urban living, alternative healing practices in the Caribbean and the importance of herbs in Caribbean cuisine. Also of relevance is the status of older people in the society and how younger people assess their knowledge. You may want to look at studies of other societies where plants and herbs for cooking and healing are part of the traditional knowledge store and still used today in their households – for example, the Amerindian groups in the Caribbean or indigenous peoples elsewhere.   (continues overleaf)

BOX 13.12 continued

Data collection

Your sample may consist of five or six persons aged perhaps 60 years and older, but you may want to seek a distinction between rural and urban living by interviewing some in the country and some in the town. Long conversational interviews that you audio tape are perhaps the best method of data collection here. (However, the longer the interview the more typing will have to be done to convert the oral information on the tape to a typed transcript that is more suitable for data analysis.) It is a good idea to have a list of areas that you are interested in to keep the interview focused, but the participants should be able to speak freely on the topics they want to discuss. Some possibilities are:

- 'When you were growing up did you learn a lot about how to use plants for medicines, say?'
- 'Nowadays people go to the pharmacy for everything; what alternatives were used when you were growing up?'
- 'Do you teach your children and grandchildren these things?'
- 'Out of all this knowledge you have, what do you actually use today?'

Data analysis

The typed transcripts of the interviews are used to analyse the data. Make several copies. Leave a wide margin on the right to write in themes you detect in the data (Fig. 13.7).

Read and re-read the transcripts several times to get a 'feel' for the different lines of analysis that may be emerging. On a separate piece of paper jot down the ideas you have about themes in the data, using one word or as few words as possible. These themes will be used to code the data. Read each transcript again and where the data may be saying something close to one of the themes you identified, note that in the wide right-hand margin. For example, if the interviewee is saying something about using herbs to cook, you could code that information as 'cook' but the person may be more specific as there are several processes involved in food preparation (e.g. preserving), so that codes and sub-codes could be identified.

The following codes may or may not be detected in each transcript. They identify parts of the text where the interviewee may be speaking generally of using herbs in cooking and more specifically to cure or preserve meats, to add unique flavours to food, to create rich colour, or to enhance its appearance.

Code/subcode: cook/cure cook/taste
cook/colour cook/garnish

The excerpt from an interview transcript in Fig. 13.7 has been coded by the researcher. It brings up ideas about criticism of the present state of health knowledge among the professionals in the society – doctors and the legal profession. It suggests that sidelining bush medicines involves us in a heavy import bill from western countries and the unwillingness to see the medicinal value in

---

Lucilla, p. 3

R: Yes. We used to use so much different thing for cold dat doctors today don't even know bout. We used to boil Christmas Bush and add a lil sugar, yes man, and dat used to go down with no problem man. And it have a thing call vervine when your blood get hot and it need to cool and calm down – ah tell you doctors today only know about Buckleys! And if yuh look good Buckleys must have some ah dat same Christmas Bush…

criticism of scientific medicine [critic–doc]

And you know in dem times marijuana, we used to use it for the wheezing. You take the leaf and make tea and dat real good for the asthma, people swear by dat. But what you think? Today dat same herb is illegal and you have to go buy medicine from foreign …

medical use [med-cold]

med-asth

critic-law

Fig. 13.7 Qualitative data analysis

BOX 13.12 continued

marijuana also involves us in medical imports from the West. The researcher has used codes to include both types of criticisms and information on the medical use of herbs for two ailments. Reading over the transcript at another time the researcher may 'see' more ideas that link up to those expressed by other respondents.

Findings

This is an example of the different formats that can be used in writing up a qualitative study and how presentation, interpretation and discussion interweave. In your version there would not be any headings like those below, it should flow as a narrative. The headings have been put in to alert you to the different voices and devices used in writing up a qualitative study.

The author's voice

Three of the participants lived in rural areas, two females and one male. They had extensive knowledge about herbs and plants for medicinal and culinary use and were eager to share this information. They came from the same general area and were all over 70 years of age. Their knowledge of herbs and plants was passed on from their parents and grandparents and they too in turn taught their children and grandchildren. As children and for most of their adult life they regularly used 'bush medicine' and even now they seldom visit a doctor. Only the male participant had had an operation. On the whole they felt that the younger members of the family did know about the different plants and what they could be used for but they tended to only use what was in the immediate vicinity, they did not know where to go to look for all the other types of plants.

Verbatim voice of participants

R1: You see all round here we have a lot of shining bush and sweet broom and de children mother does bathe dem in sweet broom to get rid of skin rash and those kind of things but only down by the river over yonder it have a lot of wormgrass and watergrass good for cooling and cleaning the body but they don't go for it. If I don't go for it, dem never go. Dem buy medicine in the pharmacy and spend a heap ah good money when dey could just pick it!

Thick description – details

The participants in town lived with their families. All were female. One spoke of how she grew up in the country and had learned bush medicine from her mother. She described how aloes was used for different purposes.

R4: De first thing you have to do when you cut the aloes is make sure you get a long piece dat full of the goodness in it, dat oozing out so to speak. You could put it just so on burns. It will cool the skin and you can just paste it on and in no time at all your skin back to good, good. If you get a cut too. And you can peel it and put it in the fridge in a jug of water and you can drink that instead of water just to cool and clean your insides.

The author's voice is interspersed throughout the account, telling the reader what has been found, interpreting and discussing it. The participants' voices are also interspersed throughout, where the author selects verbatim excerpts from the interview transcript to illustrate a point. 'Thick description' is used in qualitative studies to deepen an understanding of the context. In the case above it is a participant giving some details but the author could also decide to describe each participant in detail and their home situation to give the reader a 'feel' for the context. Other forms of text that could be used are stories and vignettes (brief portrayals, for example, of one of the participants and his or her story).

Interweaving of description, interpretation and discussion

While the participants criticized the younger members of the family, especially those in town, for abandoning the merits of bush medicine for the pharmacy, they were not sure sometimes about dosage and side effects. They felt that the younger members only put up objections like that because they had a prejudice about 'old-time ways'. The elderly were unwilling to see the side of the argument that lack of standards in brewing the herbs could be dangerous for the patient. They tended to rely on tried and tested practice, even though nothing was written down. In this situation age-old cultural knowledge is being lost – the elderly are not documenting what they know, they feel that it is the duty of the younger members to preserve and carry on traditions, and the younger members tend to be suspicious of cures that you can go outside and pick. They are being influenced by modern urban living and tend to feel that medicines should be issued by qualified people and come in a bottle with recommended doses. Between these two positions the cultural knowledge of the older heads is being steadily whittled down through lack of use. In the meantime, western medicine is becoming the norm despite all the fears about over-the-counter drugs, over-prescribing of drugs to inflate the income of the drug companies, and the medicalization of minor ailments.

Summary

The final sections of a research report include the 'Conclusion', 'Recommendations' (if any), 'References' and the 'Appendix'. The conclusion and recommendations must relate directly to the research problem, the research questions, the literature reviewed, and the findings. The appendix is useful in that related material can be placed there that would be too bulky within the study, especially if it is not critical information for that section. The list of references is standard practice for all scholarly work and great care should be taken to use a particular citation style correctly. The references give the reader valuable information about related materials and show that the writer has been informed by a range of sources. In addition, citing references shows that the writer is careful to acknowledge the sources of his or her ideas and statements, thereby safeguarding the intellectual property of others.

WRAP UP

This chapter has introduced you to the field of research, emphasizing that there is more than one way of conducting research. Whether the researcher chooses the quantitative or qualitative mode of inquiry, the research process has to be systematic, ensuring high standards of reliability and validity. You have also learned that a research study must be highly focused and that the formulation of research objectives, research questions and the statement of the problem help to keep the researcher on course. The literature review too, while being informative, emphasizes the researcher's stance on the issue. If these early aspects of the study are well thought out then the time 'in the field' (namely data collection) and the process of data analysis should go smoothly. Again, the data collected are guided and analysed by reference to the research questions. Conducting systematic research is a skill that young Caribbean scholars should develop as they seek to investigate social life and thereby make an impact on human development in the region.

PRACTICE TESTS

Structured response

1. Distinguish between (a) reliability and (b) validity in research. (4 marks)
2. Explain what is meant by 'action research'. (2 marks)
3. For an identified research problem, formulate
   (a) relevant research objectives
   (b) a problem statement
   (c) two research questions. (6 marks)
4. Distinguish between (a) quantitative and
   (b) qualitative research. (4 marks)
5. Explain what is meant by a 'hypothesis'. (2 marks)
6. Describe how the scientific method influences research in the social sciences. (4 marks)
7. For a study on the upsurge of crime in a Caribbean country list three relevant data sources. (3 marks)
8. Define the following terms
   (a) empirical data
   (b) survey research
   (c) random sampling. (6 marks)
9. List three characteristics of a well-constructed questionnaire. (3 marks)
10. For a qualitative study, describe three ways in which the researcher can reduce bias. (6 marks)

REFERENCES

American Association of University Women. (1995). *How schools shortchange girls. A study of major findings on girls and education. The AAUW report.* New York: Marlowe & Co.

Bailey, B. (2000). *Gender and education in Jamaica: what about the boys?* Kingston, Jamaica: UNESCO. (EFA in the Caribbean: Assessment 2000. Monograph Series No.15)

Barriteau, E. (2003). Requiem for the male marginalization thesis in the Caribbean: death of a non-theory. In E. Barriteau (Ed.), *Confronting power, theorizing gender: interdisciplinary perspectives in the Caribbean,* pp. 324–355. Kingston, Jamaica: UWI Press.

Brown, V. (2005). *Violence, media and health: I shot the sheriff.* Barbados: Commonwealth Broadcasting Association. Retrieved on 13 January 2006 at http://www.cba.org.uk/conference/2005/BarbadosSpeech3.htm

Evans, H. (1999). The construction of gender and achievement in secondary schools in Jamaica. *Caribbean Journal of Education*, 21 (1 &2), pp. 3–24.

Ferguson, A. (2000). *Bad boys: public schools in the making of black masculinity.* Ann Arbor, MI: University of Michigan Press.

Gigli, S. (2004). *Children, youth and media around the world: an overview of trends and issues.* A report prepared by Intermedia for UNICEF's Fourth World Summit on Media for Children and Adolescents, Rio de Janeiro, Brazil. Retrieved on 13 June 2006 at http://www.ifcw.org/rio_research_paper_on_media.htm

Gilbert, P., & Gilbert, R. (2001). Masculinity, inequality and post-school opportunities. *International Journal of Inclusive Education*, 5(1), pp. 1–13.

Gurian, M. (2001). *Boys and girls learn differently! A guide for teachers and parents.* San Francisco, CA: Jossey Bass.

Mac an Ghaill, M. (1996). What about the boys? Schooling, class and crisis masculinity. *Sociological Review*, 44, pp. 381–397.

Martino, W. (1999). 'Cool boys', 'party animals', 'squids', and 'poofters': interrogating the dynamics and politics of adolescent masculinities in school. *British Journal of Sociology of Education*, 20(2), pp. 239–263.

Moir, A., & Jessel, D. (1991). *Brain sex: the real difference between men and women.* New York: Delta.

Nilan, P. (2000). 'You're hopeless I swear to God': shifting masculinities in classroom talk. *Gender and Education*, 12(1), pp. 53–68.

Parry, O. (1996). In one ear and out the other: unmasking masculinities in the Caribbean classroom. *Sociological Research Online*, 1(2) at http://www.socresonline.org.uk/socresonline.1/2/2.html

Parry, O. (1997). 'Schooling is fooling': why do Jamaican boys underachieve in school? *Gender and Education*, 9(2), pp. 223–231.

Parsons, T., & Bales, R. (1956). *Family socialization and the interaction process.* London: Routledge & Kegan Paul.

Robinson, C. (2005). The media and victims of violence. *Jamaica Observer*, 13 February.

Sommers, C. H. (2000). *The war against boys: how misguided feminism is harming our young men.* New York: Simon & Schuster.

UNICEF. Opinion polls: What young people think. Summary of polls in East Asia and the Pacific, Europe and Central Asia, and Latin America and the Caribbean. Retrieved on 13 June 2006 at http://www.unicef.org/polls

Warrington, M., & Younger, M. (2001). Single-sex classes and equal opportunities for girls and boys: perspectives through time from a mixed comprehensive school in England. *Oxford Review of Education*, 27(3), pp. 339–356.

Weaver-Hightower, M. (2005). Dare the school build a new education for boys? *Teachers College Record,* No. 11743, 14 February 2005. Accessed at http://www.tcrecord.orgID

GLOSSARY

Note: *bold italic* type is used within definitions for terms defined elsewhere in the glossary.

aboriginal pertaining to the first or original inhabitants of a region who have established continuous cultural links there, and their descendants; sometimes referred to as *native* or *indigenous*.

acculturation the imposition of a dominant group's way of life on another group. This may or may not result in assimilation.

achieved status social position based on merit, e.g. a high-paying job based on educational qualifications.

ageism age-related *prejudices*, *stereotypes* and *discrimination*, often applied to elderly persons, which treats them as having little worth.

Apprenticeship the period between 1834 and 1838 when freedom was introduced gradually in the British Caribbean. It was not implemented in all territories and ended prematurely because of the threat of unrest (it was supposed to end in 1840 for the field slaves).

ascribed status social position based on criteria conferred on someone by virtue of birth, e.g. wealth or poverty.

assimilation the absorption of a cultural group into the *norms* and *values* of a dominant group through *acculturation.*

atmospheric pressure the force of the molecules in a unit of air pressing down on the Earth's surface. Also known as *barometric pressure* (it is measured by a barometer).

balance of payments the difference between the value of a country's imports (computers, cars, flour, loan payments) and its exports (tourism, primary products, cultural goods e.g. music), usually for a year. It measures the amount of its currency flowing out (debts) against that flowing in (credits).

beliefs the acceptance of something (idea, tenets, *dogma*) as true, inspiring confidence and trust.

bourgeoisie in *Marxist* thought refers to the *capitalist* class as a whole. *Bourgeois* is an adjective and/or the singular form. *See also* **petite bourgeoisie***.*

Bretton Woods Institutions the IMF (International Monetary Fund) and the World Bank (IBRD – International Bank for Reconstruction and Development) were formed in 1944 at a conference in the town of Bretton Woods, New Hampshire. In 1948 the General Agreement on Tariffs and Trade (GATT) was formed. All three were to assist in bringing about global economic cooperation.

capitalism the dominant economic system in the world today, in which the *means of production* are largely privately owned and capital is invested to produce and distribute goods and services. Prices are determined by *free market* forces, where competition rather than government or other controls exist.

caste social position based on *race*, colour or *ethnicity* which is the basis for stratifying the society, as in India, where it was based on lineage.

civil rights movement a movement which began in the US in the 1950s and continued into the 1960s. It was a peaceful protest aimed at ending racial segregation and securing equal opportunity and treatment for minorities, especially African-Americans.

class (social class, socio-economic class) *status* based on a ranking of groups in society in terms of their income e.g. high, middle and lower social class; also an indicator of occupational status.

classism beliefs or attitudes that relegate persons to limited options or portray them negatively because of their socio-economic *class*, e.g. when vocational guidance tutors steer lower-income students towards lower-income jobs.

colonialism the control or rule of one country by another, usually for economic exploitation. All institutions are controlled by the foreign power. *See also* **imperialism***.*

colonization the imposition of political and economic control over one country by another, which usually has superior weapons technology and is at a relatively advanced stage of development compared to the colonized peoples.

Commonwealth The 'Commonwealth of Nations' or the 'British Commonwealth' refers to a world organization of independent states and dependent territories that were once (or are) colonies of Great Britain. Countries gain through trade and other economic agreements as well as general cooperation in various areas.

communism a mode of production where every aspect is controlled by the workers. It forms the basis of an egalitarian society where everybody is treated alike. It is an *ideology* about human relationships. *See also Marxism.*

conservation protection of the environment through measures that preserve or restore it through careful management of natural resources.

constituency the geographical area or electoral district that is represented in parliament by an elected politician from that area.

constitution the *rules* and principles for governing a country. It may or may not be codified in a written document. It defines the power and duties of government bodies and officials and guarantees *rights* to the people.

constitutional monarchy a system of government in which a monarch is head of state but his or her powers are controlled by the *constitution* and laws of the country. In many instances this is a purely ceremonial position.

construct an idea that has been created to represent some aspect of social life which is not clearly evident and so needs to be made more visible to be studied and analysed. Social *class* and 'the social' are constructs.

cosmology the study of how people relate to the physical and spiritual universe. African cosmology describes the core religious ideas of a people or their world view – e.g. the world of spirits and the world of humans and how they inter-penetrate.

coup d'etat the overthrow of a government by a small group of persons (often the military) who either assassinate those in authority or forcibly remove them from office.

creedism *prejudice* and *discrimination* directed at an individual or group because of their *religion*. Afrocentric religions have in the past been the target of discriminatory acts by governments and other groups in the Caribbean.

creolization the meeting and mixing of cultures to produce something new out of the fusion, a term that tends to be specifically used to refer to Caribbean processes of mixing.

crown colony a British colony where the British Crown directly controls many aspects of government through an appointed governor. After the Morant Bay rebellion in Jamaica in 1865 the British forced the legislature to surrender its powers and Jamaica became a crown colony.

cult a small group having *beliefs* and practices that differ greatly from those of the mainstream. For example, some believe they know when the end of the world will happen, in some the leader is worshipped or believed to have special powers. They have an authoritarian structure demanding loyalty to the group.

cultural capital knowledge, skills and competencies that individuals learn by belonging to a certain social *class* or cultural group that gives them advantages in social situations.

cultural diversity different ethnic traditions (evident in *race*, language, *religion*, *customs*, family practices) found in one society or region.

cultural erasure loss of a particular cultural practice over time, to be replaced by modern ways of life.

cultural imperialism the practices whereby a dominant culture (usually a technologically superior group) attempts to promote their own culture and language over that of another (usually a country with fewer resources).

cultural pluralism different cultural or racial groups in a society mixing only to a certain extent, with limited social and cultural integration.

cultural renewal the revival of a cultural practice, possibly in relation to tourism – creating tourist packages or producing cultural artefacts.

cultural reproduction the socializing forces of the major *social institutions* that serve to reproduce a society's culture from one generation to the next. From a *Marxist* perspective, *social* reproduction happens when the younger generation remain in the same social class as their parents – there is no *social mobility*.

cultural retention the maintaining of cultural practices by a group even though another culture may be more dominant.

custom common practice that has become *institutionalized* in a society, e.g. gift giving at Christmas and wearing gender-appropriate clothes.

customary law traditional patterns of behaviour that are widely recognized in a particular society as lawful. These laws originated differently from those proclaimed by the legislative authorities (*civil law*) and sometimes clash with the latter, e.g. customary laws that privilege males in matters of inheritance.

decolonization the process whereby a colony achieves independence. The independence of Algeria from France in 1962 and Angola from Portugal in 1975 were won amidst bloody liberation wars. In the Caribbean, independence was achieved peacefully because Britain wanted to rid itself of its colonies.

dependency model a theory that explains global inequality between countries in terms of the colonial exploitation of poor societies by rich ones. Dependency theorists argue that colonial powers 'underdeveloped' their colonies while developing their own trade and economic institutions.

devaluation the reduction in the value of a country's currency, usually by government decision. Exports become less expensive for foreigners to buy and foreign products become more expensive for domestic consumers to buy. Consequently, imports are discouraged and the balance of trade improved.

diaspora the forced scattering of a people away from their homeland, e.g. Jews and Africans.

diffusion the mixing of molecules in liquids that are placed in contact. The molecules spread out from an area where they are highly concentrated to an area of less concentration. *Cultural diffusion* refers to the spreading of ideas and institutions from one culture to another.

digital divide the gap between those who have access to computers and other *ICTs*, and are computer literate, and those who cannot use computers and do not have access to them. It exists within a country as in young versus elderly users, and between countries, as in industrialized versus less-industrialized countries.

discrimination treating others unfairly, on the basis of attitudes and *beliefs*, and often as a result of *prejudice*. See also *ageism, classism, creedism, racism, sexism*.

distributive justice a concern for what is good or right in a society based on the allocation of goods. Rewards and punishments are distributed to persons depending on their relative merits. This ensures that equals are not dealt with unequally and that unequals are not treated as if they are equals.

dogma a system of *beliefs* or religious laws that believers or adherents are expected to uphold without doubt.

economic development *economic growth* resulting in an improvement in human *welfare*.

economic growth the increase in the output (value of the goods and services) produced by a country, usually measured by the annual percentage increase in its Gross Domestic Product.

economy a *social institution* which embodies the valued ideas and *beliefs* that society has about how it should organize production.

ecosystem a natural system of plants and animals which has evolved so that interactions within the system are more or less in equilibrium (or balance).

ecotourism travel and accommodation that aim to disturb the natural environment as little as possible and to promote the welfare of the local people.

ecumenism a movement to create better cooperation and understanding among the different faiths (usually Christian) in the world. *Inter-faith* is more commonly used for services and activities that include other *religions*.

electorate persons in a country who are qualified to vote in an election; e.g. those attaining the required age and those who can prove citizenship.

elites members of the highest social class or those who rank above others in terms of wealth, *status* or prestige.

emancipation in the Caribbean context, refers specifically to the freeing of the African enslaved population by their European captors.

empowerment the understanding that a person can change his or her circumstances for the better because prevailing dominant assumptions and practices are seen as challenges to be overcome.

encomienda a legal system of trusteeship whereby the Amerindian population in the New World were defined as subjects of the Spanish Crown and expected to pay tribute in taxes and labour. In return they were to be taught Christianity and protected.

enculturation the domination of a cultural group by another so that aspects of the dominant culture are adopted but they do not become *assimilated*.

endogamy marriage within one's social group according to *custom* to preserve the *norms* and culture of that group as well as property rights.

enfranchisement freedom from being oppressed or limited in some way, such as in obtaining the right to vote or to buy land so that one could become self-sufficient.

ENSO El Niño–Southern Oscillation. El Niño refers to the warming of the sea surface in the equatorial

Pacific, which leads to atmospheric changes known as the Southern Oscillation and rainfall and temperature variations globally. Since the two occur together the terms have been combined.

entrench to establish and protect ideas or a particular position so firmly that change is unlikely to happen.

entrepreneurship qualities or abilities that someone has that are likely to result in business success – innovative, risk-taker, creative thinker, visionary.

environmental degradation the deterioration of the environment caused by human activity that increases pollution of land, air and water and reduces the numbers and types of animals and plants. Natural events such as volcanic activity do not degrade the environment, but change it.

environmental disasters events that cause harm and injury to humans and their livelihood and which are largely brought about by over-use of natural resources and settlement in vulnerable areas. Flooding, landslides, hurricanes and soil erosion are natural events that could become environmental disasters.

environmental hazards natural events such as earthquakes or volcanic eruptions that could become disasters if they adversely affect human life and property.

equity fair treatment, as in a just distribution of resources or provisions whereby people have equal opportunities.

ethnic group a group of people who feel a sense of belonging together based on shared culture, language, ancestry, nationality, *religion*, *race*, skin colour or other factors.

ethnicity cultural attributes or affiliations based on the ways of life of one's *ethnic group.*

ethnocentric ideas and policies derived from (usually) a 'first world' country and imposed on a 'third world' country.

extended family a *family* unit comprising members of the older and younger generations. It may refer only to one's relatives to differentiate them from the immediate family.

false consciousness a *Marxist* term which states that the oppressed often fail to recognize that the ways in which they are exploited are of their own creation, such as when they adopt the *values* of the *elites*.

family a *social institution* which embodies the valued ideas and *beliefs* that society has about how children

should be reared and *socialized* and how human reproduction should take place.

fascism a right-wing authoritarian political *ideology* advocating a totalitarian state where citizens can have no loyalties other than to the nation. It is based on mass militarization and is violently opposed to *communism*.

federation a system of government where several states which are self-governing belong to a much larger combined state that defines the relationships between each state and the central or federal government. The US, St Kitts–Nevis and Brazil are all federal states.

feminism a movement dedicated to the attainment of political, social and economic equality of all people (men *and* women). Some activists focus on the inequalities suffered by women in a male-dominated society whilst some see *sexist* oppression as affecting both men and women.

feudalism in medieval Europe the land-owning nobles made grants of land (fiefs) to their subjects (vassals) who were obligated to provide military service. The vassal had few *rights* and was under the protection of the noble.

free market an economic system where resources are allocated based only on the forces of supply and demand. In reality, most countries place some restrictions on the market.

free trade trade between countries where there are no or minimal customs dues such as *tariffs* or taxes placed on goods and services or where there are few import quotas or foreign currency restrictions.

functionalism a sociological perspective which studies the social system as a set of harmonious relationships between all the *social institutions*. Consensus is the characteristic of society that helps it to cohere and develop.

gatekeepers those who hold power that can facilitate or obstruct others in accessing some good, e.g. those who certify dentists and doctors as eligible to practice in a country, those who control decision-making about building new schools as well as those who screen job applicants.

gender inequality a principle held by *feminists* that women occupy a subordinate position in society relative to men largely owing to *beliefs* that men and women are essentially different.

gender socialization the process by which boys and girls learn the behaviours and attitudes that their society deems appropriate for males and females.

genocide the extermination or near extermination of a race or cultural group, e.g. the Tainos.

Gini Index a ratio calculated to measure income or wealth inequality within and across countries. Inaccuracies may occur in comparisons between countries due to differences in benefits for the poor (food stamps, money, subsidized travel, etc.).

globalization the processes by which flows of trade, finance and information between countries are broadened and deepened so that they function as one global market.

hegemony the domination of a society by a group or groups whose ideas, culture, *beliefs* and *values* are regarded as legitimate by most of the people.

human capital people regarded as resources, just like land or raw materials, that could be invested in for development to take place.

human development a view of development which sees people as the means and ends of development, and that they have to be provided with the opportunities to develop themselves.

Human Development Paradigm (HDP) a model of development created by UN economists which focuses on *human development*. The focus is on broadening people's options by instituting policies to enhance equity, productivity, *empowerment* and sustainability.

hybridization the fusion of two or more groups of people or cultural practices to produce a new entity with elements of each of the parent influences, e.g. 'mixed' ethnic groupings.

ICTs (information and communications technologies) the networking of computers and other digital technologies into integrated mass information and communications systems and databases.

identity a sense of belonging constructed and negotiated in relation to a larger group or context – one's *family*, *ethnic group* or nation; an individual's conception of his or her self in relation to all the social groups in which he or she is included and excluded.

ideology a set of *beliefs* that includes a programme for the liberation of some group that feels oppressed, and which is intolerant of other ideologies.

imperialism the conquest and control of another territory for political power and prestige, e.g. the conquest of the Americas by Spain.

indentureship bonded or contract labour where the indentured labourer or servant was free to return home at the end of the period of indentureship or remain in the Caribbean and given a piece of land.

Industrial Revolution the changes in society and economy that occurred in Europe in the eighteenth and nineteenth centuries based on technological innovations and inventions resulting in mechanization, the growth of factories and industrial towns, as well as improvements in transportation and communications.

inflation a sustained rise in the cost of living in a country, with most or all goods and services increasing in price. This can give rise to *balance of payments* problems and loss of income for some groups, e.g. the elderly.

institutionalized a practice that becomes a well-established and accepted part of the system, e.g. bribery for getting things done in an inefficient bureaucracy. Also used to refer to caring for people in an institution, such as a home for elderly persons.

instrumental having *value* only if it is a means to promote some end, e.g. seeing education solely as a means of getting a good job. Having intrinsic value, on the other hand, means that something (e.g. education) is regarded as useful in itself – to increase knowledge, skills and expertise.

intelligentsia the educated and intellectual **elite** of a society, comprising a distinct social class of artists, teachers, writers, scholars, clergy and thinkers. It is felt that these persons have a responsibility to ensure good government by critical examination and discussion of issues for the public good.

interculturation the cultural mixing that occurs in a *plural society* where *ethnic groups* may live with limited mixing yet elements of their cultures become incorporated into each other's way of life.

internationalization the blurring of national borders through the capabilities of *ICTs*, e.g. distance education programmes and foreign tertiary education providers in the Caribbean operating without the need for permission from national authorities.

isobars lines on a weather map joining places of equal *atmospheric pressure* (adjusted to sea level).

joint household a household including many members of the *extended family* where each sub-family unit occupies a specific space or its own household within a larger family compound.

judiciary the system of law courts, judges and magistrates, and the police service, which work together to maintain a just society. The specific function of judges is to interpret the law and this branch of the government is separate from the executive and the *legislature*.

kin relatives by blood, marriage, tribal affiliation and fictive relationships.

legislature the branch of government that makes laws for a nation, consisting of elected representatives. The *executive* is chosen from the legislature in the British Westminster system, which has been widely adopted in the Caribbean.

legitimacy the acceptance of someone or some system of authority or power as having the right to rule. This could be based on charisma, tradition, law or the recognition, for example, that the government is following democratic principles.

leisure time that is free to do with as one may wish, usually activities associated with fun, enjoyment and *recreation*.

lingua franca a common or *hybrid* language, often not fully developed (a *pidgin*), enabling speakers of many different languages to communicate.

lobby a group advocating changes (usually in government policy), which tries to alert the public to an issue, persuading them to follow the cause, and solicits meetings and debates with government officials.

Marxism a theory of society put forward by Karl Marx in the nineteenth century. Social development was seen as occurring through changes in the economic subsystem brought on by contradictions in the *social relations of production*. *Capitalism* in this view will give way, because of inherent contradictions, to a *communist* state.

mass media forms of communication designed to reach a mass audience immediately or over a short period of time. Examples include newspapers, television, radio and the internet.

matrifocal literally focusing around the mother. In matrifocal *families*, the day-to-day lives of the household revolve around the mother. She may be the sole breadwinner or have the support of a male, but he tends to be absent or marginal to the life of the household.

means of production a *Marxist* term referring to anything that labour needs to produce goods – land, machinery, money, power, raw materials.

mercantilism economic ideas prevailing in Europe from the sixteenth to the eighteenth centuries, advocating government intervention to promote exports, to discourage imports by instituting *tariffs* on foreign goods, and to demand payment in bullion (gold and silver), the accumulation of which was believed to be a sign of wealth.

meritocracy a society where progress or upward *social mobility* is based on individual achievement (merit). The rewards of the society (power, prestige and wealth) are distributed according to the abilities and achievements of individuals, who are said to have 'earned' their various positions or *statuses*.

metropole a country where economic, cultural and technological power is concentrated and which influences society and culture in the *periphery* (the ex-colonies and present-day dependencies).

metropolitan country a country that is among the world centres of business, industry, manufacturing and *ICTs*, where the urban population far exceeds those in primary production. Through the *mass media* their lifestyles and *values* influence social life in other countries.

Middle Passage that sector of the Atlantic *slave trade* between Africa and the Americas.

minority group a group, usually an *ethnic group*, that may or may not be numerically inferior to a more dominant group, which limits their access to education, employment, health care, land and other *rights*. They have no political power and their *values* and traditions are marginal to the society.

misandry hatred and oppression of men and boys based on the belief that males are not suited to be good fathers, husbands, or even good human beings. Researchers attribute the rise of misandry to some *feminists* who advocate contempt for men. Both men and women can be misandrists.

misogyny hatred and oppression of women and girls through making them into sexual objects, as in pornography, and showing contempt for their abilities and *roles*. Such behaviours support the continued subordination of females by males. Both men and women can be misogynists.

monoculture a form of agriculture where one crop (e.g. sugar cane) is cultivated on a large scale and dominates the landscape and the economy.

monopoly the domination of one firm in the production and marketing of some good or service. For example, telecommunication providers in the Caribbean were traditionally in the hands of foreign companies who were allowed by governments to be the sole authority in providing the service and setting prices.

multilateral organizations non-governmental, international organizations set up to enable groups of countries to work together for some common goal, for example, the United Nations. However, individual powerful nations such as the US sometimes dominate these bodies or act unilaterally (without consultation).

multinational companies (MNCs) firms with their headquarters in *metropolitan countries* which carry out their operations in different countries, usually developing countries. They are also referred to as *transnational corporations (TNCs)*.

nationality the status of belonging to a country through citizenship or sharing commonalities with an *ethnic group* who may form a nation without being a state.

nationalization The act of taking control of a private firm, such as the assets of a *multinational company* in a specific country, by that country's government. This may happen if the government feels that the MNC is sending too much of its profits out of the country. The MNC may or may not be compensated.

nativism promoting the *rights* and world view of a group to which one belongs in an attempt to oppose mainstream ideas that marginalize those rights or views. Examples include women, homosexuals, the disabled, militant Muslims, ethnic minorities and indigenous peoples, as well as groups such as the Ku Klux Klan.

négritude the *ideology* largely developed by poets and writers in the French colonial countries of Africa and the Caribbean to protest against the *racism* directed at people of African origin. They advocated a celebration and discussion of 'blackness' as a rival perspective to the dominant one of white, western culture.

neo-colonial relationships between developed countries and ex-colonies that seem to hold the latter in a position of dependency and underdevelopment.

neoliberalism economic policies in western countries promoting the *free market* and removal of restrictions to trade and production. It advocates *privatization*, control of labour, the unrestricted flow of capital and corporate control of the market.

norms standards for behaviours that are valued in a society. They are cultural *rules* that carry *sanctions* – rewards or punishments. *See also sanctions*.

nuclear family a *family* unit comprising a parent and child or parents and children.

pan-Africanism an *ideology* promoting the brotherhood of all the African peoples the world over to interrogate their oppression, past and present, by using their common culture and ancestry as a force to unite and seek ways of fostering the development of Africa and African peoples.

paradigm a view of reality that is governed by assumptions agreed to by scholars and researchers in a particular field, e.g. scientific research. Another paradigm can rise to prominence and challenge an existing paradigm as providing a better way of explaining reality, e.g. qualitative research.

parliamentary government a system of government based on the Westminster or British model where the executive comprises a Cabinet with members drawn from the *legislature*, i.e. the House of Representatives and the Senate. The names given to the Houses of Parliament may differ from country to country.

patois a form of language that differs across the Caribbean and varies from the standard European languages in vocabulary, grammar, idiom and other characteristics. Today it is referred to as 'the creole' and is the first language of most Caribbean people.

patriarchy a social system where men dominate all the *social institutions* and females occupy an oppressed position.

periphery countries which do not have high levels of technological and industrial development and where trade flows are dominated by imports from the *metropole*. Examples include many of the newly independent states of the Caribbean, Africa and the Pacific.

petite bourgeoisie a social class in *Marxist* theory comprising professionals and small business owners; often used to refer to the lower middle class. While the petite bourgeoisie may employ workers, they usually work closely with them and they do not control the *means of production*.

pigementocracy *social stratification* in the Caribbean due to racial *prejudice* and *discrimination* based on skin colour. So much mixing of *ethnic groups* has occurred that there is a range of colour in all ethnicities. White and lighter skin colour are accorded more **status** and thus darker skin could exclude groups from certain jobs and associations as well as friendship groups.

planned economy an economy that is centrally planned where the government owns the **means of production**, allocates resources and fixes pricing. **Socialist** and **communist** countries tend to have planned (or command) economies.

plantation model a development theory that views Caribbean economy and society as locked into a colonial relationship with the **metropole**. Exports are mainly primary products, the bulk of manufactured goods are imported, and the society is still stratified according to **race** and **ethnicity**.

plantation society the rigidly stratified system of social and economic relations enforced on plantations in the Americas. *See also* **slave society**.

plate tectonics a theory that explains seismic, volcanic and **tectonic activity** by the movement of crustal blocks ('plates') relative to each other.

plural society one theory put forward to explain Caribbean society. A society where two or more racial or ethnic groups live but where there is limited mixing of cultures or intermarriage. Each group has maintained some form of its own institutions, e.g. **religion**, **family** and education.

pollution contamination of the natural environment by any substance that causes it harm or reduces its aesthetic appeal.

polygamy the practice of having more than one wife or husband.

polyglot usually refers to people living together but having many cultures and languages, forming a heterogeneous and diverse society.

postcolonial a society that is now independent and has to deal with the problem of the ex-colonizers' **values**, ideas and **beliefs** still being enshrined in positions of dominance in all the **social institutions** of the land.

postmodernism a perspective or attitude that seeks understanding of social life by deconstructing those theories and structures that tend to give full and certain explanations as grand narratives.

power sharing forms of governance where all political parties and groups in the population are afforded some power in making decisions and policies. This model is based on consensus, consultation and compromise, and

can vary according to the context of different countries. It is an option for deeply divided societies.

prejudice a positive or negative attitude towards particular persons or groups based on **stereotypes** rather than personal knowledge or experience of the persons or groups concerned.

privatization a process usually undertaken by governments to transfer ownership of nationally owned firms and utilities into the hands of private enterprise. *See also* **nationalization.**

proletariat a term from **Marxist** theory referring to the lowest social **class** comprising persons who only have their labour power to sell.

proprietorships a system of governance which evolved in French and British colonies. A lord or noble was granted territory such as an island by the monarch and he became the Lord Proprietor, entitled to tax the colonists; in return he was supposed to protect them and ensure good governance.

protectionism a trade policy instituted to help stimulate local production of goods. High **tariffs** imposed on certain imported goods make them more expensive on the local market compared with locally produced equivalents.

race a social construct that is used to categorize human populations based on physical features transmitted by genes from one generation to the other. So much variation exists within one category that there is little evidence to support the notion of separate races in biology.

racism **stereotypes**, **prejudice** and acts of **discrimination** based on someone's **race**.

recreation activities engaged in for their therapeutic powers – to refresh energies and to find release from work and related chores. Many forms of recreation involve interaction with others, as in **sports**, picnics and travel.

referendum a plebiscite, or when the entire electorate of a country is asked to vote on a particular issue of immediate and urgent importance to the state.

religion a **social institution** which embodies the valued ideas and **beliefs** that society has about our relationship to a divine or sacred entity and the afterlife.

reparations the act of one country making amends to another for wrongdoing, acknowledging responsibility for events like slavery or the Holocaust. In 2000, the

German government formed a Foundation to help to compensate victims who are still alive today and suffered under the Nazi regime.

republic a state where supreme authority is vested in the people and not a monarch. Citizens vote for their representatives to form the government. Power resides in the people and the government is subject to their wishes through the *rule of law*.

rights entitlements that human beings have by virtue of being human to be treated in a just and equitable manner. They are largely derived from moral reasoning about the equality of humankind and many are enshrined as laws.

risk management the analysis or assessment of exposure to risk (the possibility of incurring loss) and devising strategies to manage the risk. They include avoidance (moving away from disaster-prone areas), reducing its effects (by being insured) or mitigating the risk (having evacuation plans).

rites ceremonies or solemn *rituals* designed to commemorate important religious events such as Good Friday, or transitions in a person's life to another *status* (e.g. marriage or, in some countries, puberty).

rituals traditional practices which tend to encourage a sense of belonging and community. For example, preparations observed by a group of friends in planning to watch a major *sports* event on television; *family* celebrations associated with weddings, baptisms and the like, or even family routines.

roles a set of expectations for behaviour for someone of a certain *status*, e.g. a mother's role or that of a teacher or student. The set of expectations is based on *values* and *norms* for that social status in that society.

royalties payments to the creators of original works such as authors, inventors or composers from the sale of their works by companies authorized to sell or use the works, or from sale of the rights to use copyrighted material.

rule of law the understanding that governments and their agents must act in accordance with the established legislative framework of a country. It is meant to curb arbitrary acts, to enforce equality before the law, and to preserve law and order.

sanctions rewards or punishments (consequences) designed to encourage or discourage certain behaviours. They tend to stabilize *norms* and make them an integral part of social life.

scientific method the research model used in the natural sciences that is also dominant in the social sciences. It advocates choosing representative samples, testing hypotheses through a study of the interaction of variables under strict controls, and ensuring objectivity so that generalizations can be made.

sect an offshoot from a larger religious group, holding most of the *beliefs* of the parent group but also incorporating different elements which may be controversial.

secularization the process whereby the institution of *religion* no longer governs many aspects of social life; education and the government have taken over some of its functions. Also refers to the increasing complexity of society, allowing for *social mobility*, which influences changing traditional values.

separation of powers government where the three arms – executive, *judiciary* and *legislature* – have different kinds of authority and power, in order to minimize opportunities for abuse of power.

sexism *prejudice* and *discrimination* based on someone's sex.

shifting cultivation the practice often carried out by small farmers in tropical areas where land is farmed for a few years and then abandoned to regain its fertility.

slave society the form of social relationships that developed in territories where the plantation was the major social and economic institution. The fact that large numbers of the population were enslaved conditioned all aspects of life in society.

slave trade the Atlantic Slave Trade developed by the commercial and maritime powers of Europe which supplied an enslaved labour force for the plantations, ranches and mines of the Americas from the sixteenth to the nineteenth centuries.

social capital the advantages that some individuals within groups have because they have access to connections that are valued by others. Having these connections confers prestige on these persons. Those without these advantages suffer marginalization and are less popular.

social construction an idea or a concept used to portray some aspect of social life that has become part of the shared understandings of people even though it has no existence in fact. For example, *race* is a social construction, as are femininity and masculinity.

social contract a covenant or agreement between a government and the citizens of a country where the latter agree to give up their total freedom to act (their natural liberties) in return for protection and an organized social existence.

social exclusion social injustice experienced when groups are obstructed in accessing opportunities allowing them to live a better life. The obstruction may be deliberate or may stem from policies promoting mainstream values which ignore the needs of *minority groups*, the poor, the illiterate and rural residents.

social institutions a set of valued ideas and *beliefs* which varies from one society to another and from which members create their *social organizations*.

social justice a condition that most societies strive for where fair treatment is experienced by all groups and everyone shares equally in the benefits of the society.

social mobility the movement of an individual or a group from one socio-economic *class* to another, usually higher up in the system of *social stratification*.

social organizations arrangements that society makes to carry out its basic functions and which are based on the ideas and *beliefs* of its *social institutions*, e.g. the ideas a society has about *religion* may be reflected in organizations such as churches, Sunday School, and the separation of Church and State.

social stratification the ranking of social groups according to wealth, *status* and/or prestige.

social structure the practices, patterns, behaviours and relationships that characterize the *social institutions* and *social organizations* in a society.

socialism an *ideology* that describes, according to Marx, the state after the overthrow of *capitalism*. The state would function to uplift workers and seek their interests. The economy would be transformed and as each person learns their responsibilities to one another, there would be no need for a state and *communism* would be established.

socialization the process whereby members learn to be human – they learn the *rules* that society has devised for living and interacting in society. *Primary socialization* refers to how the very young learn the rules of society at home. *Secondary socialization* is accomplished by school, the church, the mass media and other agencies throughout life.

soil erosion the process whereby soil is removed by the forces of wind, water and moving ice. This happens

naturally but when the activities of human beings increase the amount of soil being lost, the process is called *accelerated soil erosion*.

sport physical activity undertaken as *recreation* or for competition as games where there are organized and accepted *rules* of play, but it can also be for exercise and well-being, as in walking or aerobic activities.

standard of living the quantity and quality of goods and services that the people in a country have access to that can enable them to satisfy their wants and lead more comfortable lives.

status the position occupied by someone in the social system, e.g. teacher, mother, husband, policewoman.

statute law laws passed by the legislative body of a country and written or codified (as opposed to customary law).

stereotype a belief that someone has about others that is not based on personal knowledge but on exaggeration and distortion; it could develop into *prejudices* for or against those persons or groups.

structural adjustment policies (SAPs) policies recommended by the World Bank and the IMF to heavily indebted countries to repay their debts and receive loans to re-structure a path to development. These policies include reducing inflation, opening up markets, *devaluation*, and reducing spending on health and education.

subaltern groups in *postcolonial* societies who struggle with indigenous *values* and *beliefs* and those of the ex-colonizer.

subculture a smaller group within the mainstream who are distinguished by characteristics and *values* that set them apart. Youth is a subculture based on age and a religious minority could also form a subculture. *Class*, gender, political affiliation and sexual orientation are the bases for other kinds of subcultures.

substructure a *Marxist* concept of the *economy* as the most important *social institution* in explaining social relations.

suffragette a movement in the nineteenth and early twentieth centuries in Britain and the US where women agitated, lobbied and demonstrated in order to bring attention to the fact that they were not entitled to vote. Through their efforts women in the US achieved suffrage in 1920 and those in Britain in 1928.

superstructure a *Marxist* concept describing those *social institutions* which are influenced by the *economy* so that the dominant ideas and *values* in the *family*, *religion* and politics support the dominant groups in the economy.

sustainable development a theory of development that views the process in a holistic light, encompassing social as well as *economic development* and emphasizing the importance of conserving the environment and natural resources.

syncretism the mixing of cultural practices from different *ethnic groups* to create a hybrid or a different entity fusing aspects of the original practices, e.g. music, culinary arts, *religion*.

tariffs taxes or customs duties put on goods coming into a country to raise revenue and/or to protect locally produced goods and services from cheaper imports.

tectonic activity earth movements that may result from seismic, volcanic and mountain-building activity. Plate margins are tectonically active. *See also* *plate tectonics*.

theocracy the rule of a country (e.g. Iran) according to the tenets and beliefs of a particular *religion*. Clerics form the highest authority.

total institution a sociological term to describe systems where all aspects of the lives of persons there (e.g. prison, slave society) are regulated and controlled by those in authority.

trade embargo the banning of exports to and imports from a particular country, usually imposed by one country's government on another if there is some major disagreement. It is an act of punishment designed to force compliance.

trade liberalization the removal of restrictions such as *tariffs*, taxes, customs duties, subsidies, quota systems and import licenses to allow all types of goods and services to be freely imported and exported

traditions elements of a culture and practices that are passed on from one generation to the next and form a body of *customs*.

transculturation cultural change involving the whole society, sometimes due to political upheavals. The steady import of enslaved Africans into the Caribbean drastically altered all aspects of society and culture.

transnational corporations (TNCs) *see multinational companies*.

Triangular Trade the name given to the Atlantic Slave Trade where ships left ports in Europe laden with manufactured goods to be traded on the West African coast for slaves. The ships then crossed the Atlantic (the *Middle Passage*) to trade the enslaved for rum, sugar, molasses, tobacco and cotton in the Americas and then headed back to Europe, on the final leg of a triangle.

underclass those who are extremely poor, who may or may not be employed (whether underemployed, fully employed or self-employed), and who are dependent on *welfare* assistance, where it exists.

universal adult suffrage the right of all citizens in a country to vote in national elections once they have attained the required age.

values shared ideas in society about how something should be ranked. Indigenous societies tend to place high value on communitarian and environmentally friendly behaviours, whilst western societies tend to value competitiveness and the accumulation of wealth.

welfare the provision of financial assistance or other types of aid, usually by the government of a country, to those who cannot afford on their own to buy the minimum basic amenities of life. It is based on principles of equality and *equity*.

INDEX

How to use the index: You should generally look up the most *precise* term you are interested in. For reasons of space, however, it has not been possible to provide access points from every possible angle. If you cannot find what you are looking for, try a more general heading or look under a related topic (*see* and *see also* references are provided to remind you). Remember to use the **Glossary** to look up meanings of terms. Institutions known more commonly by their abbreviated form are entered in that form only (e.g. 'IMF' rather than 'International Monetary Fund'). Alphabetical arrangement is word-by-word (this means, for example, that 'social mobility' comes before 'socialism'); words like 'and', 'in' and 'through' are ignored in the arrangement of subheadings. Page numbers in *italics* refer to diagrams and photographs.

acculturation 15, 16, 80–1
achieved criteria 86, 87, 89, 401
ACP countries 253, 254, 280
action research 417–19
Adams, Grantley *121*, 284
adaptation 47, 257–8
advertisements 316
Africa 80, 104, 337, 342
Africans
  culture 80, 81, 82, 83, 117
  diversity 106
  ethnic identity 69
  families 170, 172, 175, 359
  gender system 360–1
  languages 77, 78, 79
  mixed-race children 72–4
  oppression 112, 335
  pre-Columbian 103
  relations with Indians 69, 107, 363–4
  religion 75–7, 185, 403
  reparations movement 118
  resistance 116–18
  rights 112, 189–90, 338
  see also pan-Africanism; slavery
ageism 193, 384–8, 405
agriculture
  development 120, 238, 345
  and soil erosion 133, 134, 135, *136*
  trade terms 253, 254, 280
  water supply 141, 142
American Psychological Association 440–1
Amerindians *23*, 95–8, 115–16, 366–70
  diversity 63, 74, 96–7
  economy 111
  language 66, 367
  rights 189, 367, 369, 370, 377
  traditions 124
Anguilla 14, 15, 137–8
anomalies, in science 30
anthropology, 48–9, 66–7

Antigua and Barbuda 206, 319
appendices 441
Arawaks 96
archaeology 95, 96
Archaic peoples *94*, 95, 96
ascriptive criteria 84, 402
asiento 100
associated states 13, 15
Association of Caribbean States 6, 285–6

Baha'is 187–8
banana trade 280
Baptists *44*, 75, 185, 403
Barbados 11, 206
Barbuda 206, 319
basketball 222
Beckford, George 54
behaviour 43–4, 48, 320–1
beliefs 50, 54, 56, 167–70
  in knowledge 29, 30–1, 33
  media influence 320–1
  religious 168, 183, 184, 187–8
  see also prejudice; values
Belize
  barrier reef 143, 146
  Caribs 116
  climate 137
  ethnic composition 366
  land rights 367, 369, 377
  languages 66
  mass media 324
  punta rock 210
  see also Garifuna; Maya
Bermuda 5
Best, Lloyd 346, 347, 352–3
biodiversity 144–5
biology 47
Bird, Lester 319
Bishop, Maurice 217
Black Panthers 338, 339
Black Power 80, 217, 338, 339, 340–1, 350
blogging 293, 314

Braithwaite, Lloyd 53
Bretton Woods Institutions 277–9
Briggs, Cyril 336
Britain
  cricket 220, 221, 307
  food 214
  immigration 226
  Navigation Acts 113, 203
  political influence 191, 215–16, 218–19
  universities 289
British colonies 100–1, 102
  acculturation 15, 16, 80–1
  capitalism 350–3
  federation 14–15, 284
  governance 11, 13, 14–15, 215
  underdevelopment 352
  see also particular countries
British Empire 11, 14
British Overseas Territories 13, 14–15
buccaneers 101
Burnham, Forbes 365
Bustamante, Alexander *121*
Butler, Uriah Buzz *121*

Cable and Wireless 291
calypsos 208–10, 222
Canada 220, 226
Canadian Mission 186
cannibalism 97
capitalism
  alternatives 247–8
  Marxist analysis 40, 86, 174, 347–53
  values 129, 256
Caribbean, definitions 3–10
Caribbean Basin 3–6
Caribbean Community *see* CARICOM
Caribbean Examinations Council 290–1
Caribbean Plate 7–8, 155, *157*, 158
Caribbean Sea 4, 5, 6
Caribbean Tourism Organization 292

Caribbeans, many 10–20
Caribs 79, 95–6, 97, 116, 368, 369
CARICOM 5, 16, 282–3, 285, 287–8
    Single Market and Economy
        (CSME) 292–3
CARIFTA 282, 284–5, 304
Carmichael, Stokely 338, 339
Carnival 205, 206, 207, 229
caste system 84
Castro, Fidel 217, 247–8
cell phones 270, 272
Césaire, Aimé 342, 343
children 193, 306, 307–8, 385
    mixed race 72–4
Chinese 107, 110, 399, 400
Christianity 75–7, 184–5, 186–7, 204
citizenship 10, 12–16, 227, 360, 364–5
civil society 36
class 86–9, 182, 184–5, 191
    see also social mobility
classism 399, 400–2
climate 137–8, 147
    see also drought; rainfall
Coard, Bernard 217
colonialism 8–9, 14–16, 199–200
    challenges and resistance 69,
        114–23
    and development 256–7, 352
    see also plantation economy; slavery
colonies
    education 177–8
    governance 10–16, 122, 215
    justice system 189–91
colonization
    cultural effects 19–20, 64–70, 74–82
    racist basis 200
coloured people 72–4, 85–6
Columbus, Christopher 98, 115
common market 285, 287–8, 292–3
Commonwealth 11, 304
communalism 69
communication see ICTs; mass media
communism 10, 217, 226, 335, 336,
    348
community radio 323, 324
constitutions 188, 189, 191, 360, 378
constructs 27
consumption 202–4, 232
contested knowledge 31–2
continental drift 155
cooking 213–15, 230
coral reefs 143–8
cosmology 76
Costa Rica 136
creativity 204–15, 258–9

creedism 399, 402–4
creole 66, 72, 77–9, 90
creolization 74–80, 220–2, 258–9
    see also hybridization; language
cricket 220–2, 291, 301–2, 303, 307
crime 312, 426
crown colonies 13, 14, 122
Cuba 76, 81–2, 106, 217, 226, 247–8
culinary arts 213–15, 230
cultural assimilation 16, 81
cultural capital 182
cultural diversity 61–70
    see also hybridization
cultural erasure 79
cultural identity 17–21, 66–7, 255–9,
    307–8
    in drama 212
    see also ethnic identity; national
        identity
cultural imperialism 324–6, 327
cultural pluralism 68
cultural products 44–5, 51, 229–30,
    258–9
    foreign influence 204–15, 324–6
    see also festivals; mass media; music;
        theatre
cultural renewal 79–80
cultural retention 79, 81, 117
cultural sensitivity 56
culture 43–53
    archaeological evidence 95, 96
    Caribbean 20, 53–7
    and discrimination 399–404
    and society 38–43, 53–7
    see also beliefs; socialization; values
        and particular aspects of culture
culture sphere 257–9
curriculum 181
customary law 193

data analysis 412, 438–9, 442–4, 446
data collection 412, 414, 415, 418,
    429–37, 439, 442, 446
data sources 421–2
debt, external 254
decolonization 14–15, 119–23, 178,
    211, 340
definitions 27, 28, 31, 32, 34
deforestation 131, 132–4, 142
departements 11, 13–14, 16
dependencies 13
dependency 203, 247, 346
dependent population 240, 380, 387
destabilization 248
developed countries 238, 239

developing countries 238, 239
    loans 277, 278
development 237–40
    cultural factors 255–9
    and discrimination 387–8, 397–8,
        401–2
    economic 120, 240–1, 344–54
    economic constraints 252–5
    and education 180, 238, 242, 243,
        246
    environmental constraints 259–61
    and ideology 247–8, 249
    indicators 240–1, 245, 246, 261, 265
    and internationalization 273
    and mass media 316–26
    recommendations 275, 277–8, 279
    social constraints 249–52
    and sport 301–13
    women's role 356
    see also human development;
        sustainable development;
        underdevelopment
diaspora 20, 106, 227, 364
difference 64, 68, 70, 357–8, 384
diffusion 46
Digicel 291
digital divide 36, 272
disability 179, 300, 306
disaster mitigation 141, 153–4, 159,
    162–3, 260
discipline, in sport 308–11
discrimination 383
    ageist 384–8
    cultural 399–404
    institutionalized 400–4
    laws against 194
    sexist 357–8, 389–98
    see also prejudice
distance learning 289, 290
distributive justice 379
DNA 98
domestic violence 394–7, 398
Dominica, Caribs 116, 368, 369
drought 137–42
drug trafficking 227–8
Du Bois, W. E. B. 335, 338
Dutch colonies 11, 101, 102, 368
    see also Suriname

earthquakes 155, 157, 158–9, 161,
    162–3
East Indies 108
economic development 240–1, 301–3,
    344–54
    see also development

economic diversification 120
economic growth 240–1, 246, 252–5, 344–7
economy, systems of production 111–14, 120
ecosystems 130–1
ecotourism 223
ecumenism 188, 402
education 31, 176–83
    beliefs 50, 168, 170
    and development 180, 238, 242, 243, 246
    inequities 257, 401
    internationalization 288–90, 311
    and religion 182, 402
    research 428
    and social mobility 65, 88, 178, 179, 180–1, 251
    see also schools; students; universities
El Niño 140–2
elderly people 193, 306, 384–8, 405
elections 122, 216, 218, 365
elites 54, 341, 349
email, for research 436–7
emergency planning 154
emigration 219–20
employment
    discrimination 383, 386–7, 392, 402
    migration for 219–20
    sports-related 302–3
    see also labour
empowerment 244, 245, 251, 257
encomienda 111, 115
enculturation 46, 80–1, 325–6
enfranchisement 120–2
English language 77–8
Enlightenment 32, 33
enslavement 115
    see also slavery
ENSO 141–2, 146
entertainment 321–2
environment 47, 127–30
    degradation 130–1
    and development 243, 259–61
    protection 148
    and tourism 223, 225, 262–3, 292
environmental determinism 127–8
environmental disasters 130, 132–63, 259–60
environmental hazards 130–2
equity 243, 244, 245, 376
    see also inequality; rights
ethics, in research 414, 417, 438–9

Ethiopia 340, *341*
ethnic composition 109–10, *110*, 366
ethnic groups
    diversity 61–2
    relations between 67–71, 83, 363–5, 400
    rights 377
ethnic identity 18–19, 69, 212, 362–3, 365–6
ethnic violence 68, 71, 365
ethnicity 62, 63
    and citizenship 364–5
    and discrimination 399–404
    in politics 191, 216, 218
    see also race; racism
ethnocentrism 45, 171–2, 383
    development models 240–1, 242
    education 177, 178
    history 93, 94, 96–8, 115, 366–8
European Union 15, 253, 254, 280
Europeans 100–2
    attitudes and values 73, 129, 190, 199–200
    culture 80–1
    families 170, 171–2
    languages 9–10, 66, 77–9
    mixed-race children 72–4
    see also colonialism; colonization; ethnocentrism; slave trade
examinations 178–9, 290–1
exploitation 256–7, 348
exports 280
extended families 119, 170, 173–4

fair trade 280
fairness 376, 379–80
false consciousness 349
families 60, 168–9, 170–6, 387
    forms 170–3, 174, 176, 195–6, 359
    violence in 394–7, 398
Fanon, Frantz 342–3
farm workers 219–20
farming see agriculture
Farrakhan, Louis 338
fashion 204
fathers, role 171, 172
fault lines 158
federation 14–15, 282, 284
femininity 371, 390–1
feminism 354–62
    see also sexism; women
festivals 83, 204–5, 206, 229
feudalism 347
Fiji 68
fish 144–5, 213

fishing 146, 147, 148
flooding 134, *135*
food 213–15, 230
football (soccer) 222–3, 307, 308
France, *departements* 11, 13–14, 16
François, Elma 355
free market 248, 274, 277, 281
free press 317–20
free states 13
free trade 270, 273–6, 277–81
    in Caribbean 282–3, 284–8, 292–3
Free Trade Area of the Americas 286
freedom 238, 332
French colonies 100–1, 102
    cultural assimilation 16, 81
    food 213–14
    governance 11, 13–14, 16
    négritude 342–3
French language 78
French Revolution 190, 351
functionalism 39, *40*, 174, 177, 184, 192
Fundamentalism 186–7

Gairy, Eric 217
Galileo Galilei 31
Garifuna 74, 79, 116, 187, 210, 366, 367
Garvey, Amy Ashwood 355
Garvey, Marcus 334, 338, 339–40
gatekeepers 401
Geertz, Clifford 48, 52
gender 357
gender inequality 173, 175, 192, 354–62, 392, *393*, 428
gender relations 174–5, 359–60, 371
    see also feminism; sexism
gender stereotypes 172, 357, 390–1
gender studies 356
generalizations 28, 390–1
genetics 98
genocide 68, 98
geography 3–6, 38, 47, 127–8
geology 7, 155–61
Ghana 337
Gini Index 250, 265
Gittens, Julius 319
global warming 147
globalization 16–17, 269–72, 279–80, 282–3
    see also internationalization
gold 98, 111
Gordon, Ken 319
government
    colonies 10–16, 122, 215

economic role 247–8, 249
media ownership 318, 323
Westminster Model 191, 215–16, 218
Greater Antilles 4, 95, 115
Green Globe 225
Grenada 217
gross domestic product (GDP) 240, 246
gross national product (GNP) 240, 241
groundwater 140, 142
Guadeloupe 11, 14, 109
Guevara, Ché 217
Guyana
    Amerindians 63, 66, 366, 368, 369
    ethnic composition *110*
    ethnic identity 69, 362–3
    ethnic relations 364–5
    gender relations 360
    indentured labour 107, 108
    land rights 369
    rainfall 139, 141
    socialism 11

Haiti
    creole 78
    justice and rights 190
    revolution 118, 351
    soil erosion 133
    terracing *136*
health and fitness 304–7, 384, 386
health tourism 224
high culture 45
Hill, Anita 394
Hindi 66
Hinduism *44*, 186, 363
Hispaniola 98, 115, 133
history 8–10, 38, 47, 64–5
    ethnocentric 93, 94, 96–8, 115, 366–8
    feminist 358–9
home schooling 168, 179
homeland 19, 20
homosexuality 391
hotel ownership 224–5
human capital 180, 242
human development 241–3, 244, *245*
    and ageism 388
    and education 180, 181
    mass media role 316–26
    and sport 300, 304–7
    and tourism 263–4
Human Development Index 245, 246, 261, 265

Human Development Paradigm 241–3, 244
human rights *see* rights
human values *see* values
hurricanes 149, 149–54, 163
hybridization 70–83, 204–15
    and creativity 258–9
    religion 75–7, 183–7
    theatre arts 211–13
    see also cultural diversity
hydrological cycle *140*
hypotheses 425

ICTs 35–6, 254, 270–2, 292
    see also mass media
ideals 48
identity
    and gender 356, 357, 360–2
    see also cultural identity
ideology 247–8, 249, 281, 331–3
    see also particular ideologies e.g. pan-Africanism
IMF 273, 278–9
immigration 226
    see also migration
imperialism 199–200
import substitution 283
imports 203
income inequality 249–52, 392, *393*
indentured labour 67, 106–10, 113–14, 119, 186, 363–4
independence 14–15, 16, 119–23
    see also neocolonialism
Indians 107–10, 113–14
    citizenship 364–5
    cultural and ethnic identity 67, 69, 83, 362–4
    entrepreneurship 119
    ethnic relations 69, 107, 363–4
    families 170, 174–5
    gender system 360–2
    languages 66
    religion *44*, 175, 186, 187, 363
indigenous peoples *see* Amerindians; Caribs
industrial revolution 33, 347–8
industry 203, 252–5, 344–7, 352
inequality 84, 249–52
    see also gender inequality; social stratification
inequity 380–4
    see also racism; sexism, *etc.*
information dissemination 314–15, 316–21
information society 35–6

information sources 421–2
infrastructure 253
injustice 380–405
institutionalized discrimination 84–6, 383, 400–4
intelligence, multiple 305
intelligentsia 86
interculturation 82, 83, 361
international agreements 378
    see also United Nations
internationalization 270, 272–6, 277–81, 282
    education 288–9, 290, 311
    see also globalization
internet 314
interpretive sociology 174, 177, 184, 192
interviews 410, 416, 420, 433, 434–5, 446
investigative reporting 320
investment 253–4, 275, 276, 344–7
Islam 175, 186, 187, 363
Island Caribs 97
Italy 340, *341*

Jagan, Cheddi 365
Jamaica
    Chinese 400
    development 249
    food supply *236*
    gender violence 395
    indentured labour 107, 108
    rainfall 139–40
    reggae 208–9
    religion 75, 185
    socialism 249
    sport 307, 312
    Unique Jamaica 271
    university 289
    withdrawal from federation 284
James, C. L. R. 350–1
journalism 318, 320
justice 187–94
    see also social justice

Kincaid, Jamaica *213*
King, Martin Luther 338
kinship 173, 175
knowledge 28–34, 38
knowledge industry 272
Kuhn, Thomas 30–1

labour
    costs 107
    and free trade 274, 275

surplus 344, 346
see also employment; working class
labour movement 121–2
land redistribution 244
land rights 367, 369, 370, 377
land tenure 265
language 9, 45–6, 66
  creole 66, 72, 77–9, 90
  and education 182
  in theatre 211, 212
Latin America 6, 8–9
learning society 36
Leeward Islands 4, 14
  see also Antigua; Montserrat; St
    Kitts–Nevis
leisure 299
Lesser Antilles 4, 95, 116, 153, *157*,
  158
Lewis, William Arthur 34–6
libel 318
liberation 238
life expectancy 246
lingua franca 78–9
literature 211–13, 364
literature review *412*, 427–8, 442,
  445–6
Lomé Convention 253, 280
Lovelace, Earl *213*

McKay, Claude 336
magic 76
magma 155, 156, 158, 160
Malcolm X 338
male marginalization 361, 428
Manley, Michael 249
Manley, Norman *121*
'Many Caribbeans' 10–17
marginalization 361, 368–9, 428
marine parks/reserves 148
market, free 248, 274, 277, 281
market research 410, 411
Marley, Bob 208, 209, 229
Maroons *44*, 63, 68, 69, 117
Marson, Una 355
Martinique 11, 14, 81
Marx, Karl 86, 347, 348
Marxist analysis
  capitalism 40, *41*, 347–53
  education 177
  families 174
  feminist 358
  justice system 192
  racial discrimination 339
  religion 184
masculinity 371, 389, 390–1

mass media 202, 313–15
  American 272, 310, 324–6
  Caribbean portrayal 24, 413
  and development 316–26
  ownership 318, 323
  popular culture 44–5
  research projects 24, 413, 424, 426
  sport on 302, 309, 310–11
material culture 48, 95, 96
matriarchy 171
matrifocal families 171, 360–1
Maya 366, 367, 377
meaning systems 48, 49
meritocracy 88
mestizos 74, 367
metropolitan countries
  Caribbean culture 229–30
  migration to 219–20, 226–7
  relations with colonies 9, 12–16,
    199–202, 346
  see also colonialism
Mexico 6, 103
Middle Passage 105
migrant labour 219–20
migration 20, 93–111, 219–20, 226–7,
  229
Millennium Development Goals 246
misandry 391
miscegenation 72, 98
misogyny 391
modernization 242, 256
monoculture 114, 120
Montserrat 13, 14, 15, 160, *161*, 162
motherhood 169, 171, 172, 175
mulattoes 74
multilateral organizations 275,
  276–80
multinational companies 275, 276,
  344–7
music 83, 205–10, 222, 229, 230, 232
Muslims *see* Islam
Mussolini, Benito 340
mutual advantage model 379–80
Myalism 75

Naipaul, Vidia 53, *213*
narcotics 227–8
nation-states 282, 283
National Association for the
  Advancement of Colored
  People 335
national identity 307, 308, 362–3,
  365–6
nationalism 340
nationality 18, 63

nationalization 249
native people *see* Amerindians
nativism 404
natural disasters 130, 132–63, 259–60
natural rights *see* rights
natural sciences 28–31, 32, 33
Navigation Acts 113, 203
négritude 342–3
neo-Marxism 349–53
neocolonialism 200–1
neoliberalism 281, 283
Nettleford, R. 55
Nevis *see* St Kitts–Nevis
New World Group 346, 347
news 314, 316–17
newspapers 314, 317, 324
  pan-Africanist 334, 336, 339
Nkrumah, Kwame 337
Nonconformism 185
norms, family 168–9
nuclear families 170, 171–2, 176, 359
Nurse, Malcolm 336–7

observational data 436–7
occupation, and class 88, 89
Old Representative System 122
Olmec civilization 103
Olympic Games 309–10
Operation Urgent Fury 217
oral history 124
Organization of Eastern Caribbean
  States 16–17, 285
otherness 200, 382–3
outsourcing 271

Padmore, George 336–7, 350
pan-Africanism 331, 332, 333–44,
  350
paradigm shifts 30–1
parliament 216
patois 77, 78
patriarchy 171, 174–5, 356–62,
  389–90
peasant farming 120
Pentecostals 186–7
performance 322
physical education 300, 305, 306
pidgin languages 79
pigmentocracy 72–3
pirates 101
place, sense of 17–18
planned economy 247–8, 249
plantation economy 120, 124, 352–3
plantation society 54, 69, 84–6, 105–
  6, 112–14, 118, 346

plantocracy *85*
plate tectonics 7, 155–7, 158
play 300
plural societies 68, 69, 71, 82, 83, 400
poetry 212
political participation 257, 283
political parties 218
    ethnic basis 191, 216, 218, 364–5
political science 39
political systems 10–17, 47, 122, 215–19
    see also government
politics, and ideology 332
pollution 130–1, 147
polygamy 172, 175
popular culture 44–5
Portugal 99, 100, 102–3, 104
postcolonialism 201, 202
postmodernism 33, 128–9, 181
pottery 95, 96
poverty 250, 251
    Amerindians 368–9
    and disasters 162–3, 260
    and discrimination 401–2
    and education 177
    and family form 172, 173
    and IMF policies 278–9
    and injustice 192
    and soil erosion 133, 136–7
poverty reduction 247–8, 251, 263–4, 379–80
power 128–9, 191, 192, 359–60
prejudice 381–3
    see also discrimination
presidential government 215–16
press freedom 317–20
primary producers 252
prime ministers, power 218
privateers 101
probability 430
productive sector 252–5, 296
productivity 244, *245*, 253
proletariat 86, 351
proprietorships 101
Protestant churches 185
publishing 313
Puerto Rico 13, 344
punta rock 210

qualitative research 416–17, 438, 445–7
quantitative research 414, 415, 438, 442–5
questionnaires 415, 433, 434–5

race 62, 63, 102
    hybridization 72–4
racism 16, 84–6, 200, 383, 399–402
radio 202, 318, 319, 321, 322, 323, 324
rainfall 134, 137–40
rape 396
Rastafarianism *44*, 76, 185–6, 208, 229–30, 334, 340
recipes 214
recreation 299–300, 304, 321
references 440–1
reggae 208–9
regional integration 14–15, 281–95, 307, 323–4
Regional Security System 294
religion 43, *44*, 58, 75–7, 168, 183–8
    and education 182, 402
    festivals 204
    and rights 193
    stereotypes and discrimination 381, 399, 402–4
Renaissance 33
reparations movement 118
republics 11
research 409–15
    instruments 410, 433–7
    objectives 422–3
    problems 419–20, 425–7
    process *412*, 419–48
    purpose 413, 416, 417
    questions *412*, 423–4
    reliability 410, 417
    types 413–19
    validity 411–12, 417
resistance 185, 202, 205, 206, 403
resistance movements 114–19, 123
    Amerindian 115–16, 367, 370
    see also Maroons; revolution
responsibilities 376
retirement 193, 386, 405
revolutions 118, 190, 247–8, 351
rights 188–94, 376, 377–8
    Africans 112, 189–90, 338
    Amerindians 189, 367, 369, 370, 377
risk management 162
rites and rituals 183
Rodney, Walter 341, 351–2
Rogers, Julian 319
roles, gender-based 169, 171, 172, 356, 357, 358, 390–1
rule of law 216
rural poverty 250

St Kitts–Nevis 14, 15, 63, 64, 312
St Lucia 148
St Vincent and the Grenadines 74, 75, 116, 162, 185
sampling (in research) 414, 430–2
Santeria 76
scholarly societies 41
scholars, rivalry 30–1
Scholastic Assessment Tests (SATs) 290–1
schools 177–8
    denominational 182, 186, 402
    gender issues 428
    history 124
    indiscipline research 415, 416, 418
    sport 300, 305, 306, 307–8
    see also education
scientific knowledge 29, 30, 31, 33
scientific method 28–31, 33, 413–14, 425
    see also natural sciences
Seacole, Mary 355
Seaga, Edward 249
seasonal migration 219–20
security, regional 294
Selassie, Haile 334, 340
self, perceptions of 66–7
self-esteem 312
self-reliance 380
Senghor, Léopold 343
separation of powers 215
service sector 252
    see also tourism
sexism 357–8, 389–98
    see also feminism; women
sexual discrimination 389–98
sexual harassment 392–3, 394
shifting cultivation 134
Shiprider Agreement 227
Shouter/Spiritual Baptists *44*, 75, 185, 403
skin colour 72–4, 84–6
slander 318
slave trade 100, 102–6, 117
slavery 102, 111–13
    abolition 106, 117–18, 351, 353
    injustice 189–90
    resistance to 116–18
    transculturation through 82
    see also Africans; Maroons
slaves
    education 177
    family life 172, 359
    rebellion 117, 118
    social stratification 84–6

Smith, R.T. 53
smuggling 100
soca 209–10
soccer (football) 222–3, 307, 308
the social 27–35, 36–7, 51
social capital 204
social class 86–9, 182, 184–5, 191
social cohesion 180, 184
social constructions
    culture 51, 53, 63
    race 62, 73
    scientific knowledge 29, 30, 31, 33
    society 37
social contract 379
social distance 181
social exclusion 250–1
social groups, membership 32
social injustice 380–405
social institutions 39, 167–70, 257
    see also education; family; justice;
        religion
social justice 375–80
social life, dynamism 33–4
social location 18, 32, 36–7, 54, 56
social mobility 54, 88–9
    through education 65, 88, 178,
        179, 180–1, 251
    and migration 20
    women 361
social organizations 39, 170, 179
social relations of production 192,
    352
social sciences 31–2, 33, 38
    research see research
    societies 41
    see also particular disciplines
social stratification 54, 65, 83–8
    and development 249–50
    Marxist analysis 347
    plantation society 84–6, 112, 113,
        118
    and skin colour 72–3, 84–6
    see also class
socialism 10, 11, 348
    and development 247–8, 249
socialization 39, 45–6, 168, 322
    through education 176–7
    through enculturation 80–1
    and gender 356, 357, 359–62, 389
    and prejudice 381–2
    and values 378
societies, scholarly 41
society
    academic perspectives 38–43
    Caribbean 53–7

and culture 38–43
    definitions 32, 33, 34, 37, 42
    environmental relations 127–30
    Marxist analysis 347–53
    popular understanding 35–7
    as social construction 37
    sociological study 65–6
sociology 39–40, 43, 51–2, 65–6
    of education 177
    of family 174
    functionalist 39, 40
    of justice system 192
    Marxist 40, 41
    of religion 184
    scientific method 33
soil conservation 133, 135–6
soil erosion 132–7
Soufrière Hills 160, 161, 162
Spain 99, 100
Spanish Empire 98–100
    challenges to 101, 102
    encomienda 111, 115
    native resistance 115–16
    rights 189
    slavery 105–6
spatial perception 9–10
Spiritual (Shouter) Baptists 44, 75,
    185, 403
sport 299–301
    and development 301–13
    external influences 220–3
    sponsorship 291, 303
    see also cricket
sports scholarships 311
sports tourism 224, 301
Sri Lanka 68
Stalin, Josef 336–7
state, and society 39
    see also government
status 65, 83
    in family 169
    and skin colour 72–3, 84–6
steelbands 207, 208
stereotypes 381–3
    ageist 384–8
    cultural 399–404
    sexist 172, 357, 390–1
Stewart, Gordon 224–5
structural adjustment policies 278–9
students
    protest 341
    research project on 420, 422,
        423–4, 426
    under-achievement 181
subaltern populations 201, 202

subcultures 46
substructure 41, 349
sugar production 114, 117
Summit of the Americas 370
superstructure 41, 349
Suriname 66, 68, 109–10, 110
surveys 432–3
sustainable development 148, 241–2,
    243–5, 260
sustainable tourism 225, 262–3
symbols 45–6, 48–9, 52, 53
syncretic religions 75–7, 183–7, 403
systems of production 111–14, 120

Tainos 79, 96–7, 98, 115–16
tariffs 203, 273–5, 280, 284–5
tectonic activity 7, 155–60
telecommunications 270–1
    see also ICTs
television 202, 318, 320–1, 323, 324,
    327–8, 442–5
    sport 302, 309
theatre 211–13
theocracies 183
Thomas, Clarence 394
Tobago 143, 144, 323
Tordesillas, Treaty of 99
total institution, slavery as 112
tourism 23, 223–5, 236, 292
    coral reefs 146, 148
    and development 261–4
    research project 426–7
    and sport 224, 301
trade 203, 228, 236
    globalization 269, 270, 272
    internationalization 273–6, 277–
        81
    preferential terms 252, 253, 280
    protectionism 274, 275
    regional 281–8
    structure 255
    see also free trade; World Trade
        Organization
trade blocs 16, 285–6
trade unions 121–2, 339, 348
transculturation 81–2
transnational corporations 275, 276,
    344–7
transplanted peoples 19–20, 67–8
triangular trade 105
Trinidad and Tobago
    Carnival 206, 207
    community radio 323
    creoles 72
    ethnic composition 10

ethnic relations 69, 83, 360–5
exports *236*
football 308
gender identity 360–2
income inequality 392, *393*
indentured labour 107, 108, 186
languages 66
press harassment 319
religion 75, 186, 363, 403
state of emergency 341
steelbands 207
university 289
see also Tobago
Trotskyism 350
tsunamis 158, 159
Turks and Caicos Islands 13, 14

underdevelopment 352
see also development
United Nations
   Convention on the Rights of the
      Child 193
   Development Programme 246
   Universal Declaration of Human
      Rights 189, 377
   World Conference on
      Women 395
United States
   admiration for 204, 325
   anti-communism 217, 226
   Caribbean relations 227–8, 231,
      294
   civil rights 338, 339
   communism 336
   cultural influence 205
   elderly lobby 388
   free states in association with 13
   Grenada invasion 217
   immigration 226
   mass media 272, 310, 324–6
   multinationals 276
   pan-Africanism 334–9

presidential system 215–16
religion 186–7
sport 222, 310, 311
Supreme Court 394
tourists 223
trade 228
and World Bank 277
universal adult suffrage 122
Universal Negro Improvement
   Association 334, 338
universities 179, 288–9, 290, 311
University of the West Indies 288–9,
   341, 356
urbanisation 129
'us' and 'them' syndrome 68, 70, 322
USSR 247–8

values 48, 49, 50
   communalistic 69
   cultural 45
   and development 237–8, 256, 257,
      259, 260
   European 199–200
   family 168–9
   media influence 320–1, 325
   modern 242
   religious 183
   and rights 378
   scientific 33
   and social location 54, 56
   in sport 308–11
   see also beliefs; ideology
variables 423
violence 68, 71, 365, 394–7, 398
volcanoes 155, 158, 159–61, 162, 163

Walcott, Derek 53, 212
Washington Consensus 278
water supplies 142, 378
wealth 249, 251–2, 261
Weber, Max 86, 87–8
webs of significance 48–9, 52

welfare 246, 376, 378–80
West Indies 108
West Indies Cricket Board 291, 302
West Indies Federation 14, 284
western hegemony 200–1, 203–4
Westminster Model 191, 215–16, 218
Wider Caribbean Region 6, 8, 16–17
Williams, Eric 284, 351, 353
Williams, Henry Sylvester 333
Williams, Raymond 45
Windward Islands 4
   see also particular islands
Windward and Leeward Islands
   Associated States 15
women
   discrimination against 389–98
   diversity 358
   employment 359, 392, 397
   enslavement 359
   exploitation 174, 356
   men's hatred 391
   oppression 187, 357–8, 360–2
   rights 192, 193
   roles 169, 171, 356, 357, 358,
      390–1
   sexual harassment 392–3, 394
   social mobility 361
   stereotypes 390–1
   violence against 394–7, 398
   writers 364
   see also feminism; motherhood
working class 86–7, 348
World Bank 261, 273, 277–8
World Trade Organization 253, 275,
   279–80
writers 211–13, 364

youth
   sport 306, 307–8, 311–12
   stereotypes 385
   television viewing 442–5